PREVIOUS YEARS' SOLVED PAPERS

Environmental Science

For UGC-NET/JRF

Paper I, II and III

Atlantic Research Division

ATLANTIC

PUBLISHERS & DISTRIBUTORS (P) LTD

Published by

ATLANTIC

PUBLISHERS & DISTRIBUTORS (P) LTD

7/22, Ansari Road, Darya Ganj,
New Delhi-110002
Phones : +91-11-40775252, 23273880, 23275880, 23280451
Fax : +91-11-23285873
Web : www.atlanticbooks.com
E-mail : orders@atlanticbooks.com

Branch Office
5, Nallathambi Street, Wallajah Road,
Chennai-600002
Phones : +91-44-64611085, 32413319
E-mail : chennai@atlanticbooks.com

Printed in India at Nice Printing Press, A-33/3A, Site-IV,
Industrial Area, Sahibabad, Ghaziabad, U.P.

Preface

The University Grants Commission (UGC) conducts National Eligibility Test (N] subjects twice every year, once each in June and December, to determine eligibi and university level lectureship and for award of Junior Research Fellowship (JI nationals in order to ensure minimum standards for the entrants in the teaching research.

The book contains previous years' solved papers (objective type questions) oı Environmental Science, from June 2005 to December 2015. It covers all three paı and III). In Paper I (General Paper on Teaching and Research Aptitude), solved pa included from December 2005 and in Paper II (Elective), solved papers have beer June 2005. In Paper III (Core and Elective), solved papers of objective type quest included from June 2012, conforming to the existing UGC-NET pattern. In addit Mock Tests for Paper I, II and III have been included in the book under Practice P have been given at the end of each set for self-check.

It will be useful for those preparing for UGC-NET/JRF in the subject of Science. It will give them a feel of the type of questions asked in NET in t Multiple-choice, Matching type, True/False, Assertion-Reasoning type, etc. The in this book will enable the students to judge their own level of competence be their knowledge. It will also help them revise the important questions in the ent enhance their self-confidence. Suggestions for further improvement of the boo welcome.

Atlantic Re

Contents

JUNE–2005

Note: This paper contains Fifty (50) objective type questions, each question carrying two (2) marks. Attempt all the questions.

PAPER–II

1. For maximum biogas production following conditions are recommended:
   (a) Strict anaerobic
   (b) Strict aerobic
   (c) Only cellulose as a carbon source
   (d) Semi aerobic

2. To establish wind mill for commercial production of electricity, the optimum range of wind speeds required is:
   (a) 4 - 10 m/sec (b) 20 - 30 m/sec
   (c) 35 - 45 m/sec (d) > 100 m/sec

3. To initiate fission of ^{238}U, the kinetic energy required for neutron is:
   (a) ~ 1.5 MeV (b) ~ 0.5 MeV
   (c) ~ .025 MeV (d) ~ 1 KeV

4. The national ambient air quality standard for average annual concentration of NO_X in residential area is:
   (a) 20 $\mu g/m^3$ (b) 60 $\mu g/m^3$
   (c) 80 $\mu g/m^3$ (d) 100 $\mu g/m^3$

5. Land sea and mountain valley breezes occur on which of the following horizontal space scales:
   (a) Micro scale (b) Meso scale
   (c) Synoptic scale (d) > 40,000 km

6. Carbon dioxide absorbs radiation very strongly in which of the following wavelength ranges?
   (a) 12 - 18 μm (b) 4 - 11 μm
   (c) 0.7 - 3 μm (d) 0.8 - 1.1 μm

7. About 97% of the atmospheric mass lies in the first
   (a) 30 km above ground
   (b) 100 km above ground
   (c) 300 km above ground
   (d) 10 km above ground

8. Which is the correct chronological order (oldest to youngest) in which the following were formed:
   (I) Atlantic Ocean
   (II) Indian Ocean
   (III) Pacific Ocean
   (IV) Mediterranean sea
   Select the correct answer using the codes given below:
   Codes:
   (a) III, I, IV, II (b) III, I, II, IV
   (c) I, III, II, IV (d) I, III, IV, II

9. A seismogram records the following types of earthquake waves:
   (I) L Waves (II) P Waves
   (III) S Waves
   The correct chronological sequence of the arrival of these waves is:
   (a) II, III, I (b) II, I, III
   (c) III, II, I (d) III I II

10. In humid climate, the rate of weathering of the following types of rocks is such that:
   (a) Basalt > Dunite > Granite
   (b) Basalt > Granite > Dunite
   (c) Dunite > Granite > Basalt
   (d) Dunite > Basalt > Granite

11. Which one of the following proximate content of coal indicates the optimum by product availability during coal carbonisation:
(a) Moisture (b) Volatile matter
(c) Fixed Carbon (d) Ash

12. Match List I and List II and select the correct answer choosing the codes given below the lists:

List I	**List II**
A. Chain silicates	(i) Quartz
B. Tekto silicates	(ii) Beryl
C. Phyllo silicates	(iii) Augite
D. Cyclo silicates	(iv) Muscovite

Codes:	A	B	C	D
(a)	(i)	(ii)	(iii)	(iv)
(b)	(i)	(ii)	(iv)	(iii)
(c)	(iii)	(i)	(ii)	(iv)
(d)	(iii)	(i)	(iv)	(ii)

13. In a closed ecosystem, across its boundries,
(a) Energy can transfer but mass cannot transfer
(b) Mass can transfer but energy cannot transfer
(c) Both energy and mass cannot transfer
(d) Both energy and mass can transfer

14. Under z transformation $z = (x - \mu)/\sigma$, the normal distribution $f(x)$ with mean μ and standard deviation σ, has the standard deviation:
(a) 0 (b) 1
(c) ∞ (d) $\sqrt{\pi}$

15. The geometric mean of the following numbers 2, 3, 2, 3, 2, 3, 2, 3 is:
(a) $\sqrt{6}$ (b) 6
(c) 2.5 (d) 5.0

16. Which of the following gases has maximum global warming potential (GWP)?
(a) SF_6 (b) CH_4
(c) CO_2 (d) CFC_5

17. In India, Air (Prevention and Control of Pollution) Act came into being in which year?
(a) 1974 (b) 1981
(c) 1978 (d) 1990

18. Kyoto Protocol envisages a reduction is CO_2 concentration, below 1990 levels, by:
(a) 10.2% (b) 5.2 %
(c) 15% (d) 25%

19. Anamalous expansion of water have helped amphibious biological systems to sustain themselves in polar regions such as:
(a) Polar bear (b) Frog
(c) Eskimo (d) Seal

20. When 100 mL of 0.1M sulphuric acid is used to neutralise 0.01N NaOH, how many milli-litres of NaOH will be required?
(a) 100 (b) 500
(c) 1000 (d) 2000

21. If 100% noise dose corresponds to equivalent sound pressure level L_{eq} = 90 dB for 8 hours, then 25% dose would correspond to:
(a) 93 dB for 2 hours
(b) 90 dB for 4 hours
(c) 87 dB for 4 hours
(d) 87 dB for 2 hours

22. ^{60}Co (Cobalt sixty) is used to treat cancer as it emits:
(a) Strong gamma rays
(b) β radiations
(c) α radiations
(d) X-rays

23. Molar concentration of pure water is:
(a) 1 M (b) 18 M
(c) 55.5 M (d) 100 M

24. The internal combustion engines using petrol are mainly responsible for the generation of:
(a) Ozone (b) NO_X
(c) SO_X (d) VOCs

25. Which nod gene product interacts with flavonoids to initiate the process of root hair deformation?
(a) Nod A (b) Nod B
(c) Nod C (d) Nod D

26. Which of the materials is most preferred as a carrier for legume inoculation?
(a) Peat (b) Slag
(c) Soil (d) Anthracite

27. **Assertion (A):** The ozone layer absorbs UV radiations.
Reason (R): Part of the UV flux is used up in the formation of ozone in stratosphere.
(a) Both (A) and (R) are true and (R) is the correct explanation of (A)
(b) Both (A) and (R) are true and (R) is not the correct explanation of (A)
(c) (A) is true but (R) is false
(d) (A) is false but (R) is true

28. Match List I and List II and select the correct answer using the codes given below the lists:

List I (Characteristics)
A. Point of initial movement during the earthquakes
B. Measurement of the magnitude of earthquake
C. Measurement of solar radiation incident on earth
D. Earthquakes generated water waves in coastal areas

List II (Terms/Names)
(i) Tsunami (ii) Insolation
(iii) Richter scale (iv) Focus

Codes:	**A**	**B**	**C**	**D**
(a)	(iv)	(iii)	(ii)	(i)
(b)	(iii)	(iv)	(i)	(ii)
(c)	(ii)	(i)	(iii)	(iv)
(d)	(i)	(ii)	(iv)	(iii)

29. Which is the most common gas released from the landfills:
(a) Carbon monoxide
(b) Methane
(c) Hydrogen Sulphide
(d) Carbon dioxide

30. Trickling filters are used for the treatment of:
(a) Primary sewage
(b) Secondary sewage
(c) Tertiary sewage
(d) Quaternary sewage

31. Continuous-flow air-agitated photobioreactors are used for the removal of which compound from water?
(a) Nitrite (b) Chloride
(c) Cyanide (d) Nitrate

32. Sea water is:
(a) acidic (b) alkaline
(c) neutral (d) hypotonic

33. The tidal mouth of a river opening into the sea is termed as:
(a) Estuary (b) Littoral zone
(c) Hypoliminion (d) Abyssal zone

34. In an aquatic ecosystem, the depth to which light penetrates is called:
(a) aphotic (b) photic
(c) euphotic (d) nonphotic

35. Which of the following is used for the large scale treatment of potable water?
(a) Chlorine
(b) Potassium permagnate
(c) Ozone
(d) Potassium permagnate and UV radiation

36. High BOD values in a water sample reflects a:
(a) High biodegradable organic content
(b) Low organic content
(c) High phosphorous content
(d) High nitrogen content

37. Biological rhythm in animals is regulated by one of the following:
(a) Water (b) Air
(c) Light (d) Crowding

38. Pineal gland mediates the environmental information to animals through the day-night secretion of:
(a) Gonadotropin (b) Thyroxin
(c) Melanin (d) Melatonin

39. Zeitgeber means:
(a) Time giving
(b) Photoperiod information
(c) Temperature information
(d) Rainfall information

40. The ΔG_0 of ATP hydrolysis could not be measured directly because:
(a) one cannot determine the K_{eq}
(b) ATPase concentration could not be measured
(c) One of the reactants could not be estimated
(d) The products could not be determined

41. The corals generally grow in nutrient poor clear sea water because:
(a) Nutrients are provided through sewage
(b) Single cell algae present on the corals provide nutrients through photosynthesis
(c) They absorb nutrients from the sea water
(d) They get nutrition from the dead organisms.

42. Thermoclines of a lake mean:
(a) The upper layer with well lit, well mixed and relatively having warm water
(b) The intermediate layer in which a rapid decline in temperature occurs with depth
(c) The deep layer which is generally cold and dark
(d) The bottom layer

43. A cell is filled up with 0.6M NaCl and presumed that the membrane is more permeable to water than NaCl. In this condition if the cell is placed in 0.2M NaCl, the approach to equilibrium will be largely governed by:
(a) Osmosis
(b) Diffusion
(c) Losing salt rapidly
(d) Losing salt and water equally

44. When a low lander man is transferred to high altitudes, the oxygen consumption will:
(a) not decrease
(b) remain the same
(c) reduce mytochondrial oxygen tension
(d) Impair oxidative metabolism

45. **Assertion (A):** Cost-Benefit Analysis is an important tool in Environmental Impact Assessment.
Reason (R): It evaluates the likely return on capital inputs in a project.
(a) Both (A) and (R) are true and (R) is the correct explanation of (A)
(b) Both (A) and (R) are true but (R) is not the correct explanation of (A)
(c) (A) is true but (R) is false
(d) (A) is false but (R) is true

46. Environmental Impact Assessment (EIA) seeks to achieve goals pertaining to:
(a) Sustainable Development
(b) Prevention of pollution only
(c) Conservation of resources only
(d) Social Benefit

47. **Assertion (A):** Environmental Audit is an important aspect of post-project analysis.

Reason (R): It helps in assessment of compliance with environmental regulatory requirements.

(a) Both (A) and (R) are true and (R) is the correct explanation of (A)
(b) Both (A) and (R) are true but (R) is not the correct explanation of (A)
(c) (A) is true but R is false
(d) (A) is false but R is true

48. For the detection of Polyaromatic hydrocarbons (PAH) which of the following instruments is used?
(a) Atomic Absorption Spectrophotometer
(b) X-ray Diffractometer
(c) Gas Chromatograph
(d) Flame Photometer

49. **Assertion (A):** Land use changes have implications for climate.
Reason (R): The radiative fluxes get modified.
(a) Both (A) and (R) are true and (R) is the correct explanation of (A)
(b) Both (A) and (R) are true but (R) is not the correct explanation of (A)
(c) (A) is true but (R) is false
(d) (A) is false but (R) is true

50. Tissue protein can be estimated by:
(a) Gravimetric method
(b) Biurate method
(c) Caloriemeter
(d) Manometer

ANSWERS

1. (a)	2. (d)	3. (a)	4. (a)	5. (c)
6. (c)	7. (b)	8. (a)	9. (a)	10. (b)
11. (d)	12. (d)	13. (a)	14. (c)	15. (a)
16. (d)	17. (b)	18. (b)	19. (c)	20. (a)
21. (a)	22. (b)	23. (c)	24. (c)	25. (d)
26. (b)	27. (c)	28. (a)	29. (b)	30. (b)
31. (c)	32. (a)	33. (a)	34. (b)	35. (a)
36. (a)	37. (c)	38. (d)	39. (b)	40. (b)
41. (c)	42. (b)	43. (b)	44. (a)	45. (a)
46. (a)	47. (a)	48. (c)	49. (c)	50. (b)

DECEMBER–2005

Note: This paper contains Fifty (50) objective type questions, each question carrying two (2) marks. Attempt all the questions.

PAPER–I

1. Team teaching has the potential to develop:
   (a) Competitive spirit
   (b) Cooperation
   (c) The habit of supplementing the teaching of each other
   (d) Highlighting the gaps in each other's teaching

2. Which of the following is the most important characteristic of Open Book Examination system?
   (a) Students become serious.
   (b) It improves attendance in the classroom.
   (c) It reduces examination anxiety amongst students.
   (d) It compels students to think.

3. Which of the following methods of teaching encourages the use of maximum senses?
   (a) Problem-solving method
   (b) Laboratory method
   (c) Self-study method
   (d) Team teaching method

4. Which of the following statement is correct?
   (a) Communicator should have fine senses
   (b) Communicator should have tolerance power
   (c) Communicator should be soft spoken
   (d) Communicator should have good personality

5. An effective teacher is one who can:
   (a) control the class
   (b) give more information in less time
   (c) motivate students to learn
   (d) correct the assignments carefully

6. One of the following is not a quality of researcher:
   (a) Unison with that of which he is in search
   (b) He must be of alert mind
   (c) Keenness in enquiry
   (d) His assertion to outstrip the evidence

7. A satisfactory statistical quantitative method should not possess one of the following qualities:
   (a) Appropriateness (b) Measurability
   (c) Comparability (d) Flexibility

8. Books and records are the primary sources of data in:
   (a) historical research
   (b) participatory research
   (c) clinical research
   (d) laboratory research

9. Which of the following statement is correct?
   (a) objectives should be pinpointed
   (b) objectives can be written in statement or question form
   (c) another word for problem is variable
   (d) All of the above

10. The important pre-requisites of a researcher in sciences, social sciences and humanities are:

(a) laboratory skills, records, supervisor, topic
(b) Supervisor, topic, critical analysis, patience
(c) archives, supervisor, topic, flexibility in thinking
(d) topic, supervisor, good temperament, pre-conceived notions

Read the following passage and answer the questions 11 to 15:

Knowledge creation in many cases requires creativity and idea generation. This is especially important in generating alternative decision support solutions. Some people believe that an individual's creative ability stems primarily from personality traits such as inventiveness, independence, individuality, enthusiasm, and flexibility. However, several studies have found that creativity is not so much a function of individual traits as was once believed, and that individual creativity can be learned and improved. This understanding has led innovative companies to recognise that the key to fostering creativity may be the development of an idea-nurturing work environment. Idea-generation methods and techniques, to be used by individuals or in groups, are consequently being developed. Manual methods for supporting idea generation, such as brainstorming in a group, can be very successful in certain situations. However, in other situations, such an approach is either not economically feasible or not possible. For example, manual methods in group creativity sessions will not work or will not be effective when: (1) there is no time to conduct a proper idea-generation session; (2) there is a poor facilitator (or no facilitator at all); (3) it is too expensive to conduct an idea-generation session; (4) the subject matter is too sensitive for a face-to-face session; or (5) there are not enough participants, the mix of participants is not optimal, or there is no climate for idea generation. In such cases, computerised idea-generation methods have been tried, with frequent success.

Idea-generation software is designed to help stimulate a single user or a group to produce new ideas, options and choices. The user does all the work, but the software encourages and pushes, something like a personal trainer. Although idea-generation software is still relatively new, there are several packages on the market. Various approaches are used by idea-generating software to increase the flow of ideas to the user. Idea Fisher, for example, has an associate lexicon of the English language that cross-references words and phrases. These associative links, based on analogies and metaphors, make it easy for the user to be fed words related to a given theme. Some software packages use questions to prompt the user towards new, unexplored patterns of thought. This helps users to break out of cyclical thinking patterns, conquer mental blocks, or deal with bouts of procrastination.

11. The author, in this passage has focussed on
(a) knowledge creation
(b) idea-generation
(c) creativity
(d) individual traits

12. Fostering creativity needs an environment of
(a) decision support systems
(b) idea-nurturing
(c) decision support solutions
(d) alternative individual factors

13. Manual methods for the support of idea-generation, in certain occasions,
(a) are alternatively effective
(b) can be less expensive
(c) do not need a facilitator
(d) require a mix of optimal participants

14. Idea-generation software works as if it is a:
(a) stimulant
(b) knowledge package
(c) user-friendly trainer
(d) climate creator

15. Mental blocks, bouts of procrastination and cyclical thinking patterns can be won when:
(a) innovative companies employ electronic thinking methods
(b) idea-generation software prompts questions
(c) manual methods are removed
(d) individuals acquire a neutral attitude towards the software

16. Level C of the effectiveness of communication is defined as:
(a) channel noise
(b) semantic noise
(c) psychological noise
(d) source noise

17. Recording a television programme on a VCR is an example of:
(a) time-shifting
(b) content reference
(c) mechanical clarity
(d) media synchronisation

18. A good communicator is the one who offers to his audience:
(a) plentiful of information
(b) a good amount of statistics
(c) concise proof
(d) repetition of facts

19. The largest number of newspapers in India is published from the state of:
(a) Kerala (b) Maharashtra
(c) West Bengal (d) Uttar Pradesh

20. Insert the missing number:
8 24 12 ? 18 54
(a) 26 (b) 24
(c) 36 (d) 32

21. January 1, 1995 was Sunday. What day of the week lies on January 1, 1996?
(a) Sunday (b) Monday
(c) Saturday (d) None of these

22. The sum of a positive number and its reciprocal is twice the difference of the number and its reciprocal. The number is:
(a) $\sqrt{2}$ (b) $\frac{1}{\sqrt{2}}$
(c) $\sqrt{3}$ (d) $\frac{1}{\sqrt{3}}$

23. In a certain code, ROUNDS is written as RONUDS. How will PLEASE will be written in the same code:
(a) LPAESE (b) PLAESE
(c) LPAEES (d) PLASEE

24. At what time between 5.30 and 6.00 will the hands of an clock be at right angles?
(a) $43\frac{5}{11}$ min. past 5
(b) $43\frac{7}{11}$ min. past 5
(c) 40 min. past 5
(d) 45 min. past 5

25. **Statements:** I All students are ambitious
II All ambitious persons are hard working
Conclusions: (i) All students are hard-working
(ii) All hardly working people are not ambitious
Which of the following is correct?
(a) Only (i) is correct
(b) Only (ii) is correct
(c) Both (i) and (ii) are correct
(d) Neither (i) nor (ii) is correct

26. **Statement:** Most students are intelligent
Conclusions: (i) Some students are intelligent
(ii) All students are not intelligent

Which of the following is implied?
(a) Only (i) is implied
(b) Only (ii) is implied
(c) Both (i) and (ii) are implied
(d) Neither (i) nor (ii) is implied

27. **Statement:** Most labourers are poor
Conclusions: (i) Some labourers are poor
(ii) All labourers are not poor
Which of the following is implied?
(a) Only (i) is implied
(b) Only (ii) is implied
(c) Both (i) and (ii) are implied
(d) Neither (i) nor (ii) is implied

28. Line access and avoidance of collision are the main functions of:
(a) the CPU
(b) the monitor
(c) network protocols
(d) wide area networks

29. In the hypermedia database, information bits are stored in the form of:
(a) signals (b) cubes
(c) nodes (d) symbols

30. Communications bandwidth that has the highest capacity and is used by microwave, cable and fibre optics lines is known as:
(a) hyper-link
(b) broadband
(c) bus width
(d) carrier wave

31. An electronic bill board that has a short text or graphical advertising message is referred to as:
(a) bulletin (b) strap
(c) bridge line (d) banner

32. Which of the following is not the characteristic of a computer?
(a) computer is an electrical machine
(b) computer cannot think at its own
(c) computer processes information error free
(d) computer can hold data for any length of time

33. Bitumen is obtained from:
(a) Forests and Plants
(b) Kerosene oil
(c) Crude oil
(d) underground mines

34. Malaria is caused by:
(a) bacterial infection
(b) viral infection
(c) parasitic infection
(d) fungal infection

35. The cloudy nights are warmer compared to clear nights (without clouds) during winter days. This is because:
(a) clouds radiate heat towards the earth
(b) clouds prevent cold wave from the sky, descend on earth
(c) clouds prevent escaping of the heat radiation from the earth
(d) clouds being at great heights from earth absorb heat from the sun and send towards the earth

36. Largest soil group of India is:
(a) Red soil (b) Black soil
(c) Sandy soil (d) Mountain soil

37. Main pollutant of the Indian coastal water is:
(a) oil spill
(b) municipal sewage
(c) industrial effluents
(d) aerosols

38. Human ear is most sensitive to noise in the following frequency ranges:
(a) 1-2 KHz (b) 100-500 Hz
(c) 10-12 KHz (d) 13-16 KHz

39. Which species of chromium is toxic in water:
(a) Cr + 2 (b) Cr + 3
(c) Cr + 6 (d) Cr is non-toxic element

40. Match List I (Dams) with List II (Rivers) in the following:

List I (Dams)	List II (Rivers)
(A) Bhakra	(i) Krishna
(B) Nagarjunasagar	(ii) Damodar
(C) Panchet	(iii) Sutlej
(D) Hirakud	(iv) Bhagirathi
(E) Tehri	(v) Mahanadi

Codes:	A	B	C	D	E
(a)	v	iii	iv	ii	i
(b)	iii	i	ii	v	iv
(c)	i	ii	iv	iii	v
(d)	ii	iii	iv	i	v

41. A negative reaction to a mediated communication is described as:
(a) flak
(b) fragmented feedback
(c) passive response
(d) non-conformity

42. The launch of satellite channel by IGNOU on 26th January 2003 for technological education for the growth and development of distance education is:
(a) Eklavya channel
(b) Gyandarshan channel
(c) Rajrishi channel
(d) None of these

43. Match List I with List II and select the correct answer from the codes given below:

List I (Institutions)	List II (Locations)
(A) The Indian Council of Historical Research (ICHR)	(i) Shimla
(B) The Indian Institute of Advanced Studies (IIAS)	(ii) New Delhi
(C) The Indian Council of Philosophical Research (ICPR)	(iii) Bangalore
(D) The Central Institute of Coastal Engineering for Fisheries	(iv) Lucknow

Codes:	A	B	C	D
(a)	ii	i	iv	iii
(b)	i	ii	iii	iv
(c)	ii	iv	i	iii
(d)	iv	iii	ii	i

44. Which of the following is not a Fundamental Right?
(a) Right to equality
(b) Right against exploitation
(c) Right to freedom of speech and expression
(d) Right of free compulsory education of all children upto the age of 14

45. The Lok Sabha can be dissolved before the expiry of its normal five year term by:
(a) The Prime Minister
(b) The Speaker of Lok Sabha
(c) The President on the recommendation of the Prime Minister
(d) None of the above

Study the following graph carefully and answer Q.No. 46 to 50 given below it:

EXPORT OF TINS

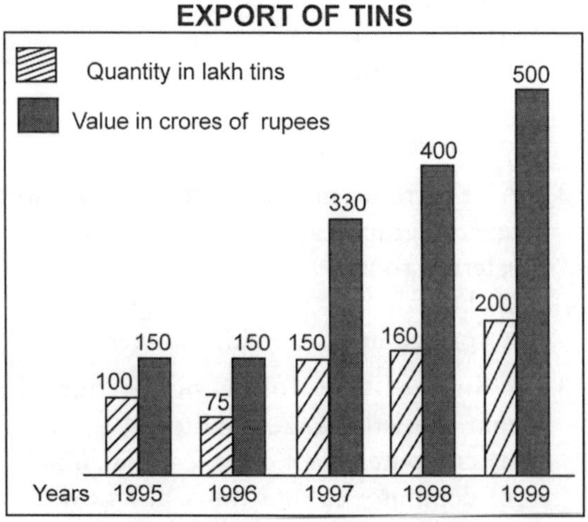

46. In which year the value per tin was minimum?
(a) 1995 (b) 1996
(c) 1998 (d) 1999

47. What was the difference between the tins exported in 1997 and 1998?
(a) 10 (b) 1000
(c) 100000 (d) 1000000

48. What was the approximate percentage increase in export value from 1995 to 1999?
(a) 350 (b) 330.3
(c) 433.3 (d) None of these

49. What was the percentage drop in export quantity from 1995 to 1996?
(a) 75 (b) 50
(c) 25 (d) None of these

50. If in 1998, the tins were exported at the same rate per tin as that in 1997, what would be the value (in crores of rupees) of export in 1998?
(a) 400 (b) 375
(c) 352 (d) 330

ANSWERS

1. (c)	2. (d)	3. (b)	4. (a)	5. (c)
6. (d)	7. (d)	8. (a)	9. (a)	10. (b)
11. (a)	12. (b)	13. (a)	14. (a)	15. (b)
16. (a)	17. (d)	18. (a)	19. (d)	20. (c)
21. (b)	22. (d)	23. (b)	24. (b)	25. (c)
26. (b)	27. (b)	28. (c)	29. (a)	30. (b)
31. (b)	32. (a)	33. (d)	34. (c)	35. (c)
36. (a)	37. (c)	38. (d)	39. (c)	40. (b)
41. (c)	42. (a)	43. (a)	44. (d)	45. (c)
46. (a)	47. (a)	48. (d)	49. (c)	50. (c)

PAPER–II

1. Air quality standards are based on:
(a) Climate and topography
(b) Ambient air quality alone
(c) Dose of a pollutant
(d) Method of measurement

2. The unleaded petrol, as an automotive fuel, should not have the lead levels exceeding:
(a) 0.05 g/L (b) 0.15 g/L
(c) 0.25 g/L (d) 0.50 g/L

3. A major part of air pollution load lies in:
(a) Troposphere (b) Stratosphere
(c) Thermosphere (d) Ionosphere

4. Which is the correct order of the degree of weathering of the following rocks:
(a) Dunite > Basalt > Granite > Rhyolite
(b) Basalt > Dunite > Granite > Rhyolite
(c) Granite > Basalt > Dunite > Rhyolite
(d) Rhyolite > Granite > Dunite > Basalt

5. Interior of the earth is inferred through:
(a) Deep continental drilling
(b) Deep ocean drilling
(c) Seismic soundings
(d) Heat flow measurements

6. The minimum thickness to be used in biodegradable carry bags should be:
(a) 5 microns (b) 10 microns
(c) 15 microns (d) 20 microns

7. The criteria indicators of water pollution are:
(a) pH, COD, BOD, DO
(b) pH, Coliform, COD, DO
(c) Coliform, COD, BOD
(d) BOD, DO, Coliform

8. The cation exchange capacity of silty loams is:
(a) 0 – 1 (b) 1 – 5
(c) 5 – 15 (d) 15 – 30

9. Air Pollution Tolerance Index (APTI) of vegetation is calculated using:
(a) Pb content, SO_2 content and NO_x content in air
(b) Ascorbic acid, total chlorophyl and pH of water content on vegetation
(c) SPM, pH of water and soil types of the area
(d) Landscape of the area; SO_2 and NO_X levels in air

10. The state having the largest forest cover in India is:
(a) Andhra Pradesh (b) Orissa
(c) Maharashtra (d) Chhattisgarh

11. Coal mine workers are prone to victims of one of the following diseases:
(a) Pneumoconiosis (b) Byssinosis
(c) Asbestosis (d) Silicosis

12. The number of oxygen molecules required for the complete combustion of 1 molecule of propane is:
(a) 2 (b) 3
(c) 4 (d) 5

13. Which one of the following is necessary for the growth and maintenance of animal bones and teeth:
(a) Hydrogen (b) Oxygen
(c) Phosphates (d) Sulphur

14. Which of the following organisms are used as components of biofertilisers:
(a) Blue green algae only
(b) Coliform bacteria and mushrooms
(c) N-fixing bacteria only
(d) Blue green algae and N-fixing bacteria

15. Which one of the following photochemical reactions is correct:
(a) $SO_2 \xrightarrow{h\nu} SO_2^*$
(b) $N_2O + h\nu \longrightarrow N_2 + O^*$
(c) $O_3 + h\nu \longrightarrow O + O_2$
(d) $O_2 + h\nu \longrightarrow O_2 + e$

16. **Assertion (A):** CFCs destroy ozone molecules in stratosphere
Reason (R): CFCs have very high global warming potential
(a) Both (A) and (R) are true and (R) is the correct explanation of (A)
(b) Both (A) and (R) are true but (R) is not the correct explanation of (A)
(c) (A) is true; (R) is false
(d) (A) is false; (R) is true

17. Match the List I and List II. Select the correct answer using the codes given below the lists:
List I
A. Environmental Protection Act
B. Air (Prevention and Control of Pollution) Act
C. Water (Prevention and Control of Pollution) Act
D. Public Liability Insurance Act
List II
(i) 1991 (ii) 1974
(iii) 1981 (iv) 1986

Codes:	A	B	C	D
(a)	(i)	(ii)	(iv)	(iii)
(b)	(iv)	(iii)	(ii)	(i)
(c)	(ii)	(iv)	(i)	(iii)
(d)	(iii)	(i)	(ii)	(iv)

18. 2 ppm of CO at 25°C and 760 mm of Hg pressure is equivalent to:
(a) 1250 $\mu g/m^3$ (b) 1145 $\mu g/m^3$
(c) 2500 $\mu g/m^3$ (d) 2290 $\mu g/m^3$

19. 1 kW-hour of energy is equivalent to:
(a) 460 KCal (b) 1250 KCal
(c) 860 KCal (d) 760 KCal

20. The dominant gas in biogas is:
(a) CH_4 (b) C_2H_5
(c) CO_2 (d) NO_2

21. Match the following List I and List II and select the correct answer using the codes given below the lists:

List I	List II
A. Fluvial	(i) Moraines
B. Shallow Marine	(ii) Loess
C. Glacial	(iii) Oxbow lake
D. Eolian	(iv) Spits and Bar

Codes:	A	B	C	D
(a)	(iii)	(iv)	(i)	(ii)
(b)	(i)	(ii)	(iii)	(iv)
(c)	(iv)	(iii)	(ii)	(i)
(d)	(iii)	(iv)	(ii)	(i)

22. Which of the following pairs is not correctly matched?
(a) Tropical zone – Hot, winterless
(b) Sub-tropical zone – Hot with cool winter
(c) Temperate zone – Warm summer with pronounced winter
(d) Alpine zone – Long summer with short severe winter

23. The hydraulic conductivity or the coefficient of permeability of which of the following media is the highest:
(a) Clay (b) Sand
(c) Gravel (d) Sandstone

24. Aquatic organisms are very sensitive to:
(a) Salinity
(b) pH
(c) Temperature
(d) Dissolved oxygen

25. Which of the following acts as a trigger for a landslide to occur:
(a) Vegetation loss
(b) Rainfall
(c) Animal movement
(d) Vehicular movement

26. After sodium chloride, which of the following compounds has the maximum concentration in sea water:
(a) Magnesium sulphate
(b) Calcium sulphate
(c) Magnesium chloride
(d) Potassium sulphate

27. The directions for the regulation, prohibition or the closure of any industry are given by:
(a) State government
(b) Central government
(c) State Pollution Control Board
(d) Central Pollution Control Board

28. Match the List I and List II. Select the correct answer using the codes given below the lists:

List I (Category of Area)
(a) Commercial area
(b) Residential area
(c) Industrial area
(d) Silence zones

List II (Daytime Noise standards in dB)
(i) 75 (ii) 50
(iii) 65 (iv) 55

Codes:	A	B	C	D
(a)	(i)	(ii)	(iv)	(iii)
(b)	(iii)	(iv)	(i)	(ii)
(c)	(iv)	(iii)	(ii)	(i)
(d)	(ii)	(i)	(iv)	(iii)

29. Which of the following sets has the maximum dispersion:
(a) 10, 11, 12, 10, 11, 10, 10, 11, 10, 11
(b) 1, 2, 1, 2, 1, 2, 1, 2, 1, 2
(c) 1, 2, 3, 4, 5, 6, 7, 8, 9, 10
(d) 5, 5, 6, 6, 5, 5, 6, 5, 6, 5

30. Which of the following methods is suitable for hypothesis testing:

(a) Two way analysis of variance
(b) t-test
(c) Cluster Analysis
(d) Correlation and regression

31. Box model is mainly employed for analysing the:
(a) dispersal of atmospheric pollutants
(b) Predictor and Prey populations
(c) Birth and death rates
(d) Discharge of a waste into groundwaters

32. The geometric mean of 2, 2, 3 and 3 is:
(a) 6 (b) $\sqrt{6}$
(c) 5 (d) 1.6

33. Match the List I and List II. Select the correct answer using the codes given below the lists:

List I	List II
(a) Tropical forest	(i) Sunderbans
(b) Conifer forest	(ii) Himachal Pradesh
(c) Mangroves	(iii) Rajasthan
(d) Deciduous forest	(iv) Silent valley

Codes:	A	B	C	D
(a)	(i)	(ii)	(iv)	(iii)
(b)	(ii)	(i)	(iv)	(iii)
(c)	(i)	(iv)	(ii)	(iii)
(d)	(iv)	(ii)	(i)	(iii)

34. Imhoff tank is used for:
(a) Filteration and Flocculation
(b) Sludge digestion and sedimentation
(c) Demineralization
(d) Distillation

35. A solar cell is basically a:
(a) p type semiconductor
(b) n type semiconductor
(c) p-n diode
(d) p-n-p transistor

36. The information system useful to identify the location of a point is:
(a) GIS (b) GPS
(c) Clinometer (d) Compass

37. The global warming potential of N_2O relative to CO_2 is:
(a) 25 (b) 10,000
(c) 0.5 (d) 230

38. The size distribution of aerosols in ambient urban environment tends to follow:
(a) Normal distribution
(b) Exponential distribution
(c) Junge's distribution
(d) Poisson distribution

39. The temperature required to fuse Deuterium and Tritium nuclei is of the order of:
(a) ~ 10^5 °k (b) ~ 10^8 °k
(c) ~ 10^4 °k (d) ~ 10^6 °k

40. Landfill sites can be permitted in:
(a) wetlands
(b) flood plains
(c) habitats of endangered species and recharge zones for local drinking water supplies
(d) abandoned mines with impermeable barrier at the bottom with a leachate recycling system

41. The satellite which has been put into orbit recently capable of producing high resolution thematic data is:
(a) IRS-2D (b) EDUSAT
(c) RESOURCESAT (d) LANDSAT

42. The atmosphere is chemically homogenous upto an altitude of:
(a) 10 km (b) 30 km
(c) 50 km (d) 80 km

43. At which stage of an ecological succession, an ecosystem exhibits total photosynthesis equal to respiration?
(a) Pioneer (b) Climax
(c) Virgin (d) Mid-seral

44. When in a community a species has the same abundance and density, the frequency of the species shall be:
(a) 20% (b) 50%
(c) 90% (d) 100%

45. For determination of primary productivity in a lake, which is the most appropriate time for sampling?
(a) 5 AM (b) 8 AM
(c) 12 Noon (d) 3 PM

46. Which is the best and simple method for determination of fluorine in ground water?
(a) Atomic Absorption spectrometry
(b) Spectrophotometry
(c) Flame photometry
(d) Ion-selective electrode

Read the passage below and answer questions that follow based on your understanding of the passage:

Forests in India are fast disappearing at a rate of about 0.6% per year equivalent to about 7.3 million ha. This renders all the closed tropical forests disappear within 177 years. At this rate of destruction of tropical forests, about 20-25% of the world's plant species would have been lost by the year 2000. By another estimate 90% of tropical forest area containing about 505 varieties of world plant species will be destroyed during the next 20 years. By another estimate 1000 species/year would become extinct. This figure is expected to rise to 10,000 species/year. During the next 20 years, about one million species are likely to disappear.

Loss of biodiversity is severe in agricultural ecosystems too. During green revolution, thousands of wild crop varieties were replaced with a few hybrid species. This resulted in slight disappearance of genetic resources of crop plants, especially of wheat and rice. With the disappearance of the plants, the associated microorganisms and fauna were also lost. Further indiscriminate use of fertilizers and insecticides reduced the microbial species diversity live stock populations are already homogenised and their diversity is extinct.

Much of the fragile breeding and feeding grounds of almost 2/3rd of the world's oceanic fish have been destroyed. Endangered marine life in India lists about 8 species of marine mammals, 5 species of marine turtles, 1 species of hemichordate, 3 species of cephalochordate, 10 species of crab, etc.

Major cause of loss of biodiversity is the expansion of agricultural practices. Biological diversity is replaced by biological uniformity or monoculture in the name of green revolution in agriculture, white revolution in dairying and blue revolution in fisheries. The purpose of all these revolutions is to ensure food security and prevent "hunger disaster".

Biodiversity is also lost due to reclamation for building dams, factories highways, mining operations, etc. in the forested regions. Illegal trade and poaching of wild life also damaged biodiversity. Thus, biodiversity is destroyed by anthropogenic activities.

47. Loss of biodiversity is primarily due to:
(a) Green revolution
(b) White revolution
(c) Blue revolution
(d) Mining Activity

48. Decrease in India's forest cover is attributed mainly to:
(a) Urbanization and Industrialisation
(b) Agriculture and Dairying
(c) Rail and Road Construction
(d) Mining and Power Plants

49. About 90% of tropical forest area containing __________ varieties of world's plant species in the next twenty years.
(a) 7.3 million (b) 505
(c) 10,000 (d) 1000

50. The reduction of microbial species is due to:
    (a) Mining operations
    (b) Application of chemical fertilizers
    (c) Loss of wildlife
    (d) Construction of highways.

ANSWERS

1. (b)	2. (a)	3. (a)	4. (c)	5. (c)
6. (c)	7. (b)	8. (c)	9. (a)	10. (d)
11. (d)	12. (c)	13. (c)	14. (d)	15. (a)
16. (a)	17. (b)	18. (b)	19. (d)	20. (a)
21. (a)	22. (d)	23. (d)	24. (d)	25. (a)
26. (a)	27. (d)	28. (b)	29. (a)	30. (d)
31. (a)	32. (b)	33. (d)	34. (a)	35. (a)
36. (b)	37. (c)	38. (d)	39. (b)	40. (c)
41. (c)	42. (b)	43. (c)	44. (b)	45. (b)
46. (a)	47. (a)	48. (b)	49. (b)	50. (b)

JUNE–2006

Note: This paper contains fifty (50) objective type questions, each question carrying two (2) marks. Attempt all the questions.

PAPER–I

1. Which of the following comprise teaching skill:
   (a) Black Board writing
   (b) Questioning
   (c) Explaining
   (d) All of the above

2. Which of the following statements is most appropriate?
   (a) Teachers can teach.
   (b) Teachers help can create in a student a desire to learn.
   (c) Lecture Method can be used for developing thinking.
   (d) Teachers are born.

3. The first Indian chronicler of Indian history was:
   (a) Megasthanese (b) Fahiyan
   (c) Huan Tsang (d) Kalhan

4. Which of the following statements is correct?
   (a) Syllabus is a part of curriculum.
   (b) Syllabus is an annexure to curriculum.
   (c) Curriculum is the same in all educational institutions affiliated to a particular university.
   (d) Syllabus is not the same in all educational institutions affiliated to a particular university.

5. Which of the two given options is of the level of understanding?
   (I) Define noun.
   (II) Define noun in your own words.
   (a) Only I (b) Only II
   (c) Both I and II (d) Neither I nor II

6. Which of the following options are the main tasks of research in modern society?
   (I) to keep pace with the advancement in knowledge.
   (II) to discover new things.
   (III) to write a critique on the earlier writings.
   (IV) to systematically examine and critically analyse the investigations/sources with objectivity.
   (a) IV, II and I (b) I, II and III
   (c) I and III (d) II, III and IV

7. Match List I (Interviews) with List II (Meaning) and select the correct answer from the codes given below:

   List I (Interviews)
   (A) Structured interviews
   (B) Unstructured interviews
   (C) Focussed interviews
   (D) Clinical interviews

   List II (Meaning)
   (i) Greater flexibility approach
   (ii) Attention on the questions to be answered
   (iii) Individual life experience
   (iv) Pre-determined question
   (v) Non-directive

Codes:	A	B	C	D
(a)	(iv)	(i)	(ii)	(iii)
(b)	(ii)	(iv)	(i)	(iii)
(c)	(v)	(ii)	(iv)	(i)
(d)	(i)	(iii)	(v)	(iv)

8. What do you consider as the main aim of inter disciplinary research?
   (a) To bring out holistic approach to research.
   (b) To reduce the emphasis of single subject in research domain.
   (c) To over simplify the problem of research.
   (d) To create a new trend in research methodology.
9. One of the aims of the scientific method in research is to:
   (a) improve data interpretation
   (b) eliminate spurious relations
   (c) confirm triangulation
   (d) introduce new variables
10. The depth of any research can be judged by:
    (a) title of the research.
    (b) objectives of the research.
    (c) total expenditure on the research.
    (d) duration of the research.

Read the following passage and answer the questions 11 to 15:

The superintendence, direction and control of preparation of electoral rolls for, and the conduct of, elections to Parliament and State Legislatures and elections to the offices of the President and the Vice-President of India are vested in the Election Commission of India. It is an independent constitutional authority.

Independence of the Election Commission and its insulation from executive interference is ensured by a specific provision under Article 324(5) of the constitution that the chief Election Commissioner shall not be removed from his office except in like manner and on like grounds as a Judge of the Supreme Court and conditions of his service shall not be varied to his disadvantage after his appointment.

In C.W.P. No. 4912 of 1998 (Kushra Bharat Vs. Union of India and others), the Delhi High Court directed that information relating to Government dues owed by the candidates to the departments dealing with Government accommodation, electricity, water, telephone and transport, etc. and any other dues should be furnished by the candidates and this information should be published by the election authorities under the commission.

11. The text of the passage reflects or raises certain questions:
    (a) The authority of the commission can not be challenged.
    (b) This would help in stopping the criminalization of Indian politics.
    (c) This would reduce substantially the number of contesting candidates.
    (d) This would ensure fair and free elections.
12. According to the passage, the Election Commission is an independent constitutional authority. This is under Article No.:
    (a) 324 (b) 356
    (c) 246 (d) 161
13. Independence of the Commission means:
    (a) have a constitutional status.
    (b) have legislative powers.
    (c) have judicial powers.
    (d) have political powers.
14. Fair and free election means:
    (a) transparency
    (b) to maintain law and order
    (c) regional considerations
    (d) role for pressure groups

15. The Chief Election Commissioner can be removed from his office under Article:
(a) 125 (b) 352
(c) 226 (d) 324

16. The function of mass communication of supplying information regarding the processes, issues, events and societal developments is known as:
(a) content supply (b) surveillance
(c) gratification (d) correlation

17. The science of the study of feedback systems in humans, animals and machines is known as:
(a) cybernetics
(b) reverse communication
(c) selectivity study
(d) response analysis

18. Networked media exist in inter-connected:
(a) social environments
(b) economic environments
(c) political environments
(d) technological environments

19. The combination of computing, telecommunications and media in a digital atmosphere is referred to as:
(a) online communication
(b) integrated media
(c) digital combine
(d) convergence

20. A dialogue between a human-being and a computer programme that occurs simultaneously in various forms is described as:
(a) man-machine speak
(b) binary chat
(c) digital talk
(d) interactivity

21. Insert the missing number:

$$\frac{16}{32}, \frac{15}{33}, \frac{17}{31}, \frac{14}{34}, ?$$

(a) $\frac{19}{35}$ (b) $\frac{19}{30}$
(c) $\frac{18}{35}$ (d) $\frac{18}{30}$

22. Monday falls on 20th March 1995. What was the day on 3rd November 1994?
(a) Thursday (b) Sunday
(c) Tuesday (d) Saturday

23. The average of four consecutive even numbers is 27. The largest of these numbers is
(a) 36 (b) 32
(c) 30 (d) 28

24. In a certain code, FHQK means GIRL. How will WOMEN be written in the same code?
(a) VNLDM (b) FHQKN
(c) XPNFO (d) VLNDM

25. At what time between 4 and 5 o'clock will the hands of a watch point in opposite directions?
(a) 45 min. past 4
(b) $40\frac{4}{11}$ min. past 4
(c) 50 min. past 4
(d) $54\frac{6}{11}$ min. past 4

26. Which of the following conclusions is logically valid based on statement given below?
Statement: Most teachers are hard working.
Conclusions: (I) Some teachers are hard working.
(II) Some teachers are not hard working.
(a) Only (I) is implied
(b) Only (II) is implied
(c) Both (I) and (II) are implied
(d) Neither (I) nor (II) is implied

27. Who among the following can be asked to make a statement in Indian Parliament?
    (a) Any MLA
    (b) Chief of Army Staff
    (c) Solicitor General of India
    (d) Mayor of Delhi

28. Which of the following conclusions is logically valid based on statement given below?
    Statement: Most of the Indian states existed before independence.
    Conclusions: (I) Some Indian States existed before independence.
    (II) All Indian States did not exist before independence.
    (a) Only (I) is implied
    (b) Only (II) is implied
    (c) Both (I) and (II) are implied
    (d) Neither (I) nor (II) is implied

29. Water is always involved with landslides. This is because it:
    (a) reduces the shear strength of rocks
    (b) increases the weight of the overburden
    (c) enhances chemical weathering
    (d) is a universal solvent

30. Direction for this question:
    Given below are two statements (a) and (b) followed by two conclusions (i) and (ii).
    Considering the statements to be true, indicate which of the following conclusions logically follow from the given statements by selecting one of the four response alternatives given below the conclusion:
    Statements: (a) all businessmen are wealthy.
    (b) all wealthy people are hard working.
    Conclusions: (i) All businessmen are hard working.
    (ii) All hardly working people are not wealthy.
    (a) Only (i) follows
    (b) Only (ii) follows
    (c) Only (i) and (ii) follows
    (d) Neither (i) nor (ii) follows

31. Using websites to pour out one's grievances is called:
    (a) cyberventing (b) cyber ranting
    (c) web hate (d) web plea

32. In web search, finding a large number of documents with very little relevant information is termed:
    (a) poor recall
    (b) web crawl
    (c) poor precision rate
    (d) poor web response

33. The concept of connect intelligence is derived from:
    (a) virtual reality
    (b) fuzzy logic
    (c) bluetooth technology
    (d) value added networks

34. Use of an ordinary telephone as an Internet applicance is called:
    (a) voicenet
    (b) voice telephone
    (c) voice line
    (d) voice portal

35. Video transmission over the Internet that looks like delayed live casting is called:
    (a) virtual video
    (b) direct broadcast
    (c) video shift
    (d) real-time video

36. Which is the smallest North-east State in India?
    (a) Tripura (b) Meghalaya
    (c) Mizoram (d) Manipur

37. Tamil Nadu coastal belt has drinking water shortage due to:
    (a) high evaporation
    (b) sea water flooding due to tsunami
    (c) over exploitation of ground water by tubewells
    (d) seepage of sea water

38. While all rivers of Peninsular India flow into the Bay of Bengal, Narmada and Tapti flow into the Arabian Sea because these two rivers:
    (a) Follow the slope of these rift valleys
    (b) The general slope of the Indian peninsula is from east to west
    (c) The Indian peninsula north of the Satpura ranges, is tilted towards the west
    (d) The Indian peninsula south of the Satpura ranges is tilted towards east

39. Soils in the Mahanadi delta are less fertile than those in the Godavari delta because of:
    (a) erosion of top soils by annual floods
    (b) inundation of land by sea water
    (c) traditional agriculture practices
    (d) the derivation of alluvial soil from red-soil hinterland

40. Which of the following institutions in the field of education is set up by the MHRD Government of India?
    (a) Indian council of world Affair, New Delhi
    (b) Mythic Society, Bangalore
    (c) National Bal Bhawn, New Delhi
    (d) India International Centre, New Delhi

41. **Assertion (A):** Aerosols have potential for modifying climate
    Reason (R): Aerosols interact with both short waves and radiation.
    (a) Both (A) and (R) are true, and (R) is the correct explanation of (A)
    (b) Both (A) and (R) are true, but (R) is not the correct explanation of (A)
    (c) (A) is true, but (R) is false
    (d) (A) is false, but (R) is true

42. 'SITE' stands for:
    (a) System for International technology and Engineering
    (b) Satellite Instructional Television Experiment
    (c) South Indian Trade Estate
    (d) State Institute of Technology and Engineering

43. What is the name of the Research station established by the Indian Government for 'Conducting Research at Antarctic?
    (a) Dakshin Gangotri
    (b) Yamunotri
    (c) Uttari Gangotri
    (d) None of the above

44. Ministry of Human Resource Development (HRD) includes:
    (a) Department of Elementary Education and Literacy
    (b) Department of Secondary Education and Higher Education
    (c) Department of Women and Child Development
    (d) All of the above

45. Parliament can legislate on matters listed in the State list:
    (a) With the prior permission of the President.
    (b) Only after the constitution is amended suitably.
    (c) In case of inconsistency among State legislatures.
    (d) At the request of two or more States.

The following pie chart indicates the expenditure of a country on various sports during a particular year. Study the pie chart and answer Question Number 46 to 50.

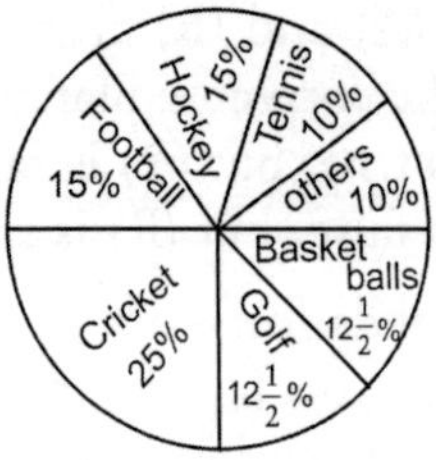

46. The ratio of the total expenditure on football to that of expenditure on hockey is:
    (a) 1 : 15 (b) 1 : 1
    (c) 15 : 1 (d) 3 : 20
47. If the total expenditure on sports during the year was ₹ 1,20,000,00 how much was spent on basket ball?
    (a) ₹ 9,50,000 (b) ₹ 10,00,000
    (c) ₹ 12,00,000 (d) ₹ 15,00,000
48. The chart shows that the most popular game of the country is:
    (a) Hockey (b) Football
    (c) Cricket (d) Tennis
49. Out of the following country's expenditure is the same on:
    (a) Hockey and Tennis
    (b) Golf and Basket ball
    (c) Cricket and Football
    (d) Hockey and Golf
50. If the total expenditure on sport during the year was ₹ 1,50,00,000 the expenditure on cricket and hockey together was:
    (a) ₹ 60,00,000 (b) ₹ 50,00,000
    (c) ₹ 37,50,000 (d) ₹ 25,00,000

ANSWERS

1. (d)	2. (b)	3. (d)	4. (a)	5. (b)
6. (a)	7. (a)	8. (a)	9. (b)	10. (b)
11. (d)	12. (a)	13. (a)	14. (b)	15. (d)
16. (a)	17. (a)	18. (d)	19. (d)	20. (d)
21. (d)	22. (a)	23. (c)	24. (c)	25. (d)
26. (c)	27. (c)	28. (b)	29. (b)	30. (a)
31. (a)	32. (a)	33. (d)	34. (c)	35. (d)
36. (c)	37. (d)	38. (a)	39. (a)	40. (c)
41. (a)	42. (b)	43. (a)	44. (d)	45. (d)
46. (b)	47. (a)	48. (c)	49. (b)	50. (a)

PAPER–II

1. The correct sequence of the decreasing order of abundance of the given elements in the Earth's crust is:
   (a) iron, oxygen, silicon, aluminium
   (b) oxygen, aluminium, silicon, iron
   (c) silicon, oxygen, iron, aluminium
   (d) oxygen, silicon, aluminium, iron
2. Consider the following statement about the Himalayan orogeny:
   (i) The orogeny resulted from the southward movement of the Indian plate
   (ii) The orogeny began about 25 million years ago
   (iii) The orogeny closed about 1 million year ago
   (iv) The Himalaya have a root of relatively light crustal rock projecting in the denser mantle

   Of the statements:
   (a) (i) and (ii) are correct
   (b) (iii) and (iv) are correct
   (c) (i) and (iii) are correct
   (d) (ii) and (iv) are correct
3. Which one of the following statement is true of braided stream?
   (a) Width of channel is less than its depth
   (b) Width and depth of a channel are equal
   (c) Width of channel is greater than the depth
   (d) Width and depth of a channel are unrelated

4. Consider the following pelagic deposits:
   (i) Diatom ooze
   (ii) Globigerina ooze
   (iii) Pteropod ooze
   (iv) Radiolarian ooze

   The correct sequence of occurrence of these pelagic deposits with increasing depth of the ocean is:
   (a) (iii), (ii), (iv), (i)
   (b) (ii), (iii), (i), (iv)
   (c) (iii), (ii), (i), (iv)
   (d) (ii), (iii), (iv), (i)

5. Which one of the following pairs of metals is commonly associated with copper ores?
   (a) Gold and molybdenum
   (b) Tin and lead
   (c) Manganese and chromium
   (d) Platinum and nickel

6. In a vertical section across a sulphide deposit, the site representing the best situation for supergene enrichment would be:
   (a) above the water table
   (b) below the water table
   (c) in the oxidation zone
   (d) in the zone rich in humus

7. Who coined the term "Chronobiology"?
   (a) Franz Halberg
   (b) M.K. Chandrasekhar
   (c) D.S. Farner
   (d) E. Bunning

8. Acid rain is due to:
   (a) production of SO_2 gas
   (b) SO_2 gas converted to H_2SO_4
   (c) production of CO_2
   (d) Hydrocarbon containing varying amount of hydrogen and carbon

9. If nocturnal animal in the light dark cycle of 12 h light and 12 h darkness is kept in constant darkness for 10 days, then what will happen to the onset of its daily activities:
   (a) start earlier than what was before
   (b) start later than what was before
   (c) no change in the activity time
   (d) activities remain on throughout the dark period

10. Whenever there is high BOD, DO is less so much that fish cannot survive, because:
    (a) Fish utilize all oxygen
    (b) Bacteria utilize all oxygen
    (c) Algae utilize all oxygen
    (d) Biological compounds are toxic to fish

11. The drinking water contaminated with *E.Coli* is not safe even after ordinary filtration, but if subjected to RO treatment it is much safe, because:
    (a) RO treatment kills bacteria
    (b) RO treatment generates O_3 that kills bacteria
    (c) There is a filtration at molecular level in RO system
    (d) RO treatment generates chlorine gas that kills bacteria

12. In a water body, there was food chain starting from planton to eagle. 0.3 PPT DDT was the concentration in the water, but in eagle's body it was found to be 25 PPM, This:
    (a) phenomenon is called as bioabsorption
    (b) phenomenon is called as biodesorption
    (c) phenomenon is called as biomagnification
    (d) phenomenon is called as biotransformation

13. For the vehicles using petrol one must carry valid PUC. To get such certificate one must have following parameters, in exhaust, below limits as prescribed by the authorities:

(a) O_2, O_3 and SPM
(b) CO, HC
(c) CO and CO_2
(d) CO, CO_2 and the temperature of the exhaust

14. You are estimating a 'X' compound by colorimetry. Final, stable colour is pink. Which filter you will use to record your reading? Filter having maximum transmission at:
(a) 420 nm (b) 540 nm
(c) 660 nm (d) 700 nm

15. Carbon moxide is poisonous to human because:
(a) It causes mutations
(b) It is very soluble in blood
(c) It is combustible gas
(d) It strongly binds to heme

16. Separation of compounds in Gas Chromatography (GC) depend upon:
(a) Molecular weight
(b) Solubility in carrier gas
(c) Solubility in stationary phase
(d) Solubility in carrier gas and liquid phase

17. To understand the 3D structure of the molecule following technique is used:
(a) X-ray diffraction
(b) Atomic absorption spectrophotometry
(c) MPTLC
(d) GC-MS/MS

18. Which element cannot be estimated by flame photometry?
(a) Na^+ (b) K
(c) Li (d) Fe

19. Electrophoresis cannot resolve molecules like:
(a) Proteins (b) Nucleic Acids
(c) DNA fragments (d) Simple lipids

20. Which of the following instrument is most suitable to estimate heavy metals from the effluent?
(a) Chromatography
(b) Atomic Absorption spectrophotometer
(c) Flame photometer
(d) Electrophoresis

21. Which compound initiates the curling of root hairs in legumes?
(a) IAA (b) Gibberellin
(c) Ethylene oxide (d) Auxin

22. Which one of the following is the microsymbiont in *Azolla-Anabaena* symbiosis?
(a) *Azolla*
(b) *Anabaena*
(c) None of the above
(d) Both (a) and (b)

23. Which of the following bacterium produces Bt toxin?
(a) *Bacillus subtilis*
(b) *Bacillus thrungenesis*
(c) *Bacillus stereothermophillus*
(d) *Bacillus thermoruber*

24. The scientist who got the first patent for genetically modified bacterium used for biodegradation of oil:
(a) Wickerham (b) Chakraborty
(c) Khurana (d) Beijernick

25. Leguminous plants are recommended for rotation of crops, because they:
(a) kill insects
(b) require little amount of water
(c) help in nitrogen fixation
(d) are cash crops

26. The compounds responsible for the proliferation of algal blooms in water bodies are:
(a) Nitrates and chlorides
(b) Nitrates and phosphates
(c) Phosphates and silicates
(d) Nitrates and carbonates

27. Which of the chlorine compound is used for the disinfection of municipal supply water?

(a) Hypochlorite
(b) Calcium chloride
(c) Potassium permanganate
(d) Magnesium chloride

28. The colour of golden rice is due to the presence of:
(a) Vitamin (b) Carotenoid
(c) Flavonoid (d) Dye

29. The fungi most commonly involved in ectomycorrhizal association are:
(a) Basidiomycetes
(b) Ascomycetes
(c) Phycomycetes
(d) Deuteromycetes

30. The pink colouration of the root nodules of leguminous plants is due to:
(a) Hemoglobin (b) Leghemoglobin
(c) Nitrosoamine (d) Bilirubin

31. Upto 100 km, the scale length of the variation in pressure with altitude is:
(a) ~ 12 km (b) ~ 1.8 km
(c) ~ 7 km (d) ~ 3.2 km

32. The third moment of the data set 1, 2, 0, 3, 4 is:
(a) 20 (b) 10
(c) 5 (d) 4

33. If the coefficient of correlation is r, then the coefficient of determination is:
(a) $\sqrt{r}$ (b) 10
(c) r (d) $\frac{1}{r^2}$

34. For a Binomial distribution if p is the probability of happening of an event and q = 1 – p, then the variance in a sample of N observations would be:
(a) Npq (b) $\sqrt{Npq}$
(c) $\sqrt{N}/pq$ (d) $pq/\sqrt{N-1}$

35. In fusion reaction involving Deuterium atoms $D + D = He^3 + n + X$, the energy released X is:
(a) ~ 17.6 MeV (b) ~ 3.2 MeV
(c) ~ 1 MeV (d) ~ 4 MeV

36. Which of the following noise indices is used in ascertaining the quality of noise environment according to WHO standards?
(a) L_{50}
(b) L_{10}
(c) L_{eq} for 8 hours
(d) Instantaneous sound pressure level

37. The contribution of CO_2 in climate change is estimated to be about:
(a) ~ 57% (b) ~ 85%
(c) ~ 90% (d) ~ 80%

38. Cost-Benefit Analysis seeks to analyse cost and benefits of a project in terms of:
(a) Monetary gains
(b) Social gain/loss
(c) Environmental and monetary gains/losses
(d) Social and Environmental costs and gains

39. The size distribution of suspended particulate matter in urban environment tends to follow which of the following distributions:
(a) Binomial (b) Poisson
(c) Normal (d) Log normal

40. An increase of 1 ppm in atmospheric concentration of CO_2 corresponds to an increase of carbon in atmosphere equivalent to an amount:
(a) ~ 5.1×10^6 Tons
(b) ~ 12.5×10^6 Tons
(c) ~ 1.4×10^9 Tons
(d) ~ 2.12 Gigatons

41. Precautionary principle is a guiding rule in:
(a) Cost benefit analysis
(b) Cost effective analysis
(c) Environmental impact analysis
(d) Environmental Audit

42. A company or organization can go to ISO 14000 certification provided it has an ongoing Environmental Management System in operation for at least:
(a) 3 months (b) 6 months
(c) 1 year (d) 5 years

43. The National ambient air quality standard for Respirable Suspended Particulate Matter (RSPM) in residential area recommends annual average concentrations in (μg/m^3) not exceeding:
(a) 100 μg/m^3 (b) 200 μg/m^3
(c) 400 μg/m^3 (d) 500 μg/m^3

44. For dumping of radio active nuclear waste which of the following is the recommended site:
(a) Saltmines (b) Oceans
(c) Deserts (d) River beds

45. Which of the following coal types has the highest calorific value?
(a) Peat (b) Lignite
(c) Anthracite (d) Bituminous

46. Which is the largest ecosystem in the world?
(a) Forests (b) Deserts
(c) Oceans (d) Rivers

47. Which is the most abundant element in hot water springs?
(a) Nitrogen (b) Sulphur
(c) Carbon (d) Phosphorous

48. **Assertion (A):** Tropospheric ozone exists in urban areas.
Reason (R): The photochemical reactions involving oxides of nitrogen produces O_3.
(a) Both (A) and (R) are true and (R) is the correct explanation of (A)
(b) Both (A) and (R) are true but (R) is not the correct explanation of (A)
(c) (A) is true but (R) is false
(d) (A) is false but (R) is true

49. A protein can be formed from any sequence of amino acids. How many different sequences can be obtained from a protein composed of 100 amino acids?
(a) 100 (b) 100^{20}
(c) 100^{40} (d) 20^{100}

50. The last Earth Summit was held in which city?
(a) Rio de Janeiro (b) Kyoto
(c) Hague (d) Johannesburg

ANSWERS

1. (d)	2. (d)	3. (c)	4. (c)	5. (d)
6. (b)	7. (a)	8. (b)	9. (d)	10. (b)
11. (c)	12. (c)	13. (c)	14. (d)	15. (b)
16. (d)	17. (a)	18. (c)	19. (d)	20. (b)
21. (a)	22. (d)	23. (b)	24. (d)	25. (c)
26. (c)	27. (c)	28. (c)	29. (b)	30. (b)
31. (d)	32. (c)	33. (a)	34. (b)	35. (a)
36. (c)	37. (a)	38. (c)	39. (c)	40. (b)
41. (c)	42. (b)	43. (a)	44. (a)	45. (c)
46. (c)	47. (b)	48. (a)	49. (d)	50. (b)

DECEMBER–2006

Note: This paper contains fifty (50) objective type questions, each question carrying two (2) marks. Attempt all the questions.

PAPER–I

1. Which of the following is not instructional material?
   (a) Over Head Projector
   (b) Audio Cassette
   (c) Printed Material
   (d) Transparency

2. Which of the following statement is not correct?
   (a) Lecture Method can develop reasoning
   (b) Lecture Method can develop knowledge
   (c) Lecture Method is one way process
   (d) During Lecture Method students are passive

3. The main objective of teaching at Higher Education Level is:
   (a) To prepare students to pass examination
   (b) To develop the capacity to take decisions
   (c) To give new information
   (d) To motivate students to ask questions during lecture

4. Which of the following statement is correct?
   (a) Reliability ensures validity
   (b) Validity ensures reliability
   (c) Reliability and validity are independent of each other
   (d) Reliability does not depend on objectivity

5. Which of the following indicates evaluation?
   (a) Ram got 45 marks out of 200
   (b) Mohan got 38 percent marks in English
   (c) Shyam got First Division in final examination
   (d) All of the above

6. Research can be conducted by a person who:
   (a) has studied research methodology
   (b) holds a postgraduate degree
   (c) possesses thinking and reasoning ability
   (d) is a hard worker

7. Which of the following statements is correct?
   (a) Objectives of research are stated in first chapter of the thesis
   (b) Researcher must possess analytical ability
   (c) Variability is the source of problem
   (d) All of the above

8. Which of the following is not the Method of Research?
   (a) Observation (b) Historical
   (c) Survey (d) Philosophical

9. Research can be classified as:
   (a) Basic, Applied and Action Research
   (b) Quantitative and Qualitative Research
   (c) Philosophical, Historical, Survey and Experimental Research
   (d) All of the above

10. The first step of research is:
    (a) Selecting a problem
    (b) Searching a problem
    (c) Finding a problem
    (d) Identifying a problem

Read the following passage and answer the question nos. 11 to 15:

After almost three decades of contemplating Swarovski-encrusted navels on increasing flat abs, the Mumbai film industry is on a discovery of India and itself. With budgets of over 30 crore each, four soon to be released movies by premier directors are exploring the idea of who we are and redefining who the other is. It is a fundamental question which the bling-bling, glam-sham and disham-disham tends to avoid. It is also a question which binds an audience when the lights go dim and the projector rolls: as a nation, who are we? As a people, where are we going?

The Germans coined a word for it, zeitgeist, which perhaps Yash Chopra would not care to pronounce. But at 72, he remains the person who can best capture it. After being the first to project the diasporic Indian on screen in Lamhe in 1991, he has returned to his roots in a new movie. Veer Zaara, set in 1986, where Pakistan, the traditional other, the part that got away, is the lover and the saviour. In Subhash Ghai's Kisna, set in 1947, the other is the English woman. She is not a memsahib, but a mehbooba. In Ketan Mehta's The Rising, the East India Englishman is not the evil oppressor of countless cardboard characterisations, which span the spectrum from Jewel in the Crown to Kranti, but an honourable friend.

This is Manoj Kumar's Desh Ki Dharti with a difference: there is culture, not contentious politics; balle balle, not bombs: no dooriyan (distance), only nazdeekiyan (closeness).

All four films are heralding a new hero and heroine. The new hero is fallible and vulnerable, committed to his dharma, but also not afraid of failure—less of a boy and more of a man. He even has a grown up name: Veer Pratap Singh in Veer Zaara and Mohan Bhargav in Swades. The new heroine is not a babe, but often a bebe, dressed in traditional Punjabi clothes, often with the stereotypical body type as well as in Bride and Prejudice of Gurinder Chadha.

11. Which word Yash Chopra would not be able to pronounce?
    (a) Bling + bling (b) Zeitgeist
    (c) Montaz (d) Dooriyan
12. Who made Lamhe in 1991?
    (a) Subhash Ghai (b) Yash Chopra
    (c) Aditya Chopra (d) Sakti Samanta
13. Which movie is associated with Manoj Kumar?
    (a) Jewel in the Crown
    (b) Kisna
    (c) Zaara
    (d) Desh Ki Dharti
14. Which is the latest film by Yash Chopra?
    (a) Deewar
    (b) Kabhi Kabhi
    (c) Dilwale Dulhaniya Le Jayenge
    (d) Veer Zaara
15. Which is the dress of the heroine in Veer Zaara?
    (a) Traditional Gujarati Clothes
    (b) Traditional Bengali Clothes
    (c) Traditional Punjabi Clothes
    (d) Traditional Madrasi Clothes
16. Which one of the following can be termed as verbal communication?
    (a) Prof. Sharma delivered the lecture in the classroom.
    (b) Signal at the cross-road changed from green to orange.
    (c) The child was crying to attract the attention of the mother.
    (d) Dipak wrote a letter for leave application.

17. Which is the 24 hours English Business news channel in India?
(a) Zee News (b) NDTV 24×7
(c) CNBC (d) India News

18. Consider the following statements in communication:
(i) Hema Malini is the Chairperson of the Children's Film Society, India.
(ii) Yash Chopra is the Chairman of the Central Board of Film Certification of India.
(iii) Sharmila Tagore is the Chairperson of National Film Development Corporation.
(iv) Dilip Kumar, Raj Kapoor and Preeti Zinta have all been recipients of Dada Saheb Phalke Award.

Which of the statements given above is/ are correct?
(a) (i) and (iii) (b) (ii) and (iii)
(c) (iv) only (d) (iii) only

19. Which of the following pair is not correctly matched?
(a) N. Ram : The Hindu
(b) Barkha Dutt : Zee News
(c) Pranay Roy : NDTV 24×7
(d) Prabhu Chawla : Aaj taak

20. "Because you deserve to know" is the punchline used by:
(a) *The Times of India*
(b) *The Hindu*
(c) *Indian Express*
(d) *Hindustan Times*

21. In the sequence of numbers 8, 24, 12, X, 18, 54 the missing number X is:
(a) 26 (b) 24
(c) 36 (d) 32

22. If A stands for 5, B for 6, C for 7, D for 8 and so on, then the following numbers stand for 17, 19, 20, 9 and 8:
(a) PLANE (b) MOPED
(c) MOTOR (d) TONGA

23. The letters in the first set have certain relationship. On the basis of this relationship what is the right choice for the second set?

AST : BRU : : NQV : ?
(a) ORW (b) MPU
(c) MRW (d) OPW

24. In a certain code, PAN is written as 31 and PAR as 35. In this code PAT is written as:
(a) 30 (b) 37
(c) 38 (d) 39

25. The sides of a triangle are in the ratio of $\frac{1}{2}:\frac{1}{3}:\frac{1}{4}$. If its perimeter is 52 cm, the length of the smallest side is:
(a) 9 cm (b) 10 cm
(c) 11 cm (d) 12 cm

26. Which one of the following statements is completely non-sensible?
(a) He was a bachelor, but he married recently.
(b) He is a bachelor, but he married recently.
(c) When he married, he was not a bachelor.
(d) When he was a bachelor, he was not married.

27. Which of the following statements are mutually contradictory?
(i) All flowers are not fragrant.
(ii) Most flowers are not fragrant.
(iii) None of the flowers is fragrant.
(iv) Most flowers are fragrant.

Choose the correct answer from the codes given below:

Codes:
(a) (i) and (ii) (b) (i) and (iii)
(c) (ii) and (iii) (d) (iii) and (iv)

28. Which of the following statements say the same thing?

(i) "I am a teacher" (said by Arvind)
(ii) "I am a teacher" (said by Binod)
(iii) "My son is a teacher" (said by Binod's father)
(iv) "My brother is a teacher" (said by Binod's sister)
(v) "My brother is a teacher" (said by Binod's only sister)
(vi) "My sole enemy is a teacher" (said by Binod's only enemy)

Choose the correct answer from the codes given below:

Codes:

(a) (i) and (ii)
(b) (ii), (iii), (iv) and (v)
(c) (ii) and (vi)
(d) (v) and (vi)

29. Which of the following are correct ways of arguing?
(i) There can be no second husband without a second wife.
(ii) Anil is a friend of Bob, Bob is a friend of Raj, hence Anil is a friend of Raj.
(iii) A is equal to B, B is equal to C, hence A is equal to C.
(iv) If everyone is a liar, then we cannot prove it.

Choose the correct answer from the codes given below:

Codes:

(a) (iii) and (iv)
(b) (i), (iii) and (iv)
(c) (ii), (iii) and (iv)
(d) (i), (ii), (iii) and (iv)

30. Which of the following statement/s are ALWAYS FALSE?
(i) The sun will not rise in the East some day.
(ii) A wooden table is not a table.
(iii) Delhi city will be drowned under water.
(iv) Cars run on water as fuel.

Choose the correct answer from the codes given below:

Codes:

(a) (i), (iii) and (iv) (b) Only (iii)
(c) (i), (ii) and (iii) (d) (ii) alone

Study the following graph and answer question numbers 31 to 33:

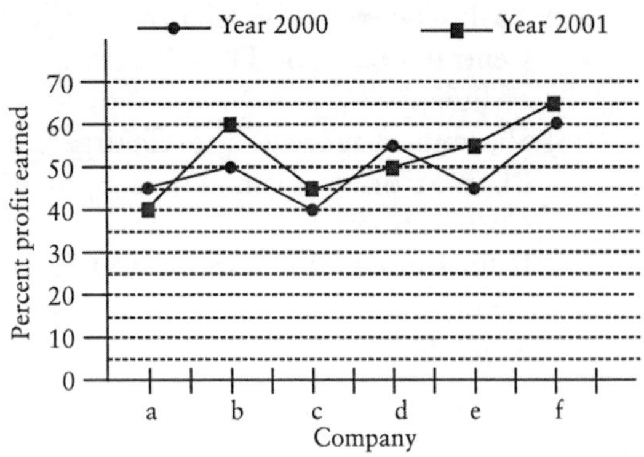

31. In the year 2000, which of the following Companies earned maximum percent profit?
(a) a (b) b
(c) d (d) f

32. In the year 2001, which of the following Companies earned minimum percent profit?
(a) a (b) c
(c) d (d) e

33. In the years 2000 and 2001, which of the following Companies earned maximum average percent profit?
(a) f (b) e
(c) d (d) b

34. Human Development Report for 'each' of the year at global level has been published by:
(a) UNDP (b) WTO
(c) IMF (d) World Bank

35. The number of students in four classes A, B, C, D and their respective mean marks obtained by each of the class are given below:

	Class A	Class B	Class C	Class D
Number of students	10	40	30	20
Arithmetic mean	20	30	50	15

The combined mean of the marks of four classes together will be:
(a) 32 (b) 50
(c) 20 (d) 15

36. LAN stands for:
(a) Local And National
(b) Local Area Network
(c) Large Area Network
(d) Live Area Network

37. Which of the following statement is correct?
(a) Modem is a software
(b) Modem helps in stabilizing the voltage
(c) Modem is the operating system
(d) Modem converts the analog signal into digital signal and vice-versa

38. Which of the following is the appropriate definition of a computer?
(a) Computer is a machine that can process information.
(b) Computer is an electronic device that can store, retrieve and process both qualitative and quantitative data quickly and accurately.
(c) Computer is an electronic device that can store, retrieve and quickly process only quantitative data.
(d) Computer is a machine that can store, retrieve and process quickly and accurately only qualitative information.

39. Information and Communication Technology includes:
(a) On line learning
(b) Learning through the use of EDUSAT
(c) Web Based Learning
(d) All of the above

40. Which of the following is the appropriate format of URL of e-mail?
(a) www_mail.com
(b) www@mail.com
(c) WWW@mail.com
(d) www.mail.com

41. The most significant impact of volcanic erouption has been felt in the form of:
(a) change in weather
(b) sinking of islands
(c) loss of vegetation
(d) extinction of animals

42. With absorption and decomposition of CO_2 in ocean water beyond desired level, there will be:
(a) decrease in temperature
(b) increase in salinity
(c) growth of phyto plankton
(d) rise in sea level

43. Arrange column II in proper sequence so as to match it with column I and choose the correct answer from the codes given below:

Column I Water Quality	Column II pH Value
(A) Neutral	(i) 5
(B) Moderately acidic	(ii) 7
(C) Alkaline	(iii) 4
(D) Injurious	(iv) 8

Codes:	(A)	(B)	(C)	(D)
(a)	(ii)	(iii)	(i)	(iv)
(b)	(i)	(iii)	(ii)	(iv)
(c)	(ii)	(i)	(iv)	(iii)
(d)	(iv)	(ii)	(iii)	(i)

44. The maximum emission of pollutants from fuel sources in India is caused by:
(a) Coal
(b) Firewood

(c) Refuse burning
(d) Vegetable waste product

45. The urbanisation process accounts for the wind in the urban centres during nights to remain:
(a) faster than that in rural areas
(b) slower than that in rural areas
(c) the same as that in rural areas
(d) cooler than that in rural areas

46. The University Grants Commission was constituted on the recommendation of:
(a) Dr. Sarvapalli Radhakrishnan Commission
(b) Mudaliar Commission
(c) Sargent Commission
(d) Kothari Commission

47. Which one of the following Articles of the Constitution of India safeguards the rights of Minorities to establish and run educational institutions of their own liking?
(a) Article 19 (b) Article 29
(c) Article 30 (d) Article 31

48. Match List I (Institutions) with List II (Functions) and select the correct answer by using the codes given below:

List I (Institutions)
(A) Parliament
(B) C & A.G.
(C) Ministry of Finance
(D) Executing Departments

List II (Functions)
(i) Formulation of Budget
(ii) Enactment of Budget
(iii) Implementation of Budget
(iv) Legality of expenditure
(v) Justification of Income

Codes:	**(A)**	**(B)**	**(C)**	**(D)**
(a)	(iii)	(iv)	(ii)	(i)
(b)	(ii)	(iv)	(i)	(iii)
(c)	(v)	(iii)	(iv)	(ii)
(d)	(iv)	(ii)	(iii)	(v)

49. Foundation training to the newly recruited IAS (Probationers) is imparted by:
(a) Indian Institute of Public Administration
(b) Administrative Staff College of India
(c) L.B.S. National Academy of Administration
(d) Centre for Advanced Studies

50. Electoral disputes arising out of Presidential and Vice-Presidential Elections are settled by:
(a) Election Commission of India
(b) Joint Committee of Parliament
(c) Supreme Court of India
(d) Central Election Tribunal

ANSWERS

1. (d)	2. (a)	3. (b)	4. (b)	5. (d)
6. (c)	7. (d)	8. (b)	9. (d)	10. (d)
11. (b)	12. (b)	13. (d)	14. (d)	15. (c)
16. (c)	17. (c)	18. (d)	19. (b)	20. (d)
21. (c)	22. (b)	23. (d)	24. (b)	25. (d)
26. (b)	27. (b)	28. (b)	29. (a)	30. (d)
31. (d)	32. (a)	33. (a)	34. (a)	35. (a)
36. (b)	37. (d)	38. (b)	39. (d)	40. (b)
41. (a)	42. (c)	43. (c)	44. (c)	45. (b)
46. (a)	47. (c)	48. (b)	49. (c)	50. (c)

PAPER–II

1. Due to Corriolis effect, wind in the:
(a) Northern Hemisphere moves to the left with respect to the rotating earth.
(b) Northern Hemisphere moves to the right.
(c) Southern Hemisphere moves northward.
(d) Both Hemispheres move independently of each other.

2. Precipitation of $CaCO_3$ may occur when:
   (a) Sea water is shallow and CO_2 is lost.
   (b) Sea water is warm and CO_2 is being lost.
   (c) Sea water is cold and CO_2 is being lost.
   (d) Sea water is deep and CO_2 is being added.

3. CO_2 in soil and CO_2 in atmosphere differ:
   (a) by a factor of 2 (b) by a factor of 1
   (c) by a factor of 3.5 (d) by a factor of 4

4. Consider the earth to be a blackbody with average temperature 15°C and surface area 5.1×10^{14} m^2. Find the rate at which energy is radiated by the earth and the wave length at which maximum power is radiated.
   (Hint: Stefan-Boltzman Constant = 5.67×10^{-8} W/m^2-K^4 and use Wien's Rule)
   (a) 4×10^{17} W, 2.02 μm
   (b) 1×10^{17} W, 5.1 μm
   (c) 1.5×10^{17} W, 7.5 μm
   (d) 2×10^{17} W, 10.1 μm

5. Trapping plume occurs when:
   (a) Temperature increases with height.
   (b) Temperature decreases with height.
   (c) Temperature remains steady with height.
   (d) Plume lies in a lapse region and sandwiched between inversion layers.

6. The pH of a solution containing hydrogen ions concentration of 10^{-5} mol/L is:
   (a) 5.0 (b) 7.0
   (c) 2.0 (d) 9.0

7. Malathion is:
   (a) Organo Phosphorus Pesticide
   (b) Organo Chloro Pesticide
   (c) Organo Carbamate Pesticide
   (d) Not a Pesticide

8. Critical point for water in a P-T diagram suggests: (One statement only is correct)
   (a) Water is unstable
   (b) Steam is the only stable phase
   (c) Both ice and steam are stable phases
   (d) Steam, liquid water and ice are stable phases

9. The range of pH for river water in India is:
   (a) 1 - 14 (b) 4 - 5
   (c) 6.5 - 8.0 (d) 7 - 12

10. In all fresh water in India, the dominant ion is:
    (a) HCO_3^- (b) Cl^-
    (c) Ca^{+2} (d) SO_4^{-2}

11. Ozone toxicity to plants is generally due to the involvement of which unsaturated hydrocarbons:
    (a) Unsaturated fatty acid
    (b) Methylene
    (c) Ethylene
    (d) None of the above

12. In vitro pollen germination is inhibited by:
    (a) SO_2 (b) O_3
    (c) Both of the above (d) None of these

13. Which one of the following is the most productive ecosystem?
    (a) Oligotrophic lake (b) High Sea
    (c) Estuary (d) Savanna

14. Vermiculture technology is used in:
    (a) Production of Fish
    (b) Animal Husbandary
    (c) Poultry Farming
    (d) Organic Farming

15. Which one of the following sequence represent increasing order of toxicity of metals?
    (a) Ca, Zn, Cd, Mn
    (b) Ca, Mn, Zn, Cd
    (c) Zn, Mn, Cd, Ca
    (d) Mn, Cd, Zn, Ca

16. Energy flow in an ecosystem is:
(a) Cyclic (b) Multidirectional
(c) Sequential (d) Unidirectional

17. Removal of key-stone species would cause:
(a) Drastic change in community composition
(b) Drastic change in ecological system
(c) Drastic change in food chain
(d) Drastic change in energy flow

18. Match List I and List II and select correct answer:

List I	**List II**
A. Mesozoic	(i) Tertiary
B. Proterozoic	(ii) Triassic
C. Cenozoic	(iii) Pre Cambrian
D. Paleozoic	(iv) Permian

Codes:	**A**	**B**	**C**	**D**
(a)	(iii)	(ii)	(i)	(iv)
(b)	(ii)	(iii)	(i)	(iv)
(c)	(ii)	(iii)	(iv)	(i)
(d)	(iii)	(ii)	(iv)	(i)

19. Correct order of increasing energy content for various types of coal is:
(a) Anthracite, Peat, Bit-coal, Lignite
(b) Lignite, Peat, Bit-coal, Anthracite
(c) Peat, Lignite, Bit-coal, Anthracite
(d) Peat, Lignite, Anthracite, Bit-coal

20. Silica content of granodiorite is in the range of:
(a) 22 - 44 % (b) 66 - 88 %
(c) 44 - 56 % (d) 44 - 66 %

21. Formation of sedimentary chalcopyrite requires:
(a) High pH, high Eh (b) Low pH, high Eh
(c) Only low Eh (d) Low Eh, low pH

22. Bowen's law basically tell us:
(a) How a sedimentary rock is formed
(b) How various igneous minerals are formed
(c) How some economic minerals are formed
(d) Both (a) and (b) are correct

23. Match the 24 hourly average ambient air quality standards from List I and List II:

List I	**List II**
A. Sulphur dioxide	(i) 100 μg/m³
B. Oxides of nitrogen	(ii) 200 μg/m³
C. Suspended particulate matter	(iii) 80 μg/m³
D. Respirable particulate matter	(iv) 20 μg/m³

Codes:	**A**	**B**	**C**	**D**
(a)	(iii)	(iv)	(ii)	(i)
(b)	(iv)	(iii)	(i)	(ii)
(c)	(iii)	(i)	(iv)	(ii)
(d)	(i)	(ii)	(iii)	(iv)

24. The most abundant alkaline component of the atmosphere is:
(a) Ammonia (b) Nitrogen
(c) Sulphur dioxide (d) Carbon dioxide

25. The faecal indicator bacteria is:
(a) *Staphylococeus aureus*
(b) *Streptococeus faecalis*
(c) *Ercherichia coli*
(d) *Salmonella typhi*

26. The maximum permissible level of BOD (mg/L) in waste water that is let into river is:
(a) 20 (b) 30
(c) 40 (d) 10

27. Coral reefs are vulnerable to:
(a) Siltation (b) Flood water
(c) Nutrients (d) Salt flow

28. **Assertion (A):** The mangroves are nursery ground for fish and larvae.
Reason (R): The mangroves are covered with mangrove plants that enrich the environment.
(a) Both (A) and (R) are true and (R) is the correct explanation of (A)
(b) Both (A) and (R) are true but (R) is not the correct explanation of (A)
(c) (A) is true but (R) is false
(d) (A) is false but (R) is true

29. In an industrial environment what is the single most important factor in an accident prevention programme?
(a) A written programme
(b) Training
(c) Safety engineers
(d) Management support

30. Match the following List I and List II and select the correct answer using the codes given below:

List I
A. Public hearing is required
B. Public hearing is not required
C. Baseline air quality data is collected
D. Baseline noise level data is collected

List II
(i) Modernisation of existing irrigation projects
(ii) Highway projects
(iii) Once in each season
(iv) 24 hourly twice a week

Codes:	A	B	C	D
(a)	(i)	(iv)	(ii)	(iii)
(b)	(ii)	(i)	(iv)	(iii)
(c)	(iii)	(i)	(iv)	(ii)
(d)	(iv)	(iii)	(i)	(ii)

31. All lands with tree cover of canopy density of 40% and above is notified as:
(a) Scrub (b) Open forest
(c) Dense forest (d) Forest cover

32. Match the List I and List II and select the correct answer using the codes given below:

List I (Power generation capacity)
A. 500 MW and more
B. 200/210 MW and above but less than 500 MW
C. less than 200/210 MW
D. steam generation capacity less than 8.5 MT

List II (Stack height (m))
(i) $H = 14 (Q)^{0.3}$ (ii) 275
(iii) 220 (iv) 9

Note: H = Physical stack height in metres
Q = Emission rate of SO_2 in kg/hr.

Codes:	A	B	C	D
(a)	(i)	(ii)	(iii)	(iv)
(b)	(ii)	(iii)	(i)	(iv)
(c)	(iii)	(iv)	(ii)	(i)
(d)	(iv)	(i)	(ii)	(iii)

33. The Water (Prevention and Control of Pollution) Act 1974 ....
(a) Regulates the discharge of hazardous pollutants into the nations surface water.
(b) Regulates the emission of hazardous air pollutants.
(c) Regulates waste disposal of sea.
(d) Regulates the transportation of hazardous materials.

34. The harmonic mean of the numbers 0, 2, 4, 6 is:
(a) 3 (b) 0
(c) 2 (d) 1

35. **Assertion (A):** Wetlands are often described as ecotones.
Reason (R): Wetlands are biologically rich dynamic zones of transition between two different ecosystems.
(a) Both (A) and (R) are true and (R) is the correct explanation of (A)
(b) Both (A) and (R) are true but (R) is not the correct explanation of (A)
(c) (A) is true but (R) is false
(d) (A) is false but (R) is true

36. The first National Park established in India is:
(a) Indira Gandhi National Park
(b) Indravati National Park
(c) Corbett National Park
(d) Kaziranga National Park

37. The main pollutant in vehicle emission is:
(a) CO (b) CO_2
(c) SO_2 (d) SO_3

38. A device fitted to the exhaust system of a petrol driven motor vehicle to reduce emissions of pollutants is called as:
(a) Conversion System
(b) Conversion Kit
(c) Catalytic Converter
(d) Catalytic Box

39. The particle A in the following equation is:

$$^{238}_{92}U + A \rightarrow ^{239}_{92}U$$

(a) p (b) e
(c) n (d) α

40. The average solar constant is:
(a) 2.2 cal/cm^2/sec
(b) 4.5 cal/cm^2/sec
(c) 2.2 k cal/cm^2/sec
(d) 1.36 kw/m^2

41. Which one of the following group of plants is most resistant to ionising radiations?
(a) Coniferous Forest
(b) Grass Land
(c) Lichen and Mosses
(d) Mixed Forest

42. How many moles of oxygen are required to burn one mole of propane?
(a) 2 (b) 3
(c) 4 (d) 5

43. What percentage of India's population lives in Urban Centres.
(a) 20 (b) 30
(c) 10 (d) 50

44. The recent asbestos controversy about the French ship going to Alang was primarily due to:
(a) Violation of Indian Coastal Zone Laws.
(b) Violation of Transnational Movement of Hazardous Waste.
(c) Gujarat State Pollution Control Laws.
(d) Indian Air Pollution Laws.

45. Due to the increasing energy use the ozone layer over the arctic is:
(a) Increasing
(b) Decreasing
(c) Not shifting in size
(d) Not affected at all

46. Ecological restoration of degraded sites are aimed to:
(a) Restore all biophysical characteristics of pristine ecosystem.
(b) Restore social desirable and economically feasible characteristics of original ecosystem.
(c) Leave it alone and allow natural regeneration.
(d) Prohibit all human activity in the area.

47. The first Environmental Law in India was enacted in:
(a) 1947 (b) 1950
(c) 1972 (d) 1982

48. The permissible Arsenic levels in drinking water is:
(a) 20 μg/L (b) 50 μg/L
(c) 75 μg/L (d) 50 mg/L

49. The mean annual rainfall in India is:
(a) 110 mm (b) 110 cm
(c) 85 cm (d) 110 m

50. The median of a set of numbers 2, 5, 8, 10, 12, 16, 20, 23:
(a) 10 (b) 12
(c) 12.5 (d) 9

ANSWERS

1. (a)	2. (a)	3. (d)	4. (b)	5. (d)	26. (d)	27. (c)	28. (b)	29. (b)	30. (b)
6. (a)	7. (a)	8. (d)	9. (c)	10. (a)	31. (b)	32. (b)	33. (a)	34. (b)	35. (c)
11. (b)	12. (b)	13. (d)	14. (d)	15. (b)	36. (c)	37. (b)	38. (c)	39. (b)	40. (d)
16. (d)	17. (a)	18. (b)	19. (c)	20. (a)	41. (c)	42. (b)	43. (b)	44. (b)	45. (b)
21. (b)	22. (d)	23. (a)	24. (b)	25. (c)	46. (a)	47. (b)	48. (a)	49. (b)	50. (b)

JUNE–2007

Note: This paper contains Fifty (50) multiple-choice questions, each question carrying two (2) marks. Attempt all of them.

PAPER–I

1. Teacher uses visual-aids to make learning
   (a) simple
   (b) more knowledgeable
   (c) quicker
   (d) interesting
2. The teacher's role at the higher educational level is to
   (a) provide information to students
   (b) promote self-learning in students
   (c) encourage healthy competition among students
   (d) help students to solve their personal problems
3. Which one of the following teachers would you like the most?
   (a) Punctual
   (b) Having research aptitude
   (c) Loving and having high idealistic philosophy
   (d) Who often amuses his students
4. Micro teaching is most effective for the student-teacher
   (a) during the practice-teaching
   (b) after the practice-teaching
   (c) before the practice-teaching
   (d) None of the above
5. Which is the least important factor in teaching?
   (a) Punishing the students
   (b) Maintaining discipline in the class
   (c) Lecturing in impressive way
   (d) Drawing sketches and diagrams on the blackboard
6. To test null hypothesis, a researcher uses
   (a) t test (b) ANOVA
   (c) χ^2 (d) factorial analysis
7. A research problem is feasible only when
   (a) it has utility and relevance
   (b) it is researchable
   (c) it is new and adds something to knowledge
   (d) All of the above
8. Bibliography given in a research report
   (a) shows vast knowledge of the researcher
   (b) helps those interested in further research
   (c) has no relevance to research
   (d) All of the above
9. Fundamental research reflects the ability to
   (a) Synthesise new ideals
   (b) Expound new principles
   (c) Evaluate the existing material concerning research
   (d) Study the existing literature regarding various topics
10. The study in which the investigators attempt to trace an effect is known as
    (a) Survey Research
    (b) *Ex-post Facto* Research

(c) Historical Research
(d) Summative Research

Read the following passage and answer the questions 11 to 15:

All political systems need to mediate the relationship between private wealth and public power. Those that fail risk a dysfunctional government captured by wealthy interests. Corruption is one symptom of such failure with private willingness-to-pay trumping public goals. Private individuals and business firms pay to get routine services and to get to the head of the bureaucratic queue. They pay to limit their taxes, avoid costly regulations, obtain contracts at inflated prices and get concessions and privatised firms at low prices. If corruption is endemic, public officials—both bureaucrats and elected officials—may redesign programs and propose public projects with few public benefits and many opportunities for private profit. Of course, corruption, in the sense of bribes, pay-offs and kickbacks, is only one type of government failure. Efforts to promote 'good governance' must be broader than anti-corruption campaigns. Governments may be honest but inefficient because no one has an incentive to work productively, and narrow elites may capture the state and exert excess influence on policy. Bribery may induce the lazy to work hard and permit those not in the inner circle of cronies to obtain benefits. However, even in such cases, corruption cannot be confined to 'functional' areas. It will be a temptation whenever private benefits are positive. It may be a reasonable response to a harsh reality but, over time, it can facilitate a spiral into an even worse situation.

11. The governments which fail to focus on the relationship between private wealth and public power are likely to become
(a) Functional
(b) Dysfunctional
(c) Normal functioning
(d) Good governance

12. One important symptom of bad governance is
(a) Corruption
(b) High taxes
(c) Complicated rules and regulations
(d) High prices

13. When corruption is rampant, public officials always aim at many opportunities for
(a) Public benefits (b) Public profit
(c) Private profit (d) Corporate gains

14. Productivity linked incentives to public/ private officials is one of the indicatives for
(a) Efficient government
(b) Bad governance
(c) Inefficient government
(d) Corruption

15. The spiralling corruption can only be contained by promoting
(a) Private profit
(b) Anti-corruption campaign
(c) Good governance
(d) Pay-offs and kickbacks

16. Press Council of India is located at
(a) Chennai (b) Mumbai
(c) Kolkata (d) Delhi

17. Adjusting the photo for publication by cutting is technically known as
(a) Photo cutting
(b) Photo bleeding
(c) Photo cropping
(d) Photo adjustment

18. Feedback of a message comes from
(a) Satellite (b) Media
(c) Audience (d) Communicator

19. Collection of information in advance before designing communication strategy is known as

(a) Feedback (b) Feed-forward
(c) Research study (d) Opinion poll

20. The aspect ratio of TV screen is
(a) 4:3 (b) 4:2
(c) 3:5 (d) 2:3

21. Which is the number that comes next in the sequence?
9, 8, 8, 8, 7, 8, 6, __
(a) 5 (b) 6
(c) 8 (d) 4

22. If in a certain language PUNCTUAL is coded as 16598623, how would ACTUPULN be coded?
(a) 834536 (b) 29861635
(c) 834530 (d) 834539

23. The question to be answered by factorial analysis of the quantitative data does not explain one of the following
(a) Is 'X' related to 'Y'?
(b) How is 'X' related to 'Y'?
(c) How does 'X' affect the dependent variable 'Y' at different levels of another independent variable 'K' or 'M'?
(d) How is 'X' by 'K' related to 'M'?

24. January 12, 1980 was Saturday, what day was January 12, 1979?
(a) Saturday (b) Friday
(c) Sunday (d) Thursday

25. How many Mondays are there in a particular month of a particular year, if the month ends on Wednesday?
(a) 5 (b) 4
(c) 3 (d) None of these

26. From the given four statements, select the two which cannot be true but yet both can be false. Choose the right pair.
1. All men are mortal
2. Some men are mortal
3. No man is mortal
4. Some men are not mortal
(a) 1 and 2 (b) 3 and 4
(c) 1 and 3 (d) 2 and 4

27. A Syllogism must have
(a) Three terms (b) Four terms
(c) Six terms (d) Five terms

28. Copula is that part of proposition which denotes the relationship between
(a) Subject and predicate
(b) Known and unknown
(c) Major premise and minor premise
(d) Subject and object

29. "E" denotes
(a) Universal Negative Proposition
(b) Particular Affirmative Proposition
(c) Universal Affirmative Proposition
(d) Particular Negative Proposition

30. 'A' is the father of 'C' and 'D' is the son of 'B'. 'E' is the brother of 'A'. If 'C' is the sister of 'D' how is 'B' related to 'E'?
(a) Daughter (b) Husband
(c) Sister-in-law (d) Brother-in-law

31. Which of the following methods will you choose to prepare choropleth map of India showing urban density of population?
(a) Quartiles (b) Quintiles
(c) Mean and SD (d) Break-point

32. Which of the following methods is best suited to show on a map the types of crops being grown in a region?
(a) Choropleth (b) Chorochromatic
(c) Choroschematic (d) Isopleth

33. A ratio represents the relation between
(a) Part and Part
(b) Part and Whole
(c) Whole and Whole
(d) All of the above

34. Out of four numbers, the average of the first three numbers is thrice the fourth number. If the average of the four numbers is 5, the fourth number is

(a) 4.5 (b) 5
(c) 2 (d) 4

35. Circle graphs are used to show
(a) How various sections share in the whole
(b) How various parts are related to the whole
(c) How one whole is related to other wholes
(d) How one part is related to other parts

36. On the keyboard of computer each character has an "ASCII" value which stands for
(a) American Stock Code for Information Interchange
(b) American Standard Code for Information Interchange
(c) African Standard Code for Information Interchange
(d) Adaptable Standard Code for Information Change

37. Which part of the Central Processing Unit (CPU) performs calculation and makes decisions
(a) Arithmetic Logic Unit
(b) Alternating Logic Unit
(c) Alternate Local Unit
(d) American Logic Unit

38. "Dpi" stands for
(a) Dots per inch
(b) Digits per unit
(c) Dots pixel inch
(d) Diagrams per inch

39. The process of laying out a document with text, graphics, headlines and photographs is involved in
(a) Deck Top Publishing
(b) Desk Top Printing
(c) Desk Top Publishing
(d) Deck Top Printing

40. Transfer of data from one application to another line is known as
(a) Dynamic Disk Exchange
(b) Dodgy Data Exchange
(c) Dogmatic Data Exchange
(d) Dynamic Data Exchange

41. Tsunami occurs due to
(a) Mild earthquakes and landslides in the oceans
(b) Strong earthquakes and landslides in the oceans
(c) Strong earthquakes and landslides in mountains
(d) Strong earthquakes and landslides in deserts

42. Which of the natural hazards have big effect on Indian people each year?
(a) Cyclones (b) Floods
(c) Earthquakes (d) Landslides

43. Comparative Environment Impact Assessment study is to be conducted for
(a) the whole year
(b) three seasons excluding monsoon
(c) any three seasons
(d) the worst season

44. Sea level rise results primarily due to
(a) Heavy rainfall
(b) Melting of glaciers
(c) Submarine volcanism
(d) Seafloor spreading

45. The plume rise in a coal based power plant depends on
1. Buoyancy
2. Atmospheric stability
3. Momentum of exhaust gases identify

Codes:
(a) Both (1) and (2)
(b) Both (2) and (3)
(c) Both (1) and (3)
(d) (1), (2) and (3)

46. Value education makes a student
(a) Good citizen
(b) Successful businessman

(c) Popular teacher
(d) Efficient manager

47. Networking of libraries through electronic media is known as
(a) Inflibnet (b) Libinfnet
(c) Internet (d) HTML

48. The University which telecasts interactive educational programmes through its own channel is
(a) B.R. Ambedkar Open University, Hyderabad
(b) I.G.N.O.U.
(c) University of Pune
(d) Annamalai University

49. The Government established the University Grants Commission by an Act of Parliament in the year
(a) 1980 (b) 1948
(c) 1950 (d) 1956

50. Universities having central campus for imparting education are called
(a) Central Universities
(b) Deemed Universities
(c) Residential Universities
(d) Open Universities

ANSWERS

1. (d)	2. (a)	3. (a)	4. (b)	5. (a)
6. (c)	7. (d)	8. (b)	9. (b)	10. (b)
11. (b)	12. (a)	13. (c)	14. (a)	15. (c)
16. (d)	17. (c)	18. (c)	19. (d)	20. (a)
21. (c)	22. (b)	23. (c)	24. (b)	25. (d)
26. (b)	27. (a)	28. (b)	29. (a)	30. (d)
31. (b)	32. (c)	33. (b)	34. (c)	35. (a)
36. (a)	37. (a)	38. (a)	39. (c)	40. (d)
41. (b)	42. (b)	43. (a)	44. (b)	45. (d)
46. (a)	47. (a)	48. (b)	49. (d)	50. (b)

PAPER–II

Note: This paper contains fifty (50) objective type questions, each question carrying two (2) marks. Attempt all the questions.

1. Which of the following statement about Fjord is incorrect?
(a) Most Fjords were formed due to raise in sea level after the melting of Pleistocene ice
(b) It is an emergent coast that was originally submerged
(c) It is a long narrow inlet of the sea bound by steep slopes
(d) It is a glaciated valley that has been inundated by the sea

2. Given 'd' as particle size and 'V' settling velocity in cm/sec., the correct relationship between 'd' and 'V' is given by:
(a) $V \propto \frac{1}{d^n}$ (b) $V \propto d^n$
(c) $V \propto d$ (d) $V = \frac{1}{d^n}$

3. Residence time of water molecule in the ocean is:
(a) 3.5 years (b) 3.5 million years
(c) 35 years (d) 35000 years

4. Hyperplasia means:
(a) excessive motility of a muscle
(b) Voracious eating
(c) Abnormal increase in number of cells
(d) An increase in size of a cell

5. Carbon dioxide absorbs radiation in the range:
(a) 5.5 and 7 microns
(b) Greater than 27 microns
(c) 8 to 13 microns
(d) 0.1 to 30 microns

6. Sodium is usually estimated by which of the following analytical technique:
   (a) Flame Photometry
   (b) Coulometry
   (c) High pressure liquid chromotography
   (d) Visible spectrophotometry

7. Which combination of the following elements constitute a major portion of earth crust:
   (a) Oxygen and Silicon
   (b) Oxygen and Iron
   (c) Silicon and Iron
   (d) Aluminium and Iron

8. **Assertion (A):** Chlorofluorocarbons deplete ozone.
   Reason (R): These compounds contain Chlorine, Bromine and Fluorine.
   (a) Both (A) and (R) are true and (R) is the correct explanation of (A)
   (b) Both (A) and (R) are true but (R) is not the correct explanation of (A)
   (c) (A) is true but (R) is false
   (d) (A) is false but (R) is true

9. The chemical composition of CFC-115 is:
   (a) C_2F_5Cl (b) C_2FCl_5
   (c) $CHClF_2$ (d) $C_2H_2F_2Cl_2$

10. Maximum Density of water is at:
    (a) 4°C (b) 0°C
    (c) 100°C (d) 272°C

11. The cause of lung cancer Mesothalemia is:
    (a) Asbestos (b) Arsenic
    (c) Mercury (d) Chromium

12. Which of the following pattern of evolution accounts for all the diversity present on earth today?
    (a) Microevolution (b) Megaevolution
    (c) Biodiversity (d) Speciation

13. Group of individuals of the same species that share common attributes are called:
    (a) Community (b) Population
    (c) Ecotype (d) Society

14. Which one of the following is the correct food chain?
    (a) Algae → Daphnia → Dragon Fly Nymph → Newt → Grass Snake
    (b) Daphnia → Dragon Fly Nymph → Newt → Algae → Grass Snake
    (c) Grass Snake → Newt → Dragon Fly Nymph → Daphnia → Algae
    (d) Newt → Grass Snake → Dragon Fly Nymph → Algae → Daphnia

15. Match the items in List I with List II and select the correct answers using codes given below:

List I	**List II**
A. Fohn wind	(i) Analogous to rainbow
B. Fog bow	(ii) Herbivorous plants
C. Forbs	(iii) Warm winds descending from mountains
D. Fore shock	(iv) Earthquake

Codes:	**A**	**B**	**C**	**D**
(a)	(i)	(ii)	(iii)	(iv)
(b)	(iii)	(ii)	(iv)	(i)
(c)	(ii)	(iii)	(i)	(iv)
(d)	(iii)	(i)	(ii)	(iv)

16. **Assertion (A):** Monsoonal rainfall is very high both on the west coast and northeast India.
    Reason (R): The duration of monsoon over west coast and northeast India is longer than other parts of India.
    (a) Both (A) and (R) are true and (R) is the correct explanation of (A)
    (b) Both (A) and (R) are true but (R) is not the correct explanation of (A)
    (c) (A) is true but (R) is false
    (d) (A) is false but (R) is true

17. Match the climatic categories in List II for places in List I using the codes given below:

List I	List II
A. Delhi	(i) Arid
B. Mumbai	(ii) Semi Arid
C. Jodhpur	(iii) Moist Sub humid
D. Shillong	(iv) Per Humid

Codes:	A	B	C	D
(a)	(ii)	(iii)	(i)	(iv)
(b)	(iv)	(ii)	(iii)	(i)
(c)	(iii)	(iv)	(ii)	(i)
(d)	(i)	(ii)	(iv)	(iii)

18. Match the items in List I with List II and select the correct answers using codes given below:

List I	List II
A. Lignite	(i) Bikaner
B. Asbestos	(ii) Chotanagpur
C. Titanium	(iii) Southern Malabar
D. Iron	(iv) Ratnagiri

Codes:	A	B	C	D
(a)	(i)	(ii)	(iii)	(iv)
(b)	(i)	(ii)	(iv)	(iii)
(c)	(ii)	(i)	(iii)	(iv)
(d)	(ii)	(i)	(iv)	(iii)

19. Which one of the following statements regarding ELNINO is not true?
    (a) It is an extension of equitorial current towards the western coast of South America.
    (b) It is an occasional warm current leading to an increase of about 10°C in subsurface water temperature.
    (c) It develops as temporary replacement of usual cold Peruvian current.
    (d) It causes an increase in plankton thriving in cold Peruvian current.

20. The process of alluviation indicates:
    (a) Removal of particles from the upper layer of soil
    (b) Removal of particles from lower layer of soil
    (c) Deposition of soil particles in sub-soil layer
    (d) Transportation of soil particles in the B-horizon

21. Which one of the following is the cleanest source of energy?
    (a) Hydropower (b) Fossil fuel
    (c) Nuclear power (d) Wind energy

22. Match the items in List I with List II and select the correct answer using codes given below:

List I	List II
A. CFC	(i) Bhopal Gas Tragedy
B. CO_2	(ii) Global Warming
C. BOD	(iii) Ozone depletion
D. MIC	(iv) Water pollution

Codes:	A	B	C	D
(a)	(iii)	(ii)	(iv)	(i)
(b)	(iv)	(iii)	(i)	(ii)
(c)	(i)	(ii)	(iii)	(iv)
(d)	(iv)	(iii)	(ii)	(i)

23. The global warming efficiency of a CFC molecule in relation to a CO_2 molecule is higher by a factor of:
    (a) 125 (b) 25
    (c) 20,000 (d) 1500

24. Arsenic problem in India is primarily due to:
    (a) Overexploitation of arsenopyrite in the hinterland
    (b) Overexploitation of coal in Bihar and Bengal
    (c) Overexploitation of ground water in the affected areas
    (d) Overexploitation of surface water in the affected areas

25. Acid rain is caused by:
    (a) CO and CO_2 (b) SO_2 and O_2
    (c) SO_2 and NO_2 (d) NO_2 and O_2

26. What will be the outcome of eutrophication of surface waters?

(a) Overproduction of biomass
(b) Decrease in nitrogen concentration
(c) Decrease in phosphorus concentration
(d) Decrease in both nitrogen and phosphorus concentrations

27. **Assertion (A):** Negatively charged soil particles attract positive ions like Ca^{++} and Mg^{++}

Reason (R): The attraction keeps the ions at soil level for ready availability.

(a) Both (A) and (R) are true and (R) is the correct explanation of (A).
(b) Both (A) and (R) are true but (R) is not the correct explanation of (A).
(c) (A) is true but (R) is false.
(d) (A) is false but (R) is true.

28. Match the items in List I with List II and select the correct answer using codes given below:

List I

A. The audible frequency range is
B. The audible sound level pressure is
C. Ratio of Intensity to a reference
D. Energy content for varying sound

List II

(i) 20mPa to 200Pa
(ii) 20 – 20,000 Hz
(iii) Equivalent continuous sound Intensity of sound expressed in level (Leq) log scale is
(iv) Decibel levels

Codes:	A	B	C	D
(a)	(ii)	(i)	(iv)	(iii)
(b)	(i)	(ii)	(iii)	(iv)
(c)	(iv)	(iii)	(ii)	(i)
(d)	(iii)	(iv)	(ii)	(i)

29. Cost Benefit analysis is required in case of proposals involving clearance of forest land:

(a) Greater than 10 ha but less than 20 ha
(b) Greater than 20 ha
(c) Greater than 5 ha but less than 10 ha
(d) Greater than 40 ha only

30. Ecologically sensitive and important areas, breeding and spawning grounds of marine life etc., are categorized in coastal Regulation Zone as:

(a) CRZ - IV (b) CRZ - II
(c) CRZ - III (d) CRZ - I

31. A management tool comprising a systematic, periodic and objective evaluation of how well an environmental organization, management and equipment are performing is known as:

(a) Raw material balance
(b) Input-output analysis
(c) Acturities at site
(d) Environmental audit

32. Choose right expansion of CITES of 1975:

(a) Centre for International Training in Endangered Species of Wild Fauna and Flora
(b) Committee on International Trade and Environment and Sustainable Development
(c) Council of Indian Trade and Environmental Survey of Wild Fauna and Flora
(d) Convention on International Trade in Endangered Species of Wild Fauna and Flora

33. Match the items in List I with List II and select the correct answer using codes given below:

List I

A. Montreal Convention
B. Rio-Summit
C. Ramsah Convention
D. Kyoto Protocol

List II

(i) Ozone depletion
(ii) Greenhouse gas
(iii) Convention on Biological diversity
(iv) Wetlands convention

Codes:	**A**	**B**	**C**	**D**
(a)	(iii)	(ii)	(i)	(iv)
(b)	(iv)	(iii)	(i)	(ii)
(c)	(i)	(iii)	(iv)	(ii)
(d)	(i)	(ii)	(iv)	(iii)

34. The least preferred technique in the disposal of municipal solid waste is:
(a) incineration (b) composting
(c) land filling (d) bricketting

35. Bacterial decomposition of biological material under aerobic condition is:
(a) Fermentation (b) Fertilization
(c) Contamination (d) Composting

36. When you go for shopping, what are you expected to do to save environment?
(a) Shop for products that have as little packaging as possible.
(b) In any store, use a bag even it is not needed.
(c) Do not reduce the frequency of shopping.
(d) Buy paper towels and napkins.

37. Match the items in List I with List II and select the correct answer using codes given below:
List I
A. polyethylene terephthalate
B. high density polyethylene
C. vinyl low density polyethylene
D. polypropylene
List II
(i) detergent bottles
(ii) beverage bottles
(iii) shampoo bottles
(iv) cooking oil bottles
Codes:
(a) (A) and (ii) (b) (B) and (iii)
(c) (C) and (i) (d) (D) and (iv)

38. In the analysis of 15 water samples, Ca and Mg gave a correlation of +0.95. It means:
(a) Ca came from soil and Mg came from biota
(b) Ca and Mg both came from the same type of water
(c) Ca and Mg are both cogenetic
(d) Ca and Mg came from different sources

39. If a piece of metal weighs 10.2 g in air, 8.6 g in water and 7.8 g in another liquid, then what will be the specific gravity of the liquid?
(a) 1.0 (b) 1.5
(c) 2.0 (d) 3.0

40. The geometric mean of the numbers 2, 4, 8, 16, 32 is:
(a) 12 (b) 16
(c) 8 (d) 32

41. The correlation coefficient between the variables X, Y as given in the following table:

X	1	3	4	6	8	9	11	14
Y	1	2	4	4	5	7	8	9

is:
(a) –0.977 (b) –0.517
(c) +0.977 (d) +0.217

42. Climatic stress is caused by insufficient and/or excessive regime of:
(a) Temperature
(b) Humidity
(c) Solar radiation
(d) All of the above

43. The chemical that is used to ripen mangoes is:
(a) Calcium sulphide
(b) Calcium carbide
(c) Calcium carbonate
(d) Calcium chloride

44. Which two of the following statements regarding ISO 14000 series of standards are true?

Answer choosing the codes given below:

(i) ISO 14000 standards are based on a principle assumption that better environmental management will lead to better environmental performance.

(ii) ISO 14000 standards are regulatory standards developed by ISO.

(iii) ISO 14000 standards are market driven and therefore are based on voluntary involvement of all interests in the market place.

(iv) The adoption of ISO 14000 is a one time commitment.

Codes:

(a) (i) and (ii) (b) (ii) and (iii)
(c) (i) and (iii) (d) (iii) and (iv)

45. Organisms that generate energy using light are:
(a) oligotrophs
(b) chaemorganotrophs
(c) chaemolithotrophs
(d) photoautotrophs

46. Conversion of $^{239}_{94}Pu$ to $^{239}_{92}U$ involves the following types of decay:
(a) α and β (b) α and γ
(c) β and γ (d) only β

47. Land use pattern is usually studied by the following technique:
(a) Aerial photography
(b) Satellite imaging
(c) Satellite imaging and G.I.S.
(d) Satellite imaging, G.I.S. and G.P.S.

48. To conserve coral reefs the Govt. of India declared one of the following as marine park:
(a) Gulf of Kutch
(b) Lakshadweep Islands
(c) Gulf of Mannar
(d) Andaman Islands

49. Which one of the following does not contribute to conservation of water?
(a) Waste water treatment
(b) Waste land development
(c) Water shed protection
(d) Rain water harvesting

50. Particle size in soil can be classified as Clay: 1-4 micron. Silt: 4-62 micron. Sand: 62-1000 micron. Boulder: >1000 micron. It is hence correct to suggest that in nature particle size distribution follows:
(a) Binomial distribution
(b) Lognormal distribution
(c) Linear distribution
(d) Normal distribution

ANSWERS

1. (d)	2. (a)	3. (c)	4. (c)	5. (a)
6. (a)	7. (a)	8. (c)	9. (a)	10. (a)
11. (b)	12. (c)	13. (c)	14. (a)	15. (d)
16. (b)	17. (a)	18. (a)	19. (a)	20. (c)
21. (d)	22. (a)	23. (a)	24. (c)	25. (c)
26. (a)	27. (a)	28. (a)	29. (a)	30. (d)
31. (d)	32. (d)	33. (c)	34. (d)	35. (a)
36. (a)	37. (c)	38. (d)	39. (c)	40. (c)
41. (c)	42. (d)	43. (b)	44. (a)	45. (d)
46. (b)	47. (b)	48. (b)	49. (b)	50. (d)

DECEMBER–2007

Note: This paper contains Fifty (50) multiple-choice questions, each question carrying two (2) marks. Attempt all of them.

PAPER–I

1. Verbal guidance is least effective in the learning of
   (a) Aptitudes (b) Skills
   (c) Attitudes (d) Relationship
2. Which is the most important aspect of the teacher's role in learning?
   (a) The development of insight into what constitutes an adequate performance
   (b) The development of insight into what constitutes the pitfalls and dangers to be avoided
   (c) The provision of encouragement and moral support
   (d) The provision of continuous diagnostic and remedial help
3. The most appropriate purpose of learning is
   (a) personal adjustment
   (b) modification of behaviour
   (c) social and political awarness
   (d) preparing oneself for employment
4. The students who keep on asking questions in the class should be
   (a) encouraged to find answer independently
   (b) advised to meet the teacher after the class
   (c) encouraged to continue questioning
   (d) advised not to disturb during the lecture
5. Maximum participation of students is possible in teaching through
   (a) discussion method
   (b) lecture method
   (c) audio-visual aids
   (d) textbook method
6. Generalised conclusion on the basis of a sample is technically known as
   (a) Data analysis and interpretation
   (b) Parameter inference
   (c) Statistical inference
   (d) All of the above
7. The experimental study is based on
   (a) The manipulation of variables
   (b) Conceptual parameters
   (c) Replication of research
   (d) Survey of literature
8. The main characteristic of scientific research is
   (a) Empirical (b) Theoretical
   (c) Experimental (d) All of the above
9. Authenticity of a research finding is its
   (a) Originality (b) Validity
   (c) Objectivity (d) All of the above
10. Which technique is generally followed when the population is finite?
    (a) Area Sampling Technique
    (b) Purposive Sampling Technique
    (c) Systematic Sampling Technique
    (d) None of the above

Read the following passage and answer the questions 11 to 15:

Gandhi's overall social and environmental philosophy is based on what human beings need rather than what they want. His early introduction to the teachings of Jains, Theosophists, Christian sermons, Ruskin and Tolstoy, and most significantly the *Bhagavad Gita*, were to have profound impact on the development of Gandhi's holistic thinking on humanity, nature and their ecological interrelation. His deep concern for the disadvantaged, the poor and rural population created an ambience for an alternative social thinking that was at once far-sighted, local and immediate. For Gandhi was acutely aware that the demands generated by the need to feed and sustain human life, compounded by the growing industrialisation of India, far outstripped the finite resources of nature. This might nowadays appear naive or commonplace, but such pronouncements were as rare as they were heretical a century ago. Gandhi was also concerned about the destruction, under colonial and modernist designs, of the existing infrastructures which had more potential for keeping a community flourishing within ecologically-sensitive traditional patterns of subsistence, especially in the rural areas, than did the incoming Western alternatives based on nature-blind technology and the enslavement of human spirit and energies.

Perhaps the moral principle for which Gandhi is best known is that of active non-violence, derived from the traditional moral restraint of not injuring another being. The most refined expression of this value is in the great epic of the *Mahabharata* (c. 100 BCE to 200 CE), where moral development proceeds through placing constraints on the liberties, desires and acquisitiveness endemic to human life. One's action is judged in terms of consequences and the impact it is likely to have on another. Jainas had generalised this principle to include all sentient creatures and biocommunities alike. Advanced Jaina monks and nuns will sweep their path to avoid harming insects and even bacteria. Non-injury is a non-negotiable universal prescription.

11. Which one of the following have a profound impact on the development of Gandhi's holistic thinking on humanity, nature and their ecological interrelations?
    (a) Jain teachings
    (b) Christian sermons
    (c) *Bhagavad Gita*
    (d) Ruskin and Tolstoy
12. Gandhi's overall social and environmental philosophy is based on human beings'
    (a) need (b) desire
    (c) wealth (d) welfare
13. Gandhiji's deep concern for the disadvantaged, the poor and rural population created an ambience for an alternative
    (a) rural policy
    (b) social thinking
    (c) urban policy
    (d) economic thinking
14. Colonial policy and modernisation led to the destruction of
    (a) major industrial infrastructure
    (b) irrigation infrastructure
    (c) urban infrastructure
    (d) rural infrastructure
15. Gandhi's active non-violence is derived from
    (a) Moral restraint of not injuring another being
    (b) Having liberties, desires and acquisitiveness
    (c) Freedom of action
    (d) Nature-blind technology and enslavement of human spirit and energies
16. DTH service was started in the year
    (a) 2000 (b) 2002
    (c) 2004 (d) 2006
17. National Press day is celebrated on
    (a) 16th November (b) 19th November
    (c) 21st November (d) 30th November

18. The total number of members in the Press Council of India are
    (a) 28 (b) 14
    (c) 17 (d) 20
19. The right to impart and receive information is guaranteed in the Constitution of India by Article
    (a) 19(2)(a) (b) 19(16)
    (c) 19(2) (d) 19(1)(a)
20. Use of radio for higher education is based on the presumption of
    (a) Enriching curriculum based instruction
    (b) Replacing teacher in the long run
    (c) Everybody having access to a radio set
    (d) Other means of instruction getting outdated
21. Find out the number which should come at the place of question mark which will complete the following series.

    5, 4, 9, 17, 35, ? = 139
    (a) 149 (b) 79
    (c) 49 (d) 69

Questions 22 to 24 are based on the following diagram in which there are three interlocking circles I, S and P, where circle I stands for Indians, circle S for Scientists and circle P for Politicians. Different regions in the figure are lettered from a to g.

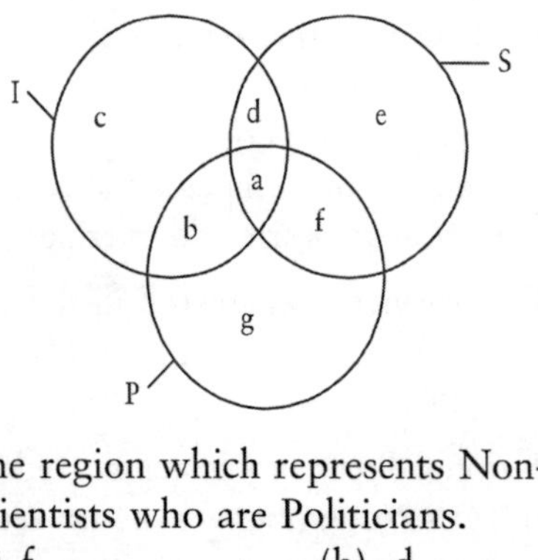

22. The region which represents Non-Indian Scientists who are Politicians.
    (a) f (b) d
    (c) a (d) c
23. The region which represents Indians who are neither Scientists nor Politicians.
    (a) g (b) c
    (c) f (d) a
24. The region which represents Politicians who are Indians as well as Scientists.
    (a) b (b) c
    (c) a (d) d
25. Which number is missing in the following series?
    2, 5, 10, 17, 26, 37, 50, ?
    (a) 63 (b) 65
    (c) 67 (d) 69
26. The function of measurement includes.
    (a) Prognosis (b) Diagnosis
    (c) Prediction (d) All of the above
27. Logical arguments are based on
    (a) Scientific reasoning
    (b) Customary reasoning
    (c) Mathematical reasoning
    (d) Syllogistic reasoning
28. Insert the missing number 4 : 17 : : 7 : ?
    (a) 48 (b) 49
    (c) 50 (d) 51
29. Choose the odd word.
    (a) Nun (b) Knight
    (c) Monk (d) Priest
30. Choose the number which is different from others in the group.
    (a) 49 (b) 63
    (c) 77 (d) 81
31. Probability sampling implies.
    (a) Stratified Random Sampling
    (b) Systematic Random Sampling
    (c) Simple Random Sampling
    (d) All of the above
32. Insert the missing number.

    $\frac{36}{62}, \frac{39}{63}, \frac{43}{61}, \frac{48}{64}, ?$

(a) $\frac{51}{65}$ (b) $\frac{56}{60}$

(c) $\frac{54}{65}$ (d) $\frac{33}{60}$

33. At what time between 3 and 4 o'clock will the hands of a watch point in opposite directions?
    (a) 40 minutes past three
    (b) 45 minutes past three
    (c) 50 minutes past three
    (d) 55 minutes past three

34. Mary has three children. What is the probability that none of the three children is a boy?

    (a) $\frac{1}{2}$ (b) $\frac{1}{3}$

    (c) $\frac{3}{4}$ (d) 1

35. If the radius of a circle is increased by 50 percent. Its area is increased by
    (a) 125 percent (b) 100 percent
    (c) 75 percent (d) 50 percent

36. CD ROM stands for
    (a) Computer Disk Read Only Memory
    (b) Compact Disk Read Over Memory
    (c) Compact Disk Read Only Memory
    (d) Computer Disk Read Over Memory

37. The 'brain' of a computer which keeps peripherals under its control is called
    (a) Common Power Unit
    (b) Common Processing Unit
    (c) Central Power Unit
    (d) Central Processing Unit

38. Data can be saved on backing storage medium known as
    (a) Compact Disk Recordable
    (b) Computer Disk Rewritable
    (c) Compact Disk Rewritable
    (d) Computer Data Rewritable

39. RAM means
    (a) Random Access Memory
    (b) Rigid Access Memory
    (c) Rapid Access Memory
    (d) Revolving Access Memory

40. www represents
    (a) who what and where
    (b) weird wide web
    (c) word wide web
    (d) world wide web

41. Deforestation during the recent decades has led to
    (a) Soil erosion
    (b) Landslides
    (c) Loss of bio-diversity
    (d) All of the above

42. Which one of the following natural hazards is responsible for causing highest human disaster?
    (a) Earthquakes
    (b) Volcanic eruptions
    (c) Snowstorms
    (d) Tsunami

43. Which one of the following is appropriate for natural hazard mitigation?
    (a) International AID
    (b) Timely Warning System
    (c) Rehabilitation
    (d) Community Participation

44. Slums in metro city are the result of
    (a) Rural to urban migration
    (b) Poverty of the city-scape
    (c) Lack of urban infrastructure
    (d) Urban-governance

45. The great Indian Bustard bird is found in
    (a) Thar Desert of India
    (b) Coastal regions of India
    (c) Temperate Forests in the Himalaya
    (d) Tarai zones of the Himalayan Foot

46. The first Indian Satellite for serving the educational sector is known as
(a) SATEDU (b) INSAT-B
(c) EDUSAT (d) INSAT-C

47. Exclusive educational channel of IGNOU is known as
(a) Gyan Darshan (b) Gyan Vani
(c) Door Darshan (d) Prasar Bharati

48. The headquarter of Mahatma Gandhi Antarrashtriya Hindi Vishwavidyalaya is situated in
(a) Sevagram (b) New Delhi
(c) Wardha (d) Ahmedabad

49. Match List I with List II and select the correct answer using the codes given below.

List I (Institutes)
A. Central Institute of English and Foreign Languages
B. Gramodaya Vishwavidyalaya
C. Central Institute of Higher Tibetan Studies
D. IGNOU

List II (Locations)
1. Chitrakoot 2. Hyderabad
3. New Delhi 4. Dharmasala

Codes:	A	B	C	D
(a)	2	1	4	3
(b)	4	3	2	1
(c)	3	4	1	2
(d)	1	2	4	3

50. The aim of vocationalisation of education is
(a) preparing students for a vocation along with knowledge
(b) converting liberal education into vocational education
(c) giving more importance to vocational than general education
(d) making liberal education job-oriented

ANSWERS

1. (b)	2. (a)	3. (b)	4. (a)	5. (a)
6. (c)	7. (c)	8. (c)	9. (d)	10. (c)
11. (c)	12. (a)	13. (b)	14. (c)	15. (a)
16. (d)	17. (a)	18. (a)	19. (d)	20. (b)
21. (d)	22. (a)	23. (b)	24. (d)	25. (b)
26. (d)	27. (d)	28. (c)	29. (b)	30. (c)
31. (d)	32. (c)	33. (c)	34. (d)	35. (a)
36. (c)	37. (d)	38. (c)	39. (a)	40. (d)
41. (d)	42. (a)	43. (b)	44. (a)	45. (a)
46. (c)	47. (a)	48. (c)	49. (a)	50. (d)

PAPER–II

Note: This paper contains fifty (50) objective type questions, each question carrying two (2) marks. All questions are compulsory.

1. Wind rose of a given location represents:
(a) Frequency distribution of wind speeds in the form of a histogram.
(b) Frequency distribution of wind speeds in percentage terms in the form of a π chart.
(c) Frequency distribution of wind speed associated with a cyclose.
(d) Frequency distribution of wind speed and direction in polar coordinates.

2. **Assertion (A):** Sustainable production of hay or green fodder is essential for uninterrupted supply of animal products.
Reason (R): Environmental concerns are detrimental for sustainable production of hay or green fodder.
(a) Both (A) and (R) are true but (R) is not the correct explanation of (A)
(b) Both (A) and (R) are true and (R) is the correct explanation of (A)

(c) (A) is true and (R) is false
(d) (A) is false and (R) is true

3. For a clear sunny day with sun higher than 60° above horizon and wind speed greater than 6 m/sec, the atmosphere is:
(a) Stable
(b) Slightly unstable
(c) Moderately unstable
(d) Very unstable

4. The mass of the earth's crust is approximately:
(a) 2.5×10^{25} g (b) 3.2×10^{20} g
(c) 2.8×10^{32} g (d) 1.8×10^{35} g

5. The time scale of meso-scale meteorological phenomenon is:
(a) Hours to a day
(b) 3-4 days
(c) Few weeks
(d) Few weeks to several months

6. The reaction is in equilibrium if Gibb's free energy (G):
(a) Increases i.e., $\Delta G > 0$
(b) Decreases i.e., $\Delta G < 0$
(c) Remains same i.e., $\Delta G = 0$
(d) Varies i.e., $\Delta G > 0$ or $\Delta G < 0$

7. How CO emitted by automobiles prevents transfer of O_2 in the body tissue:
(a) By changing O_2 into CO
(b) By destroying the haemoglobin
(c) By forming stable compound with haemoglobin
(d) By obstructing the reaction of O_2 with haemoglobin

8. In qualitative analysis the sulphides of Group-II are precipitated in presence of dilute HCl, while of Group-IV are precipitated only in the presence of NH_4OH. It is because:
(a) Solubility product of sulphides of Group-II is greater than that of Group-IV
(b) Solubility product of sulphides of Group-II is less than that of Group-IV
(c) Sulphides of Group-II are insoluble in acids
(d) Sulphides of Group-IV are insoluble in alkalies

9. Arrange the following atmospheric gases in the decreasing order of their abundance:
I. Oxygen II. Carbon dioxide
III. Argon IV. Methane
Codes:
(a) III > I > II > IV (b) II > I > III > IV
(c) I > III > II > IV (d) III > I > IV > II

10. Which of the following is equivalent to the number of substrate molecules converted to product in a given unit of time by a single enzyme molecule when the enzyme is saturated with substrate?
(a) Specific constant
(b) Michaelis constant
(c) Dissociation constant
(d) Turn-over number

11. DDT is harmful from the ecological point of view mainly because it undergoes:
(a) Biotransformation
(b) Bioaccumulation
(c) Biomagnification
(d) Biodegradation

12. Which of the following radiations continuously act on ^{14}N to produce ^{14}C isotope in the atmosphere?
(a) X-rays (b) γ-rays
(c) UV-rays (d) Cosmic rays

13. The proteins in the cell walls of microorganisms have an overall net negative charge at pH of most soil environments, because:
(a) the pH of the environment is greater than the pI
(b) the pH of the environment is less than the pI
(c) the pH of the environment is the same as pI
(d) None of the above

14. Oxidoreductases:
    (a) oxidize a substrate by removing a pair of electrons and the accompanying hydrogen atoms
    (b) break molecules apart by adding water across bonds
    (c) hydrolyse the substrate
    (d) put molecules together

15. Which of the following is a nematofungus?
    (a) *Rhizoctonia solani*
    (b) *Penicillium sp.*
    (c) *Phanerochaete chrysosporium*
    (d) *Mucor mucedo*

16. The diaatomaceous earth is used as a:
    (a) chemical insecticide
    (b) non-chemical insecticide
    (c) fungicide
    (d) bacterocide

17. **Assertion (A):** Among micro-organisms white-rot fungi most efficiently degrade lignin.
    Reason (R): White-rot fungi produce ligninolytic enzymes.
    (a) Both (A) and (R) are true and (R) is the correct explanation of (A)
    (b) Both (A) and (R) are true but (R) is not the correct explanation of (A)
    (c) (A) is true but (R) is false
    (d) (A) is false but (R) is true

18. In deep oceans the phenomenon of inverted biomass pyramid occurs mainly due to:
    I. Fast growth rate and high nutrient requirement of producers.
    II. Rapid turnover rate and short life span of producers.
    III. Slow growth rate and high nutrient requirement of herbivores.
    IV. Slow turnover and long life span of herbivores.

    Which of the following combinations is correct?
    (a) I and III (b) I and IV
    (c) II and III (d) II and IV

19. Alpha diversity represents:
    (a) species richness
    (b) species evenness
    (c) species richness and evenness
    (d) species richness and dominance

20. Populations of two species may interact in several ways. One of these called protocooperation occurs when:
    (a) One population inhibits the other
    (b) Interaction is favourable to both but not obligatory
    (c) Interaction is favourable to both but obligatory
    (d) Neither population affects the other

21. The term benthos refers to communities which grow:
    (a) Attached on the bark of trees
    (b) Attached on submerged plants
    (c) Attached at the bottom of a waterbody
    (d) Attached on submerged woody roots

22. Pelagic sediments are found in the:
    (a) continental shelf
    (b) continental slope
    (c) mid-oceanic ridges
    (d) deep oceanic plains

23. Pleistocene period began:
    (a) 5.0 million years ago
    (b) 1.7 million years ago
    (c) 10 million years ago
    (d) 28 million years ago

24. Sodium and Potassium in rock and soil materials are generally estimated by:
    (a) UV-Visible spectrophotometry
    (b) Flame photometry
    (c) HPLC
    (d) Colorimetry

25. Match the List I and List II in respect of the geochemical affinity of the elements:

List I	List II
A. Chalcophile	(i) Carbon
B. Lithophile	(ii) Nitrogen
C. Siderophile	(iii) Sulphur
D. Atmophile	(iv) Oxygen
E. Biophile	(v) Iron

Codes:	A	B	C	D	E
(a)	(v)	(iv)	(iii)	(i)	(ii)
(b)	(iii)	(iv)	(v)	(ii)	(i)
(c)	(iv)	(v)	(i)	(ii)	(iii)
(d)	(iii)	(i)	(ii)	(iv)	(v)

26. Match the List I and List II:

List I (Sedimentary Environment)	List II (Rock Material)
A. Deep Sea	(i) till
B. Lakes	(ii) loess
C. Desert	(iii) evaporite
D. Glacier Margins	(iv) ooze

Codes:	A	B	C	D
(a)	(iv)	(iii)	(ii)	(i)
(b)	(iii)	(ii)	(i)	(iv)
(c)	(iv)	(i)	(ii)	(iii)
(d)	(iii)	(ii)	(iv)	(i)

27. Chemical weathering of rock material is most effective in which of the following regions?
(a) Aravalli Hills (b) Vindhyan Hills
(c) Ladakh (d) Western Ghats

28. Fission of 1 gm of ^{235}U liberates energy equivalent to about:
(a) 1 metric ton of coal
(b) 1.5 metric ton of coal
(c) 2.2 metric ton of coal
(d) 2.7 metric ton of coal

29. Under operating conditions of maximum power output from an ideal Magnetohydrodynamic power plant, the electrical efficiency is:
(a) 50% (b) 25%
(c) 75% (d) 100%

30. The maximum value of the coefficient of performance for a wind turbine is:
(a) $\frac{3}{4}$ (b) $\frac{5}{6}$
(c) $\frac{11}{27}$ (d) $\frac{16}{27}$

31. **Assertion (A):** Electrostatic precipitators are very efficient devices for removal of particulate matter from the gas stream.
Reason (R): Corona discharge helps in charging of particulate matter which are collected on the grounded electrodes (plates).
(a) Both (A) and (R) are true and (R) is the correct explanation of (A)
(b) Both (A) and (R) are true but (R) is not the correct explanation of (A)
(c) (A) is true but (R) is false
(d) (A) is false but (R) is true

32. Stratospheric ozone is produced by electromagnetic radiations of wavelength in the range:
(a) 180-240 nm (b) 280-320 nm
(c) 320-400 nm (d) 150-180 nm

33. $PM_{2.5}$ refers to:
(a) mass of particles of size less than 2.5 μm.
(b) mass of particles of size greater than 2.5 μm.
(c) number of particles of size less than 2.5 μm.
(d) number of particles of size greater than 2.5 μm.

34. A person is exposed to noise of 87 dB for 2 hours. If 100% noise dose corresponds to 90 dB noise exposure for 8 hours, the person is subjected to a noise dose of:
(a) 50% (b) 2.5%
(c) 12.5% (d) 6.25%

35. If the EIA indicates that another state is likely to be affected, the state, in which EIA is planned, has to:
   (a) transmit to the affected state any relevant information from the EIA concerning it
   (b) keep the relevant information fully secret
   (c) handover the information to the central pollution control board
   (d) None of the above

36. The combination of primary and secondary treatment reduces the original sewage BOD by:
   (a) 30-40% (b) 50-60%
   (c) 60-70% (d) 80-90%

37. A simple and relatively inexpensive film-flow type of aerobic treatment method is:
   (a) Septic tank
   (b) Activated sludge process
   (c) Percolating filter system
   (d) All of the above

38. Which of the following is not a molecular method for the detection of microbial population from water/soil?
   (a) Dot-blot hybridization
   (b) MPN
   (c) RT-PCR
   (d) PCR

39. Under Kyoto Protocol, the percentage reduction sought to be achieved in CO_2 emissions from 1990 levels by the year 2012 is:
   (a) ~ 10% (b) ~ 5.2%
   (c) ~ 15.2% (d) ~ 20.5%

40. In a simple regression model $Y = \alpha + \beta X + \in$ (Y = dependent variable, X = independent variable, α, β are regression coefficients, $\in$ = random error), the variance of $\in$ is:
   (a) 0
   (b) $\frac{\alpha^2}{\beta^2}$
   (c) $\frac{\beta^2}{\alpha^2}$
   (d) α^2; (σ = standard deviation)

41. In the Box-model the pollutant concentration (C) over an area varies with mixing height (H) as:
   (a) $C \alpha H$ (b) $C \alpha \frac{1}{H}$
   (c) $C \alpha H^{\frac{1}{2}}$ (d) $C \alpha H^{-\frac{1}{2}}$

42. For a Binomial distribution, the first moment is:
   (a) 1 (b) 3
   (c) –1 (d) 0

43. The Harmonic mean of the data 2, 2, 1 is:
   (a) $\frac{3}{2}$ (b) $\frac{5}{3}$
   (c) 2 (d) $\frac{3}{5}$

44. For a Normal distribution, the moment coefficient of skewness is:
   (a) 0 (b) 1
   (c) 3 (d) –1

45. Which of the following water purification technology removes minerals from drinking water?
   (a) Filteration (b) Ultra-filteration
   (c) Reverse osmosis (d) UV treatment

46. Identify the correct sequence of gases in the decreasing order of their contribution to global warming:
   (a) CO_2 > CFCs > CH_4 > N_2O
   (b) CO_2 > CH_4 > N_2O > CFCs
   (c) CO_2 > CH_4 > CFCs > N_2O
   (d) CO_2 > N_2O > CH_4 > CFCs

47. Convention on Biological Diversity, adopted at the UN Conference on Environment and Development in 1992, aims to curb destruction of:
   (a) Biological species (b) Habitats
   (c) Ecosystems (d) All of the above

48. According to IPCC, during the 20th century earth's mean surface temperature has risen by:
(a) ~ 0.4°C (b) ~ 0.6°C
(c) ~ 0.8°C (d) ~ 1.0°C

49. According to US water standards, the maximum permissible coliform count (number/100 mL) in recreational waters is:
(a) 10,000 (b) 5,000
(c) 1,000 (d) 500

50. **Assertion (A):** At present in India, the use of solar energy is rather limited.
Reason (R): Large scale use of solar energy has uncertain environmental implications.
(a) Both (A) and (R) are true and (R) is the correct explanation of (A)
(b) Both (A) and (R) are true but (R) is not the correct explanation of (A)
(c) (A) is true but (R) is false
(d) (A) is false but (R) is true

ANSWERS

1. (d)	2. (a)	3. (b)	4. (b)	5. (d)
6. (b)	7. (c)	8. (a)	9. (c)	10. (b)
11. (b)	12. (d)	13. (b)	14. (a)	15. (c)
16. (b)	17. (a)	18. (d)	19. (a)	20. (b)
21. (c)	22. (d)	23. (b)	24. (c)	25. (b)
26. (a)	27. (d)	28. (d)	29. (c)	30. (a)
31. (a)	32. (b)	33. (c)	34. (a)	35. (a)
36. (c)	37. (b)	38. (b)	39. (b)	40. (a)
41. (b)	42. (d)	43. (c)	44. (a)	45. (c)
46. (b)	47. (d)	48. (c)	49. (d)	50. (c)

JUNE–2008

Note: This paper contains Fifty (50) multiple-choice questions, each question carrying two (2) marks. Attempt all of them.

PAPER–I

1. The teacher has been glorified by the phrase "Friend, philosopher and guide" because
   (a) He has to play all vital roles in the context of society
   (b) He transmits the high value of humanity to students
   (c) He is the great reformer of the society
   (d) He is a great patriot

2. The most important cause of failure for teacher lies in the area of
   (a) interpersonal relationship
   (b) lack of command over the knowledge of the subject
   (c) verbal ability
   (d) strict handling of the students

3. A teacher can establish rapport with his students by
   (a) becoming a figure of authority
   (b) impressing students with knowledge and skill
   (c) playing the role of a guide
   (d) becoming a friend to the students

4. Education is a powerful instrument of
   (a) Social transformation
   (b) Personal transformation
   (c) Cultural transformation
   (d) All of the above

5. A teacher's major contribution towards the maximum self-realisation of the student is affected through
   (a) Constant fulfilment of the students' needs
   (b) Strict control of classroom activities
   (c) Sensitivity to students' needs, goals and purposes
   (d) Strict reinforcement of academic standards

6. Research problem is selected from the stand point of
   (a) Researcher's interest
   (b) Financial support
   (c) Social relevance
   (d) Availability of relevant literature

7. Which one is called non-probability sampling?
   (a) Cluster sampling
   (b) Quota sampling
   (c) Systematic sampling
   (d) Stratified random sampling

8. Formulation of hypothesis may not be required in
   (a) Survey method
   (b) Historical studies
   (c) Experimental studies
   (d) Normative studies

9. Fieldwork based research is classified as
   (a) Empirical (b) Historical
   (c) Experimental (d) Biographical

10. Which of the following sampling method is appropriate to study the prevalence of AIDS amongst male and female in India in 1976, 1986, 1996 and 2006?

(a) Cluster sampling
(b) Systematic sampling
(c) Quota sampling
(d) Stratified random sampling

Read the following passage and answer the questions 11 to 15:

The fundamental principle is that Article 14 forbids class legislation but permits reasonable classification for the purpose of legislation which classification must satisfy the twin tests of classification being founded on an intelligible differential which distinguishes persons or things that are grouped together from those that are left out of the group and that differentia must have a rational nexus to the object sought to be achieved by the Statute in question. The thrust of Article 14 is that the citizen is entitled to equality before law and equal protection of laws. In the very nature of things the society being composed of unequals a welfare State will have to strive by both executive and legislative action to help the less fortunate in society to ameliorate their condition so that the social and economic inequality in the society may be bridged. This would necessitate a legislative application to a group of citizens otherwise unequal and amelioration of whose lot is the object of state affirmative action. In the absence of the doctrine of classification such legislation is likely to flounder on the bedrock of equality enshrined in Article 14. The Court realistically appraising the social and economic inequality and keeping in view the guidelines on which the State action must move as constitutionally laid down in Part IV of the Constitution evolved the doctrine of classification. The doctrine was evolved to sustain a legislation or State action designed to help weaker sections of the society or some such segments of the society in need of succour. Legislative and executive action may accordingly be sustained if it satisfies the twin tests of reasonable classification and the rational principle correlated to the object sought to be achieved.

The concept of equality before the law does not involve the idea of absolute equality among human beings which is a physical impossibility. All that Article 14 guarantees is a similarity of treatment contra-distinguished from identical treatment. Equality before law means that among equals the law should be equal and should be equally administered and that the likes should be treated alike. Equality before the law does not mean that things which are different shall be as though they are the same. It of course means denial of any special privilege by reason of birth, creed or the like. The legislation as well as the executive government, while dealing with diverse problems arising out of an infinite variety of human relations must of necessity have the power of making special laws, to attain any particular object and to achieve that object it must have the power of selection or classification of persons and things upon which such laws are to operate.

11. Right to equality, one of the fundamental rights, is enunciated in the Constitution under Part III, Article
(a) 12 (b) 13
(c) 14 (d) 15

12. The main thrust of Right to equality is that it permits
(a) class legislation
(b) equality before law and equal protection under the law
(c) absolute equality
(d) special privilege by reason of birth

13. The social and economic inequality in the society can be bridged by
(a) executive and legislative action
(b) universal suffrage
(c) identical treatment
(d) None of the above

14. The doctrine of classification is evolved to
    (a) Help weaker sections of the society
    (b) Provide absolute equality
    (c) Provide identical treatment
    (d) None of the above

15. While dealing with diverse problems arising out of an infinite variety of human relations, the government
    (a) must have the power of making special laws
    (b) must not have any power to make special laws
    (c) must have power to withdraw equal rights
    (d) None of the above

16. Communication with oneself is known as
    (a) Group communication
    (b) Grapevine communication
    (c) Interpersonal communication
    (d) Intrapersonal communication

17. Which broadcasting system for TV is followed in India?
    (a) NTSE (b) PAL
    (c) SECAM (d) NTCS

18. All India Radio before 1936 was known as
    (a) Indian Radio Broadcasting
    (b) Broadcasting Service of India
    (c) Indian State Broadcasting Service
    (d) All India Broadcasting Service

19. The biggest news agency of India is
    (a) PTI
    (b) UNI
    (c) NANAP
    (d) Samachar Bharati

20. Prasar Bharati was launched in the year
    (a) 1995 (b) 1997
    (c) 1999 (d) 2001

21. A statistical measure based upon the entire population is called parameter while measure based upon a sample is known as
    (a) Sample parameter
    (b) Inference
    (c) Statistics
    (d) None of these

22. The importance of the correlation co-efficient lies in the fact that
    (a) There is a linear relationship between the correlated variables
    (b) It is one of the most valid measure of statistics
    (c) It allows one to determine the degree or strength of the association between two variables
    (d) It is a non-parametric method of statistical analysis

23. The F-test
    (a) is essentially a two tailed test
    (b) is essentially a one tailed test
    (c) can be one tailed as well as two tailed depending on the hypothesis
    (d) can never be a one tailed test

24. What will be the next letter in the following series
    DCXW, FEVU, HGTS, ______
    (a) AKPO (b) JBYZ
    (c) JIRQ (d) LMRS

25. The following question is based on the diagram given below. If the two small circles represent formal classroom education and distance education and the big circle stands for university system of education, which figure represents the university systems?

    (a) 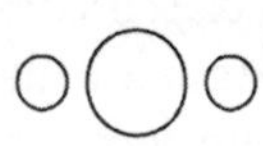 (b) 

    (c) 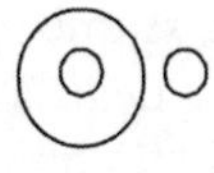 (d) 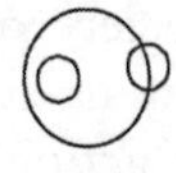

26. The statement, *To be non-violent is good* is a

(a) Moral judgement
(b) Factual judgement
(c) Religious judgement
(d) Value judgement

27. **Assertion (A):** Man is a rational being.

Reason (R): Man is a social being.
(a) Both (A) and (R) are true and (R) is the correct explanation of (A)
(b) Both (A) and (R) are true but (R) is not the correct explanation of (A)
(c) (A) is true but (R) is false
(d) (A) is false but (R) is true

28. Value Judgements are
(a) Factual Judgements
(b) Ordinary Judgements
(c) Normative Judgements
(d) Expression of public opinion

29. Deductive reasoning proceeds from
(a) general to particular
(b) particular to general
(c) one general conclusion to another general conclusion
(d) one particular conclusion to another particular conclusion

30. AGARTALA is written in code as 14168171, the code for AGRA is
(a) 1641 (b) 1416
(c) 1441 (d) 1461

31. Which one of the following is the most comprehensive source of population data?
(a) National Family Health Surveys
(b) National Sample Surveys
(c) Census
(d) Demographic Health Surveys

32. Which one of the following principles is not applicable to sampling?
(a) Sample units must be clearly defined
(b) Sample units must be dependent on each other
(c) Same units of sample should be used throughout the study
(d) Sample units must be chosen in a systematic and objective manner

33. If January 1st, 2007 is Monday, what was the day on 1st January 1995?
(a) Sunday (b) Monday
(c) Friday (d) Saturday

34. Insert the missing number in the following series
4 16 8 64 ? 256
(a) 16 (b) 24
(c) 32 (d) 20

35. If an article is sold for ₹ 178 at a loss of 11%; what would be its selling price in order to earn a profit of 11%?
(a) ₹ 222.50 (b) ₹ 267
(c) ₹ 222 (d) ₹ 220

36. WYSIWYG—describes the display of a document on screen as it will actually print
(a) What you state is what you get
(b) What you see is what you get
(c) What you save is what you get
(d) What you suggest is what you get

37. Which of the following is not a Computer language?
(a) PASCAL (b) UNIX
(c) FORTRAN (d) COBOL

38. A keyboard has at least
(a) 91 keys (b) 101 keys
(c) 111 keys (d) 121 keys

39. An E-mail address is composed of
(a) two parts (b) three parts
(c) four parts (d) five parts

40. Corel Draw is a popular
(a) Illustration program
(b) Programming language
(c) Text program
(d) None of the above

41. Human ear is most sensitive to noise in which of the following ranges
(a) 1-2 KHz (b) 100-500 Hz
(c) 10-12 KHz (d) 13-16 KHz

42. Which one of the following units is used to measure intensity of noise?

(a) decible (b) Hz
(c) Phon (d) Watts/m^2

43. If the population growth follows a logistic curve, the maximum sustainable yield
(a) is equal to half the carrying capacity
(b) is equal to the carrying capacity
(c) depends on growth rates
(d) depends on the initial population

44. Chemical weathering of rocks is largely dependent upon
(a) high temperature
(b) strong wind action
(c) heavy rainfall
(d) glaciation

45. Structure of earth's system consists of the following: Match List I with List II and give the correct answer.

List I (Zone)
A. Atmosphere B. Biosphere
C. Hydrosphere D. Lithosphere

List II (Chemical Character)
1. Inert gases
2. Salt, freshwater, snow and ice
3. Organic substances, skeleton matter
4. Light silicates

Codes:	A	B	C	D
(a)	2	3	1	4
(b)	1	3	2	4
(c)	2	1	3	4
(d)	3	1	2	4

46. NAAC is an autonomous institution under the aegis of
(a) ICSSR (b) CSIR
(c) AICTE (d) UGC

47. National Council for Women's Education was established in
(a) 1958 (b) 1976
(c) 1989 (d) 2000

48. Which one of the following is not situated in New Delhi?
(a) Indian Council of Cultural Relations
(b) Indian Council of Scientific Research
(c) National Council of Educational Research and Training
(d) Indian Institute of Advanced Studies

49. Autonomy in higher education implies freedom in
(a) Administration
(b) Policy-making
(c) Finance
(d) Curriculum development

50. Match List I with List II and select the correct answer from the codes given below

List I (Institutions)
A. Dr. Hari Singh Gour University
B. S.N.D.T. University
C. M.S. University
D. J.N. Vyas University

List II (Locations)
1. Mumbai 2. Baroda
3. Jodhpur 4. Sagar

Codes:	A	B	C	D
(a)	4	1	2	3
(b)	1	2	3	4
(c)	3	1	2	4
(d)	2	4	1	3

ANSWERS

1. (b)	2. (b)	3. (b)	4. (d)	5. (c)
6. (c)	7. (b)	8. (b)	9. (a)	10. (d)
11. (c)	12. (b)	13. (a)	14. (a)	15. (a)
16. (d)	17. (b)	18. (c)	19. (a)	20. (b)
21. (a)	22. (c)	23. (c)	24. (c)	25. (b)
26. (a)	27. (b)	28. (c)	29. (a)	30. (d)
31. (c)	32. (b)	33. (d)	34. (a)	35. (c)
36. (b)	37. (b)	38. (b)	39. (a)	40. (a)
41. (b)	42. (a)	43. (a)	44. (c)	45. (b)
46. (d)	47. (a)	48. (d)	49. (c)	50. (a)

PAPER–II

Note: This paper contains fifty (50) objective type questions, each question carrying two (2) marks. Attempt all the questions.

1. **Assertion (A):** Sustainable development is necessary for the survival of human race.
   Reason (R): Rapid economic growth without environmental concerns cannot be sustained.
   (a) (A) is true and (R) is false.
   (b) (A) is false and (R) is true.
   (c) Both (A) and (R) true but (R) is not the correct explanation.
   (d) Both (A) and (R) true and (R) is the correct explanation.

2. The spatial scale of meso scale meteorological phenomena is approximately:
   (a) 2 – 3 km to 5 – 6 km
   (b) few km to 100 km
   (c) few 100 m to few km
   (d) 10 mm to 1 km

3. The mass of the earth's mantle is approximately:
   (a) 2×10^{25} gm (b) 8.1×10^{17} gm
   (c) 4.05×10^{27} gm (d) 3.1×10^{22} gm

4. When the environmental lapse rate is less than the adiabatic lapse rate, the atmosphere is:
   (a) Stable
   (b) Moderately unstable
   (c) Highly unstable
   (d) Neutral

5. The standard hydrogen electrode, the pressure of hydrogen and hydrogen ion concentration respectively are:
   (a) 1 atm ; 10 m (b) 10 atm ; 1m
   (c) 1 atm ; 1 m (d) 1 atm ; m/10

6. Consider the following statements:
   (i) Entropy in a spontaneous reaction increases
   (ii) Free energy in a spontaneous reaction increases
   (iii) Free energy remains constant when reaction is in equilibrium
   (iv) Free energy increases in a reverse reaction Which of these are correct:
   (a) (i) and (ii) (b) (ii) and (iii)
   (c) (i), (iii) and (iv) (d) None of these

7. **Assertion (A):** Increased level of Arsenic in water is—health hazard.
   Reason (R): Arsenic has antagonistic behaviour with other metals, its dietary requirement is in trace amount and shows speciation.
   (a) Both (A) and (R) true.
   (b) Both (A) and (R) true but (R) is not the correct explanation of (A).
   (c) (A) is true but (R) is false.
   (d) (A) is false but (R) is true.

8. One liter of water contains:
   (a) $55.5 \times 6.02 \times 10^{23}$ H_2O molecules
   (b) $25.5 \times 6.02 \times 10^{23}$ H_2O molecules
   (c) $1.0 \times 6.02 \times 10^{23}$ H_2O molecules
   (d) $1000 \times 6.02 \times 10^{23}$ H_2O molecules

9. When terrestrial plant communities progress with time from successional to climax stage:
   (i) Standing crop biomass increases
   (ii) Net ecosystem productivity increases
   (iii) Gross productivity per unit of standing crop biomass decreases
   (iv) Biomass supported per unit of energy flow decreases.

   Which of the following combination is correct:
   (a) (i) and (ii) (b) (i) and (iii)
   (c) (i) and (iv) (d) (ii) and (iii)

10. **Assertion (A):** 'Hot spots' are the region showing richness of endemic species.

Reason (R): The distribution of endemic species are confined to a specific region.
(a) Both (A) and (R) are true and (R) is correct explanation of (A).
(b) Both (A) and (R) are true but (R) is not the correct explanation.
(c) (A) is true but (R) is false.
(d) (A) is false but (R) is true.

11. Trophic structure may be shown graphically by ecological pyramids; which of the following ecological pyramid will always have a true upright pyramid shape:
(a) Pyramid of numbers
(b) Pyramid of biomass
(c) Pyramid of energy
(d) All of the above

12. Species diversity is generally higher in ecosystem experiencing:
(a) No disturbance
(b) Moderate disturbance
(c) High disturbance
(d) Drastic disturbance

13. Those Planktons which have dimensions in the range of 2 – 20 μm are known as:
(a) Micro plankton (b) Nano plankton
(c) Peri plankton (d) Pico plankton

14. **Assertion (A):** Plants are not auxotrophs.
Reason (R): Plants can synthesize all the growth factors they need.
(a) Both (A) and (R) are true and (R) is the correct explanation of (A).
(b) Both (A) and (R) are true but (R) is not the correct explanation of (A).
(c) (A) is false and (R) is true.
(d) (A) is true and (R) is false.

15. **Assertion (A):** Decomposition of hydrocarbons is favoured in neutral soil.
Reason (R): Neutral pH favours the greatest populations of micro organisms.
(a) Both (A) and (R) are true and (R) is not the correct explanation of (A).
(b) Both (A) and (R) are true and (R) is the correct explanation of (A)
(c) (A) is false (R) is true
(d) (A) is true (R) is false

16. A majority of the antibiotics are derived from actinomycetes come from members of the genus:
(a) *Nocardia* (b) *Streptomyces*
(c) *Micromonospora* (d) *Actinomyces*

17. Germany's poison gas in World War I was developed by:
(a) Knowels (b) Haber
(c) Hitlor (d) Stevenson

18. Which of the following nitrogen fixers is found in philosophers?
(a) *Azotobacter*
(b) *Clostridium*
(c) *Klebsiella*
(d) *Rhodospirillum*

19. *Thiobacillus* and *Beggiatoa* play an important role in the:
(a) Water cycle on Earth
(b) Phosphorus cycle
(c) Sulphur cycle in the soil
(d) Breakdown of sewage

20. One of the purpose of secondary treatment of industrial waste water and sewage is to:
(a) increase the chlorine content
(b) reduce the BOD
(c) encourage the formation of PCBs
(d) discourage ammonification

21. AGENDA 21 specifically advocates to devise strategies to:
(a) Promote economic growth to support increasing human population with adequate environment care
(b) Control human population explosion, resource over use and deteriorating environmental quality

(c) Halt and reverse the effects of environmental degradation to promote sustainable and environmentally sound development
(d) Promote economic development and environmental with a view to reduce poverty and faster human welfare

22. Eutrophication of water bodies is triggered by:
(a) Excessive growth of phytoplanktons
(b) Excessive growth of fishes
(c) Excessive inflow of nutrients
(d) Bright sunlight

23. Under montreal protocol, developing countries are required to phase out the HCFCs by the year:
(a) 2030 (b) 2010
(c) 2020 (d) 2040

24. Identify the correct sequence of gases in the increasing order of their global warming potential:
(a) $CH_4 < N_2O < CFC < SF_6$
(b) $CO_2 < N_2O < CH_4 < CFC$
(c) $CO_2 < CH_4 < SF_6 < CFC$
(d) $N_2O < CH_4 < CO_2 < CFC$

25. In a simple regression consisting of dependent variable Y, independent variable X and random error term $\in$, $Y = \alpha + \beta X + \in$, the expectation value $< \in >$ is:
(a) 0 (b) α/β
(c) β/α (d) $(\beta - \alpha)$

26. If p and q are the probabilities of success and failure, respectively in a trial and N is the total number of trials, the variance is:
(a) $\sqrt{npq}$ (b) npq
(c) $n\frac{p}{q}$ (d) $n\frac{q}{p}$

27. If S = 4 is the standard deviation of sample size 20 drawn from a normal distribution with standard deviation σ = 2, the value of Ψ^2 (Chi-square) statistic is:
(a) 40 (b) 10
(c) 20 (d) 80

28. Under unstable atmospheric conditions, the plum rise (Δh) above the stack varies with wind speed (u) at stack height as:
(a) $\Delta h \propto u$ (b) $\Delta h \propto 1/u$
(c) $\Delta h \propto u^{1/3}$ (d) $\Delta h \propto u^{-1/3}$

29. The geometric mean of the data 2, 4, 27 is:
(a) 6 (b) $\sqrt[6]{6}$
(c) 16.5 (d) $\sqrt{33}$

30. Bulking of sewage sludge is frequently associated with:
(a) High C: N ratio
(b) High C: P ratio
(c) High dissolved oxygen
(d) All of the above

31. Which of the following is removed from waste water by:
(a) Phosphates
(b) Organic Compounds
(c) Ammonia
(d) Sulphates

32. The bacteria responsible for deposition of iron oxide in water pipes:
(a) *Gallionella* (b) *Klebsiella*
(c) *Thermococcus* (d) *Helicobacter*

33. **Assertion (A):** In electrostatic precipitator corona discharge is used for removing particulate particles from the gas stream.
Reason (R): The corona discharge creates an electric field, which makes the particles settle down.
(a) Both (A) and (R) are true and (R) is the correct explanation of (A).
(b) Both (A) and (R) are true but (R) is not the correct explanation of (A).
(c) (A) is true but (R) is false.
(d) (A) is false but (R) is true.

34. Which of the following affects the ozone concentration in troposphere:
(a) CO (b) N_2
(c) SO_2 (d) CO_2

35. **Assertion (A):** While characterizing the size of an aerosol particle aerodynamic diameter is used.
Reason (R): The aerosol particle may be of irregular shape.
(a) Both (A) and (R) are true and (R) is correct explanation of (A).
(b) Both (A) and (R) are true but (R) is not the correct explanation of (A).
(c) (A) is true but (R) is false.
(d) (A) is false but (R) is true.

36. The noise index Lgo refers to:
(a) Background noise level
(b) Peak noise level
(c) Average noise level
(d) 90%

37. Fission of 1 gm of ^{235}U liberates energy equivalent to about:
(a) 5.7 barrels of crude oil
(b) 13.7 barrels of crude oil
(c) 18.7 barrels of crude oil
(d) 22.7 barrels of crude oil

38. To increase the power output from a MHD power plant, which of the following compounds is used:
(a) ZnO (b) Fe_2O_3
(c) Cs_2O_3 (d) SiO_2

39. **Assertion (A):** Geothermal reservoirs with temperatures above 180°C are useful for generating electric power.
Reason (R): High temperature steam can be used to drive turbines to generate electricity.
(a) Both (A) and (R) are true and (R) is the ecorrect explanation of (A).
(b) Both (A) and (R) are true but (R) is not the correct explanation of (A).
(c) (A) is true but (R) is false.
(d) (A) is false but (R) is true.

40. The optimum range of wind speeds for wind power generation is:
(a) 2 – 4 m/sec (b) 1 – 2 m/sec
(c) 4 – 12 m/sec (d) 15 – 20 m/sec

41. Deep sea ferromanganese nodules are found on:
(a) Oceanic plateau (b) Oceanic ridges
(c) Oceanic islands (d) Oceanic plains

42. In ocean regime carbonate compensation depth (CCD) implies:
(a) Precipitation of carbonate
(b) Dissolution of carbonate
(c) Evaporation of carbonate
(d) Sublimation of carbonate

43. Which of the following statement is not correct:
Carcinogenic agents like pesticides are mutagens which may cause.
(a) Change in chromosome
(b) Change in nucleotide sequence in DNA of sperms or eggs, which is inherited
(c) Change in nucleotide sequence in DNA of somatic cells is inherited
(d) Change in DNA sequence may be due to generation of free radicals in the cells

44. According to the Public Liability Insurance Act 1991, what is the upper monetary limit for drawing insurance policies by the owners for handling any hazardous substance:
(a) ₹ 5 Crores (b) ₹ 50 Crores
(c) ₹ 500 Crores (d) ₹ 1000 Crores

45. Hospital waste has to be disposed off by:
(a) handing over to hazardous waste management site
(b) burrying 3 meters below the ground
(c) burrying 10 meters below the ground
(d) incineration

46. Which of the following industries do not produce hazardous waste?
(a) Electroplating (b) Chemical
(c) Sugar (d) Pharmaceutical

47. Four stages, viz. Initiation, Inventory analysis, Impact assessment and improvement assessment are associated with:
(a) LCA
(b) EIA
(c) Environmental Audit
(d) Environmental Impact - Statement

48. When industry with 'Red' category is to be established, it is necessary to have public hearing or inquiry under the procedure called as:
(a) Environmental Health Hazard (EHH)
(b) Environmental Litigation (EL)
(c) Environmental Management System (EMS)
(d) Environmental Impact Assessment (EIA)

49. The National Ambient Air Quality Standard for 1 hour average concentration (mg/m^3) of CO in restricted area is:
(a) 2 (b) 4
(c) 16 (d) 20

50. For aerosol particles of size comparable to wavelengths of either shortwave radiation or infrared radiation, the following type of scattering takes place:
(a) Rayleigh scattering
(b) Mie scattering
(c) Raman scattering
(d) Brillouin scattering

ANSWERS

1. (c)	2. (c)	3. (d)	4. (b)	5. (c)
6. (b)	7. (c)	8. (c)	9. (c)	10. (b)
11. (c)	12. (d)	13. (b)	14. (d)	15. (b)
16. (d)	17. (a)	18. (a)	19. (d)	20. (b)
21. (a)	22. (a)	23. (c)	24. (b)	25. (a)
26. (b)	27. (b)	28. (a)	29. (a)	30. (b)
31. (b)	32. (b)	33. (a)	34. (b)	35. (c)
36. (c)	37. (b)	38. (b)	39. (b)	40. (c)
41. (b)	42. (a)	43. (d)	44. (b)	45. (d)
46. (a)	47. (d)	48. (a)	49. (a)	50. (a)

DECEMBER–2008

Note: This paper contains Fifty (50) multiple-choice questions, each question carrying two (2) marks. Attempt all of them.

PAPER–I

1. According to Swami Vivekananda, teacher's success depends on
   (a) His renunciation of personal gain and service to others
   (b) His professional training and creativity
   (c) His concentration on his work and duties with a spirit of obedience to God
   (d) His mastery on the subject and capacity in controlling the students

2. Which of the following teacher will be liked most?
   (a) A teacher of high idealistic attitude
   (b) A loving teacher
   (c) A teacher who is disciplined
   (d) A teacher who often amuses his students

3. A teacher's most important challenge is
   (a) To make students do their home work
   (b) To make teaching-learning process enjoyable
   (c) To maintain discipline in the classroom
   (d) To prepare the question paper

4. Value-education stands for
   (a) making a student healthy
   (b) making a student to get a job
   (c) inculcation of virtues
   (d) all-round development of personality

5. When a normal student behaves in an erratic manner in the class, you would
   (a) pull up the student then and there
   (b) talk to the student after the class
   (c) ask the student to leave the class
   (d) ignore the student

6. The research is always
   (a) verifying the old knowledge
   (b) exploring new knowledge
   (c) filling the gap between knowledge
   (d) All of these

7. The research that applies the laws at the time of field study to draw more and more clear ideas about the problem is
   (a) Applied research
   (b) Action research
   (c) Experimental research
   (d) None of these

8. When a research problem is related to heterogeneous population, the most suitable sampling method is
   (a) Cluster Sampling
   (b) Stratified Sampling
   (c) Convenient Sampling
   (d) Lottery Method

9. The process not needed in experimental research is:
   (a) Observation
   (b) Manipulation and replication
   (c) Controlling
   (d) Reference collection

10. A research problem is not feasible only when
    (a) it is researchable
    (b) it is new and adds something to knowledge
    (c) it consists of independent and dependent variables
    (d) it has utility and relevance

Read the following passage carefully and answer the questions 11 to 15:

Radically changing monsoon patterns, reduction in the winter rice harvest and a quantum increase in respiratory diseases all part of the environmental doomsday scenario which is reportedly playing out in South Asia. According to a United Nations Environment Program report, a deadly three-kilometer deep blanket of pollution comprising a fearsome, cocktail of ash, acids, aerosols and other particles has enveloped in this region. For India, already struggling to cope with a drought, the implication of this are devastating and further crop failure will amount to a life and death question for many Indians. The increase in premature deaths will have adverse social and economic consequences and a rise in morbidities will place an unbearable burden on our crumbling health system. And there is no one to blame but ourselves. Both official and corporate India has always been allergic to any mention of clean technology. Most mechanical two wheelers roll of the assembly line without proper pollution control system. Little effort is made for R&D on simple technologies, which could make a vital difference to people's lives and the environment.

However, while there is no denying that South Asia must clean up its act, skeptics might question the timing of the haze report. The Kyoto meet on climate change is just two weeks away and the stage is set for the usual battle between the developing world and the West, particularly the United States of America. President Mr. Bush has adamantly refused to sign any protocol, which would mean a change in American consumption level. U.N. environment report will likely find a place in the U.S. arsenal as it plants an accusing finger towards controls like India and China. Yet the U.S.A. can hardly deny its own dubious role in the matter of erasing trading quotas.

Richer countries can simply buy up excess credits from poorer countries and continue to pollute. Rather than try to get the better of developing countries, who undoubtedly have taken up environmental shortcuts in their bid to catch up with the West, the USA should take a look at the environmental profigacy, which is going on within. From opening up virgin territories for oil exploration to relaxing the standards for drinking water, Mr. Bush's policies are not exactly beneficial, not even to America's interests. We realise that we are all in this together and that pollution anywhere should be a global concern otherwise there will only be more tunnels at the end of the tunnel.

11. Both official and corporate India is allergic to
    (a) Failure of Monsoon
    (b) Poverty and Inequality
    (c) Slowdown in Industrial Production
    (d) Mention of Clean Technology
12. If the rate of premature death increases it will
    (a) Exert added burden on the crumbling economy
    (b) Have adverse social and economic consequences
    (c) Make positive effect on our effort to control population
    (d) Have less job aspirants in the society
13. According to the passage, the two-wheeler industry is not adequately concerned about

(a) Passenger safety on the roads
(b) Life cover insurance of the vehicle owner
(c) Pollution control system in the vehicle
(d) Rising cost of the two wheelers

14. What could be the reason behind timing of the haze report just before the Kyoto meet?
(a) United Nations is working hand-in-glove with U.S.A.
(b) Organisers of the forthcoming meet to teach a lesson to the U.S.A.
(c) Drawing attention of the world towards devastating effects of environment degradation.
(d) U.S.A. wants to use it as a handle against the developing countries in the forthcoming meet.

15. Which of the following is the indication of environmental degradation in South Asia?
(a) Social and economic inequality
(b) Crumbling health care system
(c) Inadequate pollution control system
(d) Radically changing monsoon pattern

16. Community Radio is a type of radio service that caters to the interest of
(a) Local audience (b) Education
(c) Entertainment (d) News

17. Orkut is a part of
(a) Intrapersonal Communication
(b) Mass Communication
(c) Group Communication
(d) Interpersonal Communication

18. Match List I with List II and select the correct answer using the codes given below.

List I (Artists)
A. Amrita Shergill
B. T. Swaminathan Pillai
C. Bhimsen Joshi
D. Padma Subramaniyam

List II (Art)
1. Flute 2. Classical Song
3. Painting 4. Bharat Natyam

Codes:	A	B	C	D
(a)	3	1	2	4
(b)	2	3	1	4
(c)	4	2	3	1
(d)	1	4	2	3

19. Which is not correct in latest communication award?
(a) Salman Rushdie – Booker's Prize—July 20, 2008
(b) Dilip Sanghavi – Business Standard CEO Award, July 22, 2008
(c) Tapan Sinha – Dada Saheb Falke Award, July 21, 2008
(d) Gautam Ghosh – Osians Lifetime Achievement Award, July 11, 2008

20. Firewalls are used to protect a communication network system against
(a) Unauthorised attacks
(b) Virus attacks
(c) Data-driven attacks
(d) Fire-attacks

21. Insert the missing number in the following

$\frac{2}{7}, \frac{4}{7}, ?, \frac{11}{21}, \frac{16}{31},$

(a) $\frac{10}{8}$ (b) $\frac{6}{10}$

(c) $\frac{5}{10}$ (d) $\frac{7}{13}$

22. In a certain code, GAMESMAN is written as AGMEMSAN. How would DISCLOSE be written in that code?
(a) IDSCOLSE (b) IDCSOLES
(c) IDSCOLES (d) IDSCLOSE

23. The letters in the first set have a certain relationship. On the basis of this relationship mark the right choice for the second set : AST : BRU :: NQV: ?
(a) ORW (b) MPU
(c) MRW (d) OPW

24. On what dates of April, 1994 did Sunday fall?
(a) 2, 9, 16, 23, 30
(b) 3, 10, 17, 24
(c) 4, 11, 18, 25
(d) 1, 8, 15, 22, 29

25. Find out the wrong number in the sequence
125, 127, 130, 135, 142, 153, 165
(a) 130 (b) 142
(c) 153 (d) 165

26. There are five books A, B, C, D and E. The book C lies above D, the book E is below A and B is below E. Which is at the bottom?
(a) E (b) B
(c) A (d) C

27. Logical reasoning is based on
(a) Truth of involved propositions
(b) Valid relation among the involved propositions
(c) Employment of symbolic language
(d) Employment of ordinary language

28. Two propositions with the same subject and predicate terms but different in quality are
(a) Contradictory (b) Contrary
(c) Subaltern (d) Identical

29. The premises of a valid deductive argument
(a) Provide some evidence for its conclusion
(b) Provide no evidence for its conclusion
(c) Are irrelevant for its conclusion
(d) Provide conclusive evidence for its conclusion

30. Syllogistic reasoning is
(a) Deductive (b) Inductive
(c) Experimental (d) Hypothetical

Study the following Venn diagram and answer questions nos. 31 to 33.

Three circles representing GRADUATES, CLERKS and GOVERNMENT EMPLOYEES are intersecting. The intersections are marked A, B, C, e, f, g and h. Which part best represents the statements in questions 31 to 33?

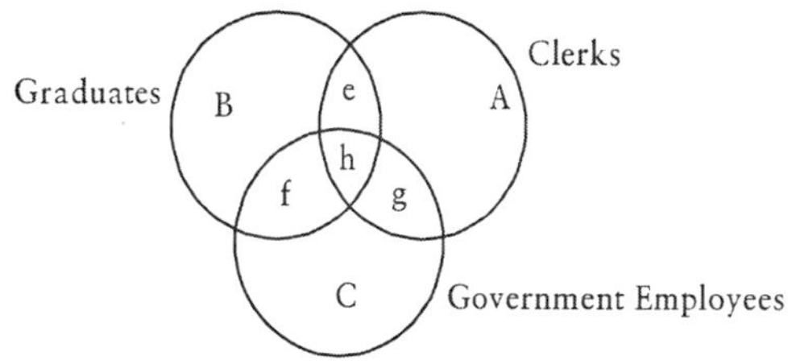

31. Some Graduates are Government employees but not as Clerks.
(a) h (b) g
(c) f (d) e

32. Clerks who are graduates as well as government employees.
(a) e (b) f
(c) g (d) h

33. Some graduates are Clerks but not Government employees.
(a) f (b) g
(c) h (d) e

Study the following graph and answer questions numbers from 34 to 35

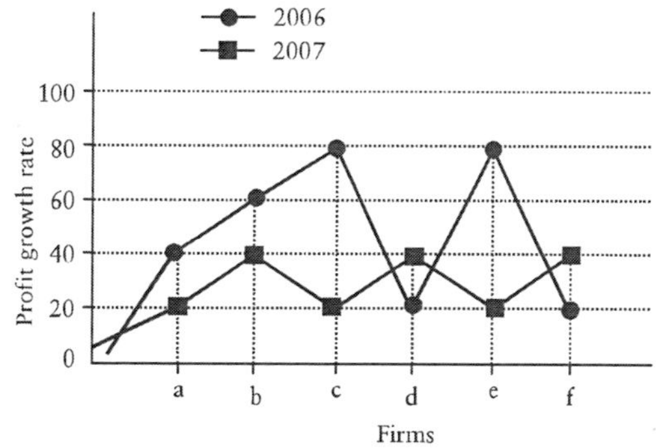

34. Which of the firms got maximum profit growth rate in the year 2006?
(a) ab (b) ce
(c) cd (d) ef

35. Which of the firms got maximum profit growth rate in the year 2007?
(a) bdf (b) acf
(c) bed (d) ace

36. The accounting software 'Tally' was developed by
(a) HCL (b) TCS
(c) Infosys (d) Wipro

37. Errors in computer programs are called
(a) Follies (b) Mistakes
(c) Bugs (d) Spam

38. HTML is basically used to design
(a) Webpage
(b) Website
(c) Graphics
(d) Tables and Frames

39. 'Micro Processing' is made for
(a) Computer
(b) Digital System
(c) Calculator
(d) Electronic Goods

40. Information, a combination of graphics, text, sound, video and animation is called
(a) Multiprogram
(b) Multifacet
(c) Multimedia
(d) Multiprocess

41. Which of the following pairs regarding typical composition of hospital wastes is incorrect?
(a) Plastic - 9-12%
(b) Metals - 1-2%
(c) Ceramic - 8-10%
(d) Biodegradable - 35-40%

42. Freshwater achieves its greatest density at
(a) –4°C (b) 0°C
(c) 4°C (d) –2.5°C

43. Which one of the following is not associated with earthquakes?
(a) Focus (b) Epicenter
(c) Seismograph (d) Swells

44. The tallest trees in the world are found in the region
(a) Equatorial region
(b) Temperate region
(c) Monsoon region
(d) Mediterranean region

45. Match List I with List II and select the correct answer from the codes given below.

List I (National Parks)
A. Periyar
B. Nandan Kanan
C. Corbett National Park
D. Sariska Tiger Reserve

List II (States)
1. Odisha
2. Kerala
3. Rajasthan
4. Uttarakhand

Codes:	A	B	C	D
(a)	2	1	4	3
(b)	1	2	4	3
(c)	3	2	1	4
(d)	1	2	3	4

46. According to Radhakrishnan Commission, the aim of Higher Education is
(a) To develop the democratic values, peace and harmony
(b) To develop great personalities who can give their contributions in politics, administration, industry and commerce
(c) Both (a) and (b)
(d) None of these

47. The National Museum at New Delhi is attached to

(a) Delhi University
(b) a Deemed University
(c) a Subordinate Office of the JNU
(d) Part of Ministry of Tourism and Culture

48. Match List I with List II and select the correct answer from the code given below.

List I (Institutions)	List II (Locations)
A. National Law Institute	1. Shimla
B. Indian Institute of Advanced Studies	2. Bhopal
C. National Judicial Academy	3. Hyderabad
D. National Savings Institute	4. Nagpur

Codes:	A	B	C	D
(a)	3	2	4	1
(b)	1	2	3	4
(c)	4	3	1	2
(d)	3	1	2	4

49. Election of Rural and Urban local bodies are conducted and ultimately supervised by
(a) Election Commission of India
(b) State Election Commission
(c) District Collector and District Magistrate
(d) Concerned Returning Officer

50. Which opinion is not correct?
(a) Education is a subject of concurrent list of VII schedule of Constitution of India
(b) University Grants Commission is a statutory body
(c) Patent, inventions, design, copyright and trade marks are the subject of concurrent list
(d) Indian Council of Social Science Research is a statutory body related to research in social sciences

ANSWERS

1. (d)	2. (c)	3. (b)	4. (c)	5. (b)
6. (d)	7. (a)	8. (b)	9. (d)	10. (b)
11. (d)	12. (b)	13. (c)	14. (c)	15. (d)
16. (a)	17. (d)	18. (a)	19. (b)	20. (a)
21. (d)	22. (a)	23. (d)	24. (b)	25. (d)
26. (b)	27. (b)	28. (a)	29. (d)	30. (a)
31. (c)	32. (d)	33. (d)	34. (b)	35. (a)
36. (b)	37. (c)	38. (a)	39. (a)	40. (c)
41. (d)	42. (c)	43. (d)	44. (b)	45. (a)
46. (c)	47. (d)	48. (d)	49. (b)	50. (c)

PAPER–II

Note: This paper contains fifty (50) objective type questions, each question carrying two (2) marks. Attempt all the questions.

1. Plants suitable for biomonitoring of SO_2 pollution are:
(a) White pine, moss and lichens
(b) Tobacco, grapes and garden bean
(c) Apricot, peach and gladiolas
(d) Tomato and lettuce

2. Which of the following survive by forming spores?
(a) *Escherichia coli* (b) *Rhizobium*
(c) *Clostridium* (d) *Salmonella*

3. *Deinococcus* and *Deinobacter* are radiation resistant bacteria because:
(a) They have effective repair mechanism for damaged DNA and have high concentration of carotenoids
(b) They do not absorb radiations
(c) They have RNA instead of DNA
(d) They grow in ice

4. The orchid seeds do not germinate under ordinary conditions because:
   (a) Orchid seeds are too large for dispersal
   (b) Orchid seeds do not have endosperm
   (c) Orchid seeds undergo a dormancy period
   (d) They germinate under very dry conditions
5. Which of the following is for rhizosphere?
   (a) Region where soil and roots make contact
   (b) Apical part of root
   (c) Epidermal part of the root
   (d) Root hairs
6. Suppose the number of individual prey population is N_1 and their intrinsic rate of population increase N_1, where:

   $r_1 = b - m$

   b = birth rate per individual

   m = mortality rate per individual, then the rate of change of the prey population (dN_1/dt) (without immigration and emigration) is as below:

   (a) $\frac{1}{2}r_1N_1$ (b) r_1N_1
   (c) $(r_1N_1)^2$ (d) $(r_1N_1)^{1/2}$
7. The photosynthetic zone is limited to the upper layers of water in the soil with a high intensity of productivity per unit volume, yielding an average of about:
   (a) 300 mg c m^{-2} hr^{-1}
   (b) 250 mg c m^{-2} hr^{-1}
   (c) 100 mg c m^{-2} hr^{-1}
   (d) 75 mg c m^{-2} hr^{-1}
8. **Assertion (A):** Copper - T is used as a contraceptive.

   Reason (R): Copper of Copper - T disrupts production of some reproductive hormone.
   (a) Both (A) and (R) are true and (R) is correct explanation of (A).
   (b) Both (A) and (R) are true, but (R) is not correct explanation of (A).
   (c) (A) is true, but (R) is false.
   (d) (A) is false, but (R) is true.
9. Asbestos use is banned in many countries. It is known to cause:
   (a) Cardiac diseases
   (b) Urinary diseases
   (c) Lung cancer
   (d) Cataract
10. Which of the following is used as a carrier for the Rhizobium biofertilization?
    (a) Peat bog (b) Salt
    (c) Sand (d) Cow dung
11. The flow in natural streams is almost always turbulent and may be assumed to be incompressible, consequently the applicable equations of motion for the fluid are the:
    (a) Bed-load equation
    (b) Reynolds equation
    (c) Lane's model
    (d) Lacey's equation
12. Suspended sediment load is that part of the sediment load which is transported within the main body flow. The primary mechanism of maintaining the sediment particles in suspension is:
    (a) Channel flow
    (b) Particle size
    (c) Turbulent diffusion
    (d) Dissolved gasses
13. A highly vesicular material derived from acidic lavas and produced in very large quantities is known as:
    (a) Scoriae (b) Volcanic bomb
    (c) Pumice (d) Tuff
14. Half life (T) of a radioactive sample is given by:

(a) $0.693/\lambda$ (b) $1.693/\lambda$
(c) $0.693/2\lambda$ (d) $1.693/2\lambda$

Where λ is the disintegration constant.

15. At the present time volcanoes are confined to certain limited areas of the Earth's surface. This special zone is called:
(a) Trans-Atlantic volcanic zone
(b) Circum-Pacific Ring of fire
(c) Central-Asian inter-continental zone
(d) Indian-Ocean volcanic belt

16. When the cavities between the mineral grains in a rock contains fluid, it is called:
(a) Permeable rock (b) Porous rock
(c) Cavernous rock (d) Fractured rock

17. Temperature in the troposphere:
(a) Decreases with height
(b) Rapidly increases with height
(c) Slowly increases with height
(d) Remains constant

18. Failure to explain the black body radiation emission spectrum in the ultraviolet region (ultraviolet catastrophe) has occurred in:
(a) Plancks radiation law
(b) Rayleigh Jeans law
(c) Wiens Displacement law
(d) Stephans Boltzmann law

19. A noise signal can be characterized through its amplitude/energy content in the signal. The signal can be expressed in various forms like root mean square value, given as:

(a) $\left[\frac{1}{T}\int_0^T a^2(t)dt\right]^{1/2}$ (b) $\left[\frac{1}{2T}\int_0^T a^2(t)dt\right]^{1/2}$

(c) $\left[\frac{1}{T}\int_0^T |a|\cdot dt\right]$ (d) $\left[\frac{1}{2T}\int_0^T |a|\cdot dt\right]$

Where T is the relevant time period over which the averaging takes place and $a(t)$ the instantaneous amplitude.

20. Sound pressure level (dB) can be expressed as:

(a) $20\ \log_{10}\left(\frac{\text{Measured pressure}}{\text{Reference pressure}}\right)$

(b) $20\ \log_{10}\left(\frac{\text{Reference pressure}}{\text{Measured pressure}}\right)$

(c) $20\ \log_{10}\left(\frac{\text{Reference pressure}}{\text{Measured pressure}}\right)^{1/2}$

(d) $20\ \log_{10}\left(\frac{\text{Measured pressure}}{\text{Reference pressure}}\right)^{1/2}$

21. Relationship regarding wave particle duality ($P = h/\lambda$, P = momentum, h = Plancks constant and λ, The wave length), was given by:
(a) Heisenberg (b) De Broglie
(c) Neils Bohr (d) Schroedinger

22. The effect of low level non-ionizing electromagnetic radiation effects on biological systems can be classified in the following category:
(a) Instantaneous (b) Delayed
(c) Not at all (d) Prolonged

23. Which of the following is a recalcitrant?
(a) Sugarcane waste (b) DDT
(c) Lignin (d) Cellulose

24. A small reduction in ozone concentration can lead to a large increase in the amount of harmful ultraviolet radiations reaching the earth in the wavelength region:
(a) 200 – 205 nm (b) 220 – 225 nm
(c) 260 – 265 nm (d) 295 – 300 nm

25. The planet nearest to the Sun is:
(a) Earth (b) Mercury
(c) Moon (d) Jupitor

26. Steel units generate which of the following air pollutants:
(a) Particulates, smoke, carbon monoxide, fluoride
(b) SO_2, acid mist

(c) NO_X, SO_2, particulates
(d) SO_2, NO_X, particulates, smoke

27. In a soil profile, O_2 concentration:
(a) Increases vertically from top to bottom
(b) Increases horizontally but not vertically
(c) Decreases vertically from top to bottom
(d) Both vertically and horizontally increases randomly

28. Mobile phone frequencies are in the range of:
(a) 1 kHz – 100 kHz
(b) 100 kHz – 100 MHz
(c) 100 MHz – 700 MHz
(d) 800 MHz – 2200 MHz

29. Elements in sea water present in order of increasing residence time:
(a) Na > Cl > Mg > Ca > K > Fe > P
(b) Cl > Na > Mg > Ca > K > P > Fe
(c) Cl > Mg > Ca > Na > K > Fe > P
(d) Mg > Ca > Cl > Na > K > P > Fe

30. **Assertion (A):** Aerosols have potential for modifying the climate.
Reason (R): Aerosols interact with both short wave and infrared radiation.
(a) Both (A) and (R) are true and (R) is the correct explanation of (A).
(b) Both (A) and (R) are true, but (R) is not the correct explanation of (A).
(c) (A) is true, but (R) is false.
(d) (A) is false, but (R) is true.

31. Out of the following which is not a greenhouse gas:
(a) CH_4 (b) CO_2
(c) N_2O (d) SO_2

32. Ozone "hole" in the stratosphere was discovered over the continent of:
(a) North America (b) Australia
(c) Antarctica (d) Greenland

33. Which of the following layers of Earth have the composition of peridotite?
(a) Upper Mantle
(b) Inner Core
(c) Outer Core
(d) Continental Crust

34. Sedimentary component which is produced *in-situ* within the pore spaces is called:
(a) Primary (b) Authigenic
(c) Allogenic (d) Orogenic

35. Stoke's law of settling velocity simplified as $V \propto \frac{1}{d^n}$ suggest that:
(a) A large particle 100 μm in diameter will settle slowly compared to a smaller 10 μm particle
(b) A large particle 100 μm in diameter, will settle faster than a smaller particle 10 μm
(c) Both a large 100 μm particle and a small 10 μm particle will settle in a column of 10 cm at the same time.
(d) Small particle 10 μm in diameter will settle faster, while coarser particle of 100 μm diameter will remain in suspension.

36. Which of these remote sensing tool is commonly used for groundwater exploration and soil moisture determinations:
(a) Colour composite imageries
(b) Band 5 spectra
(c) Infrared spectra
(d) Black and white Aerial photos

37. The atmosphere is divided in four layers. The layer in contact with the surface of the Earth is called:
(a) Stratosphere (b) Troposphere
(c) Mesosphere (d) Ionosphere

38. A ship (X) moving due North with a velocity (v) observes that another ship (Y) is moving due west, the actual velocity of (Y) is:
   (a) (v) is due East
   (b) $(\sqrt{2}v)$ is towards North West
   (c) (v) is towards South East
   (d) $(\sqrt{2}v)$ is towards North East

39. The solubility of Fe in water:
   (a) Increases with increasing pH
   (b) Decreases with increasing pH
   (c) Independent of pH
   (d) Dependent only on redox potential and not pH

40. A cube of ice with radius of 100 mm is formed at 3°C. When ice melts, the final volume will be:
   (a) 1000 cm^3 (b) 1250 cm^3
   (c) 1000 mm^3 (d) 1750 mm^3

41. Which of the following phenomena can be explained by the wave model of light, but not by the particle model?
   (a) Pressure is exerted by a light beam
   (b) All of the energy emitted by an atom, as light can later be completely transferred to another atom
   (c) A light beam changes direction when passing from one medium to another
   (d) Light can reach the geometrical shadow of an obstacle in its path

42. 2 ppm of CO at 25°C and 760 mm of Hg pressure is equivalent to:
   (a) 1250 $\mu g/m^3$ (b) 1145 $\mu g/m^3$
   (c) 2500 $\mu g/m^3$ (d) 2290 $\mu g/m^3$

43. Which waves carry most energy?
   (a) UV light
   (b) Infrared light
   (c) Microwaves
   (d) Millimeter waves

44. If one wishes to measure total As, As+3 and As+5 in a sample the most suitable analytical tool is:
   (a) Atomic Absorption spectrophotometer
   (b) Ion chromatograph
   (c) Scanning Electron Microscope
   (d) Gas chromatograph

45. The acid rains result from chemical transformation and transport of:
   (a) Sulphur dioxide and nitrogen oxide
   (b) Phosphorus pentaoxide and sulphur compound
   (c) Chlorine gas and nitrous oxide
   (d) Iron oxide and copper nitrate

46. Any particulate matter, gas, or combination thereof other than water vapour is called:
   (a) Air curtain
   (b) Air emission
   (c) Air monitoring
   (d) Air contaminant

47. The chemical system for removal of the ions of salt, is called:
   (a) Ion transfer
   (b) Ionization
   (c) Ion exchange
   (d) Ion vaporization

48. At ordinary temperatures, the molecules of a diatomic gas have only translational and rotational kinetic energies. At high temperatures, they may have vibrational energy. As a result of this, compared to lower temperatures, a diatomic gas at higher temperatures will have:
   (a) Lower molar heat capacity
   (b) Higher molar heat capacity
   (c) Lower isothermal compressibility
   (d) Higher isothermal compressibility

49. In the periodic table of elements:
    (a) Non-metallic property increases vertically
    (b) Metallic property increases from right to left
    (c) Non-metallic property increases from right to left
    (d) Metallic property increases left to right and from top to bottom
50. Polychlorinated biphenyls (PCBs) which cause environmental exposure risk have these important properties:
    (a) Very high volatility in air
    (b) Chemically unstable and highly reactive
    (c) Heat stable and have no flash or fire point
    (d) Highly soluble in water and poorly soluble in oils and organic solvents

ANSWERS

1. (a)	2. (c)	3. (b)	4. (d)	5. (d)
6. (b)	7. (a)	8. (c)	9. (c)	10. (a)
11. (d)	12. (a)	13. (c)	14. (a)	15. (b)
16. (a)	17. (a)	18. (b)	19. (c)	20. (a)
21. (d)	22. (a)	23. (c)	24. (a)	25. (b)
26. (d)	27. (c)	28. (b)	29. (a)	30. (b)
31. (d)	32. (c)	33. (b)	34. (c)	35. (d)
36. (d)	37. (b)	38. (c)	39. (b)	40. (d)
41. (c)	42. (d)	43. (b)	44. (a)	45. (a)
46. (b)	47. (c)	48. (c)	49. (d)	50. (d)

JUNE–2009

Note: This paper contains Fifty (50) multiple-choice questions, each question carrying two (2) marks. Attempt all of them.

PAPER–I

1. Good evaluation of written material should not be based on
   (a) Linguistic expression
   (b) Logical presentation
   (c) Ability to reproduce whatever is read
   (d) Comprehension of subject

2. Why do teachers use teaching aid?
   (a) To make teaching fun-filled
   (b) To teach within understanding level of students
   (c) For students' attention
   (d) To make students attentive

3. Attitudes, concepts, skills and knowledge are products of
   (a) Learning (b) Research
   (c) Heredity (d) Explanation

4. Which among the following gives more freedom to the learner to interact?
   (a) Use of film
   (b) Small group discussion
   (c) Lectures by experts
   (d) Viewing country wide classroom program on TV

5. Which of the following is not a product of learning?
   (a) Attitudes (b) Concepts
   (c) Knowledge (d) Maturation

6. How can the objectivity of the research be enhanced?
   (a) Through its impartiality
   (b) Through its reliability
   (c) Through its validity
   (d) All of these

7. Action-research is
   (a) An applied research
   (b) A research carried out to solve immediate problems
   (c) A longitudinal research
   (d) All of the above

8. The basis on which assumptions are formulated
   (a) Cultural background of the country
   (b) Universities
   (c) Specific characteristics of the castes
   (d) All of these

9. Which of the following is classified in the category of the developmental research?
   (a) Philosophical research
   (b) Action research
   (c) Descriptive research
   (d) All of the above

10. We use Factorial Analysis
    (a) To know the relationship between two variables
    (b) To test the Hypothesis
    (c) To know the difference between two variables
    (d) To know the difference among the many variables

Read the following passage and answer the questions 11 to 15:

While the British rule in India was detrimental to the economic development of the country, it did help in starting of the process of modernising Indian society and formed several progressive institutions during that process. One of the most beneficial institutions, which were initiated by the British, was democracy. Nobody can dispute that despite its many shortcomings, democracy was and is far better alternative to the arbitrary rule of the rajas and nawabs, which prevailed in India in the pre-British days.

However, one of the harmful traditions of British democracy inherited by India was that of conflict instead of cooperation between elected members. This was its essential feature. The party, which got the support of the majority of elected members, formed the government while the others constituted a standing opposition. The existence of the opposition to those in power was and is regarded as a hallmark of democracy.

In principle, democracy consists of rule by the people; but where direct rule is not possible, it's rule by persons elected by the people. It is natural that there would be some differences of opinion among the elected members as in the rest of the society.

Normally, members of any organisations have differences of opinion between themselves on different issues but they manage to work on the basis of a consensus and they do not normally form a division between some who are in majority and are placed in power, while treating the others as in opposition.

The members of an organisation usually work on consensus. Consensus simply means that after an adequate discussion, members agree that the majority opinion may prevail for the time being. Thus persons who form a majority on one issue and whose opinion is allowed to prevail may not be on the same side if there is a difference on some other issue.

It was largely by accident that instead of this normal procedure, a two-party system came to prevail in Britain and that is now being generally taken as the best method of democratic rule.

Many democratically inclined persons in India regret that such a two-party system was not brought about in the country. It appears that to have two parties in India—of more or less equal strength—is a virtual impossibility. Those who regret the absence of a two-party system should take the reasons into consideration.

When the two-party system got established in Britain, there were two groups among the rulers (consisting of a limited electorate) who had the same economic interests among themselves and who therefore formed two groups within the selected members of Parliament.

There were members of the British aristocracy (which landed interests and consisting of lord, barons, etc.) and members of the new commercial class consisting of merchants and artisans. These groups were more or less of equal strength and they were able to establish their separate rule at different times.

Answer the following questions:

11. In pre-British period, when India was ruled by the independent rulers
    (a) Peace and prosperity prevailed in the society
    (b) People were isolated from political affairs
    (c) Public opinion was inevitable for policy making
    (d) Law was equal for one and all
12. What is the distinguishing feature of the democracy practised in Britain?
    (a) End to the rule of might is right.
    (b) Rule of the people, by the people and for the people.
    (c) It has stood the test of time.
    (d) Cooperation between elected members.

13. Democracy is practised where
    (a) Elected members form a uniform opinion regarding policy matter.
    (b) Opposition is more powerful than the ruling combine.
    (c) Representatives of masses.
    (d) None of these.

14. Which of the following is true about the British rule in India?
    (a) It was behind the modernisation of the Indian society.
    (b) India gained economically during that period.
    (c) Various establishments were formed for the purpose of progress.
    (d) None of these.

15. Who became the members of the new commercial class during that time?
    (a) British Aristocrats
    (b) Lord and Barons
    (c) Political Persons
    (d) Merchants and Artisans

16. Which one of the following Telephonic Conferencing with a radio link is very popular throughout the world?
    (a) TPS (b) Telepresence
    (c) Video conference (d) Video teletext

17. Which is not 24 hours news channel?
    (a) NDTV 24×7
    (b) ZEE News
    (c) Aajtak
    (d) Lok Sabha Channel

18. The main objective of FM station in radio is
    (a) Information, Entertainment and Tourism
    (b) Entertainment, Information and Interaction
    (c) Tourism, Interaction and Entertainment
    (d) Entertainment only

19. In communication chatting on internet is
    (a) Verbal communication
    (b) Non-verbal communication
    (c) Parallel communication
    (d) Grapevine communication

20. Match List I with List II and select the correct answer using the codes given below:

    List I (Artists)
    A. Pandit Jasraj B. Kishan Maharaj
    C. Ravi Shankar D. Udai Shankar

    List II (Art)
    1. Hindustani vocalist
    2. Sitar
    3. Tabla
    4. Dance

Codes:	A	B	C	D
(a)	1	2	3	4
(b)	1	3	4	2
(c)	1	3	2	4
(d)	3	2	1	4

21. Insert the missing number in the following.
    3, 8, 18, 23, 33, ?, 48
    (a) 37 (b) 40
    (c) 38 (d) 45

22. In a certain code, CLOCK is written as KCOLC. How would STEPS be written in that code?
    (a) SPEST (b) SPSET
    (c) SPETS (d) SEPTS

23. The letters in the first set have a certain relationship. On the basis of this relationship mark the right choice for the second set
    BDFH : OMKI :: GHIK : ?
    (a) FHJL (b) RPNL
    (c) LNPR (d) LJHF

24. What was the day of the week on 1st January 2001?
    (a) Friday (b) Monday
    (c) Sunday (d) Wednesday

25. Find out the wrong number in the sequence.
52, 51, 48, 43, 34, 27, 16
(a) 27 (b) 34
(c) 43 (d) 48

26. In a deductive argument conclusion is
(a) Summing up of the premises
(b) Not necessarily based on premises
(c) Entailed by the premises
(d) Additional to the premises

27. 'No man are mortal' is contradictory of
(a) Some man are mortal
(b) Some man are not mortal
(c) All men are mortal
(d) No mortal is man

28. A deductive argument is valid if
(a) premises are false and conclusion is true
(b) premises are false and conclusion is also false
(c) premises are true and conclusion is false
(d) premises are true and conclusion is true

29. Structure of logical argument is based on
(a) Formal validity
(b) Material truth
(c) Linguistic expression
(d) Aptness of examples

30. Two ladies and two men are playing bridge and seated at North, East, South and West of a table. No lady is facing East. Persons sitting opposite to each other are not of the same sex. One man is facing South. Which direction are the ladies facing to?
(a) East and West
(b) North and West
(c) South and East
(d) None of these

Questions 31 and 32 are based on the following venn diagram in which there are three intersecting circles representing Hindi knowing persons, English knowing persons and persons who are working as teachers. Different regions so obtained in the figure are marked as a, b, c, d, e, f and g.

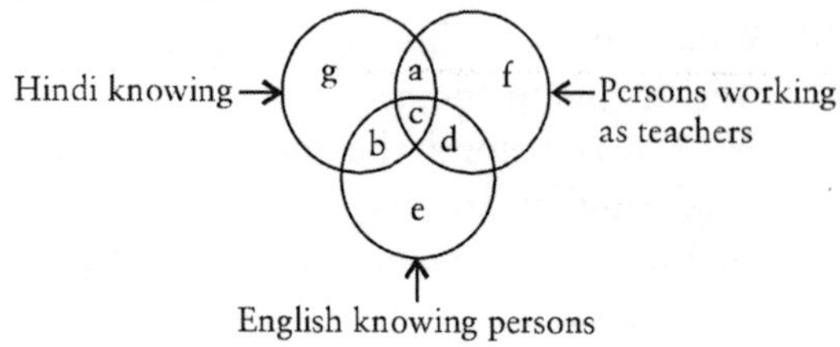

31. If you want to select Hindi and English knowing teachers, which of the following is to be selected?
(a) g (b) b
(c) c (d) e

32. If you want to select persons, who do not know English and are not teachers, which of the region is to be selected?
(a) e (b) g
(c) b (d) a

Study the following graph carefully and answer questions 33 to 35.

Export of Engineering Goods

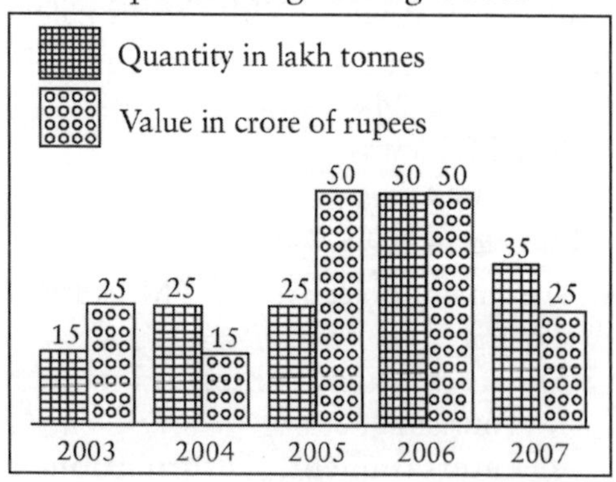

33. In which year the quantity of engineering goods' exports was maximum?
(a) 2005 (b) 2006
(c) 2004 (d) 2007

34. In which year the value of engineering goods decreased by 50 percent compared to the previous year?
(a) 2004 (b) 2007
(c) 2005 (d) 2006

35. In which year the quantity of exports was 100 percent higher than the quantity of previous year?
(a) 2004 (b) 2005
(c) 2006 (d) 2007

36. What do you need to put your web pages on the www?
(a) a connection to internet
(b) a web browser
(c) a web server
(d) All of the above

37. Which was the first company to launch mobile phone services in India?
(a) Essar (b) BPL
(c) Hutchison (d) Airtel

38. Chandrayan I was launched on 22nd October, 2008 in India from
(a) Bangalore (b) Sri Harikota
(c) Chennai (d) Ahmedabad

39. What is blog?
(a) Online music
(b) Intranet
(c) A personal or corporate website in the form of an online journal
(d) A personal or corporate Google search

40. Which is not online Indian Matrimonial website?
(a) www.jeevansathi.com
(b) www.bharatmatrimony.com
(c) www.shaadi.com
(d) www.u.k.singlemuslim.com

41. Environmental impact assessment is an objective analysis of the probable changes in
(a) physical characteristics of the environment
(b) biophysical characteristics of the environment
(c) socio-economic characteristics of the environment
(d) All of the above

42. Bog is a wetland that receives water from
(a) nearby water bodies
(b) melting
(c) only rainfall
(d) only sea

43. Which of the following region is in the very high risk zone of earthquakes?
(a) Central Indian Highland
(b) Coastal region
(c) Himalayan region
(d) Indian desert

44. Match List I with List II and select the correct answer using the codes given below.

List I (Institutes)
A. Central Arid Zone Institute
B. Space Application Centre
C. Indian Institute of Public Administration
D. Headquarters of Indian Science Congress

List II (Cities)
1. Kolkata 2. New Delhi
3. Ahmedabad 4. Jodhpur

Codes:	A	B	C	D
(a)	4	3	2	1
(b)	4	2	1	3
(c)	3	1	2	4
(d)	1	2	4	3

45. Indian coastal areas experienced Tsunami disaster in the year
(a) 2005 (b) 2004
(c) 2006 (d) 2007

46. The Kothari Commission's report was entitled
(a) Education and National Development
(b) Learning to be adventure

(c) Diversification of Education
(d) Education and socialisation in democracy

47. Which of the following is not a Dual mode University?
(a) Delhi University
(b) Bangalore University
(c) Madras University
(d) Indira Gandhi National Open University

48. Which part of the Constitution of India is known as "Code of Administrators"?
(a) Part I (b) Part II
(c) Part III (d) Part IV

49. Which article of the Constitution provides safeguards to Naga Customary and their social practices against any act of Parliament?
(a) Article 371 A (b) Article 371 B
(c) Article 371 C (d) Article 263

50. Which one of the following is not the tool of good governance?
(a) Right to Information
(b) Citizens' Charter
(c) Social Auditing
(d) Judicial Activism

ANSWERS

1. (a)	2. (a)	3. (a)	4. (b)	5. (d)
6. (d)	7. (b)	8. (a)	9. (d)	10. (d)
11. (b)	12. (d)	13. (a)	14. (c)	15. (a)
16. (b)	17. (d)	18. (b)	19. (b)	20. (c)
21. (c)	22. (c)	23. (b)	24. (b)	25. (b)
26. (c)	27. (c)	28. (d)	29. (b)	30. (b)
31. (c)	32. (b)	33. (b)	34. (b)	35. (c)
36. (d)	37. (d)	38. (b)	39. (c)	40. (d)
41. (d)	42. (a)	43. (b)	44. (a)	45. (b)
46. (a)	47. (d)	48. (d)	49. (a)	50. (d)

DECEMBER–2009

Note: This paper contains Sixty (60) multiple-choice questions, each question carrying two (2) marks. Candidate is expected to answer any Fifty (50) questions. In case more than Fifty (50) questions are attempted, only the first Fifty (50) questions will be evaluated.

PAPER–I

1. The University which telecasts interaction educational programs through its own channel is
   (a) Osmania University
   (b) University of Pune
   (c) Annamalai University
   (d) Indira Gandhi National University (IGNOU)

2. Which of the following skills are needed for present day teacher to adjust effectively with the classroom teaching?
   1. Knowledge of technology
   2. Use of technology in teaching learning
   3. Knowledge of students' needs
   4. Content mastery

   (a) 1 and 3 (b) 2 and 3
   (c) 2, 3 and 4 (d) 2 and 4

3. Who has signed as MoU for Accreditation of Teacher Education Institutions in India?
   (a) NAAC and UGC
   (b) NCTE and NAAC
   (c) UGC and NCTE
   (d) NCTE and IGNOU

4. The primary duty of the teacher is to
   (a) raise the intellectual standard of the students
   (b) improve the physical standard of the students
   (c) help all-round development of the students
   (d) imbibe value system in the students

5. Micro teaching is more effective
   (a) during the preparation for teaching-practice
   (b) during the teaching-practice
   (c) after the teaching-practice
   (d) always

6. What quality the students like the most in a teacher?
   (a) Idealist philosophy
   (b) Compassion
   (c) Discipline
   (d) Entertaining

7. A null hypothesis is
   (a) when there is no difference between the variables
   (b) the same as research hypothesis
   (c) subjective in nature
   (d) when there is difference between the variables

8. The research which is exploring new facts through the study of the past is called
   (a) Philosophical research
   (b) Historical research
   (c) Mythological research
   (d) Content analysis

9. Action research is
   (a) An applied research
   (b) A research carried out to solve immediate problems
   (c) A longitudinal research
   (d) Simulative research

10. The process not needed in Experimental Researches is
    (a) Observation (b) Manipulation
    (c) Controlling (d) Content Analysis
11. Manipulation is always a part of
    (a) Historical research
    (b) Fundamental research
    (c) Descriptive research
    (d) Experimental research
12. Which correlation co-efficient best explains the relationship between creativity and intelligence?
    (a) 1.00 (b) 0.6
    (c) 0.5 (d) 0.3

Read the following passage and answer the Question Nos. 13 to 18:

The decisive shift in British Policy really came about under mass pressure in the autumn and winter of 1945 to 46—the months which Penderel Moon while editing Wavell's Journal has perceptively described as 'The Edge of a Volcano'. Very foolishly, the British initially decided to hold public trials of several hundreds of the 20,000 I.N.A. prisoners (as well as dismissing from service and detaining without trial no less than 7,000). They compounded the folly by holding the first trial in the Red Fort, Delhi in November 1945, and putting on the dock together a Hindu, a Muslim and a Sikh (P.K. Sehgal, Shah Nawaz, Gurbaksh Singh Dhillon). Bhulabhai Desai, Tejbahadur Sapru and Nehru appeared for the defence (the latter putting on his barrister's gown after 25 years), and the Muslim League also joined the countrywide protest. On 20 November, an Intelligence Bureau note admitted that "there has seldom been a matter which has attracted so much Indian public interest and, it is safe to say, sympathy...this particular brand of sympathy cuts across communal barriers". A journalist (B. Shiva Rao) visiting the Red Fort prisoners on the same day reported that 'There is not the slightest feeling among them of Hindu and Muslim.... A majority of the men now awaiting trial in the Red Fort is Muslim. Some of these men are bitter that Mr. Jinnah is keeping alive a controversy about Pakistan.' The British became extremely nervous about the I.N.A. spirit spreading to the Indian Army, and in January the Punjab Governor reported that a Lahore reception for released I.N.A. prisoners had been attended by Indian soldiers in uniform.

13. Which heading is more appropriate to assign to the above passage?
    (a) Wavell's Journal
    (b) Role of Muslim League
    (c) I.N.A. Trials
    (d) Red Fort Prisoners
14. The trial of P.K. Sehgal, Shah Nawaz and Gurbaksh Singh Dhillon symbolises
    (a) communal harmony
    (b) threat to all religious persons
    (c) threat to persons fighting for the freedom
    (d) British reaction against the natives
15. I.N.A. stands for
    (a) Indian National Assembly
    (b) Indian National Association
    (c) Inter-national Association
    (d) Indian National Army
16. 'There has seldom been a matter which has attracted so much Indian Public Interest and, it is safe to say, sympathy... this particular brand of sympathy cuts across communal barriers.' Who sympathises to whom and against whom?
    (a) Muslims sympathised with Shah Nawaz against the British
    (b) Hindus sympathised with P.K. Sehgal against the British
    (c) Sikhs sympathised with Gurbaksh Singh Dhillon against the British
    (d) Indians sympathised with the persons who were to be trialled

17. The majority of people waiting for trial outside the Red Fort and criticising Jinnah were the
    (a) Hindus
    (b) Muslims
    (c) Sikhs
    (d) Hindus and Muslims both
18. The sympathy of Indian soldiers in uniform with the released I.N.A. prisoners at Lahore indicates
    (a) Feeling of Nationalism and Fraternity
    (b) Rebellion nature of Indian soldiers
    (c) Simply to participate in the reception party
    (d) None of the above
19. The country which has the distinction of having the two largest circulated newspapers in the world is
    (a) Great Britain
    (b) The United States
    (c) Japan
    (d) China
20. The chronological order of non-verbal communication is
    (a) Signs, symbols, codes, colours
    (b) Symbols, codes, signs, colours
    (c) Colours, signs, codes, symbols
    (d) Codes, colours, symbols, signs
21. Which of the following statements is not connected with communication?
    (a) Medium is the message.
    (b) The world is an electronic cocoon.
    (c) Information is power.
    (d) Telepathy is technological.
22. Communication becomes circular when
    (a) the decoder becomes an encoder
    (b) the feedback is absent
    (c) the source is credible
    (d) the channel is clear
23. The site that played a major role during the terrorist attack on Mumbai (26/11) in 2008 was
    (a) Orkut (b) Facebook
    (c) Amazon.com (d) Twitter
24. **Assertion (A):** For an effective classroom communication at times it is desirable to use the projection technology.
    Reason (R): Using the projection technology facilitates extensive coverage of course contents.
    (a) Both (A) and (R) are true, and (R) is the correct explanation.
    (b) Both (A) and (R) are true, but (R) is not the correct explanation.
    (c) (A) is true, but (R) is false.
    (d) (A) is false, but (R) is true.
25. January 1, 1995 was a Sunday. What day of the week lies on January 1, 1996?
    (a) Sunday (b) Monday
    (c) Wednesday (d) Saturday
26. When an error of 1% is made in the length and breadth of a rectangle, the percentage error (%) in the area of a rectangle will be
    (a) 0 (b) 1
    (c) 2 (d) 4
27. The next number in the series 2, 5, 9, 19, 37, ? will be
    (a) 74 (b) 75
    (c) 76 (d) None of these
28. There are 10 true-false questions in an examination. Then these questions can be answered in
    (a) 20 ways (b) 100 ways
    (c) 240 ways (d) 1024 ways
29. What will be the next term in the following?
    DCXW, FEVU, HGTS, ?
    (a) AKPO (b) ABYZ
    (c) JIRQ (d) LMRS
30. Three individuals X, Y, Z hired a car on a sharing basis and paid ₹ 1,040. They

used it for 7, 8, 11 hours, respectively. What are the charges paid by Y?
(a) ₹ 290 (b) ₹ 320
(c) ₹ 360 (d) ₹ 440

31. Deductive argument involves
(a) sufficient evidence
(b) critical thinking
(c) seeing logical relations
(d) repeated observation

32. Inductive reasoning is based on or presupposes
(a) uniformity of nature
(b) God created the world
(c) unity of nature
(d) laws of nature

33. To be critical, thinking must be
(a) practical
(b) socially relevant
(c) individually satisfying
(d) analytical

34. Which of the following is an analogous statement?
(a) Man is like God
(b) God is great
(c) Gandhiji is the Father of the Nation
(d) Man is a rational being

Questions from 35-36 are based on the following diagram in which there are three intersecting circles. H representing The Hindu, I representing Indian Express and T representing The Times of India. A total of 50 persons were surveyed and the number in the Venn diagram indicates the number of persons reading the newspapers.

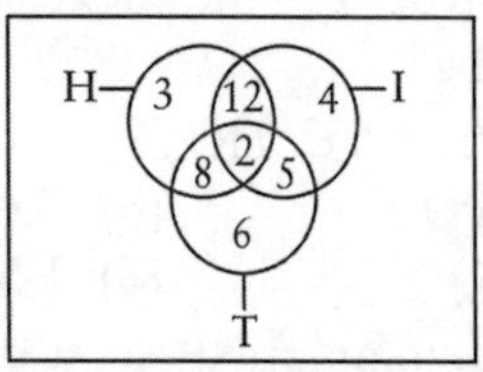

35. How many persons would be reading at least two newspapers?
(a) 23 (b) 25
(c) 27 (d) 29

36. How many persons would be reading almost two newspapers?
(a) 23 (b) 25
(c) 27 (d) 48

37. Which of the following graphs does not represent regular (periodic) behaviour of the variable f(t)?

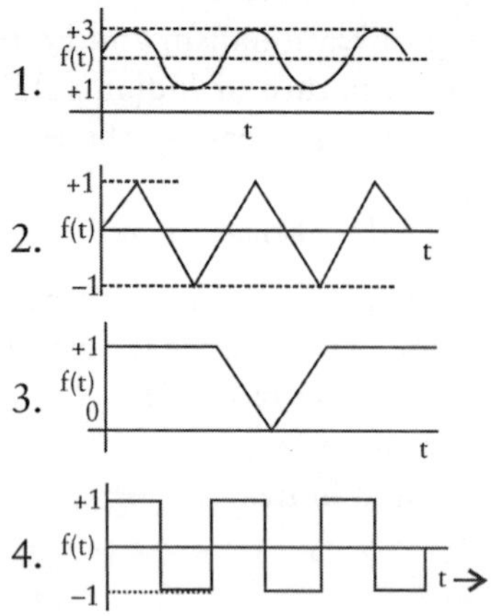

(a) 1 (b) 2
(c) 3 (d) 4

Study the following graph and answer the questions 38 to 40.

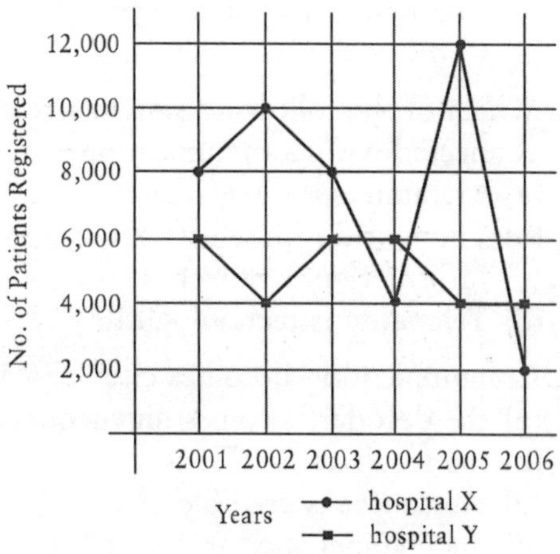

38. In which year total number of patients registered in hospital X and hospital Y was the maximum?

(a) 2003 (b) 2004
(c) 2005 (d) 2006

39. What is the maximum dispersion in the registration of patients in the two hospitals in a year?
(a) 8000 (b) 6000
(c) 4000 (d) 2000

40. In which year there was maximum decrease in registration of patients in hospital X?
(a) 2003 (b) 2004
(c) 2005 (d) 2006

41. Which of the following sources of data is not based on primary data collection?
(a) Census of India
(b) National Sample Survey
(c) Statistical Abstracts of India
(d) National Family Health Survey

42. Which of the four data sets have more dispersion?

(a)	88	91	90	92	89	91
(b)	0	1	1	0	–1	–2
(c)	3	5	2	4	1	5
(d)	0	5	8	10	–2	–8

43. Which of the following is not related to information security on the Internet?
(a) Data Encryption
(b) Water Marking
(c) Data Hiding
(d) Information Retrieval

44. Which is the largest unit of storage among the following?
(a) Terabyte (b) Megabyte
(c) Kilobyte (d) Gigabyte

45. bit stands for
(a) binary information term
(b) binary digit
(c) binary tree
(d) Bivariate Theory

46. Which one of the following is not a linear data structure?
(a) Array (b) Binary Tree
(c) Queue (d) Stack

47. Which one of the following is not a network device?
(a) Router (b) Switch
(c) Hub (d) CPU

48. A compiler is used to convert the following to object code which can be executed
(a) High-level language
(b) Low-level language
(c) Assembly language
(d) Natural language

49. The great Indian Bustard bird is found in
(a) Thar Desert of Rajasthan
(b) Malabar Coast
(c) Coastal regions of India
(d) Delta regions

50. The Sagarmanthan National Park has been established to preserve the eco-system of which mountain peak?
(a) Kanchenjunga (b) Mount Everest
(c) Annapurna (d) Dhaulavira

51. Maximum soot is released from
(a) Petrol vehicles
(b) CNG vehicles
(c) Diesel vehicles
(d) Thermal Power Plants

52. Surface Ozone is produced from
(a) Transport sector
(b) Cement plants
(c) Textile industry
(d) Chemical industry

53. Which one of the following non-conventional energy sources can be exploited most economically?
(a) Solar
(b) Wind
(c) Geothermal
(d) Ocean Thermal Energy Conversion (OTEC)

54. The most recurring natural hazard in India is
(a) Earthquakes (b) Floods
(c) Landslides (d) Volcanoes

55. The recommendation of National Knowledge Commission for the establishment of 1500 Universities is to
(a) create more teaching jobs
(b) ensure increase in student enrolment in higher education
(c) replace or substitute the privately managed higher education institutions by public institutions
(d) enable increased movement of students from rural areas to urban areas

56. According to Article 120 of the Constitution of India, the business in Parliament shall be transacted in
(a) Only English
(b) Only Hindi
(c) Both English and Hindi
(d) All the languages included in Eighth Schedule of the Constitution

57. Which of the following is more interactive and student centric?
(a) Seminar
(b) Workshop
(c) Lecture
(d) Group Discussion

58. The Parliament in India is composed of
(a) Lok Sabha and Rajya Sabha
(b) Lok Sabha, Rajya Sabha and Vice President
(c) Lok Sabha, Rajya Sabha and President
(d) Lok Sabha, Rajya Sabha with their Secretariats

59. The enrolment in higher education in India is contributed both by Formal System of Education and by System of Distance Education. Distance education contributes
(a) 50% of formal system
(b) 25% of formal system
(c) 10% of the formal system
(d) Distance education system's contribution is not taken into account while considering the figures of enrolment in higher education

60. **Assertion (A):** The UGC Academic Staff Colleges came into existence to improve the quality of teachers.
Reason (R): University and college teachers have to undergo both orientation and refresher courses.
(a) Both (A) and (R) are true and (R) is the correct explanation.
(b) Both (A) and (R) are correct but (R) is not the correct explanation of (A).
(c) (A) is correct and (R) is false.
(d) (A) is false and (R) is correct.

ANSWERS

1. (d)	2. (c)	3. (b)	4. (c)	5. (b)
6. (c)	7. (a)	8. (b)	9. (b)	10. (b)
11. (c)	12. (b)	13. (c)	14. (a)	15. (d)
16. (d)	17. (b)	18. (a)	19. (c)	20. (a)
21. (d)	22. (a)	23. (a)	24. (a)	25. (b)
26. (c)	27. (b)	28. (d)	29. (c)	30. (b)
31. (c)	32. (a)	33. (b)	34. (a)	35. (c)
36. (d)	37. (c)	38. (c)	39. (a)	40. (d)
41. (c)	42. (d)	43. (d)	44. (a)	45. (b)
46. (b)	47. (d)	48. (a)	49. (a)	50. (b)
51. (d)	52. (a)	53. (a)	54. (b)	55. (b)
56. (c)	57. (d)	58. (c)	59. (b)	60. (a)

PAPER–II

Note: This paper contains fifty (50) objective type questions, each question carrying two (2) marks. Attempt all the questions.

1. The use of anthropoid hazard chemicals like DDT causes reduction in fish population because the chemical mimics the effect of
   (a) Luteinizing hormone
   (b) Testosterone
   (c) Estrogen
   (d) All of the above
2. The ionizing radiation, which affects the activities of most of the enzymes is due to
   (a) Photoemission of electron
   (b) Interaction of α-particles, β-and γ-rays with enzymes
   (c) Interaction of electrons with body.
   (d) Interaction of radiation with tissues.
3. SDS-PAGE of tissue proteins under denaturation determines the
   (a) Hydrogen bond breakage
   (b) Sulfide bridge breakage
   (c) Subunits of protein
   (d) None of the above
4. Intake of lead may primarily cause the damage of
   (a) Brain (b) Lung
   (c) Liver (d) Kidney
5. Parallelism among the standard curves can be determined by one of the following.
   (a) ANOVA (b) Student's-t test
   (c) Chi-square test (d) ANCOVA
6. Liquid ammonia can be used in refrigeration because of its
   (a) High basicity
   (b) High dipole moment
   (c) High heat of vaporization
   (d) Non-toxic nature
7. The pair of molecules forming strongest intermolecular hydrogen bonds are
   (a) H_2O and H_2
   (b) HCOOH and CH_3COOH
   (c) CH_3COCH_3 and $CHCl_3$
   (d) SiH_4 and SiF_6
8. Which of these requires quantum nature of light for their explanation?
   (a) Diffraction
   (b) Polarisation
   (c) Black body spectrum
   (d) Interference
9. The mass of 1 mole of electron is equal to
   (a) $9.1094 \times 6.16 \times 10^{-28}$ g
   (b) $9.1094 \times 10^{-31} \times 6.023 \times 10^{23}$ kg
   (c) $(9.1094 \times 10^{-31}) / 6.023 \times 10^{23}$ kg
   (d) $(6.023 \times 10^{23}) / 6.1094 \times 10^{-28}$ gm
10. Which set of stoichiometric coefficient correctly balance the equation
   A. H_2O_2 + B. $KMnO_4$ + C. H_2SO_4 $\rightarrow$ D. K_2SO_4 + E. Mn SO_4 + F. H_2O + G. O_2

	A	B	C	D	E	F	G
(a)	1	1	1	1	1	1	1
(b)	1	2	3	1	2	4	3
(c)	2	5	3	2	1	8	5
(d)	5	2	3	1	2	8	5

11. Which of the transmutation does not take place by α-decay?
   (a) $^{238}U_{92} \longrightarrow {}^{234}Th^{90}$
   (b) $^{213}Bi_{83} \longrightarrow {}^{213}Po_{84}$
   (c) $^{226}Ra_{88} \longrightarrow {}^{222}Rn_{86}$
   (d) $^{227}Ac_{89} \longrightarrow {}^{223}Fr_{87}$
12. Which radioactive element is considered under Indoor pollutants category?
   (a) O –16 (b) N –13
   (c) Carbon 14 (d) Radon

13. Industries generating hazardous waste are classified as
(a) Brown (b) Green
(c) Yellow (d) Red

14. One of the following methods for disposal of municipal solid waste known to be scientific is
(a) Open land disposal
(b) Incerination
(c) Landfill method
(d) Sanitary landfill method

15. One of the following is not an In situ conservation for biological resources.
(a) Biosphere reserve
(b) National Parks
(c) Protected areas
(d) Breeding under confined areas

16. Solar ponds are used for
(a) Salt production (b) Aquaculture
(c) Power generation (d) All of the above

17. Biodiesel is produced in India presently from
(a) Calotropis sp (b) Catharanthus sp
(c) Jatropha sp (d) Delonix sp

18. Ozone depletion is caused by the increase in the level of
(a) Water vapour
(b) Chloroflurocarbon
(c) Oxygen
(d) Carbon monoxide

19. Thermal power generation in India is carried out by burning
(a) Natural gas (b) Coal
(c) Oil (d) All of the above

20. Biogas production is the outcome of
(a) Methanogenesis
(b) Pyrolysis
(c) Methanogenesis and Gasification
(d) Gasification

21. Mauna Loa, in Hawaii is famous for
(a) Botanical Garden
(b) Monitoring sea level rise since 1950
(c) Biggest collection of mammals fossils
(d) Continuous monitoring of atmospheric CO_2 since 1957.

22. To generate environmental awareness Paryavaran Vahini Scheme was launched in
(a) 1998 (b) 1968
(c) 1992 (d) 1994

23. General Circulation Model (GCM's) are used to
(a) predict climate
(b) predict cyclones
(c) study ocean currents
(d) study temperature on wind

24. Among the following which country has lowest per capita greenhouse gas emission?
(a) France (b) India
(c) China (d) Mexico

25. Water (Prevention & Control of Pollution) Act 1974, industries are allowed to release waste in inland water having BOD level
(a) 100 mg/L (b) 30 mg/L
(c) 150 mg/L (d) 80 mg/L

26. Richael Carsson in her book Silent Spring has raised concern on
(a) Economical and social impacts
(b) Deforestation
(c) Climate change
(d) Impacts of agrochemicals on ecological functions

27. The term oligotrophic refers to
(a) Higher nutrients in water
(b) High aquatic productivity
(c) Low nutrients and low productivity
(d) Algal blooms

28. Following initiative under International efforts made to have household eco-friendly refrigerators:
(a) Kyoto Protocol
(b) Basal Convention
(c) Montreal Protocol
(d) CITES

29. The 'mean' that stands for relative importance of different items in a data set is
(a) Weighted mean
(b) Harmonic mean
(c) Arithmetic mean
(d) Geometric mean

30. In symmetrical distribution pattern
(a) Median, Mean and Mode coincide
(b) Mean & Median coincide
(c) Mean & Mode coincide
(d) Mode & Median coincide

31. Which statistical device helps in analysing the covariation of two or more variables?
(a) Regression
(b) Correlation
(c) Standard deviation
(d) Mean of the variables

32. Stoke's Law of Settling Velocity is represented by
(a) $\upsilon \propto d$ (b) $\upsilon \propto \frac{1}{a} n$
(c) $\upsilon = \frac{1}{d}$ (d) $\upsilon = cd$

33. Correct arrangement in order of decreasing soil particle size
(a) Sand, clay, silt (b) Silt, sand, clay
(c) Sand, silt, clay (d) Clay, silt, sand

34. Comparing continental and oceanic crust
(a) the chemical composition of crust does not vary.
(b) the Fe content in continental crust is more than that of oceanic crust.
(c) the Si and Al content in continental crust is more than that of oceanic crust.
(d) the Na, Ca, Al content in oceanic crust is more than that of continental crust.

35. The size distribution of particles in soil and sediments generally follow
(a) binomial distribution
(b) normal distribution
(c) linear distribution
(d) log-normal distribution

36. Maximum density of water is at
(a) 0°C (b) 100°C
(c) – 4°C (d) 4°C

37. The geochemical weathering process can be viewed as
(a) Clay minerals + $CO_2 \rightleftharpoons$ Quartz + Al_2O_3
(b) Primary silicate + CO_2 + $H_2O \rightleftharpoons$ clay minerals + cations + $HCO_3^- + H_4SiO_4 + H^+$
(c) Primary silicate + $H_2O \rightleftharpoons Al_2O_3 + SiO_2 + CaO + H^+$
(d) Clay minerals + $H_2O \rightleftharpoons Fe_2O_3 + Al_2O_3 + SiO_2 + CaO$

38. Which group of minerals represent
(a) Polymorphic transformation
(b) Non-substitutional representation
(c) Isomorphic substitution
(d) Unmixed presence of different non silicates

39. Garnet is a metamorphic product of
(a) Feldspar (b) Quartzite
(c) Mica (d) Serpentine

40. Formation of marble can be represented by
(a) $CaSiO_3 \rightleftharpoons Ca^{+2} + SiO_3^{-2}$
(b) $CaO + CO_2 \rightleftharpoons CaCO_3$
(c) $CaCO_3 \rightleftharpoons CaO + CO_2$
(d) $CaCO_3 + SiO_2 \rightleftharpoons CaSiO_3 + CO_2$

41. For the precipitation of $CaCO_3$ from water

$Ca^{+2} + CO_3^{-2} - CaCO_3$

the equilibrium constant K is $10^{-8.3}$. This indicates that

(a) Ca^{+2} & CO_3^{-2} concentration are equal in water
(b) $m_{CO_3^{-2}} \gg m_{Ca^{+2}}$
(c) $m_{Ca^{+2}} < m_{CO_3^{-2}}$
(d) $m_{Ca^{+2}} = \dfrac{1}{m_{CO_3^{-2}}}$

42. How many sites as potential areas for biosphere reserves have been identified by the National MAB Committee for the Department of Environment?
(a) 13 (b) 23
(c) 33 (d) 43

43. Which one of the following is not a permitting cryoprotectant?
(a) Glycerol
(b) DMSO
(c) Sucrose
(d) 1, 2 – propanediol

44. The aggregation of all eco systems on the earth is referred to as
(a) Atmosphere (b) Ecosphere
(c) Stratosphere (d) Ionosphere

45. Which one of the following is not a biofertilizer?
(a) Aquatic ferns
(b) Blue-green algae
(c) Phosphate-Solubilising micro-organisms
(d) Vermicompost

46. Who first used and defined "Ecology" in 1866?
(a) H. Reiter (b) Haeckel
(c) Charles Elton (d) Odum

47. CITES has following schedules in order of priority to protect animals and plants from trade:
(a) Schedule I, II, III (b) Schedule I, I, III
(c) Schedule III, III, I (d) Schedule II, I, III

48. Methamoglobinemia is actually caused by water pollution containing
(a) NO_2 (b) NO_3^-
(c) NO_4^+ (d) NO_2^-

49. Environmental Impact Assessment is mandatory for certain developmental project under one of the following legislation:
(a) The Factories' Act
(b) Forest Act
(c) Environment (Protection) Act
(d) Air (Pollution and Control) Act

50. Which one of the following air pollution control device has highest efficiency in controlling dust?
(a) Wet Scrubber
(b) Electrostatic precipitator
(c) Venturi Scrubber
(d) Cyclonic spray scrubber

ANSWERS

1. (a)	2. (b)	3. (a)	4. (d)	5. (a)
6. (b)	7. (a)	8. (a)	9. (b)	10. (c)
11. (b)	12. (d)	13. (d)	14. (b)	15. (d)
16. (c)	17. (c)	18. (b)	19. (b)	20. (c)
21. (d)	22. (d)	23. (d)	24. (b)	25. (b)
26. (d)	27. (c)	28. (c)	29. (c)	30. (d)
31. (b)	32. (b)	33. (d)	34. (b)	35. (a)
36. (d)	37. (b)	38. (b)	39. (c)	40. (b)
41. (c)	42. (a)	43. (b)	44. (b)	45. (a)
46. (b)	47. (d)	48. (b)	49. (c)	50. (b)

JUNE–2010

Note: This paper contains Sixty (60) multiple-choice questions, each question carrying two (2) marks. Candidate is expected to answer any Fifty (50) questions. In case more than Fifty (50) questions are attempted, only the first Fifty (50) questions will be evaluated.

PAPER–I

1. Which one of the following is the most important quality of a good teacher?
   (a) Punctuality and sincerity
   (b) Content mastery
   (c) Content mastery and reactive
   (d) Content mastery and sociable

2. The primary responsibility for the teacher's adjustment lies with
   (a) The children
   (b) The principal
   (c) The teacher himself
   (d) The community

3. As per the NCTE norms, what should be the staff strength for a unit of 100 students at B.Ed. level?
   (a) 1 + 7 (b) 1 + 9
   (c) 1 + 10 (d) 1 + 5

4. Research has shown that the most frequent symptom of nervous instability among teachers is
   (a) Digestive upsets
   (b) Explosive behaviour
   (c) Fatigue
   (d) Worry

5. Which one of the following statements is correct?
   (a) Syllabus is an annexure to the curriculum.
   (b) Curriculum is the same in all educational institutions.
   (c) Curriculum includes both formal and informal education.
   (d) Curriculum does not include methods of evaluation.

6. A successful teacher is one who is
   (a) Compassionate and disciplinarian
   (b) Quite and reactive
   (c) Tolerant and dominating
   (d) Passive and active

Read the following passage carefully and answer the questions 7 to 12.

The phrase "What is it like?" stands for a fundamental thought process. How does one go about observing and reporting on things and events that occupy segments of earth space? Of all the infinite variety of phenomena on the face of the earth, how does one decide what phenomena to observe? There is no such thing as a complete description of the earth or any part of it, for every microscopic point on the earth's surface differs from every other such point. Experience shows that the things observed are already familiar, because they are like phenomena that occur at home or because they resemble the abstract images and models developed in the human mind.

How are abstract images formed? Humans alone among the animals possess language; their words symbolise not only specific things but also mental images of classes of things. People can remember what they have seen or experienced because they attach a word symbol to them.

During the long record of our efforts to gain more and more knowledge about the face of the earth as the human habitat, there has been a continuing interplay between things and events. The direct observation through the senses is described as a percept; the mental image is described as a concept. Percepts are what some people describe as reality, in contrast to mental images, which are theoretical, implying that they are not real.

The relation of Percept to Concept is not as simple as the definition implies. It is now quite clear that people of different cultures or even individuals in the same culture develop different mental images of reality and what they perceive is a reflection of these preconceptions. The direct observation of things and events on the face of the earth is so clearly a function of the mental images of the mind of the observer that the whole idea of reality must be reconsidered.

Concepts determine what the observer perceives, yet concepts are derived from the generalisations of previous percepts. What happens is that the educated observer is taught to accept a set of concepts and then sharpens or changes these concepts during a professional career. In any one field of scholarship, professional opinion at one time determines what concepts and procedures are acceptable, and these form a kind of model of scholarly behaviour.

7. The problem raised in the passage reflects on
   (a) thought process
   (b) human behaviour
   (c) cultural perceptions
   (d) professional opinion
8. According to the passage, human beings have mostly in mind
   (a) Observation of things
   (b) Preparation of mental images
   (c) Expression through language
   (d) To gain knowledge
9. Concept means
   (a) A mental image
   (b) A reality
   (c) An idea expressed in language form
   (d) All of the above
10. The relation of Percept to Concept is
    (a) Positive (b) Negative
    (c) Reflective (d) Absolute
11. In the passage, the earth is taken as
    (a) The Globe
    (b) The Human Habitat
    (c) A Celestial Body
    (d) A Planet
12. Percept means
    (a) Direct observation through the senses
    (b) A conceived idea
    (c) Ends of a spectrum
    (d) An abstract image
13. Action research means
    (a) A longitudinal research
    (b) An applied research
    (c) A research initiated to solve an immediate problem
    (d) A research with socio-economic objective
14. Research is
    (a) Searching again and again
    (b) Finding solution to any problem
    (c) Working in a scientific way to search for truth of any problem
    (d) None of the above
15. A common test in research demands much priority on
    (a) Reliability (b) Usability
    (c) Objectivity (d) All of the above
16. Which of the following is the first step in starting the research process?

(a) Searching sources of information to locate problem
(b) Survey of related literature
(c) Identification of problem
(d) Searching for solutions to the problem

17. If a researcher conducts a research on finding out which administrative style contributes more to institutional effectiveness? This will be an example of
(a) Basic Research
(b) Action Research
(c) Applied Research
(d) None of the above

18. Normal Probability Curve should be
(a) Positively skewed
(b) Negatively skewed
(c) Leptokurtic skewed
(d) Zero skewed

19. In communication, a major barrier to reception of messages is
(a) audience attitude
(b) audience knowledge
(c) audience education
(d) audience income

20. Post-modernism is associated with
(a) Newspapers (b) Magazines
(c) Radio (d) Television

21. Didactic communication is
(a) intra-porsonal (b) inter-personal
(c) organisational (d) relational

22. In communication, the language is
(a) the non-verbal code
(b) the verbal code
(c) the symbolic code
(d) the iconic code

23. Identify the correct sequence of the following:
(a) Source, channel, message, receiver
(b) Source, receiver, channel, message
(c) Source, message, receiver, channel
(d) Source, message, channel, receiver

24. **Assertion (A):** Mass media promote a culture of violence in the society.

Reason (R): Because violence sells in the market as people themselves are violent in character.

Codes:
(a) Both (A) and (R) are true and (R) is the correct explanation of (A).
(b) Both (A) and (R) are true, but (R) is not the correct explanation of (A).
(c) (A) is true, but (R) is false.
(d) Both (A) and (R) are false.

25. When an error of 1% is made in the length of a square, the percentage error in the area of a square will be
(a) 0 (b) 1/2
(c) 1 (d) 2

26. On January 12, 1980, it was a Saturday. The day of the week on January 12, 1979 was
(a) Thursday (b) Friday
(c) Saturday (d) Sunday

27. If water is called food, food is called tree, tree is called earth, earth is called world, which of the following grows a fruit?
(a) Water (b) Tree
(c) World (d) Earth

28. E is the son of A, D is the son of B, E is married to C, C is the daughter of E. How is D related to E?
(a) Brother (b) Uncle
(c) Father-in-law (d) Brother-in-law

29. If INSURANCE is coded as ECNARUSNI, how HINDRANCE will be coded?
(a) CADNIHWCE (b) HANCDEINR
(c) AENIRHDCN (d) ECNARDNIH

30. Find the next number in the following series: 2, 5, 10, 17, 26, 37, 50, ?
(a) 63 (b) 65
(c) 67 (d) 69

31. Which of the following is an example of circular argument?
    (a) God created man in his image and man created God in his own image.
    (b) God is the source of a scripture and the scripture is the source of our knowledge of God.
    (c) Some of the Indians are great because India is great.
    (d) Rama is great because he is Rama.

32. Lakshmana is a morally good person because
    (a) he is religious (b) he is educated
    (c) he is rich (d) he is rational

33. Two statements I and II given below are followed by two conclusions (A) and (B). Supposing the statements are true, which of the following conclusions can logically follow?

    Statements:
    I. Some religious people are morally good.
    II. Some religious people are rational.

    Conclusion:
    (A) Rationally religious people are good morally.
    (B) Non-rational religious persons are not morally good.
    (a) Only (A) follows
    (b) Only (B) follows
    (c) Both (A) and (B) follow
    (d) Neither (A) nor (B) follows

34. Certainty is
    (a) an objective fact
    (b) emotionally satisfying
    (c) logical
    (d) ontological

Questions from 35 to 36 are based on the following diagram in which there are three intersecting circles I, S and P where circle I stands for Indians, circle S stands for Scientists and circle P for Politicians. Different regions of the figure are lettered from a to g.

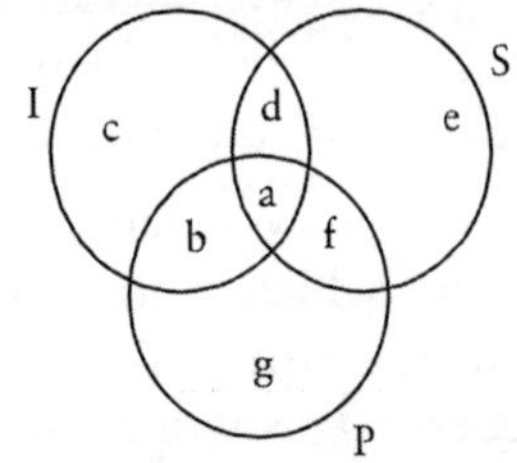

35. The region which represents non-scientists who are politicians.
    (a) f (b) d
    (c) a (d) c

36. The region which represents politicians who are Indians as well as scientists.
    (a) b (b) c
    (c) a (d) d

37. The population of a city is plotted as a function of time (years) in graphic form below:

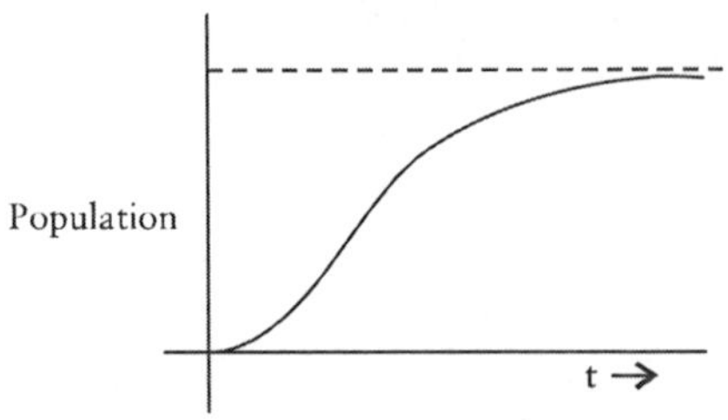

Which of the following inference can be drawn from above plot?
    (a) The population increases exponentially.
    (b) The population increases in parabolic fashion.
    (c) The population initially increases in a linear fashion and then stabilises.
    (d) The population initially increases exponentially and then stabilises.

In the following chart, the price of logs is shown in per cubic metre and that of Plywood and Saw Timber in per tonnes. Study the chart and answer the following questions 38, 39 and 40.

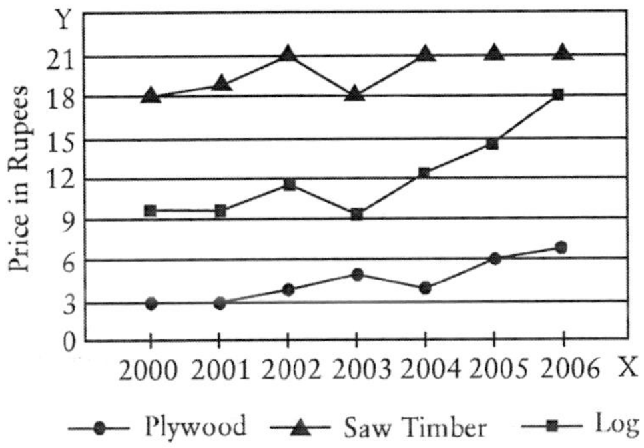

38. Which product shows the maximum percentage increase in price over the period?
(a) Saw timber (b) Plywood
(c) Log (d) None of these

39. What is the maximum percentage increase in price per cubic metre of log?
(a) 6 (b) 12
(c) 18 (d) None of these

40. In which year the prices of two products decreased and that of the third increased?
(a) 2000 (b) 2002
(c) 2003 (d) 2006

41. Which one of the following is the oldest Archival source of data in India?
(a) National Sample Surveys
(b) Agricultural Statistics
(c) Census
(d) Vital Statistics

42. In a large random data set following normal distribution, the ratio (%) of number of data points which are in the range of (mean ± standard deviation) to the total number of data points, is
(a) ~ 50% (b) ~ 67%
(c) ~ 97% (d) ~ 47%

43. Which number system is usually followed in a typical 32-bit computer?
(a) 2 (b) 8
(c) 10 (d) 16

44. Which one of the following is an example of Operating System?
(a) Microsoft Word
(b) Microsoft Excel
(c) Microsoft Access
(d) Microsoft Windows

45. Which one of the following represent the binary equivalent of the decimal number 23?
(a) 01011 (b) 10111
(c) 10011 (d) None of these

46. Which one of the following is different from other members?
(a) Google (b) Windows
(c) Linux (d) Mac

47. Where does a computer add and compare its data?
(a) CPU (b) Memory
(c) Hard disk (d) Floppy disk

48. Computers on an internet are identified by
(a) e-mail address
(b) street address
(c) IP address
(d) None of the above

49. The Right to Information Act, 2005 makes the provision of
(a) Dissemination of all types of information by all Public authorities to any person
(b) Establishment of Central, State and District Level Information Commissions as an appellate body
(c) Transparency and accountability in Public authorities
(d) All of the above

50. Which type of natural hazards cause maximum damage to property and lives?
(a) Hydrological
(b) Hydro-meteorological
(c) Geological
(d) Geo-chemical

51. Dioxins are produced from
    (a) Wastelands
    (b) Power plants
    (c) Sugar factories
    (d) Combustion of plastics

52. The slogan "A tree for each child" was coined for
    (a) Social forestry program
    (b) Clean Air program
    (c) Soil conservation program
    (d) Environmental protection program

53. The main constituents of biogas are
    (a) Methane and Carbon dioxide
    (b) Methane and Nitric oxide
    (c) Methane, Hydrogen and Nitric oxide
    (d) Methane and Sulphur dioxide

54. **Assertion (A):** In the world as a whole, the environment has degraded during past several decades.

    Reason (R): The population of the world has been growing significantly.
    (a) (A) is correct, (R) is correct and (R) is the correct explanation of (A).
    (b) (A) is correct, (R) is correct and (R) is not the correct explanation of (A).
    (c) (A) is correct, but (R) is false.
    (d) (A) is false, but (R) is correct.

55. Climate change has implications for
    1. soil moisture 2. forest fires
    3. biodiversity 4. groundwater

    Identify the correct combination according to the code:

    Codes:
    (a) 1 and 3 (b) 1, 2 and 3
    (c) 1, 3 and 4 (d) 1, 2, 3 and 4

56. The accreditation process by National Assessment and Accreditation Council (NAAC) differs from that of National Board of Accreditation (NBA) in terms of
    (a) Disciplines covered by both being the same, there is duplication of efforts.
    (b) One has institutional grading approach and the other has program grading approach.
    (c) Once get accredited by NBA or NAAC, the institution is free from renewal of grading, which is not a progressive decision.
    (d) This accreditation amounts to approval of minimum standards in the quality of education in the institution concerned.

57. Which option is not correct?
    (a) Most of the educational institutions of National repute in scientific and technical sphere fall under 64th entry of Union list.
    (b) Education, in general, is the subject of concurrent list since 42nd Constitutional Amendment Act 1976.
    (c) Central Advisory Board on Education (CABE) was first established in 1920.
    (d) India had implemented the right to Free and Compulsory Primary Education in 2002 through 86th Constitutional Amendment.

58. Which statement is not correct about the "National Education Day" of India?
    (a) It is celebrated on 5th September every year.
    (b) It is celebrated on 11th November every year.
    (c) It is celebrated in the memory of India's first Union Minister of Education, Dr. Abul Kalam Azad.
    (d) It is being celebrated since 2008.

59. Match List I with List II and select the correct answer from the codes given below:

    List I
    (Articles of the Constitution)
    A. Article 280 B. Article 324
    C. Article 323 D. Article 315

List II (Institutions)

1. Administrative Tribunals
2. Election Commission of India
3. Finance Commission at Union level
4. Union Public Service Commission

Codes:	A	B	C	D
(a)	1	2	3	4
(b)	3	2	1	4
(c)	2	3	4	1
(d)	2	4	3	1

60. Deemed Universities declared by UGC under Section 3 of the UGC Act 1956, are not permitted to
   (a) offer programs in higher education and issue degrees
   (b) give affiliation to any institute of higher education
   (c) open off-campus and off-shore campus anywhere in the country and overseas respectively without the permission of the UGC
   (d) offer distance education programs without the approval of the Distance Education Council

ANSWERS

1. (b)	2. (c)	3. (c)	4. (b)	5. (c)
6. (a)	7. (c)	8. (a)	9. (a)	10. (c)
11. (b)	12. (a)	13. (c)	14. (c)	15. (d)
16. (c)	17. (c)	18. (d)	19. (c)	20. (d)
21. (b)	22. (b)	23. (d)	24. (d)	25. (d)
26. (b)	27. (c)	28. (d)	29. (d)	30. (b)
31. (b)	32. (a)	33. (d)	34. (c)	35. (a)
36. (c)	37. (d)	38. (c)	39. (d)	40. (b)
41. (c)	42. (b)	43. (a)	44. (d)	45. (b)
46. (b)	47. (a)	48. (c)	49. (d)	50. (c)
51. (d)	52. (d)	53. (a)	54. (b)	55. (d)
56. (c)	57. (a)	58. (a)	59. (b)	60. (b)

PAPER–II

Note: This paper contains fifty (50) objective type questions, each question carrying two (2) marks. Attempt all the questions.

1. PIXEL is used in evaluation of satellite imageries. It refers to
   (a) Photo ionic radiation
   (b) Photo induced x-rays emitted light
   (c) Printed in x-radiation region
   (d) An image of 100 km × 100 km region
2. Geostationary satellites orbit above the earth at about
   (a) 10 km above the earth
   (b) 500 km above the earth
   (c) 1500 km above the earth
   (d) 5 km above the earth
3. Environmental assessment of a developmental projects follow the following sequence to achieve sustainable development.
   (a) EA $\rightarrow$ EMP $\rightarrow$ EIA
   (b) EIA $\rightarrow$ EA $\rightarrow$ EMP
   (c) EMP $\rightarrow$ EA $\rightarrow$ EIA
   (d) EIA $\rightarrow$ EMP $\rightarrow$ EA
4. Dolomite is
   (a) an isomorphic substitution between $CaCO_3$ & $MgCO_3$
   (b) a fixed composition of $Ca_{0.52}$ $Mg_{0.48}$ CO_3
   (c) a polygraph of limestone
   (d) an isomorph of calcite
5. In order of increasing cation exchange capacity
   (a) Illite > Kaolinite > Sericite > Gibbsite
   (b) Kaolinite > Gibbsite > Sericite > Illite
   (c) Kaolinite > Illite > Montmorillonite
   (d) Montmorillonite > Kaolinite > Illite

6. In order of increasing energy content
   (a) Lignite, Peat, Anthracite, Bituminous coal
   (b) Peat, Lignite, Anthracite, Bituminous coal
   (c) Anthracite, Lignite, Bituminous coal, Peat
   (d) Bituminous coal, Anthracite, Lignite, Peat
7. Agenda 21 is blue-print for environment and development. Agenda 21 was an outcome of the meeting at
   (a) Rio de Janeiro (b) Stockholm
   (c) Vienna (d) Washington
8. BOD of the effluents discharged on land for irrigation should not exceed
   (a) 30 mg/L (b) 100 mg/L
   (c) 300 mg/L (d) 60 mg/L
9. Atmospheric radioactive window permits thermal radiation of which wavelength to leave the earth?
   (a) 4.3 to 9.3 μm (b) 9.5 to 10.6 μm
   (c) 7 to 12 μm (d) 7.3 to 10.3 μm
10. Three constituents that contribute towards stratospheric ozone depletion
   (a) CFC-11, CFC-12, N_2O
   (b) CFC-11, CFC-16, NO_2
   (c) CFC-11, CFC-12, O_2
   (d) CFC-11, CFC-13, H_2
11. In an ecological succession there is a progressive change in biological community over time and space
   (a) Old species are replaced by new one.
   (b) Old species evolved into new species.
   (c) New species moves in displacing previous one.
   (d) At each stage there is a modification in the environment to adopt new species.
12. In nitrogen cycle elemental nitrogen returned to the atmosphere by the following process.
   (a) Nitrogen fixing bacteria.
   (b) Nitrogen fixation by bluegreen algae.
   (c) Nitrification process.
   (d) Denitrification process.
13. Fe & Mg silicates form ideal solid solution in
   (a) Pyroxene (b) Feldspar
   (c) Olivine (d) Mica
14. One of the following represent plygioclases:
   (a) $NaAl_2Si_2O_6$
   (b) $KAlSi_3\text{-}O_8$
   (c) $Mg_2Al_2Si_2O_6$
   (d) $Na_xK_{1-x}Al_2Si_2O_6$
15. Government of India has enacted various Acts for protection & conservation of environment. However, more inclusive Act is
   (a) Water (Prevention & Control of Pollution) Act
   (b) Air (Prevention & Control of Pollution) Act
   (c) Forest Act
   (d) Environment (Protection) Act
16. CRZ notification of Government of India specify the stretches of sea, bays, estuaries, etc. as coastal areas requires protection from developmental activities.
   (a) upto 500 metre from High Tide Level
   (b) upto 150 metre from High Tide Level
   (c) upto 500 metre from Low Tide Level
   (d) upto 100 metre from Low Tide Level
17. An objective of environmental audit is
   (a) Raw-material & Waste minimization.
   (b) Energy conservation & monitoring.
   (c) To improve technical competency.
   (d) All of the above.
18. Biome is a natural community of
   (a) Plants in a geographical area
   (b) Animals in a geographical area
   (c) Plants and animals in a geographical area
   (d) Plants in Arctic region

19. Who proposed that succession is not orderly and directional but is heterogenous?
(a) Clements (b) Egler
(c) Tansley (d) Reiter

20. In an ecosystem a food chain is represented as:

Dead organic matter → Earthworm → Sparrow → Falcon.

This is a type of
(a) Predator food chain
(b) Grazing food chain
(c) Detritus food chain
(d) Auxiliary food chain

21. The rate of biogenetic nutrients between the abiotic and biotic components of an ecosystem is often referred to as
(a) Turn over rate (b) Production rate
(c) Standing state (d) Cycling rate

22. Which of the following pair is not correctly matched regarding National Parks and their locations?
(a) Nilgiri → Tamil Nadu
(b) Sunderbans → West Bengal
(c) Nanda Devi → Uttar Pradesh
(d) Kanha → Rajasthan

23. Ecotone is
(a) ecosystem
(b) a zone of an ecosystem
(c) an ecological study
(d) a zone between two ecosystems

24. When solid becomes liquid at its melting point, the entropy
(a) increases
(b) decreases
(c) is zero
(d) remains unaltered

25. The CNS poisoning by methyl mercury is known as
(a) Methamoglobinemia
(b) Minamata disease
(c) Anemic disease
(d) All of the above

26. Topographic factors affect indirectly one of the following:
(a) Edaphic factors (b) Biotic factors
(c) Climatic factors (d) All of the above

27. Atmosphere contains various layers each having characteristic composition. The correct sequence starting from earth surface is
(a) Stratosphere → Ionosphere → Toposphere.
(b) Toposphere → Ionosphere → Stratosphere.
(c) Ionosphere → Stratosphere → Toposphere.
(d) Toposphere → Stratosphere → Ionosphere.

28. One of the following in biogeochemical cycle has not involved biological fixation:
(a) Oxygen (b) Carbon
(c) Nitrogen (d) Phosphorus

29. One of the following 'P' values indicates significance of the test:
(a) $P > 0.05$ (b) $P < 0.05$
(c) $P = 0.05$ (d) All of the above

30. The calorific value of natural gas varies from
(a) 12,000 – 14,000 kCal/m^3
(b) 13,000 – 18,000 kCal/m^3
(c) 16,000 – 18,000 kCal/m^3
(d) 10,000 – 11,000 kCal/m^3

31. Biogas is composed of
(a) Ethane, CO_2, H_2 & N_2
(b) Methane, CO_2, H_2 & N_2
(c) Methane, CO_2 & N_2
(d) Ethane, Methane & CO_2

32. Which of the following is the concentration of CO_2 in the atmosphere (water vapour free)?
(a) 0.32% (b) 0.032%
(c) 0.38% (d) 0.038%

33. Methanization is carried out by the process of
(a) Incineration
(b) Alcoholic fermentation
(c) Thermo-chemical transformation
(d) Anaerobic fermentation

34. Diesel oil is a fraction obtained between
(a) 40-120°C (b) 180-250°C
(c) 250-320°C (d) 280-360°C

35. In a trickling filter biological method of domestic waste treatment a layer of biological community growing on the substrate is
(a) Algal film
(b) Bacterial layer
(c) Protozon community
(d) Zoogloea film

36. Primary clarifier is basically designed to remove which of the following from waste water?
(a) Particulate matter
(b) Heavy materials & large size materials
(c) Particulate matter & oily substances
(d) Dissolved substances

37. Solubility of NaCl in water is 10^{-1} m/L. The concentration of Na^+ in water will be
(a) $\left[\frac{10^{-1}}{2}\right]$m/L (b) $\left[\frac{10^{1}}{2}\right]$m/L
(c) 10^{-1} m/L (d) $\left[\sqrt{10^{-1}}\right]$m/L

38. In a river with symmetric channel
(a) Maximum velocity is at the bottom
(b) Minimum velocity is at the surface
(c) Maximum velocity is at the borders
(d) Maximum velocity is at 0.7 of the depth

39. Reciprocal of arithmetic mean of the reciprocal of individual observation refers to
(a) weighted mean (b) geometric mean
(c) median mean (d) harmonic mean

40. If the size of the sample is very small, then suitable sampling method for better result is obtained by
(a) Random sampling
(b) Stratified sampling
(c) Census sampling
(d) Purposive sampling

41. In an unbalanced or skewed distribution, which measures of central tendency is leased biased?
(a) Mean (b) Median
(c) Mode (d) Range

42. Proposed fuel for controlled nuclear fusion is lithium deuteride, LiD.
Which of the following reactions would possibly contribute to energy production?
I. ${}^{6}_{3}Li + {}^{1}_{0}h \rightarrow {}^{4}_{2}He + {}^{3}_{1}H$
II. ${}^{6}_{3}Li + {}^{2}_{1}H \rightarrow 2{}^{4}_{2}He$
III. $2{}^{2}_{1}H + {}^{3}_{2}He + {}^{1}_{0}h$
(a) All of them (b) I
(c) III (d) I and II

43. What is the free energy, ΔG, when 1.0 mole of water is converted, at 100°C and 1.0 atm, to steam at 100°C and 1.0 atm in a reversible manner?
[ΔH_{vap} (H_2O) = 9.7 kCalmole^{-1}]
(a) 9700 Cal (b) 970 Cal
(c) – 970 Cal (d) 0.0 Cal

44. Silver oxalate $Ag_2(C_2O_4)$ is dissolved in pure water. The concentration of Ag^+ in the saturated solution is 2.2×10^{-4} mole liter. What is the ksp value of $Ag_2(C_2O_4)$?
(a) 5.3×10^{-12} (b) 5.0×10^{-8}
(c) 2.2×10^{-4} (d) 11×10^{-12}

45. The bond distance in A-B is 0.917 Å and the dipole moment is 1.91 D. The partial character of the bond is
(a) 43% (b) 50%
(c) 45% (d) 38.5%

46. One of the chief ores of uranium (Z = 92) is pitch blende (U_3O_8). When pitch blende is treated with nitric acid, uranyl nitrate [$UO_2(NO_3)_2$] is formed. What is the change in the oxidation number of uranium when this conversion takes place?
(a) + 6 (b) no change
(c) + 2/3 (d) + 2

47. The silicate ion in chrysotile consists of double strands of SiO_4^{-4} tetrahedra as shown below:

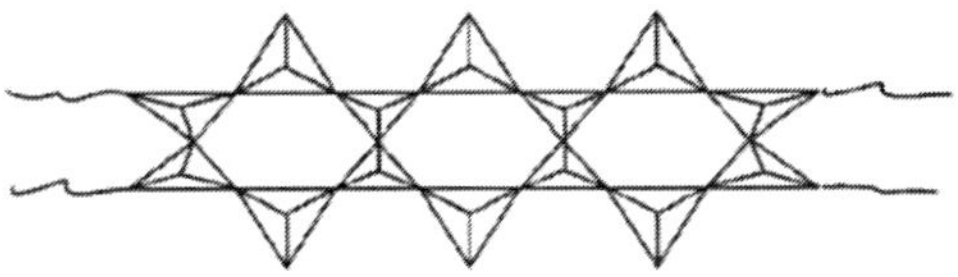

What is the general composition of the silicate ion in chrysolite?
(a) $(SiO_2)_n$ (b) $Si_2O_7^{-6}$
(c) $(Si_4O_{11})_n^{-6n}$ (d) $(SiO_3)_n^{-2n}$

48. One of the following categories of CRZ, there is no developmental activities are allowed:
(a) CRZ-II (b) CRZ-I
(c) CRZ-III (d) CRZ-IV

49. Rapid EIA is called
(a) a study of three months
(b) a study of four months
(c) a study of six months
(d) a study of one year

50. Development of 'Green Belts' around industries are
(a) to control ground leachates
(b) to mitigate the gaseous pollutant
(c) to increase bioaesthetic
(d) All of the above

ANSWERS

1. (b)	2. (c)	3. (b)	4. (a)	5. (c)
6. (b)	7. (a)	8. (a)	9. (b)	10. (a)
11. (c)	12. (a)	13. (a)	14. (b)	15. (d)
16. (a)	17. (d)	18. (c)	19. (b)	20. (a)
21. (d)	22. (c)	23. (d)	24. (a)	25. (d)
26. (a)	27. (d)	28. (b)	29. (c)	30. (a)
31. (d)	32. (b)	33. (d)	34. (c)	35. (a)
36. (b)	37. (b)	38. (b)	39. (d)	40. (d)
41. (b)	42. (c)	43. (b)	44. (a)	45. (b)
46. (b)	47. (b)	48. (b)	49. (a)	50. (d)

DECEMBER–2010

Note: This paper contains Sixty (60) multiple-choice questions, each question carrying two (2) marks. Candidate is expected to answer any Fifty (50) questions. In case more than Fifty (50) questions are attempted, only the first Fifty (50) questions will be evaluated.

PAPER–I

1. Which of the following variables cannot be expressed in quantitative terms?
   (a) Socio-economic Status
   (b) Marital Status
   (c) Numerical Aptitude
   (d) Professional Attitude

2. A doctor studies the relative effectiveness of two drugs of dengue fever. His research would be classified as
   (a) Descriptive Survey
   (b) Experimental Research
   (c) Case Study
   (d) Ethnography

3. The term 'phenomenology' is associated with the process of
   (a) Qualitative Research
   (b) Analysis of Variance
   (c) Correlational Study
   (d) Probability Sampling

4. The 'Sociogram' technique is used to study
   (a) Vocational Interest
   (b) Professional Competence
   (c) Human Relations
   (d) Achievement Motivation

Read the following passage carefully and answer questions from 5 to 10.

It should be remembered that the nationalist movement in India, like all nationalist movements, was essentially a bourgeois movement. It represented the natural historical stage of development, and to consider it or to criticise it as a working-class movement is wrong. Gandhi represented that movement and the Indian masses in relation to that movement to a supreme degree, and he became the voice of Indian people to that extent. The main contribution of Gandhi to India and the Indian masses has been through the powerful movements which he launched through the National Congress. Through nation-wide action he sought to mould the millions, and largely succeeded in doing so, and changing them from a demoralised, timid and hopeless mass, bullied and crushed by every dominant interest, and incapable of resistance, into a people with self-respect and self-reliance, resisting tyranny, and capable of united action and sacrifice for a larger cause.

Gandhi made people think of political and economic issues and every village and every bazaar hummed with argument and debate on the new ideas and hopes that filled the people. That was an amazing psychological change. The time was ripe for it, of course, and circumstances and world conditions worked for this change. But a great leader is necessary to take advantage of circumstances and conditions. Gandhi was that leader, and he released many of the bonds that imprisoned and disabled our minds, and none of us who experienced it can ever forget that great feeling of release and exhilaration that came over the Indian people.

Gandhi has played a revolutionary role in India of the greatest importance because he knew how to make the most of the objective conditions and could reach the heart of the masses, while groups with a more advanced ideology functioned largely in the air because they did not fit in with those conditions and could therefore not evoke any substantial response from the masses.

It is perfectly true that Gandhi, functioning in the nationalist plane, does not think in terms of the conflict of classes, and tries to compose their differences. But the action he has indulged and taught the people has inevitably raised mass consciousness tremendously and made social issues vital. Gandhi and the Congress must be judged by the policies they pursue and the action they indulge in. But behind this, personality counts and colours those policies and activities. In the case of very exceptional person like Gandhi the question of personality becomes especially important in order to understand and appraise him. To us he has represented the spirit and honour of India, the yearning of her sorrowing millions to be rid of their innumerable burdens, and an insult to him by the British Government or others has been an insult to India and her people.

5. Which one of the following is true of the given passage?
   (a) The passage is a critique of Gandhi's role in Indian movement for independence
   (b) The passage hails the role of Gandhi in India's freedom movement
   (c) The author is neutral on Gandhi's role in India's freedom movement
   (d) It is an account of Indian National Congress's support to the working-class movement

6. The change that the Gandhian movement brought among the Indian masses was
   (a) Physical (b) Cultural
   (c) Technological (d) Psychological

7. To consider the nationalist movement or to criticise it as a working-class movement was wrong because it was a
   (a) historical movement
   (b) voice of the Indian people
   (c) bourgeois movement
   (d) movement represented by Gandhi

8. Gandhi played a revolutionary role in India because he could
   (a) preach morality
   (b) reach the heart of Indians
   (c) see the conflict of classes
   (d) lead the Indian National Congress

9. Groups with advanced ideology functioned in the air as they did not fit in with
   (a) objective conditions of masses
   (b) the Gandhian ideology
   (c) the class consciousness of the people
   (d) the differences among masses

10. The author concludes the passage by
   (a) criticising the Indian masses
   (b) the Gandhian movement
   (c) pointing out the importance of the personality of Gandhi
   (d) identifying the sorrows of millions of Indians

11. Media that exist in an interconnected series of communication—points are referred to as
   (a) Networked media
   (b) Connective media
   (c) Nodal media
   (d) Multimedia

12. The information function of mass communication is described as

(a) diffusion (b) publicity
(c) surveillance (d) diversion

13. An example of asynchronous medium is
(a) Radio (b) Television
(c) Film (d) Newspaper

14. In communication, connotative words are
(a) explicit (b) abstract
(c) simple (d) cultural

15. A message beneath a message is labelled as
(a) embedded text (b) internal text
(c) intertext (d) subtext

16. In analogue mass communication, stories are
(a) static (b) dynamic
(c) interactive (d) exploratory

17. Determine the relationship between the pair of words ALWAYS : NEVER and then select from the following pair of words which have a similar relationship
(a) often : rarely
(b) frequently : occasionally
(c) constantly : frequently
(d) intermittently : casually

18. Find the wrong number in the sequence 52, 51, 48, 43, 34, 27, 16
(a) 27 (b) 34
(c) 43 (d) 48

19. In a certain code, PAN is written as 31 and PAR as 35, then PAT is written in the same code as
(a) 30 (b) 37
(c) 39 (d) 41

20. The letters in the first set have certain relationship. On the basis of this relationship, make the right choice for the second set:
AF : IK : : LQ : ?
(a) MO (b) NP
(c) OR (d) TV

21. If 5472 = 9, 6342 = 6, 7584 = 6, what is 9236?
(a) 2 (b) 3
(c) 4 (d) 5

22. In an examination, 35% of the total students failed in Hindi, 45% failed in English and 20% in both. The percentage of those who passed in both subjects is
(a) 10 (b) 20
(c) 30 (d) 40

23. Two statements I and II given below are followed by two conclusions (A) and (B). Supposing the statements are true, which of the following conclusions can logically follow?

Statements:
I. Some flowers are red.
II. Some flowers are blue.

Conclusions:
(A) Some flowers are neither red nor blue.
(B) Some flowers are both red and blue.
(a) Only (A) follows
(b) Only (B) follows
(c) Both (A) and (B) follows
(d) Neither (A) nor (B) follows

24. If the statement 'all students are intelligent' is true, which of the following statements are false?
(i) No students are intelligent.
(ii) Some students are intelligent.
(iii) Some students are not intelligent.
(a) (i) and (ii) (b) (i) and (iii)
(c) (ii) and (iii) (d) Only (i)

25. A reasoning where we start with certain particular statements and conclude with a universal statement is called
(a) Deductive Reasoning
(b) Inductive Reasoning
(c) Abnormal Reasoning
(d) Transcendental Reasoning

26. What is the smallest number of ducks that could swim in this formation—two ducks in front of a duck, two ducks behind a duck and a duck between two ducks?
(a) 5 (b) 7
(c) 4 (d) 3

27. Mr. A, Miss B, Mr. C and Miss D are sitting around a table and discussing their trades.
(i) Mr. A sits opposite to the cook.
(ii) Miss B sits right to the barber.
(iii) The washerman sits right to the barber.
(iv) Miss D sits opposite to Mr. C.

What are the trades of A and B?
(a) Tailor and barber
(b) Barber and cook
(c) Tailor and cook
(d) Tailor and washerman

28. Which one of the following methods serves to measure correlation between two variables?
(a) Scatter Diagram
(b) Frequency Distribution
(c) Two-way table
(d) Coefficient of Rank Correlation

29. Which one of the following is not an Internet Service Provider (ISP)?
(a) MTNL
(b) BSNL
(c) ERNET India
(d) Infotech India Ltd.

30. The hexadecimal number system consists of the symbols
(a) 0 - 7 (b) 0 - 9, A - F
(c) 0 - 7, A - F (d) None of these

31. The binary equivalent of $(-15)_{10}$ is (2's complement system is used)
(a) 11110001 (b) 11110000
(c) 10001111 (d) None of these

32. 1 GB is equal to
(a) 2^{30} bits (b) 2^{30} bytes
(c) 2^{20} bits (d) 2^{20} bytes

33. The set of computer programs that manage the hardware/software of a computer is called
(a) Compiler system
(b) Operation system
(c) Operating system
(d) None of these

34. SMIME in Internet technology stands for
(a) Secure Multipurpose Internet Mail Extension
(b) Secure Multimedia Internet Mail Extension
(c) Simple Multipurpose Internet Mail Extension
(d) Simple Multimedia Internet Mail Extension

35. Which of the following is not covered in 8 missions under the Climate Action Plan of Government of India?
(a) Solar power
(b) Waste to energy conversion
(c) Afforestation
(d) Nuclear energy

36. The concentration of Total Dissolved Solids (TDS) in drinking water should not exceed
(a) 500 mg/L (b) 400 mg/L
(c) 300 mg/L (d) 200 mg/L

37. 'Chipko' movement was first started by
(a) Arundhati Roy
(b) Medha Patkar
(c) Ila Bhatt
(d) Sunderlal Bahuguna

38. The constituents of photochemical smog responsible for eye irritation are
(a) SO_2 and O_3 (b) SO_2 and NO_2
(c) HCHO and PAN (d) SO_2 and SPM

39. **Assertion (A):** Some carbonaceous aerosols may be carcinogenic.
Reason (R): They may contain polycyclic aromatic hydrocarbons (PAHs).
(a) Both (A) and (R) are correct and (R) is the correct explanation of (A).
(b) Both (A) and (R) are correct but (R) is not the correct explanation of (A).
(c) (A) is correct, but (R) is false.
(d) (A) is false, but (R) is correct.

40. Volcanic eruptions affect
(a) atmosphere and hydrosphere
(b) hydrosphere and biosphere
(c) lithosphere, biosphere and atmosphere
(d) lithosphere, hydrosphere and atmosphere

41. India's first Defence University is in the State of
(a) Haryana (b) Andhra Pradesh
(c) Uttar Pradesh (d) Punjab

42. Most of the Universities in India
(a) conduct teaching and research only
(b) affiliate colleges and conduct examinations
(c) conduct teaching/research and examinations
(d) promote research only

43. Which one of the following is not a Constitutional Body?
(a) Election Commission
(b) Finance Commission
(c) Union Public Service Commission
(d) Planning Commission

44. Which one of the following statements is not correct?
(a) Indian Parliament is supreme.
(b) The Supreme Court of India has the power of judicial review.
(c) There is a division of powers between the Centre and the States.
(d) There is a Council of Ministers to aid and advise the President.

45. Which one of the following statements reflects the republic character of Indian democracy?
(a) Written constitution
(b) No State religion
(c) Devolution of power to local Government institutions
(d) Elected President and directly or indirectly elected Parliament

46. Who among the following appointed by the Governor can be removed by only the President of India?
(a) Chief Minister of a State
(b) A member of the State Public Service Commission
(c) Advocate-General
(d) Vice Chancellor of a State University

47. If two small circles represent the class of the 'men' and the class of the 'plants' and the big circle represents 'mortality', which one of the following figures represent the proposition 'All men are mortal'?

(a) 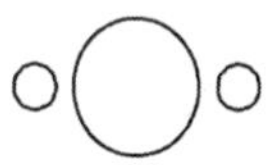
(b) 
(c) 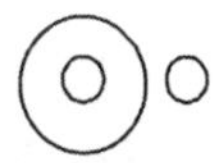
(d) 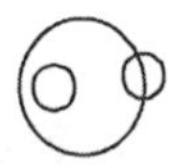

The following table presents the production of electronic items (TVs and LCDs) in a factory during the period from 2006 to 2010. Study the table carefully and answer the questions from 48 to 52:

Year	2006	2007	2008	2009	2010
TVs	6000	9000	13000	11000	8000
LCDs	7000	9400	9000	10000	12000

48. In which year, the total production of electronic items is maximum?
(a) 2006 (b) 2007
(c) 2008 (d) 2010

49. What is the difference between averages of production of LCDs and TVs from 2006 to 2008?
(a) 3000 (b) 2867
(c) 3015 (d) None of these

50. What is the year in which production of TVs is half the production of LCDs in the year 2010?
(a) 2007 (b) 2006
(c) 2009 (d) 2008

51. What is the ratio of production of LCDs in the years 2008 and 2010?
(a) 4:3 (b) 3:4
(c) 1:3 (d) 2:3

52. What is the ratio of production of TVs in the years 2006 and 2007?
(a) 6:7 (b) 7:6
(c) 2:3 (d) 3:2

53. Some students in a class exhibit great curiosity for learning. It may be because such children
(a) Are gifted
(b) Come from rich families
(c) Show artificial behaviour
(d) Create indiscipline in the class

54. The most important quality of a good teacher is
(a) Sound knowledge of subject matter
(b) Good communication skills
(c) Concern for students' welfare
(d) Effective leadership qualities

55. Which one of the following is appropriate in respect of teacher-student relationship?
(a) Very informal and intimate
(b) Limited to classroom only
(c) Cordial and respectful
(d) Indifferent

56. The academic performance of students can be improved if parents are encouraged to
(a) supervise the work of their wards
(b) arrange for extra tuition
(c) remain unconcerned about it
(d) interact with teachers frequently

57. In a lively classroom situation, there is likely to be
(a) occasional roars of laughter
(b) complete silence
(c) frequent teacher-student dialogue
(d) loud discussion among students

58. If a parent approaches the teacher to do some favour to his/her ward in the examination, the teacher should
(a) try to help him
(b) ask him not to talk in those terms
(c) refuse politely and firmly
(d) ask him rudely to go away

59. Which of the following phrases is not relevant to describe the meaning of research as a process?
(a) Systematic Activity
(b) Objective Observation
(c) Trial and Error
(d) Problem Solving

60. Which of the following is not an example of a continuous variable?
(a) Family size (b) Intelligence
(c) Height (d) Altitude

ANSWERS

1. (d)	2. (b)	3. (a)	4. (c)	5. (b)
6. (d)	7. (c)	8. (b)	9. (a)	10. (c)
11. (a)	12. (c)	13. (d)	14. (d)	15. (d)
16. (a)	17. (a)	18. (b)	19. (b)	20. (d)
21. (a)	22. (b)	23. (c)	24. (d)	25. (b)
26. (a)	27. (c)	28. (d)	29. (d)	30. (b)
31. (d)	32. (b)	33. (c)	34. (a)	35. (d)
36. (a)	37. (d)	38. (b)	39. (a)	40. (d)
41. (a)	42. (c)	43. (d)	44. (b)	45. (d)
46. (b)	47. (c)	48. (c)	49. (d)	50. (b)
51. (b)	52. (c)	53. (a)	54. (b)	55. (c)
56. (d)	57. (c)	58. (c)	59. (c)	60. (c)

PAPER–II

Note: This paper contains fifty (50) objective type questions, each question carrying two (2) marks. All questions are compulsory.

1. Across the boundaries of a closed thermodynamical system
   (a) matter flows but the energy doesn't.
   (b) energy flows but the matter doesn't.
   (c) both energy and matter flow.
   (d) both energy and matter do not flow.

2. The largest soil group in India is of
   (a) Red soil (b) Black soil
   (c) Sandy soil (d) Mountain soil

3. Sustainable development is about
   (a) Social justice and equity
   (b) Avoiding depletion of non-renewable resources
   (c) Environmental protection
   (d) All of the above

4. The mixing height is maximum in the
   (a) morning (b) noon time
   (c) evening (d) mid-night

5. Synoptic scale in meteorology is of the order of
   (a) 100 m (b) 1 km
   (c) 10 km (d) 1000 km

6. Polychlorinated biphenyls (PCBs) are known to cause
   (a) deformities in foetus
   (b) nervous disorders
   (c) liver and stomach cancer
   (d) All of the above

7. Match the List I and List II and select the correct answer from the codes given below the lists:

List I (Analytical techniques)	List II (Measured items)
A. XRF	(i) Functional groups
B. Nephelometry	(ii) Elements
C. IR spectroscopy	(iii) Turbidity
D. Gas chromatography	(iv) PAH

Codes:	A	B	C	D
(a)	(iv)	(ii)	(iii)	(i)
(b)	(i)	(iii)	(iv)	(ii)
(c)	(iii)	(ii)	(iv)	(i)
(d)	(ii)	(iii)	(i)	(iv)

8. An antibacterial chemical present in wood smoke is
   (a) Formaldehyde (b) Cellulose
   (c) Acetone (d) Methane

9. Microfilteration generally employs
   (a) thin polymer film with uniform pore size and a high pore density
   (b) thin microfilm with smaller pore size and low pore density
   (c) thin micro-bioplastic with regular pore size and a high pore density
   (d) thin membrane filter with uniform pore size and a high pore density

10. In natural waters with pH near 7.0, the redox potential lies between
    (a) .81 Volt and 0.85 Volt
    (b) –0.41 Volt and 0.06 Volt
    (c) –0.41 Volt and 0.82 Volt
    (d) 0.06 Volt and 1.23 Volt

11. BIOCLAIM®—a metal biosorbent includes microorganisms, mainly bacteria of the genus
    (a) *Bacillus* (b) *Escherichia*
    (c) *Pseudomonas* (d) *Rhizobium*

12. *Saccharomyces cerevisae* is a
    (a) Alga (b) Bacterium
    (c) Protozoan (d) Yeast

13. Method used to select growth of a specific type of bacteria in microbial ecology is
(a) FISH test
(b) Enrichment culture
(c) Biofilms
(d) DNA sequencing

14. About half of earth's photosynthesis is carried out by
(a) Cyanobacteria
(b) Rainforest flora
(c) Protists
(d) Marine phytoplankton

15. Ramsar Convention is associated with
(a) Forest conservation
(b) Soil conservation
(c) Wetland conservation
(d) Wildlife conservation

16. In tropical cyclones, mean wind speeds are
(a) between 10 to 20 knots
(b) between 20 to 40 knots
(c) between 40 to 60 knots
(d) greater than 63 knots

17. **Assertion (A):** Processes involving living organisms are associated with sedimentation which is more closely linked with hydrosphere and the atmosphere.
Reason (R): In the biosphere geochemical differentiation takes place through the metabolic action of organisms.
(a) Both (A) and (R) are correct and (R) is the correct explanation of (A).
(b) Both (A) and (R) are correct and (R) is not the correct explanation of (A).
(c) (A) is true, but (R) is false.
(d) (A) is false, but (R) is true.

18. A mountain slope of slope angle 45 corresponds to which of the following in percent slope notation?
(a) 10 % (b) 50 %
(c) 45 % (d) 100 %

19. Elastic-Rebound Theory suggests that an earthquake results due to change in the state of rock from
(a) Elastic to brittle
(b) Elastic to plastic
(c) Plastic to elastic
(d) Elastic to undeformed

20. How many Universal Transverse Mercator (UTM) zones are there on earth?
(a) 45 (b) 50
(c) 60 (d) 90

21. Match List I and List II. Identify the correct answers using the codes given below the lists:

List I	List II
A. Noamundi Mines	(i) Gold ore
B. Khetri Mines	(ii) Pb-Zn ore
C. Zawar Mines	(iii) Iron ore
D. Kolar Mines	(iv) Copper ore

Codes:	A	B	C	D
(a)	(ii)	(iv)	(i)	(iii)
(b)	(i)	(iii)	(ii)	(iv)
(c)	(iv)	(iii)	(ii)	(i)
(d)	(iii)	(iv)	(i)	(ii)

22. The second generation resource for biofuel production.
(a) Coal
(b) Petrol
(c) Corn and molasses
(d) Crop residues

23. The maximum temperature that can be obtained in a flat plate box type solar collector is between
(a) 50°C – 90°C
(b) 100°C – 150°C
(c) 200°C – 250°C
(d) 45°C – 50°C

24. At present, the total installed capacity of power generation from all sources in India is between

(a) 60 GW to 90 GW
(b) 30 GW to 60 GW
(c) 100 GW to 200 GW
(d) 200 GW to 250 GW

25. Which of the following materials is not used as moderator to slow down the fast neutrons produced in a nuclear reactor?
(a) Water (b) Heavy water
(c) Graphite (d) Lead

26. If equivalent sound pressure level of 90 dB(a) for 8 hours represents 100% dose of noise, noise dose of 25% implies
(a) 87 dB(A) for 4 hours
(b) 84 dB(A) for 4 hours
(c) 22.5 dB(A) for 8 hours
(d) 84 dB(A) for 2 hours

27. Maximum photodissociation of NO_2 molecules in atmosphere occurs due to solar radiations in the wavelength range
(a) 300 nm – 400 nm
(b) 400 nm – 500 nm
(c) 500 nm – 550 nm
(d) 550 nm – 600 nm

28. The time scale for vertical transport of pollutants in the troposphere is typically
(a) minutes
(b) minutes to hours
(c) days to weeks
(d) years

29. For domestic drinking water supply the total dissolved solids should not exceed
(a) 250 ppm (b) 500 ppm
(c) 600 ppm (d) 100 ppm

30. Which of the following sewage treatment relies on removing the suspended solids from water?
(a) Primary treatment
(b) Secondary treatment
(c) Tertiary treatment
(d) Breaking down of organic matter

31. The concept of Environmental Impact Assessment originated from
(a) Findings of a Royal Commission investigating the 'Weald Iron Mills and Furnaces' in Southern England in 1548.
(b) Report of the 'Volta Preparatory Commission' (HMSO, 1956).
(c) Discretionary guidelines of the National Environmental Policy Act in 1971.
(d) Report of copper mining in Puerto Rico commissioned in February 1967.

32. **Assertion (A):** Impact Assessment enables the planners and decision-makers to think carefully about the project proposals.
Reason (R): Impact Assessment can help in ensuring that planners and decision-makers are more accountable for their actions.
Codes:
(a) Both (A) and (R) are true and (R) is the correct explanation of (A).
(b) Both (A) and (R) are true, but (R) is not the correct explanation of (A).
(c) (A) is true, but (R) is false.
(d) (A) is false, but (R) is true.

33. Eco-auditing focuses on
(a) Assessment of actual effects of existing activities
(b) Assessment of project decisions
(c) Policy assessment
(d) Post project assessment

34. Match the List I and List II. Select the correct answer using the codes given below the lists:
List I
A. Ad-hoc Method
B. Checklist Method
C. Overlay Method
D. Matrix Method

List II
(i) Gives some measurements and describes the impacts
(ii) Limited value for scoping

(iii) Used for screening and for impact assessment, especially for impact identification
(iv) Acts as an aid in screening sites or routes for impacts

Codes:	A	B	C	D
(a)	(i)	(ii)	(iii)	(iv)
(b)	(ii)	(iii)	(i)	(iv)
(c)	(iii)	(iv)	(ii)	(i)
(d)	(ii)	(i)	(iv)	(iii)

35. Eco-labelling is governed by
(a) ISO 14001 (b) ISO 14020
(c) ISO 14010 (d) ISO 14040

36. The predominant gas emitted during the early life of a MSW landfill is
(a) CO (b) CO_2
(c) CH_4 (d) VOCs

37. Black foot disease is caused by
(a) excess of fluoride in water
(b) deficiency of iodine in water
(c) excess of arsenic in water
(d) excess of iodine in water

38. The Water Cess Act 1977 was amended in the year
(a) 1991 (b) 1978
(c) 1988 (d) 1987

39. Public Liability Insurance Act was enacted in which year?
(a) 1991 (b) 1986
(c) 1990 (d) 1984

40. In a multiple regression model $Y_i = \alpha + \beta_{1i}X_i + \beta_2 X_{2i} + \beta_{3i}X_3 + \in_i$, if $i - N$, the number of degrees of freedom required for determining the *t*-value at 5% level of significance
(a) N – 3 (b) N – 2
(c) N – 4 (d) N – 1

41. For large population sizes, the *t*-distribution approaches
(a) Normal distribution
(b) Poisson distribution
(c) Binomial distribution
(d) Chi-square distribution

42. Lotka-Volterra Model deals with
(a) Prey-Predator interactions
(b) Predicting CO_2 concentrations
(c) Study of pollutant concentration in river streams
(d) Study of pollutant concentration in atmospheric environment

43. Eigen values of the matrix $\begin{bmatrix} 1 & 1 & 1 \\ 1 & 1 & 1 \\ 1 & 1 & 1 \end{bmatrix}$ are
(a) 0, 0, 1 (b) 0, 1, 1
(c) 0, 2, 1 (d) 0, 0, 3

44. The second moment of the data set 2, 3, 7, 8, 10 is
(a) 6 (b) 378
(c) 45.2 (d) 22.51

45. In Gaussian dispersion model, the effective stack height is taken as sum of physical stack height and the plume rise ΔH. The plume rise varies with stack velocity V_S in the following manner:
(a) $\Delta H \propto V_S$ (b) $\Delta H \propto V_S^2$
(c) $\Delta H \propto V_S^{-1}$ (d) $\Delta H \propto V_S^{3/2}$

46. **Assertion (A):** A large number of districts in States of India have become water stressed.
Reason (R): The population in India has increased appreciably since independence.
Codes:
(a) Both (A) and (R) are true and (R) is the correct explanation of (A).
(b) Both (A) and (R) are true, but (R) is not the correct explanation of (A).
(c) (A) is true, but (R) is false.
(d) (A) is false, but (R) is true.

47. Copenhagen Conference on climate change was held as a sequel to
    (a) Montreal Protocol
    (b) Ramsar Convention
    (c) Basel Convention
    (d) Kyoto Protocol

48. Under the Climate Change Action Plan of Government of India which of the renewable source of energy has been identified as a priority for exploitation?
    (a) Solar energy
    (b) Wind energy
    (c) Tidal energy
    (d) Geothermal energy

49. International Ozone Day is celebrated on
    (a) 21st April (b) 5th June
    (c) 22nd April (d) 16th September

50. Sardar Sarovar Dam is built on
    (a) Sabarmati river (b) Narmada river
    (c) Tapti river (d) Chambal river

ANSWERS

1. (b)	2. (a)	3. (c)	4. (b)	5. (d)
6. (d)	7. (b)	8. (a)	9. (d)	10. (b)
11. (a)	12. (d)	13. (c)	14. (d)	15. (c)
16. (b)	17. (a)	18. (d)	19. (d)	20. (c)
21. (c)	22. (c)	23. (b)	24. (c)	25. (a)
26. (c)	27. (a)	28. (d)	29. (b)	30. (a)
31. (a)	32. (a)	33. (a)	34. (d)	35. (a)
36. (c)	37. (c)	38. (c)	39. (a)	40. (d)
41. (a)	42. (a)	43. (d)	44. (a)	45. (c)
46. (a)	47. (d)	48. (a)	49. (d)	50. (b)

JUNE–2011

Note: This paper contains Sixty (60) multiple-choice questions, each question carrying two (2) marks. Candidate is expected to answer any Fifty (50) questions. In case more than Fifty (50) questions are attempted, only the first Fifty (50) questions will be evaluated.

PAPER–I

1. A research paper is a brief report of research work based on
   (a) Primary Data only
   (b) Secondary Data only
   (c) Both Primary and Secondary Data
   (d) None of the above

2. Newton gave three basic laws of motion. This research is categorised as
   (a) Descriptive Research
   (b) Sample Survey
   (c) Fundamental Research
   (d) Applied Research

3. A group of experts in a specific area of knowledge assembled at a place and prepared a syllabus for a new course. The process may be termed as
   (a) Seminar (b) Workshop
   (c) Conference (d) Symposium

4. In the process of conducting research "Formulation of Hypothesis" is followed by
   (a) Statement of Objectives
   (b) Analysis of Data
   (c) Selection of Research Tools
   (d) Collection of Data

Read the following passage carefully and answer questions 5 to 10:

All historians are interpreters of text if they be private letters, Government records or parish birthlists or whatever. For most kinds of historians, these are only the necessary means to understanding something other than the texts themselves, such as a political action or a historical trend, whereas for the intellectual historian, a full understanding of his chosen texts is itself the aim of his enquiries. Of course, the intellectual history is particularly prone to draw on the focus of other disciplines that are habitually interpreting texts for purposes of their own, probing the reasoning that ostensibly connects premises and conclusions. Furthermore, the boundaries with adjacent subdisciplines are shifting and indistinct: the history of art and the history of science both claim a certain autonomy, partly just because they require specialised technical skills, but both can also be seen as part of a wider intellectual history, as is evident when one considers, for example, the common stock of knowledge about cosmological beliefs or moral ideals of a period.

Like all historians, the intellectual historian is a consumer rather than a producer of 'methods'. His distinctiveness lies in which aspect of the past he is trying to illuminate, not in having exclusive possession of either a corpus of evidence or a body of techniques. That being said, it does seem that the label 'intellectual history' attracts a disproportionate share of misunderstanding.

It is alleged that intellectual history is the history of something that never really mattered. The long dominance of the historical profession by political historians bred a kind of philistinism, an unspoken belief that power and its exercise was 'what mattered'. The prejudice was reinforced by the assertion that political action was never really the outcome of principles or ideas that were 'more flapdoodle'. The legacy of this precept is still discernible in the tendency to require ideas to have 'licensed' the political class before they can be deemed worthy of intellectual attention, as if there were some reasons why the history of art or science, of philosophy or literature, were somehow of interest and significance than the history of Parties or Parliaments. Perhaps in recent years the mirror-image of this philistinism has been more common in the claim that ideas of any one is of systematic expression or sophistication do not matter, as if they were only held by a minority.

Answer the following questions:

5. An intellectual historian aims to fully understand
   (a) the chosen texts of his own
   (b) political actions
   (c) historical trends
   (d) his enquiries
6. Intellectual historians do not claim exclusive possession of
   (a) conclusions
   (b) any corpus of evidence
   (c) distinctiveness
   (d) habitual interpretation
7. The misconceptions about intellectual history stem from
   (a) a body of techniques
   (b) the common stock of knowledge
   (c) the dominance of political historians
   (d) cosmological beliefs
8. What is philistinism?
   (a) Reinforcement of prejudice
   (b) Fabrication of reasons
   (c) The hold of land-owning classes
   (d) Belief that power and its exercise matter
9. Knowledge of cosmological beliefs or moral ideas of a period can be drawn as part of
   (a) literary criticism
   (b) history of science
   (c) history of philosophy
   (d) intellectual history
10. The claim that ideas of any one is of systematic expression do not matter, as if they were held by a minority, is
    (a) to have a licensed political class
    (b) a political action
    (c) a philosophy of literature
    (d) the mirror-image of philistinism
11. Public communication tends to occur within a more
    (a) complex structure
    (b) political structure
    (c) convenient structure
    (d) formal structure
12. Transforming thoughts, ideas and messages into verbal and non-verbal signs is referred to as
    (a) channelisation (b) mediation
    (c) encoding (d) decoding
13. Effective communication needs a supportive
    (a) economic environment
    (b) political environment
    (c) social environment
    (d) multi-cultural environment
14. A major barrier in the transmission of cognitive data in the process of communication is an individual's
    (a) personality (b) expectation
    (c) social status (d) coding ability
15. When communicated, institutionalised stereotypes become
    (a) myths (b) reasons
    (c) experiences (d) convictions

16. In mass communication, selective perception is dependent on the receiver's
(a) competence (b) pre-disposition
(c) receptivity (d) ethnicity

17. Determine the relationship between the pair of words NUMERATOR : DENOMINATOR and then select the pair of words from the following which have a similar relationship:
(a) fraction : decimal
(b) divisor : quotient
(c) top : bottom
(d) dividend : divisor

18. Find the wrong number in the sequence
125, 127, 130, 135, 142, 153, 165
(a) 130 (b) 142
(c) 153 (d) 165

19. If HOBBY is coded as IOBY and LOBBY is coded as MOBY; then BOBBY is coded as
(a) BOBY (b) COBY
(c) DOBY (d) OOBY

20. The letters in the first set have certain relationship. On the basis of this relationship, make the right choice for the second set

K/T : 11/20 :: J/R :?
(a) 10/8 (b) 10/18
(c) 11/19 (d) 10/19

21. If A = 5, B = 6, C = 7, D = 8 and so on, what do the following numbers stand for?
17, 19, 20, 9, 8
(a) Plane (b) Moped
(c) Motor (d) Tonga

22. The price of oil is increased by 25%. If the expenditure is not allowed to increase, the ratio between the reduction in consumption and the original consumption is
(a) 1:3 (b) 1:4
(c) 1:5 (d) 1:6

23. How many 8's are there in the following sequence which are preceded by 5 but not immediately followed by 3?
5 8 3 7 5 8 6 3 8 5 4 5 8 4 7 6
5 5 8 3 5 8 7 5 8 2 8 5
(a) 4 (b) 5
(c) 7 (d) 3

24. If a rectangle were called a circle, a circle a point, a point a triangle and a triangle a square, the shape of a wheel is
(a) Rectangle (b) Circle
(c) Point (d) Triangle

25. Which one of the following methods is best suited for mapping the distribution of different crops as provided in the standard classification of crops in India?
(a) Pie diagram
(b) Chorochromatic technique
(c) Isopleth technique
(d) Dot method

26. Which one of the following does not come under the methods of data classification?
(a) Qualitative (b) Normative
(c) Spatial (d) Quantitative

27. Which one of the following is not a source of data?
(a) Administrative records
(b) Population census
(c) GIS
(d) Sample survey

28. If the statement 'some men are cruel' is false, which of the following statements/ statement are/is true?
(i) All men are cruel.
(ii) No men are cruel.
(iii) Some men are not cruel.

(a) (i) and (iii) (b) (i) and (ii)
(c) (ii) and (iii) (d) Only (iii)

29. The octal number system consists of the following symbols
(a) 0 – 7
(b) 0 – 9
(c) 0 – 9, A – F
(d) None of the above

30. The binary equivalent of $(-19)_{10}$ in signed magnitude system is
(a) 11101100 (b) 11101101
(c) 10010011 (d) None of these

31. DNS in internet technology stands for
(a) Dynamic Name System
(b) Domain Name System
(c) Distributed Name System
(d) None of these

32. HTML stands for
(a) Hyper Text Markup Language
(b) Hyper Text Manipulation Language
(c) Hyper Text Managing Links
(d) Hyper Text Manipulating Links

33. Which of the following is type of LAN?
(a) Ethernet
(b) Token Ring
(c) FDDI
(d) All of the above

34. Which of the following statements is true?
(a) Smart cards do not require an operating system.
(b) Smart cards and PCs use some operating system.
(c) COS is smart card operating system.
(d) The communication between reader and card is in full duplex mode.

35. The Ganga Action Plan was initiated during the year
(a) 1986 (b) 1988
(c) 1990 (d) 1992

36. Identify the correct sequence of energy sources in order of their share in the power sector in India.
(a) Thermal > nuclear > hydro > wind
(b) Thermal > hydro > nuclear > wind
(c) Hydro > nuclear > thermal > wind
(d) Nuclear > hydro > wind > thermal

37. Chromium as a contaminant in drinking water in excess of permissible levels, causes
(a) Skeletal damage
(b) Gastrointestinal problem
(c) Dermal and nervous problems
(d) Liver/Kidney problems

38. The main precursors of winter smog are
(a) N_2O and hydrocarbons
(b) NO_x and hydrocarbons
(c) SO_2 and hydrocarbons
(d) SO_2 and ozone

39. Flash floods are caused when
(a) the atmosphere is convectively unstable and there is considerable vertical wind shear
(b) the atmosphere is stable
(c) the atmosphere is convectively unstable with no vertical windshear
(d) winds are catabatic

40. In mega cities of India, the dominant source of air pollution is
(a) transport sector
(b) thermal power
(c) municipal waste
(d) commercial sector

41. The first Open University in India was set up in the State of
(a) Andhra Pradesh
(b) Delhi
(c) Himachal Pradesh
(d) Tamil Nadu

42. Most of the Universities in India are funded by

(a) the Central Government
(b) the State Governments
(c) the University Grants Commission
(d) Private bodies and Individuals

43. Which of the following organisations looks after the quality of Technical and Management education in India?
(a) NCTE (b) MCI
(c) AICTE (d) CSIR

44. Consider the following statements: Identify the statement which implies natural justice.
(a) The principle of natural justice is followed by the Courts.
(b) Justice delayed is justice denied.
(c) Natural justice is an inalienable right of a citizen.
(d) A reasonable opportunity of being heard must be given.

45. The President of India is
(a) the Head of State
(b) the Head of Government
(c) both Head of the State and the Head of the Government
(d) None of the above

46. Who among the following holds office during the pleasure of the President of India?
(a) Chief Election Commissioner
(b) Comptroller and Auditor General of India
(c) Chairman of the Union Public Service Commission
(d) Governor of a State

Questions 47 to 49 are based upon the following diagram in which there are three interlocking circles A, P and S where A stands for Artists, circle P for Professors and circle S for Sportspersons. Different regions in the figure are lettered from a to g:

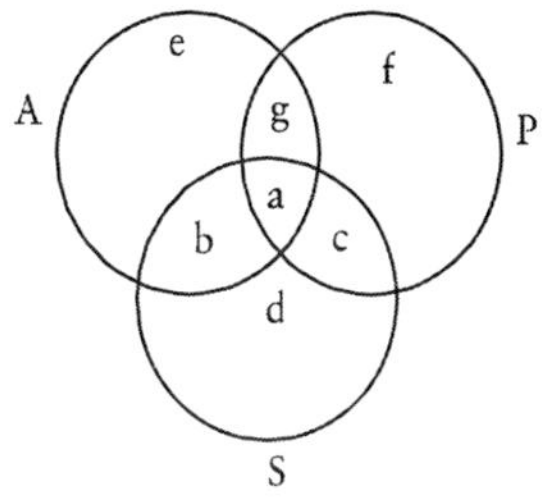

47. The region which represents artists who are neither sportsmen nor professors.
(a) d (b) e
(c) b (d) g

48. The region which represents professors, who are both artists and sportspersons.
(a) a (b) c
(c) d (d) g

49. The region which represents professors, who are also sportspersons, but not artists.
(a) e (b) f
(c) c (d) g

Questions 50 to 52 are based on the following data:

Measurements of some variable X were made at an interval of 1 minute from 10 A.M. to 10:20 A.M. The data, thus, obtained is as follows:

X: 60, 62, 65, 64, 63, 61, 66, 65, 70, 68
63, 62, 64, 69, 65, 64, 66, 67, 66, 64

50. The value of X, which is exceeded 10% of the time in the duration of measurement, is
(a) 69 (b) 68
(c) 67 (d) 66

51. The value of X, which is exceeded 90% of the time in the duration of measurement, is
(a) 63 (b) 62
(c) 61 (d) 60

52. The value of X, which is exceeded 50% of the time in the duration of measurement, is
    (a) 66 (b) 65
    (c) 64 (d) 63

53. For maintaining an effective discipline in the class, the teacher should
    (a) Allow students to do what they like.
    (b) Deal with the students strictly.
    (c) Give the students some problem to solve.
    (d) Deal with them politely and firmly.

54. An effective teaching aid is one which
    (a) is colourful and good looking
    (b) activates all faculties
    (c) is visible to all students
    (d) easy to prepare and use

55. Those teachers are popular among students who
    (a) develop intimacy with them
    (b) help them solve their problems
    (c) award good grades
    (d) take classes on extra tuition fee

56. The essence of an effective classroom environment is
    (a) a variety of teaching aids
    (b) lively student-teacher interaction
    (c) pin-drop silence
    (d) strict discipline

57. On the first day of his class, if a teacher is asked by the students to introduce himself, he should
    (a) ask them to meet after the class
    (b) tell them about himself in brief
    (c) ignore the demand and start teaching
    (d) scold the student for this unwanted demand

58. Moral values can be effectively inculcated among the students when the teacher
    (a) frequently talks about values
    (b) himself practices them
    (c) tells stories of great persons
    (d) talks of Gods and Goddesses

59. The essential qualities of a researcher are
    (a) spirit of free enquiry
    (b) reliance on observation and evidence
    (c) systematisation or theorising of knowledge
    (d) All of the above

60. Research is conducted to
    1. Generate new knowledge
    2. Not to develop a theory
    3. Obtain research degree
    4. Reinterpret existing knowledge

    Which of the above are correct?
    (a) 1, 3 & 2 (b) 3, 2 & 4
    (c) 2, 1 & 3 (d) 1, 3 & 4

ANSWERS

1. (c)	2. (c)	3. (b)	4. (c)	5. (a)
6. (b)	7. (c)	8. (d)	9. (d)	10. (d)
11. (d)	12. (c)	13. (d)	14. (c)	15. (d)
16. (b)	17. (d)	18. (d)	19. (b)	20. (b)
21. (b)	22. (c)	23. (a)	24. (c)	25. (a)
26. (b)	27. (a)	28. (b)	29. (a)	30. (d)
31. (b)	32. (a)	33. (d)	34. (c)	35. (a)
36. (b)	37. (d)	38. (c)	39. (a)	40. (a)
41. (a)	42. (c)	43. (c)	44. (d)	45. (b)
46. (d)	47. (b)	48. (a)	49. (c)	50. (c)
51. (b)	52. (d)	53. (d)	54. (b)	55. (b)
56. (b)	57. (b)	58. (b)	59. (d)	60. (d)

PAPER–II

Note: This paper contains fifty (50) objective type questions, each question carrying two (2) marks. Attempt all the questions.

1. Identify the correct sequence of energy flow through various levels of an ecosystem:
   (a) Sun's energy → Primary producers → Carnivores
   (b) Sun's energy → Primary producers → Carnivores → Herbivores
   (c) Sun's energy → Herbivores → Primary producers
   (d) Sun's energy → Primary producers → Herbivores → Carnivores
2. When environmental lapse rate is more than dry adiabatic lapse rate, the atmosphere is said to be in
   (a) Stable state
   (b) Unstable state
   (c) Neutral state
   (d) Conditionally stable state
3. Which of the following accounts for nearly 75% of the available fresh water in the world?
   (a) Groundwater (b) Glaciers
   (c) River water (d) Lakes
4. The summers in Taiga climatic zone are
   (a) hot, humid and long
   (b) warm and short
   (c) cool, rainy and short
   (d) hot and dry
5. Utilitarian conservation theory was established by
   (a) Roosevelt and Pinchot
   (b) John Muir
   (c) Rachel Carson
   (d) Brundtland
6. Ozone undergoes photolysis due to ultra-violet radiations of wavelength
   (a) < 315 nm (b) < 400 nm
   (c) < 500 nm (d) < 600 nm
7. Which of the following types of pesticides are least biodegradable?
   (a) Organo chloro compounds
   (b) Organo phosphorous compounds
   (c) Organo carbamates
   (d) All of the above
8. $MgSO_4$ can be expressed as
   (a) 120 equivalent of $CaCO_3$
   (b) 117 equivalent of $CaCO_3$
   (c) 195 equivalent of $CaCO_3$
   (d) 84 equivalent of $CaCO_3$
9. SDS-PAGE of tissue proteins under denaturation determines the
   (a) Hydrogen bond breakage
   (b) Sulphide bridge breakage
   (c) Subunits of protein
   (d) None of the above
10. In urban areas, the main constituents of photochemical smog in winter season are
    (a) SO_2 + NO_x + PAN
    (b) Hydrocarbons + CO + PAN
    (c) Hydrocarbons + SO_2 + PAN
    (d) Hydrocarbons + NO_x + O_3 + PAN
11. Redox potential in soil is governed by
    (a) strong oxidizing agent
    (b) weak oxidizing agent
    (c) organic matter
    (d) soil particle size
12. The process of invasion is completed through the following stages:
    (a) Migration and establishment of species in bare area
    (b) Migration, ecesis and aggregation
    (c) Ecesis and aggregation
    (d) Migration, aggregation and settlement of species

13. Which one is not matched correctly?
    (a) Kaziranga – Assam
    (b) Periyar – Kerala
    (c) Ranthambore – Rajasthan
    (d) Hemis High Altitude – Himachal Pradesh

14. Hyporhric biodiversity is linked with
    (a) Ecotone of surface water and groundwater
    (b) Ecotone of terrestrial and aquatic ecosystem
    (c) Groundwater
    (d) Asian region

15. *E. coli* displays diauxic growth pattern when grown in a medium containing
    (a) glucose and fructose
    (b) glucose and citrate
    (c) glucose and lactose
    (d) glucose alone

16. El Nino effect refers to the periodic extension of warm equatorial current along which coast?
    (a) Peru Coast
    (b) African Coast
    (c) East Coast of India
    (d) Somalia Coast

17. Which of the following options is correct for concentration of elements in sea water?
    (a) Na > Mg > Ca (b) Ca > Na > Mg
    (c) Mg > Na > Ca (d) Cl > Na > SO_4

18. Land use planning requires which of the following base maps?
    (a) Soil type map (b) Slope map
    (c) Soil depth map (d) All of the above

19. Gutenberg discontinuity is found at the depth of
    (a) 333 km (b) 700 km
    (c) 1500 km (d) 2900 km

20. Landslides are generally associated with heavy rainfall because
    (a) Water is universal solvent.
    (b) Water enhances chemical weathering.
    (c) Water increases the weight of overburden.
    (d) Water reduces the shear strength of rock.

21. The optimal pH for Methane production ranges between
    (a) 7 to 7.2 (b) 5 to 5.6
    (c) 8 to 9.5 (d) 2.3 to 4.5

22. Average life time (τ) and half life ($T_{½}$) of a radioactive substance are related as
    (a) $\tau = 1.44\ T_{½}$ (b) $\tau = 0.5\ T_{½}$
    (c) $\tau = 0.63\ T_{½}$ (d) $\tau = 2\ T_{½}$

23. The maximum contribution to world electricity generation from non-hydro renewable energy sources is from
    (a) Wind (b) Biomass
    (c) Solar PV (d) Geothermal

24. The maximum efficiency of a commercial solar photovoltaic cell attainable today is in the ange
    (a) 3% to 10% (b) 12% to 20%
    (c) 30% to 40% (d) 40% to 50%

25. Which of the following does not lead to global warming?
    (a) Stratospheric ozone
    (b) Tropospheric ozone
    (c) Black carbon aerosols
    (d) N_2O

26. The instrument used for determination of transparency of water is
    (a) Spectrophotometer
    (b) Ekman dredge
    (c) Conductivity bridge
    (d) Sechhi disc

27. Which of the following is an aerobic waste water treatment method?

(a) Sludge digester (b) Septic tank
(c) Percolating filter (d) Imhoff tank

28. Nitrogen Oxides (NO_x) consists of
(a) $NO + NO_2$
(b) $NO + NO_2 + N_2O$
(c) $NO + NO_2 + N_2O_5$
(d) $NO + NO_2 + N_2O + N_2O_5$

29. An increase of 10 ppm in the concentration of CO_2 in atmosphere represents approximately an addition of carbon of amount:
(a) 1.2 Kilotons
(b) 2.12 Megatons
(c) 21.2 Giga tons
(d) 2120 tons

30. Winds blowing down an incline often due to cold air drainage is called
(a) Anabatic winds
(b) Mountain winds
(c) Cyclonic winds
(d) Katabatic winds

31. ISO 14040 is related to
(a) Environmental audit
(b) Energy audit
(c) Cost benefit analysis
(d) Life cycle analysis

32. Definition of Impact Assessment was given by
(a) Kozlowski (1989)
(b) Graham Smith (1993)
(c) Heer and Hagerty (1977)
(d) Bartlett (1989)

33. **Assertion (A):** Environmental and social impact assessment never overlap with each other.
Reason (R): Environmental and social impact assessment are effectively opposite ends of the same spectrum.
Codes:
(a) Both (A) and (R) are true and (R) is the correct explanation of (A).
(b) Both (A) and (R) are true but (R) is not the correct explanation of (A).
(c) (A) is true, but (R) is false.
(d) (A) is false, but (R) is true.

34. One of the best known matrix methods for environmental impact assessment is
(a) Leopold Matrix
(b) Sphere Matrix
(c) Saratoga Matrix
(d) Component Interaction Method

35. The method for systematically evaluating alternative development schemes and weighing relevant social cost with social benefits is known as
(a) Cost – benefit analysis
(b) Social cost – benefit analysis
(c) Social benefit – cost analysis
(d) Cost – effectiveness analysis

36. Gases emitted from municipal landfill sites include
(a) SO_2 and CH_4
(b) NH_4, CO, SO_2, CH_4
(c) NH_4, H_2S, CO
(d) CH_4, H_2S, CO_2, NH_4

37. The Air (Prevention and Control of Pollution) Act, 1981 was first amended in the year
(a) 1986 (b) 1987
(c) 1988 (d) 1990

38. Identify the correct sequence of materials in order of their heating values:
(a) Methane > fuel oil > coal > wood
(b) Fuel oil > coal > methane > wood
(c) Coal > wood > fuel oil > garbage
(d) Methane > coal > garbage > wood

39. Urban air quality is basically decided by
(a) CO, SPM, SO_2, NO_2, Surface ozone
(b) SPM, NO_2, SO_2
(c) SPM, NO_2, CO
(d) SPM, SO_2, Surface ozone

40. If N is the population size at any given instant *t*, *r* its growth rate in an

environment having carrying capacity K, the environmental resistance to population growth is given by

(a) N/K (b) $1 - \frac{N}{K}$

(c) $\frac{N}{K} e^{-tr}$ (d) $\frac{N}{K} e^{tr}$

41. Which of the following statistical attributes is used to test the null hypothesis in Regression Analysis?
(a) Mean
(b) Standard deviation
(c) t-statistic
(d) χ^2-test

42. Given 'd' as particle size and 'V' setting velocity in cm/sec., the correct relationship between 'd' and 'V' is given by

(a) $V \propto \frac{1}{d^n}$ (b) $V \propto d^n$

(c) $V \propto d$ (d) $V = \frac{1}{d^n}$

43. The geometric mean of 5, 5 and 40 is
(a) 16.66 (b) 25
(c) 31.6 (d) 10

44. The Eigen values of the matrix $\begin{bmatrix} 1 & 1 \\ 1 & 1 \end{bmatrix}$ are
(a) 1, 1 (b) 0, 1
(c) 0, 2 (d) 1, –1

45. In a simple regression model $y = a + bx + E$ (where the symbols have their usual meanings), the expectation value of <E> is assumed as
(a) 0
(b) $-y$
(c) $\frac{\sigma}{\sqrt{2}}$; where σ is standard deviation
(d) σ^2

46. In the Earth Summit at Rio de Janeiro, 1992, which of the following was not an agenda?
(a) Ozone depletion
(b) Global warming
(c) CO_2 reduction targets
(d) Biodiversity conservation

47. **Assertion (A):** Most of the corporate sector in India has become conscious of the ethical dimensions pertaining to its impact on environment.
Reason (R): Indian people are increasingly becoming aware of the environmental issues.
Codes:
(a) Both (A) and (R) are true and (R) is the correct explanation of (A).
(b) Both (A) and (R) are true but (R) is not the correct explanation of (A).
(c) (A) is true, but (R) is false.
(d) (A) is false, but (R) is true.

48. 'Slash and Burn' or milpa farming is often blamed for
(a) habitat destruction
(b) forest destruction
(c) hydrological imbalance
(d) mine destruction

49. **Assertion (A):** Climate change is going to increase social tensions in India.
Reason (R): The frequency and intensity of the extreme weather events will have serious consequences for food security.
Codes:
(a) Both (A) and (R) are true and (R) is the correct explanation of (A).
(b) Both (A) and (R) are true but (R) is not the correct explanation of (A).
(c) (A) is true, but (R) is false.
(d) (A) is false, but (R) is true.

50. Snow blindness is caused due to
    (a) Ultra-violet radiations
    (b) Excessive flux of visible radiations
    (c) Infra-red radiations
    (d) Microwave radiations

ANSWERS

1. (d)	2. (b)	3. (b)	4. (c)	5. (a)
6. (a)	7. (a)	8. (a)	9. (a)	10. (d)
11. (c)	12. (b)	13. (d)	14. (a)	15. (c)
16. (a)	17. (a)	18. (d)	19. (d)	20. (d)
21. (a)	22. (a)	23. (a)	24. (b)	25. (a)
26. (d)	27. (c)	28. (a)	29. (b)	30. (b)
31. (d)	32. (c)	33. (a)	34. (a)	35. (b)
36. (d)	37. (b)	38. (a)	39. (a)	40. (a)
41. (d)	42. (a)	43. (c)	44. (c)	45. (a)
46. (c)	47. (a)	48. (b)	49. (a)	50. (a)

DECEMBER–2011

Note: This paper contains Sixty (60) multiple-choice questions, each question carrying two (2) marks. Candidate is expected to answer any Fifty (50) questions. In case more than Fifty (50) questions are attempted, only the first Fifty (50) questions will be evaluated.

PAPER–I

1. Photo bleeding means
   (a) Photo cropping
   (b) Photo placement
   (c) Photo cutting
   (d) Photo colour adjustment

2. While designing communication strategy feed-forward studies are conducted by
   (a) Audience (b) Communicator
   (c) Satellite (d) Media

3. In which language the newspapers have highest circulation?
   (a) English (b) Hindi
   (c) Bengali (d) Tamil

4. Aspect ratio of TV Screen is
   (a) 4 : 3 (b) 3 : 4
   (c) 2 : 3 (d) 2 : 4

5. Communication with oneself is known as
   (a) Organisational Communication
   (b) Grapevine Communication
   (c) Interpersonal Communication
   (d) Intrapersonal Communication

6. The term 'SITE' stands for
   (a) Satellite Indian Television Experiment
   (b) Satellite International Television Experiment
   (c) Satellite Instructional Television Experiment
   (d) Satellite Instructional Teachers Education

7. What is the number that comes next in the sequence?
   2, 5, 9, 19, 37, ___
   (a) 76 (b) 74
   (c) 75 (d) 50

8. Find the next letter for the series MPSV.....
   (a) X (b) Y
   (c) Z (d) A

9. If '367' means 'I am happy'; '748' means 'you are sad' and '469' means 'happy and sad' in a given code, then which of the following represents 'and' in that code?
   (a) 3 (b) 6
   (c) 9 (d) 4

10. The basis of the following classification is 'animal', 'man', 'house', 'book', and 'student':
    (a) Definite descriptions
    (b) Proper names
    (c) Descriptive phrases
    (d) Common names

11. **Assertion (A):** The coin when flipped next time will come up tails.
    Reason (R): Because the coin was flipped five times in a row, and each time it came up heads.

Choose the correct answer from below:
(a) Both (A) and (R) are true, and (R) is the correct explanation of (A).
(b) Both (A) and (R) are false, and (R) is the correct explanation of (A).
(c) (A) is doubtful, (R) is true, and (R) is not the correct explanation of (A).
(d) (A) is doubtful, (R) is false, and (R) is the correct explanation of (A).

12. The relation 'is a sister of' is
(a) non-symmetrical (b) symmetrical
(c) asymmetrical (d) transitive

13. If the proposition "Vegetarians are not meat eaters" is false, then which of the following inferences is correct? Choose from the codes given below:
1. "Some vegetarians are meat eaters" is true.
2. "All vegetarians are meat eaters" is doubtful.
3. "Some vegetarians are not meat eaters" is true.
4. "Some vegetarians are not meat eaters" is doubtful.

Codes:
(a) 1, 2 and 3 (b) 2, 3 and 4
(c) 1, 3 and 4 (d) 1, 2 and 4

14. Determine the nature of the following definition:
'Poor' means having an annual income of ₹ 10,000.
(a) Persuasive (b) Precising
(c) Lexical (d) Stipulative

15. Which one of the following is not an argument?
(a) If today is Tuesday, tomorrow will be Wednesday.
(b) Since today is Tuesday, tomorrow will be Wednesday.
(c) Ram insulted me so I punched him in the nose.
(d) Ram is not at home, so he must have gone to town.

16. Venn diagram is a kind of diagram to
(a) represent and assess the truth of elementary inferences with the help of Boolean Algebra of classes.
(b) represent and assess the validity of elementary inferences with the help of Boolean Algebra of classes.
(c) represent but not assess the validity of elementary inferences with the help of Boolean Algebra of classes.
(d) assess but not represent the validity of elementary inferences with the help of Boolean Algebra of classes.

17. Inductive logic studies the way in which a premise may
(a) support and entail a conclusion
(b) not support but entail a conclusion
(c) neither support nor entail a conclusion
(d) support a conclusion without entailing it

18. Which of the following statements are true? Choose from the codes given below:
1. Some arguments, while not completely valid, are almost valid.
2. A sound argument may be invalid.
3. A cogent argument may have a probably false conclusion.
4. A statement may be true or false.

Codes:
(a) 1 and 2 (b) 1, 3 and 4
(c) Only 4 (d) 3 and 4

19. If the side of the square increases by 40%, then the area of the square increases by
(a) 60% (b) 40%
(c) 196% (d) 96%

20. There are 10 lamps in a hall. Each one of them can be switched on independently. The number of ways in which hall can be illuminated is
(a) 10^2 (b) 1023
(c) 2^{10} (d) 10!

21. How many numbers between 100 and 300 begin or end with 2?
(a) 100 (b) 110
(c) 120 (d) 180

22. In a college having 300 students, every student reads 5 newspapers and every newspaper is read by 60 students. The number of newspapers required is
(a) at least 30 (b) at most 20
(c) exactly 25 (d) exactly 5

The total CO_2 emissions from various sectors are 5 mmt. In the Pie Chart given below, the percentage contribution to CO_2 emissions from various sectors is indicated.

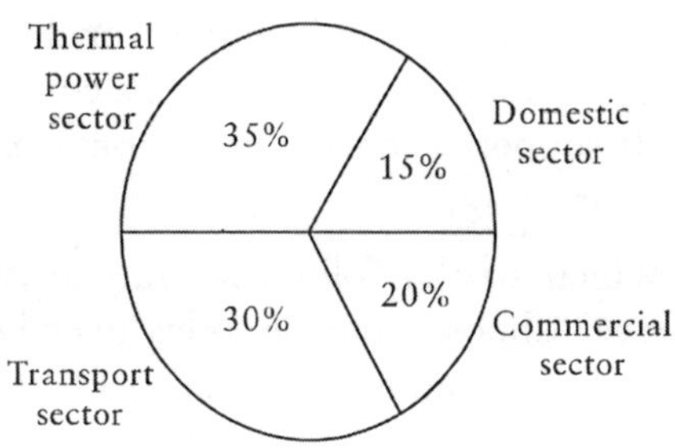

23. What is the absolute CO_2 emission from domestic sector?
(a) 1.5 mmt (b) 2.5 mmt
(c) 1.75 mmt (d) 0.75 mmt

24. What is the absolute CO_2 emission for combined thermal power and transport sectors?
(a) 3.25 mmt (b) 1.5 mmt
(c) 2.5 mmt (d) 4 mmt

25. Which of the following operating system is used on mobile phones?
(a) Windows Vista
(b) Android
(c) Windows XP
(d) All of the above

26. If $(y)_x$ represents a number y in base x, then which of the following numbers is smallest of all?
(a) $(1111)_2$ (b) $(1111)_8$
(c) $(1111)_{10}$ (d) $(1111)_{16}$

27. High level programming language can be converted to machine language using which of the following?
(a) Oracle (b) Compiler
(c) Mat lab (d) Assembler

28. HTML is used to create
(a) machine language program
(b) high level program
(c) web page
(d) web server

29. The term DNS stands for
(a) Domain Name System
(b) Defense Nuclear System
(c) Downloadable New Software
(d) Dependent Name Server

30. IPv4 and IPv6 are addresses used to identify computers on the internet. Find the correct statement out of the following:
(a) Number of bits required for IPv4 address is more than number of bits required for IPv6 address.
(b) Number of bits required for IPv4 address is same as number of bits required for IPv6 address.
(c) Number of bits required for IPv4 address is less than number of bits required for IPv6 address.
(d) Number of bits required for IPv4 address is 64.

31. Which of the following pollutants affects the respiratory tract in humans?
(a) Carbon monoxide
(b) Nitric oxide
(c) Sulphur dioxide
(d) Aerosols

32. Which of the following pollutants is not emitted from the transport sector?
    (a) Oxides of nitrogen
    (b) Chlorofluorocarbons
    (c) Carbon monoxide
    (d) Poly aromatic hydrocarbons

33. Which of the following sources of energy has the maximum potential in India?
    (a) Solar energy
    (b) Wind energy
    (c) Ocean thermal energy
    (d) Tidal energy

34. Which of the following is not a source of pollution in soil?
    (a) Transport sector
    (b) Agriculture sector
    (c) Thermal power plants
    (d) Hydropower plants

35. Which of the following is not a natural hazard?
    (a) Earthquake (b) Tsunami
    (c) Flash floods (d) Nuclear accident

36. Ecological footprint represents
    (a) area of productive land and water to meet the resources requirement
    (b) energy consumption
    (c) CO_2 emissions per person
    (d) forest cover

37. The aim of value education to inculcate in students is
    (a) the moral values
    (b) the social values
    (c) the political values
    (d) the economic values

38. Indicate the number of Regional Offices of University Grants Commission of India.
    (a) 10 (b) 07
    (c) 08 (d) 09

39. One-rupee currency note in India bears the signature of
    (a) The President of India
    (b) Finance Minister of India
    (c) Governor, Reserve Bank of India
    (d) Finance Secretary of Government of India

40. Match the List I with the List II and select the correct answer from the codes given below:

List I (Commissions and Committees)
A. First Administrative Reforms Commission
B. Paul H. Appleby Committee I
C. K. Santhanam Committee
D. Second Administrative Reforms Commission

List II (Year)
1. 2005 2. 1962
3. 1966 4. 1953

Codes:	A	B	C	D
(a)	1	3	2	4
(b)	3	4	2	1
(c)	4	2	3	1
(d)	2	1	4	3

41. Constitutionally the registration and recognition of political parties is the function performed by
    (a) The State Election Commission of respective States
    (b) The Law Ministry of Government of India
    (c) The Election Commission of India
    (d) Election Department of the State Governments

42. The members of Gram Sabha are
    (a) Sarpanch, Upsarpanch and all elected Panchas
    (b) Sarpanch, Upsarpanch and Village level worker
    (c) Sarpanch, Gram Sevak and elected Panchas
    (d) Registered voters of Village Panchayat

43. By which of the following methods the true evaluation of the students is possible?
(a) Evaluation at the end of the course
(b) Evaluation twice in a year
(c) Continuous evaluation
(d) Formative evaluation

44. Suppose a student wants to share his problems with his teacher and he visits the teacher's house for the purpose, the teacher should
(a) contact the student's parents and solve his problem
(b) suggest him that he should never visit his house
(c) suggest him to meet the principal and solve the problem
(d) extend reasonable help and boost his morale

45. When some students are deliberately attempting to disturb the discipline of the class by making mischief, what will be your role as a teacher?
(a) Expelling those students
(b) Isolate those students
(c) Reform the group with your authority
(d) Giving them an opportunity for introspection and improve their behaviour

46. Which of the following belongs to a projected aid?
(a) Blackboard (b) Diorama
(c) Epidiascope (d) Globe

47. A teacher is said to be fluent in asking questions, if he can ask
(a) meaningful questions
(b) as many questions as possible
(c) maximum number of questions in a fixed time
(d) many meaningful questions in a fixed time

48. Which of the following qualities is most essential for a teacher?
(a) He should be a learned person
(b) He should be a well-dressed person
(c) He should have patience
(d) He should be an expert in his subject

49. A hypothesis is a
(a) law (b) canon
(c) postulate (d) supposition

50. Suppose you want to investigate the working efficiency of nationalised bank in India, which one of the following would you follow?
(a) Area Sampling
(b) Multi-stage Sampling
(c) Sequential Sampling
(d) Quota Sampling

51. Controlled group condition is applied in
(a) Survey Research
(b) Historical Research
(c) Experimental Research
(d) Descriptive Research

52. Workshops are meant for
(a) giving lectures
(b) multiple target groups
(c) showcase new theories
(d) hands on training/experience

53. Which one of the following is a research tool?
(a) Graph (b) Illustration
(c) Questionnaire (d) Diagram

54. Research is not considered ethical if it
(a) tries to prove a particular point.
(b) does not ensure privacy and anonymity of the respondent.
(c) does not investigate the data scientifically.
(d) is not of a very high standard.

Read the following passage carefully and answer the questions (55 to 60):

The catalytic fact of the twentieth century is uncontrollable development, consumerist society, political materialism, and spiritual devaluation. This inordinate development has led to the transcendental 'second reality' of sacred perception that biologically transcendence is a part of human life. As the century closes, it dawns with imperative vigour that the 'first reality' of enlightened rationalism and the 'second reality' of the Beyond have to be harmonised in a worthy state of man. The *de facto* values describe what we are, they portray the 'is' of our ethic, they are *est* values (Latin *est* means is). The ideal values tell us what we ought to be, they are *esto* values (Latin *esto* 'ought to be'). Both have to be in the ebb and flow of consciousness. The ever new science and technology and the ever-perennial faith are two modes of one certainty, that is the wholeness of man, his courage to be, his share in Being.

The materialistic foundations of science have crumbled down. Science itself has proved that matter is energy, processes are as valid as facts, and affirmed the non-materiality of the universe. The encounter of the 'two cultures', the scientific and the humane, will restore the normal vision, and will be the bedrock of a 'science of understanding' in the new century. It will give new meaning to the ancient perception that quantity (measure) and quality (value) coexist at the root of nature. Human endeavours cannot afford to be humanistically irresponsible.

55. The problem raised in the passage reflects overall on
    (a) Consumerism
    (b) Materialism
    (c) Spiritual devaluation
    (d) Inordinate development

56. The *de facto* values in the passage means
    (a) What is
    (b) What ought to be
    (c) What can be
    (d) Where it is

57. According to the passage, the 'first reality' constitutes
    (a) Economic prosperity
    (b) Political development
    (c) Sacred perception of life
    (d) Enlightened rationalism

58. Encounter of the 'two cultures', the scientific and the human implies
    (a) Restoration of normal vision
    (b) Universe is both material and non-material
    (c) Man is superior to nature
    (d) Co-existence of quantity and quality in nature

59. The contents of the passage are
    (a) Descriptive (b) Prescriptive
    (c) Axiomatic (d) Optional

60. The passage indicates that science has proved that
    (a) universe is material
    (b) matter is energy
    (c) nature has abundance
    (d) humans are irresponsible

ANSWERS

1. (a)	2. (b)	3. (b)	4. (a)	5. (d)
6. (c)	7. (c)	8. (b)	9. (c)	10. (d)
11. (c)	12. (b)	13. (a)	14. (b)	15. (a)
16. (b)	17. (d)	18. (d)	19. (d)	20. (b)
21. (b)	22. (c)	23. (d)	24. (a)	25. (b)
26. (a)	27. (b)	28. (c)	29. (a)	30. (c)
31. (a)	32. (b)	33. (b)	34. (d)	35. (d)
36. (a)	37. (a)	38. (b)	39. (d)	40. (b)
41. (c)	42. (d)	43. (d)	44. (d)	45. (d)
46. (c)	47. (d)	48. (c)	49. (d)	50. (b)
51. (c)	52. (d)	53. (c)	54. (b)	55. (c)
56. (a)	57. (d)	58. (a)	59. (a)	60. (b)

PAPER–II

Note: This paper contains fifty (50) objective type questions, each question carrying two (2) marks. Attempt all the questions.

1. What are the steps necessary for sustainable management of renewable resources?
   (a) Avoiding over-exploitation and pollution of biotic systems.
   (b) Strengthening the resource base and augmenting regenerability of biotic systems.
   (c) Use of alternative resources.
   (d) All of these.
2. Fluxes of heat, water vapour and momentum are constant in
   (a) upper atmosphere
   (b) middle atmosphere
   (c) Ekman layer
   (d) surface boundary layer
3. Inversions occur when atmosphere is
   (a) unstable (b) neutral
   (c) slightly stable (d) most stable
4. When one species limits access of another species to a resource regardless of whether the resource is abundant or scarce, it is called
   (a) interspecific competition
   (b) intraspecific competition
   (c) interference competition
   (d) exploitative competition
5. Nanda Devi and Sunderbans are examples of Indian
   (a) National Parks
   (b) Sanctuaries
   (c) International heritage areas
   (d) Biosphere reserves
6. Match the List I and List II and select the correct answer from the codes given below the lists:

   List I (Analytical techniques)
   (A) XRF
   (B) Nephelometry
   (C) IR spectroscopy
   (D) UV-visible spectroscopy

   List II (Measured items)
   (i) Functional groups
   (ii) Elements
   (iii) Turbidity
   (iv) Aromatics

Codes:	A	B	C	D
(a)	(iv)	(ii)	(iii)	(i)
(b)	(i)	(iii)	(iv)	(ii)
(c)	(iii)	(ii)	(iv)	(i)
(d)	(ii)	(iii)	(i)	(iv)

7. The pH of a 0.001 M solution of HCl is
   (a) 2 (b) 4
   (c) 3 (d) 1
8. The primitive atmosphere of earth consisted of
   (a) CO_2, NO_2, NH_3, SO_2
   (b) H_2, NH_3, CH_4, H_2O
   (c) CO, N_2O_3, SO_3, H_3N
   (d) He, Ne, Ar, Kr
9. Which of the following is the major source of mercury pollution in India?
   (a) Coal based thermal power plants
   (b) Pesticides
   (c) Dental amalgam fillings
   (d) Electrical and electronic gadgets
10. Nitrite causes methaemoglobinemia by
    (a) oxidizing membrane proteins
    (b) reacting with calcium of bones
    (c) oxidizing haemoglobin
    (d) oxidizing membrane lipids

11. Solubility (S) of a sparingly soluble salt of the type AB is related to the solubility product (K_{SP}) by the relation

(a) $S = K_{SP}^2$ (b) $S = 2\ K_{SP}$

(c) $S = \sqrt{K_{SP}}$ (d) $S = K_{SP}$

12. The amount of biomass which can be sustained under steady state condition of an ecosystem is termed as
(a) Primary productivity
(b) System homeostasis
(c) Sustainable yield
(d) Carrying capacity

13. Which of the following regions generally possess large diversity in their species composition?
(a) Arctic regions
(b) Antarctic regions
(c) Snow-clad mountains
(d) Subtropical regions

14. Match the items under List I and List II and select the correct answer using codes given below:

List I
A. Tissue culture technique
B. Vermiculture technique
C. Breeding technique
D. Cryo preservation technique

List II
(i) Green revolution
(ii) Storage of propagules
(iii) Micropropagation
(iv) Organic farming

Codes:	A	B	C	D
(a)	(ii)	(iv)	(iii)	(i)
(b)	(iii)	(iv)	(i)	(ii)
(c)	(i)	(ii)	(iv)	(iii)
(d)	(iv)	(i)	(ii)	(iii)

15. Successive increase in concentration of some chemicals through different food level organisms is called
(a) Biogeochemical cycle
(b) Biological magnification
(c) Chemical production
(d) Biodegradation

16. Which of the following is a correct sequence found in a grassland ecosystem?
(a) Grasses → diatoms → deer → dog
(b) Grasses → rabbit → wolves → tiger
(c) Trees → birds → hawks → wolves
(d) Grasses → snakes → deer → dog

17. Reservoir triggered seismicity in case of hydropower projects with large pondage is most likely to occur when
(a) Thrust fault passes through the reservoir
(b) Strike-slip fault passes through the reservoir
(c) Large flood strikes the project
(d) Final reservoir level drops

18. At the present time volcanoes are confined to certain limited areas of the Earth's surface. This special zone is called
(a) Trans-Atlantic volcanic zone
(b) Circum-Pacific Ring of fire
(c) Central-Asian inter-continental zone
(d) Indian-Ocean volcanic belt

19. Given below are scales of four topographic maps. Maps of which scale will have more clarity?
(a) 1 : 50,000 (b) 1 : 25,000
(c) 1 : 250,000 (d) 1 : 1,000,000

20. Soil surveys involve which of the following?
(a) Soil series mapping
(b) Soil depth mapping
(c) Soil horizons mapping
(d) All of these

21. In which of the following frequency ranges the human era is most sensitive to noise?

(a) 1-2 KHz (b) 100-500 Hz
(c) 10-12 KHz (d) 13-16 KHz

22. The maximum value of power coefficient for a wind turbine can be
(a) 0.59 (b) 0.49
(c) 0.92 (d) 0.72

23. Average value of solar insolation $\left(\frac{w}{m^2}\right)$ at the earth's surface is
(a) 250 (b) 350
(c) 450 (d) 550

24. Fuel cells are devises that generate electricity by converting the energy released by
(a) electrochemical reactions without going through combustion process.
(b) biochemical reactions without going through combustion process.
(c) electrochemical reactions involving combustion process.
(d) biochemical reactions involving combustion process.

25. Chemically coal is composed of
(i) Carbon
(ii) Hydrogen
(iii) Oxygen
(iv) Sulphur and/or Nitrogen
(a) Only (i) and (ii)
(b) Only (i), (ii) and (iii)
(c) Only (i), (ii) and (iv)
(d) All of above

26. Which of the following gases has the maximum global warming potential (GWP)?
(a) Carbon dioxide (b) Methane
(c) Nitrous oxide (d) Water vapour

27. Acid rain has pH
(a) < 7.6 (b) > 7
(c) ≤ 5.6 (d) < 1.6

28. Which of the following gases facilitates formation of tropospheric ozone?
(a) NO_2 (b) SO_2
(c) CO (d) NH_3

29. The sound power from a voice shouting is 0.001 Watt. The sound level in dB is
(a) 90 dB (b) 60 dB
(c) 30 dB (d) 120 dB

30. According to WHO maximum permissible level of iron in drinking water is
(a) 1 mg/L (b) 5 mg/L
(c) 10 mg/L (d) 50 mg/L

31. The particle sizes associated with ambient aerosols in the atmosphere have the range
(a) $< 100\ \mu m$ (b) $5 - 10\ \mu m$
(c) $1 - 5\ \mu m$ (d) $< 1\ \mu m$

32. Which of the following indices represents the background noise level in the ambient environment?
(a) L_{dn} (b) L_{10}
(c) L_{90} (d) L_{50}

33. Which species of chromium is toxic in water?
(a) Cr^{+2} (b) Cr^{+3}
(c) Cr^{+6} (d) Cr^{0}

34. Identify the correct sequence of stages of obtaining Environmental clearance for new projects
(a) Appraisal, Screening, Scoping, Public Consultation
(b) Screening, Public Consultation, Scoping, Appraisal
(c) Screening, Appraisal, Scoping, Public Consultation
(d) Screening, Scoping, Public Consultation, Appraisal

35. **Assertion (A):** Cost benefit analysis converts the benefits from the development, damages and control measures into monetary values.
Reason (R): Cost benefit analysis compares the cost of damage caused by

developmental activity with the cost of control measures adopted and provides the optimum solution for a given environmental quality.

Which one of the following codes is correct?

Codes:

(a) Both (A) and (R) are true and (R) is the correct explanation of (A).
(b) Both (A) and (R) are true, but (R) is not the correct explanation of (A).
(c) (A) is true but (R) is false.
(d) (A) is false but (R) is true.

36. Match the items in List I with List II and select the correct answers using codes given below:

List I (Developmental project)

A. Mining Projects
B. River Valley Projects
C. Area Development Projects
D. Other Projects

List II (Validity time period for Environmental Impact Assessment Report)

(i) 10 years
(ii) 30 years
(iii) 5 years
(iv) Limited period

Codes:	A	B	C	D
(a)	(iv)	(iii)	(ii)	(i)
(b)	(i)	(ii)	(iii)	(iv)
(c)	(ii)	(i)	(iv)	(iii)
(d)	(ii)	(iii)	(i)	(iv)

37. Match the List I and List II. Identify the correct answer from the codes given below the lists:

List I (Domain)

A. Socioeconomics
B. Wildlife
C. Water quality
D. Soil environment

List II (Effects)

(i) Barrier to travel corridors
(ii) Employment opportunities
(iii) Erosivity and Erodability
(iv) BOD and COD

Codes:	A	B	C	D
(a)	(ii)	(i)	(iv)	(iii)
(b)	(i)	(iii)	(ii)	(iv)
(c)	(iv)	(ii)	(iii)	(i)
(d)	(iii)	(iv)	(i)	(ii)

38. Hazardous substances have the following attributes:
(a) Ignitability
(b) Ignitability, Reactivity and Corrosivity
(c) Reactivity and Toxicity
(d) Corrosivity and Toxicity

39. Among bio-medical wastes, human anatomical wastes fall under category
(a) 4 (b) 2
(c) 3 (d) 1

40. To test whether there is a significant difference between the means of two sets of observations, one employs the following statistical technique:
(a) Regression
(b) χ^2 test (chi-square test)
(c) t-test
(d) F-test

41. For any finite set of positive numbers, which is the correct relationship involving Harmonic Mean (HM), Geometric Mean (GM) and Arithmetic Mean (AM)?
(a) HM $\leq$ GM $\leq$ AM
(b) AM $\leq$ GM $\leq$ HM
(c) AM $\leq$ HM $\leq$ GM
(d) GM $\leq$ HM $\leq$ AM

42. The population (N) of an ecosystem follows logistic growth. If K is its carrying capacity, then the environmental resistance is

(a) $\frac{N}{K}$ (b) $1-\frac{N}{K}$
(c) $\frac{N^2}{K}$ (d) NK

43. Chemical compounds having same crystal structure are called
(a) Polymorphic (b) Pseudomorphic
(c) Isomorphic (d) None of these

44. In the Gaussian Plume Model, the plume rise, under neutral or unstable atmospheric conditions, varies with the average wind speed (u m/sec) at stack height as
(a) u (b) $\frac{1}{u}$
(c) $\frac{1}{u^2}$ (d) $\frac{1}{u^{1/3}}$

45. Micas having an atomic structure defined as continuous sheets of tetrahedrons, sharing 3-oxygen atoms, are called
(a) Inosilicate (b) Phyllosilicate
(c) Tectosilicate (d) Sorosilicate

46. Kyoto Protocol on climate change was envisaged in which year?
(a) 1992 (b) 1994
(c) 1997 (d) 2002

47. Alkalinity in river waters is caused due to
(a) Presence of SO_4^{2-}
(b) Na^+ and K^+
(c) Cl^-
(d) CO_3^- and HCO_3^-

48. 'Ring of Fire' surrounds which ocean?
(a) Indian Ocean (b) Atlantic Ocean
(c) Arctic Ocean (d) Pacific Ocean

49. **Assertion (A):** Available data suggest that the first cells on earth were anaerobic heterotrophs.
Reason (R): In the beginning, the earth's atmosphere probably lacked free oxygen.
Identify the correct answer:
Codes:
(a) Both (A) and (R) are true and (R) is the correct explanation of (A).
(b) Both (A) and (R) are true and (R) is not the correct explanation of (A).
(c) (A) is true and (R) is false.
(d) (A) is false and (R) is true.

50. Chemical formula for CFC-113 is
(a) CCl_2F_2 (b) CCl_3F_3
(c) $C_2Cl_3F_3$ (d) CCl_2F_3

ANSWERS

1. (d)	2. (d)	3. (d)	4. (c)	5. (d)
6. (d)	7. (c)	8. (b)	9. (a)	10. (c)
11. (c)	12. (d)	13. (d)	14. (b)	15. (b)
16. (b)	17. (a)	18. (b)	19. (b)	20. (d)
21. (b)	22. (a)	23. (a)	24. (a)	25. (d)
26. (a)	27. (c)	28. (d)	29. (a)	30. (a)
31. (a)	32. (d)	33. (b)	34. (d)	35. (a)
36. (c)	37. (a)	38. (b)	39. (d)	40. (c)
41. (a)	42. (a)	43. (c)	44. (b)	45. (d)
46. (c)	47. (b)	48. (d)	49. (a)	50. (c)

JUNE–2012

Note: This paper contains Sixty (60) multiple-choice questions, each question carrying two (2) marks. Candidate is expected to answer any Fifty (50) questions. In case more than Fifty (50) questions are attempted, only the first Fifty (50) questions will be evaluated.

PAPER–I

1. Video-Conferencing can be classified as one of the following types of communication:
   (a) Visual one way
   (b) Audio-Visual one way
   (c) Audio-Visual two way
   (d) Visual two way

2. MC National University of Journalism and Communication is located at
   (a) Lucknow (b) Bhopal
   (c) Chennai (d) Mumbai

3. All India Radio (A.I.R.) for broadcasting was named in the year
   (a) 1926 (b) 1936
   (c) 1946 (d) 1956

4. In India for broadcasting TV programmes which system is followed?
   (a) NTCS (b) PAL
   (c) NTSE (d) SECAM

5. The term 'DAVP' stands for
   (a) Directorate of Advertising & Vocal Publicity
   (b) Division of Audio-Visual Publicity
   (c) Department of Audio-Visual Publicity
   (d) Directorate of Advertising & Visual Publicity

6. The term "TRP" associated with TV shows stands for
   (a) Total Rating Points
   (b) Time Rating Points
   (c) Thematic Rating Points
   (d) Television Rating Points

7. Which is the number that comes next in the following sequence?
   2, 6, 12, 20, 30, 42, 56, ______
   (a) 60 (b) 64
   (c) 72 (d) 70

8. Find the next letter for the series YVSP ______.
   (a) N (b) M
   (c) O (d) L

9. Given that in a code language, '645' means 'day is warm'; '42' means 'warm spring' and '634' means 'spring is sunny'; which digit represents 'sunny'?
   (a) 3 (b) 2
   (c) 4 (d) 5

10. The basis of the following classification is:
    'first President of India' 'author of Godan' 'books in my library', 'blue things' and 'students who work hard'
    (a) Common names
    (b) Proper names
    (c) Descriptive phrases
    (d) Indefinite description

11. In the expression 'Nothing is larger than itself' the relation 'is larger than' is

(a) antisymmetric (b) asymmetrical
(c) intransitive (d) irreflexive

12. **Assertion (A):** There are more laws on the books today than ever before, and more crimes being committed than ever before.

Reason (R): Because to reduce crime we must eliminate the laws.

Choose the correct answer from below:
(a) (A) is true, (R) is doubtful and (R) is not the correct explanation of (A).
(b) (A) is false, (R) is true and (R) is the correct explanation of (A).
(c) (A) is doubtful, (R) is doubtful and (R) is not the correct explanation of (A).
(d) (A) is doubtful, (R) is true and (R) is not the correct explanation of (A).

13. If the proposition "All men are not mortal" is true then which of the following inferences is correct? Choose from the code given below:
1. "All men are mortal" is true.
2. "Some men are mortal" is false.
3. "No men are mortal" is doubtful.
4. "All men are mortal" is false.

Codes:
(a) 1, 2 and 3 (b) 2, 3 and 4
(c) 1, 3 and 4 (d) 1 and 3

14. Determine the nature of the following definition: "Abortion" means the ruthless murdering of innocent beings.
(a) Lexical (b) Persuasive
(c) Stipulative (d) Theoretical

15. Which one of the following is not an argument?
(a) Devadutt does not eat in the day so he must be eating at night.
(b) If Devadutt is growing fat and if he does not eat during the day, he will be eating at night.
(c) Devadutt eats in the night so he does not eat during the day.
(d) Since Devadutt does not eat in the day, he must be eating in the night.

16. Venn diagram is a kind of diagram to
(a) represent and assess the validity of elementary inferences of syllogistic form.
(b) represent but not assess the validity of elementary inferences of syllogistic form.
(c) represent and assess the truth of elementary inferences of syllogistic form.
(d) assess but not represent the truth of elementary inferences of syllogistic form.

17. Reasoning by analogy leads to
(a) certainty
(b) definite conclusion
(c) predictive conjecture
(d) surety

18. Which of the following statements are false? Choose from the code given below:
1. Inductive arguments always proceed from the particular to the general.
2. A cogent argument must be inductively strong.
3. A valid argument may have a false premise and a false conclusion.
4. An argument may legitimately be spoken of as 'true' or 'false'.

Codes:
(a) 2, 3 and 4 (b) 1 and 3
(c) 2 and 4 (d) 1 and 2

19. Six persons A, B, C, D, E and F are standing in a circle. B is between F and C, A is between E and D, F is to the left of D. Who is between A and F?

(a) B (b) C
(c) D (d) E

20. The price of petrol increases by 25%. By what percentage must a customer reduce the consumption so that the earlier bill on the petrol does not alter?
(a) 20% (b) 25%
(c) 30% (d) 33.33%

21. If Ram knows that y is an integer greater than 2 and less than 7 and Hari knows that y is an integer greater than 5 and less than 10, then they may correctly conclude that
(a) y can be exactly determined
(b) y may be either of two values
(c) y may be any of three values
(d) there is no value of y satisfying these conditions

22. Four pipes can fill a reservoir in 15, 20, 30 and 60 hours respectively. The first one was opened at 6 AM, second at 7 AM, third at 8 AM and the fourth at 9 AM. When will the reservoir be filled?
(a) 11 AM (b) 12 Noon
(c) 1 PM (d) 1:30 PM

The total electricity generation in a country is 97 GW. The contribution of various energy sources is indicated in percentage terms in the Pie Chart given below:

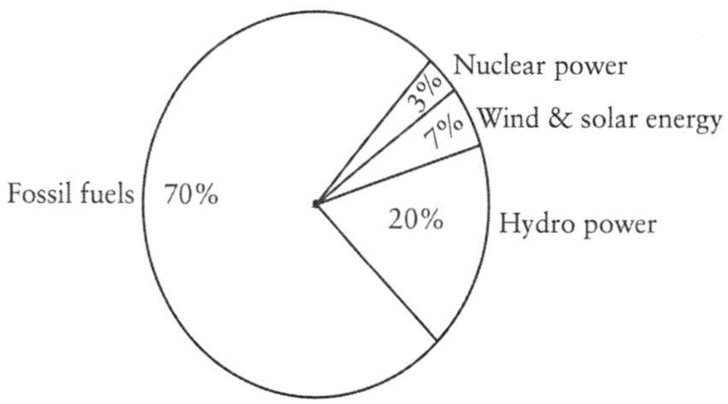

23. What is the contribution of wind and solar power in absolute terms in the electricity generation?
(a) 6.79 GW (b) 19.4 GW
(c) 9.7 GW (d) 29.1 GW

24. What is the contribution of renewable energy sources in absolute terms in the electricity generation?
(a) 29.1 GW (b) 26.19 GW
(c) 67.9 GW (d) 97 GW

25. TCP/IP is necessary if one is to connect to the
(a) Phone lines (b) LAN
(c) Internet (d) a Server

26. Each character on the keyboard of computer has an ASCII value which stands for
(a) American Stock Code for Information Interchange
(b) American Standard Code for Information Interchange
(c) African Standard Code for Information Interchange
(d) Adaptable Standard Code for Information Change

27. Which of the following is not a programming language?
(a) Pascal
(b) Microsoft Office
(c) Java
(d) C++

28. Minimum number of bits required to store any 3 digit decimal number is equal to
(a) 3 (b) 5
(c) 8 (d) 10

29. Internet explorer is a type of
(a) Operating System (b) Compiler
(c) Browser (d) IP address

30. POP3 and IMAP are e-mail accounts in which

(a) One automatically gets one's mail everyday
(b) One has to be connected to the server to read or write one's mail
(c) One only has to be connected to the server to send and receive email
(d) One does not need any telephone lines

31. Irritation in eyes is caused by the pollutant
(a) Sulphur dioxide (b) Ozone
(c) PAN (d) Nitrous oxide

32. Which is the source of chlorofluorocarbons?
(a) Thermal power plants
(b) Automobiles
(c) Refrigeration and Airconditioning
(d) Fertilizers

33. Which of the following is not a renewable natural resource?
(a) Clean air (b) Fertile soil
(c) Fresh water (d) Salt

34. Which of the following parameters is not used as a pollution indicator in water?
(a) Total dissolved solids
(b) Coliform count
(c) Dissolved oxygen
(d) Density

35. S and P waves are associated with
(a) floods (b) wind energy
(c) earthquakes (d) tidal energy

36. Match List I and List II and select the correct answer from the codes given below:

List I
(A) Ozone hole
(B) Greenhouse effect
(C) Natural hazards
(D) Sustainable development

List II
(i) Tsunami (ii) UV radiations
(iii) Methane (iv) Eco-centrism

Codes:	**A**	**B**	**C**	**D**
(a)	(ii)	(iii)	(i)	(iv)
(b)	(iii)	(ii)	(i)	(iv)
(c)	(iv)	(iii)	(i)	(ii)
(d)	(iv)	(ii)	(iii)	(i)

37. Indian Institute of Advanced Study is located at
(a) Dharmshala (b) Shimla
(c) Solan (d) Chandigarh

38. Indicate the number of Regional Offices of National Council of Teacher Education.
(a) 04 (b) 05
(c) 06 (d) 08

39. Which of the following rights was considered the "Heart and Soul" of the Indian Constitution by Dr. B.R. Ambedkar?
(a) Freedom of Speech
(b) Right to Equality
(c) Right to Freedom of Religion
(d) Right to Constitutional Remedies

40. Who among the following created the office of the District Collector in India?
(a) Lord Cornwallis
(b) Warren Hastings
(c) The Royal Commission on Decentralisation
(d) Sir Charles Metcalfe

41. The Fundamental Duties of a citizen include
1. Respect for the Constitution, the National Flag and the National Anthem.
2. To develop the scientific temper.
3. Respect for the Government.
4. To protect Wildlife.

Choose the correct answer from the codes given below:

Codes:
(a) 1, 2 and 3 (b) 1, 2 and 4
(c) 2, 3 and 4 (d) 1, 3, 4 and 2

42. The President of India takes oath
   (a) to uphold the sovereignty and integrity of India.
   (b) to bear true faith and allegiance to the Constitution of India.
   (c) to uphold the Constitution and Laws of the country.
   (d) to preserve, protect and defend the Constitution and the law of the country.

43. If you get an opportunity to teach a visually challenged student along with normal students, what type of treatment would you like to give him in the class?
   (a) Not giving extra attention because majority may suffer.
   (b) Take care of him sympathetically in the classroom.
   (c) You will think that blindness is his destiny and hence you cannot do anything.
   (d) Arrange a seat in the front row and try to teach at a pace convenient to him.

44. Which of the following is not a characteristic of a good achievement test?
   (a) Reliability (b) Objectivity
   (c) Ambiguity (d) Validity

45. Which of the following does not belong to a projected aid?
   (a) Overhead projector
   (b) Blackboard
   (c) Epidiascope
   (d) Slide projector

46. For a teacher, which of the following methods would be correct for writing on the blackboard?
   (a) Writing fast and as clearly as possible.
   (b) Writing the matter first and then asking students to read it.
   (c) Asking a question to students and then writing the answer as stated by them.
   (d) Writing the important points as clearly as possible.

47. A teacher can be successful if he/she
   (a) helps students in becoming better citizens
   (b) imparts subject knowledge to students
   (c) prepares students to pass the examination
   (d) presents the subject matter in a well-organized manner

48. Dynamic approach to teaching means
   (a) Teaching should be forceful and effective
   (b) Teachers should be energetic and dynamic
   (c) The topics of teaching should not be static, but dynamic
   (d) The students should be required to learn through activities

49. The research that aims at immediate application is
   (a) Action Research
   (b) Empirical Research
   (c) Conceptual Research
   (d) Fundamental Research

50. When two or more successive footnotes refer to the same work which one of the following expressions is used?
   (a) *ibid.* (b) *et al.*
   (c) *op. cit.* (d) *loc. cit.*

51. Nine year olds are taller than seven year olds. This is an example of a reference drawn from
   (a) Vertical study
   (b) Cross-sectional study
   (c) Time series study
   (d) Experimental study

52. Conferences are meant for
   (a) Multiple target groups
   (b) Group discussions
   (c) Show-casing new Research
   (d) All of the above

53. Ex Post Facto research means
    (a) The research is carried out after the incident.
    (b) The research is carried out prior to the incident.
    (c) The research is carried out along with the happening of an incident.
    (d) The research is carried out keeping in mind the possibilities of an incident.
54. Research ethics do not include
    (a) Honesty (b) Subjectivity
    (c) Integrity (d) Objectivity

Read the following passage carefully and answer the questions 55 to 60:

James Madison said, "A people who mean to be their own governors must arm themselves with power that knowledge gives." In India, the Official Secrets Act, 1923 was a convenient smokescreen to deny members of the public access to information. Public functioning has traditionally been shrouded in secrecy. But in a democracy in which people govern themselves, it is necessary to have more openness. In the maturing of our democracy, right to information is a major step forward; it enables citizens to participate fully in the decision-making process that affects their lives so profoundly. It is in this context that the address of the Prime Minister in the Lok Sabha is significant. He said, "I would only like to see that everyone, particularly our civil servants, should see the Bill in a positive spirit; not as a draconian law for paralyzing Government, but as an instrument for improving Government-Citizen interface resulting in a friendly, caring and effective Government functioning for the good of our People." He further said, "This is an innovative Bill, where there will be scope to review its functioning as we gain experience. Therefore, this is a piece of legislation, whose working will be kept under constant reviews."

The Commission, in its Report, has dealt with the application of the Right to Information in Executive, Legislature and Judiciary. The judiciary could be a pioneer in implementing the Act in letter and spirit because much of the work that the Judiciary does is open to public scrutiny, Government of India has sanctioned an e-governance project in the Judiciary for about ₹ 700 crores which would bring about systematic classification, standardization and categorization of records. This would help the judiciary to fulfil its mandate under the Act. Similar capacity building would be required in all other public authorities. The transformation from non-transparency to transparency and public accountability is the responsibility of all three organs of State.

55. A person gets power
    (a) by acquiring knowledge
    (b) from the Official Secrets Act, 1923
    (c) through openings
    (d) by denying public information
56. Right to Information is a major step forward to
    (a) enable citizens to participate fully in the decision-making process
    (b) to make the people aware of the Act
    (c) to gain knowledge of administration
    (d) to make the people Government friendly
57. The Prime Minister considered the Bill
    (a) to provide power to the civil servants
    (b) as an instrument for improving Government-citizen interface resulting in a friendly, caring and effective Government
    (c) a draconian law against the officials
    (d) to check the harassment of the people
58. The Commission made the Bill effective by
    (a) extending power to the executive authorities
    (b) combining the executive and legislative power

(c) recognizing Judiciary a pioneer in implementing the act in letter and spirit
(d) educating the people before its implementation

59. The Prime Minister considered the Bill innovative and hoped that
(a) It could be reviewed based on the experience gained on its functioning.
(b) The civil servants would see the Bill in a positive spirit.
(c) It would not be considered as a draconian law for paralyzing Government.
(d) All of the above.

60. The transparency and public accountability is the responsibility of three organs of the State. These three organs are
(a) Lok Sabha, Rajya Sabha and Judiciary
(b) Lok Sabha, Rajya Sabha and Executive
(c) Judiciary, Legislature and the Commission
(d) Legislature, Executive and Judiciary

ANSWERS

1. (c)	2. (b)	3. (b)	4. (b)	5. (d)
6. (a)	7. (c)	8. (b)	9. (a)	10. (c)
11. (d)	12. (a)	13. (b)	14. (b)	15. (b)
16. (a)	17. (c)	18. (c)	19. (c)	20. (a)
21. (a)	22. (c)	23. (a)	24. (b)	25. (c)
26. (b)	27. (b)	28. (d)	29. (c)	30. (c)
31. (c)	32. (c)	33. (d)	34. (d)	35. (c)
36. (a)	37. (b)	38. (a)	39. (d)	40. (b)
41. (b)	42. (d)	43. (d)	44. (c)	45. (b)
46. (d)	47. (a)	48. (d)	49. (a)	50. (a)
51. (b)	52. (d)	53. (a)	54. (b)	55. (a)
56. (a)	57. (b)	58. (c)	59. (d)	60. (d)

PAPER–II

Note: This paper contains fifty (50) objective type questions, each question carrying two (2) marks. Attempt all the questions.

1. If the standard deviation of a population is 20 and the standard error of mean is 4, then the sample size is
(a) 25 (b) 80
(c) 5 (d) 100

2. In a multiple regression model, the explained variance per d.f. is 50 and unexplained variance per d.f. is 10. The F-ratio is
(a) 2.5 (b) 5
(c) 25 (d) 0.2

3. Which one of the following is not a random sampling method?
(a) Stratified Sampling
(b) Cluster Sampling
(c) Systematic Sampling
(d) Judgement Sampling

4. In the Gaussian Plume Model, the plume size is estimated considering buoyancy of exhaust gases, stack diameter, wind speed and stability of the atmosphere. The plume size Δh depends on inside radius of stack (r) as
(a) $\Delta h \propto r$ (b) $\Delta h \propto r^{1/3}$
(c) $\Delta h \propto r^{2/3}$ (d) $\Delta h \propto r^2$

5. The acidity of normal rain water is due to
(a) CO_2 (b) Cl_2
(c) NO_2 (d) SO_2

6. Percent of water on the world's surface representing fresh water is
(a) 97 (b) 50
(c) 10 (d) 3

7. Concentration of CO_2 in present day atmosphere is
   (a) ~ 220 ppm (b) ~ 280 ppm
   (c) ~ 360 ppm (d) ~ 390 ppm
8. Hardness of diamond is due to
   (a) Coordinate bonding
   (b) Covalent bonding
   (c) Electrovalent bonding
   (d) van der Waals forces
9. In biological systems sulphur is largely bound in
   (a) Lipids
   (b) Proteins
   (c) Nucleic acids
   (d) Proteins and nucleic acids
10. pH of 0.01 M HNO_3 is
    (a) 0.1 (b) 1
    (c) 2 (d) 10
11. Which is a correct food chain in the Antarctic ecosystem?
    (a) Phytoplankton – Krill – Carnivorous Plankton – Emperor Penguin
    (b) Phytoplankton – Krill – Carnivorous Plankton – Squid – Elephant Seal – Leopard Seal
    (c) Phytoplankton – Herbivorous Zoo Plankton – Carnivorous Plankton – Adelic Penguin – Emperor Penguin
    (d) Herbivorous Zoo Plankton – Phytoplankton – Carnivorous Plankton – Elephant Seal – Leopard Seal
12. Given below are two statements, one labelled as Assertion (A) and the other labelled as Reason (R):
    Assertion (A): The phosphorous cycle in an ecosystem is a sedimentary cycle.
    Reason (R): Phosphorous does not occur naturally as gas.
    (a) Both (A) and (R) are true and (R) is the correct explanation of (A).
    (b) Both (A) and (R) are true, but (R) is not the correct explanation of (A).
    (c) (A) is true, but (R) is false.
    (d) (A) is false, but (R) is true.
13. Pyramid of trophic levels is always upright in case of
    (a) Biomass (b) Energy
    (c) Number (d) All of the above
14. Which of the following is a correct match?
    (a) Periyar – Kerala
    (b) Ranthambore – M.P.
    (c) Panna – U.P.
    (d) Bandhvgarh – Bihar
15. Replacement of existing communities by any external condition is termed
    (a) Primary succession
    (b) Secondary succession
    (c) Autogenic succession
    (d) None of the above
16. The area where two major communities meet and blend together is termed as
    (a) Ecotype (b) Biotype
    (c) Ecotone (d) Meeting place
17. Indian wolf has become an important animal because
    (a) It's name appears in Red Data Book.
    (b) It is only an important member of food chain of almost all Indian forests.
    (c) Wild dogs disappeared due to their presence.
    (d) It has been chosen as a State animal.
18. Walkley and Black rapid titration method is used for the determination of
    (a) Organic carbon content of soil
    (b) Nitrate content of soil
    (c) Phosphate content of soil
    (d) Fluoride content of soil
19. Which one of the following is an endoenzyme in soil?
    (a) Cellulase (b) Invertase
    (c) Protease (d) Dehydrogenase

20. Of the following humic groups which is not soluble in both acid and alkali?
(a) Fulvic acid (b) Humic acid
(c) Humin (d) All of the above

21. The sources of thermal pollution are
(a) Power plants
(b) Cooling forests
(c) Industrial effluents
(d) All of the above

22. Which one of the following radionuclides has the longest half life?
(a) C^{14} (b) Sr^{90}
(c) I^{131} (d) Cs^{137}

23. What is the importance of the 42nd Amendment to the Constitution brought in the year 1976?
(a) Insertion of Article 48-A
(b) Insertion of Article 51-A (g)
(c) Insertion of Article 48-A and 51-A (g)
(d) None of the above

24. Who issues the Ecomark notification?
(a) Ministry of Environment and Forest, Govt. of India
(b) Ministry of Human Health and Family Welfare, Govt. of India
(c) Department of Science and Technology, Govt. of India
(d) Bureau of Indian Standards

25. Which one of the following is a waste recycling method of solid waste management?
(a) Pelletisation
(b) Composting
(c) Incineration
(d) Sanitary Landfill

26. A hazardous waste is characterised by
(a) Ignitibility (b) Reactivity
(c) Toxicity (d) All of the above

27. How many hot spots have been identified in the world and Indian Subcontinent respectively?
(a) 17, 2 (b) 12, 3
(c) 35, 2 (d) 17, 3

28. Which one of the following chemical species of mercury is highly toxic to living system?
(a) Mercurous ion
(b) Mercuric ion
(c) Organo mercurials
(d) Atomic mercury

29. Natural gas is composed primarily of
(a) Methane
(b) n-butane
(c) n-octane
(d) A mixture of n-octane and n-butane

30. Which of the following is true regarding the Leopold interaction matrix used in Environmental Impact Assessment Process?
(a) It can be expanded.
(b) It can be contracted.
(c) It can be contracted and expanded.
(d) It cannot be contracted and expanded.

31. Which of the following can be considered in Environmental Risk Assessment?
(a) Exposure period
(b) Potency of a toxic material
(c) Quality of models
(d) All of the above

32. In India, Environmental Impact Assessment report of a proposed river valley project after environmental clearance is applicable for a maximal period of how many years?
(a) 5 (b) 10
(c) 30 (d) 2

33. An earthquake is rated as 'major' if its magnitude in Richter Scale is in the range of
(a) 4.0 – 4.9 (b) 7.0 – 7.9
(c) 6.0 – 6.9 (d) 5.0 – 5.9

34. What is the proportion of the frequency of occurrence of La Nina compared to El Nino?

(a) Half (b) One-third
(c) Twice (d) Two-third

35. An element in soil will be considered as a trace element if its concentration is
(a) 1 – 2 wt % (b) < 0.1 wt %
(c) > 2 wt % (d) < 1 wt %

36. Which of the following is correct about attribute data in Geographic Information System?
(a) Attributes are pieces of data that are connected or related to the points, lines or polygons mapped in the GIS.
(b) Attribute data can be analysed to determine patterns of importance.
(c) Attribute data is entered directly into a database where it is associated with element data.
(d) All of the above.

37. At Nadir, the LISS – IV camera in IRS-P6 has a spatial resolution of
(a) 5.8 m (b) 5.9 m
(c) 5.7 m (d) 5.6 m

38. Which one of the following can be estimated by Flame Photometer?
(a) Sodium and Potassium
(b) Cadmium and Cobalt
(c) Chlorine and Bromine
(d) Mercury and Arsenic

39. The contribution of CO_2 towards global warming has been estimated to be about
(a) 57 – 60% (b) 60 – 75%
(c) 80 – 85% (d) 45 – 55%

40. The principal components of photochemical smog in urban areas are
(a) SO_2 and NO_2
(b) SPM and CO
(c) SPM and NO_2
(d) Hydrocarbons and Ozone

41. Match Lists I and II and choose the correct answer from the codes given below:
List I (Aerosol Constituents)
A. Si
B. V
C. Benzo(a)pyrene
D. Sulfuric acid droplets
List II (Sources)
(i) Gases in the ambient atmosphere
(ii) Natural sources
(iii) Combustion of certain kinds of fuel oil
(iv) Incomplete combustion

Codes:	A	B	C	D
(a)	(ii)	(iv)	(iii)	(i)
(b)	(iii)	(i)	(ii)	(iv)
(c)	(iv)	(i)	(ii)	(iii)
(d)	(i)	(iv)	(iii)	(ii)

42. A river flowing at 20.0 m^3/sec has a tributary feeding into it with a flow rate of 5.0 m^3/sec. Upstream from the point of junction the fluoride concentration is 5 mg/L in the river and 10 mg/L in the tributary. Assuming fluoride to be conservative substance and rapid mixing in the river, the downstream concentration in the river is
(a) 6 mg/L (b) 8 mg/L
(c) 8.5 mg/L (d) 7.5 mg/L

43. The power obtained from a horizontal wind turbine operating at maximum efficiency is proportional to its diameter (D) as
(a) D (b) D^2
(c) $D^{3/2}$ (d) $\sqrt{D}$

44. Noise of 90 dB for 8 hours represents 100% dose. If the noise of 93 dB is for 1 hour duration, it represents a dose of
(a) 25% (b) 50%
(c) 75% (d) 100%

45. Scale lengths associated with mesoscale phenomenon in atmosphere are typically in the range
(a) 10 – 500 m
(b) 1 – 200 km
(c) 100 – 1000 km
(d) 1000 – 10,000 km

46. When an atmosphere has an isothermal profile, it is
(a) very stable
(b) slightly stable
(c) unstable
(d) very unstable (turbulent)

47. The wavelength range of UV-C radiation is
(a) 320 – 400 nm
(b) 280 – 320 nm
(c) 100 – 1500 nm
(d) 240 – 280 nm

48. Lightening in the atmosphere produces
(a) NO (b) CO
(c) CO_2 (d) NH_3

49. The maximum tidal energy potential in India is
(a) in Gulf of Khambhat
(b) in Gangetic delta in Sundarbans
(c) along the coast of Odisha
(d) along the coast of Chennai

50. The maximum theoretical efficiency of a silicon solar cell can be
(a) 45% (b) 30%
(c) 12% (d) 50%

ANSWERS

1. (a)	2. (b)	3. (d)	4. (c)	5. (a)
6. (d)	7. (d)	8. (b)	9. (b)	10. (c)
11. (b)	12. (b)	13. (b)	14. (a)	15. (b)
16. (c)	17. (a)	18. (a)	19. (d)	20. (c)
21. (d)	22. (d)	23. (c)	24. (a)	25. (b)
26. (d)	27. (c)	28. (c)	29. (a)	30. (c)
31. (d)	32. (b)	33. (b)	34. (a)	35. (b)
36. (d)	37. (a)	38. (a)	39. (a)	40. (d)
41. (a)	42. (a)	43. (b)	44. (a)	45. (b)
46. (b)	47. (d)	48. (a)	49. (a)	50. (a)

PAPER–III

Note: This paper contains seventy-five (75) objective type questions, each question carrying two (2) marks. All questions are compulsory.

1. If the standard deviation of a population is 20, the population and sample means are 35 and 33, respectively and the t-statistic at 95% confidence level is 2.5, the sample size is
(a) 100 (b) 125
(c) 250 (d) 625

2. For 5 degrees of freedom, the variance of 2 distribution is
(a) 10 (b) 5
(c) 16 (d) 4

3. Identify the random sampling method among the following:
(a) Judgement sampling
(b) Quota sampling
(c) Convenience sampling
(d) Stratified sampling

4. Consider a Box model for an urban area. Assuming that the pollutants are conservative and that the mixing is rapid inside the Box, the concentration (C) of pollutants varies with the mixing height as
(a) $C \propto \frac{1}{H}$ (b) $C \propto \frac{1}{H^2}$
(c) $C \propto \frac{1}{\sqrt{H}}$ (d) $C \propto H^{-3/2}$

5. At higher pH, majority of iron is present as
(a) Fe^{2+}
(b) Fe^{3+}
(c) Fe^{2+} and Fe^{3+}
(d) $Fe(OH)_2$ and $Fe(OH)_3$

6. In living organisms phosphorous is largely associated with
   (a) Carbohydrate (b) Lipids
   (c) Nucleic acids (d) Proteins
7. Molar extinction coefficient of malondialdehyde at 532 nm is 0.155 $M^{-1}cm^{-1}$. The concentration of malondialdehyde in a solution which has absorbance of 0.31 in a 1 cm curette will be
   (a) 0.5 M (b) 1.0 M
   (c) 1.5 M (d) 2.0 M
8. pOH of 0.001 M solution of HCl is
   (a) 0.1 (b) 1
   (c) 10 (d) 11
9. The molecular weight of DDT is 354.5. The quantity of DDT required to prepare one litre of 10 ppm DDT solution is
   (a) 10 mg (b) 35.45 mg
   (c) 354.5 mg (d) 354.5 g
10. Which one of the following is referred to as superoxide radical?
    (a) O (b) O^2
    (c) O_2^{o-} (d) O^3
11. The net primary productivity of an ecosystem is
    (a) the gross primary productivity minus plant respiration.
    (b) the primary productivity at herbivore level.
    (c) the primary productivity at consumer level.
    (d) the productivity at top consumer level minus respiration at all levels.
12. Which of the following habitats has not been included as Indian biodiversity hot spots?
    (a) The Eastern Ghats
    (b) The Western Ghats
    (c) North-Eastern Hills
    (d) South-Eastern Hills
13. The area of the biosphere which is protected entirely, without any experimentation and research and no biotic interference, is known as
    (a) Undisturbed zone
    (b) Buffer zone
    (c) Core zone
    (d) Principal zone
14. When a mixture of Azospirillum, Azotobacter and Vibrio was applied to rhizosphere, fixation of atmospheric nitrogen was increased. It was due to activity of
    (a) All the three
    (b) Azospirillum and Vibrio
    (c) Azotobacter and Vibrio
    (d) Azotobacter and Azospirillum
15. Which type of forests are found at an altitude of 5300 ft chiefly on mountains of Himalayas and Nilgiri?
    (a) Dry deciduous forest
    (b) Moist tropical forest
    (c) Temperate forest
    (d) Tropical moist deciduous forest
16. The sequence of events that occur during primary succession is as follows:
    (a) Nudation – Colonisation – Ecesis – Aggregation
    (b) Aggregation – Colonization – Ecesis – Nudation
    (c) Ecesis – Nudation – Aggregation – Colonization
    (d) Nudation – Ecesis – Colonization – Aggregation
17. As per Raunkaiers law of frequency, five different frequency classes (A, B, C, D and E) in a natural undisturbed community exhibit one of the following relationship:
    (a) $A < B > C \gtreqless D < E$
    (b) $A > B > C \gtreqless D < E$

(c) $A < B > C \begin{smallmatrix}\geq\\=\\<\end{smallmatrix} D > E$

(d) $A < B < C \begin{smallmatrix}\geq\\=\\<\end{smallmatrix} D > E$

18. Which one of the following category of earthworms is most suitable for Vermicomposting?
(a) Epigeic (b) Anecic
(c) Endogeic (d) All of the above

19. Which one of the following is an in situ method of biodiversity conservation?
(a) Reserve forest
(b) National parks
(c) Sanctuaries
(d) All of the above

20. Match the contaminant in Column I with the disease in Column II:

Column I
A. Mercury
B. Nitrogen
C. Cadmium
D. Coal

Column II
(i) Methamoglobinemia
(ii) Itai Itai
(iii) Silicosis
(iv) Minamata

Choose the correct code:

Codes:	A	B	C	D
(a)	(ii)	(iii)	(iv)	(i)
(b)	(iii)	(iv)	(ii)	(i)
(c)	(i)	(ii)	(iii)	(iv)
(d)	(iv)	(i)	(ii)	(iii)

21. Which of the following types of coal contains higher percentage of volatile matter?
(a) Peat (b) Lignite
(c) Bituminous (d) Anthracite

22. Carbon dioxide evolved from soil mainly comes from
(a) Microbial respiration
(b) Root respiration
(c) Soil animals respiration
(d) All of the above

23. Which one of the following pesticides persists for a long period in soil?
(a) Lindane
(b) Monocrotophos
(c) Carbaryl
(d) Parathion

24. Organic matter (OM) content of soil can be calculated from organic carbon (OC) by using the formula
(a) OM (%) = OC (%) × 1.724
(b) OM (%) = OC (%) × 1.247
(c) OM (%) = OC (%) × 1.472
(d) OM (%) = OC (%) × 1.427

25. The problem of thermal pollution can be alleviated by using
(a) Cooling ponds
(b) Cooling towers
(c) More efficient electricity generating plants
(d) All of the above

26. According to Recycled Plastics (Manufacture and Usage) Rules 1999, the minimum thickness of carry bags shall not be less than
(a) 10 microns
(b) 20 microns
(c) 30 microns
(d) 50 microns

27. Match the Act mentioned in Column I with the year of enactment mentioned in Column II:

Column I
A. The Water (Prevention and Control of Pollution) Act
B. The Air (Prevention and Control of Pollution) Act
C. The Environmental (Protection) Act
D. The Biological Diversity Act

Column II
(i) 2002 (ii) 1986
(iii) 1974 (iv) 1981

Choose the correct code:

Codes:	**A**	**B**	**C**	**D**
(a)	(i)	(iv)	(iii)	(ii)
(b)	(iii)	(iv)	(ii)	(i)
(c)	(iii)	(ii)	(i)	(iv)
(d)	(ii)	(iv)	(iii)	(i)

28. Which one of the following is not an energy recovery method of solid waste management?
(a) Pelletisation
(b) Biomethanation
(c) Pyrolysis
(d) Composting

29. The colour code of the container for collection of waste scrap generated from Hospitals is
(a) Red (b) Blue
(c) White (d) Green

30. Given below are two statements, one labelled as Assertion (A) and the other labelled as Reason (R):
Assertion (A): When quantitative probabilistic risk assessment is performed on hazardous waste sites they usually turn out to be of relatively low threats.
Reason (R): In hazardous waste sites the chance of exposure is low because of isolation of drinking water supplies and prevention of access.
Choose the correct answer:
(a) Both (A) and (R) are true and (R) is the correct explanation of (A).
(b) Both (A) and (R) are true, but (R) is not the correct explanation of (A).
(c) (A) is true, but (R) is false.
(d) (A) is false, but (R) is true.

31. In India, an Environment Impact Assessment report of a proposed mining project after environmental clearance is applicable for a maximal period of how many years?
(a) 5 years (b) 10 years
(c) 30 years (d) 2 years

32. An increase of one unit of Richter Scale represents an increase in amplitude by a factor of
(a) 10 (b) 100
(c) 1000 (d) 2

33. Which rare earth element is not present in the earth's crust but for commercial purpose comes from the Nuclear reactors?
(a) Promethium (b) Lanthanum
(c) Cerium (d) Samarium

34. To display green colour in the monitor the amount of RGB should be
(a) 255 : 0 : 0 (b) 255 : 255 : 255
(c) 0 : 0 : 0 (d) 0 : 255 : 0

35. When the temperature range in geothermal resource is generally low, electrical power generation from such resources require the use of secondary low boiling point fluid. This is generally known as
(a) Rankine cycle
(b) Production well cycle
(c) Flash stem cycle
(d) Hard Dry Rock cycle

36. The Global Warming Potential (GWP) is the least for which of the following greenhouse gases?
(a) CH_4 (b) CO_2
(c) N_2O (d) SF_6

37. The maximum specific power output (p) from a MHD power generator varies with the velocity (u) of hot ionized gas as
(a) $p \propto u$ (b) $p \propto u^2$
(c) $p \propto u^{3/2}$ (d) $p \propto u^3$

38. Given below are two statements. One labelled as Assertion (A) and the other labelled as Reason (R).
Assertion (A): Electrostatic precipitators (ESPs) can be harmful if not operated properly.

Reason (R): Corona discharge in ESPs produces ozone.

Choose the correct answer:

(a) Both (A) and (R) are correct and (R) is the correct explanation of (A).
(b) Both (A) and (R) are correct and (R) is not the correct explanation of (A).
(c) (A) is true, but (R) is false.
(d) Both (A) and (R) are false.

39. Given below are two statements. One labelled as Assertion (A) and the other labelled as Reason (R):

Assertion (A): Vegetation hedges are the best way to control noise.

Reason (R): Vegetation hedges scatter noise.

Choose the correct answer.

(a) Both (A) and (R) are correct and (R) is the correct explanation of (A).
(b) Both (A) and (R) are correct, but (R) is not the correct explanation of (A).
(c) (A) is true, but (R) is false.
(d) (A) is false, but (R) is true.

40. If w and ws are mixing ratio and saturation mixing ratio respectively; T and Td are the ambient temperature and dew point temperature respectively, then identify the correct expression of relative humidity (RH).

(a) $RH = \frac{\text{w at Td}}{\text{w at T}}$ (b) $RH = \frac{\text{w at T}}{\text{w at Td}}$

(c) $RH = \frac{\text{ws at Td}}{\text{ws at T}}$ (d) $RH = \frac{\text{ws at T}}{\text{ws at Td}}$

41. Identify mesoscale phenomenon.

(a) Tornado (b) Sea breeze
(c) Cyclone (d) Eddies

42. For elevations less than few hundred metres, if the wind speeds are u_1 and u_2 at elevations z_1 and z_2 respectively, the following equation holds $\left(\frac{u_1}{u_2}\right) = \left(\frac{z_1}{z_2}\right)^p$.

The value of the exponent p is

(a) ≤ 0.6 (b) = 1
(c) ≥ 0.6 (d) negative

43. Given below are two statements. One labelled as Assertion (A) and the other labelled as Reason (R).

Assertion (A): Noise gets attenuated more in dry atmosphere.

Reason (R): Moist air is less denser than dry air.

Choose the correct answer:

(a) Both (A) and (R) are true and (R) is the correct explanation of (A).
(b) Both (A) and (R) are true and (R) is not the correct explanation of (A).
(c) (A) is true, but (R) is false.
(d) (A) is false, but (R) is true.

44. $OH^{\bullet}$ radicals in atmosphere play a role of

(a) scavenger (b) acidifier
(c) reducing agent (d) greenhouse gas

45. The slow neutrons initiating nuclear fission with U^{235} have energies of the order of

(a) 0.25 MeV (b) 0.15 MeV
(c) 0.25 eV (d) 0.025 eV

46. The most suitable range of wind speeds for wind power generation is

(a) 1 – 5 m/s (b) 4 – 12 m/s
(c) 10 – 20 m/s (d) 20 – 50 m/s

47. For energy to be produced from nuclear fusion of Deuterium (D) and Tritium (T), the mixture of D + T has to be heated up to energies of at least

(a) 1 KeV (b) 10 KeV
(c) 500 eV (d) 1 MeV

48. Element contaminating the water body is determined and quantified by using one of the following methods:

(a) Colorimeter
(b) Spectrophotometer
(c) Atomic absorption spectrometer
(d) All of the above

49. In which type of chromatography four modes, viz., Absorption, partition, Ion exchange and exclusion, are present?
(a) HPLC
(b) Liquid-liquid chromatography
(c) Ion-exchange chromatography
(d) Absorption chromatography

50. The metal which is generally absorbed by plants along with Zn and causes "Ouch Ouch" disease in human beings is
(a) Pb (b) Cd
(c) Hg (d) Cr

51. Radioactive isotopes of which of the elements in human body decay every second?
(a) K^{40} and C^{14} (b) C^{14} and N^{6}
(c) N^{16} and K^{40} (d) None of these

52. Which of the following techniques is most appropriate for determining crystalline structure of environmental samples?
(a) Infrared spectroscopy
(b) X-ray diffraction
(c) Microspectrophotometry
(d) Raman spectroscopy

53. Which one of the following is the most predominant element in a majority of igneous rocks?
(a) Al (b) Fe
(c) O (d) Si

54. Match the entries in Group I with the process parameters in Group II:

Group I	**Group II**
A. Clark electrode	(i) Dissolved Oxygen
B. Redox Probe	(ii) pH
C. Load cell	(iii) Liquid level
D. Diaphragm gauge	(iv) Vessel pressure

Choose the correct code:

Codes:	**A**	**B**	**C**	**D**
(a)	(i)	(ii)	(iii)	(iv)
(b)	(ii)	(i)	(iv)	(iii)
(c)	(i)	(iv)	(iii)	(ii)
(d)	(iv)	(iii)	(ii)	(i)

55. Which one of the following is used to determine total organic matter by Walkley and Black method?
(a) KOH and H_2SO_4
(b) $Na_2S_2O_3$ and H_2SO_4
(c) $K_2Cr_2O_7$ and H_2SO_4
(d) HNO_3 and H_2SO_4

56. As per WHO standards the maximum permissible level of coliform organisms per 100 mL of drinking water is
(a) 10 (b) 100
(c) 150 (d) 1000

57. Progressive increase in concentration of a xenobiotic compound when it passes through the food chain is called
(a) Biomagnification
(b) Hyper accumulation
(c) Bioaccumulation
(d) None of the above

58. Highest level of biotic interaction is
(a) Mutualism (b) Predation
(c) Parasitism (d) Amensalism

59. Which one of the following is considered as indicator of aquatic pollution?
(a) Rotifers (b) Copepods
(c) Mysids (d) Calanoids

60. Poorly nourished lakes are known as
(a) Oligotrophic (b) Eutrophic
(c) Mesotrophic (d) Xerotrophic

61. Identify a sampling method which is not non-destructive.
(a) Sub-surface coring
(b) Using of neutron probes to measure soil water
(c) Fourier transform infrared spectroscopy
(d) Time domain refractometry to measure soil water

62. Ministry of Environment and Forests amended the EIA notification making public hearing mandatory for environmental clearance on

(a) 27th January 1996
(b) 10th April 1997
(c) 27th January 1997
(d) None of the above

63. The allochthonous microorganisms of an ecosystem are
(a) Indigenous microorganisms
(b) Migrant
(c) Parasitic
(d) Pathogenic

64. The rate of evaporation of oil spilled into the sea depends on
(a) The elemental concentration of sea water
(b) The composition of sea water microflora
(c) Composition of the crude oil
(d) The temperature of the sea

65. The most dangerous and heat resistant spoilage organism in canning industry is
(a) Clostridium cellulolyticum
(b) Bacillus subtilis
(c) E.coli
(d) Clostridium botulinum

66. Oxygen concentrations in compost developed in static piles usually
(a) Ten times lower than in ambient air
(b) Five times lower than in ambient air
(c) Two times more than in ambient air
(d) Five times more than in ambient air

67. If a bacterium with a 20 minute generation time is grown under optimal conditions (37°C), one cell would multiply to 10^3 (1000) cells in 3.3 hours, then how much time it will take to multiply to 106 cells?
(a) 5.3 hrs. (b) 6.6 hrs.
(c) 9.9 hrs. (d) 6.3 hrs.

68. The biodegradation of plant material is slow because of presence of
(a) Cellulose (b) Xylene
(c) Extension/protein (d) Lignin

69. The widely used aerobic suspension type of liquid waste treatment system is
(a) Rotating Biological Contactor (RBC)
(b) Percolating filter
(c) Activated sludge process
(d) Septic tank

70. The treatment designed to remove non-biodegradable organic pollutants and mineral nutrients from waste water is
(a) Lagoons
(b) Imhoff tank
(c) Secondary treatment
(d) Tertiary treatment

71. An ecotype is
(a) Genetically different forms of the same organisms
(b) Genetically similar forms of the same organisms
(c) Morphologically different forms of the same organisms
(d) Both (a) and (b)

72. Ultraviolet radiations are lethal due to inactivation of
(a) Proteins, nucleic acids and pigments
(b) Minerals, water and air
(c) Carbohydrates, fats and vitamins
(d) O_2, CO_2 and water

73. The following are the characters of species diversity:
(i) More richness (ii) More evenness
(iii) More dominance (iv) Less dominance
(v) Less richness (vi) Less evenness

Point out the combination of conditions in which species diversity of an ecosystem will be more.
(a) (i), (ii) and (iii) (b) (v), (ii) and (iii)
(c) (i), (ii) and (iv) (d) (i), (vi) and (iv)

74. Given below are two statements, one labelled as Assertion (A) and the other labelled as Reason (R).
Assertion (A): If natality is greater than mortality, it leads to population explosion.
Reason (R): The scientific study of various species of human population is called demography.
Choose the correct answer:
(a) Both (A) and (R) are true and (R) is the correct explanation of (A).
(b) Both (A) and (R) are true, but (R) is not the correct explanation of (A).
(c) (A) is true, but (R) is false.
(d) Both (A) and (R) are false.

75. Match Column I with Column II:
Column I
A. Chipko Movement
B. Narmada Bacchao Andolan
C. Climate Change
D. Silent Spring
Column II
(i) Medha Patkar
(ii) Al Gore
(iii) Rachel Carson
(iv) Sundarlal Bahuguna

Choose the correct code:

Codes:	**A**	**B**	**C**	**D**
(a)	(i)	(ii)	(iii)	(iv)
(b)	(ii)	(iii)	(iv)	(i)
(c)	(iv)	(i)	(ii)	(iii)
(d)	(iii)	(iv)	(i)	(ii)

ANSWERS

1. (d)	2. (a)	3. (d)	4. (a)	5. (d)
6. (c)	7. (d)	8. (d)	9. (a)	10. (c)
11. (a)	12. (d)	13. (c)	14. (d)	15. (c)
16. (a)	17. (b)	18. (a)	19. (d)	20. (d)
21. (a)	22. (a)	23. (a)	24. (a)	25. (d)
26. (b)	27. (b)	28. (d)	29. (b)	30. (a)
31. (c)	32. (a)	33. (a)	34. (d)	35. (a)
36. (b)	37. (b)	38. (a)	39. (d)	40. (c)
41. (b)	42. (a)	43. (b)	44. (a)	45. (d)
46. (b)	47. (b)	48. (d)	49. (a)	50. (b)
51. (a)	52. (b)	53. (c)	54. (a)	55. (c)
56. (a)	57. (a)	58. (b)	59. (a)	60. (a)
61. (a)	62. (b)	63. (b)	64. (c)	65. (d)
66. (b)	67. (b)	68. (d)	69. (c)	70. (d)
71. (a)	72. (a)	73. (c)	74. (b)	75. (c)

DECEMBER–2012

Note: This paper contains Sixty (60) multiple-choice questions, each question carrying two (2) marks. Candidate is expected to answer any Fifty (50) questions. In case more than Fifty (50) questions are attempted, only the first Fifty (50) questions will be evaluated.

PAPER–I

1. The English word 'Communication' is derived from the words
   (a) Communis and Communicare
   (b) Communist and Commune
   (c) Communism and Communalism
   (d) Communion and Common sense

2. Chinese Cultural Revolution leader Mao Zedong used a type of communication to talk to the masses is known as
   (a) Mass line communication
   (b) Group communication
   (c) Participatory communication
   (d) Dialogue communication

3. Conversing with the spirits and ancestors is termed as
   (a) Transpersonal communication
   (b) Intrapersonal communication
   (c) Interpersonal communication
   (d) Face-to-face communication

4. The largest circulated daily newspaper among the following is
   (a) *The Times of India*
   (b) *The Indian Express*
   (c) *The Hindu*
   (d) *The Deccan Herald*

5. The pioneer of the silent feature film in India was
   (a) K.A. Abbas
   (b) Satyajit Ray
   (c) B.R. Chopra
   (d) Dada Sahib Phalke

6. Classroom communication of a teacher rests on the principle of
   (a) Infotainment (b) Edutainment
   (c) Entertainment (d) Power equation

7. The missing number in the series:
   0, 6, 24, 60, 120, ?, 336, is
   (a) 240 (b) 220
   (c) 280 (d) 210

8. A group of 7 members having a majority of boys is to be formed out of 6 boys and 4 girls. The number of ways the group can be formed is
   (a) 80 (b) 100
   (c) 90 (d) 110

9. The number of observations in a group is 40. The average of the first 10 members is 4.5 and the average of the remaining 30 members is 3.5. The average of the whole group is
   (a) 4 (b) 15/2
   (c) 15/4 (d) 6

10. If MOHAN is represented by the code KMFYL, then COUNT will be represented by
    (a) AMSLR (b) MSLAR
    (c) MASRL (d) SAMLR

11. The sum of the ages of two persons A and B is 50. 5 years ago, the ratio of their ages was 5/3. The present age of A and B are
    (a) 30, 20 (b) 35, 15
    (c) 38, 12 (d) 40, 10

12. Let *a* means minus (–), *b* means multiplied by (×), C means divided by (÷) and D means plus (+). The value of 90 D 9 *a* 29 C 10 *b* 2 is
    (a) 8 (b) 10
    (c) 12 (d) 14

13. Consider the Assertion I and Assertion II and select the right code given below:
    Assertion I: Even Bank-lockers are not safe. Thieves can break them and take away your wealth. But thieves cannot go to heaven. So you should keep your wealth in heaven.
    Assertion II: The difference of skin-colour of beings is because of the distance from the sun and not because of some permanent traits. Skin-colour is the result of body's reaction to the sun and its rays.
    Codes:
    (a) Both the assertions I and II are forms of argument.
    (b) The assertion I is an argument but the assertion II is not.
    (c) The assertion II is an argument but the assertion I is not.
    (d) Both the assertions are explanations of facts.

14. By which of the following proposition, the proposition 'some men are not honest' is contradicted?
    (a) All men are honest.
    (b) Some men are honest.
    (c) No men are honest.
    (d) All of the above.

15. A stipulative definition is
    (a) always true
    (b) always false
    (c) sometimes true sometimes false
    (d) neither true nor false

16. Choose the appropriate alternative given in the codes to replace the question mark.
    Examiner – Examinee, Pleader – Client, Preceptor – ?
    (a) Customer (b) Path-finder
    (c) Perceiver (d) Disciple

17. If the statement 'most of the students are obedient' is taken to be true, which one of the following pair of statements can be claimed to be true?
    I. All obedient persons are students.
    II. All students are obedient.
    III. Some students are obedient.
    IV. Some students are not disobedient.
    Codes:
    (a) I and II (b) II and III
    (c) III and IV (d) II and IV

18. Choose the right code:
    A deductive argument claims that:
    I. The conclusion does not claim something more than that which is contained in the premises.
    II. The conclusion is supported by the premise/premises conclusively.
    III. If the conclusion is false, then premise/premises may be either true or false.
    IV. If premise/combination of premises is true, then conclusion must be true.
    Codes:
    (a) I and II (b) I and III
    (c) II and III (d) All of the above

On the basis of the data given in the following table, give answers to questions from 19 to 24:

Government Expenditures on Social Services
(As percent of total expenditure)

Sl.No.	Items	2007-08	2008-09	2009-10	2010-11
	Social Services	11.06	12.94	13.06	14.02
(a)	Education, sports & youth affairs	4.02	4.04	3.96	4.46
(b)	Health & family welfare	2.05	1.91	1.90	2.03
(c)	Water supply, housing, etc.	2.02	2.31	2.20	2.27
(d)	Information & broadcasting	0.22	0.22	0.20	0.22
(e)	Welfare to SC/ST & OBC	0.36	0.35	0.41	0.63
(f)	Labour and employment	0.27	0.27	0.22	0.25
(g)	Social welfare & nutrition	0.82	0.72	0.79	1.06
(h)	North-eastern areas	0.00	1.56	1.50	1.75
(i)	Other social services	1.29	1.55	1.87	1.34
	Total Government expenditure	100.00	100.00	100.00	100.00

19. How many activities in the social services are there where the expenditure has been less than 5 percent of the total expenditures incurred on the social services in 2008-09?
    (a) One (b) Three
    (c) Five (d) All of the above

20. In which year, the expenditures on the social services have increased at the highest rate?
    (a) 2007-08 (b) 2008-09
    (c) 2009-10 (d) 2010-11

21. Which of the following activities remains almost stagnant in terms of share of expenditures?
    (a) North-eastern areas
    (b) Welfare to SC/ST & OBC
    (c) Information & broadcasting
    (d) Social welfare and nutrition

22. Which of the following item's expenditure share is almost equal to the remaining three items in the given years?
    (a) Information & broadcasting
    (b) Welfare to SC/ST and OBC
    (c) Labour and employment
    (d) Social welfare & nutrition

23. Which of the following items of social services has registered the highest rate of increase in expenditures during 2007-08 to 2010-11?
    (a) Education, sports & youth affairs
    (b) Welfare to SC/ST & OBC
    (c) Social welfare & nutrition
    (d) Overall social services

24. Which of the following items has registered the highest rate of decline in terms of expenditure during 2007-08 to 2009-10?
    (a) Labour and employment
    (b) Health and family welfare
    (c) Social welfare and nutrition
    (d) Education, sports and youth affairs

25. ALU stands for
    (a) American Logic Unit
    (b) Alternate Local Unit
    (c) Alternating Logic Unit
    (d) Arithmetic Logic Unit

26. A Personal Computer uses a number of chips mounted on a circuit board called
    (a) Microprocessor (b) System Board
    (c) Daughter Board (d) Mother Board

27. Computer Virus is a
(a) Hardware (b) Bacteria
(c) Software (d) None of these

28. Which one of the following is correct?
(a) $(17)_{10} = (17)_{16}$
(b) $(17)_{10} = (17)_8$
(c) $(17)_{10} = (10111)_2$
(d) $(17)_{10} = (10001)_2$

29. The file extension of MS-Word document in Office 2007 is ______.
(a) .pdf (b) .doc
(c) .docx (d) .txt

30. ______ is a protocol used by e-mail clients to download e-mails to your computer.
(a) TCP (b) FTP
(c) SMTP (d) POP

31. Which of the following is a source of methane?
(a) Wetlands
(b) Foam Industry
(c) Thermal Power Plants
(d) Cement Industry

32. 'Minamata disaster' in Japan was caused by pollution due to
(a) Lead (b) Mercury
(c) Cadmium (d) Zinc

33. Biomagnification means increase in the
(a) concentration of pollutants in living organisms
(b) number of species
(c) size of living organisms
(d) biomass

34. Nagoya Protocol is related to
(a) Climate change
(b) Ozone depletion
(c) Hazardous waste
(d) Biodiversity

35. The second most important source after fossil fuels contributing to India's energy needs is
(a) Solar energy (b) Nuclear energy
(c) Hydropower (d) Wind energy

36. In case of earthquakes, an increase of magnitude 1 on Richter Scale implies
(a) a ten-fold increase in the amplitude of seismic waves.
(b) a ten-fold increase in the energy of the seismic waves.
(c) two-fold increase in the amplitude of seismic waves.
(d) two-fold increase in the energy of seismic waves.

37. Which of the following is not a measure of Human Development Index?
(a) Literacy Rate
(b) Gross Enrolment
(c) Sex Ratio
(d) Life Expectancy

38. India has the highest number of students in colleges after
(a) the U.K. (b) the U.S.A.
(c) Australia (d) Canada

39. Which of the following statement(s) is/are not correct about the Attorney General of India?
1. The President appoints a person, who is qualified to be a Judge of a High Court, to be the Attorney General of India.
2. He has the right of audience in all the Courts of the country.
3. He has the right to take part in the proceedings of the Lok Sabha and the Rajya Sabha.
4. He has a fixed tenure.

Select the correct answer from the codes given below:

Codes:
(a) 1 and 4 (b) 2, 3 and 4
(c) 3 and 4 (d) 3 only

40. Which of the following prefix President Pranab Mukherjee desires to be

discontinued while interacting with Indian dignitaries as well as in official notings?

1. His Excellency 2. Mahamahim
3. Hon'ble 4. Shri/Smt.

Select the correct answer from the codes given below:

Codes:

(a) 1 and 3 (b) 2 and 3
(c) 1 and 2 (d) 1, 2 and 3

41. Which of the following can be done under conditions of financial emergency?
 1. State Legislative Assemblies can be abolished.
 2. Central Government can acquire control over the budget and expenditure of States.
 3. Salaries of the Judges of the High Courts and the Supreme Court can be reduced.
 4. Right to Constitutional Remedies can be suspended.

Select the correct answer from the codes given below:

Codes:

(a) 1, 2 and 3 (b) 2, 3 and 4
(c) 1 and 2 (d) 2 and 3

42. Match List I with List II and select the correct answer from the codes given below:

List I

(A) Poverty Reduction Programme
(B) Human Development Scheme
(C) Social Assistance Scheme
(D) Minimum Need Scheme

List II

(i) Mid-day Meals
(ii) Indira Awas Yojana (IAY)
(iii) National Old Age Pension (NOAP)
(iv) MNREGA

Codes:	A	B	C	D
(a)	(iv)	(i)	(iii)	(ii)
(b)	(ii)	(iii)	(iv)	(i)
(c)	(iii)	(iv)	(i)	(ii)
(d)	(iv)	(iii)	(ii)	(i)

43. For an efficient and durable learning, learner should have
 (a) ability to learn only
 (b) requisite level of motivation only
 (c) opportunities to learn only
 (d) desired level of ability and motivation

44. Classroom communication must be
 (a) Teacher centric
 (b) Student centric
 (c) General centric
 (d) Textbook centric

45. The best method of teaching is to
 (a) impart information
 (b) ask students to read books
 (c) suggest good reference material
 (d) initiate a discussion and participate in it

46. Interaction inside the classroom should generate
 (a) Argument (b) Information
 (c) Ideas (d) Controversy

47. "Spare the rod and spoil the child", gives the message that
 (a) punishment in the class should be banned.
 (b) corporal punishment is not acceptable.
 (c) undesirable behaviour must be punished.
 (d) children should be beaten with rods.

48. The type of communication that the teacher has in the classroom, is termed as
 (a) Interpersonal
 (b) Mass communication
 (c) Group communication
 (d) Face-to-face communication

49. Which one of the following is an indication of the quality of a research journal?
 (a) Impact factor (b) h-index
 (c) g-index (d) i10-index

50. Good 'research ethics' means
   (a) Not disclosing the holdings of shares/stocks in a company that sponsors your research.
   (b) Assigning a particular research problem to one Ph.D./research student only.
   (c) Discussing with your colleagues confidential data from a research paper that you are reviewing for an academic journal.
   (d) Submitting the same research manuscript for publishing in more than one journal.

51. Which of the following sampling methods is based on probability?
   (a) Convenience sampling
   (b) Quota sampling
   (c) Judgement sampling
   (d) Stratified sampling

52. Which one of the following references is written according to American Psychological Association (APA) format?
   (a) Sharma, V. (2010). Fundamentals of Computer Science.
   New Delhi: Tata McGraw Hill
   (b) Sharma, V. 2010. Fundamentals of Computer Science.
   New Delhi: Tata McGraw Hill
   (c) Sharma, V. 2010. Fundamentals of Computer Science.
   New Delhi: Tata McGraw Hill
   (d) Sharma, V. (2010), Fundamentals of Computer Science.
   New Delhi: Tata McGraw Hill

53. Arrange the following steps of research in correct sequence:
   1. Identification of research problem
   2. Listing of research objectives
   3. Collection of data
   4. Methodology
   5. Data analysis
   6. Results and discussion

   (a) 1, 2, 3, 4, 5, 6 (b) 1, 2, 4, 3, 5, 6
   (c) 2, 1, 3, 4, 5, 6 (d) 2, 1, 4, 3, 5, 6

54. Identify the incorrect statement:
   (a) A hypothesis is made on the basis of limited evidence as a starting point for further investigations.
   (b) A hypothesis is a basis for reasoning without any assumption of its truth.
   (c) Hypothesis is a proposed explanation for a phenomenon.
   (d) Scientific hypothesis is a scientific theory.

Read the following passage carefully and answer the questions (55 to 60):

The popular view of towns and cities in developing countries and of urbanization process is that despite the benefits and comforts it brings, the emergence of such cities connotes environmental degradation, generation of slums and squatters, urban poverty, unemployment, crimes, lawlessness, traffic chaos, etc. But what is the reality? Given the unprecedental increase in urban population over the last 50 years from 300 million in 1950 to 2 billion in 2000 in developing countries, the wonder really is how well the world has coped, and not how badly.

In general, the urban quality of life has improved in terms of availability of water and sanitation, power, health and education, communication and transport. By way of illustration, a large number of urban residents have been provided with improved water in urban areas in Asia's largest countries such as China, India, Indonesia and Philippines. Despite that, the access to improved water in terms of percentage of total urban population seems to have declined during the last decade of 20th century, though in absolute numbers, millions of additional urbanites, have been provided improved services. These countries have made significant progress in the provision of sanitation services too, together, providing for an additional population of more than 293 million citizens within a decade (1990-2000). These improvements must be viewed against the backdrop of rapidly increasing urban population, fiscal crunch and strained human resources and efficient and quality-oriented public management.

55. The popular view about the process of urbanization in developing countries is
    (a) Positive (b) Negative
    (c) Neutral (d) Unspecified
56. The average annual increase in the number of urbanites in developing countries, from 1950 to 2000 A.D. was close to
    (a) 30 million (b) 40 million
    (c) 50 million (d) 60 million
57. The reality of urbanization is reflected in
    (a) How well the situation has been managed.
    (b) How badly the situation has gone out of control.
    (c) How fast has been the tempo of urbanization.
    (d) How fast the environment has degraded.
58. Which one of the following is not considered as an indicator of urban quality of life?
    (a) Tempo of urbanization
    (b) Provision of basic services
    (c) Access to social amenities
    (d) All of the above
59. The author in this passage has tried to focus on
    (a) Extension of Knowledge
    (b) Generation of Environmental Consciousness
    (c) Analytical Reasoning
    (d) Descriptive Statement
60. In the above passage, the author intends to state
    (a) The hazards of the urban life
    (b) The sufferings of the urban life
    (c) The awareness of human progress
    (d) The limits to growth

ANSWERS

1. (a)	2. (d)	3. (a)	4. (a)	5. (d)
6. (b)	7. (d)	8. (b)	9. (c)	10. (a)
11. (a)	12. (d)	13. (a)	14. (a)	15. (d)
16. (c)	17. (c)	18. (d)	19. (d)	20. (d)
21. (c)	22. (d)	23. (d)	24. (b)	25. (d)
26. (d)	27. (c)	28. (d)	29. (b)	30. (d)
31. (a)	32. (b)	33. (a)	34. (d)	35. (c)
36. (a)	37. (c)	38. (b)	39. (d)	40. (c)
41. (c)	42. (a)	43. (d)	44. (b)	45. (d)
46. (c)	47. (c)	48. (c)	49. (a)	50. (a)
51. (d)	52. (a)	53. (b)	54. (d)	55. (b)
56. (a)	57. (a)	58. (a)	59. (d)	60. (d)

PAPER–II

Note: This paper contains fifty (50) objective type questions, each question carrying two (2) marks. All questions are compulsory.

1. **Assertion (A):** Biosphere constitutes an excellent life-support system which is sustainable and can fulfil all human needs.
   Reason (R): The size and productivity of the Biosphere is limited by availability of water, nutrients and environmental conditions.
   Identify the correct code:
   Codes:
   (a) Both (A) and (R) are true and (R) is the correct explanation of (A).
   (b) Both (A) and (R) are true, but (R) is not the correct explanation of (A).

(c) (A) is true but (R) is false.
(d) (A) is false but (R) is true.

2. Geostrophic wind occurs when pressure gradient force balances
(a) Coriolis force
(b) Frictional force
(c) Centripetal force
(d) Coriolis and frictional force together

3. Scales of Meteorology are in the following order starting from the least
(a) Macro –, Micro –, Meso –
(b) Macro –, Meso –, Micro –
(c) Meso –, Macro –, Micro –
(d) Micro –, Meso –, Macro –

4. When the full potential of physical, chemical and biological factors, a species can use if there is no competition, it is called
(a) Fundamental niche
(b) Ecological niche
(c) Realized niche
(d) Competitive exclusion

5. The uppermost zone of atmosphere of earth, where shortwave ultraviolet radiations are absorbed, is
(a) Troposphere (b) Stratosphere
(c) Mesosphere (d) Thermosphere

6. Which of the following oxides of nitrogen is the major air pollutant released from automobile exhausts?
(a) NO (b) N_2O
(c) NO_2 (d) N_2O_3

7. Match List I with List II which contains pollutant gases and their threshold (safe limit) values as per WHO standards:

List I (Pollutant gas)	List II (Thresholds)
A. CO	(i) 2 ppm
B. SO_2	(ii) 50 ppm
C. NO	(iii) 0.08 ppm
D. PAN	(iv) 25 ppm

Identify the correct code:

Codes:	A	B	C	D
(a)	(ii)	(iii)	(i)	(iv)
(b)	(iv)	(ii)	(i)	(iii)
(c)	(ii)	(i)	(iv)	(iii)
(d)	(iii)	(iv)	(ii)	(i)

8. The band labelled as UV-C which is lethal to micro-organisms is
(a) 0.29 – V0.32 μm (b) 0.2 – V0.29 μm
(c) 0.17 – V0.2 μm (d) 0.07 – V0.21 μm

9. Which of the following species in the atmosphere is called atmospheric detergent?
(a) Chlorine radical
(b) Hydroxyl radical
(c) Methyl radical
(d) Ozone radical

10. The pOH of a 0.001 M solution of HCl is
(a) 12 (b) 10
(c) 11 (d) 13

11. Identify the pair (element-health effect) which is correctly matched:
(a) Lead – Methaemoglobinemia
(b) Arsenic – Kidney damage
(c) Mercury – Nervous disorder
(d) PAN – Hypoxemia

12. Which of the following organisms can act as primary consumer, secondary consumer, tertiary consumer or scavenger in different types of food chains?
(a) Raven
(b) Tiger
(c) Snake
(d) Phytoplanktones

13. The tendency of biological systems to resist change and to remain in a state of equilibrium is called
(a) Homeostatis
(b) Feedback mechanism
(c) Ecological efficiency
(d) Carrying capacity

14. If different categories of threatened species are written in a sequence, what is the correct order?
(a) Extinct → Vulnerable → Rare → Endangered
(b) Vulnerable → Rare → Endangered → Extinct
(c) Vulnerable → Rare → Extinct → Endangered
(d) Rare → Vulnerable → Endangered → Extinct

15. Which of the following is not a type of ex situ conservation method?
(a) Botanical garden
(b) Zoological park
(c) Wildlife sanctuaries
(d) Gene banks

16. As a consequence of succession the P/B ratio (Gross production/Standing crop biomass) is changed. It is
(a) high during developmental stages and low at mature stage.
(b) low during developmental stages and high at mature stage.
(c) > 1 or < 1 at developmental stages and approximately 1 at mature stage.
(d) remaining unchanged at all stages.

17. Preparation of hazard-zoning map in case of landslide prone regions involves comprehensive investigation of
(a) details of structural and lithological settings.
(b) geomorphic features relating to instability of slopes.
(c) seismicity pattern of the region.
(d) All of the above.

18. If ap = specified value of peak acceleration, N = mean rate of occurrence of earthquake per year, t_{ep} = time interval of consideration (exposure period) and F_{ap} = probability that an observed acceleration is less than or equal to ap, then the cumulative probability distribution of peak acceleration for epoch—dependent seismic hazard map is given by which formula?
(a) $F_{max}\ t_{ep} = \exp\{-Nt(1 - F_{ap})\}$
(b) $F_{max} = \exp\{-Nt(1 - F_{ap})\} \cdot t_{ep}$
(c) $F_{max}\ t_{ep} = \exp\{-t(1 - F_{ap})N\}$
(d) All of the above

19. **Assertion (A):** In oceans, Na has the longest residence time, within an order of magnitude of the age of the oceans.
Reason (R): The long residence time of Na reflects a lack of reactivity of sodium in the marine environment by not being readily incorporated in the common sedimentary minerals, nor being removed by biological reactions.
Identify the correct code:
Codes:
(a) Both (A) and (R) are true and (R) is the correct explanation of (A).
(b) Both (A) and (R) are true, but (R) is not the correct explanation of (A).
(c) (A) is true, but (R) is false.
(d) (A) is false, but (R) is true.

20. According to Goldieh the decreasing order of stability of following minerals of igneous rocks towards weathering is
(a) Muscovite > Quartz > Potash feldspar > Biotite
(b) Biotite > Potash feldspar > Muscovite > Quartz
(c) Quartz > Muscovite > Potash feldspar > Biotite
(d) Potash feldspar > Quartz > Muscovite > Biotite

21. In universal polar stereographic coordinate system the eastings and northings are computed using which projection method?
(a) Polar aspect stereographic projection
(b) Non-polar aspect stereographic projection

(c) Polar aspect mercator projection
(d) Non-polar aspect mercator projection

22. Pitchblende is an ore of
(a) Nickel (b) Chromium
(c) Molybdenum (d) Uranium

23. Copper (Cu) is classified according to its geochemical affinity as
(a) Siderophile element
(b) Chalcophile element
(c) Lithophile element
(d) Atmophile element

24. If 'a' is the fractional wind speed decrease at the wind turbine, the maximum extraction of power from the wind occurs when 'a' is equal to
(a) 1/2 (b) 1/3
(c) 1 (d) 3/5

25. In the following fusion energy reaction

$$D + T = {}_0n^1 + X$$

identify X
(a) Li (b) H_2
(c) He_3 (d) He_4

26. **Assertion (A):** Natural gas is a very attractive ecofriendly fuel.
Reason (R): It produces few pollutants and less carbon dioxide per unit energy than any other fossil fuel on combustion.
Identify the correct answer:
Codes:
(a) Both (A) and (R) are true and (R) is the correct explanation of (A).
(b) Both (A) and (R) are true and (R) is not the correct explanation of (A).
(c) (A) is true but (R) is false.
(d) (A) is false but (R) is true.

27. **Assertion (A):** Solar photovoltaic cells are expensive.
Reason (R): Solar photovoltaic cells are fabricated from crystalline silicon and operate only at 10-12% efficiency.
Identify the correct answer:
Codes:
(a) Both (A) and (R) are true and (R) is the correct explanation of (A).
(b) Both (A) and (R) are true and (R) is not the correct explanation of (A).
(c) (A) is true but (R) is false.
(d) (A) is false but (R) is true.

28. Human activities add 7-9 gigatons of CO_2 per annum into the atmosphere. Major contributor to this CO_2 is
(a) Burning of fossil fuels
(b) Clearing of forests for agriculture
(c) Fermentation industries
(d) Cement industries

29. According to WHO, maximum permissible level of chlorides in drinking water is
(a) 100 mg/L (b) 200 mg/L
(c) 600 mg/L (d) 800 mg/L

30. Wilting coefficient of a loam represents
(a) the minimum water content of the soil at which plants can no longer obtain water
(b) water holding capacity
(c) capillary water
(d) field capacity

31. Which one of the following techniques can be used for determining the level of cadmium in soil?
(a) UV – Visible spectrophotometer
(b) Atomic Absorption Spectrophotometer
(c) XRD
(d) IR spectrometer

32. For noise control in automobiles, the exhaust muffler attenuates sound by
(a) Absorption
(b) Destructive interference
(c) Reducing velocity of hot gases
(d) Absorption and destructive interference

33. Five particles (< 2-3 μm) can be effectively collected from industrial stacks by

(a) Fabric filters
(b) Cyclone separators
(c) Venturi scrubbers
(d) Settling chambers

34. Soil fulvic acids are strong chelators of
(a) Iron (II)
(b) Iron (III)
(c) Both Iron (II) and Iron (III)
(d) $Fe(OH)_3$

35. Natural source of polycyclic aromatic hydrocarbons (PAHs) is
(a) Root exudates
(b) Anaerobic bacteria
(c) Aerobic bacteria
(d) Grass fires

36. Match the 'phase' with the 'activity' in Environmental Audit. Identify the correct answer from the codes given below the lists:

List I (Phase)
A. Pre-Audit
B. On-site Audit
C. Post Audit

List II (Activity)
(i) Human input-output analysis in relation to economy
(ii) Reviewing audit-check lists
(iii) Records/Documents Review

Codes:	A	B	C
(a)	(ii)	(iii)	(i)
(b)	(i)	(iii)	(ii)
(c)	(i)	(ii)	(iii)
(d)	(iii)	(ii)	(i)

37. Match the Impact Assessment Methodologies (List II) with the corresponding environments (List I). Identify the correct answer from the codes given below the lists.

List I	List II
A. Air	(i) Ecosystem models
B. Biological	(ii) Gaussian models
C. Water	(iii) Mass balance approach
D. Land	(iv) G.I.S.

Codes:	A	B	C	D
(a)	(ii)	(i)	(iii)	(iv)
(b)	(i)	(ii)	(iv)	(iii)
(c)	(iii)	(iv)	(ii)	(i)
(d)	(iv)	(iii)	(i)	(ii)

38. Public hearing is conducted
(a) Prior to site selection
(b) Prior to approval of Terms of Reference
(c) After preparation of EIA
(d) After environmental clearance

39. IAIA stands for
(a) International Association of Impact Assessment
(b) Indian Association of Impact Assessment
(c) International Assembly of Impact Assessment
(d) Indian Assembly of Impact Assessment

40. Municipal Solid Wastes (MSWs) have the heating value typically in the range
(a) 9,300 to 12,800 kJ/kg
(b) 1000 to 2500 kJ/kg
(c) 1780 to 2830 kJ/kg
(d) 530 to 780 kJ/kg

41. The Motor Vehicles Act 1938 was amended in which year?
(a) 1972 (b) 1980
(c) 1988 (d) 1986

42. The following statistical test is used to ascertain whether there is significant difference between the variances of two sets of observations:
(a) t-test (b) F-test
(c) Chi-square test (d) Regression

43. The population (N) of an ecosystem obeys the growth equation

$$\frac{dN}{dt} = \alpha N - \beta N^2$$

where α and β are constants. The maximum sustainable yield of this ecosystem will be

(a) $\alpha - \beta N$ (b) α/β
(c) $\alpha/2\beta$ (d) α^2/β

44. The geometric mean of the following data:

4, 10, 25, 10

is

(a) 10 (b) 5
(c) 12.25 (d) $\frac{100}{49}$

45. If the mean and variance of a Poisson distribution are μ and σ, then the following relation is correct.

(a) $\sigma = \mu^2$ (b) $\sigma = \sqrt{\mu}$
(c) $\sigma^2 = \mu$ (d) $\sigma = 2\mu$

46. In the Gaussian Plume Model, the plume rise varies with Buoyancy Flux Parameter F as

(a) F (b) $F^{\frac{1}{2}}$
(c) $F^{\frac{1}{3}}$ (d) $F^{\frac{1}{4}}$

47. United Nations Conference on Environment, also termed as Earth Summit, was held in 1992 in which city?

(a) Rio de Janeiro (b) Kyoto
(c) Stockholm (d) Copenhagen

48. In which part of India, the tropical Western Ghats are situated?

(a) Punjab (b) Rajasthan
(c) Gujarat (d) Kerala

49. Variety of different species, genetic variability among individuals within each species and variety of ecosystems constitute the so-called

(a) Species diversity
(b) Genetic diversity
(c) Biological diversity
(d) Ecological diversity

50. Baba Amte was the leader of

(a) Appiko Movement
(b) Chipko Movement
(c) Narmada Bachao Andolan
(d) Tehri Dam Movement

ANSWERS

1. (d)	2. (a)	3. (d)	4. (a)	5. (d)
6. (a)	7. (c)	8. (b)	9. (b)	10. (c)
11. (d)	12. (a)	13. (a)	14. (b)	15. (c)
16. (a)	17. (d)	18. (a)	19. (a)	20. (c)
21. (a)	22. (d)	23. (b)	24. (b)	25. (d)
26. (a)	27. (a)	28. (a)	29. (c)	30. (a)
31. (b)	32. (c)	33. (c)	34. (c)	35. (d)
36. (a)	37. (a)	38. (c)	39. (a)	40. (a)
41. (c)	42. (b)	43. (c)	44. (a)	45. (a)
46. (c)	47. (a)	48. (d)	49. (c)	50. (c)

PAPER–III

Note: This paper contains seventy-five (75) objective type questions of two (2) marks each. All questions are compulsory.

1. In a multiple regression model, the f-ratio is used to test the

(a) Variance of the data
(b) Standard error of mean
(c) R^2 value
(d) Overall goodness of fit of the model.

2. If the mean of a sample is 20, the standard error of mean is 1 and the t-statistic for 95% level of confidence is 2.5, the population mean will be in the range

(a) 17.5 to 22.5 (b) 15 to 25
(c) 20 to 25 (d) 15 to 20

3. The third moment about the mean of a distribution of a set of observations is a measure of
(a) Mode (b) Skewness
(c) Kurtosis (d) Variance

4. Consider an air shed over a city in the form of a rectangular box. The wind velocity is 5 m/sec normal to left face of the box. The length of the box along the direction of wind is 10 km and mixing height is 1 km. Assuming rapid mixing of the pollutants which are conservative in nature, the concentration of the pollutants in the city would reach 63% of its final value in
(a) 2,000 sec (b) 5,000 sec
(c) 10,000 sec (d) 1,000 sec

5. Which one of the following states of mercury is volatile?
(a) Organic (b) Ionic
(c) Atomic (d) All of the above

6. Molar extinction coefficient of H_2O_2 at 240 nm is 0.04 $M^{-1}cm^{-1}$. The concentration of H_2O_2 in a solution which has absorbance of 0.6 in a 3 cm curette will be
(a) 5 M (b) 10 M
(c) 15 M (d) 20 M

7. A reference solution is to be prepared with 5 PPM parabenzopyrene (molecular weight = 252). The quantity of parabenzopyrene required for preparing one litre 5 PPM solution is
(a) 252 mg (b) 25.2 mg
(c) 5 mg (d) 252 μg

8. Which one of the following is a peroxyl radical?
(a) OH° (b) R°
(c) RO° (d) ROO°

9. Depending upon the amount of net primary productivity the various ecosystems can be arranged in a decreasing sequence of yield.
(a) Tropical seasonal forest – Tropical rain forest – Temperate Grassland – Woodland and Shrubland
(b) Tropical seasonal forest – Tropical rain forest – Woodland and Shrubland – Temperate Grassland
(c) Tropical rain forest – Temperate Grassland – Woodland and Shrubland – Tropical seasonal forest
(d) Tropical rain forest – Tropical seasonal forest – Woodland and Shrubland – Temperate Grassland

10. Which of the following is a correct sequence of secondary seral vegetation development on any habitat?
(a) Ecesis – Invasion – Aggregation – Stabilization
(b) Ecesis – Aggregation – Invasion – Stabilization
(c) Aggregation – Invasion – Ecesis – Stabilization
(d) Invasion – Ecesis – Aggregation – Stabilization

11. What is common feature among the following?
Abies delavayi
Aconitum diennorrhzum
Adinandra griffthii
Aglaia perviridis
(a) All have been extinct.
(b) All are gymnosperms.
(c) All are identified as endangered species.
(d) All are angiosperms.

12. Raunkiaer's normal biological spectrum for phanerogamic flora of the world exhibits one of the following sequence of occurrence (%) of different life forms.
(a) Phanerophytes, Hemicryptophytes, Therophytes, Cryptophytes, Chaemophytes.

(b) Phanerophytes, Hemicryptophytes, Therophytes, Chaemophytes, Cryptophytes.
(c) Phanerophytes, Hemicryptophytes, Cryptophytes, Chaemophytes, Therophytes.
(d) Phanerophytes, Chaemophytes, Hemicryptophytes, Cryptophytes, Therophytes.

13. One of the following categories of earthworms is most suitable for wasteland reclamation.
(a) Epigeic
(b) Anecic
(c) Endogeic
(d) None of the above

14. How many mega-bio-diverse countries have been identified in the world?
(a) 2 (b) 12
(c) 17 (d) 35

15. Which one of the following is an *Ex-situ* method of biodiversity conservation?
(a) Seed storage (b) DNA Bank
(c) Tissue culture (d) All of the above

16. Which one of the following is a methyl isocyanate (MIC) based pesticide?
(a) Sevin (Carbaryl)
(b) Temix (Aldicarb)
(c) Furadon (Carbofuran)
(d) All of the above

17. The sequence of fossil fuels in the order of higher to lower heating value is as follows:
(a) Coal, Petroleum, Natural Gas, Hydrogen.
(b) Hydrogen, Natural Gas, Petroleum, Coal.
(c) Hydrogen, Coal, Natural Gas, Petroleum.
(d) Natural Gas, Petroleum, Coal, Hydrogen.

18. Natural ore of radioactive materials does not contain which one of the following isotope?
(a) U^{235} (b) Pu^{239}
(c) U^{238} (d) Th^{232}

19. The process of splitting bigger hydrocarbon into smaller hydrocarbon molecules is called
(a) Pyrolysis
(b) Thermal decomposition
(c) Cracking
(d) Combustion

20. Which one of the following is a complex in organic fertilizer?
(a) Urea
(b) Super phosphate
(c) Potash
(d) NPK

21. The sequence of ease of decomposition of organic compounds in soil is
(a) Lignin – Hemicellulose – Starch – Crude protein – Fat
(b) Crude protein – Starch – Fat – Lignin – Hemicellulose
(c) Starch – Crude protein – Hemicellulose – Fat – Lignin
(d) Fat – Starch – Lignin – Hemicellulose – Crude protein

22. Which one of the following radionuclides has the lowest half life period?
(a) C^{14} (b) Sr^{90}
(c) I^{131} (d) Cs^{137}

23. Match the rules mentioned in Column I with year of enforcement mentioned in Column II.

Column I

A. Hazardous Wastes (Management and Handling) Rules
B. Biomedical Solid Wastes (Management and Handling) Rules

C. Municipal Solid Wastes (Management and Handling) Rules
D. The Water (Prevention and Control of Pollution) Cess Rules

Column II
1. 2000
2. 1978
3. 1989
4. 1998

Choose the correct code:

Codes:	A	B	C	D
(a)	3	4	1	2
(b)	4	1	2	3
(c)	2	4	3	1
(d)	1	3	4	2

24. Average composition of biodegradable waste in Municipal Solid Waste (MSW) of India is
(a) 30 – 35% (b) 40 – 45%
(c) 55 – 65% (d) 60 – 70%

25. The treatment method recommended for the human anatomical waste generated from hospitals is
(a) Chemical disinfection
(b) Autoclaving
(c) Incineration
(d) All of the above

26. Match the waste class mentioned in Column I with Color Code of the Collection Container mentioned in Column II.

Column I
A. Human Anatomica Waste
B. Waste Scrap
C. Discarded glass ware
D. Disposable plastics

Column II
1. Blue
2. Green
3. Red
4. White

Choose the correct code:

Codes:	A	B	C	D
(a)	2	3	1	4
(b)	4	2	3	1
(c)	1	2	3	4
(d)	3	1	4	2

27. Which of the following is true when frequency of occurrence of risk is remote but possible?
(a) Risk is acceptable.
(b) Risk reduction measures should be implemented.
(c) Risk is unacceptable.
(d) Both (a) and (b) are true.

28. Given below are two statements, one labelled as Assertion (A) and the other labelled as Reason (R).
Assertion (A): Indirect impacts are more difficult to measure, but can ultimately be more important.
Reason (R): In areas where wildlife is plentiful, such as Africa, new roads often lead to the rapid depletion of animals.
Choose the correct answer.
Codes:
(a) Both (A) and (R) are true and (R) is the correct explanation.
(b) Both (A) and (R) are true, but (R) is not the correct explanation.
(c) (A) is true, but (R) is false.
(d) (A) is false, but (R) is true.

29. An earthquake measuring over 8 on Richter Scale is rated as
(a) Destructive (b) Major
(c) Great (d) Damaging

30. Given below are two statements, one labelled as Assertion (A) and the other labelled as Reason (R).
Assertion (A): It is difficult to judge how changes in localized gas samples represent more general conditions in the Volcano.

Reason (R): The composition of the juvenile gases emitted from volcanic vents often show considerable variation over short periods and distances.

Choose the correct answer.

Codes:

(a) Both (A) and (R) are true and (R) is the correct explanation of (A).

(b) Both (A) and (R) are true, but (R) is not the correct explanation of (A).

(c) (A) is true, but (R) is false.

(d) (A) is false, but (R) is true.

31. In a false-color set, human visual perception is limited to how many independent coordinates?

(a) Three (b) Four

(c) One (d) Five

32. If D = Detector Dimension, F = Focal Length, H = Flying Height, then Ground Resolution Element (GRE) is equal to

(a) (D/F) × H (b) D/F

(c) H/F (d) D/H

33. Darkest level of the associated color (RGB) would have brightness value equal to

(a) 0 (b) 256

(c) 255 (d) 2047

34. The efficiency of a MHD power generator for applied electric field $\vec{E}$, magnetic field $\vec{B}$ and velocity of hot ionized gas $\vec{U}$ is

(a) $\frac{|\vec{E}|}{|\vec{U}||\vec{B}|}$ (b) $\frac{|\vec{U}||\vec{B}|}{|\vec{E}|}$

(c) $\frac{|\vec{E}|^2}{|\vec{U}||\vec{B}|}$ (d) $\frac{|\vec{E}|^2}{|\vec{U}||\vec{B}|^2}$

35. Match the List I with List II and choose the correct answer from the codes given below:

List I (Constituents of Particulate matter)

A. Si

B. PAH

C. SO_4^{2-}

D. Pb

List II (Sources)

1. Natural Resources
2. Incomplete combustion of fossil fuels
3. Elements largely introduced by Human Activities
4. Reactions of a gas in atmosphere

Choose the correct code:

Codes:	A	B	C	D
(a)	1	2	4	3
(b)	2	3	4	1
(c)	2	4	1	3
(d)	3	4	2	1

36. For aerosol particles having sizes > 1 μm, the terminal settling velocity (V_T) of an aerosol particle varies with its diameter (D) as

(a) $V_T \propto D$ (b) $V_T \propto D^2$

(c) $V_T \propto D^3$ (d) $V_T \propto D^{3/2}$

37. Scale lengths associated with synoptic scale phenomenon in atmosphere are typically in the range

(a) 10 – 100 km

(b) 200 – 40,000 km

(c) 10,000 – 100,000 km

(d) 1 – 10 km

38. Assume that the atmosphere is isothermal at 25°C and the estimated maximum daily surface temperature is 35°C, the mixing height is (take adiabatic lapse rate to be 1°C per 100 m)

(a) 3.5 km (b) 2.5 km

(c) 1.5 km (d) 1 km

39. The wavelengths of UV-A radiations are in the range

(a) 200 – 240 nm (b) 240 – 280 nm

(c) 280 – 320 nm (d) 320 – 400 nm

40. Two sounds of 80 dB and 85 dB superimpose at a location. What is the resultant sound at that location?
(a) ~ 82 dB (b) ~ 87 dB
(c) ~ 91 dB (d) ~ 165 dB

41. The coefficient of performance of a wind turbine for maximum power output is
(a) 13/18 (b) 5/8
(c) 16/27 (d) 11/17

42. Which of the following does not have a direct role in climate change?
(a) Sulphate and nitrate aerosols
(b) Black carbon aerosols
(c) Surface ozone
(d) Nitric oxide

43. Which method is used to separate molecules on the basis of their sizes?
(a) Ion exchange chromatography
(b) Molecular exclusion chromatography
(c) Adsorption chromatography
(d) Thin layer chromatography

44. Which type of support media is used in different types of electrophoresis?
(a) Agarose gel
(b) Polyacrylamide gel
(c) Sodium dedecyl sulphate polyacrylamide gel
(d) All of the above

45. Which of the following categories of plants get benefitted more due to elevation of CO_2 level?
(a) C_3 plants (b) C_4 plants
(c) CAM plants (d) All of the above

46. Aquifers that extend continuously from the land surface through material of high permeability are
(a) Aquitards
(b) Auicludes
(c) Confined aquifers
(d) Unconfined aquifers

47. Which one of the following is used to determine ambient concentration of suspended particulate matter?
(a) Cascade impactor
(b) Kjeldahl's Flask
(c) Sacchi Disk
(d) Folin-Wu method

48. Which of the following laws states that the solubility of a gas in a liquid is proportional to the partial pressure of that gas in contact with liquid?
(a) Hick's law
(b) Henry's law
(c) Hardy-Weinburg law of equilibrium
(d) 2nd Law of Newton

49. Maximum CaO is found in
(a) Bauxite (b) Limonite
(c) Lime Stone (d) Siderite

50. The sequence of chemical constituents in order of their abundance in a majority of sedimentary rocks is
(a) $SiO_2 > TiO_2 > Al_2O_3 > Fe_2O_3$
(b) $SiO_2 > Al_2O_3 > Fe_2O_3 > TiO_2$
(c) $SiO_2 > Fe_2O_3 > Al_2O_3 > TiO_2$
(d) $SiO_2 > Fe_2O_3 > TiO_2 > Al_2O_3$

51. The primary producers in the marine ecosystem are
(a) Eubacteria and Algae
(b) Cyanobacteria and Algae
(c) Algae and Protozoans
(d) All of the above

52. Mycorrhizae can be used as biofertilizers because they
(a) fix nitrogen
(b) fix CO_2
(c) solubilise phosphate
(d) kill pathogens

53. Given below are two statements, one labelled as Assertion (A) and the other labelled as Reason (R).

Assertion (A): Some plants with mycorrhizal fungi are able to occupy habitats that otherwise could not inhabit.
Reason (R): The importance of mycorrhizal plant interaction is attested by the fact that 95% of all plants have mycorrhizae.
Choose the correct answer:
Codes:
(a) Both (A) and (R) are true and (R) is the correct explanation of (A).
(b) Both (A) and (R) are true but (R) is not the correct explanation of (A).
(c) (A) is true, but (R) is false.
(d) (A) is false, but (R) is true.

54. An interactive association between two populations in which one population benefits from the association, while the other is not affected, is
(a) Mutualism (b) Neutralism
(c) Commensalism (d) Symbiosis

55. The method for downstreaming of ethanol from fermentation broth is
(a) Filtration
(b) Flow cytometry
(c) Distillation
(d) Flame Photometry

56. The country which uses maximum nuclear power is
(a) U.S.A. (b) Japan
(c) France (d) Germany

57. Which bacteria removes copper from low grade copper ore?
(a) *Thiobacillus sp*
(b) *Bacillus thuringiensis*
(c) *Rhizobium sp*
(d) All of the above

58. Which of the following is not a part of Geographic Information System (GIS)?
(a) Projection
(b) Overlay
(c) Reclassification
(d) Measuring distance and connectivity

59. Ultrafiltration can remove
(a) Suspended solids (b) Bacteria
(c) Protozoa (d) All of the above

60. A good automobile fuel, in addition to having high calorific value, should have
(a) High ignition temperature
(b) High viscosity
(c) Low ignition temperature
(d) Moderate ignition temperature

61. Reserve food material in algae is
(a) Starch (b) Cellulose
(c) Protein (d) None of these

62. The biodegradability of xenobiotics can be characterized by
(a) Rate of CO_2 formation
(b) Rate of O_2 consumption
(c) Ratio of BOD to COD
(d) All of the above

63. The soil borne plant pathogens could be controlled by
(a) Lowering pH (b) Increasing pH
(c) Adding lime (d) All of the above

64. A selective Lignin degrading fungus belongs to
(a) Soft – rot (b) Brown – rot
(c) White – rot (d) Red – rot

65. The drastic reduction in the number of intestinal pathogens during activated sludge process is the overall result of
(a) Competition
(b) Competition and adsorption
(c) Predation, competition and adsorption
(d) Competition, adsorption, predation and settling

66. Which of the following disinfection method does not result in synthesis of organochlorine?

(a) Chlorination
(b) Chloroamination
(c) Ozonation
(d) None of the above

67. An organism's niche is
(a) the way the organism uses the range of physical and biological conditions in which it lives.
(b) all the biological and physical factors in the organism's environment.
(c) the function role played by the organism where it lives.
(d) the range of temperature that the organism needs to live.

68. The pyramid of biomass is invented in
(a) Forest ecosystem
(b) Greenland ecosystem
(c) Aquatic ecosystem
(d) All of the above

69. Which of the following chemicals of anthropogenic origin mimics the effect of estrogen in animals?
(a) Alkyl phenol
(b) Polychlorinated biphenyl
(c) O, p' - DDT
(d) All of the above

70. "Black Foot" disease in human beings is caused due to use of water contaminated with
(a) Mercury (b) Cadmium
(c) Silver (d) Arsenic

71. Largest amount of fresh water is present in
(a) Lakes (b) Rivers
(c) Glaciers (d) Polar Ice

72. A threatened species is
(a) only endangered species
(b) only vulnerable species
(c) only rare species
(d) All of the above

73. Given below are two statements, one labelled as Assertion (A) and the other labelled as Reason (R).
Assertion (A): Animals adopt various strategies to survive in hostile environment.
Reason (R): Praying mantis is green in color which emerges with plant foliage.
Choose the correct code:
Codcs:
(a) Both (A) and (R) are true, with (R) being the correct explanation of (A).
(b) Both (A) and (R) are true but (R) is not correct explanation of (A).
(c) (A) is true, but (R) is false.
(d) Both (A) and (R) are false.

74. Given below are two statements, one labelled as Assertion (A) and the other labelled as Reason (R).
Assertion (A): Increasing temperature in the environment influences gonadal growth in fish.
Reason (R): Increase in day length causes increase in environmental temperature in summer.
Choose the correct code:
Codes:
(a) Both (A) and (R) are true, and (R) is the correct explanation of (A).
(b) Both (A) and (R) are true, but (R) is not the correct explanation of (A).
(c) (A) is true, and (R) is wrong.
(d) (A) and (R) are wrong.

75. Match Column I with Column II:

Column I
A. The Rio Summit
B. Johannesburg Earth Summit
C. Kyoto Protocol
D. The Stockholm Conference

Column II

1. 1997 2. 1972
3. 1992 4. 2002

Codes:	A	B	C	D
(a)	3	4	1	2
(b)	1	2	3	4
(c)	4	3	2	1
(d)	2	1	4	3

ANSWERS

1. (d)	2. (a)	3. (b)	4. (a)	5. (c)
6. (a)	7. (c)	8. (d)	9. (d)	10. (b)
11. (c)	12. (b)	13. (c)	14. (c)	15. (d)
16. (d)	17. (b)	18. (b)	19. (c)	20. (d)
21. (c)	22. (c)	23. (a)	24. (b)	25. (c)
26. (d)	27. (a)	28. (b)	29. (c)	30. (a)
31. (a)	32. (a)	33. (a)	34. (a)	35. (a)
36. (b)	37. (b)	38. (d)	39. (d)	40. (a)
41. (c)	42. (d)	43. (b)	44. (d)	45. (a)
46. (d)	47. (a)	48. (b)	49. (c)	50. (b)
51. (b)	52. (c)	53. (a)	54. (c)	55. (c)
56. (c)	57. (a)	58. (a)	59. (d)	60. (d)
61. (a)	62. (d)	63. (a)	64. (c)	65. (d)
66. (c)	67. (c)	68. (c)	69. (d)	70. (d)
71. (d)	72. (d)	73. (c)	74. (a)	75. (a)

JUNE–2013

Note: This paper contains Sixty (60) multiple-choice questions, each question carrying two (2) marks. Candidate is expected to answer any Fifty (50) questions. In case more than Fifty (50) questions are attempted, only the first Fifty (50) questions will be evaluated.

PAPER–I

1. Which one of the following references is written as per Modern Language Association (MLA) format?
   (a) Hall, Donald. Fundamentals of Electronics, New Delhi: Prentice Hall of India, 2005
   (b) Hall, Donald, Fundamentals of Electronics. New Delhi: Prentice Hall of India, 2005
   (c) Hall, Donald, Fundamentals of Electronics, New Delhi: Prentice Hall of India, 2005
   (d) Hall, Donald. Fundamentals of Electronics. New Delhi: Prentice Hall of India, 2005

2. A workshop is
   (a) a conference for discussion on a topic.
   (b) a meeting for discussion on a topic.
   (c) a class at a college or a university in which a teacher and the students discuss a topic.
   (d) a brief intensive course for a small group emphasizing the development of a skill or technique for solving a specific problem.

3. A working hypothesis is
   (a) a proven hypothesis for an argument.
   (b) not required to be tested.
   (c) a provisionally accepted hypothesis for further research.
   (d) a scientific theory.

Read the following passage carefully and answer the questions (4 to 9):

The Taj Mahal has become one of the world's best known monuments. This domed white marble structure is situated on a high plinth at the southern end of a four-quartered garden, evoking the gardens of paradise, enclosed within walls measuring 305 by 549 metres. Outside the walls, in an area known as Mumtazabad, were living quarters for attendants, markets, serais and other structures built by local merchants and nobles. The tomb complex and the other imperial structures of Mumtazabad were maintained by the income of thirty villages given specifically for the tomb's support. The name Taj Mahal is unknown in Mughal chronicles, but it is used by contemporary Europeans in India, suggesting that this was the tomb's popular name. In contemporary texts, it is generally called simply the Illuminated Tomb (Rauza-i-Munavvara).

Mumtaz Mahal died shortly after delivering her fourteenth child in 1631. The Mughal court was then residing in Burhanpur. Her remains were temporarily buried by the griefstricken emperor in a spacious garden known as Zainabad on the bank of the river Tapti. Six months later her body was transported to Agra, where it was interred in land chosen for the mausoleum. This land, situated south of the Mughal city on the bank of the Jamuna, had belonged to the Kachhwaha rajas since the time of Raja Man Singh and was purchased from the then current raja, Jai Singh. Although contemporary chronicles indicate Jai Singh's willing cooperation in this exchange, extant *farmans* (imperial commands) indicate that the final price was not settled until almost two years after the mausoleum's commencement. Jai Singh's further cooperation was insured by imperial orders issued between 1632 and 1637 demanding that he provide stone masons and carts to transport marble from the mines at Makrana, within his "ancestral domain", to Agra where both the Taj Mahal and Shah Jahan's additions to the Agra fort were constructed concurrently.

Work on the mausoleum was commenced early in 1632. Inscriptional evidence indicates much of the tomb was completed by 1636. By 1643, when Shah Jahan most lavishly celebrated the 'Urs ceremony for Mumtaz Mahal', the entire complex was virtually complete.

4. Marble stone used for the construction of the Taj Mahal was brought from the ancestral domain of Raja Jai Singh. The name of the place where mines of marble is
   (a) Burhanpur (b) Makrana
   (c) Amber (d) Jaipur
5. The popular name Taj Mahal was given by
   (a) Shah Jahan
   (b) Tourists
   (c) Public
   (d) European travellers
6. Point out the true statement from the following:
   (a) Marble was not used for the construction of the Taj Mahal.
   (b) Red sand stone is non-visible in the Taj Mahal complex.
   (c) The Taj Mahal is surrounded by a four-quartered garden known as Chahr Bagh.
   (d) The Taj Mahal was constructed to celebrate the 'Urs ceremony for Mumtaz Mahal'.
7. In the contemporary texts the Taj Mahal is known
   (a) Mumtazabad
   (b) Mumtaz Mahal
   (c) Zainabad
   (d) Rauza-i-Munavvara
8. The construction of the Taj Mahal was completed between the period
   (a) 1632 – 1636 A.D.
   (b) 1630 – 1643 A.D.
   (c) 1632 – 1643 A.D.
   (d) 1636 – 1643 A.D.
9. The documents indicating the ownership of land, where the Taj Mahal was built, known as
   (a) Farman
   (b) Sale Deed
   (c) Sale-Purchase Deed
   (d) None of the above
10. In the process of communication, which one of the following is in the chronological order?
    (a) Communicator, Medium, Receiver, Effect, Message
    (b) Medium, Communicator, Message, Receiver, Effect
    (c) Communicator, Message, Medium, Receiver, Effect
    (d) Message, Communicator, Medium, Receiver, Effect
11. Bengal Gazette, the first Newspaper in India was started in 1780 by
    (a) Dr. Annie Besant
    (b) James Augustus Hicky
    (c) Lord Cripson
    (d) A.O. Hume

12. Press censorship in India was imposed during the tenure of the Prime Minister
(a) Rajeev Gandhi
(b) Narasimha Rao
(c) Indira Gandhi
(d) Deve Gowda

13. Communication via New media such as computers, teleshopping, internet and mobile telephony is termed as
(a) Entertainment
(b) Interactive communication
(c) Developmental communication
(d) Communitarian

14. Classroom communication of a teacher rests on the principle of
(a) Infotainment
(b) Edutainment
(c) Entertainment
(d) Enlightenment

15. _______ is important when a teacher communicates with his/her student.
(a) Sympathy (b) Empathy
(c) Apathy (d) Antipathy

16. In a certain code GALIB is represented by HBMJC. TIGER will be represented by
(a) UJHFS (b) UHJSF
(c) JHUSF (d) HUJSF

17. In a certain cricket tournament 45 matches were played. Each team played once against each of the other teams. The number of teams participated in the tournament is
(a) 8 (b) 10
(c) 12 (d) 14

18. The missing number in the series 40, 120, 60, 180, 90, ?, 135 is
(a) 110 (b) 270
(c) 105 (d) 210

19. The odd numbers from 1 to 45 which are exactly divisible by 3 are arranged in an ascending order. The number at 6th position is
(a) 18 (b) 24
(c) 33 (d) 36

20. The mean of four numbers a, b, c, d is 100. If c = 70, then the mean of the remaining numbers is
(a) 30 (b) $\frac{85}{2}$
(c) $\frac{170}{3}$ (d) 110

21. If the radius of a circle is increased by 50%, the perimeter of the circle will increase by
(a) 20% (b) 30%
(c) 40% (d) 50%

22. If the statement 'some men are honest' is false, which among the following statements will be true. Choose the correct code given below:
(i) All men are honest.
(ii) No men are honest.
(iii) Some men are not honest.
(iv) All men are dishonest.

Codes:
(a) (i), (ii) and (iii)
(b) (ii), (iii) and (iv)
(c) (i), (iii) and (iv)
(d) (ii), (i) and (iv)

23. Choose the proper alternative given in the codes to replace the question mark.
Bee – Honey, Cow – Milk, Teacher –?
(a) Intelligence (b) Marks
(c) Lessons (d) Wisdom

24. P is the father of R and S is the son of Q and T is the brother of P. If R is the sister of S, how is Q related to T?
(a) Wife
(b) Sister-in-law
(c) Brother-in-law
(d) Daughter-in-law

25. A definition put forward to resolve a dispute by influencing attitudes or stirring emotions is called
(a) Lexical (b) Persuasive
(c) Stipulative (d) Precisions

26. Which of the codes given below contains only the correct statements?
Statements:
(i) Venn diagram is a clear method of notation.
(ii) Venn diagram is the most direct method of testing the validity of categorical syllogisms.
(iii) In Venn diagram method the premises and the conclusion of a categorical syllogism is diagrammed.
(iv) In Venn diagram method the three overlapping circles are drawn for testing a categorical syllogism.

Codes:
(a) (i), (ii) and (iii)
(b) (i), (ii) and (iv)
(c) (ii), (iii) and (iv)
(d) (i), (iii) and (iv)

27. Inductive reasoning presupposes
(a) unity in human nature
(b) integrity in human nature
(c) uniformity in human nature
(d) harmony in human nature

Read the table below and based on this table answer questions from 28 to 33:

Area under Major Horticulture Crops
(in lakh hectares)

Year	Fruits	Vegetables	Flowers	Total Horti-culture Area
2005-06	53	72	1	187
2006-07	56	75	1	194
2007-08	58	78	2	202
2008-09	61	79	2	207
2009-10	63	79	2	209

28. Which of the following two years have recorded the highest rate of increase in area under the total horticulture?
(a) 2005-06 & 2006-07
(b) 2006-07 & 2008-09
(c) 2007-08 & 2008-09
(d) 2006-07 & 2007-08

29. Shares of the area under flowers, vegetables and fruits in the area under total horticulture are respectively:
(a) 1, 38 and 30 percent
(b) 30, 38 and 1 percent
(c) 38, 30 and 1 percent
(d) 35, 36 and 2 percent

30. Which of the following has recorded the highest rate of increase in area during 2005-06 to 2009-10?
(a) Fruits
(b) Vegetables
(c) Flowers
(d) Total horticulture

31. Find out the horticultural crop that has recorded an increase of area by around 10 percent from 2005-06 to 2009-10
(a) Fruits
(b) Vegetables
(c) Flowers
(d) Total horticulture

32. What has been the share of area under fruits, vegetables and flowers in the area under total horticulture in 2007-08?
(a) 53 percent (b) 68 percent
(c) 79 percent (d) 100 percent

33. In which year, area under fruits has recorded the highest rate of increase?
(a) 2006-07 (b) 2007-08
(c) 2008-09 (d) 2009-10

34. 'www' stands for
(a) work with web
(b) word wide web
(c) world wide web
(d) worth while web

35. A hard disk is divided into tracks which is further subdivided into
(a) Clusters (b) Sectors
(c) Vectors (d) Heads

36. A computer program that translates a program statement by statement into machine language is called a/an
(a) Compiler (b) Simulator
(c) Translator (d) Interpreter

37. A Gigabyte is equal to
(a) 1024 Megabytes
(b) 1024 Kilobytes
(c) 1024 Terabytes
(d) 1024 Bytes

38. A Compiler is a software which converts
(a) characters to bits
(b) high level language to machine language
(c) machine language to high level language
(d) words to bits

39. Virtual memory is
(a) an extremely large main memory.
(b) an extremely large secondary memory.
(c) an illusion of extremely large main memory.
(d) a type of memory used in super computers.

40. The phrase 'tragedy of commons' is in the context of
(a) tragic event related to damage caused by release of poisonous gases.
(b) tragic conditions of poor people.
(c) degradation of renewable free access resources.
(d) climate change.

41. Kyoto Protocol is related to
(a) Ozone depletion
(b) Hazardous waste
(c) Climate change
(d) Nuclear energy

42. Which of the following is a source of emissions leading to the eventual formation of surface ozone as a pollutant?
(a) Transport sector
(b) Refrigeration and Airconditioning
(c) Wetlands
(d) Fertilizers

43. The smog in cities in India mainly consists of
(a) Oxides of sulphur
(b) Oxides of nitrogen and unburnt hydrocarbons
(c) Carbon monoxide and SPM
(d) Oxides of sulphur and ozone

44. Which of the following types of natural hazards have the highest potential to cause damage to humans?
(a) Earthquakes
(b) Forest fires
(c) Volcanic eruptions
(d) Droughts and Floods

45. The percentage share of renewable energy sources in the power production in India is around
(a) 2-3% (b) 22-25%
(c) 10-12% (d) < 1%

46. In which of the following categories the enrolment of students in higher education in 2010-11 was beyond the percentage of seats reserved?
(a) OBC students
(b) SC students
(c) ST students
(d) Woman students

47. Which one of the following statements is not correct about the University Grants Commission (UGC)?

(a) It was established in 1956 by an Act of Parliament.
(b) It is tasked with promoting and coordinating higher education.
(c) It receives Plan and Non-Plan funds from the Central Government.
(d) It receives funds from State Governments in respect of State Universities.

48. Consider the statement which is followed by two arguments (I) and (II):
Statement: Should India switch over to a two party system?
Arguments: (I) Yes, it will lead to stability of Government.
(II) No, it will limit the choice of voters.
(a) Only argument (I) is strong.
(b) Only argument (II) is strong.
(c) Both the arguments are strong.
(d) Neither of the arguments is strong.

49. Consider the statement which is followed by two arguments (I) and (II):
Statement: Should persons with criminal background be banned from contesting elections?
Arguments: (I) Yes, it will decriminalise politics.
(II) No, it will encourage the ruling party to file frivolous cases against their political opponents.
(a) Only argument (I) is strong.
(b) Only argument (II) is strong.
(c) Both the arguments are strong.
(d) Neither of the arguments is strong.

50. Which of the following statement(s) is/are correct about a Judge of the Supreme Court of India?
1. A Judge of the Supreme Court is appointed by the President of India.
2. He holds office during the pleasure of the President.
3. He can be suspended, pending an inquiry.
4. He can be removed for proven misbehaviour or incapacity.

Select the correct answer from the codes given below:
Codes:
(a) 1, 2 and 3 (b) 1, 3 and 4
(c) 1 and 3 (d) 1 and 4

51. In the warrant of precedence, the Speaker of the Lok Sabha comes next only to
(a) The President
(b) The Vice-President
(c) The Prime Minister
(d) The Cabinet Ministers

52. The blackboard can be utilised best by a teacher for
(a) putting the matter of teaching in black and white
(b) making the students attentive
(c) writing the important and notable points
(d) highlighting the teacher himself

53. Nowadays the most effective mode of learning is
(a) self study
(b) face-to-face learning
(c) e-learning
(d) blended learning

54. At the primary school stage, most of the teachers should be women because they
(a) can teach children better than men.
(b) know basic content better than men.
(c) are available on lower salaries.
(d) can deal with children with love and affection.

55. Which one is the highest order of learning?
(a) Chain learning
(b) Problem-solving learning

(c) Stimulus-response learning
(d) Conditioned-reflex learning

56. A person can enjoy teaching as a profession when he
(a) has control over students.
(b) commands respect from students.
(c) is more qualified than his colleagues.
(d) is very close to higher authorities.

57. "A diagram speaks more than 1000 words." The statement means that the teacher should
(a) use diagrams in teaching.
(b) speak more and more in the class.
(c) use teaching aids in the class.
(d) not speak too much in the class.

58. A research paper
(a) is a compilation of information on a topic.
(b) contains original research as deemed by the author.
(c) contains peer-reviewed original research or evaluation of research conducted by others.
(d) can be published in more than one journal.

59. Which one of the following belongs to the category of good 'research ethics'?
(a) Publishing the same paper in two research journals without telling the editors.
(b) Conducting a review of the literature that acknowledges the contributions of other people in the relevant field or relevant prior work.
(c) Trimming outliers from a data set without discussing your reasons in a research paper.
(d) Including a colleague as an author on a research paper in return for a favour even though the colleague did not make a serious contribution to the paper.

60. Which of the following sampling methods is not based on probability?
(a) Simple Random Sampling
(b) Stratified Sampling
(c) Quota Sampling
(d) Cluster Sampling

ANSWERS

1. (d)	2. (d)	3. (c)	4. (b)	5. (d)
6. (c)	7. (d)	8. (c)	9. (a)	10. (c)
11. (b)	12. (c)	13. (b)	14. (b)	15. (b)
16. (a)	17. (b)	18. (b)	19. (c)	20. (d)
21. (d)	22. (b)	23. (d)	24. (b)	25. (b)
26. (b)	27. (c)	28. (d)	29. (a)	30. (c)
31. (b)	32. (b)	33. (a)	34. (c)	35. (b)
36. (d)	37. (a)	38. (b)	39. (c)	40. (c)
41. (c)	42. (a)	43. (b)	44. (d)	45. (c)
46. (a)	47. (d)	48. (c)	49. (a)	50. (d)
51. (c)	52. (c)	53. (d)	54. (d)	55. (d)
56. (b)	57. (c)	58. (c)	59. (b)	60. (c)

PAPER–II

Note: This paper contains fifty (50) objective type questions, each question carrying two (2) marks. All questions are compulsory.

1. **Assertion (A):** Every country should integrate the principles of sustainable development into its policies and programmes.
Reason (R): Environmental resources are a Nation's wealth.
Choose the correct code from the following:

(a) Both (A) and (R) are true and (R) is the correct explanation of (A).
(b) Both (A) and (R) are true, but (R) is not the correct explanation of (A).
(c) (A) is true, but (R) is false.
(d) (A) is false, but (R) is true.

2. Wind rose represents statistical distribution of
(a) Wind velocity in vector form
(b) Wind speeds in scalar form
(c) Wind speeds in π diagram
(d) Wind speeds in the form of histograms

3. In the redox reaction given below, which one of the sub-strates in forward reaction is oxidized?

$$2Fe^{3+} + H_2 \rightarrow 2Fe^{2+} + 2H^+$$

(a) Fe^{3+} (b) H_2
(c) H^+ (d) Fe^{2+}

4. If soil in a given area is wetted and allowed to drain till percolation is stopped, the amount of water thus retained is called
(a) Storage capacity
(b) Capillary capacity
(c) Hygroscopic capacity
(d) Field capacity

5. Quantity of 5M HCl required for preparing 1000 mL of 0.1 M HCl is,
(a) 20 mL (b) 2 mL
(c) 200 mL (d) 100 mL

6. The method which can be used for the softening of water having high calcium, high magnesium-carbonate hardness and some non-carbonate hardness
(a) single-stage lime process.
(b) excess lime process.
(c) single-stage lime-soda ash process.
(d) excess lime-soda ash process.

7. Spotted deer, Asiatic wild ass, Black buck are:
(a) Endangered species
(b) Vulnerable species
(c) Threatened species
(d) Key species

8. Specific mortality of members of a population is expressed by
(a) Life table
(b) Survivorship curve
(c) Rate of mortality
(d) Rate of fecundity

9. Which group of vertebrate comprises maximum number of endangered species?
(a) Fish (b) Amphibia
(c) Reptiles (d) Birds

10. Under anaerobic condition denitrifying *Pseudomonas* changes,
(a) Nitrate to molecular nitrogen
(b) Nitrate to ammonia
(c) Nitrate to Nitrite
(d) Nitrite to Nitrate

11. The Phenomenon of having higher number of species in ecotone is called
(a) Dominance effect (b) Edge effect
(c) Abundance (d) Frequency

12. Which specific common feature is not found in zooplankton and rabbit?
(a) Both are animals
(b) Both are primary consumers
(c) Both are carnivores
(d) Both are herbivores

13. The following exogenous and endogenous factors are the cause of extinction of animal species:
I. Ecological niche.
II. Decrease in reproductive potency.
III. Lesser adaptability to fluctuating environment.

Choose the correct answer from the codes given below:

Codes:
(a) I only (b) II only
(c) I and II (d) I, II and III

14. Positive mass balance of glaciers has been recently reported from
    (a) Eastern Himalayas
    (b) Nepal Himalayas
    (c) Western Himalayas
    (d) Karakoram

15. Which of the following will lead to reduction in greenhouse gases in atmosphere?
    (a) Increased chemical weathering of rocks
    (b) Volcanic eruption
    (c) Lowering of mean sea level
    (d) An increase in melting of glacial ice

16. The unconsolidated material with highest permeability is
    (a) Landslide with clayey component
    (b) Altered volcanic ash
    (c) Well-sorted alluvial sand
    (d) Buried mud flows

17. Which of the following component of cryosphere has the longest life?
    (a) Sea ice (b) Icebergs
    (c) Valley glaciers (d) Ice sheets

18. Aerobic bacteria is most active in
    (a) Moist and saturated soil
    (b) Moist and non-saturated soil
    (c) Alluvial soil
    (d) Permafrost

19. Andisols are formed by
    (a) Biological activity
    (b) Erosion by wind
    (c) Erosion by waves
    (d) Volcanoes

20. In case of photovoltaic cell, the maximum theoretical efficiency of conversion is
    (a) ~ 45% (b) ~ 30%
    (c) ~ 25% (d) ~ 50%

21. Consider an ideal wind power generator, if the wind speed increases 3 times, the power output would increase by how many times?
    (a) 3 (b) 9
    (c) 27 (d) 81

22. Identify the correct sequence in increasing order of total CO_2 emissions from various countries at present.
    (a) Britain < India < China < USA
    (b) India < Britain < China < USA
    (c) Britain < USA < India < China
    (d) Britain < India < USA < China

23. Arsenic compounds cause
    (a) Dwarfism
    (b) Dermatitis
    (c) Thyrotoxicosis
    (d) Wilson's disease

24. What is the pE value in an acid mine water sample having
    $[Fe^{2+}] = 7.03 \times 10^{-3}$ M and
    $[Fe^{3+}] = 3.71 \times 10^{-4}$ M
    (a) 10.5 (b) 12.5
    (c) 14.5 (d) 18.5

25. **Assertion (A):** Chronic exposure to ozone is a possible contributor to forest decline.
    Reason (R): Surface ozone is a greenhouse gas.
    Identify the correct code:
    (a) Both (A) and (R) are true and (R) is the correct explanation of (A).
    (b) Both (A) and (R) are true, but (R) is not the correct explanation of (A).
    (c) (A) is true, but (R) is false.
    (d) (A) is false, but (R) is true.

26. Identify the most dominant pollutant in terms of its concentration levels in urban atmosphere.
    (a) Oxides of nitrogen
    (b) Oxides of sulphur
    (c) Particulate matter
    (d) Carbon monoxide

27. The main constituents of photochemical smog are
    (a) Oxides of sulphur and CO
    (b) Oxides of sulphur and hydrocarbons

(c) Oxides of nitrogen and CO
(d) Oxides of nitrogen, hydrocarbons and ozone

28. The air borne fraction of carbon is
(a) ~ 0.72 (b) ~ 0.62
(c) ~ 0.46 (d) ~ 0.38

29. The noise index L_{eq} is used for noise standards in ambient environment of urban areas. The prescribed duration of the integration associated with L_{eq} is
(a) 12 hours (b) 8 hours
(c) 1 hour (d) 30 minutes

30. In alkaline soils, which of the following is not present in soluble state?
(a) Phosphorous (b) Calcium
(c) Nitrates (d) Potassium

31. Which one of the following is not a post-audit activity under environmental audit process?
(a) Review of draft report by Law department.
(b) Issue of final report to functional specialist.
(c) Develop action plan to establish responsibility.
(d) Report audit findings.

32. Which one of the following pairs is correctly matched?

(a) Specification for environmental management system	ISO 14001
(b) Environmental performance evaluation	ISO 14040
(c) Guidelines for environmental auditing	ISO 14000
(d) Environmental labels and declaration	ISO 14004

33. In accordance with the Indian EIA notification 2006, within how many days if Environmental Appraisal Committee do not specify the Terms of Reference, the proponent can go ahead with its own Terms of Reference?
(a) 15 days (b) 45 days
(c) 60 days (d) 90 days

34. Which is the correct sequence for impact assessment process in EIA?
(a) Description of Environment → Identification of impacts → Prediction of impacts → Evaluation of impacts → Identification of mitigation needs.
(b) Identification of impacts → Prediction of impacts → Evaluation of impacts → Identification of mitigation needs.
(c) Identification of impacts → Description of Environment → Prediction of impacts → Evaluation of impacts → Identification of mitigation needs.
(d) Prediction of impacts → Identification of impacts → Description of environment → Evaluation of impacts → Identification of mitigation needs.

35. Quantifying the energy and raw material requirement as a part of life cycle assessment, is termed as
(a) Life Cycle improvement analysis.
(b) Life Cycle impact analysis.
(c) Life Cycle inventory.
(d) Life Cycle pre-requisites.

36. Which of the following pertains to "high-waste approach" in dealing with the solid and hazardous wastes?
(a) Burying and burning
(b) Recycling
(c) Composting
(d) Reusing

37. **Assertion (A):** Dumping of sewage to river water may decrease oxygen even below 4 mg/L.
Reason (R): Dumping of sewage pollutes river water heavily.

Identify the correct answer:

(a) Both (A) and (R) are true with (R) being the correct explanation.
(b) Both (A) and (R) are true, but (R) is not the correct explanation.
(c) (A) is true, but (R) is wrong.
(d) Both (A) and (R) are wrong.

38. In most of the studies, a large sample size is anticipated to
(a) get a low level of precision.
(b) maximize the sampling error.
(c) get a high level of precision.
(d) maximize the standard deviation.

39. The geometric mean of 4, 8 and 16 is
(a) 9.3 (b) 8.0
(c) 4.8 (d) 10.2

40. The covariance between two data of N observations each represented by variables X and Y is given by

(a) $\frac{\Sigma(X-\overline{X})(Y-\overline{Y})}{N^2}$

(b) $\frac{\Sigma(X-\overline{X})^2(Y-\overline{Y})^2}{N}$

(c) $\frac{\Sigma(X-\overline{X})^2(Y-\overline{Y})^2}{N^2}$

(d) $\frac{\Sigma(X-\overline{X})(Y-\overline{Y})}{N}$

41. The mean and standard deviation of a Binomial distribution are 9 and 1, respectively. The first moment of the distribution is
(a) 9 (b) 3
(c) 1 (d) 0

42. Which one of the following is used in manufacturing flexible plastic bags and sheets?
(a) Polystyrene (PS)
(b) Polyethylene terephthalate (PET)
(c) Low density polyethylene (LDPE)
(d) TEFLON

43. Which one of the following is a non-formal environment education and awareness programme?
(a) Environmental appreciation courses.
(b) National Environment Awareness Campaign.
(c) Environmental Education in School System.
(d) Environmental Management Business Studies.

44. Bioparks are conceived, developed and managed with a goal of conservation of biodiversity through
(i) development of educational and scientific activities.
(ii) promoting silviculture and monoculture.
(iii) promoting local community welfare without harming the natural habitat.

Choose the correct answer from the codes:

Codes:
(a) (i) and (ii) (b) (ii) and (iii)
(c) (i) and (iii) (d) (i), (ii) and (iii)

45. In about a 7 metre deep pond the series of vegetation development will be
(a) Submerged → Floating → Reed → Herb
(b) Floating → Submerged → Reed → Herb
(c) Floating → Reed → Submerged → Herb
(d) Submerged → Reed → Floating → Herb

46. In terrestrial ecosystems, roughly how much NPP ends up being broken down by decomposers?
(a) 90% (b) 70%
(c) 50% (d) 10%

47. Which of the following BOD level waste water is permitted to be released inlands by industries under water (Prevention and Control of Pollution) Act, 1974?

(a) 30 mg/L (b) 80 mg/L
(c) 100 mg/L (d) 150 mg/L

48. Hydraulic conductivity is a function of
(a) medium alone
(b) fluid alone
(c) either fluid or medium
(d) both fluid and medium

49. Dachigam sanctuary is associated with
(a) Hangul (b) Rhinoceros
(c) Barking deer (d) Leopard

50. Rio + 20 summit was held in
(a) Durban (b) Johannesburg
(c) Rio de Janeiro (d) Cancun

ANSWERS

1. (b)	2. (a)	3. (b)	4. (d)	5. (a)
6. (d)	7. (b)	8. (b)	9. (d)	10. (a)
11. (b)	12. (c)	13. (d)	14. (d)	15. (a)
16. (c)	17. (d)	18. (b)	19. (d)	20. (a)
21. (c)	22. (d)	23. (b)	24. (c)	25. (b)
26. (d)	27. (d)	28. (c)	29. (b)	30. (a)
31. (d)	32. (a)	33. (c)	34. (a)	35. (c)
36. (a)	37. (a)	38. (c)	39. (b)	40. (a)
41. (d)	42. (c)	43. (b)	44. (c)	45. (a)
46. (a)	47. (a)	48. (d)	49. (a)	50. (c)

PAPER–III

Note: This paper contains seventy-five (75) objective type questions of two (2) marks each. All questions are compulsory.

1. Most of the day-to-day weather changes are associated with which scale in meteorology?
(a) Micro scale (b) Meso scale
(c) Synoptic scale (d) Planetary scale

2. Match the List I with List II and choose the correct answer from the codes given below:
List I (Date)
A. 5th June
B. 2nd December
C. 22nd May
D. 21st March
List II (Event)
(i) National Pollution Prevention Day
(ii) World Environment Day
(iii) World Forest Day
(iv) Bio-diversity Day

Codes:	A	B	C	D
(a)	(ii)	(i)	(iv)	(iii)
(b)	(iii)	(ii)	(iv)	(i)
(c)	(iv)	(iii)	(ii)	(i)
(d)	(i)	(iv)	(iii)	(ii)

3. 'Fanning' smoke stack plumes are observed when
(a) there is an inversion above the ground surface.
(b) there is unstable atmosphere.
(c) there is neutrally stable atmosphere.
(d) the stack height is below an inversion layer.

4. The cyclonic winds are generated by the approximate balance between
(a) Pressure gradient force and coriolis force.
(b) Centrifugal force and coriolis force.
(c) Centrifugal force, coriolis force and frictional drag force.
(d) Centrifugal force and pressure gradient force.

5. Mixing height is determined by
(a) adiabatic lapse rate and environmental lapse rate.
(b) vertical profile of wind speeds and adiabatic lapse rate.

(c) vertical profiles of wind speeds and ambient temperature.
(d) wind speeds and solar insolation.

6. United Nations has declared "UN Decade of Education for Sustainable Development" and the decade identified for this education is
(a) 2006 – 2015 (b) 2005 – 2014
(c) 2011 – 2020 (d) 2012 – 2021

7. Halon-1301 is a
(a) Fire extinguisher
(b) Solvent
(c) Refrigerant
(d) Aerosol propellant

8. Which of the following is a primary pollutant in atmospheric air?
(a) Cl_2 (b) SO_3
(c) Nitrates (d) Sulphates

9. Hardness is expressed on the Mohs scale, which ranges from
(a) 1 to 10 (b) 1 to 14
(c) –14 to 14 (d) 1 to 100

10. The halon H-1211 has the following chemical composition:
(a) CF_2 Cl Br (b) CCl_2 FBr
(c) CCl_2 F_2 (d) CBr_2 Cl F

11. The most toxic among the chlorinated hydrocarbons is
(a) Aldrin (b) DDT
(c) Endrin (d) Heptachlor

12. Agent orange is a
(a) Weedicide (b) Fungicide
(c) Nematicide (d) Rodenticide

13. Major source of SO_2 is
(a) Cement Industry
(b) Forest fires
(c) Thermal Power Stations
(d) Volcanic activity

14. Match each water contaminant in Column I with its preferred method of removal in Column II.

Column I
A. Mn^{2+}
B. Ca^{2+} and HCO_3^-
C. Trihalomethane
D. Mg^{2+}

Column II
(i) Activated Carbon
(ii) Raise pH by addition of Na_2CO_3
(iii) Addition of lime
(iv) Oxidation

Codes:	A	B	C	D
(a)	(iv)	(iii)	(i)	(ii)
(b)	(iii)	(ii)	(iv)	(i)
(c)	(ii)	(iv)	(iii)	(i)
(d)	(i)	(ii)	(iv)	(iii)

15. Reverse Osmosis (RO) operated at 200-1200 psig removes particles ranging from
(a) 0.0001 to 0.001 μm
(b) 0.01 to 10 μm
(c) 0.1 to 1.0 μm
(d) 0.1 to 2.0 μm

16. Coagulation is a chemical process, in which charged particles or colloids undergo
(a) Stabilization (b) Destabilization
(c) Attraction (d) Precipitation

17. Water has the following chemical composition:

$[Ca^{2+}]$ = 15 mg/L;

$[Mg^{2+}]$ = 10 mg/L;
$[SO_4^{2-}]$ = 30 mg/L;

The total hardness of water will be
(a) 80 mg/L as $CaCO_3$
(b) 55 mg/L as $CaCO_3$
(c) 160 mg/L as $CaCO_3$
(d) 40 mg/L as $CaCO_3$

18. Two water samples were collected.
Sample # 1 : pH = 9, but no carbonate or other dissolved proton donors or acceptors.

Sample # 2 : pH = 8.3, but it contains dissolved $NaHCO_3$ at a concentration of 0.01/mg/L

Which of the following is true based on the above observations?

(a) Sample # 1 will have more alkalinity.
(b) Sample # 2 will have more alkalinity.
(c) Sample # 1 and sample # 2 will have exactly same alkalinity.
(d) Alkalinity cannot be estimated.

19. Two soil samples, A and B, at different soil moisture levels are placed in contact with each other. Water will more likely move from soil A to soil B if their water potential, expressed in kPa, are:

(a) A = –5; B = +5
(b) A = –5; B = –5
(c) A = –20; B = –10
(d) A = –30; B = – 40

20. Blue baby syndrome is caused by

(a) Carbon monoxide
(b) Nitrate
(c) Fluoride
(d) Mercury

21. **Assertion (A):** For solar cell fabrication, those semiconducting materials which have band-gap energies in the range 1-1.8 eV are most suitable.

Reason (R): The maximum solar irradiance is around a wavelength corresponding to 1.5 eV.

Identify the correct code:

(a) Both (A) and (R) are correct and (R) is the correct explanation of (A).
(b) Both (A) and (R) are correct and (R) is not the correct explanation of (A).
(c) (A) is true, but (R) is false.
(d) (A) is false, but (R) is true.

22. **Assertion (A):** State factors (external factors) control the overall structure of an ecosystem and the way things work within it.

Reason (R): The state factors are not themselves influenced by the ecosystem.

Identify the correct code:

(a) (A) is correct (R) is incorrect.
(b) Both (A) and (R) are correct, but (R) is not correct explanation of (A).
(c) Both (A) and (R) are correct and (R) is correct explanation of (A).
(d) Both (A) and (R) are incorrect.

23. **Assertion (A):** When energy is transferred between trophic levels, the successive level in the pathway have lesser available energy compared to the preceding level.

Reason (R): Whenever energy is transformed, there is loss of energy through the release of heat.

(a) Both (A) and (R) are true and (R) is the correct explanation.
(b) Both (A) and (R) are true and (R) is not the correct explanation.
(c) (A) is true and (R) is false.
(d) (A) is false and (R) is true.

24. **Assertion (A):** The ecosystem surrounding a river gets damaged due to construction of a dam.

Reason (R): The area gets inundated with large volume of water.

Identify the correct answer:

(a) Both (A) and (R) are true, with (R) being the correct explanation.
(b) Both (A) and (R) are true, but (R) is not the correct explanation.
(c) (A) is true, but (R) is wrong.
(d) Both (A) and (R) are wrong.

25. **Assertion (A):** Soils rich in clay minerals have high levels of organic matter.

Reason (R): Clay soils tend to have low decomposition rates.

Identify the correct answer:

(a) Both statements are correct and (R) is correct explanation of (A).
(b) Both statements are correct, but (R) is not correct explanation of (A).

(c) Statement (A) is correct, but (R) is incorrect.
(d) Statement (A) is incorrect, but (R) is correct.

26. **Assertion (A):** Nitrogen cycle is an endogenic biogeochemical cycle.
Reason (R): Atmospheric N_2 can be fixed by certain prokaryotes in the soil.
Choose correct answer:
(a) Both (A) and (R) are true and (R) is the correct explanation of (A).
(b) Both (A) and (R) are true, but (R) is not the correct explanation of (A).
(c) (A) is true, but (R) is false.
(d) (A) is false, but (R) is true.

27. Match the following:
Column I
A. Nekton
B. Neuston
C. Benthos
D. Plankton
Column II
(i) Associated with surface film water.
(ii) Found at the bottom of an aquatic ecosystem.
(iii) Active swimmer, against water current.
(iv) Incapable of independent movement.

Choose the correct answer from the codes:

Codes:	A	B	C	D
(a)	(i)	(iii)	(iv)	(ii)
(b)	(ii)	(iv)	(i)	(iii)
(c)	(iii)	(i)	(ii)	(iv)
(d)	(iv)	(ii)	(iii)	(i)

28. Which of the following is not a major biome of India?
(a) Tropical rain forest biomes
(b) Tropical deciduous forest biomes
(c) Temperate needle leaf forest biomes
(d) Mountains and glaciers

29. To survive and avoid competition for the same resources, a species usually occupies only part of its fundamental niche in a particular community or ecosystem. This is called
(a) Geographic isolation
(b) Mutualism
(c) Realized Niche
(d) Broad Niche

30. Which of the following is not a characteristic feature of community?
(a) Populations of different species occupying a particular place.
(b) Complex interacting network of plants, animals and microbes.
(c) Different species interacting with one another and with their environment of matter and energy.
(d) Groups of interacting individuals of different species.

31. Which of the following food chains is correct?
(a) Krill → Adelie Penguins → Emperor Penguins → Leopard Seal
(b) Krill → Crabeater Seal → Leopard Seal → Killer Whale
(c) Krill → Leopard Seal → Emperor Penguins → Killer Whale
(d) Krill → Crabeater Seal → Killer Whale → Leopard Seal

32. The observation that individuals of a population are uniformly distributed suggests that
(a) density of population is low.
(b) resources are distributed unevenly.
(c) the members of the population are neither attracted to nor repelled by one another.
(d) the members of the population are competing for access to a resource.

33. Which of the following biomes is correctly paired with the description of its climate?

(a) Tropical forests – nearly constant day length and temperature
(b) Tundra – long summers, mild winters
(c) Savanna – cool temperature year-round, uniform precipitation during the year
(d) Temperate grasslands – relatively short growing season, mild winters

34. Cellulose and hemicellulose are not resistant to decay but are broken down more slowly. They are considered
(a) Labile
(b) Moderately labile
(c) Recalcitrant
(d) Non-labile

35. The parasitic gall formation is related to
(a) Host-specific antibodies
(b) Parasite specific cysts
(c) Parasite specific enzymes
(d) Host specific hormones

36. What is the estimate of volume of water yield for saturated pond aquifer of 1 metre width and 2 metre depth and length of 4 metre. Consider the porosity of sand to be 35% and specific yield to be 25%?
(a) 2.8 m^3 (b) 28 m^3
(c) 0.28 m^3 (d) 280 m^3

37. Arrange the following climate proxies in ascending order of time scales:
(i) Lithological records
(ii) Pollens
(iii) Tree rings
(iv) Historical records
(a) (iv), (iii), (i), (ii)
(b) (iv), (iii), (ii), (i)
(c) (iv), (ii), (i), (iii)
(d) (iv), (i), (iii), (ii)

38. Acid drainage is more in mining of
(a) Granite
(b) Bauxite
(c) Lime stone
(d) Base metal sulphide

39. Geothermal gradient in Earth is
(a) uniform throughout.
(b) higher in continental lithosphere.
(c) higher in subduction zones.
(d) lower at mid-oceanic ridges.

40. Coal mining areas are affected by
(i) Land subsidence
(ii) Fire hazard
(iii) Radioactive waste
(iv) Air pollution
(a) (i) and (ii)
(b) (i), (ii) and (iii)
(c) (i), (ii) and (iv)
(d) (i), (ii), (iii) and (iv)

41. Radioactive elements are concentrated in
(a) Earth's core
(b) Earth's mantle
(c) Mid-Oceanic ridges
(d) Earth's crust

42. What led to maximum number of fatalities during Indonesian 2004 Earthquake?
(a) Death on account of openings on surface
(b) Fires generated due to earthquake
(c) Epidemic diseases
(d) Tsunami

43. Maximum carbon in the world is found in
(a) Oceans (b) Coal mines
(c) Antarctica (d) Forests

44. The highest seismic domain in India is
(a) The Himalayas
(b) The Western ghats
(c) The Indogangetic plains
(d) The Dharwar craton

45. Earth's core is mainly composed of
(a) Iron (b) Nitrogen
(c) Carbon (d) Magnesium

46. Gasification is
(a) the high temperature (~ 750 – 850°C) conversion of solid, carbonaceous fuel into flammable gas mixtures.
(b) the high temperature (~ 750 – 850°C) conversion of solid, carbonaceous fuel into liquid.
(c) the low temperature (~ 250 – 350°C) conversion of solid, carbonaceous fuel into flammable gas mixture.
(d) the low temperature (~ 250 – 350°C) conversion of solid, carbonaceous fuel into liquid.

47. In case of magneto hydrodynamic power generation, for maximum power output, the efficiency is
(a) 0.25 (b) 0.5
(c) 0.75 (d) 0.4

48. Which combination of radiative fluxes plays the all important role in climate change?
(a) Visible and infrared
(b) Visible and UV
(c) Visible, UV and infrared
(d) UV, microwaves and infrared

49. The climate sensitivity parameter is defined as the rate of change of
(a) surface temperature with albedo of earth.
(b) surface temperature with CO_2 concentration in atmosphere.
(c) precipitation with earth's temperature.
(d) surface temperature with radiative forcing.

50. Which of the following fuels has highest carbon intensity?
(a) Natural gas (b) Oil
(c) Bituminous coal (d) Biomass

51. Solid waste treatment by pyrolysis involves
(a) Autoclaving
(b) Heating in presence of air
(c) Heating in presence of acetic acid
(d) Heating in absence of air

52. In which year Wildlife Protection Act was enacted?
(a) 1962 (b) 1972
(c) 1982 (d) 1992

53. According to National Ambient Air Quality Standards, the annual average concentration of Sulphur dioxide in residential areas in India is
(a) 20 $\mu g/m^3$ (b) 40 $\mu g/m^3$
(c) 60 $\mu g/m^3$ (d) 80 $\mu g/m^3$

54. Which of the following statements is correct in the context of Environmental Impact Assessment?
(a) The process considers broad range of potential alternatives.
(b) It provides early warning of cumulative effects.
(c) Focusses on sustainability agenda.
(d) Focusses on standard agenda.

55. Match the List I with List II and choose the correct answer from the codes given below:

List I (Components)
A. Equitable utilization of natural resources
B. Benefit to disadvantaged group
C. Creation of additional value
D. Elimination of toxic substances

List II (Dimensions)
(i) Social dimensions
(ii) Economic dimensions
(iii) Environmental dimensions
(iv) Political dimensions

Codes:	A	B	C	D
(a)	(iv)	(i)	(ii)	(iii)
(b)	(iv)	(i)	(iii)	(ii)
(c)	(iii)	(ii)	(i)	(iv)
(d)	(ii)	(iv)	(i)	(iii)

56. Among the following, which one does not belong to EIA process?
(a) Establishment of base line environmental condition.
(b) Identification, prediction and assessment of impact.
(c) Suggesting the mitigation measures.
(d) Developing EMS auditing procedures.

57. According to Gaussian Plume Model, the ground level concentration (C) of a pollutant varies with effective height (H) as (σ is the vertical dispersion coefficient):
(a) $C \propto \frac{1}{H}$ (b) $C \propto e^{-}\frac{H^2}{\sigma^2}$
(c) $C \propto e^{-}\frac{H}{\sigma}$ (d) $C \propto H^{-2}$

58. In a multiple regression analysis, an examination of variances revealed that explained sum of squares per degree of freedom and residual sum of squares per degree of freedom were 250 and 100, respectively. What is the F-ratio?
(a) 6.25 (b) 5.25
(c) 0.4 (d) 2.5

59. A source of air pollution is emitting a pollutant at the rate S(mg/hours) inside a room of volume V(m^3). The air of the room is being changed n times per hour. If k is pollutant decay rate constant, the concentration C(t) of the pollutant at any given instant of time under well-mixed conditions is given by
(a) $C(t) = \left(\frac{S}{nV}\right)(1 - e^{-nt})$
(b) $C(t) = \left(\frac{S/V}{n+k}\right)(1 - e^{-nt})$
(c) $C(t) = (S/nV)(n + k)$
(d) $C(t) = \left(\frac{nV}{S}\right)(1 - e^{-nk})$

60. Which one of the following is not an eigen value of the matrix?
$$\begin{bmatrix} -1 & 2 & 2 \\ 2 & 2 & 2 \\ -3 & -6 & -6 \end{bmatrix}$$
(a) 0 (b) –2
(c) –3 (d) 3

61. A sample of 17 measurements of the diameter of a spherical particle gave a mean = 5 μm and a standard deviation = 0.5 μm. Assuming t-statistic for 16 degrees of freedom $t_{0.05} \approx 2$, the 95% confidence limits of actual diameter are
(a) 4.75 and 5.25 μm.
(b) 4.00 and 6.00 μm.
(c) 4.9 and 5.1 μm.
(d) 4.5 and 5.5 μm.

62. "Hot spots" are areas
(i) extremely rich in species
(ii) with high endemism
(iii) extremely scarce in species
(iv) under constant threat
Choose the correct answer from the codes:
Codes:
(a) (i) and (ii)
(b) (ii) and (iii)
(c) (ii), (iii) and (iv)
(d) (i), (ii) and (iv)

63. A paddy field is an example of
(a) Fresh water ecosystem
(b) Terrestrial ecosystem
(c) Auto ecosystem
(d) Engineered ecosystem

64. Which pyramid cannot be inverted in a stable ecosystem?
(a) Pyramid of energy
(b) Pyramid of biomass
(c) Pyramid of number
(d) Pyramid of dry weight

65. Which one of the following environmental factors is responsible for cyclomorphism in animals?

(a) Moisture (b) Temperature
(c) Photoperiod (d) Wind

66. Sr^{90} can enter and accumulate in the body through
(a) Drinking water
(b) Inhaling contaminated air
(c) Food chain
(d) Skin

67. Which one of the following is a neurotoxic?
(a) Organophosphate
(b) Nitric oxide
(c) 2, 4-D
(d) Cuprous oxide

68. If 0.05 M proline-ninhydine complex has an absorbance of 0.15 at 520 nm in a 1 cm curvette, its molar extinction coefficient will be
(a) 50 m M^{-1} cm^{-1} (b) 0.1 M^{-1} cm^{-1}
(c) 1 M^{-1} cm^{-1} (d) 3 M^{-1} cm^{-1}

69. Which bacterium found in soil is anaerobic?
(a) *Clostridium Sp* (b) *Azatobacter Sp*
(c) *Bacillus Sp* (d) *Thiobacillus Sp*

70. Particles of sizes <1 μm are most efficiently removed by
(a) Cyclones
(b) Scrubbers
(c) Bag filter
(d) Electrostatic Precipitator

71. The attenuation of sound by reactive type silencers is based on
(a) absorption of sound waves
(b) scattering of sound waves
(c) impedance discontinuity
(d) interference of sound waves

72. "Farmer's lung" is a classic example for
(a) Psittacosis
(b) Extrinsic allergic alveolitis
(c) Legionnaire's disease
(d) Aspergillosis

73. The lichen and moss stages occur in
(a) Lithosere (b) Psamosere
(c) Hydrosere (d) Hydrarch

74. The mean of a data following Poisson distribution is 4. The second moment of the distribution is:
(a) 4 (b) 2
(c) 1 (d) 0

75. Which of the following rivers has maximum melt water component in its discharge?
(a) Indus (b) Ganges
(c) Brahmaputra (d) Narmada

ANSWERS

1. (c)	2. (a)	3. (a)	4. (d)	5. (a)
6. (b)	7. (a)	8. (a)	9. (a)	10. (a)
11. (c)	12. (a)	13. (d)	14. (a)	15. (a)
16. (b)	17. (a)	18. (b)	19. (d)	20. (b)
21. (a)	22. (b)	23. (b)	24. (b)	25. (a)
26. (d)	27. (c)	28. (d)	29. (c)	30. (c)
31. (b)	32. (d)	33. (a)	34. (b)	35. (c)
36. (a)	37. (b)	38. (c)	39. (b)	40. (c)
41. (d)	42. (d)	43. (a)	44. (a)	45. (a)
46. (a)	47. (b)	48. (a)	49. (d)	50. (c)
51. (d)	52. (b)	53. (c)	54. (d)	55. (a)
56. (d)	57. (b)	58. (d)	59. (a)	60. (d)
61. (a)	62. (d)	63. (d)	64. (a)	65. (b)
66. (c)	67. (a)	68. (d)	69. (a)	70. (d)
71. (c)	72. (b)	73. (a)	74. (a)	75. (a)

DECEMBER–2013

Note: This paper contains Sixty (60) multiple-choice questions, each question carrying two (2) marks. Candidate is expected to answer any Fifty (50) questions. In case more than Fifty (50) questions are attempted, only the first Fifty (50) questions will be evaluated.

PAPER–I

1. The post-industrial society is designated as
   (a) Information society
   (b) Technology society
   (c) Mediated society
   (d) Non-agricultural society

2. The initial efforts for internet based communication was for
   (a) Commercial communication
   (b) Military purposes
   (c) Personal interaction
   (d) Political campaigns

3. Internal communication within institutions is done through
   (a) LAN (b) WAN
   (c) EBB (d) MMS

4. Virtual reality provides
   (a) Sharp pictures
   (b) Individual audio
   (c) Participatory experience
   (d) Preview of new films

5. The first virtual university of India came up in
   (a) Andhra Pradesh
   (b) Maharashtra
   (c) Uttar Pradesh
   (d) Tamil Nadu

6. Arrange the following books in chronological order in which they appeared. Use the codes given below:
   (i) Limits to Growth
   (ii) Silent Spring
   (iii) Our Common Future
   (iv) Resourceful Earth
   Codes:
   (a) (i), (iii), (iv), (ii)
   (b) (ii), (iii), (i), (iv)
   (c) (ii), (i), (iii), (iv)
   (d) (i), (ii), (iii), (iv)

7. Which one of the following continents is at a greater risk of desertification?
   (a) Africa (b) Asia
   (c) South America (d) North America

8. "Women are closer to nature than men." What kind of perspective is this?
   (a) Realist (b) Essentialist
   (c) Feminist (d) Deep ecology

9. Which one of the following is not a matter a global concern in the removal of tropical forests?
   (a) Their ability to absorb the chemicals that contribute to depletion of ozone layer.
   (b) Their role in maintaining the oxygen and carbon balance of the earth.
   (c) Their ability to regulate surface and air temperatures, moisture content and reflectivity.
   (d) Their contribution to the biological diversity of the planet.

10. The most comprehensive approach to address the problems of man-environment interaction is one of the following:

(a) Natural Resource Conservation Approach
(b) Urban-industrial Growth Oriented Approach
(c) Rural-agricultural Growth Oriented Approach
(d) Watershed Development Approach

11. The major source of the pollutant gas, carbon mono-oxide (CO), in urban areas is
(a) Thermal power sector
(b) Transport sector
(c) Industrial sector
(d) Domestic sector

12. In a fuel cell driven vehicle, the energy is obtained from the combustion of
(a) Methane (b) Hydrogen
(c) LPG (d) CNG

13. Which one of the following Councils has been disbanded in 2013?
(a) Distance Education Council (DEC)
(b) National Council for Teacher Education (NCTE)
(c) National Council of Educational Research and Training (NCERT)
(d) National Assessment and Accreditation Council (NAAC)

14. Which of the following statements are correct about the National Assessment and Accreditation Council?
1. It is an autonomous institution.
2. It is tasked with the responsibility of assessing and accrediting institutions of higher education.
3. It is located in Delhi.
4. It has regional offices.

Select the correct answer from the codes given below:

Codes:
(a) 1 and 3 (b) 1 and 2
(c) 1, 2 and 4 (d) 2, 3 and 4

15. The power of the Supreme Court of India to decide disputes between two or more States falls under its
(a) Advisory Jurisdiction
(b) Appellate Jurisdiction
(c) Original Jurisdiction
(d) Writ Jurisdiction

16. Which of the following statements are correct?
1. There are seven Union Territories in India.
2. Two Union Territories have Legislative Assemblies.
3. One Union Territory has a High Court.
4. One Union Territory is the capital of two States.

Select the correct answer from the codes given below:

Codes:
(a) 1 and 3
(b) 2 and 4
(c) 2, 3 and 4 only
(d) 1, 2, 3 and 4

17. Which of the following statements are correct about the Central Information Commission?
1. The Central Information Commission is a statutory body.
2. The Chief Information Commissioner and other Information Commissioners are appointed by the President of India.
3. The Commission can impose a penalty upto a maximum of ₹ 25,000/-
4. It can punish an errant officer.

Select the correct answer from the codes given below:

Codes:
(a) 1 and 2 (b) 1, 2 and 4
(c) 1, 2 and 3 (d) 2, 3 and 4

18. Who among the following conducted the CNN-IBN-The Hindu 2013 Election Tracker Survey across 267 constituencies in 18 States?
   (a) The Centre for the Study of Developing Societies (CSDS)
   (b) The Association for Democratic Reforms (ADR)
   (c) CNN and IBN
   (d) CNN, IBN and The Hindu

19. In certain code TEACHER is written as VGCEJGT. The code of CHILDREN will be
   (a) EKNJFTGP (b) EJKNFTGP
   (c) KNJFGTP (d) None of these

20. A person has to buy both apples and mangoes. The cost of one apple is ₹ 7/- whereas that of a mango is ₹ 5/-. If the person has ₹ 38, the number of apples he can buy is
   (a) 1 (b) 2
   (c) 3 (d) 4

21. A man pointing to a lady said, "The son of her only brother is the brother of my wife". The lady is related to the man as
   (a) Mother's sister
   (b) Grandmother
   (c) Mother-in-law
   (d) Sister of father-in-law

22. In this series
   6, 4, 1, 2, 2, 8, 7, 4, 2, 1, 5, 3, 8, 6, 2, 2, 7, 1, 4, 1, 3, 5, 8, 6, how many pairs of successive numbers have a difference of 2 each?
   (a) 4 (b) 5
   (c) 6 (d) 8

23. The mean marks obtained by a class of 40 students is 65. The mean marks of half of the students is found to be 45. The mean marks of the remaining students is
   (a) 85 (b) 60
   (c) 70 (d) 65

24. Anil is twice as old as Sunita. Three years ago, he was three times as old as Sunita. The present age of Anil is
   (a) 6 years (b) 8 years
   (c) 12 years (d) 16 years

25. Which of the following is a social network?
   (a) amazon.com (b) eBay
   (c) gmail.com (d) Twitter

26. The population information is called parameter while the corresponding sample information is known as
   (a) Universe
   (b) Inference
   (c) Sampling design
   (d) Statistics

Read the following passage carefully and answer questions 27 to 32:

Heritage conservation practices improved worldwide after the International Centre for the Study of the Preservation and Restoration of Cultural Property (ICCROM) was established with UNESCO's assistance in 1959. The inter-governmental organisation with 126 member states has done a commendable job by training more than 4,000 professionals, providing practice standards, and sharing technical expertise. In this golden jubilee year, as we acknowledge its key role in global conservation, an assessment of international practices would be meaningful to the Indian conservation movement. Consistent investment, rigorous attention, and dedicated research and dissemination are some of the positive lessons to imbibe. Countries such as Italy have demonstrated that prioritising heritage with significant budget provision pays. On the other hand, India, which is no less endowed in terms of cultural capital, has a long way to go. Surveys indicate that in addition to the 6,600 protected monuments, there are over 60,000 equally valuable heritage structures that await attention. Besides the small group in the service of Archaeological Survey of India, there are only about 150 trained conservation professionals. In order to overcome this severe shortage the emphasis has been on setting up dedicated labs and training institutions. It would make much better sense for conservation to be made part of mainstream research and engineering institutes, as has been done in Europe.

Increasing funding and building institutions are the relatively easy part. The real challenge is to redefine international approaches to address local contexts. Conservation cannot limit itself to enhancing the art-historical value of the heritage structures, which international charters perhaps overemphasise. The effort has to be broad-based: It must also serve as a means to improving the quality of life in the area where the heritage structures are located. The first task therefore is to integrate conservation efforts with sound development plans that take care of people living in the heritage vicinity. Unlike in western countries, many traditional building crafts survive in India, and conservation practices offer an avenue to support them. This has been acknowledged by the Indian National Trust for Art and Cultural Heritage charter for conservation but is yet to receive substantial state support. More strength for heritage conservation can be mobilised by aligning it with the green building movement. Heritage structures are essentially eco-friendly and conservation could become a vital part of the sustainable building practices campaign in future.

27. The outlook for conservation heritage changed
    (a) after the establishment of the International Centre for the Study of the Preservation and Restoration of Cultural Property.
    (b) after training the specialists in the field.
    (c) after extending UNESCO's assistance to the educational institutions.
    (d) after ASI's measures to protect the monuments.

28. The inter-government organization was appreciated because of
    (a) increasing number of members to 126.
    (b) imparting training to professionals and sharing technical expertise.
    (c) consistent investment in conservation.
    (d) its proactive role in renovation and restoration.

29. Indian conservation movement will be successful if there would be
    (a) Financial support from the Government of India.
    (b) Non-governmental organisations role and participation in the conservation movement.
    (c) consistent investment, rigorous attention, and dedicated research and dissemination of awareness for conservation.
    (d) Archaeological Survey of India's meaningful assistance.

30. As per the surveys of historical monuments in India, there is very small number of protected monuments. As per given the total number of monuments and enlisted number of protected monuments, percentage comes to
    (a) 10 percent (b) 11 percent
    (c) 12 percent (d) 13 percent

31. What should India learn from Europe to conserve our cultural heritage?
    (i) There should be significant budget provision to conserve our cultural heritage.
    (ii) Establish dedicated labs and training institutions.
    (iii) Force the government to provide sufficient funds.
    (iv) Conservation should be made part of mainstream research and engineering institutes.

    Choose correct answer from the codes given below:

    Codes:
    (a) (i), (ii), (iii), (iv)
    (b) (i), (ii), (iv)
    (c) (i), (ii)
    (d) (i), (iii), (iv)

32. INTACH is known for its contribution for conservation of our cultural heritage. The full form of INTACH is
    (a) International Trust for Art and Cultural Heritage
    (b) Intra-national Trust for Art and Cultural Heritage
    (c) Integrated Trust for Art and Cultural Heritage
    (d) Indian National Trust for Art and Cultural Heritage

33. While delivering lecture if there is some disturbance in the class, a teacher should
    (a) keep quiet for a while and then continue.
    (b) punish those causing disturbance.
    (c) motivate to teach those causing disturbance.
    (d) not bother of what is happening in the class.

34. Effective teaching is a function of
    (a) Teacher's satisfaction.
    (b) Teacher's honesty and commitment.
    (c) Teacher's making students learn and understand.
    (d) Teacher's liking for professional excellence.

35. The most appropriate meaning of learning is
    (a) Acquisition of skills
    (b) Modification of behaviour
    (c) Personal adjustment
    (d) Inculcation of knowledge

36. Arrange the following teaching process in order:
    (i) Relate the present knowledge with previous one
    (ii) Evaluation
    (iii) Reteaching
    (iv) Formulating instructional objectives
    (v) Presentation of instructional materials

    Codes:
    (a) (i), (ii), (iii), (iv), (v)
    (b) (ii), (i), (iii), (iv), (v)
    (c) (v), (iv), (iii), (i), (ii)
    (d) (iv), (i), (v), (ii), (iii)

37. CIET stands for
    (a) Centre for Integrated Education and Technology
    (b) Central Institute for Engineering and Technology
    (c) Central Institute for Education Technology
    (d) Centre for Integrated Evaluation Techniques.

38. Teacher's role at higher education level is to
    (a) provide information to students.
    (b) promote self learning in students.
    (c) encourage healthy competition among students.
    (d) help students to solve their problems.

39. The Verstehen School of Understanding was popularised by
    (a) German Social Scientists
    (b) American Philosophers

(c) British Academicians
(d) Italian Political Analysts

40. The sequential operations in scientific research are
(a) Co-variation, Elimination of Spurious Relations, Generalisation, Theorisation
(b) Generalisation, Co-variation, Theorisation, Elimination of Spurious Relations
(c) Theorisation, Generalisation, Elimination of Spurious Relations, Co-variation
(d) Elimination of Spurious Relations, Theorisation, Generalisation, Co-variation.

41. In sampling, the lottery method is used for
(a) Interpretation
(b) Theorisation
(c) Conceptualisation
(d) Randomisation

42. Which is the main objective of research?
(a) To review the literature
(b) To summarize what is already known
(c) To get an academic degree
(d) To discover new facts or to make fresh interpretation of known facts

43. Sampling error decreases with the
(a) decrease in sample size
(b) increase in sample size
(c) process of randomization
(d) process of analysis

44. The principles of fundamental research are used in
(a) action research
(b) applied research
(c) philosophical research
(d) historical research

45. Users who use media for their own ends are identified as
(a) Passive audience
(b) Active audience
(c) Positive audience
(d) Negative audience

46. Classroom communication can be described as
(a) Exploration
(b) Institutionalisation
(c) Unsignified narration
(d) Discourse

47. Ideological codes shape our collective
(a) Productions (b) Perceptions
(c) Consumptions (d) Creations

48. In communication, myths have power, but are
(a) uncultural (b) insignificant
(c) imprecise (d) unpreferred

49. The first multi-lingual news agency of India was
(a) Samachar
(b) API
(c) Hindustan Samachar
(d) Samachar Bharati

50. Organisational communication can also be equated with
(a) intra-personal communication.
(b) inter-personal communication.
(c) group communication.
(d) mass communication.

51. If two propositions having the same subject and predicate terms are such that one is the denial of the other, the relationship between them is called
(a) Contradictory (b) Contrary
(c) Sub-contrary (d) Sub-alternation

52. Ananya and Krishna can speak and follow English. Bulbul can write and speak Hindi as Archana does. Archana talks with Ananya also in Bengali. Krishna cannot follow Bengali. Bulbul talks with Ananya in Hindi. Who can speak and follow English, Hindi and Bengali?

(a) Archana (b) Bulbul
(c) Ananya (d) Krishna

53. A stipulative definition may be said to be
(a) Always true
(b) Always false
(c) Sometimes true, sometimes false
(d) Neither true nor false

54. When the conclusion of an argument follows from its premise/premises conclusively, the argument is called
(a) Circular argument
(b) Inductive argument
(c) Deductive argument
(d) Analogical argument

55. Saturn and Mars are planets like the earth. They borrow light from the Sun and moves around the Sun as the Earth does. So those planets are inhabited by various orders of creatures as the earth is. What type of argument is contained in the above passage?
(a) Deductive (b) Astrological
(c) Analogical (d) Mathematical

56. Given below are two premises. Four conclusions are drawn from those two premises in four codes. Select the code that states the conclusion validly drawn.

Premises:
(i) All saints are religious. (major)
(ii) Some honest persons are saints. (minor)

Codes:
(a) All saints are honest.
(b) Some saints are honest.
(c) Some honest persons are religious.
(d) All religious persons are honest.

Following table provides details about the Foreign Tourist Arrivals (FTAs) in India from different regions of the world in different years. Study the table carefully and answer questions from 57 to 60 based on this table.

Region	**Number of Foreign Tourist Arrivals**		
	2007	2008	2009
Western Europe	1686083	1799525	1610086
North America	1007276	1027297	1024469
South Asia	982428	1051846	982633
South East Asia	303475	332925	348495
East Asia	352037	355230	318292
West Asia	171661	215542	201110
Total FTAs in India	5081504	5282603	5108579

57. Find out the region that contributed around 20 percent of the total foreign tourist arrivals in India in 2009.
(a) Western Europe
(b) North America
(c) South Asia
(d) South East Asia

58. Which of the following regions has recorded the highest negative growth rate of foreign tourist arrivals in India in 2009?
(a) Western Europe
(b) North America
(c) South Asia
(d) West Asia

59. Find out the region that has been showing declining trend in terms of share of foreign tourist arrivals in India in 2008 and 2009.
(a) Western Europe
(b) South East Asia
(c) East Asia
(d) West Asia

60. Identify the region that has shown hyper growth rate of foreign tourist arrivals than the growth rate of the total FTAs in India in 2008.
(a) Western Europe
(b) North America
(c) South Asia
(d) East Asia

ANSWERS

1. (a)	2. (b)	3. (a)	4. (c)	5. (d)
6. (c)	7. (a)	8. (b)	9. (a)	10. (d)
11. (b)	12. (b)	13. (a)	14. (b)	15. (c)
16. (d)	17. (c)	18. (a)	19. (b)	20. (d)
21. (d)	22. (c)	23. (a)	24. (c)	25. (d)
26. (d)	27. (a)	28. (b)	29. (c)	30. (b)
31. (b)	32. (d)	33. (c)	34. (c)	35. (b)
36. (d)	37. (c)	38. (b)	39. (a)	40. (a)
41. (d)	42. (d)	43. (b)	44. (b)	45. (b)
46. (d)	47. (b)	48. (c)	49. (c)	50. (c)
51. (a)	52. (c)	53. (d)	54. (c)	55. (c)
56. (c)	57. (b)	58. (d)	59. (a)	60. (c)

PAPER–II

Note: This paper contains fifty (50) objective type questions, each question carrying two (2) marks. All questions are compulsory.

1. Mesoscale Meteorological Phenomena occur over areas of horizontal distance in the range (km)
(a) 100 – 200 km (b) 1 – 100 km
(c) 10 – 50 km (d) 1 – 10 km

2. The Indian monsoon period is from
(a) October to November
(b) December to February
(c) June to September
(d) March to May

3. Which of the following is not a reactive oxygen species?
(a) Hydrogen peroxide
(b) Hydroxyl ion
(c) Singlet oxygen
(d) Superoxide anion

4. If air quality standard for carbon monoxide is 9.0 ppmV, the percentage as in mg/m^3 at 1 atm. at 25°C is
(a) 10.3 mg/m^3 (b) 15.2 mg/m^3
(c) 20.0 mg/m^3 (d) 5.6 mg/m^3

5. Azaridine, Ethylene dibromide, Bis (chloromethyl) ether are
(a) Alkylating agents
(b) Hydrocarbons
(c) Hydrazines
(d) Aromatic amines

6. Normality of 0.25 M phosphoric acid is
(a) 0.25 (b) 0.50
(c) 0.75 (d) 2.50

7. Match List I with List II and choose the correct answer from the codes given below:

List I (Air Pollutants)
A. Carbon monoxide
B. Nitrogen oxide
C. Sulphur dioxide
D. Ozone

List II (Sources/Activities)
(i) Coal burning
(ii) Cigarette Smoking
(iii) Chemical reaction with VOCs
(iv) Power and Industrial Plant

Codes:	A	B	C	D
(a)	(ii)	(iv)	(i)	(iii)
(b)	(i)	(ii)	(iii)	(iv)
(c)	(iii)	(i)	(iv)	(ii)
(d)	(iv)	(iii)	(ii)	(i)

8. The gaseous material which is used for the synthesis of Methyl isocyanate is

(a) Chloranil (b) Sevin
(c) Phosgene (d) Chlorine

9. During the determination of COD, sulphanilic acid is added, because
(a) it maintains the acidic nature
(b) it precipitates the mercury ions
(c) it oxidises nitrites to nitrates
(d) it reacts with ferrous ammonium sulphate

10. Which year was declared as International Year of Biodiversity?
(a) 2002 (b) 2010
(c) 2020 (d) 1972

11. The forest biome characterised by 3-4 tree species/km^2 is
(a) Tropical (b) Temperate
(c) Boreal (d) Taiga

12. Which of the following is a type of biodiversity extinction caused primarily due to anthropogenic activities?
(a) Carboniferous rain forest collapse
(b) Permian-Triassic extinction
(c) Cretaceous paleogene extinction
(d) Holocene extinction

13. The chemical used in a fermenter with molasses as a substrate is
(a) Diammonium sulphate
(b) Diammonium phosphate
(c) Diammonium nitrate
(d) Diammonium chloride

14. Which of the following is an example of lotic ecosystem?
(a) Stream ecosystem
(b) Pond ecosystem
(c) Bog ecosystem
(d) Wetland ecosystem

15. Which pyramid is always straight?
(a) Pyramid of biomass
(b) Pyramid of number
(c) Pyramid of energy
(d) Pyramid of number and biomass

16. Which of the following type of materials present in a landslide suggest that the movement was rotational?
(a) Rockflow, Debris flow, Earthflow
(b) Rock slump, Debris slump, Earth slump
(c) Rockfall, Debris fall, Earth fall
(d) Rock topple, Debris topple, Earth topple

17. Which of the following parameters is not a good indicator of contamination in ground water?
(a) BOD (b) Nitrates
(c) Silica (d) Chlorides

18. On an aerial photograph, the distance between the principal point and the conjugate principal point is called
(a) Relief (b) Tilt
(c) Photo-base (d) Focal length

19. An equatorial west to east remote sensing satellite orbiting the earth at an altitude of 36,000 km is called
(a) Sun-synchronous satellite
(b) Geostationary satellite
(c) Space shuttle
(d) Stereo imager

20. Which state of Cr (Chromium) is most toxic?
(a) Cr^{4+} (b) Cr^{3+}
(c) Cr^{5+} (d) Cr^{6+}

21. **Assertion (A):** Groundwater may get seriously contaminated in coastal areas.
Reason (R): Groundwater overdrafts near coastal areas can contaminate groundwater supplies by allowing salt water to intrude into freshwater aquifers.
Codes:
(a) Both (A) and (R) are true and (R) is the correct explanation of (A).
(b) Both (A) and (R) are true, but (R) is not the correct explanation of (A).

(c) (A) is true and (R) is false.
(d) (A) is false and (R) is true.

22. **Assertion (A):** Tropical and subtropical seas are most suitable for OTEC.
Reason (R): There is a certain minimum vertical gradient (> 25°C/km) required for OTEC to become feasible.
Codes:
(a) Both (A) and (R) are true and (R) is the correct explanation.
(b) Both (A) and (R) are true, but (R) is not the correct explanation.
(c) (A) is true, but (R) is false.
(d) (A) is false, but (R) is true.

23. On burning a certain amount of fuel a total of 500 million tonnes of CO_2 is released to the atmosphere. If the entire amount of CO_2 remains in the atmosphere, what will be the rise in the concentration of CO_2 in ppm?
(a) ~0.236 ppm (b) ~0.128 ppm
(c) ~2.312 ppm (d) ~1.216 ppm

24. A thermal power station has a heat rate of 12 mJ/kWh. Its thermal efficiency is
(a) 30% (b) 36%
(c) 40% (d) 25%

25. Assume that world coal production is 6.1 billion tons per year and estimated total recoverable resources of coal is 1.1 trillion tons. How long it would take to use up those reserves at current rate of production?
(a) ~180 years (b) ~150 years
(c) ~120 years (d) ~90 years

26. In a salt gradient solar pond, the salinity generally varies from top to bottom of the pond as
(a) < 5% to ~ 20%
(b) ~ 10% to ~ 30%
(c) ~ 20% to ~ 35%
(d) ~ 20% to ~ 40%

27. Which region among the following is not Atmospheric Brown Cloud (ABC) hotspot?
(a) East Asia
(b) South Africa
(c) Amazon Basin in South America
(d) Australia

28. Prolonged exposure to high levels of noise causes
(i) Hearing loss
(ii) Constriction of blood vessels
(iii) Gastric ulcers
(iv) Toxicity
Identify the correct answer:
(a) (i), (ii) and (iv) only
(b) (i), (iii) and (iv) only
(c) (i), (ii) and (iii) only
(d) (i), (ii), (iii) and (iv)

29. *Azolla pinnata* is a
(a) Blue green algae
(b) Green algae
(c) Red algae
(d) Fern

30. **Assertion (A):** Eruption of the volcano Mt. Pinatobu in 1991 spewed sulphur clouds into the upper reaches of the atmosphere. The following three years were cooler.
Reason (R): Sulphate aerosols reflect sunlight away from the Earth.
Codes:
(a) Both (A) and (R) are correct and (R) is correct explanation of (A).
(b) Both (A) and (R) are correct and (R) is not correct explanation of (A).
(c) (A) is correct (R) is incorrect.
(d) Both (A) and (R) are incorrect.

31. Photolysis of NO_2 occurs due to radiations of wavelength
(a) < 600 nm (b) < 550 nm
(c) < 480 nm (d) < 390 nm

32. The efficiency of removing SO_2 from the flue gas by limestone in wet scrubbers can be as high as
(a) 30% (b) 50%
(c) 70% (d) 90%

33. The depth of the oxidation ponds is typically
(a) 1 – 2 m (b) 2 – 5 m
(c) 5 – 10 m (d) 10 – 20 m

34. In EIA the baseline data describes
(a) The environmental consequences by mapping
(b) Existing environmental status of the identified study area
(c) Assessment of risk on the basis of proposal
(d) Demographic and socio-economic data

35. Which one of the following does not belong to EIA methods used for assessing the impacts of developmental activities on the environment?
(a) Checklist (b) Adhoc
(c) Network (d) Flexible

36. The EIA report of a hydropower project would be valid upto how many years after the environmental clearance of the project?
(a) 5 years (b) 6 years
(c) 30 years (d) 10 years

37. If in the screening stage of EIA, the impact level of a developmental project is not discernible, then what step should be adopted?
(a) Scoping stage is to be followed.
(b) A rapid EIA study is to be conducted.
(c) Detail EIA study is to be conducted.
(d) The project should be given Environmental Clearance.

38. The Committee which reviews the Environmental Impact Assessment and Environmental Management plan reports of a developmental project in Ministry of Environment and Forest is called
(a) Project Assessment Committee
(b) Project Appraisal Committee
(c) Project Evaluation Committee
(d) Project Estimate Committee

39. In a typical municipal solid waste, least percentage of Ash is found in
(a) Textiles (b) Plastic
(c) Leather (d) Rubber

40. Highly inflammable liquid/chemicals have flash point
(a) lower than 23°C
(b) between 23 and 26°C
(c) between 27 and 31°C
(d) between 32 and 40°C

41. Which one of the following does not contribute to climate change?
(a) NO (b) O_3
(c) SF_6 (d) HFCs

42. A population (X) in an ecosystem follows logistic growth curve. If the carrying capacity of the system is K, the growth realisation factor is
(a) $\frac{K-X}{X}$ (b) $\frac{K-X}{K}$
(c) $\frac{K-X}{K^2}$ (d) $(K - X)$

43. Which one of the following conditions would indicate that the dataset is not bell shaped?
(a) The mean is much smaller than median.
(b) The range is equal to five times the standard deviation.
(c) The range is larger than interquartile range.
(d) The range is twice the standard deviation.

44. For degrees of freedom (df) > 1, the mean (μ) of the t-distribution is
(a) zero (b) 1
(c) depends on df (d) 2

45. Which of the following is an eigen value of the matrix $\begin{bmatrix} 3 & -1 \\ 4 & -2 \end{bmatrix}$?
(a) 2 (b) 0
(c) 1 (d) 3

46. Suppose a 70 kg person drinks 2L of water everyday for 70 years with a chloroform concentration of 0.10 mg/L (the drinking water standard), upper bound cancer risk for these individual will be
(a) 17 in 1 million (b) 25 in 1 million
(c) 37 in 1 million (d) 5 in 1 million

47. What is Ecomark?
(a) Label given to recycled products
(b) Label given to an environment friendly products
(c) Land mark indicating the boundaries of bioparks
(d) Label given to non-recyclable products

48. An important source of Arsenic in Municipal Solid Water (MSW) is
(a) Pigments in plastics
(b) Rubber products
(c) Batteries
(d) Household pesticides

49. Which of the following is not a non-formal Environment Education and Awareness Programme?
(a) Global Learning and Observations to Benefit the Environment (GLOBE)
(b) National Environment Awareness Campaign (NEAC)
(c) Eco-clubs
(d) Environmental Education in School System

50. REDD stands for
(a) Recurring Emission from Deforestation and Forest Degradation
(b) Reducing Environmental Degradation and Forest Degradation
(c) Reducing Emissions from Deforestation and Forest Degradation
(d) Reducing Emissions from Degradable Deposits of Wastes

ANSWERS

1. (b)	2. (c)	3. (b)	4. (a)	5. (a)
6. (c)	7. (a)	8. (c)	9. (c)	10. (b)
11. (b)	12. (d)	13. (b)	14. (a)	15. (c)
16. (b)	17. (c)	18. (c)	19. (b)	20. (d)
21. (a)	22. (a)	23. (a)	24. (a)	25. (a)
26. (a)	27. (d)	28. (c)	29. (d)	30. (a)
31. (d)	32. (d)	33. (a)	34. (b)	35. (d)
36. (d)	37. (b)	38. (b)	39. (a)	40. (a)
41. (a)	42. (b)	43. (a)	44. (a)	45. (a)
46. (a)	47. (b)	48. (d)	49. (d)	50. (c)

PAPER–III

Note: This paper contains seventy-five (75) objective type questions of two (2) marks each. All questions are compulsory.

1. For an overcast day or night, the atmosphere is
(a) stable (b) neutral
(c) slightly stable (d) unstable

2. **Assertion (A):** The energy flow in an ecosystem follows the law of thermodynamics.
Reason (R): The energy flow in an ecosystem is unidirectional and during the transformation of energy from one

trophic level to the other, 80-90% of energy is lost.

Codes:

(a) Both (A) and (R) are true and (R) is the correct explanation of (A).
(b) Both (A) and (R) are true, but (R) is not the correct explanation of (A).
(c) (A) is true, but (R) is false.
(d) (A) is false, but (R) is true.

3. Match the List I with List II and identify the correct answer from the given codes:

List I (Thermodynamic Variables)
(Symbols have their usual meanings.)

(A) ΔG (B) $\Delta G°$
(C) ΔS (D) ΔH

List II (Expression)

(i) $\Delta E + P\Delta V$ (ii) $- n FE°$
(iii) $RT\, ln\frac{V_1}{V_2}$ (iv) $nR\, ln\frac{V_2}{V_1}$

Codes:	A	B	C	D
(a)	(ii)	(iv)	(i)	(iii)
(b)	(iii)	(ii)	(iv)	(i)
(c)	(iii)	(i)	(iv)	(ii)
(d)	(ii)	(iii)	(iv)	(i)

4. The environmental lapse rate during day time is governed by
(i) Wind speed
(ii) Sunlight
(iii) Topographical features
(iv) Cloud cover
The correct answer is
(a) (i) and (ii) only
(b) (ii) and (iii) only
(c) (i), (ii) and (iii) only
(d) (i) and (iv) only

5. The wavelength range of UV–C radiations is
(a) 200 – 280 nm (b) 180 – 240 nm
(c) 320 – 400 nm (d) 240 – 300 nm

6. In a gas chromatography experiment, the retention factor (R_f) values for pollutant 'A' and pollutant 'B' in a mixture of pollutants were 0.5 and 0.125, respectively. If the distance travelled by solvent front is 12 cms, the distance (in cms) travelled by pollutant 'A' and pollutant 'B' will be
(a) 6 and 1.5 (b) 3 and 1.5
(c) 0.5 and 0.125 (d) 1.5 and 3

7. Using the following equations, which can be determined correctly?

$$Ca(HCO_3)_2 \xrightarrow{\Delta} CaCO_3 + H_2O + CO_2$$
(by heating)

or $Ca(HCO_3)_2 + Ca(OH)_2 \longrightarrow$
$2CaCO_3 + 2H_2O$ (by addition of lime)

(a) Carbon dioxide
(b) Carbonates
(c) Bicarbonates
(d) Carbonates and Bicarbonates

8. Assume that a river having dissolved oxygen 0.5 g/m^3, BOD 0.3 g/m^3 flowing at 80 m^3/sec. converge with another river having Dissolved Oxygen 0.7 g/m^3. BOD 0.6 g/m^3 flowing at a rate of 60 m^3/sec. If after the confluence the Dissolved Oxygen is 0.59 g/m^3, then the BOD is
(a) 0.83 g/m^3 (b) 0.43 g/m^3
(c) 0.73 g/m^3 (d) 0.92 g/m^3

9. Cells grown in a medium containing phosphorous –32 will show radio labelling in
(a) Starch (b) Glycogen
(c) Proteins (d) Nucleic acids

10. C^{14} has a half-life of 5700 years. The fraction of the C^{14} atoms that decays per year is
(a) 1.216×10^{-4} (b) 0.52×10^{-3}
(c) 0.78×10^{-4} (d) 2.81×10^{-4}

11. **Assertion (A):** Marine biodiversity tends to be highest in midlatitudes in all oceans and along coasts in the Western Pacific.

Reason (R): Sea surface temperature along coasts in the Western Pacific is highest.

Codes:

(a) Both (A) and (R) are true and (R) is the correct explanation of (A).
(b) Both (A) and (R) are true, but (R) is not the correct explanation of (A).
(c) (A) is true, but (R) is false.
(d) (A) is false, but (R) is true.

12. "Double digging" is a method of
(a) Bio-intensive agriculture
(b) Deforestation
(c) Aforestation
(d) Water conservation

13. The rate of replacement of species along a gradient of habitats pertains to
(a) Alpha diversity
(b) Beta diversity
(c) Gamma diversity
(d) Species diversity

14. Match the List I and List II. Choose the correct answer from the given codes:

List I (Vegetation development)
(A) On a rock
(B) On sand
(C) In aquatic habitat
(D) In dry habitat

List II (Nomenclature of succession)
(i) Psammosere (ii) Lithosere
(iii) Xerosere (iv) Hydrosere

Codes:	A	B	C	D
(a)	(ii)	(i)	(iv)	(iii)
(b)	(i)	(ii)	(iii)	(iv)
(c)	(iii)	(iv)	(ii)	(i)
(d)	(iv)	(iii)	(i)	(ii)

15. If individuals of a species remain alive only in captivity or other human controlled conditions, the species is said to be
(a) Ecologically extinct
(b) Mass extinct
(c) Wild extinct
(d) Anthropogenic extinct

16. Which of the following symbolises correct sequence in hydrosere?
(a) Diatoms → Wolffia → Hydrilla → Cyperus → Populus
(b) Hydrilla → Wolffia → Cyperus → Populus → Diatoms
(c) Cyperus → Diatoms → Hydrilla → Wolffia → Populus
(d) Diatoms → Hydrilla → Wolffia → Cyperus → Populus

17. Which of the following is not a class of aquatic ecosystems based on salinity levels?
(a) Stagnant water ecosystem
(b) Freshwater ecosystem
(c) Brackish ecosystem
(d) Marine ecosystem

18. The K-strategists are
(i) large organisms which have relatively longer life
(ii) provide care for their offsprings
(iii) organisms that stabilise their population at carrying capacity for the area

Choose the correct answer:
(a) (i) and (ii) only
(b) (i) and (iii) only
(c) (ii) and (iii) only
(d) (i), (ii) and (iii)

19. Limnetic zone in freshwater ecosystem is characterised by
(a) Presence of rooted vegetation
(b) Absence of rooted vegetation
(c) Presence of large proportion of lime
(d) Absence of phytoplankton

20. Match the List I with List II, choose the correct answer from the given codes:

List I (Plants)
(A) *Camellia caduca*
(B) *Picea brachytyla*

(C) *Colchicum luteum*
(D) *Arachnantha clarkei*

List II (Family)
(i) Orchidaceae (ii) Theaceae
(iii) Pinaceae (iv) Liliaceae

Codes:	A	B	C	D
(a)	(iv)	(ii)	(iii)	(i)
(b)	(i)	(ii)	(iii)	(iv)
(c)	(ii)	(i)	(iv)	(iii)
(d)	(ii)	(iii)	(iv)	(i)

21. Vegetation cover shows maximum reflectance in which of the following regions of the electromagnetic radiation spectrum?
(a) Ultraviolet (b) Near infrared
(c) Middle infrared (d) Visible

22. During remote sensing of the vegetation cover, the spectral reflection of vegetation over electromagnetic radiation spectrum depends upon
(a) Pigmentation in the leaf
(b) Structure of the leaf
(c) Moisture content of the leaf
(d) All the above characters

23. Given below are statements in the context of biogeochemical cycles:
(i) Ecosystems are black boxes for many of the processes that take place within them.
(ii) Ecosystem boundaries are permeable to some degree or other.
(iii) The energy and nutrients can be transferred to and from one ecosystem to another via imports and exports.
Identify the correct answer from the codes given below:
(a) (i) and (ii) only
(b) (ii) and (iii) only
(c) (i) and (iii) only
(d) (i), (ii) and (iii)

24. The volume of ejecta and the column height for a volcano are $10^{8.5}$ m^3 and 24 km, respectively. What is its volcanic explosivity index value?
(a) 2 (b) 8
(c) 7 (d) 4

25. In the context of material balance in hydrological cycle, which of the following equations is correct for oceans?
(a) Input + change in storage = output
(b) Precipitation + inflow = evaporation
(c) Input – change in storage = output
(d) Precipitation – inflow = evaporation

26. In disaster management which steps are followed in post-disaster recovery phase?
(a) Relief, rehabilitation, reconstruction, learning–review.
(b) Risk Assessment, mitigation, preparedness, emergency plans.
(c) Relief, mitigation, emergency plans.
(d) Learning–review, emergency plans, preparedness.

27. Permafrost represents
(a) permanently frozen subsurface soil
(b) frozen leaves of Oak trees
(c) frozen needles of pine trees
(d) temporarily frozen subsurface soil

28. **Assertion (A):** Estuaries are productive ecosystems.
Reason (R): Large amounts of nutrients are introduced into the basin from the rivers that run into them.
Choose the correct answer:
(a) Both (A) and (R) are true, and (R) is the correct explanation of (A).
(b) Both (A) and (R) are true, but (R) is not the correct explanation of (A).
(c) (A) is true and (R) is false.
(d) (A) is false and (R) is true.

29. A confined aquifer of thickness 25 m has two wells 200 m apart along the direction of flow of water. The difference in their hydraulic heads is 1 m. If hydraulic conductivity is 50 m/day, the rate of flow

of water per day per metre of distance perpendicular to the flow of water is
(a) 25 m^3/day per metre
(b) 50 m^3/day per metre
(c) 5 m^3/day per metre
(d) 1 m^3/day per metre

30. Which of the following material has the highest hydraulic conductivity?
(a) Clay (b) Sandstone
(c) Limestone (d) Quartzite

31. Which of the following energy sources is not renewable on human time scale?
(a) Solar (b) Hydrothermal
(c) Geothermal (d) Biomass

32. For a solar flat plate collector the following data is given: Useful heat gain = 28 watts/m^2 per hour, solar radiation intensity = 350 watts/m^2 per hour and the factor to convert beam radiation to that on the plane of the collector = 1.2. The collector efficiency is
(a) ~ 6.6 % (b) ~ 4.8 %
(c) ~ 12.2 % (d) ~ 15.2 %

33. For the reaction in a hydrogenoxygen fuel cell,

$$H_2 + \frac{1}{2}O_2 = H_2O\ (l)$$

Given $\Delta G°$ = 240 kJ/gm – mole of H_2 and Faraday's constant = 96,500 Coulomb/gm mole.

The developed voltage in the fuel cell will be
(a) ~ 1.13 Volts (b) ~ 2.13 Volts
(c) ~ 1.51 Volts (d) ~ 1.24 Volts

34. Identify the correct sequence of the fuels in order of their increasing carbon intensity:
(a) Natural gas < Oil < Bituminous coal < Nuclear
(b) Oil < Coal < Natural gas < Nuclear
(c) Nuclear < Coal < Natural gas < Oil
(d) Nuclear < Natural gas < Oil < Bituminous coal

35. In nuclear thermal reactors, which of the following is not used as moderator?
(a) Normal water (b) Heavy water
(c) Graphite (d) Liquid Helium

36. The minimum temperature gradient (°C/km) required for OTEC is about
(a) 20 (b) 10
(c) 40 (d) 60

37. A solar pond has electricity generating capacity of 600 MWe. If the efficiency of solar energy to electric generation process was 2% and solar energy supply rate was 300 W/m^2, what is the area of solar pond?
(a) 100 km^2 (b) 90 km^2
(c) 60 km^2 (d) 180 km^2

38. Which of the following causes warming of atmosphere but cooling of the earth's surface?
(a) Ozone
(b) Black carbon aerosols
(c) All Greenhouse gases
(d) Sulphates and nitrates

39. **Assertion (A):** For noise level surveys in urban areas, weighting A is used for measurements.
Reason (R): Weighting A filters out unwanted signals.
Codes:
(a) Both (A) and (R) are true and (R) is the correct explanation of (A).
(b) Both (A) and (R) are true, but (R) is not the correct explanation of (A).
(c) (A) is true, but (R) is false.
(d) Both (A) and (R) are false.

40. Noise levels of 80 dB refers to a sound pressure level of

(a) 0.2 Pa (b) 0.02 Pa
(c) 20 Pa (d) 200 Pa

41. Asphyxiation is caused by
(a) HCN, $COCl_2$ (b) NO_X
(c) $CHCl_3$ (d) AsH_3

42. Sequence of a typical sewage treatment plant operation process will be
(a) Aeration → Flocculation → Sedimentation → Recarbonation → Filtration → Disinfection
(b) Aeration → Sedimentation → Flocculation → Filtration → Recarbonation → Disinfection
(c) Flocculation → Aeration → Recarbonation → Sedimentation → Filtration → Disinfection
(d) Sedimentation → Flocculation → Aeration → Filtration → Recarbonation → Disinfection

43. Which one of the following isotopes has maximum half-life period?
(a) Rn^{222} (b) Pb^{210}
(c) Ti^{210} (d) Bi^{210}

44. Match the List I with List II and identify the correct answer from given codes:
List I (Aerosols)
(A) Dust
(B) Mist
(C) Smoke
(D) Atmospheric Brown Cloud

List II (Constituents)
(i) Small gas borne particles resulting from combustion
(ii) Black carbon
(iii) Suspended small liquid droplets
(iv) Solid suspended particles

Codes:	A	B	C	D
(a)	(iv)	(iii)	(ii)	(i)
(b)	(iii)	(iv)	(i)	(ii)
(c)	(ii)	(i)	(iii)	(iv)
(d)	(i)	(ii)	(iii)	(iv)

45. **Assertion (A):** Chloroflurocarbons deplete ozone.
Reason (R): These compounds contain chlorine, bromine and fluorine.
Codes:
(a) Both (A) and (R) are true and (R) is the correct explanation of (A).
(b) Both (A) and (R) are true, but (R) is not the correct explanation of (A).
(c) (A) is true, but (R) is false.
(d) (A) is false, but (R) is true.

46. Which of the following organic compounds is not of biogenic origin?
(a) Isoprene (b) α-pinene
(c) Myrcene (d) Acrolein

47. Which of the following is used as plant indicator for detection of presence of SO_2 and HF in air?
(a) Lichen (b) Orchid
(c) Apricot (d) Tobacco

48. Integrated Gasification Combined Cycle (IGCC) technology is best at removing
(a) NO_2 and CO
(b) CO and SO_2
(c) Particulates and sulphur
(d) NO_2 and SO_2

49. A wastewater treatment plant in a city treats 50,000 m^3 wastewater generated per day. For an average flow rate of 25 m^3 per day per sq. metre, what should be the diameter of the circular primary settling tank?
(a) 50.4 m (b) 30.6 m
(c) 20 m (d) 25.8 m

50. An Electrostatic Precipitator (ESP) with collector plate area = 5000 m^2 treats a flue gas with drift velocity = 0.12 m/s with 98% efficiency. The volumetric flow rate (m^3/s) of the flue gas is
(a) ~ 175.2 (b) ~ 213.5
(c) ~ 153.4 (d) ~ 198.9

51. **Assertion (A):** Urban heat islands contribute to build up of pollutants in cities.
Reason (R): Urban heat islands produce a somewhat stable air mass in the city's atmosphere.
Codes:
(a) Both (A) and (R) are correct and (R) is the correct explanation of (A).
(b) Both (A) and (R) are correct, but (R) is not the correct explanation of (A).
(c) (A) is true, but (R) is false.
(d) Both (A) and (R) are false.

52. Match List I with List II and choose the correct answer from the codes given below:
List I (Analytical functions)
(A) Defining scope of EIA
(B) Identification of impacts
(C) Prediction of Impacts
(D) Impact Evaluation and Analysis
List II (Activity under the function)
(i) Critical Assessment of impacts
(ii) Estimation of the probability that a particular impact will occur
(iii) Description of the existing environment system
(iv) Deciding important issues and concerns

Codes:	A	B	C	D
(a)	(iii)	(iv)	(i)	(ii)
(b)	(iv)	(iii)	(ii)	(i)
(c)	(ii)	(i)	(iii)	(iv)
(d)	(i)	(ii)	(iv)	(iii)

53. A drawback of checklists is
(a) Preliminary analysis is available in scaling checklist
(b) Checklists are too general or incomplete
(c) Checklists summarises information to make it available to experts
(d) Ecosystem functions can be clearly understood from weighting methods

54. If EIU_j = environmental impact units for j^{th} alternative, EQ_{ij} = environmental – quality – scale value for i^{th} factor and j^{th} alternative, PIU_i = parameter importance units for i^{th} factor, then what is the correct formulation for the index expressed in environmental impact units (EIU_i)?
(a) $EIU_i = \sum_{i=1}^{n}\left(\frac{E}{Q_{ij}}\right)PIU_i$
(b) $EIU_i = \sum_{i=1}^{n}\left(\frac{Q_{ij}}{E}\right)PIU_i$
(c) $EIU_i = \sum_{i=1}^{n} EQ_{ij}\, PIU_i$
(d) $EIU_i = \sum_{i=1}^{n} \frac{PIU_i}{EQ_{ij}}$

55. Match List I with List II and choose the correct answer from the codes given below:
List I (Scales used in EIA methods)
(A) Nominal (B) Ordinal
(C) Interval (D) Ratio
List II (Example)
(i) Temperature (degrees)
(ii) Species classification
(iii) Map scale
(iv) Worst to best

Codes:	A	B	C	D
(a)	(i)	(ii)	(iii)	(iv)
(b)	(iv)	(iii)	(ii)	(i)
(c)	(iii)	(i)	(iv)	(ii)
(d)	(ii)	(iv)	(i)	(iii)

56. Risk assessment in EIA does not involve
(a) Maximum credible analysis
(b) Hazard and operability studies
(c) Preparation of disaster management plan
(d) Assessment of economic benefit arising out of a project

57. In a gravity flow autoclave, medical waste is subjected to a temperature
   (a) > 120°C (b) < 100°C
   (c) > 300°C (d) > 800°C

58. Hierarchy of priorities in hazardous waste management is
   (a) Eliminate generation → Reduce generation → Recycle/Reuse → Treatment → Disposal
   (b) Reduce generation → Eliminate generation → Recycle/Reuse → Treatment → Disposal
   (c) Eliminate generation → Reduce generation → Treatment → Recycle/Reuse → Disposal
   (d) Reduce generation → Eliminate generation → Treatment → Recycle/Reuse → Disposal

59. Public Liability Insurance Act was enacted in the year
   (a) 1991 (b) 1993
   (c) 1995 (d) 1997

60. Match List I with List II and choose the correct answer from the codes given below:

   List I (Convention)
   (A) Convention for the protection of the ozone layer
   (B) Conservation of migratory species of wild animals
   (C) Kyoto protocol
   (D) UN Convention on the law of the sea

   List II (Year)
   (i) 1979 (ii) 1985
   (iii) 1982 (iv) 1997

Codes:	A	B	C	D
(a)	(ii)	(i)	(iv)	(iii)
(b)	(ii)	(iv)	(iii)	(i)
(c)	(iii)	(i)	(ii)	(iv)
(d)	(i)	(ii)	(iii)	(iv)

61. Match List I with List II and choose the correct answer from the codes given below:

   List I (Acts)
   (A) Wildlife Protection Act
   (B) Forest Conservation Act
   (C) Air (Prevention and Control of Pollution) Act
   (D) Water (Prevention and Control of Pollution) Act

   List II (Year when enacted)
   (i) 1980 (ii) 1972
   (iii) 1974 (iv) 1981

Codes:	A	B	C	D
(a)	(ii)	(i)	(iv)	(iii)
(b)	(i)	(ii)	(iii)	(iv)
(c)	(iii)	(ii)	(i)	(iv)
(d)	(iv)	(iii)	(ii)	(i)

62. **Assertion (A):** χ^2 distribution is a non-parametric distribution.
   Reason (R): χ^2 is a sample statistic having no corresponding population parameter.
   Codes:
   (a) Both (A) and (R) are correct and (R) is the correct explanation of (A).
   (b) Both (A) and (R) are correct, but (R) is not the correct explanation of (A).
   (c) (A) is true, but (R) is false.
   (d) Both (A) and (R) are false.

63. In a simple regression analysis of y on x, the standard error of estimate of y on x, $S_{yx} = 5$, number of observations N is 30, and $\Sigma y^2 = 2000$. The unexplained variance is
   (a) 1500 (b) 750
   (c) 500 (d) 250

64. Two normal populations have variances $\sigma_1^2 = 10$ and $\sigma_2^2 = 20$. Two random samples of sizes 25 and 20, independently selected from these populations have

variances of $S_1^2 = 8$ and $S_2^2 = 15$, respectively. What is the $F_{(24,19)}$ statistic?
(a) 1 (b) 2
(c) 2.81 (d) 3.6

65. **Assertion (A):** A matrix is nonsingular if and only if none of its eigen values is zero.
Reason (R): The product of the eigen values equals the determinant of a matrix.
Codes:
(a) Both (A) and (R) are correct and (R) is the correct explanation of (A).
(b) Both (A) and (R) are correct, but (R) is not the correct explanation of (A).
(c) (A) is correct, but (R) is false.
(d) Both (A) and (R) are false.

66. In Gaussian Plume Model assume $\sigma_z = cx$ where c is a constant and ratio of σ_y to σ_z to be a constant. If H is the effective height of the stack, the maximum concentration at a distance (x) from the stack is proportional to
(a) H^{-1} (b) H^{-2}
(c) $\exp(-H^2)$ (d) $H^{-3/2}$

67. The Pearson Linear correlation coefficient (r) for the following paired data (x, y): (2, 1.4) (4, 1.8), (8, 2.1), (8, 2.3), (9, 2.6) is
(a) 0.623 (b) – 0.572
(c) 0.957 (d) 0.823

68. In a rough terrain the wind speed at a height of 10 m is 2.5 m/s. The wind speed at an elevation of 300 m will be
(a) 4.9 m/s (b) 1.2 m/s
(c) 3.6 m/s (d) 7.9 m/s

69. In the context of REDD$^+$ initiatives the land clearing in forest areas is primarily concerned with
(a) Physical resources of the area
(b) Ecology of the area
(c) Carbon budget of the area
(d) Water resources of the area

70. What was the objective of Basel Convention (1989) under UNEP?
I. Minimize generation of hazardous wastes in terms of quantity and hazardousness
II. Disposal of hazardous wastes as close to the source of generation as possible.
III. Reduce the movement of hazardous wastes.
Choose the correct codes:
(a) I and II only (b) II and III only
(c) I, II and III (d) I only

71. Global Warming Potential (GWP) of a greenhouse gas (GHG) is a comparison of global warming impact between
(a) 1 kg of GHG and 1 kg of methane
(b) 1 kg of GHG and 1 kg of CO_2
(c) 1 kg of GHG and 1 kg of N_2O
(d) 1 kg of GHG and 1 kg of CFC-11

72. Which of the following mixture of gases is called biogas?
(a) CO_2, CH_4, NH_3, H_2S, H_2O (vapour)
(b) CO, CH_4, NH_3, H_2S, H_2O (vapour)
(c) CO_2, CH_4, N_2O, NH_3, H_2O (vapour)
(d) CO_2, NO_x, H_2O, CH_4

73. Environmental ethics deal with moral relationship of human beings to
(a) the value and moral status of the environment and its non-human contents
(b) the values that are important to development and economic growth
(c) the conservation values of selected species
(d) the development of genetically modified organisms

74. The major source of BaP (Benzo-a-pyrene) in atmospheric environment is
   (a) residential wood burning
   (b) gasoline
   (c) coal tar
   (d) cooked meat

75. Match the List I with List II and choose the correct answer from the codes given below:

   List I (Materials)
   (A) Trichloroethylene
   (B) Toluene
   (C) Zinc
   (D) Phenol

   List II (Applications)
   (i) Gasoline
   (ii) Wood treatment
   (iii) Dry cleaning
   (iv) Mining

Codes:	A	B	C	D
(a)	(iii)	(i)	(iv)	(ii)
(b)	(ii)	(iii)	(i)	(iv)
(c)	(i)	(iv)	(ii)	(iii)
(d)	(iv)	(ii)	(iii)	(i)

ANSWERS

1. (b)	2. (a)	3. (b)	4. (c)	5. (a)
6. (a)	7. (d)	8. (b)	9. (d)	10. (a)
11. (a)	12. (a)	13. (b)	14. (a)	15. (c)
16. (d)	17. (a)	18. (d)	19. (b)	20. (d)
21. (b)	22. (d)	23. (d)	24. (d)	25. (b)
26. (a)	27. (a)	28. (a)	29. (c)	30. (b)
31. (c)	32. (a)	33. (d)	34. (d)	35. (d)
36. (a)	37. (a)	38. (b)	39. (c)	40. (a)
41. (a)	42. (a)	43. (b)	44. (a)	45. (c)
46. (d)	47. (a)	48. (c)	49. (a)	50. (c)
51. (a)	52. (b)	53. (b)	54. (c)	55. (d)
56. (d)	57. (a)	58. (a)	59. (a)	60. (a)
61. (a)	62. (a)	63. (b)	64. (a)	65. (a)
66. (b)	67. (c)	68. (a)	69. (c)	70. (c)
71. (b)	72. (a)	73. (a)	74. (a)	75. (a)

JUNE–2014

Note: This paper contains Sixty (60) multiple-choice questions, each question carrying two (2) marks. Candidate is expected to answer any Fifty (50) questions. In case more than Fifty (50) questions are attempted, only the first Fifty (50) questions will be evaluated.

PAPER–I

1. Breakdown in verbal communication is described as
   (a) Short circuit
   (b) Contradiction
   (c) Unevenness
   (d) Entropy
2. The Telephone Model of Communication was first developed in the area of
   (a) Technological theory
   (b) Dispersion theory
   (c) Minimal effects theory
   (d) Information theory
3. The Dada Saheb Phalke Award for 2013 has been conferred on
   (a) Karan Johar (b) Amir Khan
   (c) Asha Bhonsle (d) Gulzar
4. Photographs are not easy to
   (a) publish (b) secure
   (c) decode (d) change
5. The grains that appear on a television set when operated are also referred to as
   (a) sparks (b) green dots
   (c) snow (d) rain drops
6. In circular communication, the encoder becomes a decoder when there is
   (a) noise (b) audience
   (c) criticality (d) feedback
7. In a post-office, stamps of three different denominations of ₹ 7, ₹ 8, ₹ 10 are available. The exact amount for which one cannot buy stamps is
   (a) 19 (b) 20
   (c) 23 (d) 29
8. In certain coding method, the word QUESTION is encoded as DOMESTIC. In this coding, what is the code word for the word RESPONSE?
   (a) OMESUCEM
   (b) OMESICSM
   (c) OMESICEM
   (d) OMESISCM
9. If the series 4, 5, 8, 13, 14, 17, 22, ... is continued in the same pattern, which one of the following is not a term of this series?
   (a) 31 (b) 32
   (c) 33 (d) 35
10. Complete the series BB, FE, II, ML, PP, ... by choosing one of the following option given.
   (a) TS (b) ST
   (c) RS (d) SR
11. A man started walking from his house towards south. After walking 6 km, he turned to his left and walked 5 km. Then he walked further 3 km after turning left. He then turned to his left and continued

his walk for 9 km. How far is he away from his house?

(a) 3 km (b) 4 km
(c) 5 km (d) 6 km

12. One writes all numbers from 50 to 99 without the digits 2 and 7. How many numbers have been written?

(a) 32 (b) 36
(c) 40 (d) 38

13. "If a large diamond is cut up into little bits, it will lose its value just as an army is divided up into small units of soldiers, it loses its strength."
The argument put above may be called as

(a) Analogical (b) Deductive
(c) Statistical (d) Causal

14. Given below are some characteristics of logical argument. Select the code which expresses a characteristic which is not of inductive in character.

(a) The conclusion is claimed to follow from its premises.
(b) The conclusion is based on causal relation.
(c) The conclusion conclusively follows from its premises.
(d) The conclusion is based on observation and experiment.

15. If two propositions having the same subject and predicate terms can both be true but cannot both be false, the relation between those two propositions is called

(a) contradictory (b) contrary
(c) subcontrary (d) subaltern

16. Given below are two premises and four conclusions drawn from those premises. Select the code that expresses conclusion drawn validly from the premises (separately or jointly).

Premises:
(a) All dogs are mammals.
(b) No cats are dogs.

Conclusions:
(i) No cats are mammals.
(ii) Some cats are mammals.
(iii) No dogs are cats.
(iv) No dogs are non-mammals.

Codes:
(a) (i) only (b) (i) and (ii)
(c) (iii) and (iv) (d) (ii) and (iii)

17. Given below is a diagram of three circles A, B and C inter-related with each other. The circle A represents the class of Indians, the circle B represents the class of scientists and circle C represents the class of politicians. p, q, r, s...represent different regions. Select the code containing the region that indicates the class of Indian scientists who are not politicians.

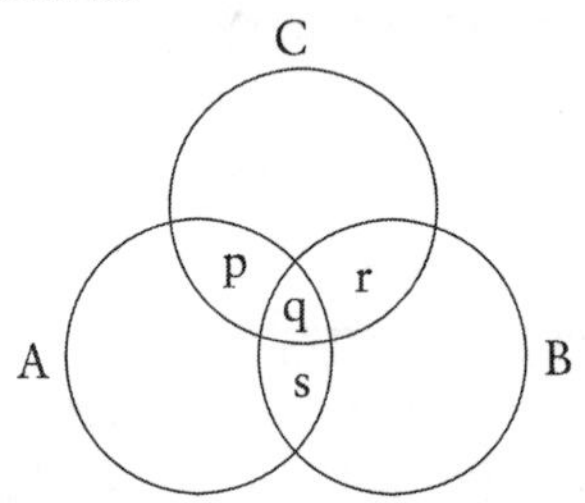

Codes:
(a) q and s only (b) s only
(c) s and r only (d) p, q and s only

Read the following table carefully. Based upon this table answer questions from 18 to 22:

Net Area under Irrigation by sources in a country (Thousand Hectares)

Year	Government canals	Private canals	Tanks	Tube wells & other wells	Other sources	Total
1997-98	17117	211	2593	32090	3102	55173
1998-99	17093	212	2792	33988	3326	57411

1999-00	16842	194	2535	34623	2915	57109
2000-01	15748	203	2449	33796	2880	55076
2001-02	15031	209	2179	34906	4347	56672
2002-03	13863	206	1802	34250	3657	53778
2003-04	14444	206	1908	35779	4281	56618
2004-05	14696	206	1727	34785	7453	58867
2005-06	15268	207	2034	35372	7314	60196

18. Which of the following sources of irrigation has registered the largest percentage of decline in Net area under irrigation during 1997-98 and 2005-06?
   (a) Government canals
   (b) Private canals
   (c) Tanks
   (d) Other sources

19. Find out the source of irrigation that has registered the maximum improvement in terms of percentage of Net irrigated area during 2002-03 and 2003-04.
   (a) Government canals
   (b) Tanks
   (c) Tube wells and other wells
   (d) Other sources

20. In which of the following years, Net irrigation by tanks increased at the highest rate?
   (a) 1998-99 (b) 2000-01
   (c) 2003-04 (d) 2005-06

21. Identify the source of irrigation that has recorded the maximum incidence of negative growth in terms of Net irrigated area during the years given in the table.
   (a) Government canals
   (b) Private canals
   (c) Tube wells and other wells
   (d) Other sources

22. In which of the following years, share of the tube wells and other wells in the total net irrigated area was the highest?
   (a) 1998-99 (b) 2000-01
   (c) 2002-03 (d) 2004-05

23. The acronym FTP stands for
   (a) File Transfer Protocol
   (b) Fast Transfer Protocol
   (c) File Tracking Protocol
   (d) File Transfer Procedure

24. Which one of the following is not a/an image/graphic file format?
   (a) PNG (b) GIF
   (c) BMP (d) GUI

25. The first web browser is
   (a) Internet Explorer
   (b) Netscape
   (c) World Wide Web
   (d) Firefox

26. When a computer is booting, BIOS is loaded to the memory by
   (a) RAM (b) ROM
   (c) CD-ROM (d) TCP

27. Which one of the following is not the same as the other three?
   (a) MAC address
   (b) Hardware address
   (c) Physical address
   (d) IP address

28. Identify the IP address from the following:
   (a) 300 · 215 · 317 · 3
   (b) 302 · 215@ · 417 · 5
   (c) 202 · 50 · 20 · 148
   (d) 202 - 50 - 20 - 148

29. The population of India is about 1.2 billion. Take the average consumption of energy per person per year in India as 30 Mega Joules. If this consumption is met by carbon based fuels and the rate of carbon emissions per kilojoule is 15×10^6 kgs, the total carbon emissions per year from India will be
   (a) 54 million metric tons
   (b) 540 million metric tons

(c) 5400 million metric tons
(d) 2400 million metric tons

30. Which of the following cities has been worst affected by urban smog in recent times?
(a) Paris (b) London
(c) Los Angeles (d) Beijing

31. The primary source of organic pollution in fresh water bodies is
(a) run-off urban areas
(b) run-off from agricultural forms
(c) sewage effluents
(d) industrial effluents

32. 'Lahar' is a natural disaster involving
(a) eruption of large amount of material
(b) strong winds
(c) strong water waves
(d) strong winds and water waves

33. In order to avoid catastrophic consequences of climate change, there is general agreement among the countries of the world to limit the rise in average surface temperature of earth compared to that of pre-industrial times by
(a) 1.5°C to 2°C
(b) 2.0°C to 3.5°C
(c) 0.5°C to 1.0°C
(d) 0.25°C to 0.5°C

34. The National Disaster Management Authority functions under the Union Ministry of
(a) Environment
(b) Water Resources
(c) Home Affairs
(d) Defence

35. Match List I and List II and select the correct answer from the codes given below:

List I
A. Flood B. Drought
C. Earthquake D. Volcano

List II
1. Lack of rainfall of sufficient duration
2. Tremors produced by the passage of vibratory waves through the rocks of the earth
3. A vent through which molted substances come out
4. Excess rain and uneven distribution of water

Codes:	A	B	C	D
(a)	4	1	2	3
(b)	2	3	4	1
(c)	3	4	2	1
(d)	4	3	1	2

36. Which one of the following greenhouse gases has the shortest residence time in the atmosphere?
(a) Chlorofluorocarbon
(b) Carbon dioxide
(c) Methane
(d) Nitrous oxide

37. Consider the following statements and select the correct answer from the codes given below:
i. Rajasthan receives the highest solar radiation in the country.
ii. India has the fifth largest installed wind power in the world.
iii. The maximum amount of wind power is contributed by Tamil Nadu.
iv. The primary source of uranium in India is Jaduguda.

Codes:
(a) i and ii
(b) i, ii and iii
(c) ii and iii
(d) i and iv

38. Who among the following is the de facto executive head of the Planning Commission?
    (a) Chairman
    (b) Deputy Chairman
    (c) Minister of State for Planning
    (d) Member Secretary

39. Education as a subject of legislation figures in the
    (a) Union List
    (b) State List
    (c) Concurrent List
    (d) Residuary Powers

40. Which of the following are Central Universities?
    1. Pondicherry University
    2. Vishwa Bharati
    3. H.N.B. Garhwal University
    4. Kurukshetra University

    Select the correct answer from the codes given below:

    Codes:

    (a) 1, 2 and 3 (b) 1, 3 and 4
    (c) 2, 3 and 4 (d) 1, 2 and 4

41. Consider the statement which is followed by two arguments (i) and (ii).

    Statement: India should have a very strong and powerful Lokpal.

    Arguments: (i) Yes, it will go a long in eliminating corruption in bureaucracy.
    (ii) No, it will discourage honest officers from making quick decisions.

    Codes:

    (a) Only argument (i) is strong.
    (b) Only argument (ii) is strong.
    (c) Both the arguments are strong.
    (d) Neither of the arguments is strong.

42. Which of the following universities has adopted the meta university concept?
    (a) Assam University
    (b) Delhi University
    (c) Hyderabad University
    (d) Pondicherry University

43. Which of the following statements are correct about a Central University?
    1. Central University is established under an Act of Parliament.
    2. The President of India acts as the visitor of the University.
    3. The President has the power to nominate some members to the Executive Committee or the Board of Management of the University.
    4. The President occasionally presides over the meetings of the Executive Committee or Court.

    Select the correct answer from the codes given below:

    Codes:

    (a) 1, 2 and 4 (b) 1, 3 and 4
    (c) 1, 2 and 3 (d) 1, 2, 3 and 4

44. Which one of the following is considered a sign of motivated teaching?
    (a) Students asking questions
    (b) Maximum attendance of the students
    (c) Pin drop silence in the classroom
    (d) Students taking notes

45. Which one of the following is the best method of teaching?
    (a) Lecture (b) Discussion
    (c) Demonstration (d) Narration

46. Dyslexia is associated with
    (a) mental disorder
    (b) behavioural disorder
    (c) reading disorder
    (d) writing disorder

47. The e-content generation for undergraduate courses has been assigned

by the Ministry of Human Resource Development to

(a) INFLIBNET
(b) Consortium for Educational Communication
(c) National Knowledge Commission
(d) Indira Gandhi National Open University

48. Classroom communication is normally considered as

(a) effective (b) cognitive
(c) affective (d) selective

49. Who among the following, propounded the concept of paradigm?

(a) Peter Haggett (b) Von Thunen
(c) Thomas Kuhn (d) John K. Wright

50. In a thesis, figures and tables are included in

(a) the appendix
(b) a separate chapter
(c) the concluding chapter
(d) the text itself

51. A thesis statement is

(a) an observation (b) a fact
(c) an assertion (d) a discussion

52. The research approach of Max Weber to understand how people create meanings in natural settings is identified as

(a) positive paradigm
(b) critical paradigm
(c) natural paradigm
(d) interpretative paradigm

53. Which one of the following is a non-probability sampling?

(a) Simple random
(b) Purposive
(c) Systematic
(d) Stratified

54. Identify the category of evaluation that assesses the learning progress to provide continuous feedback to the students during instruction.

(a) Placement (b) Diagnostic
(c) Formative (d) Summative

55. The research stream of immediate application is

(a) Conceptual research
(b) Action research
(c) Fundamental research
(d) Empirical research

Read the following passage carefully and answer questions 56 to 60:

Traditional Indian values must be viewed both from the angle of the individual and from that of the geographically delimited agglomeration of peoples or groups enjoying a common system of leadership which we call the 'State'. The Indian 'State's' special feature is the peaceful, or perhaps mostly peaceful, co-existence of social groups of various historical provenances which mutually adhere in a geographical, economic, and political sense, without ever assimilating to each other in social terms, in ways of thinking, or even in language. Modern Indian law will determine certain rules, especially in relation to the regime of the family, upon the basis of how the loin-cloth is tied, or how the turban is worn, for this may identify the litigants as members of a regional group, and therefore as participants in its traditional law, though their ancestors left the region three or four centuries earlier. The use of the word 'State' above must not mislead us. There was no such thing as a conflict between the individual and the State, atleast before foreign governments became established, just as there was no concept of state 'sovereignty' or of any church-and-state dichotomy.

Modern Indian 'secularism' has an admittedly peculiar feature: It requires the state to make a fair distribution of attention and support amongst all religions. These blessed aspects of India's famed tolerance (Indian kings so rarely persecuted religious groups that the exceptions prove the rule) at once struck Portuguese and other European visitors to the West Coast of India in the sixteenth century, and the impression made upon them in this and other ways gave rise, at one remove, to the basic constitution of Thomas More's Utopia. There is little about modern India that strikes one at once as Utopian: but the insistence upon the inculcation of norms, and the absence of bigotry and institutionalized exploitation of human or natural resources, are two very different features which link the realities of India and her tradition with the essence of all Utopians.

56. Which of the following is a special feature of the Indian State?
    (a) Peaceful co-existence of people under a common system of leadership
    (b) Peaceful co-existence of social groups of different historical provenances attached to each other in a geographical, economic and political sense
    (c) Social integration of all groups
    (d) Cultural assimilation of all social groups.
57. The author uses the word 'State' to highlight
    (a) Antagonistic relationship between the state and the individual throughout the period of history.
    (b) Absence of conflict between the state and the individuals upto a point in time.
    (c) The concept of state sovereignty.
    (d) Dependence on religion.
58. Which one is the peculiar feature of modern Indian 'Secularism'?
    (a) No discrimination on religious considerations
    (b) Total indifference to religion
    (c) No space for social identity
    (d) Disregard for social law
59. The basic construction of Thomas More's Utopia was inspired by
    (a) Indian tradition of religious tolerance.
    (b) Persecution of religious groups by Indian rulers.
    (c) Social inequality in India.
    (d) European perception of Indian State.
60. What is the striking feature of modern India?
    (a) A replica of Utopian State
    (b) Uniform laws
    (c) Adherence to traditional values
    (d) Absence of Bigotry

ANSWERS

1. (d)	2. (d)	3. (d)	4. (c)	5. (c)
6. (d)	7. (a)	8. (c)	9. (c)	10. (a)
11. (c)	12. (a)	13. (a)	14. (c)	15. (c)
16. (c)	17. (b)	18. (c)	19. (d)	20. (d)
21. (a)	22. (c)	23. (a)	24. (d)	25. (c)
26. (b)	27. (d)	28. (c)	29. (b)	30. (d)
31. (c)	32. (a)	33. (a)	34. (c)	35. (a)
36. (c)	37. (d)	38. (b)	39. (c)	40. (a)
41. (a)	42. (b)	43. (c)	44. (a)	45. (c)
46. (c)	47. (b)	48. (c)	49. (c)	50. (d)
51. (c)	52. (d)	53. (b)	54. (c)	55. (b)
56. (b)	57. (d)	58. (a)	59. (a)	60. (d)

PAPER–II

Note: This paper contains fifty (50) objective type questions of two (2) marks each. All questions are compulsory.

1. For a clear night and with windspeeds < 3 m/s, the atmosphere is
   (a) stable
   (b) slightly unstable
   (c) neutral
   (d) slightly stable

2. **Assertion (A):** Chemosynthesis plays an important role in 'S' cycle.
   Reason (R): In chemosynthesis, some sulphur compounds act as source of energy.
   Codes:
   (a) Both (A) and (R) are true and (R) is the correct explanation.
   (b) Both (A) and (R) are true and (R) is not the correct explanation.
   (c) (A) is true but (R) is false.
   (d) (A) is false but (R) is true.

3. Which of the following is NOT a correct statement?
   (a) Tropics are the warmest and wettest regions.
   (b) Subtropical high pressure zones create dry zones at about 30 N and S.
   (c) Temperature and precipitation are lowest at the poles.
   (d) Temperature is lowest and precipitation is highest at the poles.

4. Protecting nature and the wilderness for its own sake is referred as
   (a) Deep ecology
   (b) Shallow ecology
   (c) Self ecology
   (d) Selfless ecology

5. For the analysis of oxides of Nitrogen, which of the following set of reagents are used?
   (a) Sulphanilic acid, NEDA, H_2O_2, HNO_3
   (b) Sulphamic acid, NEDA, H_2O_2, HNO_3
   (c) Sulphamic acid, Nicotine, H_2O, HNO_3
   (d) Sulphomolybdic acid, NEDA, H_2O_2, H_2SO_4

6. Number of ions of cadmium present in 3n moles of cadmium nitrate is
   (a) 18.069×10^{23} (b) 18.069×10^{20}
   (c) 18.069×10^{17} (d) 18.069×10^{14}

7. Which one of the following organisms is a free living nitrogen fixer?
   (a) *Rhizobium* (b) *Azotobacter*
   (c) *Frankia* (d) *Dorylimes*

8. Which one of the following has highest bioconcentration factor (BCF)?
   (a) DDT (b) DDE
   (c) Chlordane (d) Heptachlor

9. Consider an Ocean Thermal Energy Conversion (OTEC) process operating between 30 °C and 5 °C. What would be the maximum possible efficiency for an electricity generator station operating with these temperatures?
   (a) 8% (b) 15%
   (c) 25% (d) 40%

10. The process of 'Nebulisation' in Atomic Absorption Spectrophotometry is to
    (a) convert the liquid sample to gaseous form.
    (b) convert the liquid sample into small droplets.
    (c) sublimate the sample.
    (d) solubilization of the solute.

11. Individuals of a plant species occurring in a particular area constitute
    (a) fauna (b) flora
    (c) flora and fauna (d) population

12. A local population genetically, structurally and functionally adapted to its local environment is called
    (a) ecotype (b) ecophene
    (c) ecad (d) ecocline
13. Mycorrhizae is an example of
    (a) Ammensalism (b) Commensalism
    (c) Parasitism (d) Symbiosis
14. The entire series of communities of biotic succession from pioneer to climax community is known as
    (a) Troph (b) Sere
    (c) Population (d) Biome
15. In which of the following ecosystems the pyramid of biomass is inverted?
    (a) Forest (b) Grassland
    (c) Pond (d) Desert
16. The first National Park established in India is
    (a) Kaziranga National Park
    (b) The Jim Corbett National Park
    (c) Hazaribagh National Park
    (d) Gir National Park
17. The animals that rest or swim on the surface of the lakes are called
    (a) Nektons (b) Neustons
    (c) Benthos (d) Peritons
18. Which of the following is an example of *in situ* conservation of biodiversity?
    (a) Captive breeding
    (b) Seed bank
    (c) National park
    (d) Pollen bank
19. A biome contains
    (a) many ecosystems
    (b) many communities
    (c) many populations
    (d) a single ecosystem
20. In Bhopal gas tragedy, the quantity of Methyl Isocyanate leaked into the atmosphere was around
    (a) ~ 180 tonnes (b) ~ 60 tonnes
    (c) ~ 112 tonnes (d) ~ 40 tonnes
21. What is the sequence of arrival of seismic waves at a recording station?
    (a) P-wave, S-wave, L-wave, R-wave.
    (b) S-wave, P-wave, R-wave, L-wave.
    (c) R-wave, L-wave, P-wave, S-wave.
    (d) S-wave, L-wave, R-wave, P-wave.
22. The presence of ammonia in groundwater may indicate a nearby
    (a) coal mine
    (b) municipal solid waste dumping site
    (c) thermal power plant
    (d) granite quarry
23. Given below are statements in the context of a truly vertical aerial photograph:
    1. The principal point, nadir point and isocentre coincide.
    2. Isocentre is the centre from where the radial displacements of images take place.
    3. Tilt is a character of vertical aerial photograph.

    Identify the correct answer from the codes given below:
    (a) 1 only (b) 1 and 2 only
    (c) 1 and 3 only (d) 2 and 3 only
24. Kaolinite is a type of clay Mineral with layers of silicon and aluminium in the ratio of
    (a) 1 : 1 (b) 1 : 2
    (c) 2 : 1 (d) 3 : 1
25. In an ideal Magneto Hydro Dynamic Power Generator, the separation between the plates = 0.5 m, magnetic flux density = 2 Wb/m^2 and average fuel velocity

= 500 m/sec. The voltage developed across the plates will be
(a) 500 V (b) 1000 V
(c) 2000 V (d) 5000 V

26. If the wind speed in a certain area increases by a factor of 2 from 4 m/s to 8 m/s, the power output from an ideal wind mill will increase by a factor of
(a) 4 (b) 8
(c) 16 (d) 2

27. Under Jawaharlal Nehru Solar Mission of Government of India, a total of 20,000 MW of utility Grid Power (including roof to solar power) is sought to be installed by the year
(a) 2020 (b) 2022
(c) 2025 (d) 2030

28. In which country dry steam deposits have been used as such for electricity generation?
(a) Italy (b) Iceland
(c) Austria (d) New Zealand

29. The resources which are unlimited and where quality is not degraded are termed as
(a) renewable (b) reusable
(c) immutable (d) exhaustible

30. The most toxic form of mercury in water is
(a) 2 Hg^+ (b) Hg^{2+}
(c) $H_3C - Hg^+$ (d) Hg^o

31. Hardness of water is due to the presence of
(a) Calcium and Magnesium ions
(b) Strontium and Nitrate ions
(c) Sodium and Chloride ions
(d) Potassium and Nitrite ions

32. Principal constituents of atmospheric brown clouds are
1. Soot
2. Soil dust
3. Fly ash
4. Sulphates and Nitrates

Identify the correct code:
(a) 1 and 2 only (b) 1 and 4 only
(c) 2, 3 and 4 only (d) 1, 2, 3 and 4

33. The famous 'London Smog' was observed in the year
(a) 1750 (b) 1952
(c) 1972 (d) 2000

34. The permissible limit of day time industrial noise as recommended by WHO is
(a) 80 dB (b) 75 dB
(c) 90 dB (d) 76 dB

35. Surface litter layer on ground soil is also known as
(a) 'O' horizon (b) 'A' horizon
(c) 'B' horizon (d) 'C' horizon

36. Which one of the following represents the correct Uranium decay series?
(a) Uranium → Radium → Radon → Polonium
(b) Uranium → Radon → Radium → Polonium
(c) Uranium → Radium → Polonium → Radon
(d) Uranium → Radon → Polonium → Radium

37. Hydropower projects with large reservoirs affect the environment by release of
(a) CO (b) CO_2
(c) CH_4 (d) NO_2

38. Terms of reference is fixed at which stage of EIA process?
(a) Screening stage
(b) Scoping stage
(c) Detailed EIA stage
(d) Project Appraisal stage

39. Arrange the functions associated with EIA in a sequential manner
   (i) Identification
   (ii) Prediction
   (iii) Defining the scope
   (iv) Impact evaluation and analysis

Codes:

(a)	(i)	(iii)	(iv)	(ii)
(b)	(ii)	(iv)	(i)	(iii)
(c)	(iii)	(i)	(ii)	(iv)
(d)	(iv)	(ii)	(iii)	(i)

40. The role of State Pollution Control Board in EIA is
   1. Public hearing/consultation
   2. Issue of NOC
   3. Collecting environmental data
   4. Survey of fauna and flora

Codes:

(a) 1 and 2 only (b) 1 and 2 only
(c) 3 and 4 only (d) 2 and 3 only

41. Percentage of carbon in a typical municipal solid waste ranges from
(a) 50-60 % (b) 40-50 %
(c) 30-40 % (d) 20-30 %

42. Which one of the following has maximum destruction and removable efficiency?
(a) Incineration
(b) Biological Treatment
(c) Chemical Treatment
(d) Landfill

43. Wastes are known to be corrosive if the pH is
(a) ≤ 2 (b) ≤ 3
(c) ≤ 4 (d) ≤ 5

44. Hazardous Waste Management and Handling Rule was enacted in the year
(a) 1989 (b) 1979
(c) 1969 (d) 1999

45. For a given set of data 5, 8, 12, 15 and 20, the comparison of geometric $(\bar{G})$, harmonic $(\bar{H})$, and arithmetic mean $(\bar{X})$ will be
(a) $\bar{H} > \bar{G} > \bar{X}$ (b) $\bar{H} > \bar{G} < \bar{X}$
(c) $\bar{H} < \bar{G} < \bar{X}$ (d) $\bar{H} < \bar{G} > \bar{X}$

46. Algal bloom follows a population growth pattern, which is
(a) J-shaped (b) S-shaped
(c) Exponential (d) Linear

47. t-distribution is approximately normal for sample size η
(a) ≥ 30 (b) ≥ 10
(c) ≥ 15 (d) ≥ 20

48. Two sets of data consisting of 10 and 20 observations have same mean 8 with standard deviations of 1 and 2, respectively. If the two data sets are combined, then the variance is
(a) 3 (b) 2
(c) 5 (d) 1.5

49. Match the List I with List II and choose the correct answer from the given codes:

List I (Event)	List II (Date)
(A) Earth Day	(i) 5th June
(B) World Environment Day	(ii) 3rd October
(C) Ozone Day	(iii) 22nd April
(D) World Nature Day	(iv) 16th September

Codes:	A	B	C	D
(a)	(i)	(ii)	(iv)	(iii)
(b)	(iii)	(i)	(iv)	(ii)
(c)	(ii)	(i)	(iii)	(iv)
(d)	(iv)	(iii)	(ii)	(i)

50. CBD stands for
(a) Convention on Biological Diversity
(b) Conservation Biodiversity Development

(c) Conservation Association for Biodiversity and Management
(d) Cumulative Plan for Biological Diversity

ANSWERS

1. (a)	2. (a)	3. (d)	4. (a)	5. (a)
6. (d)	7. (b)	8. (a)	9. (a)	10. (b)
11. (d)	12. (a)	13. (d)	14. (b)	15. (c)
16. (b)	17. (b)	18. (c)	19. (a)	20. (d)
21. (a)	22. (b)	23. (a)	24. (a)	25. (a)
26. (b)	27. (b)	28. (a)	29. (c)	30. (c)
31. (a)	32. (d)	33. (b)	34. (b)	35. (a)
36. (a)	37. (c)	38. (b)	39. (c)	40. (b)
41. (a)	42. (a)	43. (a)	44. (a)	45. (c)
46. (a)	47. (a)	48. (a)	49. (b)	50. (a)

PAPER–III

Note: This paper contains seventy-five (75) objective type questions of two (2) marks each. All questions are compulsory.

1. Chemosynthesis involves CO_2 fixation using energy derived from
   (a) Sunlight
   (b) Infrared radiation
   (c) UV-radiation
   (d) Inorganic and Organic compounds

2. Wind in the mountain-valley regions are of
   (a) Microscale (b) Mesoscale
   (c) Macroscale (d) Synoptic scale

3. In tropical region an aircraft is flying at an altitude of 10 km. At that altitude the temperature is – 40 °C. What is the ambient temperature on the ground?
   (a) 24 °C (b) 40 °C
   (c) 30 °C (d) 20 °C

4. **Assertion (A):** Upper atmosphere shields life on earth.
   Reason (R): Ultraviolet radiations are absorbed in the upper atmosphere.
   Choose the correct answer:
   Codes:
   (a) Both (A) and (R) are true and (R) is the correct explanation of (A).
   (b) Both (A) and (R) are true, but (R) is not the correct explanation of (A).
   (c) (A) is true and (R) is false.
   (d) (A) is false and (R) is true.

5. The molar extinction coefficient of proline ninhydrin complex at 520 nm is 0.34 $\mu M^{-1} Cm^{-1}$. A solution of the proline ninhydrin complex has an absorbance of 0.68 in a one centimeter cuvette. The concentration (μM) of proline is
   (a) 0.5 (b) 0.2312
   (c) 2.312 (d) 2

6. The principal components of photochemical smog in urban areas are
   (a) SO_2 and NO_2
   (b) SPM and CO
   (c) SPM and NO_2
   (d) Oxides of Nitrogen, Hydrocarbons and Ozone.

7. The amount of a particular gas dissolved in water depends on
   1. its solubility in water.
   2. its partial pressure at the air/water interface or sediment/water interface.
   3. the water temperature.
   4. the levels of salts in the water.

   Identify the correct answer:
   (a) 1 and 2 only (b) 2, 3 and 4 only
   (c) 1, 2 and 3 only (d) 1, 2, 3 and 4

8. A 50 ml solution of pH = 1 is mixed with a 50 ml solution of pH = 2. The pH of the mixture will be nearly
   (a) 0.76 (b) 1.26
   (c) 1.76 (d) 2.26

9. The solubility product of the following type of reaction:
   $$Al(OH)_3 \longrightarrow Al^{3+} + 3\overset{\ominus}{O}H \text{ is}$$
   (a) Ksp = (Al) (OH)
   (b) Ksp = $(Al^{3+})\ (3\overset{\ominus}{O}H)$
   (c) Ksp = $(Al^{3+})\ (\overset{\ominus}{O}H)^3$
   (d) Ksp = $(Al^{3+})\ (\overset{\ominus}{O}H)$

10. Cells grown in medium containing isotope sulphur 35 will show radio labelling in
    (a) membrane lipids
    (b) membrane proteins
    (c) glycogen
    (d) nucleic acid

11. A stream flowing at 10.0 m^3/s has a tributary feeding it with a flow of 5.0 m^3/s. The stream concentration of chloride upstream at the junction is 20.0 mg/L and the tributary chloride concentration is 40 mg/L. Treating chloride as a conservative substance and assuming complete mixing of the two streams, find the down stream concentration.
    (a) 26.7 mg/L (b) 30.2 mg/L
    (c) 22.6 mg/L (d) 35.2 mg/L

12. Assume that dilution factor p for an unseeded mixture of waste and water is 0.03. The DO of the mixture is initially 9.0 mg/L and after 5 days, it has dropped to 3.0 mg/L. The reaction rate constant 'K' has been found to be 0.22/day. Five day BOD of the water will be
    (a) 200 mg/L (b) 150 mg/L
    (c) 100 mg/L (d) 75 mg/L

13. Nudation is generally caused by
    (a) migration of species
    (b) climate change
    (c) invasion of foreign species
    (d) modification of habitat

14. Which one of the following is the best tool to study the interacting residues in protein-ligand interaction?
    (a) X-ray crystallography
    (b) Circular dichroism spectroscopy
    (c) UV - V is spectroscopy
    (d) Fluorescence spectroscopy

15. During centrifugation, if the centrifugal force is F_C, buoyant force is F_b, and frictional force is F_f, which of the following equations expresses the sedimentation of the molecule?
    (a) $F_C = F_b - F_f$ (b) $F_C = F_b + F_f$
    (c) $F_C = \frac{F_b - F_f}{2}$ (d) $F_C = \frac{F_b + F_f}{2}$

16. Match the List I with List II and choose the correct answer from the given codes:
    List I (Lakes)
    (A) Oligotrophic lakes
    (B) Dystrophic lakes
    (C) Eutrophic lakes
    (D) Volcanic lakes
    List II (Characteristics)
    (i) More nutrient concentration
    (ii) Magmatic water
    (iii) Low nutrient concentration
    (iv) Low pH and high humic acid conditions

Codes:	A	B	C	D
(a)	(i)	(ii)	(iii)	(iv)
(b)	(ii)	(i)	(iv)	(iii)
(c)	(iii)	(iv)	(i)	(ii)
(d)	(iv)	(iii)	(ii)	(i)

17. The earthworm used for composting is
    1. *Crassiclitellata excavata*
    2. *Octochaetona serrata*
    3. *Lumbricus terrestris*
    4. *Eisenia foetida*

    Choose the correct answer:
    (a) 1 and 2 only (b) 2 and 4 only
    (c) 2 and 3 only (d) 1 and 4 only

18. The amount of the living material present in different trophic levels at a given time is called
    1. standing crop 2. standing state
    3. biomass 4. biosphere

    Choose the correct answer:
    (a) 1 and 3 are correct.
    (b) 4 is correct.
    (c) 2 is correct.
    (d) 3 and 2 are correct.

19. Many orchids use trees as a surface to grow. This is an example of
    (a) Commensalism (b) Mutualism
    (c) Parasitism (d) Predation

20. The *r*- strategist is a
    (a) small organism that has a short life, produces many offsprings and does not reach carrying capacity.
    (b) small organism that has a longer life, produces offsprings and does not reach carrying capacity.
    (c) small organism that has a short life, produces numerous offsprings and reach carrying capacity.
    (d) medium organism that has a short life, produces numerous offsprings and reach carrying capacity.

21. Under the Rhino relocation project, during 1987, Rhinoes were introduced in
    (a) Assam
    (b) Meghalaya
    (c) West Bengal
    (d) Madhya Pradesh

22. Which of the following is an endangered bird species?
    (a) Kashmir stag
    (b) Great Indian Bustard
    (c) Hangul
    (d) Black buck

23. In India, Crocodile breeding project started for the first time in
    (a) Tamil Nadu (b) West Bengal
    (c) Odisha (d) Goa

24. Identify the correct sequence of materials in terms of their porosity.
    (a) Sand > clay > gravel
    (b) Clay > sand > gravel
    (c) Gravel > sand > clay
    (d) Gravel > clay > sand

25. For an aquifer of gravel having cross sectional area of 4 m^2 and a depth of 2.5 m, how much water could potentially be extracted? (The porosity and specific yield of gravel are 25% and 20% respectively.)
    (a) 0.5 m^3 (b) 0.25 m^3
    (c) 0.125 m^3 (d) 1 m^3

26. The layers formed by thermal stratification in lakes are
    (a) Epilimnion, Midlimnion, Hypolimnion
    (b) Epilimnion, Oligolimnion, Hypolimnion
    (c) Epilimnion, Dystrolimnion, Hypolimnion
    (d) Epilimnion, Thermocline, Hypolimnion

27. On an aerial photograph, the focal length (f) of the camera lens is 6 inches and flying height (H) over the datum line is 15,000 ft. What is scale of the aerial photograph?
    (a) 1: 30,000 (b) 1: 10,000
    (c) 1: 5,000 (d) 1: 25,000

28. Which of the following substrate will have highest reflectance value?
   (a) Silt loam with 20% moisture.
   (b) Clay with 36% moisture.
   (c) Silt loam with 0.8% moisture.
   (d) Clay with 2% moisture.

29. **Assertion (A):** For sustainable development of a region, proper land use planning is required.
   Reason (R): Land use planning involves inputs of soil types, rock types, seismicity, weather pattern and socio-economic conditions of a region.
   Codes:
   (a) Both (A) and (R) are true and (R) is the correct explanation of (A).
   (b) Both (A) and (R) are true, but (R) is not the correct explanation of (A).
   (c) (A) is true and (R) is false.
   (d) (A) is false and (R) is true.

30. Tundra is a biome characterized by
   (a) stunted trees and permanently frozen sub-surface soil.
   (b) coniferous trees and permanently frozen sub-surface soil.
   (c) lack of trees and permanently frozen sub-surface soil.
   (d) evergreen trees and permanently frozen sub-surface soil.

31. Acid mine drainage occurs when
   (a) the combined action of O_2, H_2O and certain bacteria cause sulphur in coal to form H_2SO_4.
   (b) the combined action of H_2O and certain bacteria cause sulphur in coal to form H_2SO_4.
   (c) the combined action of O_2 and certain bacteria cause sulphur in coal to form H_2SO_4.
   (d) the combined action of SO_2 and certain bacteria with coal to form H_2SO_4.

32. In accordance with the Saffir-Simpson hurricane scale, a cyclonic storm of category 5 should have wind speeds
   (a) > 69 ms^{-1} (b) 50 – 58 ms^{-1}
   (c) 59 – 69 ms^{-1} (d) 33 – 42 ms^{-1}

33. **Assertion (A):** Large scale OTEC development may not be good for environment.
   Reason (R): Release of CO_2 from ocean depths into the atmosphere could exacerbate GHG effect.
   Codes:
   (a) Both (A) and (R) are true and (R) is the correct explanation of (A).
   (b) Both (A) and (R) are true, but (R) is not the correct explanation of (A).
   (c) (A) is true, but (R) is false.
   (d) Both (A) and (R) are false.

34. In a methane fuel cell, what will be the voltage of the cell and its efficiency?
   (Given: $\Delta G° = 8 \times 10^5$ Joules/gm – mole
   $\Delta H° = 8.8 \times 10^5$ Joules/gm – mole and Faraday's constant = 96500 coulomb/ gm-mole)
   (a) ~ 1.23 Volts, ~ 90.9%
   (b) ~ 1.04 Volts, ~ 90.9%
   (c) ~ 1.15 Volts, ~ 11%
   (d) ~ 2.13 Volts, ~ 92%

35. The coefficient of performance for an ideal wind mill is
   (a) 3/8 (b) 5/16
   (c) 2/5 (d) 16/27

36. Assume that the energy released during the combustion of methane is 900 kJ/ mol. Its carbon intensity is
   (a) 13.3 gc/MJ (b) 15.3 gc/MJ
   (c) 19.7 gc/MJ (d) 24.2 gc/MJ

37. In a nuclear fusion reactor it is envisaged to use a liquid blanket of Li to absorb fast neutrons from D+T reaction. How

many neutrons are produced as a result of ${}^{7}_{3}Li + {}^{1}_{0}n$?

(a) 1 (b) 2
(c) 3 (d) 4

38. In an ideal MHD power plant, the electrical efficiency corresponding to maximum power production is
(a) 50% (b) 75%
(c) 25% (d) 100%

39. Energy intensity is a measure of
(a) effectiveness of energy utilisation
(b) energy produced per unit area
(c) energy produced per unit volume
(d) energy produced per unit area per unit time

40. One of the criteria for characterizing a region as ABC hotspot is that the annual mean anthropogenic Aerosol Optical Depth (AOD) is greater than
(a) 0.3 (b) 0.5
(c) 0.8 (d) 0.1

41. The resultant of two noise levels of 50 dB and 55 dB is
(a) 58 db (b) 55.41 dB
(c) 52.5 dB (d) 56.19 dB

42. Which of the following is used as a coagulant for removal of phosphates in water?
(a) Aluminium sulphate
(b) Iron sulphate
(c) Copper sulphate
(d) Potassium chromate

43. Which of the following radionuclides has the longest half-life?
(a) C^{14} (b) Sr^{90}
(c) I^{131} (d) Cs^{137}

44. Under anaerobic conditions nitrogenase catalises
(a) breakdown of atmospheric nitrogen
(b) oxidation of atmospheric nitrogen
(c) reduction of atmospheric nitrogen
(d) hydrolysis of nitrogenous compounds

45. Size range of atmospheric aerosols is
(a) 5nm – 100μm
(b) 100μm – 150μm
(c) 150μm – 200μm
(d) 0.01nm – 5nm

46. Which one of the following is used as microbial indicator of water contamination?
(a) Coliform bacteria
(b) Giardia
(c) Cryptosporidium
(d) Tobacco mosaic virus

47. Elevated salt and Na^{+} concentrations in soils are highly toxic to many plants, but relatively high tolerance level (to this toxicity) is seen in
(a) Sugarbeet (b) Sugarcane
(c) Onion (d) Lettuce

48. Which of the following hydrocarbons is emitted by vegetation?
(a) Ocimene
(b) Xylene
(c) Acrolein
(d) 1, 3 - Pentadions

49. For particles of size > 5 μm, the efficiency of cyclones can be as high as
(a) 50% (b) 60%
(c) 80% (d) 90%

50. Given the following parameters of a primary settling chamber:

Diameter = 50m, Depth = 2.5m, average detention time = 2 hours. How much quantity of waste water is being treated?
(a) ~ 58928 m^3/day (b) ~ 48321 m^3/day
(c) ~ 45321 m^3/day (d) ~ 25321 m^3/day

51. A flat surface type electrostatic precipitator (ESP) has the following parameters: collector plate area A = 4600 m^2, volumetric flow rate Q = 200 m^3/s and effective drift velocity of flue gas = 0.15 m/s. What is the efficiency of the ESP?
(a) ~ 0.968 (b) ~ 0.981
(c) ~ 0.975 (d) ~ 0.922

52. **Assertion (A):** Cost-benefit analysis for assessment of natural systems is not merely concerned with the effects on environmental quality but seeks the conditions for sustainable use of the natural resources of a region.
Reason (R): Cost-benefit analysis is not useful for small scale development projects, but is better suited for the analysis and evaluation of a regional development plan.
Identify the correct answer:
Codes:
(a) Both (A) and (R) are true and (R) is the correct explanation.
(b) Both (A) and (R) are true but (R) is not the correct explanation.
(c) (A) is true and (R) is wrong.
(d) Both (A) and (R) are wrong.

53. Battelle-Columbus weighting-scaling checklist methodology for water-resources projects obtains base line data on how many environmental parameters?
(a) 40 (b) 78
(c) 68 (d) 50

54. Match List I with List II and choose the correct answer from the codes given below:
List I
(A) Checklists methods
(B) Overlays methods
(C) Adhoc methods
(D) Matrices methods
List II
(i) Involve preparation of a set of transparent maps, which represent the spatial distribution of an environmental characteristics
(ii) Highly structured approaches involving importance weightings for factors and application of scaling techniques
(iii) Identification and evaluation of interactions between various activities and environmental parameters
(iv) Indicate broad areas of possible impacts by listing composite environmental parameters

Codes:	A	B	C	D
(a)	(i)	(ii)	(iii)	(iv)
(b)	(iv)	(ii)	(i)	(iii)
(c)	(ii)	(i)	(iv)	(iii)
(d)	(iii)	(iv)	(ii)	(i)

55. Match List I with List II and choose the correct answer from the codes given below:
List I (Criteria of EIA Methodology)
(A) Impact identification
(B) Impact measurement
(C) Impact communication
(D) Impact interpretation
List II (Component)
(i) Magnitude
(ii) Specificity
(iii) Depth of analysis
(iv) Comprehensive overall perspective

Codes:	A	B	C	D
(a)	(i)	(iv)	(iii)	(ii)
(b)	(ii)	(i)	(iv)	(iii)
(c)	(iii)	(iv)	(i)	(ii)
(d)	(iv)	(iii)	(ii)	(i)

56. Significant hazard/accident factor to be considered under risk assessment of distillaries are
(a) toxic gas release and human accident
(b) pressure wave and heat radiation
(c) toxic gas release and radiation
(d) pressure wave and toxic gas release

57. If 'I' is the impact of the population on the environment, 'P' is the size of the population, 'A' is the per capita affluence or consumption and 'T' is the damage caused by technologies, then which of the following equation is correct?
(a) $I = (P \times A)/T$ (b) $I = P \times A \times T$
(c) $I = T/(P \times A)$ (d) $I = P/(A \times T)$

58. According to Environment (Protection) Act, 1986 permissible limits of oil and grease in the effluents to be discharged into public sewers is
(a) 10 mg/*l* (b) 20 mg/*l*
(c) 25 mg/*l* (d) 30 mg/*l*

59. 'Reed swamp stage' is also referred to as
(a) submerged stage
(b) woodland stage
(c) rooted floated stage
(d) amphibious stage

60. Match List I with List II and choose the correct answer from the given codes:

List I (Ecosystem types)	List II (Characteristics)
(A) Coral reefs	(i) Still water
(B) Deltas	(ii) Saline water
(C) Wetlands	(iii) Brackish water
(D) Rivers	(iv) Fresh water

Codes:	A	B	C	D
(a)	(i)	(ii)	(iii)	(iv)
(b)	(ii)	(iii)	(i)	(iv)
(c)	(ii)	(i)	(iv)	(iii)
(d)	(iii)	(iv)	(i)	(ii)

61. Maximum energy content (KJ/kg) in a typical municipal solid waste is found in
(a) Plastic (b) Leather
(c) Wood (d) Textile

62. Public Liability Insurance Act was enacted in the year
(a) 1991 (b) 1993
(c) 1995 (d) 1997

63. A sample size of 17 observations is selected from a normal population with mean = 50. The sample mean and variance are 48 and 8 respectively. The value of t-statistic is
(a) 0.25 (b) – 2.82
(c) – 2.2 (d) 0.71

64. A class has equal number of boys and girls. The mean and standard deviation of their weights are $\bar{X}_g = 40$ kg, $S_g = 2$ kg for girls and $\bar{X}_b = 50$ kg, $S_b = 2$ kg for boys. What is the combined variance of the weights of the whole class?
(a) 29 (b) 16
(c) 8 (d) 19

65. For a simple regression analysis involving the dependent variable Y and explanatory variable X, the following data is given: No. of observations N = 40, $\Sigma X^2 = 2000$, $\Sigma Y^2 = 2000$, $\bar{X} = 20$, $\bar{Y} = 5$, standard error of estimate of Y on X, $S_{YX} = 4$. The explained variance is
(a) 360 (b) 860
(c) 500 (d) 580

66. A Ψ^2 distribution with 10 degrees of freedom has variance
(a) 10 (b) 20
(c) 5 (d) 40

67. The rank of the matrix

$$\begin{bmatrix} 1 & 1 & 1 \\ 1 & -1 & -1 \\ 3 & 1 & 1 \end{bmatrix} \text{ is}$$

(a) 2
(b) 3
(c) 1
(d) Not possible to determine.

68. Which of the following is not an eigenvector of the matrix $\begin{bmatrix} 2 & 0 \\ 0 & 5 \end{bmatrix}$?

(a) $\begin{bmatrix} 1 \\ 0 \end{bmatrix}$ (b) $\begin{bmatrix} 0 \\ 1 \end{bmatrix}$
(c) $\begin{bmatrix} 0 \\ 2 \end{bmatrix}$ (d) $\begin{bmatrix} 1 \\ 1 \end{bmatrix}$

69. **Assertion (A):** Ground level concentration of pollutants decreases when taller stacks are used.
Reason (R): The ground level concentration varies inversely proportional to the height of the stacks.
Codes:
(a) Both (A) and (R) are correct and (R) is the correct explanation of (A).
(b) Both (A) and (R) are correct, but (R) is not the correct explanation of (A).
(c) (A) is true and (R) is false.
(d) Both (A) and (R) are false.

70. Assume that 5.3 billion people live in less developed countries, where average birth rate is 23 and infant mortality rate is 53. Then the total death due to infant mortality are
(a) 6.5×10^6/year
(b) 5.3×10^6/year
(c) 7.3×10^6/year
(d) 8.5×10^6/year

71. Which of the following act as 'natural sink for carbon'?
1. Trees
2. Oceans
3. Soils

Choose the correct code:
(a) 1 only (b) 1 and 2 only
(c) 1, 2 and 3 (d) 2 and 3 only

72. Match List I with List II and choose the correct answer from the codes given below:

List I (GHGs)	List II (Atmospheric Lifetime) (Yrs)
(A) CFC–12	(i) 12
(B) Methane	(ii) 50-200
(C) CO_2	(iii) 114
(D) N_2O	(iv) 100

Codes:	**A**	**B**	**C**	**D**
(a)	(iii)	(iv)	(i)	(ii)
(b)	(ii)	(iii)	(iv)	(i)
(c)	(iv)	(i)	(ii)	(iii)
(d)	(i)	(ii)	(iii)	(iv)

73. REDD$^+$ initiatives include
1. Forest carbon partnership facility
2. Forest investment programme
3. Sanitation for all
4. Food security for all

Choose the correct code:
(a) 1 and 4 only (b) 1 and 2 only
(c) 1, 2 and 3 only (d) 3 and 4 only

74. Match List I with List II and choose the correct answer from the codes given below:

List I (Environment Related Treaties)	List I (Year)
(A) CITES	(i) 1989
(B) Basel	(ii) 1973

(C) UNFCCC (iii) 1997
(D) Kyoto Protocol (iv) 1992

Codes:	**A**	**B**	**C**	**D**
(a)	(iii)	(ii)	(i)	(iv)
(b)	(iv)	(iii)	(ii)	(i)
(c)	(i)	(iv)	(iii)	(ii)
(d)	(ii)	(i)	(iv)	(iii)

75. Identify the correct sequence with reference to sensitization about environmental problems.
   (a) Knowledge → Awareness → Attitude → Skill → Evaluation ability → Participation
   (b) Knowledge → Awareness → Skill → Attitude → Participation → Evaluation ability
   (c) Awareness → Knowledge → Attitude Skill → Evaluation ability → Participation
   (d) Awareness → Knowledge → Participation → Attitude → Skill → Evaluation ability

ANSWERS

1. (d)	2. (b)	3. (a)	4. (b)	5. (d)
6. (d)	7. (d)	8. (b)	9. (c)	10. (b)
11. (a)	12. (a)	13. (b)	14. (a)	15. (b)
16. (c)	17. (b)	18. (a)	19. (a)	20. (a)
21. (a)	22. (b)	23. (c)	24. (b)	25. (a)
26. (d)	27. (a)	28. (c)	29. (a)	30. (c)
31. (a)	32. (a)	33. (a)	34. (b)	35. (d)
36. (a)	37. (b)	38. (a)	39. (a)	40. (a)
41. (d)	42. (a)	43. (d)	44. (c)	45. (a)
46. (a)	47. (a)	48. (a)	49. (d)	50. (a)
51. (a)	52. (a)	53. (b)	54. (c)	55. (b)
56. (b)	57. (b)	58. (a)	59. (d)	60. (b)
61. (a)	62. (a)	63. (b)	64. (a)	65. (a)
66. (b)	67. (a)	68. (d)	69. (c)	70. (a)
71. (c)	72. (c)	73. (b)	74. (d)	75. (c)

DECEMBER–2014

Note: This paper contains Sixty (60) multiple-choice questions, each question carrying two (2) marks. Candidate is expected to answer any Fifty (50) questions. In case more than Fifty (50) questions are attempted, only the first Fifty (50) questions will be evaluated.

PAPER–I

1. The term 'Yellow Journalism' refers to
   (a) sensational news about terrorism and violence
   (b) sensationalism and exaggeration to attract readers/viewers.
   (c) sensational news about arts and culture
   (d) sensational news prints in yellow paper.

2. In the classroom, the teacher sends the message either as words or images. The students are really
   (a) Encoders (b) Decoders
   (c) Agitators (d) Propagators

3. Media is known as
   (a) First Estate (b) Second Estate
   (c) Third Estate (d) Fourth Estate

4. The mode of communication that involves a single source transmitting information to a large number of receivers simultaneously, is called
   (a) Group Communication
   (b) Mass Communication
   (c) Intrapersonal Communication
   (d) Interpersonal Communication

5. A smart classroom is a teaching space which has
   (i) Smart portion with a touch panel control system.
   (ii) PC/Laptop connection and DVD/VCR player.
   (iii) Document camera and specialized software.
   (iv) Projector and screen.
   Select the correct answer from the codes given below:
   (a) (i) and (ii) only
   (b) (ii) and (iv) only
   (c) (i), (ii) and (iii) only
   (d) (i), (ii), (iii) and (iv)

6. Digital Empowerment means
   (i) Universal digit literacy.
   (ii) Universal access to all digital resources.
   (iii) Collaborative digital platform for participative governance.
   (iv) Probability of all entitlements for individuals through cloud.
   Choose the correct answer from the codes given below:
   (a) (i) and (ii) only
   (b) (ii) and (iii) only
   (c) (i), (ii) and (iii) only
   (d) (i), (ii), (iii) and (iv)

7. The next term in the series:
   2, 7, 28, 63, 126, ____ is
   (a) 215 (b) 245
   (c) 276 (d) 296

8. The next term in the series:
   AB, ED, IH, NM, ______ is

(a) TS (b) ST
(c) TU (d) SU

9. If STREAMERS is coded as UVTGALDQR, then KNOWLEDGE will be coded as
(a) MQPYLCDFD (b) MPQYLDCFD
(c) PMYQLDFCD (d) YMQPLDDFC

10. A is brother of B. B is the brother of C. C is the husband of D. E is the father of A. D is related to E as
(a) Daughter
(b) Daughter-in-law
(c) Sister-in-law
(d) Sister

11. Two numbers are in the ratio 3 : 5. If 9 is subtracted from the numbers, the ratio becomes 12 : 23. The numbers are
(a) 30, 50 (b) 36, 60
(c) 33, 55 (d) 42, 70

12. The mean of the ages of father and his son is 27 years. After 18 years, father will be twice as old as his son. Their present ages are
(a) 42, 12 (b) 40, 14
(c) 30, 24 (d) 36, 18

Read the following passage carefully and answer questions 13 to 17:

The literary distaste for politics, however, seems to be focused not so much on the largely murky practice of politics in itself as a subject of literary representation but rather more on how it is often depicted in literature, i.e., on the very politics of such representation. A political novel often turns out to be not merely a novel about politics but a novel with a politics of its own, for it seeks not merely to show us how things are but has fairly definite ideas about how things should be, and precisely what one should think and do in order to make things move in that desired direction. In short, it seeks to convert and enlist the reader to a particular cause or ideology; it often is (in an only too familiar phrase) not literature but propaganda. This is said to violate the very spirit of literature which is to broaden our understanding of the world and the range of our sympathies rather than to narrow them down through partisan commitment. As John Keats said, "We hate poetry that has a palpable design upon us".

Another reason why politics does not seem amenable to the highest kind of literary representation seems to arise from the fact that politics by its very nature is constituted of ideas and ideologies. If political situations do not lend themselves to happy literary treatment, political ideas present perhaps an even greater problem in this regard. Literature, it is argued, is about human experiences rather than about intellectual abstractions; it deals in what is called the 'felt reality' of human flesh and blood, and in sap and savour (*rasa*) rather than in arid and lifeless ideas. In an extensive discussion of the matter in her book *Ideas and the Novel*, the American novelist Mary McCarthy observed that 'ideas are still today felt to be unsightly in the novel' though that was not so in 'former days', i.e., in the 18th and 19th centuries. Her formulation of the precise nature of the incompatibility between ideas on the one hand and the novel on the other betrays perhaps a divided conscience in the matter and a sense of dilemma shared by many writers and readers: "An idea cannot have loose ends, but a novel, I almost think, needs them. Nevertheless, there is enough in common for the novelists to feel...the attraction of ideas while taking up arms against them—most often with weapons of mockery."

13. According to the passage, a political novel often turns out to be a
(a) Literary distaste for politics
(b) Literary representation of politics

(c) Novel with its own politics
(d) Depiction of murky practice of politics

14. A political novel reveals
(a) Reality of the things
(b) Writer's perception
(c) Particular ideology of the readers
(d) The spirit of literature

15. The constructs of politics by its nature is
(a) Prevalent political situation
(b) Ideas and ideologies
(c) Political propaganda
(d) Understanding of human nature

16. Literature deals with
(a) Human experiences in politics
(b) Intellectual abstractions
(c) Dry and empty ideas
(d) Felt reality of human life

17. The observation of the novelist, Mary McCarthy reveals
(a) unseen felt ideas of today in the novel
(b) dichotomy of conscience on political ideas and novels
(c) compatibility between idea and novel
(d) endless ideas and novels

18. When in a group of propositions, one proposition is claimed to follow from the others, that group of propositions is called
(a) An argument
(b) A valid argument
(c) An explanation
(d) An invalid argument

19. Namita and Samita are brilliant and studious. Anita and Karabi are obedient and irregular. Babita and Namita are irregular but brilliant. Samita and Kabita are regular and obedient. Who among them is/are brilliant, obedient, regular and studious?
(a) Samita alone
(b) Namita and Samita
(c) Kabita alone
(d) Anita alone

20. Warrior is related to sword, carpenter is related to saw, farmer is related to plough. In the same way, the author is related to
(a) Book (b) Fame
(c) Reader (d) Pen

21. Given below is a diagram of three circles A, B and C over-lapping each other. The circle A represents the class of honest people, the circle B represents the class of sincere people and circle C represents the class of politicians. p, q, r, s, U, X, Y represent different regions. Select the code that represents the region indicating the class of honest politicians who are not sincere.

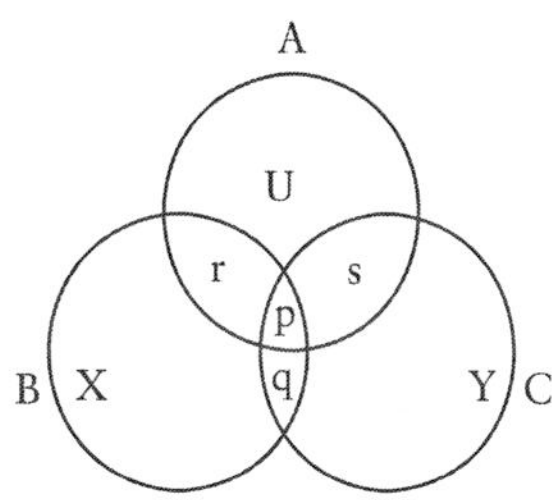

Codes:
(a) X (b) q
(c) p (d) s

22. "A man ought no more to value himself for being wiser than a woman if he owes his advantage to a better education, than he ought to boast of his courage for beating a man when his hands were tied."
The above passage is an instance of
(a) Deductive argument
(b) Hypothetical argument
(c) Analogical argument
(d) Factual argument

23. By which of the following proposition, the proposition 'wise men are hardly afraid of death' is contradicted?
   (a) Some wise men are afraid of death.
   (b) All wise men are afraid of death.
   (c) No wise men is afraid of death.
   (d) Some wise men are not afraid of death.

For a country CO_2 emissions (million metric tons) from various sectors are given in the following table. Answer the questions (24 to 29) based on the data given:

CO_2 emissions (million metric tons)					
Year/Sector	Power	Industry	Commercial	Agriculture	Domestic
2005	500	200	150	80	100
2006	600	300	200	90	110
2007	650	320	250	100	120
2008	700	400	300	150	150
2009	800	450	320	200	180

24. What is the percentage (%) growth of CO_2 emissions from power sector during 2005 to 2009?
   (a) 60 (b) 50
   (c) 40 (d) 80
25. Which sector has recorded maximum growth in CO_2 emissions during 2005 to 2009?
   (a) Power (b) Industry
   (c) Commercial (d) Agriculture
26. By what percentage (%), the total emissions of CO_2 have increased from 2005 to 2009?
   (a) ~89.32% (b) ~57.62%
   (c) ~40.32% (d) ~113.12%
27. What is the average annual growth rate of CO_2 emissions in power sector?
   (a) ~12.57% (b) ~16.87%
   (c) ~30.81% (d) ~50.25%
28. What is the percentage contribution of power sector to total CO_2 emissions in the year 2008?
   (a) ~30.82% (b) ~41.18%
   (c) ~51.38% (d) ~60.25%
29. In which year, the contribution (%) of industry to total sectoral CO_2 emissions was minimum?
   (a) 2005 (b) 2006
   (c) 2007 (d) 2009
30. Symbols A-F are used in which one of the following?
   (a) Binary number system
   (b) Decimal number system
   (c) Hexadecimal number system
   (d) Octal number system
31. Which one of the following is not a search engine?
   (a) Google (b) Chrome
   (c) Yahoo (d) Bing
32. CSS stands for
   (a) Cascading Style Sheets
   (b) Collecting Style Sheets
   (c) Comparative Style Sheets
   (d) Comprehensive Style Sheets
33. MOOC stands for
   (a) Media Online Open Course
   (b) Massachusetts Open Online Course
   (c) Massive Open Online Course
   (d) Myrind Open Online Course
34. Binary equivalent of decimal number 35 is
   (a) 100011 (b) 110001
   (c) 110101 (d) 101011
35. gif, jpg, bmp, png are used as extensions for files which store
   (a) audio data (b) image data
   (c) video data (d) text data
36. Which of the anthropogenic activity accounts for more than two-third of global water consumption?
   (a) Agriculture
   (b) Hydropower generation

(c) Industry
(d) Domestic and Municipal usage

37. One of the anthropogenic sources of gaseous pollutants chlorofluorocarbons (CFCs) in air is
(a) Cement industry
(b) Fertiliser industry
(c) Foam industry
(d) Pesticide industry

38. In terms of total CO_2 emissions from a country, identify the correct sequence:
(a) U.S.A. > China > India > Russia
(b) China > U.S.A. > India > Russia
(c) China > U.S.A. > Russia > India
(d) U.S.A. > China > Russia > India

39. Match List-I and List-II and identify the correct code:

List I
(A) World Health Day
(B) World Population Day
(C) World Ozone Day
(D) World AIDS Day

List II
(i) 16th September (ii) 1st December
(iii) 11th July (iv) 7th April

Codes:	**A**	**B**	**C**	**D**
(a)	(i)	(ii)	(iii)	(iv)
(b)	(iv)	(iii)	(i)	(ii)
(c)	(ii)	(iii)	(iv)	(i)
(d)	(iii)	(iv)	(ii)	(i)

40. The cyclone 'Hudhud' hit the coast of which State?
(a) Andhra Pradesh (b) Karnataka
(c) Kerala (d) Gujarat

41. Which of the following is not a renewable natural resource?
(a) Clean air (b) Fresh water
(c) Fertile soil (d) Salt

42. The maximum number of fake institutions/universities as identified by the UGC in the year 2014 are in the State/Union territory of
(a) Bihar (b) Uttar Pradesh
(c) Tamil Nadu (d) Delhi

43. Which of the following institutions are empowered to confer or grant degrees under the UGC Act, 1956?
1. A university established by an Act of Parliament.
2. A university established by an Act of Legislature.
3. A university/institution established by a linguistic minority.
4. An institution which is a deemed to be university.

Select the correct answer from the codes given below:
(a) 1 and 2 (b) 1, 2 and 3
(c) 1, 2 and 4 (d) 1, 2, 3 and 4

44. Which of the following are the tools of good governance?
1. Social Audit
2. Separation of Powers
3. Citizen's Charter
4. Right to Information

Select the correct answer from the codes given below:
(a) 1, 3 and 4 (b) 2, 3 and 4
(c) 1 and 4 (d) 1, 2, 3 and 4

45. Which of the following powers, the President has in relation to Lok Sabha?
1. Summoning
2. Adjournment—sine die
3. Prorogation
4. Dissolution

Select the correct answer from the codes given below:
(a) 1 and 4 (b) 1, 2 and 3
(c) 1, 3 and 4 (d) 1, 2, 3 and 4

46. The interval between two sessions of Parliament must not exceed
    (a) 3 months (b) 6 months
    (c) 4 months (d) 100 days
47. Right to Privacy as a Fundamental Right is implied in
    (a) Right to Freedom
    (b) Right to Life and Personal Liberty
    (c) Right to Equality
    (d) Right against Exploitation
48. Which of the following organizations deals with 'capacity building program' on Educational Planning?
    (a) NCERT (b) UGC
    (c) NAAC (d) NUEPA
49. "Education is the manifestation of perfection already in man" was stated by
    (a) M.K. Gandhi
    (b) R.N. Tagore
    (c) Swami Vivekanand
    (d) Sri Aurobindo
50. Which of the following is not a prescribed level of teaching?
    (a) Memory (b) Understanding
    (c) Reflective (d) Differentiation
51. Maximum participation of students during teaching is possible through
    (a) Lecture method
    (b) Demonstration method
    (c) Inductive method
    (d) Textbook method
52. Diagnostic evaluation ascertains
    (a) Students performance at the beginning of instructions.
    (b) Learning progress and failures during instructions.
    (c) Degree of achievement of instructions at the end.
    (d) Causes and remedies of persistent learning problems during instructions.
53. Instructional aids are used by the teacher to
    (a) glorify the class
    (b) attract the students
    (c) clarify the concepts
    (d) ensure discipline
54. Attitude of the teacher that affects teaching pertains to
    (a) Affective domain
    (b) Cognitive domain
    (c) Connative domain
    (d) Psychomotor domain
55. When planning to do as social research, it is better to
    (a) approach the topic with an open mind
    (b) do a pilot study before getting stuck into it
    (c) be familiar with literature on the topic
    (d) forget about theory because this is a very practical
56. When academicians are called to deliver lecture or presentation to an audience on certain topics or a set of topics of educational nature, it is called
    (a) Training Program
    (b) Seminar
    (c) Workshop
    (d) Symposium
57. The core elements of a dissertation are
    (a) Introduction; Data Collection; Data Analysis; Conclusions and Recommendations
    (b) Executive Summary; Literature review; Data gathered; Conclusions; Bibliography
    (c) Research Plan; Research Data; Analysis; References
    (d) Introduction; Literature Review; Research Methodology; Results; Discussion and Conclusion

58. What is a Research Design?
    (a) A way of conducting research that is not grounded in theory.
    (b) The choice between using qualitative or quantitative methods.
    (c) The style in which you present your research findings e.g. a graph.
    (d) A framework for every stage of the collection and analysis of data.
59. 'Sampling Cases' means
    (a) Sampling using a sampling frame
    (b) Identifying people who are suitable for research
    (c) Literally the researcher's brief case
    (d) Sampling of people, newspapers, television programmes etc.
60. The frequency distribution of a research data which is symmetrical in shape similar to a normal distribution but center peak is much higher, is
    (a) Skewed (b) Mesokurtic
    (c) Leptokurtic (d) Platykurtic

ANSWERS

1. (b)	2. (b)	3. (d)	4. (b)	5. (d)
6. (d)	7. (a)	8. (a)	9. (b)	10. (b)
11. (c)	12. (a)	13. (c)	14. (b)	15. (b)
16. (d)	17. (a)	18. (a)	19. (a)	20. (d)
21. (d)	22. (c)	23. (b)	24. (a)	25. (d)
26. (a)	27. (a)	28. (b)	29. (a)	30. (c)
31. (b)	32. (a)	33. (c)	34. (a)	35. (b)
36. (a)	37. (c)	38. (b)	39. (b)	40. (a)
41. (d)	42. (b)	43. (c)	44. (a)	45. (c)
46. (b)	47. (b)	48. (d)	49. (c)	50. (d)
51. (b)	52. (d)	53. (c)	54. (a)	55. (c)
56. (b)	57. (d)	58. (d)	59. (d)	60. (c)

PAPER–II

Note: This paper contains fifty (50) objective type questions of two (2) marks each. All questions are compulsory.

1. Thermal stratification of aquatic ecosystems takes place in
    (a) tropical lakes
    (b) temperate lakes
    (c) glacier lakes
    (d) meandering rivers
2. The scale length of pressure variations in atmosphere in vertical direction is about
    (a) 3 km (b) 4.8 km
    (c) 7 km (d) 12 km
3. Which radioactive element is considered as an indoor pollutant?
    (a) Oxygen-18 (b) Nitrogen-15
    (c) Carbon-13 (d) Radon
4. In a closed thermodynamic system, across its boundaries
    (a) no transfer of heat is possible.
    (b) no transfer of work is possible.
    (c) transfer of heat is possible but not of work.
    (d) transfer of heat and work is possible.
5. In an urban area, moist air at 27 °C has a mixing ratio of 50 gm per kg. Its virtual temperature is
    (a) 33.69 °C (b) 38.15 °C
    (c) 36.15 °C (d) 32.30 °C
6. Under aerobic biodegradation of DDT, which of the following compound is formed?
    (a) DDD (b) DDE
    (c) DDN (d) DDS
7. Among the following heavy metals, which has highest concentration in earth's crust?

(a) Chromium (b) Copper
(c) Nickel (d) Zinc

8. Composition-wise halons are related to
(a) CFCs (b) Halides
(c) Hydrocarbons (d) Peptides

9. Which of the following gases has highest absorption co-efficient for solubility in water?
(a) Hydrogen (b) Nitrogen
(c) Oxygen (d) Carbon dioxide

10. Quantity of glucose (MW 180) required to prepare 1000 ml of 5% solution is
(a) 5 g (b) 50 g
(c) 900 g (d) 9000 g

11. Endemic species are
(a) Uniformly distributed across the landscape
(b) Widely distributed
(c) Restricted to a particular area
(d) Continuously distributed globally

12. Which of the following is the *in-situ* biodiversity conservation site?
(a) Arboretum
(b) Botanical garden
(c) Biosphere reserve
(d) Orchidarium

13. The largest unit of climax communities representing well defined climatic zone is referred to as
(a) Biosphere (b) Biome
(c) Biota (d) Landscape

14. An active, adaptive control process which is able to maintain the overall balance is known as
(a) Bohr's Hypothesis
(b) Miller Hypothesis
(c) Gaia Hypothesis
(d) Kepler's Law

15. Niche of an organism is
(a) Address (b) Profession
(c) Location (d) Range

16. Out of the total fresh water volume of the frozen form constitutes
(a) 60 % (b) 70 %
(c) 80 % (d) 50 %

17. If Q = stream flow, P = precipitation, E = evapotranspiration, ΔS = net change in storage and ΔT = net underground transfers, then the basic water balance equation is
(a) $Q = (P + E) - (\Delta S + \Delta T)$
(b) $Q = (P - E) - (\Delta S + \Delta T)$
(c) $Q = (P - E) + (\Delta S + \Delta T)$
(d) $Q = (P - E) - (\Delta S - \Delta T)$

18. Particles with a diameter smaller than 0.002 mm are classed as
(a) Cobble (b) Pebble
(c) Silt (d) Colloids

19. Water storage capacity of which soil is maximum?
(a) Sandy loam (b) Loam
(c) Clay loam (d) Heavy clay

20. Which among the following is not a hot desert?
(a) Sahara (b) Kalahari
(c) Thar (d) Gobi

21. In an ideal MHD power generator, the maximum power P output varies with the velocity (u) of conducting fuel as
(a) $P_{max} \propto u$ (b) $P_{max} \propto u^2$
(c) $P_{max} \propto u^3$ (d) $P_{max} \propto u^{3/2}$

22. Which is the most efficient energy source for producing electricity?
(a) Nuclear power (b) Hydro power
(c) Wind power (d) Solar power

23. Which of the following types of coal has highest water content?

(a) Anthracite
(b) Bituminous coal
(c) Lignite
(d) Subbituminous coal

24. Energy intensity is the amount of energy
(a) produced per unit gross domestic product
(b) consumed per unit gross domestic product
(c) produced per year per unit area of the country
(d) consumed per year per unit area of the country

25. Which is the cleanest fuel for power generation?
(a) Coal (b) Uranium
(c) Hydrogen (d) Water

26. The mountain that rises a kilometre or more above the surrounding sea floor is called
(a) Oceanic island (b) Atoll
(c) Seamount (d) Island arc

27. Which form of As is most toxic?
(a) As^{+3} (b) As^{+2}
(c) As^{+6} (d) As^{+4}

28. Noise climate is represented by
(a) $L_{10} - L_{90}$ (b) L_{eq}
(c) L_{50} (d) $(L_{10} - L_{90})^2/60$

29. The classical smog is mainly composed of
(a) NO_x and smoke particulates
(b) O_3 and SO_2
(c) SO_2 and NO_x
(d) SO_2 and smoke particulates

30. According to National Ambient Air Quality Standards the annual average concentration of SPM in a residential area should not exceed
(a) 80 μg/m^3 (b) 100 μg/m^3
(c) 140 μg/m^3 (d) 200 μg/m^3

31. "Blue baby syndrome" is caused due to intake of water high in
(a) Ammonia (b) Nitrates
(c) Sulphates (d) Sulphides

32. EIA of mining activities involve impact assessment on
1. Geological Environment
2. Biological Environment
3. Aerial Environment

Codes:
(a) 1 only (b) 2 and 3 only
(c) 1 and 3 only (d) 1, 2 and 3

33. Accreditation of Environmental Consultant Organizations in India is done by
(a) Ministry of Environment, Forest and Climate Change
(b) Central Pollution Control Board
(c) Ministry of Earth Sciences
(d) Quality Council of India

34. Life Cycle Assessment (LCA) does not include
(a) Life Cycle Inventory of the product
(b) Quantitative improvement in the process of the product
(c) Life Cycle Impact Analysis
(d) Emergency Preparedness Plan

35. A developmental project requires both environmental clearance as well as approval under
(a) Water Act, 1974
(b) Forest (Conservation) Act, 1980
(c) National Environmental Tribunal Act, 1995
(d) Air Act, 1981

36. The best practice of disposal of construction and demolition (C & D) debris is
    (a) Incineration
    (b) Recycling
    (c) Land fills
    (d) Solidification

37. Pyrolysis of Solid Waste refers to
    (a) High temperature aerobic incineration
    (b) High temperature anaerobic distillation of waste for energy generation
    (c) Ambient aerobic distillation
    (d) Ambient anaerobic distillation

38. Kyoto Protocol of 1997 introduced the concept of carbon trading in the year of
    (a) 2000 (b) 2004
    (c) 2001 (d) 2002

39. Citizen's Charter on Environment in the Constitution of India is embodied in
    (a) Article 48 (b) Article 48A
    (c) Article 49A (d) Article 51A

40. United Nation's Conference on Environment and Development was held in
    (a) December, 1993
    (b) June, 1992
    (c) December, 1995
    (d) November, 1996

41. The geometric mean of the numbers 4, 6 and 9 is
    (a) 6 (b) 8
    (c) 5 (d) 7

42. A complete enumerate of all items in the population is
    (a) Unrestricted sampling
    (b) Non-probability sampling
    (c) Census
    (d) Sample survey

43. The term 'parameter' is an attribute associated with the data pertaining to
    (a) sample
    (b) population
    (c) descriptive statistics
    (d) sampling technique

44. A solar cell of surface area = 5 cm^2 delivers a current of 0.1 A at 0.6 V. If the intensity of solar radiation impinging on the solar cell is 1.0 kW/m^2, the efficiency of the solar cell is
    (a) 6 % (b) 3 %
    (c) 30 % (d) 12 %

45. **Assertion (A):** Living systems exposed to drought salinity and freezing show enhanced levels of osmolytes.
    Reason (R): Drought, salinity and freezing stress induce water deficit.
    In the context of the two statements, which one of the following is correct?
    (a) Both (A) and (R) are true and (R) is the correct explanation of (A).
    (b) Both (A) and (R) are true, but (R) is not the correct explanation of (A).
    (c) (A) is true, but (R) is false.
    (d) (A) is false, but (R) is true.

46. UN Decade of Education for Sustainable Development is
    (a) 2000-2009 (b) 2005-2014
    (c) 2010-2019 (d) 2020-2031

47. Two kinds of the values distinguished in environmental ethics are
    (a) Instrumental value and intrinsic value
    (b) Direct use values and social values
    (c) Social values and existence value
    (d) Indirect use value and aesthetic value

48. The natural sources of methyl bromide in the atmosphere is
    (a) Ocean (b) Volcanoes
    (c) Landslide (d) Vegetation

49. The part of an actual resource which can be developed profitably in the future is
    (a) Non-renewable resources
    (b) Potential resources
    (c) Reserved resources
    (d) Stock resources

50. Trophic state index of aquatic ecosystem is determined by the concentration of
    (a) Chlorophyll-a (b) NO_3^-
    (c) PO_4^{3} (d) NO_2

ANSWERS

1. (b)	2. (c)	3. (d)	4. (d)	5. (c)
6. (b)	7. (b)	8. (a)	9. (d)	10. (b)
11. (c)	12. (c)	13. (b)	14. (c)	15. (b)
16. (b)	17. (c)	18. (d)	19. (d)	20. (d)
21. (b)	22. (b)	23. (c)	24. (b)	25. (c)
26. (c)	27. (a)	28. (a)	29. (d)	30. (c)
31. (b)	32. (d)	33. (d)	34. (d)	35. (b)
36. (c)	37. (b)	38. (d)	39. (d)	40. (b)
41. (a)	42. (c)	43. (b)	44. (d)	45. (a)
46. (b)	47. (a)	48. (a)	49. (c)	50. (a)

PAPER–III

Note: This paper contains seventy-five (75) objective type questions of two (2) marks each. All questions are compulsory.

1. Which of the following ranges of scale lengths represents meso-scale motions in atmosphere?
   (a) 30 km-400 km (b) 500 m-10 km
   (c) 1 km-2 km (d) 100 m-1 km

2. Rayleigh scattering in the atmosphere is caused by
   (a) molecules larger than the wavelength
   (b) molecules equal to the size of wavelength
   (c) molecules whose size is much smaller than the wavelength
   (d) molecules and particles of all sizes

3. Wind rose is a
   (a) graphical representation of wind velocity vector over a period of time in a polar diagram.
   (b) graphical representation of wind velocity vector in a spherical coordinate system over a period of time.
   (c) graphical representation of horizontal and vertical wind speeds over a period of time in polar diagram.
   (d) graphical representation of instantaneous wind velocity at a particular time.

4. The key groups of organic molecules that help in chelation of metal ions are
   1. – COOH 2. – SH
   3. CH_3 4. – CHO
   Choose the correct answer from the codes given below:
   (a) 1 only (b) 1 and 2 only
   (c) 2, 3 and 4 only (d) 1, 2 and 4 only

5. Geostrophic winds are the result of the balance between
   (a) coriolis force and pressure gradient force
   (b) coriolis force and centrifugal force
   (c) pressure gradient force and frictional force
   (d) pressure gradient force and centrifugal force

6. A possible mechanism for photochemical smog inhibition is to add compounds like diethylhydroxylamine (DEHA) as it reacts with

(a) hydrocarbon
(b) nitrogen dioxide
(c) PAN
(d) hydroxyl radicals

7. In the determination of sulphur dioxide by p-rosaniline method, the end product is
(a) p-rosaniline sulfonic acid
(b) methyl p-rosaniline
(c) p-rosaniline methyl sulfonic acid
(d) sulfo methyl p-rosaniline

8. Number of molecuels present in 10 ml of proline is
(a) 6.023×10^{23} (b) 6.023×10^{20}
(c) 6.023×10^{18} (d) 6.023×10^{17}

9. Nitrogenous biochemical oxygen demand refers to the quantity of O_2 needed to convert
(a) N_2 to NO_3^-
(b) N_2 to NH_4^+
(c) NH_4^+ to NO_3^-
(d) Protein to $CO_2 + H_2O + NO_2$

10. Beer-Lambert's law defines
(a) The degree of absorption of monochromatic light by a homogeneous medium
(b) Atomic absorption spectrophotometry
(c) Atomic emission spectrophotometry
(d) Gas chromatography

11. Chemically phytochelatins are
(a) Proteins
(b) Polysaccharides
(c) Lipids
(d) Polypeptides

12. Mixture of organic pollutants X and Y were separated using paper chromatography and the R_f values obtained for X and Y were 0.75 and 0.25, respectively. Which relationship holds good for the solubility of these pollutants in mobile phase?
(a) X > Y (b) X < Y
(c) X = Y (d) X + Y = 1

13. Overall reaction of Winkler's method is
$$4S_2O_3^{2-} + 4H^+ + O_2 \rightarrow 2S_4O_6^{2-} + 2H_2O$$
This equation indicates:
(a) One mole of O_2 is equivalent to one mole of thiosulphate.
(b) One mole of O_2 is equivalent to two moles of thiosulphate.
(c) One mole of O_2 is equivalent to three moles of thiosulphate.
(d) One mole of O_2 is equivalent to four moles of thiosulphate.

14. Return of an ecosystem to a condition prior to disturbance refers to as
(a) Rehabilitation (b) Restoration
(c) Rejuvenation (d) Reclaimation

15. **Assertion (A):** Shade loving species show better natural regeneration under highly disturbed condition.
Reason (R): Heliophilic species needs more exposure to light for better natural regeneration.
In the context of the two statements, which one of the following is correct?
(a) Both (A) and (R) are true and (R) is the correct explanation of (A).
(b) Both (A) and (R) are true, but (R) is not the correct explanation of (A).
(c) (A) is true, but (R) is false.
(d) (A) is false, but (R) is true.

16. Which one of the following enzymes work under strict anaerobic conditions to fix atmospheric nitrogen?
(a) Nitrate reductase
(b) Nitrite reductase
(c) Transaminase
(d) Nitrogenase

17. Predatory strategy followed by an alligator for hunting is
(a) Chase (b) Stalk
(c) Ambush (d) Camouflage

18. In a tropical peat forest, the carbon storage (tonnes/ha) is typically in the range
(a) 3000-6000 (b) 13000-16000
(c) 300-600 (d) 300-1600

19. Which one of the following bacterial species convert NO_2^- to NO_3^-?
(a) *Nitrosomonas* (b) *Nitrobacter*
(c) *Rhizobium* (d) *Azospirillum*

20. **Assertion (A):** Living system adapted to low temperatures invariably show higher unsaturated to saturated fatty acid in membrane lipids.
Reason (R): Fluidity of membranes is directly proportional to unsaturated to saturated fatty acids in membrane lipids.
In the context of the two statements, which one of the following is correct?
(a) Both (A) and (R) are true and (R) is the correct explanation of (A).
(b) Both (A) and (R) are true, but (R) is not the correct explanation of (A).
(c) (A) is true, but (R) is false.
(d) (A) is false, but (R) is true.

21. Which of the following(s) are produced during fermentation?
1. Ethanol 2. Citrate
3. Lactate 4. Succinate
Choose the correct answer from the codes given below:
(a) 1 only (b) 1 and 2 only
(c) 1 and 3 only (d) 2 and 4 only

22. Salinity of the ocean varies from 2.0 % to 4.2 % in
(a) Red Sea and Gulf of Kachchh
(b) Black Sea and Omura Bay
(c) Baltic Sea and Persian Gulf
(d) Mediterranean Sea and Bay of Fundy

23. Uranium in Indian agricultural soils is mainly contributed by
(a) Weathering of Uranium rich minerals
(b) Excess addition of NPK fertilizers
(c) Excess addition of pesticides
(d) Excess addition of fungicides

24. Loamy sand contains
(a) > 80 % silt and > 80 % clay
(b) 10 % silt and 5 % clay
(c) 15 to 30 % silt and 10 to 15 % clay
(d) > 80 % silt and < 20% clay

25. Spectral reflectance of leaf is highest for which band?
(a) Blue (b) Green
(c) Near infrared (d) Middle infrared

26. Match the List I with List II and choose the correct answer from the given codes:

List I (Elements)	List II (Concentration in Earth's Crust by weight %)
(A) Oxygen	(i) 8.13
(B) Aluminium	(ii) 46.60
(C) Iron	(iii) 27.72
(D) Silicon	(iv) 5.00

Identify the correct code:

Codes:	(A)	(B)	(C)	(D)
(a)	(i)	(iv)	(iii)	(ii)
(b)	(iii)	(ii)	(i)	(iv)
(c)	(ii)	(i)	(iv)	(iii)
(d)	(iv)	(iii)	(ii)	(i)

27. Indian Microwave Remote Sensing Satellite is
(a) RISAT (b) Resourcesat
(c) IRS (d) Bhaskara

28. Mount Etna in Sicily and Mauna Loa in Hawaiian Islands are the most noteworthy examples of

(a) shield volcanoes
(b) plug dome
(c) strato volcanoes
(d) pyroclastic cones

29. Match the List I with List II and choose the correct answer from the given codes:

List I (Mineral Deposit)	List II (Top producer)
(A) Bauxite	(i) Peru
(B) Copper	(ii) India
(C) Mica	(iii) USA
(D) Guano	(iv) Australia

Identify the correct code:

Codes:	(A)	(B)	(C)	(D)
(a)	(i)	(ii)	(iii)	(iv)
(b)	(iv)	(iii)	(ii)	(i)
(c)	(iii)	(i)	(iv)	(ii)
(d)	(ii)	(iv)	(i)	(iii)

30. Which of the following fuels has the highest HHV carbon intensity?
(a) Natural gas (b) Oil
(c) Bituminous coal (d) Nuclear fuel

31. If fission of 1 atom of U^{235} produces 200 MeV energy, how much energy will be produced by 1 metric ton of U^{235}?
(a) 4.1×10^7 MJ (b) 8.2×10^7 MJ
(c) 1.23×10^8 MJ (d) 2×10^5 MJ

32. The Green Climate Fund recently set up to help poor countries adapt to climate impacts envisages financial support to the extent of (in $ per year)
(a) 100 bn (b) 30 bn
(c) 10 bn (d) 3 bn

33. Which of the following biomass conversion processes produces biogas from crop residues?
(a) Anaerobic digestion
(b) Fermentation
(c) Pyrolysis
(d) Aerobic digestion

34. Which among the following is superior carbon fixer per unit area for bioenergy generation?
(a) Trees
(b) Shrubs
(c) Blue-green algae
(d) Crops

35. Energy flow in ecosystem is governed by
(a) First law of thermodynamics
(b) Second law of thermodynamics
(c) Planck's law
(d) Kirchoff's law

36. Average number of carbon in diesel ranges between
(a) $C_{18} - C_{24}$ (b) $C_{10} - C_{16}$
(c) $C_4 - C_6$ (d) $C_{25} - C_{30}$

37. Knocking effect in the gasoline cannot be reached by one of the following additives:
(a) $(C_2H_5)_4Pb$ (b) BTX
(c) Kerosene (d) n-Butane

38. Radioactive mineral available in the Indian coastal region is
(a) Rutile (b) Monazite
(c) Apatite (d) Magnetite

39. Thermal pollution in the coastal region is caused by
1. Atomic power plants
2. Thermal power plants
3. Industrial plants
4. Tourism industry

Choose the correct answer from the codes given below:
Codes:
(a) 1, 2, 3 only (b) 1 and 2 only
(c) 3 and 4 only (d) 2 and 3 only

40. **Assertion (A):** Metallic contaminants are toxic to the microorganism.
Reason (R): Heavy metal tends to precipitate in the form of phosphatic compounds and decrease soil fertility.

In the context of the two statements, which one of the following is correct?

(a) Both (A) and (R) are true and (R) is the correct explanation of (A).
(b) Both (A) and (R) are true, but (R) is not the correct explanation of (A).
(c) (A) is true, but (R) is false.
(d) (A) is false, but (R) is true.

41. A point source of sound produces a noise of 70 dB at a distance of 20 m from it. What will be the noise level at 80 m from it?

(a) 35 dB (b) 64 dB
(c) 58 dB (d) 52 dB

42. Stratospheric ozone absorbs UV radiations principally in the wavelength range

(a) 320-400 nm (b) 230-320 nm
(c) < 290 nm (d) 180-240 nm

43. If Γ_d, Γ_s and Γ represent dry adiabatic, saturated adiabatic lapse rate and environmental lapse rate, respectively, the condition for unstable atmosphere is

(a) $\Gamma > \Gamma_d$ (b) $\Gamma < \Gamma_d$
(c) $\Gamma < \Gamma_s$ (d) $\Gamma < \Gamma_s < \Gamma_d$

44. At initial time (t_0) number of *E. coli* per ml was 10. If generation time is 30 minutes, what would be number of cells per ml after a duration of 4 hours?

(a) 256 (b) 2560
(c) 240 (d) 300

45. Emission inventories involved in urban air quality assessment include parameters on

1. SO_2, NO_x, particulate matter pollutants
2. Industry, traffic, domestic sources
3. Fuel type, gasoline, wood as energy carrier

Choose the correct answer from codes given below:

Codes:

(a) 1 and 2 only (b) 2 and 3 only
(c) 1 and 3 only (d) 1, 2 and 3

46. **Assertion (A):** Leopold matrix can be expanded or contracted.

Reason (R): Leopold matrix is a checklist designed to show possible interactions between developmental activities and set of environmental characteristics.

In the context of the two statements, which one of the following is correct?

(a) Both (A) and (R) are true and (R) is the correct explanation of (A).
(b) Both (A) and (R) are true, but (R) is not the correct explanation of (A).
(c) (A) is true, but (R) is false.
(d) (A) is false, but (R) is true.

47. In Battele environment evaluation system the total parameter importance units is lowest for

(a) Ecology
(b) Environmental Pollution
(c) Aesthetics
(d) Human interest

48. ISO 14040 is

(a) Environmental Management: Life cycle assessment principle and framework.
(b) Environmental Management - environmental assessment of sites and organization.
(c) Guidelines for environmental audit - general principle.
(d) Environmental Management - vocabulary.

49. Given below are stages within each tier of risk assessment:

1. identification of consequences
2. hazard identification
3. probability assessment
4. assessment of consequences as well as significance of risk
5. magnitude assessment for consequences

Which one of the following code represent correct sequences?

(a) 2, 1, 5, 3, 4 (b) 1, 2, 3, 4, 5
(c) 3, 2, 4, 5, 1 (d) 4, 2, 1, 3, 5

50. Ecolabels are indicators of
1. Acceptable level of environmental impact of a product.
2. Environmental performance of a product.
3. Claims of environmental friendliness of a product.

Choose the correct answer from the codes given below:

(a) 1, 2, 3 (b) 1, 2 only
(c) 1 only (d) 2 only

51. Ecosystem diversity can be best studied using the
(a) Topographical maps
(b) Geoinformatics
(c) Geodesy
(d) Geology

52. Biennial assessment of forest cover in India is done by
(a) Indian Institute of Remote Sensing, Dehradun
(b) Forest Research Institute, Dehradun
(c) Indian Institute of Forest Management, Bhopal
(d) Forest Survey of India, Dehradun

53. Soil moisture using remote sensing techniques is determined best in
(a) Optical region
(b) Thermal region
(c) Microwave region
(d) Infrared region

54. Which one of the following statements is not connected to ISO 14000 series of Environmental Management?
(a) Promotes eco-labelling of the product
(b) It is based on the recommendation of TC-207 committee
(c) Make the environmental audit mandatory
(d) Promotes human rights and women empowerment

55. As per colour coding of plastic bags for biomedical wastes, match the List I with List II and choose the correct answer from the codes given below:

List I (Colour Code)
(A) Yellow plastic bags
(B) Black plastic bags
(C) Blue/White plastic bags
(D) Red plastic bags

List II (Option for disposal)
(i) Disposal in secured land fills
(ii) Incineration and deep burials
(iii) Autoclaving and chemical treatment
(iv) Microwave treatments and destruction

Codes:	(A)	(B)	(C)	(D)
(a)	(iv)	(iii)	(ii)	(i)
(b)	(i)	(iv)	(iii)	(ii)
(c)	(ii)	(i)	(iv)	(iii)
(d)	(iii)	(ii)	(i)	(iv)

56. Given below is a list of natural disasters:
1. Hudhud cyclone
2. Chernobyl nuclear plant disaster
3. Tsunami in Indian Ocean
4. Bhopal gas tragedy

Which is the correct chronological sequence for the above events in the codes given below?

Codes:

(a) 3, 1, 2, 4 (b) 2, 3, 1, 4
(c) 4, 2, 3, 1 (d) 1, 2, 3, 4

57. Benchmarking in environmental management refers to
   (a) Potential risk assessment.
   (b) Reporting of environmental performance.
   (c) Assessment of organization's business processes against the best-in-class operations to improve the performance.
   (d) Setting of environmental standards to be followed by environmental managers.

58. Basel convention is related to
   (a) Control of ozone depletion.
   (b) Control of water pollution.
   (c) Transboundary movement of hazardous wastes and their disposal.
   (d) Environmental auditing.

59. Concept of intergenerational equity on natural resources refers to
   (a) Legal obligations of present generation to future generations.
   (b) Moral obligation of the present generation to future generation.
   (c) Equitable responsibility of pollution generating industries.
   (d) Prudent use of resources inherited from previous generation.

60. Which among the following is not correct in regard to the sources of nitrate in the soils?
   1. Microbial breakdown of soil organic matter, organic manure and plant residues.
   2. Fertilizers which add nitrate and that formed by microbial oxidation of NH_4^+ from ammonium fertilizers or urea.
   3. Addition from the atmosphere.
   4. Pesticides containing nitrogen atoms.

   Choose the correct answer from the following codes:

   Codes:

   (a) 1 (b) 2
   (c) 3 (d) 4

61. Which one of the following protozoan is related to water borne disease?
   (a) *Spumella sp.*
   (b) *Entamoeba histolytica*
   (c) *Paramoecium*
   (d) *Plasmodium vivax*

62. Match the List I with List II, choose the correct answer from the given codes:

   List I (Group of Analysis)
   (A) Unidimensional analysis
   (B) Multivariate analysis
   (C) Interferential analysis
   (D) Bivariate analysis

   List II (Test)
   (i) Testing of hypothesis
   (ii) Measure of central tendency
   (iii) Two-way ANOVA
   (iv) Canonical analysis

Codes:	(A)	(B)	(C)	(D)
(a)	(i)	(iii)	(iv)	(ii)
(b)	(ii)	(iv)	(i)	(iii)
(c)	(iii)	(i)	(ii)	(iv)
(d)	(iv)	(ii)	(iii)	(i)

63. The differences between crude birth rate and crude death rate in a population is called
   (a) Population momentum
   (b) Demographic transition rate
   (c) Net migration rate
   (d) Rate of natural increase

64. Which set of stoichiometric coefficient correctly balance the equation?

(a) H_2O_2 + (b) $KMnO_4$ + (c) $H_2SO_4 \rightarrow$
(d) K_2SO_4 + (e) $MnSO_4$ + (f) H_2O + (g) O_2

Select the correct answer from the codes given below:

Codes:

	a	b	c	d	e	f	g
(a)	1	1	1	1	1	1	1
(b)	1	2	3	1	2	4	3
(c)	2	5	3	2	1	8	5
(d)	5	2	3	1	2	8	5

65. **Assertion (A):** The hypothesis testing can proceed on the basis of null hypothesis.
Reason (R): If null hypothesis is true probabilities to different possible sample result can be assigned to it.
In the context of the two statements, which one of the following is correct?
(a) Both (A) and (R) are true and (R) is the correct explanation of (A).
(b) Both (A) and (R) are true, but (R) is not the correct explanation of (A).
(c) (A) is true, but (R) is false.
(d) (A) is false, but (R) is true.

66. The advantage of Leslie matrices are
1. Stable age distribution is not required for valid population projections.
2. Can derive finite rate of population change.
3. Requires large amount of data on population structure.
Choose the correct answer from the codes given below:
Codes:
(a) 1 and 3 only (b) 1 only
(c) 1 and 2 only (d) 2 and 3 only

67. Important characteristics of χ^2 test are
1. As a non-parametric test, it is based on frequencies.
2. It is not useful for estimation and to test hypothesis.
3. Can be applied to a complex contingency table.
Choose the correct answer from the codes given below:
Codes:
(a) 1 and 2 only (b) 1 and 3 only
(c) 2 and 3 only (d) 1, 2 and 3

68. The quantity of 0.2% solution needed to prepare 1000 mL of 10 ppm solution is
(a) 5 mL (b) 10 mL
(c) 20 mL (d) 200 mL

69. Which one of the following international events was not related to climate change?
(a) UN framework convention on climate change, 1992.
(b) Montreal Protocol, 1987
(c) Stockholm conference on "Human and Environment", 1972
(d) Kyoto Protocol, 1997

70. Which of the following has the lowest Ozone depletion potential?
(a) HCFC-22 (b) HCFC-123
(c) Halon-1211 (d) CFC-12

71. **Assertion (A):** Rain water harvesting, primarily aims at artificial recharge of ground water to uplift the ground water table.
Reason (R): Under rain water harvesting, the primary aim is to let the rain water infiltrate into the underground aquifer.
In the context of the two statements, which one of the following is correct?
(a) Both (A) and (R) are true and (R) is the correct explanation of (A).
(b) Both (A) and (R) are true, but (R) is not the correct explanation of (A).
(c) (A) is true, but (R) is false.
(d) (A) is false, but (R) is true.

72. For environmental mass awareness, Paryavaran Vahini Scheme was launched in the year

(a) 1988 (b) 2003
(c) 1992 (d) 1998

73. Disaster Management Act in India came into existence in the year
(a) 2003 (b) 2005
(c) 1998 (d) 2006

74. Which one of the following is most reactive oxygen species?
(a) $^1O_2$ (b) O_2^-
(c) H_2O_2 (d) $\dot{O}H$

75. If we move through the group I elements from top to bottom we first encounter Lithium, Sodium and Potassium. If we move further which elements we will encounter in sequence?
(a) Caesium, Calcium, Rubidium
(b) Rubidium, Caesium, Francium
(c) Rubidium, Caesium, Rhodium
(d) Magnesium, Rubidium, Francium

ANSWERS

1. (a)	2. (c)	3. (a)	4. (d)	5. (a)
6. (d)	7. (c)	8. (z)	9. (c)	10. (a)
11. (d)	12. (a)	13. (d)	14. (b)	15. (d)
16. (d)	17. (c)	18. (a)	19. (b)	20. (a)
21. (c)	22. (z)	23. (b)	24. (b)	25. (c)
26. (c)	27. (a)	28. (2)	29. (b)	30. (c)
31. (z)	32. (a)	33. (a)	34. (c)	35. (b)
36. (b)	37. (z)	38. (b)	39. (b)	40. (a)
41. (c)	42. (b)	43. (a)	44. (b)	45. (d)
46. (a)	47. (c)	48. (a)	49. (a)	50. (b)
51. (b)	52. (d)	53. (c)	54. (d)	55. (c)
56. (c)	57. (c)	58. (c)	59. (b)	60. (d)
61. (b)	62. (b)	63. (d)	64. (b)	65. (a)
66. (c)	67. (b)	68. (a)	69. (c)	70. (b)
71. (b)	72. (c)	73. (b)	74. (d)	75. (b)

JUNE–2015

Note: This paper contains Sixty (60) multiple-choice questions, each question carrying two (2) marks. Candidate is expected to answer any Fifty (50) questions. In case more than Fifty (50) questions are attempted, only the first Fifty (50) questions will be evaluated.

PAPER–I

1. Which of the following is the highest level of cognitive ability?
   (a) Knowing (b) Understanding
   (c) Analysing (d) Evaluating
2. Which of the following factors does not impact teaching?
   (a) Teacher's knowledge
   (b) Classroom activities that encourage learning
   (c) Socio-economic background of teachers and students
   (d) Learning through experience
3. Which of the following statements about teaching aids are correct?
   (1) They help in retaining concepts for longer duration.
   (2) They help students learn better.
   (3) They make teaching learning process interesting.
   (4) They enhance rote learning.
   Select the correct answer from the codes given below:
   (a) (1), (2), (3) and (4)
   (b) (1), (2) and (3)
   (c) (2), (3) and (4)
   (d) (1), (2) and (4)
4. Techniques used by a teacher to teach include:
   (1) Lecture
   (2) Interactive lecture
   (3) Group work
   (4) Self study
   Select the correct answer from the codes given below:
   (a) (1), (2) and (3)
   (b) (1), (2), (3) and (4)
   (c) (2), (3) and (4)
   (d) (1), (2) and (4)
5. Achievement tests are commonly used for the purpose of:
   (a) Making selections for a specific job
   (b) Selecting candidates for a course
   (c) Identifying strengths and weaknesses of learners
   (d) Assessing the amount of learning after teaching
6. A good teacher is one who:
   (a) gives useful information
   (b) explains concepts and principles
   (c) gives printed notes to students
   (d) inspires students to learn
7. Which of the following statements regarding the meaning of research are correct?
   (1) Research refers to a series of systematic activity or activities undertaken to find out the solution of a problem.
   (2) It is a systematic, logical and an unbiased process wherein verification

of hypothesis, data analysis, interpretation and formation of principles can be done.
(3) It is an intellectual enquiry or quest towards truth.
(4) It leads to enhancement of knowledge.
Select the correct answer from the codes given below:
(a) (1), (2) and (3)
(b) (2), (3) and (4)
(c) (1), (3) and (4)
(d) (1), (2), (3) and (4)

8. A good thesis writing should involve:
(a) reduction of punctuation and grammatical errors to a minimum.
(b) careful checking of references.
(c) consistency in the way the thesis is written.
(d) a clear and well-written abstract.
Select the correct answer from the codes given below:
(a) (1), (2), (3) and (4)
(b) (1), (2) and (3)
(c) (1), (2) and (4)
(d) (2), (3) and (4)

9. Jean Piaget gave a theory of cognitive development of humans on the basis of his:
(a) Fundamental Research
(b) Applied Research
(c) Action Research
(d) Evaluation Research

10. "Male and female students perform equally well in a numerical aptitude test." This statement indicates a:
(a) research hypothesis
(b) null hypothesis
(c) directional hypothesis
(d) statistical hypothesis

11. The conclusions/findings of which type of research cannot be generalized to other situations?
(a) Historical Research
(b) Descriptive Research
(c) Experimental Research
(d) Causal Comparative Research

12. Which of the following steps are required to design a questionnaire?
(1) Writing primary and secondary aims of the study.
(2) Review of the current literature.
(3) Prepare a draft of questionnaire.
(4) Rcvision of the draft.
Select the correct answer from the codes given below:
(a) (1), (2) and (3)
(b) (1), (3) and (4)
(c) (2), (3) and (4)
(d) (1), (2), (3) and (4)

Read the following passage carefully and answer questions 13 to 18.

Story telling is not in our genes. Neither it is an evolutionary history. It is the essence of what makes us Human.

Human beings progress by telling stories. One event can result in a great variety of stories being told about it. Sometimes those stories differ greatly. Which stories are picked up and repeated and which ones are dropped and forgotten often determines how we progress. Our history, knowledge and understanding are all the collections of the few stories that survive. This includes the stories that we tell each other about the future. And how the future will turn out depends partly, possibly largely, on which stories we collectively choose to believe.

Some stories are designed to spread fear and concern. This is because some story-tellers feel that there is a need to raise some tensions. Some stories are frightening, they are like totemic warnings: "Fail to act now and we are all doomed." Then there are stories that indicate that all will be fine so long as we leave everything upto a few especially able adults. Currently, this trend is being led by those who call themselves "rational optimists". They tend to claim that it is human nature to compete and to succeed and also to profit at the expense of others. The rational optimists however, do not realize how humanity has progressed overtime through amiable social networks and how large groups work in less selfishness and in the process accommodate rich and poor, high and low alike. This aspect in story-telling is considered by the 'Practical Possibles', who sit between those who say all is fine and cheerful and be individualistic in your approach to a successful future, and those who ordain pessimism and fear that we are doomed.

What the future holds for us is which stories we hold on to and how we act on them.

Answer the following questions:

13. Our knowledge is a collection of:
    (a) all stories that we have heard during our life-time
    (b) some stories that we remember
    (c) a few stories that survive
    (d) some important stories
14. Story telling is:
    (a) an art
    (b) a science
    (c) in our genes
    (d) the essence of what makes us human
15. How the future will turn out to be, depends upon the stories?
    (a) We collectively choose to believe in
    (b) Which are repeatedly narrated
    (c) Designed to spread fear and tension
    (d) Designed to make prophecy
16. Rational optimists:
    (1) Look for opportunities.
    (2) Are sensible and cheerful.
    (3) Are selfishly driven.

    Identify the correct answer from the codes given below:
    (a) (1), (2) and (3) (b) (1) only
    (c) (1) and (2) only (d) (2) and (3) only
17. Humans become less selfish when:
    (a) they work in large groups
    (b) they listen to frightening stories
    (c) they listen to cheerful stories
    (d) they work in solitude
18. 'Practical Possibles' are the ones who:
    (a) follow Midway Path
    (b) are doom-mongers
    (c) are self-centred
    (d) are cheerful and carefree
19. Effectiveness of communication can be traced from which of the following?
    (1) Attitude surveys
    (2) Performance records
    (3) Students attendance
    (4) Selection of communication channel

    Select the correct answer from the codes given below:
    (a) (1), (2), (3) and (4)
    (b) (1), (2) and (3)
    (c) (2), (3) and (4)
    (d) (1), (2) and (4)
20. **Assertion (A):** Formal communication tends to be fast and flexible.
    Reason (R): Formal communication is a systematic and orderly flow of information.
    (a) Both (A) and (R) are correct and (R) is correct explanation of (A)
    (b) Both (A) and (R) are correct, but (R) is not correct explanation of (A)
    (c) (A) is correct, but (R) is false
    (d) (A) is false, but (R) is correct
21. Which of the following are the characteristic features of communication?
    (1) Communication involves exchange of ideas, facts and opinions.

(2) Communication involves both information and understanding.
(3) Communication is a continuous process.
(4) Communication is a circular process.

Select the correct answer from the codes given below:
(a) (1), (2) and (3)
(b) (1), (2) and (4)
(c) (2), (3) and (4)
(d) (1), (2), (3) and (4)

22. The term 'grapevine' is also known as:
(a) Downward communication
(b) Informal communication
(c) Upward communication
(d) Horizontal communication

23. Which of the following is not a principle of effective communication?
(a) Persuasive and convincing dialogue
(b) Participation of the audience
(c) One-way transfer of information
(d) Strategic use of grapevine

24. In communication, the language is:
(a) The verbal code
(b) Intrapersonal
(c) The symbolic code
(d) The non-verbal code

25. The next term in the series is:
2, 5, 9, 19, 37, ?
(a) 73 (b) 75
(c) 78 (d) 80

26. In certain code MATHURA is coded as JXQEROX. The code of HOTELS will be:
(a) LEQIBP (b) ELQBIP
(c) LEBIQP (d) ELIPQB

27. One day Prakash left home and walked 10 km towards south, turned right and walked 5 km, turned right and walked 10 km and turned left and walked 10 km. How many km will he have to walk to reach his home straight?
(a) 10 (b) 20
(c) 15 (d) 30

28. A girl introduced a boy as the son of the daughter of the father of her uncle. The boy is related to the girl as:
(a) Brother (b) Uncle
(c) Nephew (d) Son

29. In an examination 10,000 students appeared. The result revealed the number of students who have:
passed in all five subjects = 5583
passed in three subjects only = 1400
passed in two subjects only = 1200
passed in one subject only = 735
failed in English only = 75
failed in Physics only = 145
failed in Chemistry only = 140
failed in Mathematics only = 200
failed in Bio-science only = 157
The number of students passed in at least four subjects is:
(a) 6300 (b) 6900
(c) 7300 (d) 7900

30. At present a person is 4 times older than his son and is 3 years older than his wife. After 3 years the age of the son will be 15 years. The age of the person's wife after 5 years will be:
(a) 42 (b) 48
(c) 45 (d) 50

31. If we want to seek new knowledge of facts about the world, we must rely on reason of the type:
(a) Inductive (b) Deductive
(c) Demonstrative (d) Physiological

32. A deductive argument is invalid if:
(a) Its premises and conclusions are all false
(b) Its premises are true but its conclusion is false

(c) Its premises are false but its conclusion is true
(d) Its premises and conclusions are all true

33. Inductive reasoning is grounded on:
(a) Integrity of nature
(b) Unity of nature
(c) Uniformity of nature
(d) Harmony of nature

34. Among the following statements two are contradictory to each other. Select the correct code that represents them:
Statements:
(1) All poets are philosophers.
(2) Some poets are philosophers.
(3) Some poets are not philosophers.
(4) No philosopher is a poet.
Codes:
(a) (1) and (2) (b) (1) and (4)
(c) (1) and (3) (d) (2) and (3)

35. Which of the codes given below contains only the correct statements? Select the code:
Statements:
(1) Venn diagram represents the arguments graphically.
(2) Venn diagram can enhance our understanding.
(3) Venn diagram may be called valid or invalid.
(4) Venn diagram is clear method of notation.
Codes:
(a) (1), (2) and (3) (b) (1), (2) and (4)
(c) (2), (3) and (4) (d) (1), (3) and (4)

36. When the purpose of a definition is to explain the use or to eliminate ambiguity the definition is called:
(a) Stipulative (b) Theoretical
(c) Lexical (d) Persuasive

Question numbers 37 to 42 are based on the tabulated data given below:

A company has 20 employees with their age (in years) and salary (in thousand rupees per month) mentioned against each of them:

S.No.	Age (in years)	Salary (in thousand rupees per month)
1.	44	35
2.	32	20
3.	54	45
4.	42	35
5.	31	20
6.	53	60
7.	42	50
8.	51	55
9.	34	25
10.	41	30
11.	33	30
12.	31	35
13.	30	35
14.	37	40
15.	44	45
16.	36	35
17.	34	35
18.	49	50
19.	43	45
20.	45	50

37. Classify the data of age of each employee in class interval of 5 years. Which class interval of 5 years has the maximum average salary?
(a) 35-40 years (b) 40-45 years
(c) 45-50 years (d) 50-55 years

38. What is the frequency (%) in the class interval of 30-35 years?
(a) 20% (b) 25%
(c) 30% (d) 35%

39. What is the average age of the employees?
(a) 40.3 years (b) 38.6 years
(c) 47.2 years (d) 45.3 years

40. What is the fraction (%) of employees getting salary ≥ 40,000 per month?
(a) 45% (b) 50%
(c) 35% (d) 32%

41. What is the average salary (in thousand per month) in the age group 40-50 years?
(a) 35 (b) 42.5
(c) 40.5 (d) 36.5

42. What is the fraction of employees getting salary less than the average salary of all the employees?
(a) 45% (b) 50%
(c) 55% (d) 47%

43. Encoding or scrambling data for transmission across a network is known as:
(a) Protection (b) Detection
(c) Encryption (d) Decryption

44. Which of the following is not an output device?
(a) Printer (b) Speaker
(c) Monitor (d) Keyboard

45. Which of the following represents one billion characters?
(a) Kilobyte (b) Megabyte
(c) Gigabyte (d) Terabyte

46. Which of the following is not open source software?
(a) Internet explorer
(b) Fedora Linux
(c) Open office
(d) Apache HTTP server

47. Which one of the following represents the binary equivalent of the decimal number 25?
(a) 10101 (b) 01101
(c) 11001 (d) 11011

48. Which is an instant messenger that is used for chatting?
(a) Altavista (b) MAC
(c) Microsoft Office (d) Google Talk

49. In which of the countries per capita use of water is maximum?
(a) USA (b) European Union
(c) China (d) India

50. India's contribution to total global carbon dioxide emissions is about:
(a) ~ 3% (b) ~ 6%
(c) ~ 10% (d) ~ 15%

51. Two earthquakes A and B happen to be of magnitude 5 and 6 respectively on Richter Scale. The ratio of the energies released E_B/E_A will be approximately:
(a) ~ 8 (b) ~ 16
(c) ~ 32 (d) ~ 64

52. Which of the following combinations represent renewable natural resources?
(a) Fertile soil, fresh water and natural gas
(b) Clean air, phosphates and biological diversity
(c) Fishes, fertile soil and fresh water
(d) Oil, forests and tides

53. In the recently launched Air Quality Index in India, which of the following pollutants is not included?
(a) Carbon monoxide
(b) Fine particulate matter
(c) Ozone
(d) Chlorofluorocarbons

54. The factors which are most important in determining the impact of anthropogenic activities on environment are:
(a) Population, affluence per person, land available per person
(b) Population, affluence per person and the technology used for exploiting resources

(c) Atmospheric conditions, population and forest cover
(d) Population, forest cover and land available per person

55. The session of the parliament is summoned by:
(a) The President
(b) The Prime Minister
(c) The Speaker of the Lok Sabha
(d) The Speaker of the Lok Sabha and the Chairman of the Rajya Sabha

56. Civil Service Day is celebrated in India on:
(a) 21st April (b) 24th April
(c) 21st June (d) 7th July

57. The South Asia University is situated in the city of:
(a) Colombo (b) Dhaka
(c) New Delhi (d) Kathmandu

58. The University Grants Commission was established with which of the following aims?
(1) Promotion of research and development in higher education
(2) Identifying and sustaining institutions of potential learning
(3) Capacity building of teachers
(4) Providing autonomy to each and every higher educational institution in India
Select the correct answer from the codes given below:
(a) (1), (2), (3) and (4)
(b) (1), (2) and (3)
(c) (2), (3) and (4)
(d) (1), (2) and (4)

59. The Gross Enrolment Ratio (GER) in institutions of higher education in India at present (2015) is about:
(a) 8 percent (b) 12 percent
(c) 19 percent (d) 23 percent

60. The total number of central universities in India in April 2015 was:
(a) 08 (b) 14
(c) 27 (d) 43

ANSWERS

1. (d)	2. (c)	3. (b)	4. (b)	5. (d)
6. (d)	7. (d)	8. (b)	9. (a)	10. (b)
11. (c)	12. (b)	13. (c)	14. (d)	15. (a)
16. (d)	17. (a)	18. (a)	19. (d)	20. (d)
21. (d)	22. (b)	23. (c)	24. (a)	25. (b)
26. (b)	27. (c)	28. (a)	29. (a)	30. (d)
31. (d)	32. (b)	33. (c)	34. (b)	35. (b)
36. (b)	37. (d)	38. (b)	39. (a)	40. (a)
41. (b)	42. (c)	43. (c)	44. (d)	45. (c)
46. (a)	47. (c)	48. (d)	49. (a)	50. (b)
51. (c)	52. (a)	53. (d)	54. (c)	55. (a)
56. (a)	57. (c)	58. (b)	59. (c)	60. (d)

PAPER–II

Note: This paper contains fifty (50) objective type questions of two (2) marks each. All questions are compulsory.

1. An endotherm's basal metabolic rate stays constant throughout a range of environmental temperatures known as the:
   1. Lower critical temperature zone
   2. Thermoneutral zone
   3. Higher critical temperature zone
   Choose the correct answer:
   (a) 1 only (b) 2 only
   (c) 1 and 2 only (d) 2 and 3 only

2. Which state has the largest coastline in India?
(a) West Bengal (b) Karnataka
(c) Gujarat (d) Odisha

3. Indicators for sustainable development are:

1. environmental pressures
2. environmental quality
3. society's response

Choose the correct answer:

(a) 1 and 2 only (b) 2 and 3 only
(c) 1 and 3 only (d) 1, 2 and 3

4. Stoichiometric calculations are based on:
(a) Moles (b) Atomic weight
(c) Atomic number (d) Loss of mass

5. BOD of the effluents discharged on land for irrigation should not exceed:
(a) 30 mg/L (b) 100 mg/L
(c) 300 mg/L (d) 60 mg/L

6. Which of the following adds to the carbon dioxide concentration in atmosphere?
1. Volcanic action
2. Respiration
3. Photosynthesis
4. Decay of organic matter

Choose the correct answer:

(a) 1 and 3 only (b) 2 only
(c) 1, 2 and 4 only (d) 1, 2, 3 and 4

7. Corrosion normally occurs when an electrochemical cell is set up on a metal surface. The corroded area is:
(a) cathode
(b) anode
(c) electrolyte
(d) entire metal surface

8. Acid sulphate soils are characteristic of marine coastal plains in areas rich in:
1. Organic matter
2. Brackish water
3. Mangrove swamps

Choose the correct answer:

(a) 1 only (b) 1 and 2 only
(c) 2 only (d) 1, 2 and 3

9. The amount of energy at one trophic level divided by the amount of energy at the trophic level immediately below it is termed as:
(a) Trophic efficiency
(b) Consumption efficiency
(c) Assimilation efficiency
(d) Production efficiency

10. Blue Whale is placed under the catagory of:
(a) Endangered species
(b) Critically endangered species
(c) Vulnerable species
(d) Extinct species

11. Maximum density of detritivorus micro organisms in pond ecosystem are present in:
(a) Limnetic zone (b) Photic zone
(c) Littoral zone (d) Benthic zone

12. Species diversity show a marked pattern as one moves from equator to the poles. Species diversity:
(a) increases as one moves towards the poles from the equator
(b) decreases as one moves from equator to poles
(c) remains constant as one moves from equator to poles
(d) is highest in the arctic antartic regions

13. Coral reefs are mainly distributed globally in:
(a) Temperate waters
(b) Tropical waters
(c) Antartic waters
(d) Arctic waters

14. Most common soil borne bacterial pathogen that manipulates plant by injecting its DNA segment into plant cell is:
(a) *Acidaminococcus fermentans*
(b) *Clostridium thermoacetium*
(c) *Rhizobium leguminosarum*
(d) *Agrobacterium tumefaciens*

15. Which among the following are the best tools/techniques to study landscaps fragmentation?

1. Remote sensing
2. Geodesy
3. Cartography
4. Geographical Information System

Choose the correct answer:

(a) 1 and 2 only (b) 1, 3 and 4 only
(c) 2, 3 and 4 only (d) 1, 2, 3 and 4

16. An earthquake's epicentre is:
(a) usually in the lower part of the mantle
(b) determined by analysing S-wave arrival time at seismic stations
(c) determined by analysing P-wave arrival time at seismic station
(d) a point on the surface directly above the focus

17. Water entrapped at the time of formation of the sedimentary rocks is called:
(a) Meteoric water (b) Connate water
(c) Juvenile water (d) Ground water

18. Which of the following pairs of igneous rocks have the same mineral composition?
(a) Granite - basalt
(b) Andesite - rhyolite
(c) Basalt - gabbro
(d) Pumic - basalt

19. Traps for petroleum and natural gas formed by deformation such as folding and fracturing of rocks are known as:
(a) Lithification traps
(b) Reservoir traps
(c) Structural traps
(d) Stratigraphic traps

20. In which one of the following areas does radiant drainage fully develop?
(a) On a point bar
(b) Around an ox-bow lake
(c) Near a delta
(d) Around a volcano

21. Which of the following countries produce highest amount of hydropower?
(a) Australia (b) Canada
(c) Italy (d) India

22. A solar cell of area 10 cm × 10 cm produces a voltage of 0.6 V and a current upto 2 A. If solar insolation is 1000 Wm^{-2}, the efficiency of the solar cell is:
(a) 15% (b) 12%
(c) 25% (d) 24%

23. An ocean wave has a height of 3 m and has time period of 10 sec. The power available for extraction from this wave in the units of kW per meter of the wavefront is approximately:
(a) 30 (b) 45
(c) 90 (d) 300

24. In the case of Silicon solar cell (Eg = 1.12 eV), the maximum wavelength of solar radiations for production of electron-hole pairs is:
(a) ~ 560 nm (b) ~ 480 nm
(c) ~ 720 nm (d) ~ 1100 nm

25. The share of India in the total annual GHG emissions of the world is approximately:
(a) 5-7% (b) 10-12%
(c) 17-20% (d) 20-25%

26. In biogas, the percentage (%) of methane is in the range of:
(a) 50-70% (b) 30-40%
(c) 70-90% (d) 40-50%

27. Indira Gandhi canal passes through the following state:
1. Punjab
2. Haryana
3. Uttar Pradesh
4. Rajasthan

Choose the correct answer:

(a) 1, 2 only (b) 1, 2, 3 only
(c) 1, 2, 4 only (d) 1, 2, 3, 4

28. Trichloromonofluoromethane is:
    1. Freon-II
    2. A spray can propellent
    3. A chlorofluorocarbon

    Choose the correct answer:
    (a) 1 only (b) 2 and 3 only
    (c) 1 and 3 only (d) 1, 2 and 3

29. Which of the following air pollutants are released by thermal power plants?
    1. Oxides of nitrogen
    2. Oxides of sulphur
    3. Ammonia
    4. Carbon monoxide

    Choose the correct answer:
    (a) 1, 3 and 4 only (b) 2 and 3 only
    (c) 1, 2 and 4 only (d) 1, 2, 3 and 4

30. The Noise Index L_{eq} for a specific duration is a measure of:
    (a) acoustic energy content
    (b) average noise amplitude
    (c) sum of instantaneous sound pressure levels
    (d) fluctuations in noise levels

31. When DDT enters the human body, it is:
    (a) water soluble and easily excreted in urine
    (b) stored in the bones
    (c) fat soluble and stored in fat tissues
    (d) processed by enzymes and becomes a different compound which is toxic

32. In which EIA guidelines notification, developmental projects were categorized as 'A' and 'B' in India?
    (a) EIA guidelines notification, 1994
    (b) EIA guidelines notification, 1986
    (c) EIA guidelines notification, 2006
    (d) EIA guidelines notification, 2000

33. Three important rivers of Indian sub-continent have their source near the Mansarovar lake in Tibet. These rivers are:
    (a) Indus, Jhelum, Ganga
    (b) Indus, Sutlej, Yamuna
    (c) Indus, Sutlej, Brahmaputra
    (d) Yamuna, Brahmaputra, Gandak

34. Which state in India has the highest area of wastelands under barren/stony/rock category?
    (a) Jammu and Kashmir
    (b) Himachal Pradesh
    (c) Arunachal Pradesh
    (d) Uttarakhand

35. During clearance of any developmental project, the minimum distance required for site selection from eco-sensitive zone is:
    (a) 5 km (b) 10 km
    (c) 15 km (d) 20 km

36. Which of the following are true regarding 'Jhum' cultivation in India?
    1. It is largely practiced in N-E India
    2. Fertility is exhausted in a few years
    3. It is referred as 'Slash and Burn' technique

    Choose the correct answer:
    (a) 1, 2 and 3 (b) 1 and 2 only
    (c) 2 and 3 only (d) 1 and 3 only

37. Compensatory afforestation provisions are covered under the Environment Act name as:
    (a) Indian Forest Act (Revised), 1982
    (b) Environment Protection Act, 1986
    (c) Forest Conservation Act, 1980
    (d) Public Liability Insurance Act, 1981

38. When a disaster has occurred, the early action in a Disaster Management Plan could be:
    (a) Response and Rescue
    (b) Warning and preparedness
    (c) Relief and Rehabilitation
    (d) Shelter and Food supply

39. An environmental problem associated with landfill waste disposal site is:
   1. Methane production
   2. Ground water pollution
   3. Incomplete decomposition

   Choose the correct answer:
   (a) 1 and 2 only (b) 1, 2 and 3
   (c) 1 and 3 only (d) 2 and 3 only

40. Eco-labelling of commercial products is regulated by:
   (a) ISO 14020 (b) ISO 14010
   (c) ISO 14030 (d) ISO 14040

41. Which one of the following is not a part of 'Waste Reduction' strategy?
   (a) Reduced use of raw material
   (b) Material Reuse
   (c) Recycling of waste
   (d) Decreased toxicity

42. The expanded form of ISWM is:
   (a) International Standards of Waste Management
   (b) Indian Standards for Waste Material
   (c) Integrated Solid Waste Management
   (d) International Solid Waste Management

43. Municipal Solid Waste (Handling and Management) rule and Biomedical Waste (Handling and Management) rule were implemented in the years respectively:
   (a) 2000 and 1998 (b) 1998 and 2002
   (c) 1996 and 1998 (d) 1990 and 1985

44. If a phosphorous limited lake having surface area equal to 80×10^6 m^2 is fed by stream with flow rate 20 m^3/s that has phosphorous concentration of 0.01 mg/L, then the phosphorous loading from the incoming stream is:
   (a) 4.0 g/s (b) 0.2 g/s
   (c) 0.4 g/s (d) 0.6 g/s

45. If K is the carrying capacity of a population N in an ecosystem following the logistic growth, its growth rate becomes zero when:
   (a) N/K = 0
   (b) Mortality > Natality
   (c) N/K = 1
   (d) N = Half of the carrying capacity of the habitat

46. A good sample design should result in:
   (a) A truely representative sample
   (b) Highly varied sampling error
   (c) Low level of confidence
   (d) Unsystemic bias

47. The mean of a Poisson's distribution is 8. Its standard deviation is:
   (a) 2 (b) $2\sqrt{2}$
   (c) 4 (d) $\frac{8}{5}$

48. Destructive powers of Tsunami result mainly from its:
   (a) Incredible Height
   (b) Unpredictability
   (c) Momentum and long wavelength
   (d) Cold water

49. Which one of the following is not correct for drip irrigation?
   (a) Drip consists of a network of perforated plastic tubing below the ground surface
   (b) Drip irrigation increases fertilizer use and water pollution from fertilizer run-off
   (c) Small holes in the tubing drops off water at a slow rate close to plant roots
   (d) This technique was developed in Israel in the 1960s

50. The non-formal Environmental Education in India provides support to:
   1. Eco-clubs
   2. GLOBE
   3. Environmental appreciation courses

Choose the correct answer:
(a) 1 and 2 only (b) 2 and 3
(c) 1 and 3 only (d) 1, 2 and 3

ANSWERS

1. (a)	2. (c)	3. (d)	4. (a)	5. (a)
6. (c)	7. (b)	8. (d)	9. (a)	10. (a)
11. (d)	12. (b)	13. (b)	14. (d)	15. (b)
16. (d)	17. (b)	18. (c)	19. (c)	20. (d)
21. (b)	22. (b)	23. (c)	24. (d)	25. (a)
26. (a)	27. (c)	28. (d)	29. (c)	30. (a)
31. (c)	32. (c)	33. (c)	34. (c)	35. (b)
36. (a)	37. (c)	38. (a)	39. (b)	40. (a)
41. (d)	42. (c)	43. (a)	44. (b)	45. (c)
46. (a)	47. (b)	48. (c)	49. (b)	50. (a)

PAPER–III

Note: This paper contains seventy-five (75) objective type questions of two (2) marks each. All questions are compulsory.

1. Biological zonation in the ocean is determined by:
   1. Ocean depth
   2. Light availability
   3. Bottom substrate

   Choose the correct answer:
   (a) 1 only (b) 1 and 2 only
   (c) 1, 2 and 3 (d) 2 and 3 only

2. Given below are two statements. One labeled as Assertion (A) and the other labeled as Reason (R):
   Assertion (A): Methanogenic archae (methanogens) grow in swamps and sewage.
   Reason (R): Methanogens are obligate anaerobes

   Choose the correct answer:
   (a) Both (A) and (R) are true and (R) is the correct explanation of (A).
   (b) Both (A) and (R) are true but (R) is not the correct explanation of (A).
   (c) (A) is true, but (R) is false.
   (d) (A) is false, but (R) is true.

3. Filamentous Cyanobacteria differentiate 5 to 10% of their vegetative cells into heterocysts. Heterocysts are characterized by:
   1. Thick cell wall
   2. Only PSI activity
   3. Nitrogenase activity

   Choose the correct answer:
   (a) 1 only (b) 1 and 2 only
   (c) 2 and 3 only (d) 1, 2 and 3

4. A critically endangered species:
   (a) Do not exist in wild habitat
   (b) Face extremely high risk of extinction in immediate future
   (c) Face high risk of extinction in the medium term future
   (d) Will not face any risk of extinction in future 1000 years

5. Which of the following characteristics of desert animals are physiological adaptation to conserve water?
   1. Thick outer covering
   2. Release dry faeces
   3. Avoid exposure to direct sunlight

   Choose the correct answer:
   (a) 1 and 3 only (b) 2 and 3 only
   (c) 1 and 2 only (d) 1, 2 and 3

6 The balance between photosynthesis and photorespiration is related to:
   1. The ratio of O_2 and CO_2 in the atmosphere
   2. Temperature
   3. Kranz anatomy
   4. The ratio of CO_2 and H_2O

Choose the correct answer:
(a) 1 and 2 only (b) 2, 3 and 4 only
(c) 1, 2 and 3 only (d) 1, 2, 3 and 4

7. Individual organism respond to environmental change through short-term adjustment(s) by:
(a) Physiological changes
(b) Cytological changes
(c) Genetic changes
(d) Phytochemical and genetic alterations

8. The hurricanes have spatial scale of:
(a) 100 Km-1000 Km
(b) 10 Km-100 Km
(c) 100m-100 Km
(d) 100m-10 Km

9. In SDS-PAGE:
(a) Polymeric proteins are not only converted into monomers, but monomers are also denatured by SDS.
(b) Polymeric proteins converted into monomeric units, but monomers are not denatured.
(c) Polymeric proteins are retained as single unit.
(d) SDS do not have any negative impact on native structure of monomers.

10. Which of the following is the major source of mercury pollution in India?
(a) Coal based thermal power plants
(b) Pesticides manufacturing
(c) Dental amalgam fillings
(d) Electrical and electronic gadgets

11. A non-metal 'X' occurs in nature in free state. It combines with hydrogen to form a gas, which is colourless and highly toxic. Apart from this, 'X' is oxidized to 'XO_2' which is a colourless, pungent and irritating gas. 'X' represents:
(a) Sulphur (b) Carbon
(c) Phosphorus (d) Nitrogen

12. Elemental carbon influences the regional climate because:
(a) It influences the radiative flux in the atmosphere due to its absorbing properties.
(b) It reacts with other pollutants.
(c) It coagulates with other atmospheric pollutants.
(d) Its concentration is usually more in the atmosphere.

13. Bioremediation of xenobiotics (like melathion) through hydrolysis involves their detoxification by:
(a) Removal of water
(b) Addition of water
(c) Both removal and addition of water
(d) Removal of phosphate

14. To determine the cation-exchange capacity, it is necessary to calculate the total positive charge associated with ions like:
(a) Ca^{2+}, Mg^{2+}, K^{+}, Na^{+}
(b) Ca^{2+}, Mn^{2+}, Fe^{3+}, Cr^{3+}
(c) Mg^{2+}, Fe^{3+}, Ni^{2+}, Cd^{2+}
(d) K^{+}, Bo^{2+}, Pb^{2+}, Hg^{2+}

15. Given below are two statements. One labeled as Assertion (A) and the other labeled as Reason (R):
Assertion (A): Organometals/organometalloids such as trimethylarsine and dimethylmercury are more toxic to living systems (including humans) compared to their inorganic forms.
Reason (R): Organometals/organometalloids are more hydrophilic than their inorganic forms and hence can move easily across lipid bilayer.
Choose the correct answer:
(a) Both (A) and (R) are true and (R) is the correct explanation of (A).
(b) Both (A) and (R) are true but (R) is not the correct explanation of (A).

(c) (A) is true, but (R) is false.
(d) (A) is false, but (R) is true.

16. Project elephant was launched in the year:
(a) 1973 (b) 1985
(c) 1992 (d) 1998

17. Biological communities in a stream vary based on:
1. Water velocity
2. Allochthnous material
3. Size of the particle on the stream bed
4. Depth of the stream
Choose the correct answer:
(a) 1 and 2 only (b) 1, 2 and 3 only
(c) 2, 3 and 4 only (d) 1, 2, 3 and 4

18. Champion and Seth (1968) classify Indian forests based on:
1. Floristic Composition
2. Precipitation
3. Distance from Sea
Choose the correct answer:
(a) 1 only (b) 1 and 2 only
(c) 2 only (d) 1, 2 and 3

19. Which one of the following statements is not correct?
(a) The solubility of gases varies considerably with pressure.
(b) Hydrocarbons chiefly occur in coal, natural gas and petroleum.
(c) Polynuclear aromatic hydrocarbons are present in coal tar and fossil fuels.
(d) All hydrocarbons are hydrophilic in nature.

20. Gauss exclusion principle states that:
(a) Complete competitors co-exist
(b) Complete competitors cannot co-exist
(c) Complete competitors tend to co-operate
(d) Symbionts evolve into complete competitors

21. Parasites in a population/community can:
1. Influence host population cycles
2. Change ecological communities
3. Change community structure
Choose the correct answer:
(a) 1, 2 and 3 (b) 2 and 3 only
(c) 3 only (d) 1 only

22. Long-term patterns of evolution are shaped by large scale process(s) such as:
1. Speciation
2. Mass extinction
3. Adaptive radiation
Choose the correct answer:
(a) 1 only (b) 2 and 3 only
(c) 1 and 3 only (d) 1, 2 and 3

23. Match the List I with List II. Identify the correct answer from the codes given below the lists:
List I (Organism)
(A) *Albugo* an Indian mustard
(B) *Penicillium* and *Staphyllococcus*
(C) Lichens
(D) Barnacles and whales
List II (Interaction)
(i) Symbiosis (ii) Ammensalism
(iii) Commensalism (iv) Parasitism

Codes:	A	B	C	D
(a)	(i)	(ii)	(iii)	(iv)
(b)	(ii)	(i)	(iv)	(iii)
(c)	(iv)	(ii)	(i)	(iii)
(d)	(iv)	(iii)	(ii)	(i)

24. Extreme of seasonal variation (as much as 80°C swing) from summer to winter is represented by:
(a) Boreal forest
(b) Tropical forests
(c) Deciduous forest
(d) Evergreen forest

25. Aeromycoflora can be trapped and quantified by:

(a) Rotorod air sampler
(b) Anderson air sampler
(c) Gregory air sampler
(d) Respirable dust sampler

26. Which among the following frequencies in microwave region of electromagnetic spectrum is better suited for determination of tree height?
(a) C-band (4-8 GHz)
(b) X-band (8-12.5 GHz)
(c) P-band (0.3-1.0 GHz)
(d) K-band (18-26.5 GHz)

27. Which of the common mineral is not a silicate?
(a) Quartz (b) Calcite
(c) Pyroxene (d) Feldspar

28. Which among the following is the best model in GIS spatial relationships?
(a) Spaghetti model
(b) Topological model
(c) Relational database model
(d) Parent-child model

29. One of the warning signs of an impending volcanic eruption is volcanic tremor, which is:
(a) A change in ground levels
(b) Inflation of a volcano as magma rises
(c) Ground shaking lasting for minutes or hours
(d) Emission of large quantities of gases

30. Time slot for measuring thermal inertia (TI) differences between land and water is:
(a) 1000 hrs. (b) 1100 hrs.
(c) 1200 hrs. (d) 1400 hrs.

31. Slump is a complex side which consists of:
(a) Curved shear surface
(b) Curved and planar shear surfaces
(c) Planar shear surface
(d) No definite shear surface

32. In rainwater harvesting, the purpose of percolation tank is:
(a) Recharge groundwater only
(b) Surface water supply for irrigation
(c) Both surface water supply and groundwater recharge
(d) Drinking water supply

33. Which of the following minerals causes fluoride pollution in the groundwater?
(a) Fluorite and Apatite
(b) Olivine and Haematite
(c) Calcite and Magnetite
(d) Quartz and Orthoclase

34. Indian monsoon is greatly influenced by:
1. Sea surface temperature in pre-monsoon season
2. El Nino
3. La Nina
4. Depression over Tibet
Choose the correct answer:
(a) 1 and 2 only (b) 2 and 3 only
(c) 3 and 4 only (d) 4 only

35. The important continental silicate mimeral weathering process of lowering carbon dioxide levels is:
(a) Hydrolysis (b) Oxidation
(c) Carbonation (d) Reduction

36. The set of processes by which soil and rock are loosened and move downhill are called:
(a) Erosion (b) Saltation
(c) Weathering (d) Abrasion

37. Wind mills are most suited for:
1. Deserts 2. Offshore
3. High altitude 4. Roof tops
Choose the correct answer:
(a) 1 and 2 only (b) 2 and 3 only
(c) 1 and 3 only (d) 2, 3 and 4 only

38. Main source of energy for a tropical cyclone formation comes from:

1. Heat of condensation of water vapours in the atmosphere
2. Torrential rains
3. Large ocean waves

Choose the correct answer:

(a) 1 only (b) 2 only
(c) 3 and 2 only (d) 1 and 3 only

39. In the following nuclear fusion reaction $^2_1D + ^2_1D = ^3_2He + ^1_0n + E$ the value of the energy E is:

(a) 17.6 MeV (b) 18.3 MeV
(c) 4.03 MeV (d) 3.27 MeV

40. Fast neutrons produced in nuclear fission reaction involving ^{235}U have average energy of the order of:

(a) 2 MeV (b) 5 MeV
(c) 100 MeV (d) 200 MeV

41. As the population growth rate increases the doubling time:

(a) Increase (b) Double
(c) Remain constant (d) Decrease

42. A tidal estuary of tidal range 2 m has trapped water area 5000 m^2. If g = 9.8 m/s^2, the maximum energy available per tidal cycle is:

(a) 2.45 kW (b) 9.8 kW
(c) 98 kW (d) 19.6 kW

43. The power (P) from an ocean wave varies with time period (T) of the wave as:

(a) $P \propto T$ (b) $P \propto T^2$
(c) $P \propto \frac{1}{T}$ (d) $P \propto \frac{1}{T^2}$

44. With reference to pre-industrial times, the present day average global surface temperature is higher approximately by:

(a) ~ 0.56°C (b) ~ 0.85°C
(c) ~ 1.3°C (d) ~ 1.5°C

45. Burning of 1 mol of CH_4 liberates 890 kJ of energy and 1 mol of CO_2. Since 1 mol of CO_2 has 12 g of carbon, the higher heating value (HHV) of methane is:

(a) 13.5 gC/MJ (b) 18.5 gC/MJ
(c) 12.0 gC/MJ (d) 10.0 gC/MJ

46. pH of 1 mM HCl is:

(a) 1 (b) 2
(c) 3 (d) 11

47. Priority air pollutants included in the air quality index for urban areas in India are:

(a) CO, NO_x, PM_{10} and $PM_{2.5}$, SO_x, O_3, ammonia and Pb
(b) CO, NO_x, SO_x and Pb
(c) NO_x, SO_x, O_3, and Pb
(d) PM_{10} and $PM_{2.5}$, NO_x, SO_x, O_3, and Pb

48. Present day advanced anaerobic digestors can generate power in the range:

(a) 2-10 MW (b) 20-100 MW
(c) 100-200 MW (d) 200-500 MW

49. Cement dust is characterized by very fine particulates. Which of the following air pollution control devices is appropriate for removing them from hot exhaust gases emanating from cement kiln?

(a) Baghouse
(b) Cyclones
(c) Venturi scrubber
(d) Electrostatic precipitator

50. The sources of aliphatic hydrocarbons in indoor environment are:

(a) Paints, adhesives and gasoline
(b) Aerosol sprays and solvents
(c) Spirits and cleansers
(d) Solvents and vinyl flooring

51. Given the following data of sound pressure levels measured at equal intervals: 60 dB, 62 dB, 63 dB, 59 dB, 60 dB, 80 dB, 58 dB, 59 dB, 65 dB, 57 dB, 62 dB. The value of the background noise level (L_{90}) is:

(a) 62.5 dB (b) 57 dB
(c) 61 dB (d) 58 dB

52. The air-to-fuel ratio (A/F) for complete combustion in an internal combustion engine is about:
(a) 14.6 (b) 11.2
(c) 12.1 (d) 15.5

53. Phytovolatalization of mercuric pollutants involves volatalization of mercury in:
(a) Elemental state
(b) Ionic state
(c) Organic state
(d) Both ionic and organic states

54. Match the List I with List II. Identify the correct answer from the codes given below the lists:

List I

(A) Texture (B) Profile
(C) Erosion (D) Conservation

List II

(i) Vertical zonation
(ii) Land degradation
(iii) Planting tree
(iv) Mineral particle size

Codes:	A	B	C	D
(a)	(iv)	(i)	(ii)	(iii)
(b)	(i)	(ii)	(iii)	(iv)
(c)	(ii)	(iii)	(iv)	(i)
(d)	(iii)	(iv)	(i)	(ii)

55. Environmental Management Plan is associated with:
(a) EIS
(b) Environmental audit
(c) ISO 14000
(d) LCA

56. ISO 14000 is connected with:
(a) Adoption of environmental safety guideline
(b) Energy audit in industries
(c) Adoption of clean development
(d) Adoption of environmental management system in industry/organisation

57. CAPART in India stands for:
(a) Committee for Advancement and Promotion of Rural Technology
(b) Council for Advancement of Rural Technology
(c) Council for Advancement of People's Action and Rural Technology
(d) Committee for Advancement and Privatization of Rural Technology

58. EIA of Port and Harbour projects involve impact assessment on:
1. Biological environment
2. Air environment
3. Soil environment
4. Social environment

Choose the correct answer:
(a) 1 only (b) 2 only
(c) 3 only (d) 1, 2 and 4 only

59. Which act provided provisions for enforcing levy and collection of a tax on water consumed by industries?
(a) Water (prevention and control of pollution) Act 1974
(b) Water (prevention and control of pollution) Cess Act 1977
(c) Environment (protection) Act 1986
(d) Public Liability Insurance Act 1991

60. Disaster risk reduction in degraded wilderness areas is better achieved using:
(a) People's participation
(b) Ecosystem based management
(c) Strenthening of people's economic conditions
(d) Afforestation

61. The major convenltions of Rio Earth Summit are:
(a) CBD and climate change
(b) Kyoto protocol and Montreal protocol

(c) CDM and Nagoya protocol
(d) Basel convention and Bameco convention

62. If $\Gamma_s < \Gamma_e < \Gamma_d$ where Γ_s, Γ_e and Γ_d are saturated adiabatic lapse rate, environmental lapse rate and dry adiabatic lapse rate, the atmosphere is:
(a) Stable
(b) Conditionally unstable
(c) Unstable
(d) Neutral

63. Match the List I with List II. Identify the correct answer from the codes given below the lists:
List I (Tests)
(A) Z-test
(B) t-test
(C) Chi-square (χ^2) test
(D) F-test
List II (Application)
(i) Judging the significance of differences between means of two small samples
(ii) Judging the significance of mean, median, mode
(iii) Compare the variance of two independent samples
(iv) Compare sample variance to a theoretical population variance

Codes:	A	B	C	D
(a)	(ii)	(i)	(iv)	(iii)
(b)	(iii)	(ii)	(i)	(iv)
(c)	(iv)	(iii)	(ii)	(i)
(d)	(i)	(iv)	(iii)	(ii)

64. Chocolates of 250 g produced in a factory were observed to have standard deviation of 2 g. A random sample of 20 chocolate showed a standard deviation of 1.5 g. What is the χ^2 value for the sample?
(a) 7.2 (b) 6.0
(c) 12.0 (d) 33.3

65. Which one of the following would indicate that a dataset is not distributed in a bell-shape?
(a) The range is equal to 5 standard deviation
(b) The range is larger than the inter quartile range
(c) The mean is much smaller than the median
(d) There are no outliers

66. In a random sample of x = 16, the mean $(\bar{X})$ is 40, and the standard deviation (sd) is 4.0. The 95% confidence interval (Z = 1.96) for the mean is:
(a) ± 4.0 (b) ± 1.96
(c) ± 0.25 (d) ± 0.30

67. The title of the Brundtland report is:
(a) Caring for Earth
(b) Caring of Biosphere
(c) Our Common Future
(d) The Silent Spring

68. According to Gaussian Plume Model, the maximum ground level concentration (C) varies with height (H) of chimney:
(a) $C \propto \frac{1}{H}$ (b) $C \propto H^{-2}$
(c) $C \propto H^{-1/2}$ (d) $C \propto H^{-3/2}$

69. Given below are two statements. One labeled as Assertion (A) and the other labeled as Reason (R):
Assertion (A): A wetland of international importance is brought under the 'Montreux Record'.
Reason (R): The country in which the wetland is located should enact a law to prohibit any human activity within five kilometers from the edge of the wetland.
Choose the correct answer:
(a) Both (A) and (R) are true and (R) is the correct explanation of (A).

(b) Both (A) and (R) are true but (R) is not the correct explanation of (A).
(c) (A) is true, but (R) is false.
(d) (A) is false, but (R) is true.

70. Which of the following methods related to fly ash utilization has future ecofriendly and economic benefits?
1. Direct application to cropland
2. Converting to Bricks
3. Using as a road-sub-base material

Codes:
(a) 1 and 2 only (b) 2 and 3 only
(c) 1 and 3 only (d) 1, 2 and 3

71. Which of the following is not one of the twelve principles of green chemistry?
(a) Minimize or eliminate the need for waste cleanup by emphasizing waste prevention
(b) Minimize energy consumption
(c) Maximize use of products from green plants
(d) Avoid the use and generation of hazardous substances that may harm humans or the environment

72. Match the List I with List II. Identify the correct answer from the codes given below the lists:

List I (Halocarbons)	List II (Atmospheric residence time)
(A) CF_4	(i) ~ 50 years
(B) CF_2Cl_2	(ii) ~ 50,000 years
(C) $CFCl_3$	(iii) ~ 65 years
(D) CF_3Br	(iv) ~ 102 years

Codes:	A	B	C	D
(a)	(ii)	(iv)	(i)	(iii)
(b)	(iii)	(i)	(ii)	(iv)
(c)	(iv)	(ii)	(iii)	(i)
(d)	(i)	(iii)	(iv)	(ii)

73. Climate change has become a buzz word throughout the world. In case of the Himalayas the best way to infer whether there is a climate change or not is to:
1. Monitor tree line
2. Monitor migration of glaciers
3. Study alteration in species composition

Choose the correct answer:
(a) 1 only (b) 1 and 2 only
(c) 2 only (d) 1, 2 and 3

74. Landslide hazards in the Himalayan region are the consequence of:
1. Road cutting
2. Seismic activity
3. Deforestation
4. Urbanization

Choose the correct answer:
(a) 1 only (b) 1 and 2 only
(c) 1, 2 and 3 only (d) 1, 2, 3 and 4

75. Consider the following International agreements.
1. The international Treaty on Plant Genetic Resources for Food and Agriculture
2. The United Nations Convention to Combat Desertification
3. The World Heritage Convention

Which of the above has/have a bearing on the biodiversity?

Choose the correct answer:
(a) 1 and 2 only (b) 3 only
(c) 1 and 3 only (d) 1, 2 and 3

ANSWERS

1. (c)	2. (a)	3. (d)	4. (b)	5. (c)
6. (c)	7. (a)	8. (a)	9. (a)	10. (a)
11. (a)	12. (a)	13. (b)	14. (a)	15. (c)
16. (c)	17. (d)	18. (b)	19. (d)	20. (b)
21. (a)	22. (d)	23. (c)	24. (a)	25. (b)
26. (c)	27. (b)	28. (b)	29. (c)	30. (d)
31. (b)	32. (a)	33. (a)	34. (a)	35. (a)
36. (a)	37. (a)	38. (a)	39. (d)	40. (a)
41. (d)	42. (c)	43. (a)	44. (b)	45. (a)
46. (c)	47. (a)	48. (a)	49. (d)	50. (a)
51. (d)	52. (a)	53. (a)	54. (a)	55. (a)
56. (d)	57. (c)	58. (d)	59. (b)	60. (b)
61. (a)	62. (b)	63. (a)	64. (a)	65. (c)
66. (b)	67. (b)	68. (b)	69. (c)	70. (b)
71. (c)	72. (a)	73. (d)	74. (d)	75. (d)

DECEMBER–2015

Note: This paper contains Sixty (60) multiple-choice questions, each question carrying two (2) marks. Candidate is expected to answer any Fifty (50) questions. In case more than Fifty (50) questions are attempted, only the first Fifty (50) questions will be evaluated.

PAPER–I

1. Greater the handicap of the students coming to the educational institutions, greater the demand on the
   (a) Family (b) Society
   (c) Teacher (d) State

2. What are the characteristics of Continuous and Comprehensive Evaluation?
   1. It increases the workload on students by taking multiple tests.
   2. It replaces marks with grades.
   3. It evaluates every aspect of the student.
   4. It helps in reducing examination phobia.

   Select the correct answer from the codes given below:
   Codes:
   (a) 1, 2, 3 and 4 (b) 2 and 4
   (c) 1, 2 and 3 (d) 2, 3 and 4

3. Which of the following attributes denote great strengths of a teacher?
   1. Full-time active involvement in the institutional management
   2. Setting examples
   3. Willingness to put assumptions to the test
   4. Acknowledging mistakes

   Select the correct answer from the codes given below:
   Codes:
   (a) 1, 2 and 4 (b) 2, 3 and 4
   (c) 1, 3 and 4 (d) 1, 2, 3 and 4

4. Which one of the following statements is correct in the context of multiple-choice type questions?
   (a) They are more objective than true-false type questions.
   (b) They are less objective than essay type questions.
   (c) They are more subjective than short-answer type questions.
   (d) They are more subjective than true-false type questions.

5. As Chairman of an independent commission on education, Jacques Delors report to UNESCO was titled:
   (a) International Commission on Education Report
   (b) Millennium Development Report
   (c) Learning: The Treasure Within
   (d) World Declaration on Education for All

6. What are required for good teaching?
   1. Diagnosis 2. Remedy
   3. Direction 4. Feedback

   Select the correct answer from the codes given below:
   Codes:
   (a) 1, 2, 3 and 4 (b) 1 and 2
   (c) 2, 3 and 4 (d) 3 and 4

7. Which of the following statements is not true in the context of participatory research?
   (a) It recognizes knowledge as power.
   (b) It emphasises on people as experts.

(c) It is a collective process of enquiry.
(d) Its sole purpose is production of knowledge.

8. Which of the following statements is true in the context of the testing of a hypothesis?
(a) It is only the alternative hypothesis, that can be tested.
(b) It is only the null hypothesis, that can be tested.
(c) Both, the alternative and the null hypotheses can be tested.
(d) Both, the alternative and the null hypotheses cannot be tested.

9. Which of the following are the basic rules of APA style of referencing format?
1. Italicize titles of shorter works such as journal articles or essays
2. Invert authors' names (last name first)
3. Italicize titles of longer works such as books and journals
4. Alphabetically index reference list

Select the correct answer from the codes given below:

Codes:
(a) 1 and 2 (b) 2, 3 and 4
(c) 3 and 4 (d) 1, 2, 3 and 4

10. Which of the following are the characteristics of a seminar?
1. It is a form of academic instruction.
2. It involves questioning, discussion and debates.
3. It involves large groups of individuals.
4. It needs involvement of skilled persons.

Select the correct answer from the codes given below:

Codes:
(a) 2 and 3 (b) 2 and 4
(c) 2, 3 and 4 (d) 1, 2 and 4

11. A researcher is interested in studying the prospects of a particular political party in an urban area. What tool should he prefer for the study?
(a) Rating scale (b) Interview
(c) Questionnaire (d) Schedule

12. Ethical norms in research do not involve guidelines for:
(a) Thesis format
(b) Copyright
(c) Patenting policy
(d) Data sharing policies

Read the following passage carefully and answer question numbers 13 to 17.

I did that thing recently where you have to sign a big card—which is a horror unto itself, especially as the keeper of the Big Card was leaning over me at the time. Suddenly I was on the spot, a rabbit in the headlights, torn between doing a fun message or some sort of in-joke or a drawing. Instead overwhelmed by the myriad options available to me, I decided to just write "Good luck, best, Joel".

It was then that I realised, to my horror, that I had forgotten how to write. My entire existence is "tap letters into computer". My shopping lists are hidden in the notes function of my phone. If I need to remember something I send an e-mail to myself. A pen is something I chew when I'm struggling to think. Paper is something I pile beneath my laptop to make it a more comfortable height for me to type on.

A poll of 1,000 teens by the stationers, Bic found that one in 10 don't own a pen, a third have never written a letter, and half of 13 to 19 years-old have never been forced to sit down and write a thank you letter. More than 80% have never written a love letter, 56% don't have letter paper at home. And a quarter have never known the unique torture of writing a birthday card. The most a teen ever has to use a pen is on an exam paper.

Bic, have you heard of mobile phones? Have you heard of e-mail, facebook and snap chatting? This is the future. Pens are dead. Paper is dead. Handwriting is a relic.

"Handwriting is one of the most creative outlets we have and should be given the same importance as other art forms such as sketching, painting or photography."

Answer the following questions:

13. When confronted with signing a big card, the author felt like "a rabbit in the headlight".
    What does this phrase mean?
    (a) A state of confusion
    (b) A state of pleasure
    (c) A state of anxiety
    (d) A state of pain

14. According to the author, which one is not the most creative outlet of pursuit?
    (a) Handwriting (b) Photography
    (c) Sketching (d) Reading

15. The entire existence of the author revolves round:
    1. Computer
    2. Mobile phone
    3. Typewriter
    Identify the correct answer from the codes given below:
    (a) 2 only (b) 1 and 2 only
    (c) 1, 2 and 3 (d) 2 and 3 only

16. How many teens, as per the Bic survey, do not own a pen?
    (a) 800 (b) 560
    (c) 500 (d) 100

17. What is the main concern of the author?
    (a) That the teens use social networks for communication.
    (b) That the teens use mobile phones.
    (c) That the teens use computer.
    (d) That the teens have forgotten the art of handwriting.

18. The main objectives of student evaluation of teachers are:
    1. To gather information about student weaknesses.
    2. To make teachers take teaching seriously.
    3. To help teachers adopt innovative methods of teaching.
    4. To identify the areas of further improvement in teacher traits.
    Identify the correct answer from the codes given below:
    (a) 1 and 2 only
    (b) 2, 3 and 4 only
    (c) 1, 2 and 3 only
    (d) 1 only

19. Using the central point of the classroom communication as the beginning of a dynamic pattern of ideas is referred to as:
    (a) Systemisation
    (b) Problem-orientation
    (c) Idea protocol
    (d) Mind mapping

20. Aspects of the voice, other than the speech are known as:
    (a) Physical language
    (b) Personal language
    (c) Para language
    (d) Delivery language

21. Every type of communication is affected by its:
    (a) Reception (b) Transmission
    (c) Non-regulation (d) Context

22. Attitudes, actions and appearances in the context of classroom communication are considered as:
    (a) Verbal (b) Non-verbal
    (c) Impersonal (d) Irrational

23. Most often, the teacher-student communication is:
    (a) Spurious
    (b) Critical
    (c) Utilitarian
    (d) Confrontational

24. In a classroom, a communicator's trust level is determined by:
(a) the use of hyperbole
(b) the change of voice level
(c) the use of abstract concepts
(d) eye contact

25. The next term in the series
2, 5, 10, 17, 26, 37, __?__ is:
(a) 50 (b) 57
(c) 62 (d) 72

26. A group of 210 students appeared in some test. The mean $\frac{1}{3}$rd of students is found to be 60. The mean of the remaining students is found to be 78. The mean of the whole group will be:
(a) 80 (b) 76
(c) 74 (d) 72

27. Anil after travelling 6 km towards East from his house realized that he has travelled in a wrong direction. He turned and travelled 12 km towards West, turned right and travelled 8 km to reach his office. The straight distance of the office from his house is:
(a) 20 km (b) 14 km
(c) 12 km (d) 10 km

28. The next term in the series
B2E, D5H, F12K, H27N, __?__ is:
(a) J56I (b) I62Q
(c) Q62J (d) J58Q

29. A party was held in which a grandmother, father, mother, four sons, their wives and one son and two daughters to each of the sons were present. The number of females present in the party is:
(a) 12 (b) 14
(c) 18 (d) 24

30. P and Q are brothers. R and S are sisters. The son of P is brother of S. Q is related to R as:
(a) Son (b) Brother
(c) Uncle (d) Father

31. Consider the argument given below:
'Pre-employment testing of teachers is quite fair because doctors, architects and engineers who are now employed had to face such a testing.'
What type of argument it is?
(a) Deductive (b) Analogical
(c) Psychological (d) Biological

32. Among the following propositions two are related in such a way that they can both be true although they cannot both be false. Which are those propositions? Select the correct code.
Propositions:
1. Some priests are cunning.
2. No priest is cunning.
3. All priests are cunning.
4. Some priests are not cunning.
Codes:
(a) 1 and 2 (b) 3 and 4
(c) 1 and 3 (d) 1 and 4

33. A Cluster of propositions with a structure that exhibits some inference is called:
(a) An inference
(b) An argument
(c) An explanation
(d) A valid argument

34. Consider the following assertion (A) and reason (R) and select the correct code given below:
(A): No man is perfect.
(R): Some men are not perfect.
(a) Both (A) and (R) are true but (R) does not provide sufficient reason for (A).
(b) Both (A) and (R) are true and (R) provides sufficient reason for (A).
(c) (A) is true but (R) is false.
(d) (A) is false but (R) is true.

35. A definition that has a meaning that is deliberately assigned to some symbol is called:
(a) Lexical (b) Precising
(c) Stipulative (d) Persuasive

36. If the proposition 'No men are honest' is taken to be false which of the following proposition/propositions can be claimed certainly to be true?
Propositions:
(a) All men are honest
(b) Some men are honest
(c) Some men are not honest
(d) No honest person is man

Given below in the table is the decadal data of Population and Electrical Power Production of a country.

Year	Population (million)	Electrical Power Production (GW)*
1951	20	10
1961	21	20
1971	24	25
1981	27	40
1991	30	50
2001	32	80
2011	35	100

* 1 GW = 1000 million watt

Based on the above table, answer the questions from Sl. No. 37 to 42.

37. Which decade registered the maximum growth rate (%) of population?
(a) 1961-71 (b) 1971-81
(c) 1991-2001 (d) 2001-11

38. Average decadal growth rate (%) of population is:
(a) ~ 12.21% (b) ~ 9.82%
(c) ~ 6.73% (d) ~ 5%

39. Based on the average decadal growth rate, what will be the population in the year 2021?
(a) 40.34 million (b) 38.49 million
(c) 37.28 million (d) 36.62 million

40. In the year 1951, what was the power availability per person?
(a) 100 W (b) 200 W
(c) 400 W (d) 500 W

41. In which decade, the average power availability per person was maximum?
(a) 1981-1991 (b) 1991-2001
(c) 2001-2011 (d) 1971-1981

42. By what percentage (%) the power production increased from 1951 to 2011?
(a) 100% (b) 300%
(c) 600% (d) 900%

43. NMEICT stands for:
(a) National Mission on Education through ICT
(b) National Mission on E-governance through ICT
(c) National Mission on E-commerce through ICT
(d) National Mission on E-learning through ICT

44. Which of the following is an instant messaging application?
1. WhatsApp
2. Google Talk
3. Viber

Select the correct answer from the codes given below:
Codes:
(a) 1 and 2 only (b) 2 and 3 only
(c) 1 only (d) 1, 2 and 3

45. In a Computer a byte generally consists of:
(a) 4 bits (b) 8 bits
(c) 16 bits (d) 10 bits

46. Which of the following is not an input device?
(a) Microphone (b) Keyboard
(c) Joystick (d) Monitor

47. Which of the following is an open source software?
(a) MS Word (b) Windows
(c) Mozilla Firefox (d) Acrobat Reader

48. Which of the following enables us to send the same letter to different persons in MS Word?
(a) Mail join (b) Mail copy
(c) Mail insert (d) Mail merge

49. Inside rural homes, the source/sources of Nitrogen Oxide Pollution may be
1. Unvented gas stoves
2. Wood stoves
3. Kerosene heaters

Choose the correct code

Codes:
(a) 1 and 2 only (b) 2 and 3 only
(c) 2 only (d) 1, 2 and 3

50. Which of the following pollutants can cause cancer in humans?
(a) Pesticides (b) Mercury
(c) Lead (d) Ozone

51. **Assertion (A):** People population control measures do not necessarily help in checking environmental degradation.

Reason (R): The relationship between population growth and environmental degradation is rather complex.

Choose the correct answer from the following:
(a) Both (A) and (R) are true and (R) is the correct explanation of (A).
(b) Both (A) and (R) are true but (R) is not the correct explanation of (A).
(c) (A) is true but (R) is false.
(d) (A) is false but (R) is true.

52. Which of the following phenomena is not a natural hazard?
(a) Wildfire
(b) Lightning
(c) Landslide
(d) Chemical contamination

53. As part of National Climate Change Policy, Indian Government is planning to raise the installed capacity of renewable energy by the year 2030 to
(a) 175 GW (b) 200 GW
(c) 250 GW (d) 350 GW

54. At present, in terms of per capita energy consumption (kWh/year), identify the correct sequence.
(a) Brazil > Russia > China > India
(b) Russia > China > India > Brazil
(c) Russia > China > Brazil > India
(d) China > Russia > Brazil > India

55. Which of the following are the objectives of Rashtriya Uchchatar Shiksha Abhiyan (RUSA)?
1. To improve the overall quality of state institutions.
2. To ensure adequate availability of quality faculty.
3. To create new institutions through upgradation of existing autonomous colleges.
4. To downgrade universities with poor infrastructure into autonomous colleges.

Select the correct answer from the codes given below:

Codes:
(a) 1, 2, 3 and 4 (b) 1, 2 and 3
(c) 1, 3 and 4 (d) 1, 2 and 4

56. The grounds on which discrimination in admission to educational institutions is constitutionally prohibited are
1. Religion 2. Sex
3. Place of birth 4. Nationality

Select the correct answer from the codes given below:

Codes:

(a) 2, 3 and 4 (b) 1, 2 and 3
(c) 1, 2 and 4 (d) 1, 2, 3 and 4

57. Which of the following statements are correct about Lok Sabha?
    1. The Constitution puts a limit on the size of the Lok Sabha.
    2. The size and shape of the Parliamentary Constituencies is determined by the Election Commission.
    3. First-past-the Post electoral system is followed.
    4. The Speaker of Lok Sabha does not have a casting vote in case of an equality of votes.

    Select the correct answer from the codes given below:

    Codes:

    (a) 1 and 3 (b) 1, 2 and 3
    (c) 1, 3 and 4 (d) 1, 2, 3 and 4

58. Public Order as an item in the Constitution figures in
    (a) the Union List
    (b) the State List
    (c) the Concurrent List
    (d) the Residuary Powers

59. The term of office of the Advocate General of a State is
    (a) 4 years
    (b) 5 years
    (c) 6 years or 65 years of age whichever is earlier
    (d) not fixed

60. Which among the following States has the highest number of seats in the Lok Sabha?
    (a) Maharashtra (b) Rajasthan
    (c) Tamil Nadu (d) West Bengal

ANSWERS

1. (c)	2. (d)	3. (b)	4. (a)	5. (c)
6. (a)	7. (d)	8. (b)	9. (b)	10. (d)
11. (c)	12. (a)	13. (a)	14. (d)	15. (b)
16. (d)	17. (d)	18. (c)	19. (d)	20. (c)
21. (d)	22. (b)	23. (c)	24. (d)	25. (a)
26. (d)	27. (d)	28. (d)	29. (b)	30. (c)
31. (b)	32. (d)	33. (b)	34. (a)	35. (c)
36. (b)	37. (a)	38. (b)	39. (b)	40. (d)
41. (c)	42. (d)	43. (a)	44. (d)	45. (b)
46. (d)	47. (c)	48. (d)	49. (d)	50. (a)
51. (a)	52. (d)	53. (d)	54. (c)	55. (b)
56. (b)	57. (a)	58. (b)	59. (d)	60. (a)

PAPER–II

Note: This paper contains fifty (50) objective type questions, each question carrying two (2) marks. All questions are compulsory.

1. Which one of the following elements contributes maximum to the earth crust by weight?
   (a) Iron (b) Silicon
   (c) Oxygen (d) Carbon

2. The lowest temperature is observed in which layer of the atmosphere?
   (a) Troposphere (b) Stratosphere
   (c) Mesosphere (d) Thermosphere

3. Which of the following gases has the lowest residence time?
   (a) CO_2 (b) N_2O
   (c) CFCs (d) CH_4

4. Which of the following statements is incorrect?
   (a) Chromium (VI) is highly toxic
   (b) Methyl mercury is most toxic mercury species
   (c) Arsenic (III) is more toxic than arsenic (V)
   (d) Cadmium is a criteria pollutant

5. The most abundant functional group present in fulvic acid, commonly found in soils, is:
   (a) Peptide group
   (b) Carboxylate group
   (c) Phenolic group
   (d) Amino group

6. The source of Stratospheric NO_x is:
   (a) Atmospheric N_2
   (b) Tropospheric N_2O
   (c) Tropospheric NO
   (d) Tropospheric NO_2

7. In troposphere, which of the following processes does not generate hydroxyl radical?
   (a) $O(^1D) + H_2O$ (b) $O(^3P) + H_2O$
   (c) $HCHO + h\nu$ (d) $HNO_2 + h\nu$

8. The most common form of lead present in pesticide is:
   (a) Lead acetate (b) Lead arsenate
   (c) Lead azide (d) Lead telluride

9. Consider the following four statements about benzo[a]pyrene:
   1. It is a group 1 carcinogen
   2. It is a polycyclic aromatic hydrocarbon
   3. Its molecular formula is $C_{20}H_{12}$
   4. It has four benzene rings

   Choose the correct code:

   Codes:
   (a) 1 and 2 only (b) 1, 2 and 3 only
   (c) 2, 3 and 4 only (d) 1, 2, 3 and 4

10. Given below are two statements. One labelled as Assertion (A) and the other labelled as Reason (R):

    Assertion (A): Radon is an inert gas and it is radioactive.

    Reason (R): All inert gases are radioactive.

    Choose the correct answer:
    (a) Both (A) and (R) are correct and (R) is the correct explanation of (A).
    (b) Both (A) and (R) are correct and (R) is not the correct explanation of (A).
    (c) (A) is true, but (R) is false.
    (d) (A) is false, but (R) is true.

11. Most of Epiphytes are examples of type of biotic interactions called:
    (a) Mutualism (b) Coevolution
    (c) Commensalism (d) Parasitism

12. Inhalation of airborne mold spore leads to disease in man such as:
    (a) Bronchitis
    (b) Allergy
    (c) Cardiac congestion
    (d) Eye irritation

13. Biological diversity is mainly a function of:
    1. Latitude
    2. Longitude
    3. Distance from sea

    Choose the correct answer:
    (a) 1 only (b) 1 and 2 only
    (c) 2 and 3 only (d) 1, 2 and 3

14. The ability of a living system to be restored through secondary succession after a more severe disturbance is known as:
    (a) Rehabilitation
    (b) Resistance
    (c) Resilience
    (d) Restoration

15. The characteristic feature of the background extinction is disappearance of a species at a:
    (a) low rate (b) fast rate
    (c) lapse rate (d) intrinsic rate

16. Speciation means:
    (a) Natural process of extinction of different species
    (b) Artificial process of extinction of different species
    (c) One species splits into two or more different species naturally
    (d) Characterisation of different species

17. Topological modelling is a well-organized cluster of functions in GIS to process:
    1. Spatial data
    2. Attribute data
    3. Physico-chemical data
    4. Species richness data

    Choose the correct code:

    Codes:

    (a) 1 and 2 only (b) 2 and 3 only
    (c) 1, 2 and 3 only (d) 1, 2, 3 and 4

18. A rock body or formation which may be porous enough to hold enough quantity of water but which by virtue of its other properties does not allow an easy and quick flow through it, is called:
    (a) Aquitard (b) Aquifuge
    (c) Aquiclude (d) Aquifer

19. For many decades, geologists noted the high number of earthquakes and active volcanoes occurring around the rim of the Pacific Ocean basin. This is called:
    (a) Volcanic ring
    (b) Ring of fire
    (c) Earthquake zone
    (d) Volcanic hot spot

20. Inversion that occurs near Earth's Surface is called:
    (a) Radiation inversion
    (b) Advectional inversion
    (c) Subsidence inversion
    (d) Cold-air-drainage inversion

21. The radiation flux emitted per unit solid angle in a specified direction by a unit area of source is called:
    (a) irradiance (b) radiance
    (c) exitance (d) radiant flux

22. Mean residence time of soil organic matter in an ecosystem is maximum in:
    (a) Tropical rain forest
    (b) Boreal forest
    (c) Temperate coniferous forest
    (d) Dry deciduous forest

23. Worst affected area by Indian Ocean Tsunami of December 2004 in India was:
    (a) Andaman and Nicobar Islands
    (b) Tamil Nadu
    (c) Andhra Pradesh
    (d) Odisha

24. Consider solar insolatioof 400 W/m^2 incident on a single solar cell of area 100 cm^2. If only 15% of the photons cause electron-hole pairs and the average energy of incident photons is ~1 eV, the short circuit current of the cell is:
    (a) 1.2 A (b) 1.5 A
    (c) 1.6 A (d) 1.8 A

25. For which of the following renewable resources of energy, sun is not directly responsible?
    (a) Wind (b) Biomass
    (c) OTEC (d) Tidal

26. In terms of the calorific value, identify the correct sequence:
    (a) Methane > hydrogen > ethanol > methanol
    (b) Hydrogen > methane > ethanol > methanol
    (c) Methane > hydrogen > methanol > ethanol
    (d) Hydrogen > ethanol > methane > methanol

27. At a given location the wind speeds are predominantly in the range 6 to 6.4 m/s. This location's wind power class will be termed as:

(a) Fair (b) Good
(c) Excellent (d) Outstanding

28. Which of the following nuclides does not undergo fission with low energy (slow) neutrons?
(a) 235 U (b) 238 U
(c) 239 Pu (d) 233 U

29. According to CPCB standards, the annual average concentration of $PM_{2.5}$ should not exceed:
(a) 60 $\mu g\ m^{-3}$ (b) 40 $\mu g\ m^{-3}$
(c) 80 $\mu g\ m^{-3}$ (d) 100 $\mu g\ m^{-3}$

30. Which of the following is a secondary aerosol?
(a) Pollens
(b) Virus
(c) Sodium Chloride
(d) Ammonium Sulphate

31. In the colorimetric determination of ambient SO_2 by WEST-GAEKE method, the absorbance of the colored complex should be measured at which of the following wavelengths?
(a) 550 nm (b) 650 nm
(c) 450 nm (d) 350 nm

32. A healthy human ear, before experiencing pain, can detect sound pressure levels as high as:
(a) 50 Pa (b) 100 Pa
(c) 200 Pa (d) 1000 Pa

33. The resultant of two noise levels of 80 dB and 50 dB will be about:
(a) ~ 80 dB (b) ~ 82 dB
(c) ~ 60 dB (d) ~ 130 dB

34. The half life of radioactive iodine –131 is:
(a) 30 years (b) 15 years
(c) 5 years (d) 8 years

35. Which of the following best describes the function of the environmental management plan as a part of the environental statement?
(a) It describes the environmental impacts of the proposal.
(b) It describes the baseline environmental data.
(c) It describes the project proposal in detail.
(d) It describes the actions and auditing procedures needed.

36. India submitted its INDCs related to climate change to the UN recently. What does INDCs stand for?
(a) Intended Nationally Devoted Contributions
(b) Intended Nationally Determined Contributions
(c) Intended Notified Decisive Contributions
(d) India's Nationally Determined Contributions

37. Formal EIA became an integral part of Environmental Management in India by a Notification for the first time in:
(a) 1988 (b) 1990
(c) 1992 (d) 1994

38. EIA is necessary because:
1. Development is not good for environment
2. Environmental impacts of development are in public interest
3. There is growing interest in sustainability

Choose the correct answer:
(a) 1 only (b) 2 only
(c) 2 and 3 only (d) 1, 2 and 3

39. A moist air parcel at 24°C has a mixing ratio of 10 g per kg. Its virtual temperature is:
(a) ~ 25.81°C (b) ~ 20.68°C
(c) ~ 31.25°C (d) ~ 28.12°C

40. The Vienna Convention is basically related to:
(a) International trade in endangered species

(b) Protection of O_3 layer
(c) Biodiversity conservation
(d) Preservation of cultural environment

41. According to Wildlife Protection Act in India, who is the authority to issue permission to hunt rogue animals?
(a) Chief Minister of the State
(b) Chief Wildlife Warden
(c) Conservator of Forest
(d) Deputy Commissioner

42. According to MOEF (now MOEFCC) notification of 1992, for labelling cosmetics as environment-friendly product, the presence of fluoride (F) in tooth paste/powder should not exceed:
(a) 20 ppm (b) 50 ppm
(c) 100 ppm (d) 10 ppm

43. Which one of the following methods converts decomposed liquid or solid hazardous organic waste effectively?
(a) Open incineration
(b) Plasma incineration
(c) Sanitory landfill
(d) Bioremidiation

44. For a bi-variate sample, the correlation coefficient is 0.25 and it is found to be significantly different from zero at 5% level of significance. Given $t_{0.05} = 1.645$, what is the minimum size of the sample?
(a) 43 (b) 50
(c) 55 (d) 63

45. Which one of the following is non-probability sampling?
(a) Convenience probability
(b) Stratified
(c) Cluster
(d) Systemic

46. A parametric test generally used to compare sample variance to a theoretical population variance, is:
(a) F-test (b) Z-test
(c) t-test (d) χ^2-text

47. From a random sample of 36 fish caught in a sample, the mean length $(\bar{X})$ and sample standard deviation (sd) were found to be 30 cm and 6 cm respectively. If at 95% confidence level z is 1.96, then the mean length of fish in this population is in the range:
(a) $27 < X < 33$ (b) $27.5 < X < 32.5$
(c) $24 < X < 36$ (d) $28.04 < X < 32$

48. One of the natural causes of occurrence of inland soil alkalinity is the presence of:
(a) Sodium hypochlorite
(b) Potassium nitrate
(c) Sodium chloride
(d) Sodium carbonate

49. The Supreme Court of India directed the government to implement environmental education in all educational institutions as compulsory subject in:
(a) 1976 (b) 2003
(c) 1988 (d) 2014

50. Organic wetland soils have:
(a) high cation capacity
(b) high bulk density
(c) low porosity
(d) high nutrient availability

ANSWERS

1. (c)	2. (c)	3. (d)	4. (d)	5. (b)
6. (b)	7. (b)	8. (b)	9. (b)	10. (c)
11. (c)	12. (b)	13. (a)	14. (c)	15. (a)
16. (c)	17. (a)	18. (c)	19. (b)	20. (a)
21. (b)	22. (b)	23. (a)	24. (a)	25. (d)
26. (b)	27. (c)	28. (b)	29. (b)	30. (d)
31. (a)	32. (c)	33. (a)	34. (d)	35. (d)

36. (b)	37. (d)	38. (c)	39. (a)	40. (b)
41. (b)	42. (d)	43. (b)	44. (a)	45. (a)
46. (d)	47. (d)	48. (d)	49. (b)	50. (a)

PAPER–III

Note: This paper contains seventy-five (75) objective type questions of two (2) marks each. All questions are compulsory.

1. Which one of the following statements is not true in the case of point source Gaussian Plume Model?
   (a) Wind speeds are constant in time.
   (b) Pollutants are conservative
   (c) Rate of emission of pollutants from the stack is constant
   (d) The ground level concentration is inversely proportional of effective stack height

2. Consider the simple regression equation Y = a + bX between the variables Y and X. If the standard deviation S_X and S_Y are 3 and 2 respectively and correlation coefficient r = 0.75, the estimate of b is:
   (a) 0.25 (b) 0.5
   (c) 1.125 (d) 1.5

3. Consider two normal population with variances of 10 and 20, respectively. If two independent random sample drawn from the two populations are of the sizes 30 and 24 and their variances 10 and 15 respectively, the value of static $F_{(29,23)}$ is:
   (a) 1.33 (b) 2.50
   (c) 1.56 (d) 3.0

4. A normal population has $\sigma^2 = 6$. The sum of squares of deviations of 15 sample values from their mean being 120, what is the χ^2 (chi-square) value?
   (a) 9 (b) 48
   (c) 20 (d) 1.33

5. Choose the correct sequence of phases associated with a population growth that exhibits logistic model represented by $\frac{dN}{dt} = rN\left(1-\frac{N}{k}\right)$.
   (a) Stationary phase → Exponential phase → Lag phase
   (b) Lag phase → Stationary phase → Exponential phase
   (c) Lag phase → Exponential phase → Stationary phase
   (d) Exponential phase → Stationary phase → Lag phase

6. The toxic substances of special concern emitted during incineration process from waste to energy plants are:
   1. Carbon monoxide
   2. Carbon dioxide
   3. Dioxins
   4. Furans

   Choose the correct answer:
   (a) 1 and 2 only (b) 2 and 3 only
   (c) 1 and 4 only (d) 3 and 4 only

7. Sanitary land fills have following properties. They:
   1. reduce trash volume in a short time
   2. release CH_4 and CO_2
   3. eventually produce leachate which contaminate ground water

   Choose the correct answer:
   (a) 1 and 2 only (b) 2 only
   (c) 1 and 3 only (d) 1, 2 and 3

8. For providing information related to environment to decision makers, policy makers, scientists and environmental engineers all over the country, ENVIS was established in the year belonging to:
   (a) Sixties (b) Seventies
   (c) Eighties (d) Nineties

9. The total radiative forcing of all major and minor greenhouse gases in the year 2014 is estimated to be:

(a) ~ 2.51 W/m^2 (b) ~ 2.93 W/m^2
(c) ~ 1.87 W/m^2 (d) ~ 2.7 W/m^2

10. For the range of temperatures observed in the earth's atmosphere, the saturation mixing ratio (W_s) and the total pressure are related as:
(a) $W_s \propto \frac{1}{p}$ (b) $W_s \propto p$
(c) $W_s \propto p^{3/2}$ (d) $W_s \propto p^{-3/2}$

11. A thermal power plant based on coal produces 100 MW of electrical power with conversion efficiency of 30%. If the ash content of coal is 5% and net heating value is 30 MJ per kg, how much ash is produced daily?
(a) 48 metric tons (b) 24 metric tons
(c) 90 metric tons (d) 60 metric tons

12. Under which section of Wildlife (Protection) Act, 1972, the state government can declare an area closed to hunting for a specified period?
(a) Section 35 (b) Section 27
(c) Section 38-A (d) Section 37

13. Which one of the following criteria should not contribute to the process of establishing significance of the impact of a developmental project on environment?
(a) Sensitivity of surrounding environment
(b) Probability of the impact occurring
(c) Views and values of the developer
(d) Views and suggestions of the public

14. The following benefits may accrue as a result of environmental audit:
1. Material audit leads to improvement in the production efficiency and cost
2. Pollution monitoring leads to environmental quality improvement
3. Approach towards zero discharge and zero emission leads to clean development
4. Incentive for pollution abatement in the form of reduction in import tax leads to cleaner environment

Choose the correct answer:
(a) 1 only (b) 2 and 3 only
(c) 2 and 4 only (d) 1, 2, 3 and 4

15. Environmental Impact Assessment (EIA) was incorporated under which one of the following legislations?
(a) Air (Prevention and Control of Pollution) Act, 1981
(b) Wildlife (Protection) Act, 1981
(c) Indian Forest Act, 1927
(d) Environmental (Protection) Act, 1986

16. A company operating a vehicle manufacturing plant has developed Environmental Management System (EMS) to enhance its performance and to improve quality of its products. The key aspects of this EMS would include:
(a) Audit of manufacturing plant safety procedure
(b) Maximizing returns to stakeholders of the company
(c) The development of an overall framework for environmental affairs of the company
(d) The aspects of costs involved in developing an environmental policy

17. Best practice in scoping requires:
1. A site visit
2. Relevant experience of other similar developmental projects
3. Employing formal scoping techniques

Choose the correct answer:
(a) 1 only (b) 1 and 2 only
(c) 2 and 3 only (d) 1, 2 and 3

18. Match the List I and List II. Identify the correct answer from the codes given below:

List I (Stages in EIA)
(A) Screening
(B) Scoping

(C) Baseline description
(D) Mitigation measures

List II (Actions in EIA)

(i) Reduce or avoid the impacts
(ii) Establish present and future stages of environment
(iii) Early indication of crucial impacts
(iv) Narrowing the application of EIA

Codes:	A	B	C	D
(a)	(iv)	(iii)	(ii)	(i)
(b)	(i)	(iv)	(iii)	(ii)
(c)	(ii)	(i)	(iv)	(iii)
(d)	(iii)	(ii)	(i)	(iv)

19. The decision-making process in EIA generally does not include:
(a) Cost-benefit analysis
(b) Procedural information
(c) Socio-economic aspects
(d) Operational management

20. Which of the following actions may be recommended for acidified lakes?
(a) Ammoniation
(b) Liming
(c) Ozonation
(d) Chlorination

21. Given below are two statements. One labelled as Assertion (A) and the other labelled as Reason (R):
Assertion (A): All types of aerosols contribute to radiative forcing.
Reason (R): Aerosol effectively absorb electromagnetic radiations.
Choose the correct answer:
(a) Both (A) and (R) are correct and (R) is the correct explanation of (A).
(b) Both (A) and (R) are correct and (R) is not the correct explanation of (A).
(c) (A) is true, but (R) is false.
(d) (A) is false, but (R) is true.

22. Given below are two statements. One labelled as Assertion (A) and the other labelled as Reason (R):
Assertion (A): The efficiency of fuel cells is not limited by the second law of thermodynamics.
Reason (R): There is no intermediate heat to work conversion in a fuel cell.
Choose the correct answer:
(a) Both (A) and (R) are correct and (R) is the correct explanation of (A).
(b) Both (A) and (R) are correct and (R) is not the correct explanation of (A).
(c) (A) is true, but (R) is false.
(d) (A) is false, but (R) is true.

23. Given below are two statements. One labelled as Assertion (A) and the other labelled as Reason (R):
Assertion (A): A wind rose with approximately equal length spokes (or petals) represents great variation of wind direction over a given duration.
Reason (R): The length of the spokes is a measure of wind speeds in a given duration.
Choose the correct answer:
(a) Both (A) and (R) are correct and (R) is the correct explanation of (A).
(b) Both (A) and (R) are correct and (R) is not the correct explanation of (A).
(c) (A) is true, but (R) is false.
(d) (A) is false, but (R) is true.

24. Given below are two statements. One labelled as Assertion (A) and the other labelled as Reason (R):
Asscrtion (A): Largc scalc OTEC development may exacerbate the greenhouse effect.
Reason (R): Methane is a greenhouse gas.
Choose the correct answer:
(a) Both (A) and (R) are correct and (R) is the correct explanation of (A).
(b) Both (A) and (R) are correct and (R) is not the correct explanation of (A).

(c) (A) is true, but (R) is false.
(d) (A) is false, but (R) is true.

25. In a spectrophotometric cell of 2.0 cm pathlength, the solution of a substance shows the absorbance value of 1.0. If the molar absorptivity of the compound is 2×10^4 L mol^{-1} cm^{-1}, calculate the concentration of the substance in solution. What is the concentration of the substance in that solution?
(a) 2.5×10^{-5} mol L^{-1}
(b) 4.0×10^4 mol L^{-1}
(c) 1.0×10^{-4} mol L^{-1}
(d) 5.0×10^{-4} mol L^{-1}

26. In order to obtain useful fusion energy from a thermonuclear fusion reactor, if the confinement time of the D+T Plasma ions is 1 μ sec, the ion density (per m^3) must be:
(a) $\geq 10^{26}$ m^{-3} (b) $\geq 10^{23}$ m^{-3}
(c) $\geq 10^{20}$ m^{-3} (d) $\geq 10^{14}$ m^{-3}

27. Which of the following is not a detrivore?
(a) Vultures (b) Earthworms
(c) Insects (d) Hydrilla

28. Secondary succession begins at:
(a) base rock
(b) newly cooled lava
(c) burnt forest
(d) newly created shallow pond

29. Given below are two statements. One labelled as Assertion (A) and the other labelled as Reason (R):
Assertion (A): It is generally agreed that life on earth began between 3.5 and 4.5 billion years ago.
Reason (R): The first form of life was the anaerobic bacteria as environment was devoid of oxygen.
Choose the correct answer:
(a) Both (A) and (R) are correct and (R) is the correct explanation of (A).
(b) Both (A) and (R) are correct and (R) is not the correct explanation of (A).
(c) (A) is true, but (R) is false.
(d) (A) is false, but (R) is true.

30. The total number of Sustainable Development Goals (SDGs) announced by UN in 2015 are:
(a) 15 (b) 17
(c) 19 (d) 21

31. The total area of productive ecosystem required to support the population sustainably is known as:
(a) Ecological footprint
(b) Ecological handprint
(c) Carrying capacity
(d) Ecological services

32. Carrying capacity of a population determines that a particular habitat for a given species can sustain:
(a) Minimum Population
(b) Maximum Population
(c) Average Population
(d) A Fraction of Migrating Population

33. Which one of the following is the most productive ecosystem?
(a) Lakes and streams
(b) Estuaries
(c) Continental shelf
(d) Open ocean

34. A measure that combines the number of species and their relative abundances compared with one another is termed:
(a) Species richness
(b) Species evenness
(c) Species diversity
(d) Species relationships

35. The figures of humanity's global footprint (million hectares) for different countries estimated by WWF and Global Footprint Network in 2008 fall in the sequence:
(a) US > China > European Union > Japan > India

(b) China > US > Japan > India > European Union
(c) European Union > US > China > Japan > India
(d) US > European Union > China > India > Japan

36. A common features of the synoptic and mesoscale motions in the atmosphere is that their:
(a) Vertical motion component is more in magnitude than the horizontal wind component.
(b) Vertical motion component is roughly comparable to horizontal wind component.
(c) Vertical motion component is an order of magnitude smaller than the horizontal wind component.
(d) Properties can be studied by conventional synoptic networks.

37. The shape of a plume from a tall stack located on a flat terrain is found to be of "fanning" type. It implies that the atmosphere is under the condition of:
(a) Strong lapse rate
(b) Weak lapse rate
(c) Inversion
(d) Weak lapse rate below inversion

38. Given below are two statements. One labelled as Assertion (A) and the other labelled as Reason (R):
Assertion (A): Thunderstorm is a violent convective event accompanied by thunder and lightening.
Reason (R): Thunderstorm is not associated with vertical air movement, humidity and instability.
Choose the correct answer:
(a) Both (A) and (R) are correct and (R) is the correct explanation of (A).
(b) Both (A) and (R) are correct and (R) is not the correct explanation of (A).
(c) (A) is true, but (R) is false.
(d) (A) is false, but (R) is true.

39. According to National Ambient Air Quality Standards in India, the permissible 24 hour average concentration of lead in ambient air of an industrial area is
(a) 1.0 $\mu g/m^3$ (b) 2.0 $\mu g/m^3$
(c) 3.03 $\mu g/m^3$ (d) 4.0 $\mu g/m^3$

40. Peat soils, which have undergone prolonged drought in the forest are prone for:
1. ground forest fire
2. underground forest fire
3. tree crown fire
Choose the correct code:
(a) 1 only (b) 2 only
(c) 1 and 2 only (d) 1, 2 and 3

41. Insect pests can be controlled by the use of:
1. Insecticide
2. Pheromones
3. Juvenile Hormones
4. Nitrophosphate
Choose the correct answer:
(a) 1 only (b) 1 and 2 only
(c) 1, 2 and 3 only (d) 1, 2, 3 and 4

42. Dioxins and Furans are two toxic gaseous pollutants which can be measured by:
(a) GC-MS (b) TLC
(c) ICP-AES (d) AAS

43. Based on the pE value for four water samples given below, the concentration of dissolved oxygen shall be highest in:
(a) pE = – 4.1 (b) pE = 13.9
(c) pE = 1.0 (d) pE = 7.0

44. A total of 10 instantaneous sound pressure level measurements at 10 sec intervals for a traffic site are given in the table below:

S.No.	1	2	3	4	5	6	7	8	9	10
SPL(dB)	71	75	70	78	80	84	76	74	75	74

The estimated L_{90} from these measurement is:

(a) ~ 71 dB (b) ~ 70 dB
(c) ~ 74 dB (d) ~ 75 dB

45. The composition of rhizospheric micro organisms are dependent on the soil:
    1. Texture 2. Organic matter
    3. pH 4. Elasticity

    Choose the correct answer:

    (a) 1 only (b) 1 and 2 only
    (c) 1, 2 and 3 (d) 1, 2, 3 and 4

46. Given below are two statements. One labelled as Assertion (A) and the other labelled as Reason (R):

    Assertion (A): The fundamental goal of a dose-response assessment is to obtain a mathematical relationship between the amount of a toxicant that a human is exposed to the risk that there will be.

    Reason (R): To apply dose-response data obtained from animal bioassay to humans, a scaling factor must be introduced.

    Choose the correct answer:

    (a) Both (A) and (R) are correct and (R) is the correct explanation of (A).
    (b) Both (A) and (R) are correct and (R) is not the correct explanation of (A).
    (c) (A) is true, but (R) is false.
    (d) (A) is false, but (R) is true.

47. Tropical grasslands with scattered trees are also known as:

    (a) Taigas (b) Steppe
    (c) Savannas (d) Meadows

48. On 18th April 2015, Global Alliance to Eliminate Lead Paint (GAELP) announced the goal of eliminating lead paint around the world by:

    (a) 2020 (b) 2025
    (c) 2028 (d) 2022

49. The form of coal/fuel in the ascending order of heating value can be best represented as:

    (a) Lignite < Peat < Bituminous < Anthracite
    (b) Bituminous < Lignite < Peat < Anthracite
    (c) Peat < Lignite < Bituminous < Anthracite
    (d) Peat < Lignite < Anthracite < Bituminous

50. In India wetland conservation is presently done by the Ministry of Environment, Forest and Climate Change under:

    (a) National Wetland Conservation Programme
    (b) National Plan for Conservation of Aquatic Ecosystems
    (c) National Lake Conservation Programme
    (d) Coastal Regulation Zone

51. Soil salination is not caused by:

    (a) Agricultural area with high ground water irrigation
    (b) Coastal swampy area
    (c) Flood prone area
    (d) Upland lateritic area with waste water irrigation

52. Ground water occurs under:
    1. Unconfined condition in shallow aquifers
    2. Semi Confined aquifers
    3. Confined aquifers

    Choose the correct answer:

    (a) 1 only (b) 1 and 2 only
    (c) 2 and 3 only (d) 1, 2 and 3

53. DEM (Digital Elevation Model) is best represented using:

    (a) Vector Data Models
    (b) Raster Data Models
    (c) Coverage Data Structure
    (d) Non-Topological Data Structure

54. Delta are classified into six basic types taking cognissance and importance of:

1. Rivers
2. Waves
3. Tides

Choose the correct answer:

(a) 1 only (b) 1 and 2 only
(c) 1 and 3 only (d) 1, 2 and 3

55. Large elongated depression with steep walls formed by the downward displacement of a block of the earth surface between nearly parallel faults or fault system:

(a) Thrust faults (b) Horst
(c) Grabben (d) Rift Valley

56. Which form of scattering in visible region in the atmosphere is not dependent on wavelength?

1. Rayleigh
2. Mie
3. Non-Selective

Choose the correct answer:

(a) 1 only (b) 1 and 2 only
(c) 3 only (d) 2 and 3 only

57. Best spatial configuration for designing a core natural area is:

(a) Circular (b) Rectangular
(c) Square (d) Triangle

58. Ecosystem resilience is the capacity of an ecosystem to sustain its:

1. Fundamental function
2. Structure
3. Feedbacks in the face of a spectrum of shock and perturbations

Choose the correct answer:

(a) 1 and 2 only (b) 2 and 3 only
(c) 1 and 3 only (d) 1, 2 and 3

59. With regard to ozone depletion over Antarctica, select the false statement:

(a) Circumpolar vortex acts as a reaction chamber
(b) Polar Stratospheric Clouds (PSCs) are formed within the vortex
(c) There is very low temperature inside the vortex
(d) The heterogenous reaction $ClONO_2(s) + HCl(g) \rightarrow Cl_2(g) + HNO_3(s)$ takes over PSCs

60. Match List I with List II. Choose the correct answer from the codes given below:

List I (Horizon)

(A) A - horizon (B) O - horizon
(C) C - horizon (D) B - horizon

List II (Type/Characteristics)

(i) Subsoil (ii) Leaf litter
(iii) Parent material (iv) Top soil

Codes:	A	B	C	D
(a)	(iv)	(ii)	(iii)	(i)
(b)	(i)	(iii)	(iv)	(ii)
(c)	(ii)	(iv)	(i)	(iii)
(d)	(iii)	(i)	(ii)	(iv)

61. A laboratory analysis of a waste water sample indicated BOD of 750 mg L^{-1} with rate constant (K) 0.20 day^{-1} at 20°C. The 5-day BOD at 20°C is:

(a) 675 mg L^{-1} (b) 650 mg L^{-1}
(c) 400 mg L^{-1} (d) 600 mg L^{-1}

62. A stream with a flow of 0.2 m^3/sec and a chloride concentration of 50 mg/L receives a discharge of mine drainage water with a flow of 0.05 m^3/sec and chloride concentration of 1500 mg/L. The downstream concentration of chloride is:

(a) 150 mg/L (b) 200 mg/L
(c) 340 mg/L (d) 380 mg/L

63. Four students (List A) working independently in a chromatographic analysis (List B) reported the Retention Factor (R_f) values:

List A (Students)		**List B (R_f Values)**
(A) R	→	(i) 0
(B) S	→	(ii) 0.5
(C) T	→	(iii) 1.3
(D) U	→	(iv) 1.0

The result of which student(s) is (are) definitely incorrect:

(a) R and U (b) S and T
(c) S, T and U (d) T

64. The mechanism of the formation of gaseous N_2O_5 from NO_2 and O_2 gases in the gas phase within clouds is:

$NO_2(g) + O_3(g) \rightarrow NO_3(g) + O_2(g)$ (i)

$NO_3(g) + NO_2(g) \rightarrow NO_2O_5(g)$ (ii)

The experimentally determined rate law is

$$- d [NO_2(g)]/dt = K [NO_2(g)] [O_3(g)]$$

Based on the information provided which of the following statement is incorrect?

(a) Overall reaction is: $2NO(g) + O_3(g) \rightarrow N_2O_5(g) + O_2(g)$
(b) The reaction intermediate is NO_3
(c) The rate determining step is reaction (i)
(d) The rate reaction (ii) is slower than the rate of reaction (i)

65. In a rain water sample of pH=8.45, the dominant species of dissolved sulphur dioxide shall be:

(a) $SO_2 \cdot H_2O$ (b) HSO_3^-
(c) SO_3^{2-} (d) $S_2O_5^{2-}$

66. An aquifer of sand has a saturated column of cross-sectional area 0.2 × 5 m and a depth of 3 m. If the specific yield of sand is 25%, how much water can be extracted from the aquifer?

(a) 0.5 m^3 (b) 0.75 m^3
(c) 1.2 m^3 (d) 1.5 m^3

67. Atmospheric life times of CFCs is typically in the range:

(a) 50-102 years (b) 140-200 years
(c) 200-400 years (d) 152-210 years

68. With respect to CO_2, Global Warming Potential (GWP) for N_2O over a time horizon of 100 years is estimated to be:

(a) 156 (b) 210
(c) 296 (d) 240

69. The greenhouse gas N_2O strongly absorbs infra-red radiations of wavelength(s):

(a) ~ 4.5 μm
(b) ~ 7.8 μm and 8.6 μm
(c) ~ 9.6 μm
(d) ~ 10.6 μm

70. By the year 2022, Indian government has set a new target of Solar Power generation of:

(a) 4 GW (b) 60 GW
(c) 75 GW (d) 100 GW

71. Match the List I and List II. Identify the correct answer from the codes given below the lists.

List I (Causes)

(A) Soil organisms
(B) Phosphorous assimilation
(C) Water pollution
(D) Air pollution

List II (Effects)

(i) Algal bloom
(ii) Chronic obstructive pulmonary diseases
(iii) Decomposition
(iv) Complexing agent

Codes:	A	B	C	D
(a)	(i)	(ii)	(iii)	(iv)
(b)	(iii)	(iv)	(i)	(ii)
(c)	(ii)	(iii)	(iv)	(i)
(d)	(iv)	(ii)	(i)	(iii)

72. The Wavelengths that are most important in the context of stratospheric ozone depletion are:

(a) 280-320 nm (b) 400-700 nm
(c) 700-900 nm (d) > 900 nm

73. Remote sensing satellites such as RESOURCESAT are usually placed in polar:

1. Low Earth Polar orbit
2. Sunsynchronous orbit
3. Geosynchronous orbit

Choose the correct answer:
(a) 2 and 3 only
(b) 1 and 2 only
(c) 1 and 3 only
(d) 1, 2 and 3

74. Gills of marine fishes perform the functions of the following:
(a) Water loss and salt excretion
(b) Water gain and salt excretion
(c) Water uptake and solute uptake
(d) Water loss and solute uptake

75. The instrument used for determination of soil water loss by percolation, evapotranspiration and run off is called:
(a) Lysimeter
(b) Rain Gauze
(c) Soil moisture meter
(d) Soil porosity meter

ANSWERS

1. (d)	2. (b)	3. (a)	4. (c)	5. (c)
6. (d)	7. (b)	8. (c)	9. (b)	10. (a)
11. (a)	12. (d)	13. (c)	14. (d)	15. (d)
16. (c)	17. (d)	18. (a)	19. (d)	20. (b)
21. (c)	22. (a)	23. (c)	24. (b)	25. (a)
26. (a)	27. (d)	28. (c)	29. (b)	30. (b)
31. (a)	32. (b)	33. (b)	34. (c)	35. (d)
36. (c)	37. (c)	38. (c)	39. (a)	40. (c)
41. (c)	42. (a)	43. (b)	44. (a)	45. (c)
46. (b)	47. (c)	48. (a)	49. (c)	50. (b)
51. (c)	52. (d)	53. (b)	54. (d)	55. (d)
56. (c)	57. (a)	58. (d)	59. (d)	60. (a)
61. (a)	62. (c)	63. (d)	64. (d)	65. (c)
66. (b)	67. (a)	68. (c)	69. (b)	70. (d)
71. (b)	72. (a)	73. (b)	74. (a)	75. (a)

PRACTICE PAPERS

MOCK TEST-1
PAPER-I

1. A teacher is called the leader of the class because
   (a) he is autocratic emperor of his class
   (b) he masters the art of oratory like a political leader
   (c) he is a maker of the future of his students
   (d) he belongs to a recognised teachers' union

2. The aim of introducing career courses in schools and colleges is to
   (a) increase G.K. in students
   (b) develop the ability to make the intelligent choice of jobs
   (c) provide professional knowledge to students
   (d) All of the above

3. The most effective attribute for a teacher is
   (a) Teaching skills (b) Knowledge
   (c) Feedback (d) Management

4. Those teachers are preferred most by students who
   (a) are themselves disciplined
   (b) give important questions before examination
   (c) dictate notes in the class
   (d) can clear their difficulties regarding subject-matter

5. The qualities of a teacher is/are:
   (i) He must not give any false promise
   (ii) He must not have any bad habits
   (iii) He should be mentally and physically fit
   (iv) He must not be superstitious about his class and students
   (a) (iii), (iv) and (ii)
   (b) (iv), (i) and (ii)
   (c) (i), (iii) and (iv)
   (d) All of the above

6. A teacher is more effective who can
   (a) motivate students to learn
   (b) control the class
   (c) correct the assignments carefully
   (d) give more information in less time

7. A teacher ought to know the problems prevalent in the field of education because
   (a) he can tell the government about it
   (b) with this knowledge, he can have information about education
   (c) he can tell about the same to another teacher
   (d) only he can do something about solving them

8. We can judge the quality of a research by the
   (a) experience of researcher
   (b) relevance of research
   (c) depth of the research
   (d) methodology followed in conducting the research

9. The theory or model developed through the fundamental research to the actual solution of the problems is applied in
   (a) educational research
   (b) action research

(c) applied research
(d) basic research

10. A write-up based on studies of the census data of a given area is called
(a) Research paper (b) Article
(c) Research report (d) Thesis

Direction: (11-16) Study the following passage and give answer to the questions based on it.

Knowledge creation in many cases requires creativity and idea generation. This is especially important in generating alternative decision support solutions. Some people believe that an individual's creative ability stems primarily from personality traits such as inventiveness, independence, individuality, enthusiasm, and flexibility. However, several studies have found that creativity is not so much a function of individual traits as was once believed, and that individual creativity can be learned and improved. This understanding has led innovative companies to recognise that the key to fostering creativity may be the development of an idea-nurturing work environment. Idea-generation methods and techniques, to be used by individuals or in groups, are consequently being developed. Manual methods for supporting idea generation, such as brain-storming in a group, can be very successful in certain situations. However, in other situations, such an approach is either not economically feasible or not possible. For example, manual methods in group creativity sessions will not work or will not be effective when: (a) there is no time to conduct a proper idea-generation session; (b) there is a poor facilitator (or no facilitator at all); (c) it is too expensive to conduct an idea-generation session; (d) the subject matter is too sensitive for a face-to-face session; or (e) there are not enough participants, the mix of participants is not optimal, or there is no climate for idea generation. In such cases, computerised idea-generation methods have been tried, with frequent success. Idea-generation software is designed to help stimulate a single user or a group to produce new ideas, options and choices. The user does all the work, but the software encourages and pushes, something like a personal trainer. Although idea-generation software is still relatively new, there are several packages on the market. Various approaches are used by idea-generating software to increase the flow of ideas to the user. Idea Fisher, for example, has an associate lexicon of the English language that cross-references words and phrases. These associative links, based on analogies and metaphors, make it easy for the user to be fed words related to a given theme. Some software packages use questions to prompt the user towards new, unexplored patterns of thought. This helps users to break out of cyclical thinking patterns, conquer mental blocks, or deal with bouts of procrastination.

11. The author, in this passage has focused on
(a) individual traits
(b) knowledge creation
(c) creativity
(d) idea-generation

12. Idea-generation software works as if it is a
(a) user-friendly trainer
(b) stimulant
(c) climate creator
(d) knowledge package

13. Which among the following personality traits is not believed to be a factor contributing to an individual's creative ability?
(a) Flexibility (b) Individuality
(c) Sophistication (d) Enthusiasm

14. In certain occasions, manual methods for the support of idea-generation
(a) can be less expensive
(b) do not need a facilitator

(c) require a mix of optimal participants
(d) are alternatively effective

15. Mental blocks, bouts of procrastination and cyclical thinking patterns can be won when
(a) idea-generation software prompts questions
(b) individuals acquire a neutral attitude towards the software
(c) manual methods are removed
(d) innovative companies employ electronic thinking methods

16. Fostering creativity needs an environment of
(a) decision support systems
(b) alternative individual factors
(c) idea-nurturing
(d) decision support solutions

17. For controlling noise in a classroom, the best method of communication is
(a) remaining calm and just looking at student
(b) saying 'don't talk'
(c) continue teaching without caring for noise
(d) raising one's voice above students voice

18. In India, Education TV was first introduced in the year
(a) 1978 (b) 1959
(c) 1987 (d) 1998

19. The failure of the teacher to communicate his ideas well to students may result into:
I. Classroom indiscipline.
II. Decrease in attendance in class.
III. Loss of student's interest in class.
(a) Only II (b) Only III
(c) Only I (d) All of these

20. Visualisation in the instructional process cannot increase
(a) curiosity and concentration
(b) interest and motivation
(c) stress and boredom
(d) retention and adaptation

21. Communication helps in
(a) entertainment
(b) integration of country
(c) cultural promotion
(d) All of these

22. "Because you deserve to know" is the punchline used by
(a) *Hindustan Times*
(b) *The Telegraph*
(c) *The Times of India*
(d) *India Today*

23. Find the odd man out from the following groups of letters.
(a) UlmnE (b) AbcdE
(c) ApqrL (d) IfghO

24. The ambitious computerisation program of the Government of India aimed at connecting 60,000 government schools through internet is known as
(a) Vidya Vahini (b) Gyan Vahini
(c) Kalpana project (d) Vidya Vani

25. Find the wrong number in the following sequence.
225, 336, 447, 557, 669, 771
(a) 669 (b) 557
(c) 336 (d) 771

26. In this question two words are given which have certain relationship followed by four paired lettered words. Select the paired words, that has the same relation as original pair.
ROOF : FOUNDATION
(a) Plateau : Valley
(b) Peak : Valley
(c) Mountain : Grassland
(d) Hill : Mountain

27. "Communication is a verbal process by which we understand each other and reduce uncertainty through the use of

symbol." Who is the author of this statement?
(a) David K. Barlo
(b) Dance
(c) P.S.K. Serichavenko
(d) K.J. Newman

28. Find out the missing number:
8 24 12 ? 18 54
(a) 28 (b) 32
(c) 36 (d) 38

29. A D C F
C F E H
O R ? ?
(a) JK (b) RN
(c) SU (d) QT

30. 3, 12, 27, 48, 75, (?), 147.
(a) 111 (b) 108
(c) 117 (d) 122

31. In this question four words have been given, out of which three are alike in some manner and the fourth one is different. Choose the odd one out.
(a) Epigraphy (b) Ecology
(c) Archaeology (d) Palaeontology

32. Which of the following figures will represent the right relationship between, societies, societies who run schools, DPS society.

(a) 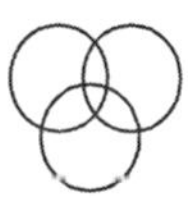 (b) 

(c)  (d) 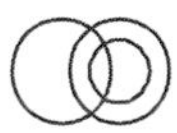

33. **Statements:**
I. All students are ambitious.
II. All ambitious persons are hard working.

Conclusions:
(i) All students are hard-working.
(ii) All hardly working people are not ambitious.

Which of the following is correct?
(a) Only (i) is correct
(b) Only (ii) is correct
(c) Both (i) and (ii) are correct
(d) Neither (i) nor (ii) is correct

34. In a certain code language:
'pit dit mit' means: 'Reena went to Delhi'.
'dit ket set' means: 'Delhi is closing'.
'mit set un' means: 'Reena' is educated.
Then what is the code for 'went'?
(a) dit (b) mit
(c) pit (d) None of these

35. EDITOR : MAGAZINE
Choose the pair from the answer choices that best expresses the relationship similar to that expressed by the question pair.
(a) Novel : Writer
(b) Director : Film
(c) Poem : Poet
(d) Chair : Carpenter

36. Should education in India be made free?
Arguments:
I. Yes, this is the only way to improve the level of literacy.
II. No, this would add already heavy burden on the exchequer.
(a) Only argument I is strong
(b) Only argument II is strong
(c) Both the arguments are strong
(d) None of these

Direction: (37-41) Study the table and answer the questions:

Export of Pulses and Import of Onion (in ₹ crores)

Year	Export of Pulses (in ₹ crores)	Import of Onion (in ₹ crores)
1998-99	44	58
1999-00	45	50

2000-01	60	54
2001-02	56	60
2002-03	92	68
2003-04	100	78
2004-05	68	60

37. During which year there was a maximum fall in export?
(a) 2004-05 (b) 2001-02
(c) 2003-04 (d) None of these

38. The percent of increase of imports in 2003-04 over 2002-03 is
(a) 14.9% (b) 14.7%
(c) 18.4% (d) 18.9%

39. In 1999-2000, the ratio of export to the import is
(a) 19:11 (b) 11:9
(c) 13:17 (d) 9:10

40. During which year there was maximum increase in import over its preceding year?
(a) 2003-04 (b) 2000-01
(c) 2001-02 (d) 2002-03

41. During which year there was minimum increase in import over its preceding year?
(a) 2003-04 (b) 2002-03
(c) 2001-02 (d) None of these

42. The sum of a positive number and its reciprocal is twice the difference of the number and its reciprocal. The number is:
(a) $\sqrt{3}$ (b) $\sqrt{2}$
(c) $\frac{1}{\sqrt{2}}$ (d) $\frac{1}{\sqrt{3}}$

43. Which one of the following states has the maximum number of Wildlife Sanctuaries (National Park and Sanctuaries)?
(a) Madhya Pradesh
(b) Rajasthan
(c) Uttar Pradesh
(d) West Bengal

Directions: (44-48) Answer the following questions based on the graph given below:

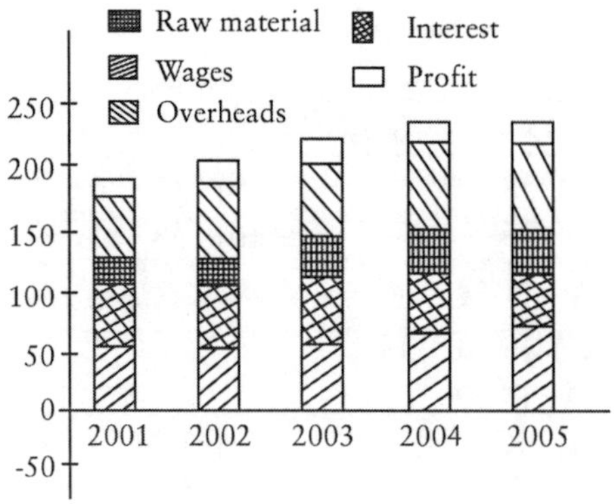

44. Which component of the cost of production has remained almost unchanged over the period 2001-2005?
(a) Wages (b) Interest
(c) Raw material (d) Overheads

45. In which year was the increase in raw material maximum?
(a) 2004 (b) 2002
(c) 2003 (d) 2001

46. What percent of costs did the profits form over the period?
(a) 7% (b) 5%
(c) 2% (d) 1%

47. In which period was the change in profit maximum?
(a) 2002-03 (b) 2001-02
(c) 2004-05 (d) 2003-04

48. If the interest component is not included in the total cost calculation, which year would show the maximum profit per unit cost?
(a) 2001 (b) 2002
(c) 2003 (d) 2005

49. How many types of emergencies have been envisaged by the constitution?

(a) One (b) Two
(c) Three (d) Four

50. Photocopying and other electrical equipments produce
(a) methane
(b) ethane
(c) ozone
(d) hydrogen dioxide

PAPER-II

1. The use of anthropoid hazard chemicals like DDT causes reduction in fish population because the chemical mimics the effect of
(a) Luteinizing hormone
(b) Testosterone
(c) Estrogen
(d) All of the above

2. Correct arrangement in order of decreasing soil particle size
(a) Sand, clay, silt (b) Silt, sand, clay
(c) Sand, silt, clay (d) Clay, silt, sand

3. Geostationary satellites orbit above the earth at about
(a) 10 km above the earth
(b) 500 km above the earth
(c) 1500 km above the earth
(d) 5 km above the earth

4. In a river with symmetric channel
(a) Maximum velocity is at the bottom
(b) Minimum velocity is at the surface
(c) Maximum velocity is at the borders
(d) Maximum velocity is at 0.7 of the depth

5. Rapid EIA is called
(a) a study of three months
(b) a study of four months
(c) a study of six months
(d) a study of one year

6. Match the List I and List II and select the correct answer from the codes given below the lists:

List I (Analytical techniques)	List II (Measured items)
A. XRF	(i) Functional groups
B. Nephelometry	(ii) Elements
C. IR spectroscopy	(iii) Turbidity
D. Gas chromatography	(iv) PAH

Codes:	A	B	C	D
(a)	(iv)	(ii)	(iii)	(i)
(b)	(i)	(iii)	(iv)	(ii)
(c)	(iii)	(ii)	(iv)	(i)
(d)	(ii)	(iii)	(i)	(iv)

7. Which of the following materials is not used as moderator to slow down the fast neutrons produced in a nuclear reactor?
(a) Water (b) Heavy water
(c) Graphite (d) Lead

8. Under the Climate Change Action Plan of Government of India which of the renewable source of energy has been identified as a priority for exploitation?
(a) Solar energy
(b) Wind energy
(c) Tidal energy
(d) Geothermal energy

9. Identify the correct sequence of energy flow through various levels of an ecosystem:
(a) Sun's energy → Primary producers → Carnivores
(b) Sun's energy → Primary producers → Carnivores Herbivores
(c) Sun's energy → Herbivores → Primary producers
(d) Sun's energy → Primary producers → Herbivores → Carnivores

10. In urban areas, the main constituents of photochemical smog in winter season are
(a) SO_2 + NO_x + PAN
(b) Hydrocarbons + CO + PAN
(c) Hydrocarbons + SO_2 + PAN
(d) Hydrocarbons + NO_x + O_3 + PAN

11. Which of the following options is correct for concentration of elements in sea water?
(a) Na > Mg > Ca (b) Ca > Na > Mg
(c) Mg > Na > Ca (d) Cl > Na > SO_4

12. The instrument used for determination of transparency of water is
(a) Spectrophotometer
(b) Ekman dredge
(c) Conductivity bridge
(d) Sechhi disc

13. The primitive atmosphere of earth consisted of
(a) CO_2, NO_2, NH_3, SO_2
(b) H_2, NH_3, CH_4, H_2O
(c) CO, N_2O_3, SO_3, H_3N
(d) He, Ne, Ar, Kr

14. Given below are scales of four topographic maps. Maps of which scale will have more clarity?
(a) 1 : 50,000 (b) 1 : 25,000
(c) 1 : 250,000 (d) 1 : 1,000,000

15. Identify the correct sequence of stages of obtaining Environmental clearance for new projects
(a) Appraisal, Screening, Scoping, Public Consultation
(b) Screening, Public Consultation, Scoping, Appraisal
(c) Screening, Appraisal, Scoping, Public Consultation
(d) Screening, Scoping, Public Consultation, Appraisal

16. To test whether there is a significant difference between the means of two sets of observations, one employs the following statistical technique:
(a) Regression
(b) χ^2 test (Chi-square test)
(c) t-test
(d) F-test

17. Chemical formula for CFC-113 is
(a) CCl_2F_2 (b) CCl_3F_3
(c) $C_2Cl_3F_3$ (d) CCl_2F_3

18. In a multiple regression model, the explained variance per d.f. is 50 and unexplained variance per d.f. is 10. The F-ratio is
(a) 2.5 (b) 5
(c) 25 (d) 0.2

19. Which is a correct food chain in the Antarctic ecosystem?
(a) Phytoplankton – Krill – Carnivorous Plankton – Emperor Penguin
(b) Phytoplankton – Krill – Carnivorous Plankton – Squid – Elephant Seal – Leopard Seal
(c) Phytoplankton – Herbivorous Zoo Plankton – Carnivorous Plankton – Adelic Penguin – Emperor Penguin
(d) Herbivorous Zoo Plankton – Phytoplankton – Carnivorous Plankton – Elephant Seal – Leopard Seal

20. In the Gaussian Plume Model, the plume size is estimated considering buoyancy of exhaust gases, stack diameter, wind speed and stability of the atmosphere. The plume size Δh depends on inside radius of stack (r) as
(a) $\Delta h \propto r$ (b) $\Delta h \propto r^{1/3}$
(c) $\Delta h \propto r^{2/3}$ (d) $\Delta h \propto r^2$

21. Pyramid of trophic levels is always upright in case of
(a) Biomass (b) Energy
(c) Number (d) All of the above

22. Replacement of existing communities by any external condition is termed
(a) Primary succession
(b) Secondary succession

(c) Autogenic succession
(d) None of the above

23. What is the importance of the 42nd Amendment to the Constitution brought in the year 1976?
(a) Insertion of Article 48-A
(b) Insertion of Article 51-A (g)
(c) Insertion of Article 48-A and 51-A (g)
(d) None of the above

24. A hazardous waste is characterised by
(a) Ignitibility (b) Reactivity
(c) Toxicity (d) All of the above

25. An earthquake is rated as 'major' if its magnitude in Richter Scale is in the range of
(a) 4.0 – 4.9 (b) 7.0 – 7.9
(c) 6.0 – 6.9 (d) 5.0 – 5.9

26. At Nadir, the LISS – IV camera in IRS-P6 has a spatial resolution of
(a) 5.8 m (b) 5.9 m
(c) 5.7 m (d) 5.6 m

27. Match List I and List II and choose the correct answer from the codes given below:

List I (Aerosol Constituents)
A. Si
B. V
C. Benzo(a)pyrene
D. Sulfuric acid droplets

List II (Sources)
(i) Gases in the ambient atmosphere
(ii) Natural sources
(iii) Combustion of certain kinds of fuel oil
(iv) Incomplete combustion

Codes:	A	B	C	D
(a)	(ii)	(iv)	(iii)	(i)
(b)	(iii)	(i)	(ii)	(iv)
(c)	(iv)	(i)	(ii)	(iii)
(d)	(i)	(iv)	(iii)	(ii)

28. Which of the following is true regarding the Leopold interaction matrix used in Environmental Impact Assessment Process?
(a) It can be expanded.
(b) It can be contracted.
(c) It can be contracted and expanded.
(d) It cannot be contracted and expanded.

29. The wavelength range of UV-C radiation is
(a) 320 – 400 nm (b) 280 – 320 nm
(c) 100 – 1500 nm (d) 240 – 280 nm

30. The maximum theoretical efficiency of a silicon solar cell can be
(a) 45% (b) 30%
(c) 12% (d) 50%

31. Consider a Box model for an urban area. Assuming that the pollutants are conservative and that the mixing is rapid inside the Box, the concentration (C) of pollutants varies with the mixing height as
(a) $C \propto \frac{1}{H}$ (b) $C \propto \frac{1}{H^2}$
(c) $C \propto \frac{1}{\sqrt{H}}$ (d) $C \propto H^{-3/2}$

32. The molecular weight of DDT is 354.5. The quantity of DDT required to prepare one litre of 10 ppm DDT solution is
(a) 10 mg (b) 35.45 mg
(c) 354.5 mg (d) 354.5 g

33. As per Raunkaiers law of frequency, five different frequency classes (A, B, C, D and E) in a natural undisturbed community exhibit one of the following relationship:
(a) $A < B > C \gtreqless D < E$
(b) $A > B > C \gtreqless D < E$
(c) $A < B > C \gtreqless D > E$
(d) $A < B < C \gtreqless D > E$

34. Which of the following types of coal contains higher percentage of volatile matter?
(a) Peat (b) Lignite
(c) Bituminous (d) Anthracite

35. Which type of forests are found at an altitude of 5300 ft chiefly on mountains of Himalayas and Nilgiri?
(a) Dry deciduous forest
(b) Moist tropical forest
(c) Temperate forest
(d) Tropical moist deciduous forest

36. Organic matter (OM) content of soil can be calculated from organic carbon (OC) by using the formula
(a) OM (%) = OC (%) × 1.724
(b) OM (%) = OC (%) × 1.247
(c) OM (%) = OC (%) × 1.472
(d) OM (%) = OC (%) × 1.427

37. Given below are two statements, one labelled as Assertion (A) and the other labelled as Reason (R):
Assertion (A): When quantitative probabilistic risk assessment is performed on hazardous wastesites they usually turn out to be of relatively low threats.
Reason (R): In hazardous waste sites the chance of exposure is low because of isolation of drinking water supplies and prevention of access.
Choose the correct answer:
(a) Both (A) and (R) are true and (R) is the correct explanation of (A).
(b) Both (A) and (R) are true, but (R) is not the correct explanation of (A).
(c) (A) is true, but (R) is false.
(d) (A) is false, but (R) is true.

38. If w and w_s are mixing ratio and saturation mixing ratio respectively; T and T_d are the ambient temperature and dew point temperature respectively, then identify the correct expression of relative humidity (RH).
(a) $RH = \frac{w \text{ at } T_d}{w \text{ at } T}$ (b) $RH = \frac{w \text{ at } T}{w \text{ at } T_d}$
(c) $RH = \frac{w_s \text{ at } T_d}{w_s \text{ at } T}$ (d) $RH = \frac{w_s \text{ at } T}{w_s \text{ at } T_d}$

39. The maximum specific power output (p) from a MHD power generator varies with the velocity (u) of hot ionized gas as
(a) $p \propto u$ (b) $p \propto u^2$
(c) $p \propto u^{3/2}$ (d) $p \propto u^3$

40. Which rare earth element is not present in the earth's crust but for commercial purpose comes from the Nuclear reactors?
(a) Promethium (b) Lanthanum
(c) Cerium (d) Samarium

41. According to Recycled Plastics (Manufacture and Usage) Rules 1999, the minimum thickness of carry bags shall not be less than
(a) 10 microns (b) 20 microns
(c) 30 microns (d) 50 microns

42. When the temperature range in geothermal resource is generally low, electrical power generation from such resources require the use of secondary low boiling point fluid. This is generally known as
(a) Rankine cycle
(b) Production well cycle
(c) Flash stem cycle
(d) Hard Dry Rock cycle

43. For elevations less than few hundred metres, if the wind speeds are u_1 and u_2 at elevations z_1 and z_2 respectively, the following equation holds $\left(\frac{u_1}{u_2}\right) = \left(\frac{z_1}{z_2}\right)^p$.
The value of the exponent p is
(a) < 0.6 (b) = 1
(c) > 0.6 (d) negative

44. In India, an Environment Impact Assessment report of a proposed mining

project after environmental clearance is applicable for a maximal period of how many years?
(a) 5 years (b) 10 years
(c) 30 years (d) 2 years

Read the following passage carefully and answer the questions (45 to 50):

The popular view of towns and cities in developing countries and of urbanization process is that despite the benefits and comforts it brings, the emergence of such cities connotes environmental degradation, generation of slums and squatters, urban poverty, unemployment, crimes, lawlessness, traffic chaos, etc. But what is the reality? Given the unprecedental increase in urban population over the last 50 years from 300 million in 1950 to 2 billion in 2000 in developing countries, the wonder really is how well the world has coped, and not how badly.

In general, the urban quality of life has improved in terms of availability of water and sanitation, power, health and education, communication and transport. By way of illustration, a large number of urban residents have been provided with improved water in urban areas in Asia's largest countries such as China, India, Indonesia and Philippines. Despite that, the access to improved water in terms of percentage of total urban population seems to have declined during the last decade of 20th century, though in absolute numbers, millions of additional urbanites, have been provided improved services. These countries have made significant progress in the provision of sanitation services too, together, providing for an additional population of more than 293 million citizens within a decade (1990-2000). These improvements must be viewed against the backdrop of rapidly increasing urban population, fiscal crunch and strained human resources and efficient and quality-oriented public management.

45. The popular view about the process of urbanization in developing countries is
(a) Positive (b) Negative
(c) Neutral (d) Unspecified

46. The average annual increase in the number of urbanites in developing countries, from 1950 to 2000 A.D. was close to
(a) 30 million (b) 40 million
(c) 50 million (d) 60 million

47. The reality of urbanization is reflected in
(a) How well the situation has been managed.
(b) How badly the situation has gone out of control.
(c) How fast has been the tempo of urbanization.
(d) How fast the environment has degraded.

48. Which one of the following is not considered as an indicator of urban quality of life?
(a) Tempo of urbanization
(b) Provision of basic services
(c) Access to social amenities
(d) All of the above

49. The author in this passage has tried to focus on
(a) Extension of Knowledge
(b) Generation of Environmental Consciousness
(c) Analytical Reasoning
(d) Descriptive Statement

50. In the above passage, the author intends to state
(a) The hazards of the urban life
(b) The sufferings of the urban life
(c) The awareness of human progress
(d) The limits to growth

PAPER-III

1. Climate in a region is
   (a) the long-term, prevailing atmospheric conditions.
   (b) determined only by seasonal daylight hours.
   (c) the atmospheric conditions on a given day.
   (d) never affected by ocean currents.
2. The visible light lies in the wavelength range of
   (a) 400-750 mμ (b) 390-560 mμ
   (c) 400-860 mμ (d) none.
3. Which of the following types of waves has greatest killing effect on the organisms?
   (a) Ultraviolet rays
   (b) Infrared rays
   (c) Electromagnetic waves
   (d) None of the above
4. What percent of solar radiation is used in photosynthesis?
   (a) 2% (b) 10%
   (c) 8% (d) 4%
5. The rate of photosynthesis is greater in
   (a) infrared region
   (b) ultraviolet region
   (c) intermittent light
   (d) Continuous light
6. Which of the following would be symptom of acute toxicity?
   (a) asthma (b) kidney damage
   (c) cancer (d) dizziness
7. When a solid melts, there is
   (a) no change in enthalpy
   (b) no change in entropy
   (c) decrease in enthalpy
   (d) increase in enthalpy
8. Hydrides that can displace H_2 from water are
   (a) Saline hydrides
   (b) Metallic hydrides
   (c) Covalent hydrides
   (d) Polymetic hydrides.
9. Which of the following sets has Lewis acid character for all the components
   (a) BF_3
   (b) BF_3, SiF_4, PF_5
   (c) SiF_4, PF_5
   (d) BF_3, PF_5
10. Which of the following moves fastest when produced during radioactive decay?
    (a) α-particle
    (b) β-particle
    (c) γ-ray
    (d) Positron
11. Match List I and List II and select the correct answer using the codes given below the lists:

    List I (Ecological Terms)
    A. Ecosphere
    B. Population
    C. Biogeocoenosis
    D. Biocoenosis

    List II (Respective Equivalents)
    (i) Biotic Community
    (ii) Ecosystems
    (iii) Groups of individuals of any one kind of organism
    (iv) Biosphere

Codes:	**A**	**B**	**C**	**D**
(a)	(iv)	(iii)	(ii)	(i)
(b)	(ii)	(iii)	(iv)	(i)
(c)	(iii)	(iv)	(ii)	(i)
(d)	(iv)	(iii)	(i)	(ii)

12. The major types of flora and fauna found in aquatic ecosystems are determined primarily by
    (a) temperature (b) salinity
    (c) pH (d) light
13. The idea of spontaneous generation was first refuted by

(a) F. Redi (b) L. Spallanzani
(c) L. Pasteur (d) S.L. Miller

14. Which of the following is a primary consumer?
(a) Cow (b) Euglena
(c) Frog (d) Wolf

15. The animal communities living in a desert are called
(a) Biomass (b) Biotic factor
(c) Food web (d) Biome

16. Which of the following has the most destructive effects on ocean floor ecosystems?
(a) trawl fishing (b) sport fishing
(c) boat anchors (d) shipwrecks

17. The process of extracting and separating gold in remote regions often results in environmental contamination with which of the following?
(a) Ozone (b) Cyanide
(c) CFCs (d) Asbestos

18 Match List I and List II and select the correct answer using the codes given below the lists:

List I (Climatic Region)	List II (Average Rainfall)
A. Wet zone	(i) 100 cm
B. Dry zone	(ii) 50 cm
C. Arid zone	(iii) 200 cm
D. Intermediate	(iv) 50 to 100 cm

Codes:	A	B	C	D
(a)	(i)	(ii)	(iii)	(iv)
(b)	(iii)	(iv)	(ii)	(i)
(c)	(iii)	(iv)	(ii)	(i)
(d)	(iv)	(iii)	(i)	(ii)

19. Which of the following mode of energy transfer has little effect on the atmosphere?
(a) Conduction (b) Convection
(c) Radiation (d) All of the above

20. With an increase in altitude, the temperature generally
(a) increases (b) decreases
(c) Both (a) and (b) (d) None

21. Which of the following can cause depletion of ozone?
(a) H_2S (b) NO
(c) Smoke (d) Aerosols

22. Every individual person inhales air daily about
(a) 1 kg (b) 15-22 kg
(c) 100 litres (d) 1 litre

23. Which of the following causes damage to the blood?
(a) Calcium (b) Magnesium
(c) Arsenic (d) Lead

24. Which of the following level of noise can be tolerated by human era?
(a) 20 decibels (b) 100 decibels
(c) 80 decibels (d) 120 decibels

25. In petrol-based vehicles, the major pollutant parts are
(a) carburettor (b) fuel tank
(c) crankcase (d) All of the above

26. After 200 million years, only 1/16 of the original amount of a particular radioactive waste will remain. The half-life of this radioactive waste is how many million years?
(a) 12.5 (b) 25
(c) 50 (d) 75

27. Which of the following in coal decreases its calorific value?
(a) Carbon (b) Hydrogen
(c) Oxygen (d) Sulphur

28. Main constituent of natural gas is
(a) carbon monoxide
(b) methane
(c) hydrogen
(d) ethane

29. Which of the following is renewable?
(a) Minerals
(b) Forests
(c) Soil
(d) Underground water

30. Atomic power is derived from
(a) Uranium (b) Platinum
(c) Silver (d) Gold

31. Which of the following parameters are needed to estimate human's impact on the environmental?
(a) population
(b) consumption
(c) affluence
(d) population and consumption are both necessary

32. Which of the following is an impact of SPM
(a) Corrodes metals (b) Irritates eyes
(c) Obscures vision (d) Causes cancer

33. Which of the following is an important water contaminant?
(a) Heavy metals
(b) Nitrogen oxides
(c) Carbon monoxide
(d) Hydrocarbons

34. Which of the following pairs regarding the air quality monitoring technique is correctly matched?
(a) SO_2...........Diffusion tube
(b) Ozone...........Ultraviolet photometry
(c) NO_2...........Infrared absorption
(d) Metals...........Polyurethane filter

35. Consider the following statements:
1. The developmental projects are required to prepare an Environmental Impact Statement
2. The developmental project does not overdraw from its ecological and environmental assests
3. Only a few countries have enacted suitable legislation regarding EIA

Of these statements
(a) only 1 is correct
(b) 2 and 3 are correct
(c) 1 and 2 are correct
(d) 1, 2 and 3 are correct

36. Which of the following criteria land filling shall meet in the disposal of solid wastes?
(a) Waste containing recoverable meterial shall follow the route of recycling
(b) Waste at the disposal site shall not be burnt
(c) The landfill storage facilities shall be daily attended for clearing wastes
(d) None of the above

37. The process of interception means
(a) holding of precipitation on different parts of the plants
(b) running of precipitation from the earth surface to lakes, rivers and marshes
(c) the condensation of water vapours
(d) None of the above

38. Particle size of waste material can be expressed by
(a) $L_w = (l + w)/2$
(b) $L_w = (l + w + h)/3$
(c) $L_w = (l + w)^{1/2}$
(d) All of the above

39. The typical composition of MSW do not depend upon
(a) locality
(b) season of the year
(c) landuse
(d) None of these

40. Which of the following pairs with respect to standard of liquid waste is incorrectly matched?
(a) pH......................6.3-9.0
(b) BOD......................30 mg/L
(c) COD......................250 mg/L
(d) Oil and grease........100 mg/L

41. What do you know about hypothesis?
    (a) Solution to a problem
    (b) Tentative solution to a problem
    (c) Blue print of a research project
    (d) Tool for data collection

42. In which type of research hypothesis is occasionally used?
    (a) Applied (b) Experimental
    (c) Historical (d) Observational

43. Product moment coefficient of correlation measures which particular type of relationship between two variables?
    (a) Linear (b) Curvilinear
    (c) Parabolic (d) Circular

44. Which statistical device helps in analysing the covariation of two or more variables?
    (a) Regression
    (b) Median
    (c) Standard Devision
    (d) Correlation

45. The formula 3 Median –2 mean is used to compute?
    (a) arithmetic mean (b) weighted mean
    (c) median (d) mode

46. Which of the following factors is an important as population in determining the environmental impact of humans?
    (a) climate (b) wealth
    (c) development (d) consumption

47. Most of the wetlands that are lost are used for
    (a) mining
    (b) urban development
    (c) agriculture
    (d) forestry

48. Which of the following greenhouse gases has the greatest heat trapping ability per molecule?
    (a) Carbon dioxide
    (b) Carbon monoxide
    (c) Chlorofluorocabon
    (d) Methane

49. What are most of the POPs listed in the Stockholm Convention "Dirty Dozen" used for?
    (a) insecticides
    (b) fungicides
    (c) herbicides
    (d) industrial solvents

50. **Assertion (A):** The stomata generally remained opened in the light and closed in the dark.
    Reason (R): The opening of stomata increases the gaseous exchange and also increases the rate of transpiration during day period.
    Codes:
    (a) Both (A) and (R) are true and (R) is the correct explanation of (A).
    (b) Both (A) and (R) are true but (R) is not a correct explanation of (A).
    (c) (A) is true, but (R) is false.
    (d) (A) is false, but (R) is true.

ANSWERS SHEET

PAPER—I

1. (c)	2. (c)	3. (a)	4. (d)	5. (d)
6. (a)	7. (d)	8. (b)	9. (c)	10. (b)
11. (d)	12. (a)	13. (c)	14. (c)	15. (a)
16. (c)	17. (a)	18. (b)	19. (a)	20. (c)
21. (d)	22. (a)	23. (c)	24. (a)	25. (b)
26. (b)	27. (b)	28. (c)	29. (d)	30. (b)
31. (b)	32. (c)	33. (a)	34. (c)	35. (b)
36. (b)	37. (a)	38. (b)	39. (d)	40. (a)
41. (d)	42. (c)	43. (a)	44. (b)	45. (c)
46. (b)	47. (d)	48. (b)	49. (c)	50. (c)

PAPER—II

1. (a)	2. (d)	3. (c)	4. (b)	5. (a)
6. (b)	7. (a)	8. (a)	9. (c)	10. (a)
11. (d)	12. (d)	13. (b)	14. (c)	15. (d)
16. (d)	17. (b)	18. (b)	19. (b)	20. (c)
21. (b)	22. (b)	23. (c)	24. (d)	25. (d)
26. (a)	27. (a)	28. (c)	29. (d)	30. (a)
31. (a)	32. (a)	33. (b)	34. (a)	35. (c)
36. (a)	37. (a)	38. (c)	39. (b)	40. (a)
41. (b)	42. (a)	43. (a)	44. (c)	45. (b)
46. (a)	47. (a)	48. (a)	49. (c)	50. (d)

PAPER—III

1. (a)	2. (a)	3. (a)	4. (a)	5. (c)
6. (d)	7. (d)	8. (a)	9. (a)	10. (c)
11. (a)	12. (d)	13. (a)	14. (a)	15. (d)
16. (a)	17. (b)	18. (b)	19. (c)	20. (c)
21. (d)	22. (b)	23. (d)	24. (c)	25. (d)
26. (c)	27. (c)	28. (b)	29. (b)	30. (a)
31. (b)	32. (c)	33. (a)	34. (b)	35. (b)
36. (c)	37. (d)	38. (d)	39. (d)	40. (d)
41. (b)	42. (b)	43. (a)	44. (d)	45. (d)
46. (d)	47. (c)	48. (c)	49. (a)	50. (b)

MOCK TEST–2
PAPER–I

1. Minimum program of guidance includes
   (a) occupational information service
   (b) data collector service
   (c) counselling service
   (d) All of these

2. If majority of students in a class is weak, a teacher should
   (a) not care about intelligent students
   (b) keep his speed of teaching fast so that students comprehension level may increase
   (c) keep his teaching slow which can also be helpful-to bright students
   (d) keep his teaching slow along with some extra guidance to bright students

3. If the principal of your institution is not satisfied with your performance and charges you with the act of negligence of duties, how would you behave with him?
   (a) You would neglect him
   (b) You would take revenge by giving physical and mental agony to him
   (c) You would keep yourself alert and make his efforts unfruitful
   (d) You would take a tough stand against the charges

4. What makes people to undertake research?
   (a) Desire to get intellectual joy of doing some creative work
   (b) Desire to get a research degree along with its consequential benefits
   (c) Desire to face the challenge in solving the unsolved problems
   (d) All of these

5. Which of the following aims at probing into the phenomenon to formulate a more precise research problem or to develop a new hypothesis?
   (a) Descriptive research
   (b) Conclusive research
   (c) Diagnostic research
   (d) Exploratory research

6. Which of the following is not instructional material?
   (a) Transparency
   (b) Overhead projector
   (c) Printed material
   (d) Audio cassette

7. Of great importance in determining the amount of transference that occurs in the process of learning is the
   (a) knowledge of the teacher
   (b) IQ of the teacher
   (c) presence of identical elements
   (d) use of appropriate elements
8. The characteristic(s) of hypothesis is/are:
   I. It can be tested.
   II. It must consist of known facts.
   III. It must be objective and specific.
   (a) I and III (b) I and II
   (c) Only I (d) All of these
9. The guide for the research requires which of the following qualities?
   (a) Interdisciplinary expertise
   (b) Subject matter expertise
   (c) Methodological expertise
   (d) All of these
10. Which of the following indicates evaluation?
   (a) Seema got 195 marks out of 200
   (b) Sapna got 72 percent marks in English
   (c) Asha got First Division in final examination
   (d) All of the above

Direction: (11-16) Study the following passage and give answer to the questions based on it.

Much of the theoretical literature of archeology in the 1980s devotes considerable energy to bashing the 1970s, and the target often turns out to be the so-called New or Processual Archeology. While many of the attacks come from recent theorists who are attempting to replace it with post-processual archeology, some criticism comes from within what was New Archeology even from the hand of its original champion, Lewis Binford. If scholars from both outside and inside the theoretical developments of the 1970s are rejecting the New Archeology, why am I defending its importance to us today? The answer is very simple...for better or worse, it is us! As Alison Whylie has recently said the New Archeology of the 1960s quickly became everybody's archeology in the 1970s. Most of today's faculty members and senior archeologists were the people who, in one way or another, adopted the teachings of New Archeology. Although most archeologists did not claim to agree with all aspects of New Archeology nor could more than two or three people agree on what it was, virtually one rejected it outright. Typically, each one presented her or his version, often using a New Archeology text as a starting point for pedagogical purposes. Few wanted to be left out of the exciting new theoretical movement of those years, and New Archeology was passed on to the succeeding generation of students who reached maturity in the 1980s and are today's young professionals.

Criticisms now leveled against the New Archeology of the seventies do have merit, but by discounting that era as misguided, critics have overlooked its crucial importance. New Archeology has an important historical role in the developments of the field we have today and it has continuing importance because it is still guiding archeology's trajectory into the future. Equally troubling is that some critics ask us to reject the basic tenets of New Archeology and to replace them with a system often called post processualist archeology. I believe this is rhetoric that not only misrepresents the achievements of the New Archeology of the seventies, but also does not successfully articulate the potential contributions of its own position.

To put the New Archeology of the seventies into perspective, it is important to review the decades leading up to its development. In the first years following World War II, archeology was still a small field, but by the fifties and the sixties, it was expanding rapidly and taking itself quite seriously. Since the launching of Sputnik in 1957 there had emerged a frenzy in the United States to make all disciplines more scientific. Great strides were made in bringing science into archeology through new dating techniques a multidisciplinary approach, early experiments with the use of statistics, and devoting substantial attention to increasing the precision of artifact classification. The sixties provided the nation with both the optimistic Kennedy years, with an emphasis on science and the conviction that we were capable of accomplishing wondrous; things, and the cynical Vietnam era. Coming on the heels of a decade of civil rights unrest, the widespread dissatisfaction with the Vietnam conflict in the late sixties molded a generation of young Americans who were distrustful of established authority. In academic life, there was an increasing emphasis on environment, other cultures, and people oriented disciplines. Anthropology and archeology grew markedly because of these trends. Archeologists were urged to become concerned with sociological issues—the people behind the artifacts.

It was during these decades of rapid change that many of the core concepts of the New Archeology entered the literature. However, they were not, at first, assembled into a program for action that attracted a solid following. Water Taylor advocated the conjuctive approach with little effect, while Leslie White's evolutionism and Julian Styeward's cultural ecology attracted some attention, but largely among cultural anthropologists. Albert Spaulding led a one-man campaign to bring science and statistics into archeology. But the individual whose work catalyzed the New Archeology movement was Lewis Binford, who incorporated these earlier lines of thinking together with an explicit concern for scientific methods and field research designs. Much of Binford's thinking probably crystallised while he was at the University of Michigan, but was during his relatively few years at the University of Chicago that he changed the direction of modern archeology.

11. New Archeology refers to
    (a) newer techniques used in Archeology
    (b) newer inventions used in Archeology
    (c) newer theoretical foundations in Archeology
    (d) None of these
12. The author defends the Archeology of the 1970's because
    (a) he has a nostalgic feeling about it
    (b) it has research value
    (c) it paved way for newer traditions
    (d) it has historical value
13. The author suggests that
    (a) We should respect new Archeology as a movement in Archeology
    (b) We should go back to the tenets of processual Archeology
    (c) We should treat tenets of new Archeology with respect
    (d) All of the above
14. The importance of Archeology arose from
    (a) the end of World War II
    (b) an increasing scientific outlook
    (c) the launch of Sputnik in 1957
    (d) All of these
15. Which one of the following is not an area of focus for archeologist?
    (a) Study the interaction of people of small group
    (b) Studying cultures of other people
    (c) Study the social structure of the past societies
    (d) Study the man-environment relationship in the past
16. An archeologist is concerned with
    (a) classification of artefacts
    (b) maintenance of museums
    (c) digging of ancient cities
    (d) All of these

17. Rhetorics means
    (a) study of the technique and rules for using language effectively
    (b) using language effectively to please or persuade
    (c) excessive use of verbal ornamentation
    (d) All of the above

18. If a receiver replying on 'hmm-mm' or 'Isee'. This type of reply is known as
    (a) positive feedback
    (b) ambiguous feedback
    (c) negative feedback
    (d) None of these

19. Which of the following FM radio stations is owned by the Times of India group?
    (a) AIR
    (b) Radio Rainbow
    (c) Radio Mirchi
    (d) Red FM

20. Find the next number in the following sequence:
    9, 8, 25, 12, 49, 18, 121, 26, ??
    (a) 142, 36 (b) 169, 36
    (c) 225, 36 (d) 196, 36

21. **Statement:** Should there be complete ban on pouched tobacco products (like Gutka) in India?
    Arguments:
    (i) Yes, it is the most important cause of mouth cancer and mouth ulcer in our country.
    (ii) No, there are many people employed in this industry right from manufacturing to retailing. This ban will hamper their livelihood.
    (a) Only argument (i) is strong
    (b) Only argument (ii) is strong
    (c) Both the arguments (i) and (ii) are strong
    (d) Neither (i) nor (ii) is strong

22. The relationship between Animal, Cows, Dogs can be shown by

    (a) 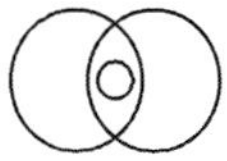 (b) 

    (c) 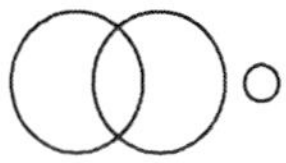 (d) 

23. If in a certain code:
    'nso prt kli chn' means 'sharma gets marriage gift'. 'pit lnm wop chn' means 'wife gives marriage gift'. 'tti wop nhi' means 'he gives nothing'. What would mean gives:
    (a) kli (b) tti
    (c) wop (d) lnm

24. Characteristics of all informal and formal communications are
    (a) Same (b) Structured
    (c) Different (d) None of these

25. Three of the following four are alike in a certain way and so form a group. Find the one which doesn't belong to that group?
    (a) Dog (b) Tiger
    (c) Horse (d) Lion

26. What is research design?
    (a) The methods used in analysis and finding the final conclusion is known as research design
    (b) A researcher needs to prepare a plan of action for his study which is known as research design
    (c) The presentation of final data is known as research design
    (d) None of these

27. Recording a television program on a Set Top Box is an example of
    (a) content reference
    (b) time-shifting
    (c) media synchronisation
    (d) mechanical clarity

28. Which of the following statements say the same thing?

(i) "I am a teacher" (said by Arvind)
(ii) "I am a teacher" (said by Binod)
(iii) "My son is a teacher" (said by Binod's father)
(iv) "My brother is a teacher" (said by Binod's sister)
(v) "My brother is a teacher" (said by Binod's only sister)
(vi) "My sole enemy is a teacher" (said by Binod's only enemy)

Choose the correct answer from the codes given below:

Codes:

(a) (v) and (vi)
(b) (i) and (ii)
(c) (ii) and (vi)
(d) (ii), (iii), (iv) and (v)

29. In this question there are two statements followed by four conclusions numbered I, II, III and IV.

Statements:

A. All books are trees.
B. All trees are lions.

Conclusions:

I. All books are lions.
II. All lions are books.
III. All trees are books.
IV. Some lions are books.

Choose the correct answer.

(a) I and IV follow
(b) II and III follow
(c) None of conclusions follow
(d) All conclusion follows

Directions: (30-34) Answer the questions based on following table.

Machines X and Y can independently produce either product P or product Q. The time taken by machines X and Y (in minutes) to produce one unit of product P and Q are given in the table below. (Each machine works 8 hours per day.)

Product	X	Y
P	10	8
Q	6	6

30. If the number of units of P is to be three times that of Q, what is the maximum idle time to maximise total units manufactured?
(a) 8 minutes (b) 0 minute
(c) 12 minutes (d) None of these

31. If X works at half its normal efficiency, what is the maximum number of units produced, if at least one unit of each must be produced?
(a) 119 (b) 135
(c) 127 (d) 136

32. What is the maximum number of units that can be manufactured in one day?
(a) 250 (b) 160
(c) 270 (d) 195

33. If equal quantities of both are to be produced, then out of four choice given below the least efficient way would be
(a) 59 of each with 8 min. idle
(b) 71 of each with 9 min. idle
(c) 53 of each with 10 min. idle
(d) 48 of each with 4 min. idle

34. What is the least number of machine hours required to produce 30 pieces of P and 25 pieces of Q respectively?
(a) 6 hr 30 min. (b) 9 hr 30 min.
(c) 6 hr 40 min. (d) 8 hr 30 min.

35. Telematic is a combination of
(a) Telecommunication and computer
(b) Telecommunication and information
(c) Television and computer
(d) All of the above

36. Following is a part of balance sheet of Timas Pvt. Ltd. Study the table and give answer to the question given below:

All values in ₹ crore

Year	Expenditure	Income
1990	3400	4000
1995	3800	4500
2000	4500	5400
2005	6400	8000

Which of the following conclusions is not true?

(a) There has been a steady growth in % profit of the company
(b) There is around 90% increase in expenditure of the firm from 1990 to 2005
(c) Income of the company is doubled in 15 years
(d) Percentage profit in 2000 was 18%

37. If EFGHUK is coded as VUTSRQ then LIMIT can be coded as
(a) KNRNC (b) ORNRG
(c) JKOKG (d) RSTSG

38. The more is 'Resolution Power' of a printer better is its
(a) Speed (b) Colour
(c) Memory (d) Quality

39. Laterite soil develops due to
(a) deposits of alluvial
(b) deposition of loess
(c) leaching
(d) continued vegetation cover

40. Line access and avoidance of collision are the main functions of
(a) network protocols
(b) wide area networks
(c) the CPU
(d) the monitor

41. Communication satellites are placed in
(a) Geostationary Orbit
(b) Polar Orbit
(c) Both (a) and (b)
(d) None of these

42. DLL stands for
(a) Data Deriving Language
(b) Data Definition Language
(c) Data Design Language
(d) All of the above

43. Transistors were first used in
(a) 2nd generation computers
(b) 3rd generation computers
(c) 4th generation computers
(d) None of these

44. Which of the following is not provided in the Constitution?
(a) Planning Commission
(b) Election Commission
(c) Finance Commission
(d) Public Service Commission

45. The 1st satellite launched in space was
(a) Early Bird (b) Sputnik-1
(c) Skylab (d) Aryabhatta-1

46. At what time between 5.30 and 6.00 will the hands of a clock be at right angles?
(a) 45 minutes past 5
(b) $43\frac{5}{11}$ minutes past 5
(c) $43\frac{7}{11}$ minutes past 5
(d) 40 minutes past 5

47. A person can be a member of Council of Ministers without being a member of Parliament for a maximum period of
(a) 45 days (b) 90 days
(c) 180 days (d) one year

48. Many engineers and architects use a different type of pen called a
(a) Pointer pen
(b) Computer pen
(c) Light pen
(d) Logical pen

49. Which of the following are wrongly matched?

Name of Volcano	Country
(a) Mt. Spur	USA
(b) Mt. Fuego	Guatemala
(c) Mt. Ag'ung	Indonesia
(d) Mt. Lascor	Equador

50. How many types of emergency can be declared by the President of India?
(a) 1 (b) 2
(c) 3 (d) 4

PAPER—II

1. The mass of 1 mole of electron is equal to
(a) $9.1094 \times 6.16 \times 10^{-28}$ g
(b) $9.1094 \times 10^{-31} \times 6.023 \times 10^{23}$ kg
(c) $(9.1094 \times 10^{-31}) / 6.023 \times 10^{23}$ kg
(d) $(6.023 \times 10^{23}) / 6.1094 \times 10^{-28}$ gm

2. Among the following which country has lowest per capita green house gas emission?
(a) France (b) India
(c) China (d) Mexico

3. CRZ notification of Government of India specify the stretches of sea, bays, estuaries, etc. as coastal areas requires protection from developmental activities.
(a) upto 500 metre from High Tide Level
(b) upto 150 metre from High Tide Level
(c) upto 500 metre from Low Tide Level
(d) upto 100 metre from Low Tide Level

4. In a multiple regression model $Y_i = \alpha + \beta_{1i}X_i + \beta_2 X_{2i} + \beta_{3i}X_3 + \epsilon_i$, if i = N, the number of degrees of freedom required for determining the t-value at 5% level of significance
(a) N – 3 (b) N – 2
(c) N – 4 (d) N – 1

5. Urban air quality is basically decided by
(a) CO, SPM, SO_2, NO_2, Surface ozone
(b) SPM, NO_2, SO_2
(c) SPM, NO_2, CO
(d) SPM, SO_2, Surface ozone

6. Snow blindness is caused due to
(a) Ultra-violet radiations
(b) Excessive flux of visible radiations
(c) Infrared radiations
(d) Microwave radiations

7. Ministry of Environment and Forests amended the EIA notification making public hearing mandatory for environmental clearance on
(a) 27th January 1996
(b) 10th April 1997
(c) 27th January 1997
(d) None of the above

8. Consider an air shed over a city in the form of a rectangular box. The wind velocity is 5 m/sec normal to left face of the box. The length of the box along the direction of wind is 10 km and mixing height is 1 km. Assuming rapid mixing of the pollutants which are conservative in nature, the concentration of the pollutants in the city would reach 63% of its final value in
(a) 2,000 sec (b) 5,000 sec
(c) 10,000 sec (d) 1,000 sec

9. The sequence of fossil fuels in the order of higher to lower heating value is as follows:
(a) Coal, Petroleum, Natural Gas, Hydrogen.
(b) Hydrogen, Natural Gas, Petroleum, Coal.
(c) Hydrogen, Coal, Natural Gas, Petroleum.
(d) Natural Gas, Petroleum, Coal, Hydrogen.

10. Given below are two statements, one labelled as Assertion (A) and the other labelled as Reason (R).

Assertion (A): Indirect impacts are more difficult to measure, but can ultimately be more important.

Reason (R): In areas where wildlife is plentiful, such as Africa, new roads often lead to the rapid depletion of animals.

Choose the correct answer.

Codes:

(a) Both (A) and (R) are true and (R) is the correct explanation.
(b) Both (A) and (R) are true, but (R) is not the correct explanation.
(c) (A) is true, but (R) is false.
(d) (A) is false, but (R) is true.

11. The efficiency of a MHD power generator for applied electric field $\vec{E}$, magnetic field $\vec{B}$ and velocity of hot ionized gas $\vec{U}$ is

(a) $\frac{|\vec{E}|}{|\vec{U}||\vec{B}|}$ (b) $\frac{|\vec{U}||\vec{B}|}{|\vec{E}|}$

(c) $\frac{|\vec{E}|^2}{|\vec{U}||\vec{B}|}$ (d) $\frac{|\vec{E}|^2}{|\vec{U}||\vec{B}|^2}$

12. The sequence of chemical constituents in order of their abundance in a majority of sedimentary rocks is

(a) $SiO_2 > TiO_2 > Al_2O_3 > Fe_2O_3$
(b) $SiO_2 > Al_2O_3 > Fe_2O_3 > TiO_2$
(c) $SiO_2 > Fe_2O_3 > Al_2O_3 > TiO_2$
(d) $SiO_2 > Fe_2O_3 > TiO_2 > Al_2O_3$

13. A good automobile fuel, in addition to having high calorific value, should have

(a) High ignition temperature
(b) High viscosity
(c) Low ignition temperature
(d) Moderate ignition temperature

14. Under anaerobic condition denitrifying *Pseudomonas* changes,

(a) Nitrate to molecular nitrogen
(b) Nitrate to ammonia
(c) Nitrate to Nitrite
(d) Nitrite to Nitrate

15. Identify the correct sequence in increasing order of total CO_2 emissions from various countries at present.

(a) Britain < India < China < USA
(b) India < Britain < China < USA
(c) Britain < USA < India < China
(d) Britain < India < USA < China

16. Which is the correct sequence for impact assessment process in EIA?

(a) Description of Environment → Identification of impacts → Prediction of impacts → Evaluation of impacts → Identification of mitigation needs.
(b) Identification of impacts → Prediction of impacts → Evaluation of impacts → Identification of mitigation needs.
(c) Identification of impacts → Description of Environment → Prediction of impacts → Evaluation of impacts → Identification of mitigation needs.
(d) Prediction of impacts → Identification of impacts → Description of environment → Evaluation of impacts → Identification of mitigation needs.

17. The covariance between two data of N observations each represented by variables X and Y is given by

(a) $\frac{\Sigma(X-\overline{X})(Y-\overline{Y})}{N^2}$

(b) $\frac{\Sigma(X-\overline{X})^2(Y-\overline{Y})^2}{N}$

(c) $\frac{\Sigma(X-\overline{X})^2(Y-\overline{Y})^2}{N^2}$

(d) $\frac{\Sigma(X-\overline{X})(Y-\overline{Y})}{N}$

18. Two water samples were collected.
Sample # 1 : pH = 9, but no carbonate or other dissolved proton donors or acceptors.
Sample # 2 : pH = 8.3, but it contains dissolved $NaHCO_3$ at a concentration of 0.01/mg/L
Which of the following is true based on the above observations.
(a) Sample # 1 will have more alkalinity.
(b) Sample # 2 will have more alkalinity.
(c) Sample # 1 and sample # 2 will have exactly same alkalinity.
(d) Alkalinity cannot be estimated.

19. A source of air pollution is emitting a pollutant at the rate S(mg/hours) inside a room of volume V(m^3). The air of the room is being changed *n* times per hour. If *k* is pollutant decay rate constant, the concentration C(*t*) of the pollutant at any given instant of time under well mixed conditions is given by
(a) $C(t) = \left(\frac{S}{nV}\right)(1 - e^{-nt})$
(b) $C(t) = \left(\frac{S/V}{n+k}\right)(1 - e^{-nt})$
(c) $C(t) = (S/nV)(n + k)$
(d) $C(t) = \left(\frac{nV}{S}\right)(1 - e^{-nk})$

20. Which pyramid cannot be inverted in a stable ecosystem?
(a) Pyramid of energy
(b) Pyramid of biomass
(c) Pyramid of number
(d) Pyramid of dry weight

Read the following passage carefully and answer questions 21 to 26:

All historians are interpreters of text if they be private letters, Government records or parish birthlists or whatever. For most kinds of historians, these are only the necessary means to understanding something other than the texts themselves, such as a political action or a historical trend, whereas for the intellectual historian, a full understanding of his chosen texts is itself the aim of his enquiries. Of course, the intellectual history is particularly prone to draw on the focus of other disciplines that are habitually interpreting texts for purposes of their own, probing the reasoning that ostensibly connects premises and conclusions. Furthermore, the boundaries with adjacent subdisciplines are shifting and indistinct: the history of art and the history of science both claim a certain autonomy, partly just because they require specialised technical skills, but both can also be seen as part of a wider intellectual history, as is evident when one considers, for example, the common stock of knowledge about cosmological beliefs or moral ideals of a period.

Like all historians, the intellectual historian is a consumer rather than a producer of 'methods'. His distinctiveness lies in which aspect of the past he is trying to illuminate, not in having exclusive possession of either a corpus of evidence or a body of techniques. That being said, it does seem that the label 'intellectual history' attracts a disproportionate share of misunderstanding.

It is alleged that intellectual history is the history of something that never really mattered. The long dominance of the historical profession by political historians bred a kind of philistinism, an unspoken belief that power and its exercise was 'what mattered'. The prejudice was reinforced by the assertion that political action was never really the outcome of principles or ideas that were 'more flapdoodle'. The legacy of this precept is still discernible in the tendency to require ideas to have 'licensed' the political class before they can be deemed worthy of intellectual attention, as if there were some reasons why the history of art or science, of philosophy or literature, were somehow of interest and significance than the history of Parties or Parliaments. Perhaps in recent years the mirror-image of this philistinism has been more common in the claim that ideas of any one is of systematic expression or sophistication do not matter, as if they were only held by a minority.

21. An intellectual historian aims to fully understand
    (a) the chosen texts of his own
    (b) political actions
    (c) historical trends
    (d) his enquiries
22. Intellectual historians do not claim exclusive possession of
    (a) conclusions
    (b) any corpus of evidence
    (c) distinctiveness
    (d) habitual interpretation
23. The misconceptions about intellectual history stem from
    (a) a body of techniques
    (b) the common stock of knowledge
    (c) the dominance of political historians
    (d) cosmological beliefs
24. What is philistinism?
    (a) Reinforcement of prejudice
    (b) Fabrication of reasons
    (c) The hold of land-owning classes
    (d) Belief that power and its exercise matter
25. Knowledge of cosmological beliefs or moral ideas of a period can be drawn as part of
    (a) literary criticism
    (b) history of science
    (c) history of philosophy
    (d) intellectual history
26. The claim that ideas of any one is of systematic expression do not matter, as if they were held by a minority, is
    (a) to have a licensed political class
    (b) a political action
    (c) a philosophy of literature
    (d) the mirror-image of philistinism
27. Which of the following statement about Fjord is incorrect?
    (a) Most Fjords were formed due to raise in sea level after the melting of Pleistocene ice
    (b) It is an emergent coast that was originally submerged
    (c) It is a long narrow inlet of the sea bound by steep slopes
    (d) It is a glaciated valley that has been inundated by the sea
28. Match the items in List I with List II and select the correct answers using codes given below:

List I	**List II**
A. Fohn wind	(i) Analogous to rainbow
B. Fog bow	(ii) Herbivorous plants
C. Forbs	(iii) Warm winds descending from mountains
D. Fore shock	(iv) Earthquake

Codes:	A	B	C	D
(a)	(i)	(ii)	(iii)	(iv)
(b)	(iii)	(ii)	(iv)	(i)
(c)	(ii)	(iii)	(i)	(iv)
(d)	(iii)	(i)	(ii)	(iv)

29. When you go for shopping, what are you expected to do to save environment?
    (a) Shop for products that have as little packaging as possible
    (b) In any store, use a bag even if it is not needed
    (c) Do not reduce the frequency of shopping
    (d) Buy paper towels and napkins.
30. Which one of the following does not contribute to conservation of water:
    (a) Waste water treatment
    (b) Waste land development

(c) Water shed protection
(d) Rain water harvesting

31. For a clear sunny day with sun higher than 60° above horizon and wind speed greater than 6 m/sec, the atmosphere is:
(a) Stable
(b) Slightly unstable
(c) Moderately unstable
(d) Very unstable

32. Populations of two species may interact in several ways. One of these called protocooperation occurs when:
(a) One population inhibits the other
(b) Interaction is favourable to both but not obligatory
(c) Interaction is favourable to both but obligatory
(d) Neither population affects the other

33. The maximum value of the coefficient of performance for a wind turbine is:
(a) $\frac{3}{4}$ (b) $\frac{5}{6}$
(c) $\frac{11}{27}$ (d) $\frac{16}{27}$

34. Identify the correct sequence of gases in the decreasing order of their contribution to global warming:
(a) CO_2 > CFCs > CH_4 > N_2O
(b) CO_2 > CH_4 > N_2O > CFCs
(c) CO_2 > CH_4 > CFCs > N_2O
(d) CO_2 > N_2O > CH_4 > CFCs

35. Consider the following statement about the Himalayan orogeny:
(i) The orogeny resulted from the southward movement of the Indian plate
(ii) The orogeny began about 25 million years ago
(iii) The orogeny closed about 1 million year ago
(iv) The Himalayas have a root of relatively light crustal rock projecting in the denser mantle

Of the statements:
(a) (i) and (ii) are correct.
(b) (iii) and (iv) are correct.
(c) (i) and (iii) are correct.
(d) (ii) and (iv) are correct.

36. In a water body, there was food chain starting from planton to eagle. 0.3 PPT DDT was the concentration in the water, but in eagle's body it was found to be 25 PPM, This:
(a) phenomenon is called as bioabsorption
(b) phenomenon is called as biodesorption
(c) phenomenon is called as biomagnification
(d) phenomenon is called as biotransformation

37. The compounds responsible for the proliferation of algal blooms in water bodies are:
(a) Nitrates and chlorides
(b) Nitrates and phosphates
(c) Phosphates and silicates
(d) Nitrates and carbonates

38. The size distribution of suspended particulate matter in urban environment tends to follow which of the following distributions:
(a) Binomial (b) Poisson
(c) Normal (d) Log normal

39. Consider the earth to be a blackbody with average temperature 15°C and surface area 5.1×10^{14} m^2. Find the rate at which energy is radiated by the earth and the wave length at which maximum power is radiated.
(Hint: Stefan-Boltzman Constant = 5.67×10^{-8} W/m^2-K^4 and use Wien's Rule)
(a) 4×10^{17} W, 2.02 μm
(b) 1×10^{17} W, 5.1 μm
(c) 1.5×10^{17} W, 7.5 μm
(d) 2×10^{17} W, 10.1 μm

40. **Assertion (A):** The mangroves are nursery ground for fish and larvae.
Reason (R): The mangroves are covered with mangrove plants that enrichs the environment.
Codes:
(a) Both (A) and (R) are true and (R) is the correct explanation of (A).
(b) Both (A) and (R) are true but (R) is not the correct explanation of (A).
(c) (A) is true, but (R) is false.
(d) (A) is false, but (R) is true.

41. Ecological restoration of degraded sites are aimed to:
(a) Restore all biophysical characteristics of pristine ecosystem.
(b) Restore social desirable and economically feasible characteristics of original ecosystem.
(c) Leave it alone and allow natural regeneration.
(d) Prohibit all human activity in the area.

42. The mean annual rainfall in India is:
(a) 110 mm (b) 110 cm
(c) 85 cm (d) 110 m

43. For maximum biogas production following conditions are recommended:
(a) Strict anaerobic
(b) Strict aerobic
(c) Only cellulose as a carbon source
(d) Semi aerobic

44. In humid climate, the rate of weathering of the following types of rocks is such that:
(a) Basalt > Dunite > Granite
(b) Basalt > Granite > Dunite
(c) Dunite > Granite > Basalt
(d) Dunite > Basalt > Granite

45. The geometric mean of the following numbers 2, 3, 2, 3, 2, 3, 2, 3 is:
(a) $\sqrt{6}$ (b) 6
(c) 2.5 (d) 5.0

46. Thermoclines of a lake mean:
(a) The upper layer with well lit, well mixed and relatively having warm water
(b) The intermediate layer in which a rapid decline in temperature occurs with depth
(c) The deep layer which is generally cold and dark
(d) The bottom layer

47. Environmental Impact Assessment (EIA) seeks to achieve goals pertaining to:
(a) Sustainable Development
(b) Prevention of pollution only
(c) Conservation of resources only
(d) Social Benefit

48. Which is the correct order of the degree of weathering of the following rocks:
(a) Dunite > Basalt > Granite > Rhyolite
(b) Basalt > Dunite > Granite > Rhyolite
(c) Granite > Basalt > Dunite > Rhyolite
(d) Rhyolite > Granite > Dunite > Basalt

49. Which of the following sets has the maximum dispersion:
(a) 10, 11, 12, 10, 11, 10, 10, 11, 10, 11
(b) 1, 2, 1, 2, 1, 2, 1, 2, 1, 2
(c) 1, 2, 3, 4, 5, 6, 7, 8, 9, 10
(d) 5, 5, 6, 6, 5, 5, 6, 5, 6, 5

50. Which is the best and simple method for determination of fluorine in ground water?
(a) Atomic Absorption spectrometry
(b) Spectrophotometry
(c) Flame photometry
(d) Ion-selective electrode

PAPER–III

1. Which of the following correctly states an observation that helps to explain circulation patterns in the atmosphere?
   (a) Cold air rises and warms as it rises
   (b) Warm air rises and cools as it rises
   (c) Cold air can hold more water vapour than warm air
   (d) All of the above

2. Which of the following would not be a consequence of a rise in global temperature?
   (a) rising sea level
   (b) increased polar ice mass
   (c) increased frequency of major or storms
   (d) increased frequency of major droughts

3. Match the List I and List II and select the correct answer from the codes given below the lists:

   List I (Environmental Factor)

   A. Light B. Temperature
   C. Water D. Wind

   List II (Effect on Vegetation)

   1. Decreases the growth of vegetation by way of reducing the moisture content of the air
   2. Affects the development of plastids and pigments
   3. Affects the development and growth of flowering
   4. Wipe out the vegetation by way of removing the top soil

Codes:	A	B	C	D
(a)	(i)	(ii)	(iii)	(iv)
(b)	(ii)	(iii)	(iv)	(i)
(c)	(iii)	(iv)	(ii)	(i)
(d)	(iv)	(iii)	(i)	(ii)

4. Any activity of the living organisms which may cause marked effects upon the living and their environment is referred to as
   (a) physical effect
   (b) edaphic effect
   (c) biotic effect
   (d) physiographic effect

5. Which of the following pairs with respect to geographical zones is incorrectly matched?
   (a) Polar zones........lies between 75° latitude and the poles
   (b) Arctic zones.........lies astride the Arctic and Antarctic circles
   (c) Equatorial zone....lies astride the poles and extends to 10° latitude south
   (d) None of the above

6. Mercury is particularly hazardous to human health because
   (a) it bioaccumulates high up the food chain.
   (b) as a heavy metal, it can cause serious impact injury.
   (c) it is light and volatile, and so is widely dispersed through the environment by wind.
   (d) as a pure metal it is very soluble in water, hence easily absorbed through drinking water.

7. The directions for the regulation, prohibition or the closure of any industry are given by:
   (a) State government
   (b) Central government
   (c) State Pollution Control Board
   (d) Central Pollution Control Board

8. In developed countries, the two most deadly sources of indoor pollution are
   (a) pesticides and cleaning agents
   (b) synthetic furniture materials and radiation from electronic equipment
   (c) radiation from electronic equipment and pesticides
   (d) radon and cigarette smoke

9. A reaction is not feasible, if
   (a) ΔH is negative and ΔS is negative
   (b) ΔH is positive and ΔS is positive
   (c) ΔH is positive and ΔS is negative
   (d) ΔH is negative and ΔS is positive.

10. Mixing height is:
   (a) the height of ground based inversion
   (b) the height at which geostrophic balance occurs
   (c) the height of contant solar flux layer
   (b) the height upto which atmosphere is churned by convection

11. Which of the following is the best example of a keystone species?
   (a) Sea otter (b) Sea urchin
   (c) Spotted owl (d) Snail darter

12. Species that serve as early warnings of environmental damage are called
   (a) keystone species
   (b) native species
   (c) specialist species
   (d) indicator species

13. A specialist faces _______ competition for resources and has _____ ability to environmental changes. A generalist faces ____ competition for resources and has _____ ability to adapt to environmental changes.
   (a) less, greater, great, less
   (b) greater, less, less, greater
   (c) less, less, greater, greater
   (d) greater, greater, less, less

14. Which of the following statements is incorrect?
   (a) About 5,000 species of plants are exclusively found in India
   (b) India has been divided into four ecological sub-regions
   (c) According to Red Data Book of IUCN, more than 1000 creatures are threatened with extinctions
   (d) Rhinoceros, the Royal Bengal and Siberian Tigers are facing most immediate danger.

15. An intimate association of two organisms of different species, for mutual benefit, involving an organic union between the two and the individuals may not be able to live separately, is called
   (a) symbiosis
   (b) commensalism
   (c) parasitism
   (d) food dependability

16. What is CITES?
   (a) a treaty banning barrier island development
   (b) a treaty banning trade in endangered species
   (c) a treaty banning dumping plastic in the ocean
   (d) a treaty banning overfishing

17. When fish populations are temporarily reduced due to overfishing, they are said to be
   (a) locally extinct
   (b) commercially extinct
   (c) economically extinct
   (d) biologically extinct

18. Groundwater can be protected least by
   (a) banning disposal of hazardous wastes in sanitary landfills and deep-injection wells.
   (b) monitoring aquifers near landfills and underground tanks.
   (c) using advanced sewage treatment.
   (d) requiring liability insurance for old and new underground tanks.

19. Which of the following statements is incorrect?
   (a) Earth surface emits long wavelength radiation
   (b) The water vapour and carbon dioxide present in the atmosphere absorb a large fraction of the long wave radiation
   (c) The heat carried by the water vapour is transmitted to the air
   (d) All the short wave radiations are absorbed by the atmospheric gases.

20. Consider the following statements regarding flow of matter:
    1. Nutrient cycles closely parallel the routes of energy flow within the biotic components
    2. The movement of material is cyclic
    3. The nutrient cycle is conservative

    Of these statements
    (a) only 1 is correct
    (b) 2 and 3 are correct
    (c) 1 and 3 are correct
    (d) All are correct

21. **Assertion (A):** There is an increase in temperature with altitude in the stratosphere.
    Reason (R): Ozone present in this layer absorbs most of the harmful ultraviolet rays from the sun.
    Codes:
    (a) Both (A) and (R) are true and (R) is the correct explanation of (A).
    (b) Both (A) and (R) are true but (R) is not a correct explanation of (A).
    (c) (A) is true, but (R) is false.
    (d) (A) is false, but (R) is true.

22. Which of the following is not an advantage of gaseous fuels over solid and liquid fuels?
    (a) They can easily be conveyed through pipelines to the actual place of use
    (b) They can be lighted at moment's notice
    (c) They cannot be pre-heated by the heat of the hot waste gases
    (d) Their combustion can readily be controlled.

23. The maximum temperature reached, when the coal is completely burnt in the theoretical amount of air, is called
    (a) fusion temperature
    (b) calorific intensity
    (c) ignition temperature
    (d) None of the above

24. Peat is
    (a) soft brown coloured
    (b) brown jelly-like mass
    (c) pitch-black coal
    (d) last stage of coalification.

25. Suitability of a diesel fuel is determined by
    (a) octane number
    (b) percentage of carbon
    (c) length of hydrocarbon chain
    (d) cetane number.

26. Petroleum is a mixture of
    (a) sulphur and nitrogen
    (b) hydrocarbons
    (c) oxygen and water
    (d) nitrogen and silver.

27. The Coriolis effect contributes to
    (a) global wind patterns
    (b) global warming
    (c) increased acidic deposition
    (d) a reduction in eutrophication.

28. Peru decided for a short time to discontinue chlorination the country's drinking water because
    (a) it was concerned that chlorine gave the water a bad taste
    (b) it was concerned over the increased risk of cancer
    (c) chlorinate was too costly
    (d) chlorine bleached the water.

29. The concept of environment is based on
    1. environmental degradation
    2. dimensions of totality of the environment
    3. shift in the interest
    4. globality

    Of these
    (a) only 1 is correct
    (b) 1, 2 and 3 are correct
    (c) 2, 3 and 4 are correct
    (d) None of the above.

30. Very toxic gas which causes headache, visual difficulty, paralysis and even death in the human being is
(a) carbon dioxide
(b) ozone
(c) carbon monoxide
(d) None of the above

31. Most poisonous pollutant in water is
(a) zinc (b) phosphate
(c) arsenic (d) carbon dioxide

32. The comprehensive legislation that is truly a milestone in the field of environmental protection was enacted in
(a) 1974 (b) 1981
(c) 1978 (d) 1985

33. The EIA clearance in the prescribed format shall be accompanied by
(a) project report
(b) environmental impact assessment report
(c) environmental management plan
(d) All of the above

34. Silence zone is defined as areas upto
(a) 100 m around such premises as hospitals, educational institutions and courts
(b) 200 m around such premises as hospitals, educational institutions and courts
(c) 500 m around such premises as hospitals, educational institutions and courts
(d) None of the above

35. MoEF amended the EIA notification making public hearing mandatory for environmental clearance on
(a) 27 January, 1996
(b) 10 April, 1997
(c) 27 January, 1997
(d) None of the above

36. The Schedule I of EIA guidelines 1994 consists of
(a) an application form
(b) details of the EAC
(c) listing of the projects requiring environmental clearance
(d) None of the above

37. What is greenhouse effect?
(a) It is rapid global heating
(b) It is the rise in temperature on earth as certain gases in the atmosphere trap energy
(c) It is dramatic increase in greenhouse emissions
(d) None of the above

38. The global warming will lead to which of the following situations?
(a) Massive extinction of species
(b) Increase in greenhouse gas emission
(c) Collapse of biological and ecological systems
(d) All of the above

39. Field capacity of a solid waste is defined as
(a) the total amount of moisture
(b) the amount that affects the quantity of leachate
(c) the moisture available in solid wastes
(d) the total amount of moisture that can be held in a waste sample under gravitational force

40. An integrated solid waste management system include
(a) generation of solid wastes
(b) collection of solid wastes
(c) wastes minimization at source
(d) None of the above

41. The formula to compute the combustion efficiency is

(a) $$\text{C.E.} = \frac{\%CO_2}{\%CO_2 + \%CO} \times 100$$

(b) $$\text{C.E.} = \frac{\%CO_2 + \%CO}{\%CO_2} \times 100$$

(c) $C.E. = \dfrac{\%CO_2}{\%CO_2 - \%CO} \times 100$

(d) None of the above

42. Solid waste is material
(a) that is cheaper to throw away
(b) cheaper to throw away than to store or use
(c) recycled and reused
(d) None of the above

43. If the size of the sample is very small which method of sampling gives better results?
(a) Stratified (b) Purposive
(c) Random (d) Census

44. The term which indicates 'relationship existing between parts of measures' is
(a) standard deviation
(b) correlation
(c) degree of freedom
(d) range

45. The number of elements in the obtained sample is called
(a) sampling frame (b) sampling unit
(c) sample design (d) sample size

46. Which of the following is a non-probability sampling
(a) Snowball sampling
(b) Stratified sampling
(c) Cluster sampling
(d) Simple random sampling

47. In testing of hypothesis, research and null hypothesis
(a) exist together (b) one at a time
(c) are invalid (d) are same

48. The best long-range strategy to reduce beach erosion is
(a) building groins
(b) preventing development on beach areas or allowing development only behind protective dunes
(c) importing sand
(d) extensive building on barrier beaches.

49. What are most of the POPs listed in the Stockholm Convention "Dirty Dozen" used for?
(a) insecticides
(b) fungicides
(c) herbicides
(d) industrial solvents

50. Which of the following global environmental concern is most directly linked to poverty?
(a) global warming
(b) desertification
(c) ozone pollution
(d) threatened oceans

ANSWERS SHEET

PAPER—I

1. (d)	2. (d)	3. (c)	4. (d)	5. (d)
6. (a)	7. (b)	8. (d)	9. (d)	10. (d)
11. (d)	12. (c)	13. (c)	14. (b)	15. (a)
16. (d)	17. (d)	18. (b)	19. (c)	20. (b)
21. (a)	22. (b)	23. (c)	24. (c)	25. (c)
26. (b)	27. (b)	28. (c)	29. (b)	30. (b)
31. (a)	32. (b)	33. (c)	34. (a)	35. (b)
36. (d)	37. (b)	38. (d)	39. (c)	40. (a)
41. (a)	42. (b)	43. (a)	44. (a)	45. (b)
46. (c)	47. (c)	48. (c)	49. (d)	50. (c)

PAPER—II

1. (b)	2. (b)	3. (a)	4. (d)	5. (a)
6. (a)	7. (b)	8. (a)	9. (b)	10. (b)
11. (a)	12. (b)	13. (d)	14. (a)	15. (d)
16. (a)	17. (a)	18. (b)	19. (b)	20. (a)

21. (a)	22. (d)	23. (d)	24. (d)	25. (d)
26. (d)	27. (d)	28. (d)	29. (a)	30. (c)
31. (b)	32. (b)	33. (a)	34. (b)	35. (d)
36. (c)	37. (c)	38. (c)	39. (b)	40. (b)
41. (a)	42. (b)	43. (a)	44. (b)	45. (a)
46. (b)	47. (a)	48. (b)	49. (a)	50. (a)

PAPER—III

1. (b)	2. (b)	3. (b)	4. (c)	5. (c)
6. (a)	7. (d)	8. (d)	9. (c)	10. (c)
11. (a)	12. (d)	13. (c)	14. (b)	15. (a)
16. (b)	17. (b)	18. (c)	19. (d)	20. (d)
21. (a)	22. (c)	23. (b)	24. (b)	25. (d)
26. (b)	27. (a)	28. (b)	29. (a)	30. (c)
31. (c)	32. (d)	33. (d)	34. (a)	35. (b)
36. (c)	37. (b)	38. (d)	39. (d)	40. (c)
41. (a)	42. (b)	43. (b)	44. (b)	45. (d)
46. (a)	47. (b)	48. (a)	49. (a)	50. (b)

MOCK TEST–3
PAPER–I

1. In the large group communications, effectively used media is
   (a) Radio
   (b) Television
   (c) Overhead Projector
   (d) Computer

2. A child may be suffering from hearing impairment if
   (a) he generally says 'please repeat' to the teacher
   (b) he speaks loudly unusually
   (c) he comes nearer to the speaker during conversation
   (d) All of the above

3. If a student is absent from the classes for a long time
   (a) Teacher should try to know the cause of his absence
   (b) Teacher should try to solve his problems or help him
   (c) Teacher should go to his home to meet him
   (d) Both (a) and (b)

4. The telecast materials are used to
   (a) increase retention power
   (b) enhance concentration and learning
   (c) reduce the burden of the teacher
   (d) All of the above

5. The main function of educational psychology is to provide prospective teacher with
   (a) how to deal with students and everyday class situation
   (b) research procedures for evaluating current teaching procedure
   (c) insight into the needs, problems and styles of behaviour of teacher
   (d) insight into various aspects of modern teaching education

6. Which of the following is not a method of research?
   (a) Historical (b) Observation
   (c) Philosophical (d) Survey

7. The communication which transpires inside a person is known as
   (a) group communication
   (b) intrapersonal communication
   (c) interpersonal communication
   (d) mass communication

8. The word research is derived from
   (a) Greek word (b) French word
   (c) Spanish word (d) Latin word

9. Educational quality is
   (a) Only a legal right
   (b) Fundamental right

(c) Only a customary right
(d) None of these

10. A good teacher is one who
(a) has genuine interest in his student
(b) is highly intelligent
(c) lives simple life
(d) has mastery over his teaching subject

11. Which of the following institutions is responsible for the implemation of reforms in teaching profession?
(a) National Institute of Educational Planning and Administration
(b) University Grants Commission
(c) National Council for Teacher's Education
(d) National Council for Educational Research and Training

12. The most important characteristic of Open Book Examination system is that
(a) it compels students to think
(b) students become serious
(c) it improves attendance in the classroom
(d) it reduces examination anxiety amongst students

13. Discussion in the class will be more effective if the topic of discussion is
(a) informed to the student well in advance
(b) not introduced
(c) stated before the start of discussion
(d) written on the board without introducing it

14. A person is not a successful communicator
(a) who presents material in a precise and clear way
(b) who sometimes becomes informal before the receiver and developes rapport
(c) who knows a lot but is somewhat reserve in his attitude
(d) who is able to adapt himself according to the language of communication

15. Which of the following provides more freedom for the learners to interact actively?
(a) Small group discussions
(b) Lecture by experts
(c) Viewing of the TV
(d) Use of film projector

16. In this question, four words are given, out of which three are alike in some manner and one is different. Choose the odd one out.
(a) Diamond (b) Graphite
(c) Coal (d) Pearl

17. Two objects or events are related in some way. Pick out that option which has the same type of relationship stated in the given two words:

HANDS : FINGERS :: ?
(a) Competition : Victory
(b) Head : Hair
(c) Skin : Colour
(d) Machine : Tools

18. Human ear is most sensitive to noise in the range
(a) 1-2 kHz (b) 100-500 Hz
(c) 10-12 kHz (d) 13-16 kHz

Direction: (19-23) Study the following passage and give answer to the questions based on it.

A recent report in *News Week* says that in American colleges, students of Asian origin outperform not only the minority group students but the majority Whites as well. Many of these students might be of Indian origin, and their achievement is something that we can be really proud of. It is unlikely that these talented youngsters will come back to India, and that is the familiar brain drain problem. However, recent statements by the nation's policymakers indicate that the perception of this issue is changing. 'Brain Bank' and not the 'Brain Drain' is the more appropriate idea, they suggest that since the expertise of Indians abroad is only deposited in other places and not lost.

This may be so, but this brain bank, like most of other banks, is one that primarily serves customers in its neighbourhood. The skills of Asians now excelling in America's colleges will mainly help the USA. No matter how significant, what non-resident Indians do for India and what their counterparts do for other Asian lands is only a by-product.

But it is also necessary to ask, or be reminded why Indians study more fruitfully when abroad. The Asians whose accomplishments *News Week* records would have probably had a very different fate if they had studied in India. In America, they found an elbow room, books and facilities not available and not likely to be available here. The need to prove themselves in their new country and the competition of an international standard they faced there must have cured mental and physical laziness. But other things helping them in America can be obtained if we achieve a change in social attitudes, especially towards youth.

We need to learn to value individuals and their unique qualities more than conformity and respectability. We need to learn the language of encouragement to add to our skill in flattery. We might also learn to be less liberal with blame and less tight-fisted with appreciation, especially to those showing signs of independence.

19. It is a general belief that the talented young Indians studying in America
    (a) will not return to pursue their careers in India
    (b) have a reputation for being hard-working
    (c) have an opportunity to contribute in India's development
    (d) can solve the brain drain problem because of recent changes in policy

20. Among the many groups of students in American colleges, Asian students
    (a) have only a minority status like the blacks
    (b) are often written about in magazines like *News Week*
    (c) are the most successful academically
    (d) have proved that they are as goods as Whites

21. There is talk of the 'Brain Bank', this idea
    (a) is based on plan to utilise foreign exchange remittances to stimulate research and development
    (b) is a solution to the brain drain problem
    (c) is a new problem caused partly by the brain drain
    (d) is a new way of looking at the role of qualified Indians living abroad

22. The students of Asian origin in America include
    (a) Indians who are the most hard-working of all
    (b) a fair number from India
    (c) a small group from India
    (d) persons from India who are very proud

23. Which of the following most appropriately sums up the intent of the author?
    (a) USA has excelled just because of the contributions from talented immigrants
    (b) We need to look at 'Brain Drain' in a positive way as 'Brain Bank'
    (c) Indians should take pride in the fact that fellow Indians have excelled in foreign lands against all odds
    (d) We need to think of the ways to help grow and retain the talent of our land

24. What should come in place of the question mark (?) in the following series?

102, 99, 104, 97, 106 ?

(a) 106 (b) 59
(c) 95 (d) 64

25. **Statement:** Let us increase the taxes to cover the deficit.

Conclusions:

I. If the taxes are not increased, the deficit cannot be met.
II. The present taxes are very low.
III. Deficit in the budget are not desirable.

Choose the correct option.

(a) II and III are implicit
(b) I and III are implicit
(c) I and II are implicit
(d) All are implicit

26. **Statements:**

A. Some dogs are cats.
B. None of the cats is a cow.

Conclusions:

I. Some cats are not dogs.
II. Some cats are dogs.
III. Some cows are dogs.
IV. No dog is a cow.

Choose the correct option.

(a) Only II follows
(b) Only III follows
(c) I and III follow
(d) Only IV follows

Directions: (27-30) Using the following table answer the questions given below.

Yearly income (in ₹ '000)

Name/Year	2008	2009	2010	2011
Mahesh	1200	1600	2000	2400
Suresh	1000	1400	1600	2000
Ganesh	900	1200	1500	2000
Seema	2000	2500	3000	3700
Sapna	1200	1200	1500	1700

27. Whose average income for all the four years is ₹ 1400000?

(a) Mahesh alone
(b) Ganesh and Sapna both
(c) Mahesh and Suresh
(d) Sapna alone

28. How high is the total average income for four years of men as compared to that of women?

(a) 2133340 (b) 3500440
(c) 4320540 (d) 5440820

29. What is the round figure, the ratio between the total income of men and that of women for all years?

(a) 16:14 (b) 14:15
(c) 15:16 (d) 23:21

30. Can we say women earn more than men?

(a) No
(b) Yes
(c) Not sure
(d) Difference is not so significant

Directions: (31-35) Using the following graph answer the questions given below.

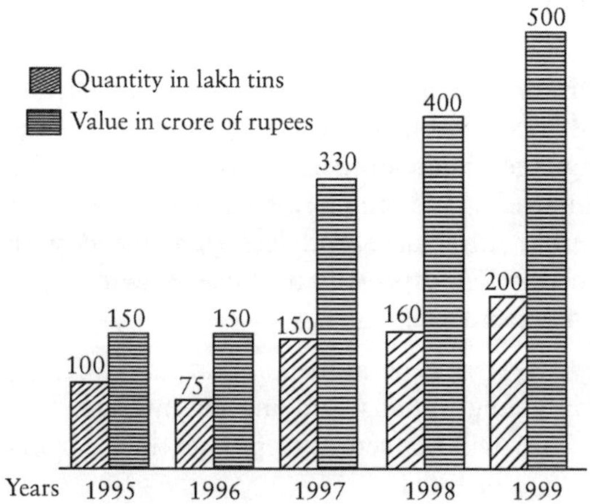

31. What was the approximate percentage increase in export value from 1995 to 1999?

(a) 435 (b) 395.5
(c) 422.8 (d) None of these

32. If in 1998, the tins were exported at the same rate per tin as that in 1997, what would be the value (in ₹ crores) of export in 1998?
(a) 375 (b) 352
(c) 395 (d) 392

33. In which year the value per tin was minimum?
(a) 1996 (b) 1998
(c) 1995 (d) 1999

34. What was the percentage drop in export quantity from 1995 to 1996?
(a) 25 (b) 46
(c) 52 (d) None of these

35. What was the difference between the tins exported in 1997 and 1998?
(a) 10 (b) 1000
(c) 100000 (d) 1000000

36. Which of the following statements is/are true about ozone layer?
(a) It is depleting due to human activities
(b) It is found in upper atmosphere, which absorbs UV rays
(c) It causes skin cancer and genetic disorder
(d) Both (a) and (b)

37. Study the figure and find the region which represents the students who study Physics and Chemistry but not Mathematics.

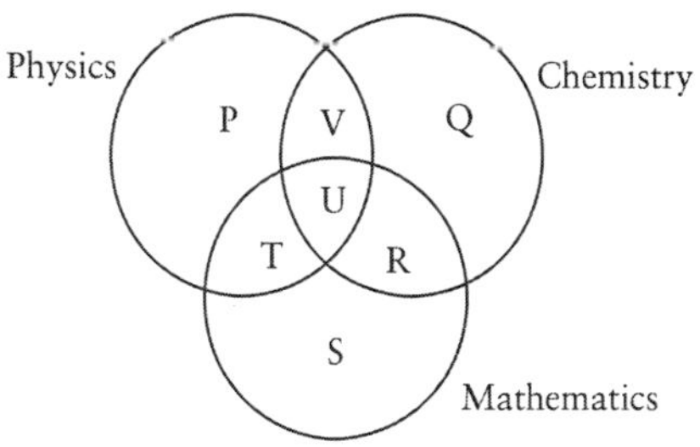

(a) P + T + S + R + U + V
(b) T
(c) P + T + S
(d) V

38. Which of the following is a non-point source of water pollution?
(a) Factories (b) Lawn
(c) Coal mines (d) None of these

39. The depletion of ozone layer causes
I. Skin cancer.
II. Damage to our immune system.
III. Damage to our eyes.
(a) Only III (b) I and II
(c) I and III (d) All of the above

40. **Statements:**
I. All the fruits are stones.
II. No tree is fruit.
III. All stones are rains.

Conclusions:
(a) Some rain is fruit
(b) No stone is a tree
(c) No rain is a tree
(d) None is true

41. Web designer is also known as
(a) Web maintainer (b) Web editor
(c) Web master (d) Web author

42. Which of the following schedule of our Constitution is related to languages?
(a) Sixth (b) Eighth
(c) Seventh (d) Tenth

43. In the hypermedia database, information bits are stored in the form of
(a) Symbols (b) Signals
(c) Cubes (d) Nodes

44. Explosive volcanic eruption is caused by
(a) High water content in ground
(b) Low viscosity of magma
(c) High viscosity of magma
(d) None of these

45. The VIRUS is a
(a) Device
(b) Software program

(c) Hardware
(d) anti-piracy software

46. Appropriation Act of the General Budget is
(a) a Constitution Amendment Bill
(b) a Finance Bill
(c) a Money Bill
(d) an Ordinary Bill

47. If in a certain language, GERMANY is coded as HGUQFTF then how will you code NEOMAN?
(a) OFQQFT (b) OFQPES
(c) OGRQFT (d) None of these

48. Which of the following is biggest fresh-water lake in India?
(a) Loktak (b) Dal
(c) Sukhna (d) None of these

49. Different memories can be classified according to the concept of
(a) Transfer Rate
(b) Access mode/capacity
(c) Access Time
(d) All of the above

50. Which of the following diagrams represents the relation between red, clothes and roses most appropriately?

(a) 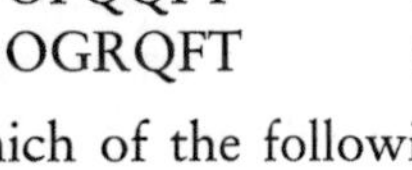 (b) 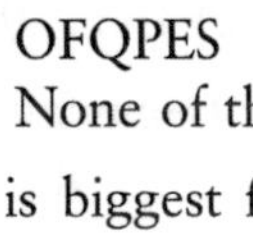

(c) 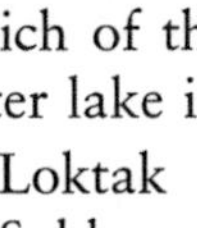 (d) 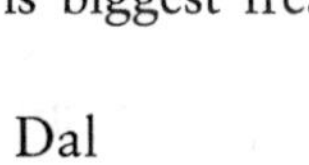

PAPER–II

Read the passage below and answer questions that follow based on your understanding of the passage:

Forests in India are fast disappearing at a rate of about 0.6% per year equivalent to about 7.3 million ha. This renders all the closed tropical forests disappear within 177 years. At this rate of destruction of tropical forests, about 20-25% of the worlds plant species would have been lost by the year 2000. By another estimate 90% of tropical forest area containing about 505 varieties of world plant species will be destroyed during the next 20 years. By another estimate 1000 species/year would become extinct. This figure is expected to rise to 10,000 species/year. During the next 20 years, about one million species are likely to disappear.

Loss of biodiversity is severe in agricultural ecosystems too. During green revolution, thousands of wild crop varieties were replaced with a few hybrid species. This resulted in slight disappearance of genetic resources of crop plants, especially of wheat and rice. With the disappearance of the plants, the associated microorganisms and fauna were also lost. Further indiscriminate use of fertilizers and insecticides reduced the microbial species diversity live stock populations are already homogenised and their diversity is extinct.

Much of the fragile breeding and feeding grounds of almost 2/3rd of the world's oceanic fish have been destroyed. Endangered marine life in India lists about 8 species of marine mammals, 5 species of marine turtles, 1 species of hemichordate, 3 species of cephalochordate, 10 species of crab, etc.

Major cause of loss of biodiversity is the expansion of agricultural practices. Biological diversity is replaced by biological uniformity or monoculture in the name of green revolution in agriculture, white revolution in dairying and blue revolution in fisheries. The purpose of all these revolutions is to ensure food security and prevent "hunger disaster".

Biodiversity is also lost due to reclamation for building dams, factories highways, mining operations, etc. in the forested regions. Illegal trade and poaching of wild life also damaged biodiversity. Thus, biodiversity is destroyed by anthropogenic activities.

1. Loss of biodiversity is primarily due to:
   (a) Green revolution
   (b) White revolution
   (c) Blue revolution
   (d) Mining Activity
2. Decrease in India's forest cover is attributed mainly to:
   (a) Urbanization and Industrialization
   (b) Agriculture and Dairying
   (c) Rail and Road Construction
   (d) Mining and Power Plants
3. About 90% of tropical forest area containing ________ varieties of world's plant species in the next twenty years.
   (a) 7.3 million (b) 505
   (c) 10,000 (d) 1000
4. The reduction of microbial species is due to:
   (a) Mining operations
   (b) Application of chemical fertilizers
   (c) Loss of wildlife
   (d) Construction of highways
5. Air quality standards are based on:
   (a) Climate and topography
   (b) Ambiet air quality alone
   (c) Dose of a pollutant
   (d) Method of measurement
6. For the detection of Polyaromatic hydrocarbons (PAH) which of the following instruments is used?
   (a) Atomic Absorption Spectrophotometer
   (b) X-ray Diffractometer
   (c) Gas Chromatograph
   (d) Flame Photometer
7. The ΔG_0 of ATP hydrolysis could not be measured directly because:
   (a) one cannot determine the K_{eq}
   (b) ATPase concentration could not be measured
   (c) One of the reactants could not be estimated
   (d) The products could not be determined
8. Match Lists I and II and select the correct answer using the codes given below the lists:

   List I (Characteristics)
   A. Point of initial movement during the earthquakes
   B. Measurement of the magnitude of earthquake
   C. Measurement of solar radiation incident on earth
   D. Earthquakes generated water waves in coastal areas

   List II (Terms/Names)
   (i) Tsunami (ii) Insolation
   (iii) Richter scale (iv) Focus

Codes:	A	B	C	D
(a)	(iv)	(iii)	(ii)	(i)
(b)	(iii)	(iv)	(i)	(ii)
(c)	(ii)	(i)	(iii)	(iv)
(d)	(i)	(ii)	(iv)	(iii)
9. The recent asbestos controversy about the French ship going to Alang was primarily due to:
   (a) Violation of Indian Coastal Zone Laws.
   (b) Violation of Transnational Movement of Hazardous Waste.
   (c) Gujarat State Pollution Control Laws.
   (d) Indian Air Pollution Laws.
10. The Water (Prevention and Control of Pollution) Act 1974 ....
   (a) Regulates the discharge of hazardous pollutants into the nations surface water.
   (b) Regulates the emission of hazardous air pollutants.
   (c) Regulates waste disposal of sea.
   (d) Regulates the transportation of hazardous materials.

11. Due to Corriolis effect, wind in the:
    (a) Northern Hemisphere moves to the left with respect to the rotating earth.
    (b) Northern Hemisphere moves to the right.
    (c) Southern Hemisphere moves northward.
    (d) Both Hemispheres moves independent of each other.

12. Removal of key-stone species would cause:
    (a) Drastic change in community composition
    (b) Drastic change in ecological system
    (c) Drastic change in food chain
    (d) Drastic change in energy flow

13. The correct sequence of the decreasing order of abundance of the given elements in the Earth's crust is:
    (a) iron, oxygen, silicon, aluminium
    (b) oxygen, aluminium, silicon, iron
    (c) silicon, oxygen, iron, aluminium
    (d) oxygen, silicon, aluminium, iron

14. If nocturnal animal in the light dark cycle of 12 h light and 12 h darkness kept in constant darkness for 10 days, then what will happen to the onset of its daily activities:
    (a) start earlier than what was before
    (b) start later than what was before
    (c) no change in the activity time
    (d) activities remain on throughout the dark period

15. Cost-Benefit Analysis seeks to analyse cost and benefits of a project in terms of:
    (a) Monetary gains
    (b) Social gain/loss
    (c) Environmental and monetary gains/ losses
    (d) Social and Environmental costs and gains

16. **Assertion (A):** Tropospheric ozone exists in urban areas.
    Reason (R): The photochemical reactions involving oxides of nitrogen produces O_3.
    Codes:
    (a) Both (A) and (R) are true and (R) is the correct explanation of (A).
    (b) Both (A) and (R) are true but (R) is not the correct explanation of (A).
    (c) (A) is true, but (R) is false.
    (d) (A) is false, but (R) is true.

17. Which of the following coal types has the highest calorific value?
    (a) Peat (b) Lignite
    (c) Anthracite (d) Bituminous

18. Wind rose of a given location represents:
    (a) Frequency distribution of wind speeds in the form of a histogram.
    (b) Frequency distribution of wind speeds in percentage terms in the form of a π chart.
    (c) Frequency distribution of wind speed associated with a cyclose.
    (d) Frequency distribution of wind speed and direction in polar coordinates.

19. In qualitative analysis the sulphides of Group-II are precipitated in presence of dilute HCl, while of Group-IV are precipitated only in the presence of NH_4OH. It is because:
    (a) Solubility product of sulphides of Group-II is greater than that of Group-IV
    (b) Solubility product of sulphides of Group-II is less than that of Group-IV
    (c) Sulphides of Group-II are insoluble in acids
    (d) Sulphides of Group-IV are insoluble in alkalies

20. In deep oceans the phenomenon of inverted biomass pyramid occurs mainly due to:

I. Fast growth rate and high nutrient requirement of producers.
II. Rapid turnover rate and short life span of producers.
III. Slow growth rate and high nutrient requirement of herbivores.
IV. Slow turnover and long life span of herbivores.

Which of the following combinations is correct?

(a) I and III (b) I and IV
(c) II and III (d) II and IV

21. If the EIA indicates that another state is likely to be affected, the state, in which EIA is planned, has to:
(a) transmit to the affected state any relevant information from the EIA concerning it
(b) keep the relevant information fully secret
(c) handover the information to the central pollution control board
(d) None of the above

22. **Assertion (A):** Chlorofluorocarbons deplete ozone.
Reason (R): These compounds contain Chlorine, Bromine and Fluorine.
Codes:
(a) Both (A) and (R) are true and (R) is the correct explanation of (A).
(b) Both (A) and (R) are true but (R) is not the correct explanation of (A).
(c) (A) is true, but (R) is false.
(d) (A) is false, but (R) is true.

23. Match the items in List I with List II and select the correct answers using codes given below:

List I	**List II**
A. Lignite	(i) Bikaner
B. Asbestos	(ii) Chotanagpur
C. Titanium	(iii) Southern Malabar
D. Iron	(iv) Ratnagiri

Codes:	**A**	**B**	**C**	**D**
(a)	(i)	(ii)	(iii)	(iv)
(b)	(i)	(ii)	(iv)	(iii)
(c)	(ii)	(i)	(iii)	(iv)
(d)	(ii)	(i)	(iv)	(iii)

24. The process of alluviation indicates:
(a) Removal of particles from the upper layer of soil
(b) Removal of particles from lower layer of soil
(c) Deposition of soil particles in sub-soil layer
(d) Transportation of soil particles in the B-horizon

25. Arsenic problem in India is primarily due to:
(a) Overexploitation of arsenopyrite in the hinterland
(b) Overexploitation of coal in Bihar and Bengal
(c) Overexploitation of ground water in the affected areas
(d) Overexploitation of surface water in the affected areas

26. The orchid seeds do not germinate under ordinary conditions because:
(a) Orchid seeds are too large for dispersal
(b) Orchid seeds do not have endosperm
(c) Orchid seeds undergo a dormancy period
(d) They germinate under very dry conditions

27. Sound pressure level (dB) can be expressed as:

(a) $20 \log_{10}\left(\frac{\text{Measured pressure}}{\text{Reference pressure}}\right)$

(b) $20 \log_{10}\left(\frac{\text{Reference pressure}}{\text{Measured pressure}}\right)$

(c) $20 \log_{10}\left(\frac{\text{Reference pressure}}{\text{Measured pressure}}\right)^{1/2}$

(d) $20 \log_{10}\left(\frac{\text{Measured pressure}}{\text{Reference pressure}}\right)^{1/2}$

28. Stoke's law of settling velocity simplified as $V \propto \frac{1}{d^n}$ suggest that:
(a) A large particle 100 μm in diameter will settle slowly compared to a smaller 10 μm particle
(b) A large particle 100 μm in diameter, will settle faster than a smaller particle 10 μm
(c) Both a large 100 μm particle and a small 10 μm particle will settle in a column of 10 cm at the same time.
(d) Small particle 10 μm in diameter will settle faster, while coarser particle of 100 μm diameter will remain in suspension.

29. At ordinary temperatures, the molecules of a diatomic gas have only translational and rotational kinetic energies. At high temperatures, they may have vibrational energy. As a result of this, compared to lower temperatures, a diatomic gas at higher temperatures will have:
(a) Lower molar heat capacity
(b) Higher molar heat capacity
(c) Lower isothermal compressibility
(d) Higher isothermal compressibility

30. When terrestrial plant communities progress with time from successional to climax stage:
(i) Standing crop biomass increases
(ii) Net ecosystem productivity increases
(iii) Gross productivity per unit of standing crop biomass decreases
(iv) Biomass supported per unit of energy flow decreases.
Which of the following combination is correct:
Codes:
(a) (i) and (ii) (b) (i) and (iii)
(c) (i) and (iv) (d) (ii) and (iii)

31. Trophic structure may be shown graphically by ecological pyramids; which of the following ecological pyramid will always have a true upright pyramid shape:
(a) Pyramid of numbers
(b) Pyramid of biomass
(c) Pyramid of energy
(d) All of the above

32. **Assertion (A):** In electrostatic precipitator corona discharge is used for removing particulate particles from the gas stream.
Reason (R): The corona discharge creates an electric field, which makes the particles settle down.
Codes:
(a) Both (A) and (R) are true and (R) is the correct explanation of (A).
(b) Both (A) and (R) are true but (R) is not the correct explanation of (A).
(c) (A) is true, but (R) is false.
(d) (A) is false, but (R) is true.

33. Fission of 1 gm of ^{235}U liberates energy equivalent to about:
(a) 5.7 barrels of crude oil
(b) 13.7 barrels of crude oil
(c) 18.7 barrels of crude oil
(d) 22.7 barrels of crude oil

34. Which of the following statement is not correct:
Carcinogenic agents like pesticides are mutagens which may cause.
(a) Change in chromosome
(b) Change in nucleotide sequence in DNA of sperms or eggs, which is inherited
(c) Change in nucleotide sequence in DNA of somatic cells is inherited
(d) Change in DNA sequence may be due to generation of free radicals in the cells

35. The ionizing radiation, which affects the activities of most of the enzymes is due to
(a) Photoemission of electron
(b) Interaction of α-particles, β- and γ-rays with enzymes
(c) Interaction of electron with body.
(d) Interaction of radiation with tissues.

36. Which set of stoichiometric coefficient correctly balance the equation
A. H_2O_2 + B. $KMnO_4$ + C. H_2SO_4
D. K_2SO_4 + E. Mn SO_4 + F. H_2O + G. O_2

	A	B	C	D	E	F	G
(a)	1	1	1	1	1	1	1
(b)	1	2	3	1	2	4	3
(c)	2	5	3	2	1	8	5
(d)	5	2	3	1	2	8	5

37. Comparing continental and oceanic crust
(a) the chemical composition of crust does not vary.
(b) the Fe content in continental crust is more than that of oceanic crust.
(c) the Si and Al content in continental crust is more than that of oceanic crust.
(d) the Na, Ca, Al content in oceanic crust is more than that of continental crust.

38. The geochemical weathering process can be viewed as
(a) Clay minerals + $CO_2 \rightleftharpoons$ Quartz + Al_2O_3
(b) Primary silicate + CO_2 + $H_2O \rightleftharpoons$ clay minerals + cations + HCO_3^- + H_4SiO_4 + H^+
(c) Primary silicate + $H_2O \rightleftharpoons Al_2O_3$ + SiO_2 + CaO + H^+
(d) Clay minerals + $H_2O \rightleftharpoons Fe_2O_3$ + Al_2O_3 + SiO_2 + CaO

39. In order of increasing cation exchange capacity
(a) Illite > Kaolinite > Sericite > Gibbsite
(b) Kaolinite > Gibbsite > Sericite > Illite
(c) Kaolinite > Illite > Montmorillonite
(d) Montmorillonite > Kaolinite > Illite

40. In an ecological succession there is a progressive change in biological community over time and space
(a) Old species are replaced by new one.
(b) Old species evolved into new species.
(c) New species moves in displacing previous one.
(d) At each stage there is a modification in the environment to adopt new species.

41. Government of India has enacted various Acts for protection and conservation of environment. However, more inclusive Act is
(a) Water (Prevention & Control of Pollution) Act
(b) Air (Prevention & Control of Pollution) Act
(c) Forest Act
(d) Environment (Protection) Act

42. Atmosphere contains various layers each having characteristic composition. The correct sequence starting from earth surface is
(a) Stratosphere → Ionosphere → Toposphere.
(b) Toposphere → Ionosphere → Stratosphere.
(c) Ionosphere → Stratosphere → Toposphere.
(d) Toposphere → Stratosphere → Ionosphere.

43. Solubility of NaCl in water is 10^{-1} m/L. The concentration of Na^+ in water will be
(a) $\left[\frac{10^{-1}}{2}\right]$ m/L (b) $\left[\frac{10^{1}}{2}\right]$ m/L
(c) 10^{-1} m/L (d) $\left[\sqrt{10^{-1}}\right]$ m/L

44. Proposed fuel for controlled nuclear fusion is lithium deuteride, LiD.
Which of the following reactions would possibly contribute to energy production?

I. ${}^{6}_{3}\text{Li} + {}^{1}_{0}\text{h} \rightarrow {}^{4}_{2}\text{He} + {}^{3}_{1}\text{H}$

II. ${}^{6}_{3}\text{Li} + {}^{2}_{1}\text{H} \rightarrow 2\,{}^{4}_{2}\text{He}$

III. $2\,{}^{2}_{1}\text{H} + {}^{3}_{2}\text{He} + {}^{1}_{0}\text{h}$

Codes:

(a) All of them (b) I
(c) III (d) I and II

45. The silicate ion in chrysotile consists of double strands of SiO_4^{-4} tetrahedra as shown below:

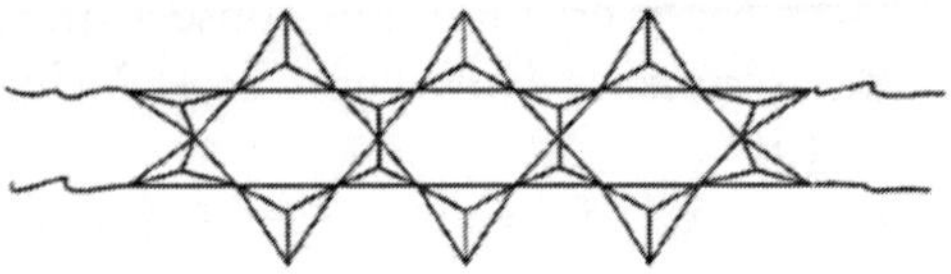

What is the general composition of the silicate ion in chrysolite?

(a) $(SiO_2)_n$ (b) $Si_2O_7^{-6}$
(c) $(Si_4O_{11})_n^{-6n}$ (d) $(SiO_3)_n^{-2n}$

46. Microfilteration generally employs
(a) thin polymer film with uniform pore size and a high pore density
(b) thin microfilm with smaller pore size and low pore density
(c) thin micro-bioplastic with regular pore size and a high pore density
(d) thin membrane filter with uniform pore size and a high pore density

47. The concept of Environmental Impact Assessment originated from
(a) Findings of a Royal Commission investigating the 'Weald Iron Mills and Furnaces' in Southern England in 1548.
(b) Report of the 'Volta Preparatory Commission' (HMSO, 1956).
(c) Discretionary guidelines of the National Environmental Policy Act in 1971.
(d) Report of copper mining in Puerto Rico commissioned in February 1967.

48. Match the List I and List II. Select the correct answer using the codes given below the lists:

List I
A. Ad-hoc Method
B. Checklist Method
C. Overlay Method
D. Matrix Method

List II
(i) Gives some measurements and describes the impacts
(ii) Limited value for scoping
(iii) Used for screening and for impact assessment, especially for impact identification
(iv) Acts as an aid in screening sites or routes for impacts

Codes:	A	B	C	D
(a)	(i)	(ii)	(iii)	(iv)
(b)	(ii)	(iii)	(i)	(iv)
(c)	(iii)	(iv)	(ii)	(i)
(d)	(ii)	(i)	(iv)	(iii)

49. **Assertion (A):** Climate change is going to increase social tensions in India.
Reason (R): The frequency and intensity of the extreme weather events will have serious consequences for food security.
Codes:
(a) Both (A) and (R) are true and (R) is the correct explanation of (A).
(b) Both (A) and (R) are true but (R) is not the correct explanation of (A).
(c) (A) is true but (R) is false.
(d) (A) is false but (R) is true.

50. In the Earth Summit at Rio de Janeiro, 1992, which of the following was not an agenda?
(a) Ozone depletion
(b) Global warming
(c) CO_2 reduction targets
(d) Biodiversity conservation

PAPER–III

1. Which of the following best describes measurements of CO_2 levels in the atmosphere since 1958?
   (a) Levels of CO_2 were steady until the mid-1970s, when they began to increase rapidly.
   (b) Measurements of CO_2 have shown a steady increase since accurate measurements began.
   (c) CO_2 levels are higher in winter and lower in summer, but the winter "highs" have increased each year and the summer "lows" have not fallen as far.
   (d) CO_2 levels are higher in winter and lower in summer, but the winter "highs" are higher each year and the summer "lows" are lower each year.

2. Which of the following does not address how oceans affect climatic conditions on land?
   (a) Water cools Earth because it reflects the most sunlight.
   (b) Oceans are the source of most water that falls as precipitation.
   (c) Coastal areas have more moderate climates than inland areas.
   (d) Ocean currents redistribute warm and cold masses of water.

3. As the amount of ozone in the stratosphere decreases,
   (a) more ultraviolet light is able to reach Earth's surface.
   (b) less solar energy is able to reach Earth's surface.
   (c) the amount of methane in the atmosphere increases.
   (d) the amount of phytoplankton in the ocean increases.

4. The photochemical activity is greatest at
   (a) the infrared end
   (b) violet end
   (c) visible region
   (d) None of the above

5. Which of the following statements is incorrect?
   (a) Temperature increases the rate of transpiration by way of causing the stomata to open
   (b) Light affects the shape of the plants by way of suppressing the production of auxins, the growth hormones
   (c) High temperature reduces the rate of metabolism by way of reducing the activity of enzyme
   (d) Wind decreases the growth of plants by way of reducing the moisture content of air.

6. The two major processes involved in the carbon cycle are
   (a) weathering and erosion
   (b) photosynthesis and respiration
   (c) evaporation and transpiration
   (d) erosion and deposition

7. Tropospheric ozone
   (a) protects Earth from most of the harmful UV radiation
   (b) binds with hemoglobin, preventing binding with oxygen in red blood cells
   (c) is produced through the interaction of heat and light, with nitrogen oxides and other carbon-containing compounds
   (d) is a primary pollutant

8. The Arrhenius equation of effect of temperature on the rate constant of a reaction is
   (a) $k = A.e^{-Ea/RT}$ (b) $k = \log \frac{E_a}{RT}$
   (c) $k = e^{-Ea/R^2T}$ (d) $k = \frac{E_a}{RT}$

9. Which of the following statements is incorrect?
   (a) Most of the gases are soluble in water to a more or less extent
   (b) The solubility is expressed in terms of absorption coefficient
   (c) The absorption coefficient for gas solubility was introduced by Bunsen
   (d) The nature of gas plays a significant role in its solubility, the gases which are easily liquified are least soluble in water.

10. Match the List I and List II and select the correct answer from the codes given below the lists:

List I	List II
A. Hard acid	(i) SO_4^{2-}
B. Soft acid	(ii) RS^+
C. Hard base	(iii) $S_2O_3^{2-}$
D. Soft base	(iv) SO_3

Codes:	A	B	C	D
(a)	(iv)	(i)	(ii)	(iii)
(b)	(iv)	(ii)	(i)	(iii)
(c)	(iii)	(ii)	(i)	(iv)
(d)	(iii)	(ii)	(iv)	(i)

11. The main difference between primary and secondary succession is that
    (a) primary succession occurs in the year before secondary succession
    (b) primary succession occurs on barren, rock areas and secondary succession does not
    (c) secondary succession ends in a climax species and primary succession ends in a pioneer species
    (d) secondary succession occurs on barren, rocky areas and primary succession does not

12. Which one of the following statements is false?
    (a) When environmental conditions are hanging rapidly, a generalist is usually better off than a specialist.
    (b) The fundamental niche of a special is the full range of physical, chemical, and the biological factors it could use if there were no competition,
    (c) The competitive exclusion principle states that no two species with the same fundamental niche can indefinitely occupy the same habitat.
    (d) Interspecific competition is competition between two members of the same species.

13. Which of the following is a true microecosystem?
    (a) ½ litre of water from a pond kept in an air tight flask
    (b) 1 litre of tap water in a flask covered over by cotton plug
    (c) 1½ litre of boiled pond water covered over by a lid
    (d) 1 litre of pond water closed with cork having gas exchange.

14. The rate of storage of organic matter in the plant tissues that is extra to its own respiratory needs by the green plants during a given period of measurement is called
    (a) gross primary productivity
    (b) net primary productivity
    (c) secondary productivities
    (d) net community productivity.

15. The synecology is
    (a) the ecological study of groups of plant or animal
    (b) the ecological studies of two distinct species living in separate but similar environmental conditions
    (c) the ecology of bottom dwelling forms
    (d) the ecological role of sunlight

16. Which of the following is not one of the reasons that protecting aquatic biodiversity especially difficult?
    (a) Lack, of public support for protection
    (b) The human ecological footprint is expanding

(c) The damage to oceans is not visible to most people.
(d) Many people view the ocean as an inexhaustible resource.

17. Drinking water quality at source after conventional treatment and disinfection should have some of the following characteristics
(a) Total coliform organisms (MPN/100 mL) 500 or less
(b) pH between 5.5 – 6.5
(c) dissolved oxygen 10 mg/litre or above
(d) B.O.D. at 20°C 3 mg/litre or less
Identify the correct combination
Codes:
(a) (a) and (d) (b) (a) and (b)
(c) (c) and (d) (d) (a) and (c)

18. Match the List I and List II and select the correct answer from the codes given below the lists:
List I
A. Ozone depletion
B. CO_2 reduction
C. Sustainable development
D. Hazardous waste
List II
(i) Basel convention
(ii) Kyoto Protocol
(iii) Rio Summit
(iv) Montreal Protocol

Codes:	A	B	C	D
(a)	(i)	(iv)	(iii)	(ii)
(b)	(iv)	(ii)	(iii)	(i)
(c)	(ii)	(iii)	(iv)	(i)
(d)	(iv)	(iii)	(ii)	(i)

19. Water is the most common and the most important chemical compounds for the livings for which of the following reasons?
1. The life has been originated in the waters of the oceans
2. It makes a large proportions of the animal tissues
3. Livings use aqueous solutions like blood and digestive juices as media for carrying out their biological functions

Select the correct answer using the codes given below:
Codes:
(a) 1, 2 and 3 (b) 1 and 2
(c) 1 and 3 (d) 2 and 3

20. The damage to land can be prevented by
(a) preparing accurate landuse data through remote sensing
(b) framing a time bound nation wide landuse planning
(c) preparing management plans for land amelioration
(d) All of the above

21. **Assertion (A):** The temperature is lowest about –90°C at a height of about 85 km.
Reason (R): Inversion of temperature takes place in the mesosphere.
Codes:
(a) Both (A) and (R) are true and (R) is the correct explanation of (A).
(b) Both (A) and (R) are true but (R) is not a correct explanation of (A).
(c) (A) is true, but (R) is false.
(d) (A) is false, but (R) is true.

22. A good fuel should possess
(a) high ignition temperature
(b) moderate ignition temperature
(c) high calorific value
(d) Both (b) and (c)

23. The calorific value of a coal sample is higher, it its
(a) moisture content is high
(b) ash content is high
(c) volatile matter is high
(d) fixed carbon is high

24. Consider the following statements:
1. The radiation reflected back to the atmosphere is called albedo
2. The atmosphere is essential in maintaining the heat balance of the body

3. The heat and sunlight both passes through the atmosphere

Of these statements

(a) Only 1 is correct
(b) 2 and 3 are correct
(c) 1 and 2 are correct
(d) 1, 2 and 3 are correct

25. Petroleum products are more widely used then coal, mainly because they
(a) are indispensable for transport on land sea and air
(b) are cheaper than coal
(c) do not leave any residue
(d) are easily available

26. Largest producer of natural gas in the world is
(a) Canada (b) U.S.A.
(c) China (d) Rusia

27. Colourless, odourless and non-corrosive air pollutants is
(a) sulphur dioxide
(b) carbon monoxide
(c) carbon dioxide
(d) ozone

28. The presence of which of the following gases in the air checks the ultraviolet light from sunlight?
(a) Sulphur dioxide
(b) Carbon monoxide
(c) Nitrogen oxide
(d) Ozone

29. Match the List I and List II. Select the correct answer using the codes given below the lists:

List I (Category of Area)
A. Commercial area
B. Residential area
C. Industrial area
D. Silence zones

List II (Daytime Noise Standards in dB)
(i) 75 (ii) 50
(iii) 65 (iv) 55

Codes:	A	B	C	D
(a)	(i)	(ii)	(iv)	(iii)
(b)	(iii)	(iv)	(i)	(ii)
(c)	(iv)	(iii)	(ii)	(i)
(d)	(ii)	(i)	(iv)	(iii)

30. A carcinogen which causes cancer of liver is
(a) toluene
(b) benzene
(c) vinyl chloride
(d) All of the above

31. Which of the following is not a green house gas?
(a) Carbon dioxide
(b) CFC's
(c) Carbon Monoxide
(d) None of the above

32. Which of the following pairs with respect to air quality standard in industrial and mixed use is incorrectly matched?
(a) SO_2..................120 μg/m^2
(b) NO_x..................80
(c) CO....................5000
(d) None of the above

33. Which of the following practices would have the biggest impact on achieving global sustainability?
(a) Recycling aluminium cans
(b) Using fuel-efficient vehicles
(c) Replanting deforested areas
(d) Reducing human population size

34. Which of the following is an example of reconciliation ecology?
(a) Restoring a native coastal estuary by planting native vegetation
(b) Purchasing development rights of coastal ecosystems
(c) Negotiating land disputes among competing parties
(d) Having a restaurant owner cooperate with local conservation efforts in ecotourism.

35. All major project plan should be examined to ensure
(a) public health and safety
(b) quality of environment
(c) Both (a) and (b)
(d) None of the above

36. How many projects in the list of Schedule I of EIA guidelines require environmental clearance from MoEF?
(a) 29 (b) 27
(c) 17 (d) None

37. Technique to assign PIU in an objective manner is
(a) baseline technique
(b) Delphi technique
(c) Both (a) and (b)
(d) None of the above

38. The most important cause for the loss of biodiversity is
(a) global warming
(b) climate change
(c) ozone depletion
(d) None of these

39. Which of the following is not determined by proximate analysis?
(a) fixed carbon
(b) ash content
(c) volatile combustible matter
(d) percentage of various chemical constituents

40. The Ministry of Environment and Forests has classified biomedical wastes into
(a) 10 categories
(b) 12 categories
(c) 21 categories
(d) None

41. Well known British practices (BPEFO and BATNEEC) can be adopted for deciding upon the management of
(a) solid wastes
(b) liquid wastes
(c) hazardous wastes
(d) None of the above

42. The Residential and Commercial wastes mainly consist of
(a) food wastes
(b) cardboard
(c) packaging material
(d) None of the above

43. Soil texture is determined by the
(a) relative proportion of mineral particles of different sizes
(b) soil organisms
(c) varying degree of weathering of parental rock
(d) None of the above

44. Consider the following statements.
I. The granite and gneiss give rise to red soil from weathering.
II. The laterite soil contains the hydrated oxides of iron and aluminium.
III. Both the red and laterite soils are poor in nitrogen rich in potash and phosphorus.

Which of the statements given above is/ are correct?
(a) I and II (b) Only II
(c) I and III (d) I, II and III

45. Colour of sedimentary rocks is primarily due to presence of
(a) organic matter
(b) copper oxide
(c) iron oxide
(d) manganese oxide

46. Laterite soil is rich in
(a) calcium
(b) iron and aluminium
(c) silicates
(d) sodium and potassium

47. Aquifer is defined as
(a) a geologic formation that yields significant quantities of water
(b) specific yields for various geological materials

(c) a geologic formation, which stores water but does not transmit
(d) All of the above

48. The very first theory about the origin of life accepted and vague in the form of
(a) life comes from another planet
(b) god's grace
(c) theory of spontaneous generation
(d) All of the above

49. Miller with the help of his experiment found
(a) nucleic
(b) protein
(c) amino acid and organic matter
(d) All of the above

50. Standing state is used to show
(a) the amount of organic substances present in an ecosystem
(b) the amount of inorganic substances present in an ecosystem
(c) the amount of dead material present in an ecosystem
(d) the biomass present in an ecosystem

ANSWERS SHEET

PAPER—I

1. (d)	2. (d)	3. (c)	4. (d)	5. (d)
6. (a)	7. (b)	8. (d)	9. (d)	10. (d)
11. (d)	12. (c)	13. (c)	14. (b)	15. (a)
16. (d)	17. (d)	18. (b)	19. (c)	20. (b)
21. (a)	22. (b)	23. (c)	24. (c)	25. (c)
26. (b)	27. (b)	28. (c)	29. (b)	30. (b)
31. (a)	32. (b)	33. (c)	34. (a)	35. (b)
36. (d)	37. (b)	38. (d)	39. (c)	40. (a)
41. (a)	42. (b)	43. (a)	44. (a)	45. (b)
46. (c)	47. (c)	48. (c)	49. (d)	50. (c)

PAPER—II

1. (b)	2. (b)	3. (a)	4. (d)	5. (a)
6. (a)	7. (b)	8. (a)	9. (b)	10. (b)
11. (a)	12. (b)	13. (d)	14. (a)	15. (d)
16. (a)	17. (a)	18. (b)	19. (b)	20. (a)
21. (a)	22. (d)	23. (d)	24. (d)	25. (d)
26. (d)	27. (d)	28. (d)	29. (a)	30. (c)
31. (b)	32. (b)	33. (a)	34. (b)	35. (d)
36. (c)	37. (c)	38. (c)	39. (b)	40. (b)
41. (a)	42. (b)	43. (a)	44. (b)	45. (a)
46. (b)	47. (a)	48. (b)	49. (a)	50. (a)

PAPER—III

1. (c)	2. (a)	3. (a)	4. (b)	5. (a)
6. (b)	7. (c)	8. (a)	9. (d)	10. (b)
11. (b)	12. (d)	13. (d)	14. (b)	15. (a)
16. (a)	17. (c)	18. (b)	19. (b)	20. (b)
21. (b)	22. (d)	23. (d)	24. (c)	25. (a)
26. (d)	27. (d)	28. (d)	29. (b)	30. (c)
31. (b)	32. (b)	33. (d)	34. (d)	35. (c)
36. (c)	37. (b)	38. (b)	39. (d)	40. (a)
41. (c)	42. (a)	43. (a)	44. (d)	45. (c)
46. (b)	47. (a)	48. (c)	49. (b)	50. (b)

MOCK TEST–4
PAPER–I

1. Dewry defines education as a
(a) theoretical need
(b) social need
(c) personal need
(d) psychological need

2. All of the following statements about a teacher are correct except the one.

(a) A teacher changes his/her attitudes and behaviour according to the need of the society
(b) A teacher is a friend, guide and philosopher
(c) A teacher distinguishes between students
(d) A teacher is the leader in the class

3. A person cannot be an effective teacher if he
(a) teaches moral values
(b) is a strict disciplinarian
(c) knows his subject well
(d) has no interest in teaching

4. The most important signal factor in underlying the success of a teacher is
(a) organisational ability
(b) scholarship
(c) communicative ability
(d) personality and his ability to relate to the class and to the pupils

5. If you are irritated and show rashness because of the inadequate behaviour of another teachers, what do you think about your own behaviour?
(a) Your behaviour is also a sign of maladjustment and so try to control yourself when you are maltreated
(b) It is justified because behaviours are choice
(c) Your behaviour is not good because elders have the right to behave you in this way
(d) All of the above

6. The term 'SITE' stands for
(a) Satellite Instructional Teachers Education
(b) Satellite International Television Experiment
(c) Satellite Instructional Television Experiment
(d) Satellite Indian Television Experiment

7. Team teaching has the potential to develop
(a) highlighting the gaps in each other's teaching
(b) competitive spirit
(c) cooperation
(d) the habit of supplementing the teaching of each other

8. In any research one should
(a) not try out anything blindly but wait until a sudden flash appears in his mind
(b) know everything in the area without bothering to learn the details of any
(c) know more and more about less and less in certain specific sub area
(d) None of these

9. Determine the nature of the following definition:
'Poor' means having an annual income of ₹ 10,000.
(a) Lexical (b) Persuasive
(c) Precising (d) Stipulative

10. Which of the following methods implies the collection of information by way of investigators own examination without interviewing the respondents?
(a) Random probability sampling
(b) Observation
(c) Posting questionnaire
(d) Schedule method

11. Why do teachers use teaching aid?
(a) For students' attention
(b) To make teaching fun-filled
(c) To make students attentive
(d) To teach within understanding level of students

12. On which of the following statements there is consensus among educators?
(a) Disciplinary cases should be totally neglected in the class
(b) Disciplinary cases should be sent to the principal only when other means have failed

(c) Disciplinary cases should never be sent to principal's office
(d) None of these

13. Good evaluation of written material should not be based on
(a) Logical presentation
(b) Comprehension of subject
(c) Linguistic expression
(d) Ability to reproduce whatever is read

14. A good researcher lays his hands on
(a) any area as long as manpower and fundings are available in plenty
(b) a specific area and tries to understand in minute details
(c) several areas and tries to understand them at fundamental level
(d) None of these

15. The basis on which assumptions are formulated
(a) Universities
(b) Cultural background of the country
(c) Specific characteristics of the castes
(d) All of these

Read the following passage and answer the questions 16 to 20:

India is dedicated to free institutions and principles of democracy. We are striving to give everyone an opportunity and raise the standard of living for all. A democracy is one where people have the right to live their own lives and develop themselves in their own way under the guidance of their chosen representatives. If our political democracy is to succeed, it is essential that it be buttressed by steps towards economic equality or what has been referred to as the 'socialistic pattern of society'. Poverty and unemployment hold the biggest threat to the successful working of our democratic system.

16. One may infer from the paragraph that in a socialistic pattern of society
(a) to provide employment to all is the greatest problem
(b) the socialist party dominates
(c) all the inhabitants are treated equal
(d) None of these

17. The successful working of Indian democratic system is under a threat of
(a) economic inequality
(b) poverty
(c) unemployment
(d) All of the above

18. In a democratic system
(a) commodities are freely bought and sold
(b) government serves the people
(c) the government is run by the people themselves
(d) people do not have political freedom

19. The word buttressed in the paragraph means
(a) Supported (b) Dictating
(c) Declared (d) Guided

20. Democracy can fail if there is
(a) opportunity for development
(b) a weak government
(c) economic inequality
(d) unemployment

21. Aspect ratio of TV Screen is
(a) 4:3 (b) 3:4
(c) 2:3 (d) 2:4

22. Which of the following is not a product of learning?
(a) Knowledge (b) Attitudes
(c) Maturation (d) Concepts

23. The first paper for the human beings was developed by
(a) The Aryans
(b) The Babilonians
(c) The Chinese
(d) The Sumerians

24. Which sequence in turn will lead one to face the west direction from which one starts turning?
(a) Right, right, left, right, left right
(b) Left, right, left, left, right, right
(c) Right, right left, left, right, right
(d) Left, left, right, left, right, left

25. Fill in the blank with the most appropriate choice
_____ is the supreme medium to express yesterday, today and tomorrow with its own unique language.
(a) Television (b) Cinema
(c) Radio (d) Newspaper

26. In which language the newspapers have highest circulation?
(a) Tamil (b) English
(c) Bengali (d) Hindi

27. Amit is the son of Rahul. Sarika, Rahul's sister has a son Sonu and a daughter Rita. Raja is the maternal uncle of Sonu. How is Rita related to Raja.
(a) Aunt (b) Sister
(c) Daughter (d) Niece

28. **Statements:** A man must be wise to be a good wrangler. Good wrangler's are all talkative and boring.

Conclusions:
I. All the wise persons are boring.
II. All the wise persons are good wranglers.

Choose the correct option.
(a) Only conclusion I follows
(b) Only conclusion II follows
(c) Both I and II follow
(d) None of these

29. What is the number that comes next in the sequence?
2, 5, 9, 19, 37, ...
(a) 74 (b) 75
(c) 76 (d) 78

30. Match List I with List II and select the correct answer using the codes given below:

List I	List II
A. Pandit Jasraj	(i) Hindustani vocalist
B. Kishan Maharaj	(ii) Sitar
C. Ravi Shankar	(iii) Tabla
D. Udai Shankar	(iv) Dance

Codes:	A	B	C	D
(a)	(i)	(ii)	(iii)	(iv)
(b)	(i)	(iii)	(iv)	(ii)
(c)	(i)	(iii)	(ii)	(iv)
(d)	(iii)	(ii)	(i)	(iv)

31. Who developed the ability to speak?
(a) Aryans (b) Neanderthal
(c) Cro-Magnon (d) Dravidians

32. In what way does communication in small group differ from that in the large group?
(a) Large group communication provides better feedback
(b) Small group provides far more interaction among the participants
(c) Interaction in small group is more restrictive
(d) Small group takes less time to convey the message

33. What is the main aim and objective of provision for feedback in communication system?
(a) Understand more about the content
(b) To make communication better by adjusting at both ends of Encoder and Decoder
(c) Identify the defect of communication
(d) Make necessary modification in communication system

34. Communications bandwidth that has the highest capacity and is used by microwave, cable and fibre optics lines is known as

(a) Carrier wave (b) Hyper-link
(c) Broadband (d) Bus width

35. In a certain code, CLOCK is written as KCOLC. How would STEPS be written in that code?
(a) SPETS (b) SPEST
(c) SPSET (d) SEPTS

36. Which one of the following is not an argument?
(a) Ram is not at home, so he must have gone to town
(b) Ram insulted me so I punched him in the nose
(c) If today is Tuesday, tomorrow will be Wednesday
(d) Since today is Tuesday, tomorrow will be Wednesday.

Direction: (37-41) Study the following pie chart and answer the questions based on it. Following pie chart represents the investment done by Timas Finance Ltd. in the various sectors. (All investments are in ₹ crores)

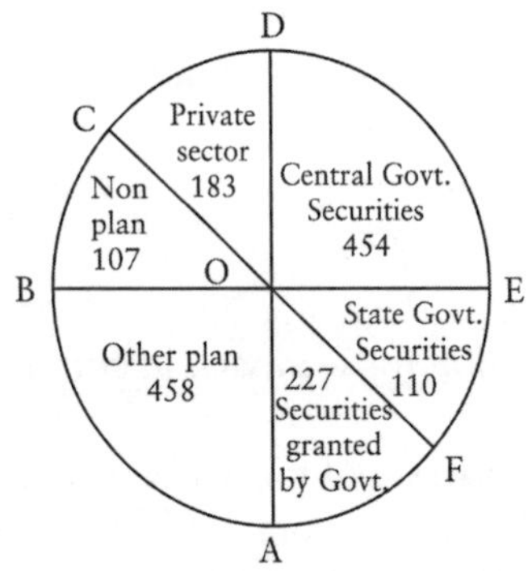

37. The percentage or gross investment in state government securities is nearly
(a) 7.1% (b) 9.2%
(c) 8.6% (d) 7.8%

38. The investment in plan and non-plan sector together is more or less than the investment in government securities (Central and State) by
(a) less, 106 crores (b) more, 4 crores
(c) more, 1 crores (d) more, 111 crores

39. The magnitude of ∠AOC is nearly
(a) 132° (b) 123°
(c) 126° (d) 115°

40. The ratio of area of the circle above ∠COF to the area of the circle below it is about
(a) 1 (b) 0.92
(c) 0.94 (d) 0.96

41. The investment in private sector is nearly what percent higher than the investment in State Government Security?
(a) 44% (b) 66%
(c) 54% (d) 46%

42. How many numbers between 100 and 300 begin or end with 2?
(a) 120 (b) 110
(c) 100 (d) 180

43. Which of the following operating system is used on mobile phones?
(a) Windows XP
(b) Windows Vista
(c) Android
(d) All of the above

44. Structure of logical argument is based on
(a) Linguistic expression
(b) Material truth
(c) Formal validity
(d) Aptness of examples

45. HTML is used to create
(a) machine language program
(b) high level program
(c) web page
(d) web server

46. Which of the following pollutants affects the respiratory tract in humans?
(a) Aerosols
(b) Sulphur dioxide

(c) Nitric oxide
(d) Carbon monoxide

47. Which of the following sources of energy has the maximum potential in India?
(a) Wind energy
(b) Solar energy
(c) Ocean thermal energy
(d) Tidal energy

48. In a deductive argument conclusion is
(a) Additional to the premises
(b) Entailed by the premises
(c) Summing up of the premises
(d) Not necessarily based on premises

49. What is the range of the numbers which can be stored in an eight bit register?
(a) –127 to +128 (b) –127 to +127
(c) –128 to +128 (d) –128 to +127

50. Universal Product Code (UPC), a pattern of bars printed on merchandise can be read by
(a) Product Code Reader
(b) Bar Code Reader
(c) Code Reader
(d) Card Reader

PAPER–II

1. Bioparks are conceived, developed and managed with a goal of conservation of biodiversity through,
(i) development of educational and scientific activities.
(ii) promoting silviculture and monoculture.
(iii) promoting local community welfare without harming the natural habitat.

Choose the correct answer from the codes:

Codes:
(a) (i) and (ii) (b) (ii) and (iii)
(c) (i) and (iii) (d) (i), (ii) and (iii)

2. The method which can be used for the softening of water having high calcium, high magnesium-carbonate hardness and some noncarbonate hardness
(a) single-stage line process.
(b) excess lime process.
(c) single stage lime-soda ash process.
(d) excess lime-soda ash process.

3. Which one of the following pairs is correctly matched?

(a)	Specification for environmental management system	ISO 14001
(b)	Environmental performance evaluation	ISO 14040
(c)	Guidelines for environmental auditing	ISO 14000
(d)	Environmental labels and declaration	ISO 14004

4. Which of the following will lead to reduction in greenhouse gases in atmosphere?
(a) Increased chemical weathering of rocks.
(b) Volcanic eruption
(c) Lowering of mean sea level
(d) An increase in melting of glacial ice

5. Match each water contaminant in Column I with its preferred method of removal in Column II.

Column I
A. Mn^{2+}
B. Ca^{2+} and HCO_3^-
C. Trihalomethane
D. Mg^{2+}

Column II
(i) Activated Carbon
(ii) Raise pH by addition of Na_2CO_3
(iii) Addition of lime
(iv) Oxidation

Codes:	A	B	C	D
(a)	(iv)	(iii)	(i)	(ii)
(b)	(iii)	(ii)	(iv)	(i)

(c)	(ii)	(iv)	(iii)	(i)
(d)	(i)	(ii)	(iv)	(iii)

6. **Assertion (A):** When energy is transferred between trophic levels, the successive level in the pathway have lesser available energy compared to the preceding level.
   Reason (R): Whenever energy is transformed, there is loss of energy through the release of heat.
   (a) Both (A) and (R) are true and (R) is the correct explanation.
   (b) Both (A) and (R) are true and (R) is not the correct explanation.
   (c) (A) is true and (R) is false.
   (d) (A) is false and (R) is true.

7. Match the following:
   Column I
   A. Nekton
   B. Neuston
   C. Benthos
   D. Plankton
   Column II
   (i) Associated with surface film water.
   (ii) Found at the bottom of an aquatic ecosystem.
   (iii) Active swimmer, against water current.
   (iv) Incapable of independent movement.

   Choose the correct answer from the Codes:

Codes:	A	B	C	D
(a)	(i)	(iii)	(iv)	(ii)
(b)	(ii)	(iv)	(i)	(iii)
(c)	(iii)	(i)	(ii)	(iv)
(d)	(iv)	(ii)	(iii)	(i)

8. Which of the following is not a characteristic feature of community?
   (a) Populations of different species occupying a particular place.
   (b) Complex interacting network of plants, animals and microbes.
   (c) Different species interacting with one another and with their environment of matter and energy.
   (d) Groups of interacting individuals of different species.

9. Gasification is
   (a) the high temperature (~ 750 – 850°C) conversion of solid, carbonaceous fuel into flammable gas mixtures.
   (b) the high temperature (~ 750 – 850°C) conversion of solid, carbonaceous fuel into liquid.
   (c) the low temperature (~ 250 – 350°C) conversion of solid, carbonaceous fuel into flammable gas mixture.
   (d) the low temperature (~ 250 – 350°C) conversion of solid, carbonaceous fuel into liquid.

10. The band labelled as UV-C which is lethal to micro-organisms is
    (a) 0.29 – 0.32 μm (b) 0.2 – 0.29 μm
    (c) 0.17 – 0.2 μm (d) 0.07 – 0.21 μm

11. If ap = specified value of peak acceleration, N = mean rate of occurrence of earthquake per year, t_{ep} = time interval of consideration (exposure period) and F_{ap} = probability that an observed acceleration is less than or equal to ap, then the cumulative probability distribution of peak acceleration for epoch—dependent seismic hazard map is given by which formula?
    (a) $F_{max}\ t_{ep} = \exp\{-Nt(1\ F_{ap})\}$
    (b) $F_{max} = \exp\{-Nt(1 - F_{ap})\}$. tep
    (c) $F_{max}\ t_{ep} = \exp\{-t(1 - F_{ap})^N\}$
    (d) All of the above

12. According to Goldieh the decreasing order of stability of following minerals of igneous rocks towards weathering is
    (a) Muscovite > Quartz > Potash feldspar > Biotite
    (b) Biotite > Potash feldspar > Muscovite > Quartz

(c) Quartz > Muscovite > Potash feldspar > Biotite
(d) Potash feldspar > Quartz > Muscovite > Biotite

13. Raunkiaer's normal biological spectrum for phanerogamic flora of the world exhibits one of the following sequence of occurrence (%) of different life forms.
(a) Phanerophytes, Hemicryptophytes, Therophytes, Cryptophytes, Chaemophytes.
(b) Phanerophytes, Hemicryptophytes, Therophytes, Chaemophytes, Cryptophytes.
(c) Phanerophytes, Hemicryptophytes, Cryptophytes, Chaemophytes, Therophytes.
(d) Phanerophytes, Chaemophytes, Hemicryptophytes, Cryptophytes, Therophytes.

14. Given below are two statements, one labelled as Assertion (A) and the other labelled as Reason (R).
Assertion (A): Indirect impacts are more difficult to measure, but can ultimately be more important.
Reason (R): In areas where wildlife is plentiful, such as Africa, new roads often lead to the rapid depletion of animals.
Choose the correct answer.
Codes:
(a) Both (A) and (R) are true and (R) is the correct explanation.
(b) Both (A) and (R) are true, but (R) is not the correct explanation.
(c) (A) is true, but (R) is false.
(d) (A) is false, but (R) is true.

15. Given below are two statements, one labelled as Assertion (A) and the other labelled as Reason (R).
Assertion (A): Increasing temperature in the environment influences gonadal growth in fish.
Reason (R): Increase in day length causes increase in environmental temperature in summer.
Choose the correct codes:
Codes:
(a) Both (A) and (R) are true, and (R) is the correct explanation of (A).
(b) Both (A) and (R) are true, but (R) is not the correct explanation of (A).
(c) (A) is true, and (R) is wrong.
(d) (A) and (R) are wrong.

16. Which one of the following is not a random sampling method?
(a) Stratified Sampling
(b) Cluster Sampling
(c) Systematic Sampling
(d) Judgement Sampling

17. Which of the following is correct about attribute data in Geographic Information System?
(a) Attributes are pieces of data that are connected or related to the points, lines or polygons mapped in the GIS.
(b) Attribute data can be analysed to determine patterns of importance.
(c) Attribute data is entered directly into a database where it is associated with element data.
(d) All of the above.

18. The net primary productivity of an ecosystem is
(a) the gross primary productivity minus plant respiration
(b) the primary productivity at herbivore level
(c) the primary productivity at consumer level
(d) the productivity at top consumer level minus respiration at all levels

19. The sequence of events that occur during primary succession is as follows:

(a) Nudation – Colonisation – Ecesis – Aggregation
(b) Aggregation – Colonization – Ecesis – Nudation
(c) Ecesis – Nudation – Aggregation – Colonization
(d) Nudation – Ecesis – Colonization – Aggregation

20. For elevations less than few hundred metres, if the wind speeds are u_1 and u_2 at elevations z_1 and z_2 respectively, the following equation holds $\left(\frac{u_1}{u_2}\right) = \left(\frac{z_1}{z_2}\right)^p$.
The value of the exponent p is
(a) < 0.6 (b) = 1
(c) > 0.6 (d) negative

21. What are the steps necessary for sustainable management of renewable resources?
(a) Avoiding over-exploitation and pollution of biotic systems.
(b) Strengthening the resource base and augmenting regenerability of biotic systems.
(c) Use of alternative resources.
(d) All of these.

22. When one species limits access of another species to a resource regardless of whether the resource is abundant or scarce, it is called
(a) interspecific competition
(b) intraspecific competition
(c) interference competition
(d) exploitative competition

23. Fuel cells are devices that generate electricity by converting the energy released by
(a) electrochemical reactions without going through combustion process.
(b) biochemical reactions without going through combustion process.
(c) electrochemical reactions involving combustion process
(d) biochemical reactions involving combustion process

24. Identify the correct sequence of stages of obtaining Environmental clearance for new projects
(a) Appraisal, Screening, Scoping, Public Consultation
(b) Screening, Public Consultation, Scoping, Appraisal
(c) Screening, Appraisal, Scoping, Public Consultation
(d) Screening, Scoping, Public Consultation, Appraisal

25. The process of invasion is completed through the following stages:
(a) Migration and establishment of species in bare area
(b) Migration, ecesis and aggregation
(c) Ecesis and aggregation
(d) Migration, aggregation and settlement of species

26. Gases emitted from municipal landfill sites include
(a) SO_2 and CH_4
(b) NH_4, CO, SO_2, CH_4
(c) NH_4, H_2S, CO
(d) CH_4, H_2S, CO_2, NH_4

27. Across the boundaries of a closed thermodynamical system
(a) matter flows but the energy doesn't.
(b) energy flows but the matter doesn't.
(c) both energy and matter flow.
(d) both energy and matter do not flow.

28. Match List I and List II. Identify the correct answers using the codes given below the lists:

List I	List II
A. Noamundi Mines	(i) Gold ore
B. Khetri Mines	(ii) Pb-Zn ore
C. Zawar Mines	(iii) Iron ore
D. Kolar Mines	(iv) Copper ore

Codes:	A	B	C	D
(a)	(ii)	(iv)	(i)	(iii)
(b)	(i)	(iii)	(ii)	(iv)
(c)	(iii)	(iv)	(ii)	(i)
(d)	(iv)	(iii)	(i)	(ii)

29. **Assertion (A):** Impact Assessment enables the planners and decision-makers to think carefully about the project proposals.
Reason (R): Impact Assessment can help in ensuring that planners and decision-makers are more accountable for their actions.
Codes:
(a) Both (A) and (R) are true and (R) is the correct explanation of (A).
(b) Both (A) and (R) are true, but (R) is not the correct explanation of (A).
(c) (A) is true, but (R) is false.
(d) (A) is false, but (R) is true.

30. In Gaussian dispersion model, the effective stack height is taken as sum of physical stack height and the plume rise ΔH. The plume rise varies with stack velocity V_S in the following manner:
(a) $\Delta H \propto V_S$ (b) $\Delta H \propto V_S^2$
(c) $\Delta H \propto V_S^{-1}$ (d) $\Delta H \propto V_S^{3/2}$

31. In order of increasing energy content
(a) Lignite, Peat, Anthracite, Bituminous coal
(b) Peat, Lignite, Anthracite, Bituminous coal
(c) Anthracite, Lignite, Bituminous coal, Peat
(d) Bituminous coal, Anthracite, Lignite, Peat

32. In a river with symmetric channel
(a) Maximum velocity is at the bottom
(b) Minimum velocity is at the surface
(c) Maximum velocity is at the borders
(d) Maximum velocity is at 0.7 of the depth

33. Which of the transmutation does not take place by α-decay?
(a) $^{238}U_{92} \longrightarrow {}^{234}Th^{90}$
(b) $^{213}Bi_{83} \longrightarrow {}^{213}Po_{84}$
(c) $^{226}Ra_{88} \longrightarrow {}^{222}Rn_{86}$
(d) $^{227}Ac_{89} \longrightarrow {}^{223}Fr_{87}$

34. Formation of marble can be represented by
(a) $CaSiO_3 \rightleftharpoons Ca^{+2} + SiO_3^{-2}$
(b) $CaO + CO_2 \rightleftharpoons CaCO_3$
(c) $CaCO_3 \rightleftharpoons CaO + CO_2$
(d) $CaCO_3 + SiO_2 \rightleftharpoons CaSiO_3 + CO_2$

35. Species diversity is generally higher in ecosystem experiencing:
(a) No disturbance
(b) Moderate disturbance
(c) High disturbance
(d) Drastic disturbance

36. When industry with 'Red' category is to be established, it is necessary to have public hearing or inquiry under the procedure called as:
(a) Environmental Health Hazard (EHH)
(b) Environmental Litigation (EL)
(c) Environmental Management System (EMS)
(d) Environmental Impact Assessment (EIA)

37. Elements in sea water present in order of increasing residence time:
(a) Na > Cl > Mg > Ca > K > Fe > P
(b) Cl > Na > Mg > Ca > K > P > Fe
(c) Cl > Mg > Ca > Na > K > Fe > P
(d) Mg > Ca > Cl > Na > K > P > Fe

38. Which of the following phenomena can be explained by the wave model of light, but not by the particle model?

(a) Pressure is exerted by a light beam
(b) All of the energy emitted by an atom, as light can later be completely transferred to another atom
(c) A light beam changes direction when passing from one medium to another
(d) Light can reach the geometrical shadow of an obstacle in its path

39. Which one of the following is the correct food chain?
(a) Algae → Daphnia → Dragon Fly Nymph → Newt → Grass Snake
(b) Daphnia → Dragon Fly Nymph → Newt → Algae → Grass Snake
(c) Grass Snake → Newt → Dragon Fly Nymph → Daphnia → Algae
(d) Newt → Grass Snake → Dragon Fly Nymph → Algae → Daphnia

40. Choose right expansion of CITES of 1975:
(a) Centre for International Training in Endangered Species of Wild Fauna and Flora
(b) Committee on International Trade and Environment and Sustainable Development
(c) Council of Indian Trade and Environmental Survey of Wild Fauna and Flora
(d) Convention on International Trade in Endangered Species of Wild Fauna and Flora

41. In the analysis of 15 water samples, Ca and Mg gave a correlation of +0.95. It means:
(a) Ca came from soil and Mg came from biota
(b) Ca and Mg both came from the same type of water
(c) Ca and Mg are both cogenetic
(d) Ca and Mg came from different sources.

42. Which two of the following statements regarding ISO 14000 series of standards are true? Answer choosing the codes given below:
(i) ISO 14000 standards are based on a principle assumption that better environmental management will lead to better environmental performance.
(ii) ISO 14000 standards are regulatory standards developed by ISO.
(iii) ISO 14000 standards are market driven and therefore are based on voluntary involvement of all interests in the market place.
(iv) The adoption of ISO 14000 is a one time commitment.

Codes:
(a) (i) and (ii) (b) (ii) and (iii)
(c) (i) and (iii) (d) (iii) and (iv)

43. Wind rose of a given location represents:
(a) Frequency distribution of wind speeds in the form of a histogram.
(b) Frequency distribution of wind speeds in percentage terms in the form of a π chart.
(c) Frequency distribution of wind speed associated with a cyclose.
(d) Frequency distribution of wind speed and direction in polar coordinates.

44. DDT is harmful from the ecological point of view mainly because it undergoes:
(a) Biotransformation
(b) Bioaccumulation
(c) Biomagnification
(d) Biodegradation

45. Which one of the following statement is true of braided stream?
(a) Width of channel is less than its depth
(b) Width and depth of a channel are equal
(c) Width of channel is greater than the depth
(d) Width and depth of a channel are unrelated

46. The drinking water contaminated with E.Coli is not safe even after ordinary filtration, but if subjected to RO treatment it is much safe, because:
   (a) RO treatment kills bacteria
   (b) RO treatment generates that kills bacteria
   (c) There is a filtration at molecular level in RO system
   (d) RO treatment generate chlorine gas that kills bacteria

47. The faecal indicator bacteria is:
   (a) *Staphylococeus aureus*
   (b) *Streptococeus faecalis*
   (c) *Escherichia coli*
   (d) *Salmonella typhi*

48. Match the List I and List II and select the correct answer using the codes given below:

   List I (Power generation capacity)
   A. 500 MW and more
   B. 200/210 MW and above but less than 500 MW
   C. less than 200/210 MW
   D. steam generation capacity less than 8.5 MT

   List II (Stack height (m))
   (i) $H = 14 (Q)^{0.3}$ (ii) 275
   (iii) 220 (iv) 9

   Note: H = Physical stack height in metres
   Q = Emission rate of SO_2 in kg/hr.

Codes:	A	B	C	D
(a)	(i)	(ii)	(iii)	(iv)
(b)	(ii)	(iii)	(i)	(iv)
(c)	(iii)	(iv)	(ii)	(i)
(d)	(iv)	(i)	(ii)	(iii)

49. When a low lander man is transferred to high altitudes, the oxygen consumption will:
   (a) not decrease
   (b) remain the same
   (c) reduce mytochondrial oxygen tension
   (d) Impair oxidative metabolism

50. Landfill sites can be permitted in:
   (a) wetlands
   (b) flood plains
   (c) habitats of endangered species and recharge zones for local drinking water supplies
   (d) abandoned mines with impermeable barrier at the bottom with a leachate recycling system

PAPER–III

1. The critical difference between today's global warming and Earth's previous climate changes is that
   (a) human-made chemicals such as CFCs do not influence global warming.
   (b) previous changes in climate were dramatic but very short-lived.
   (c) scientists can now save all species from extinction by genetic engineering,
   (d) global warming may occur much more rapidly than it did during previous climate changes.

2. Air near Earth's surface tends to be
   (a) warmer and wetter; then it rises, expanding and cooling
   (b) warmer and drier; then it rises, condensing and gathering moisture
   (c) cooler and wetter; then it rises, is warmed by the sun, and sinks again
   (d) cooler and drier; it rises when it is displaced by sinking warm air

3. Match the List I and List II and select the correct answer from the codes given below the lists:

   List I
   A. Parasitism B. Predation
   C. Amensalism D. Symbiosis

List II

1. An association between two populations in which one inhibits the other while remaining unaffected itself
2. An association between two organisms in which one acquires food and shelter at the expense of the other
3. An association between two interdependent organisms who do not harm each other
4. Interaction of two or more species, of the eaters and being eaten

Codes:	A	B	C	D
(a)	2	4	1	3
(b)	2	3	4	1
(c)	3	4	2	1
(d)	4	3	1	2

4. Which of the following is the characteristics of heterosphere?
   (a) Molecular mass of the atmosphere remains constant
   (b) The molecular mass of the gaseous mixture decreases gradually in this region
   (c) This region extends upto a height of 100 km
   (d) None of the above.

5. In the scheme of life, soil is an essential resource of life as it plays the following roles:
   1. It is the medium for growth of food and energy for the animal world
   2. It is a reservoir of carbon
   3. It is a natural reservoir for huge amounts of water
   4. It provides oxygen to the biotic community

   Select the correct answer from the codes given below:

   Codes:

   (a) 1, 2 and 3 (b) 2, 3 and 4
   (c) 1, 3 and 4 (d) 1, 2 and 4

6. The organic components of soil are significant because
   1. they give its characteristics properties and its value as the abode of life
   2. it is heterogenous mixture of products resulting from microbial and chemical transformation of organic material
   3. it imparts the soil most of the life sustaining attributes
   4. they can cause decrease in the rate of flocculation

   Select the correct answer from the codes given below:

   Codes:

   (a) 1, 2 and 3 (b) 2, 3 and 4
   (c) 1, 3 and 4 (d) all are correct

7. **Assertion (A):** NO_2 plays a significant role in the formation of photochemical smog.
   Reason (R): In presence of sunlight NO_2 reacts with hydrocarbons to produce photochemical pollutants.

   Codes:

   (a) Both (A) and (R) are true and (R) is the correct explanation of (A).
   (b) Both (A) and (R) are true but (R) is not a correct explanation of (A).
   (c) (A) is true, but (R) is false.
   (d) (A) is false, but (R) is true.

8. Which of the following statements is incorrect?
   (a) Centrifugation is a sedimentation technique, wherein individual constituents are separated by an applied centrifugal force
   (b) Centrifugal force during centrifugation is opposed by frictional drag
   (c) For a non-spherical particle, sedimentation depends not only on its mass but also on its size and shape
   (d) None of the above.

9. The molecules can be resolved on the basis of their distribution between a gas

and either a liquid or solid by separation method known as
(a) gas chromatography
(b) filtration
(c) centrifugation
(d) HPLC

10. Consider the following statements regarding the biochemical aspects of mercury
 1. Major sources of mercury are mining, industrial effluents and pesticides.
 2. Chronic mercury poisoning may result from occupational inhalation of mercury vapours, dusts and volatile mercurials.
 3. Mercury poisoning causes progressive weakening of muscles, loss of vision, impairment of the cerebra functions, eventual paralysis.

 Of these statements
 (a) Only 3 is correct
 (b) 1 and 2 are correct
 (c) 2 and 3 are correct
 (d) All are correct

11. Match the List I and List II and select the correct answer from the codes given below the lists:

 List I

 A. Parasitism B. Predation
 C. Amensalism D. Symbiosis

 List II

 (i) An association between two populations in which one inhibits the other while remaining unaffected itself
 (ii) An association between two organisms in which one acquires food and shelter at the expense of the other
 (iii) An association between two interdependent organisms who do not harm each other
 (iv) Interaction of two or more species of the eaters and being eaten

Codes:	**A**	**B**	**C**	**D**
(a)	(ii)	(iv)	(i)	(iii)
(b)	(ii)	(iii)	(iv)	(i)
(c)	(iii)	(iv)	(ii)	(i)
(d)	(iv)	(iii)	(i)	(ii)

12. Which of the following is the correct sequence of the food chain?
 (a) grass → insect → bird → snake
 (b) grass → snake → insect → deer
 (c) bacteria → grass → deer → buffalo
 (d) grass → wolf → deer → buffalo

13. Consider the following statements regarding airborne allergies
 1. Typical airborne allergic symptoms include sneezing, runny nose, and nasal congestion
 2. Airborne pollens can also cause skin allergies
 3. Pollen gains can remain airborne for hundreds of miles.

 Of these statements
 (a) Only 3 is correct
 (b) 1 and 2 are correct
 (c) 2 and 3 are correct
 (d) All are correct

14. Which of the following statements regarding biofertilizers is incorrect?
 (a) The use of biofertilizers is environment friendly
 (b) Azolla is the main source of algal biofertilizer in south and southeast Asia
 (c) BGA inoculation with composite cultures of algal genera have been found more effective
 (d) None of the above

15. A field is abandoned, and an invasive plant that can live in nutrient-poor soil into the field. If the land is later cleared of this invasive species and it is discovered that the soil has an abundance of nitrogen compounds, what conclusion can best be made?

(a) The plants used up all of the phosphorus and potassium and left the nitrogen behind
(b) Primary succession always produces an abundance of nitrogen
(c) Bacteria in soil and in root nodules converted free nitrogen
(d) The plants were able to produce nitrogen in their leaves

16. When it is no longer profitable to continue fishing an affected species, ___ is said to have occurred.
(a) economic depletion
(b) commercial depletion
(c) ecological depletion
(d) political depletion

17. The magnitude of solar radiation reaching the surface of the earth depends on
(a) time of the year
(b) time of the day
(c) orientation of land surface with respect to sun
(d) All of the above

18. Match the List I and List II and select the correct answer from the codes given below the lists:

List I

A. Flood B. Droughts
C. Earthquake D. Volcano

List II

(i) Lack of rainfall of sufficient duration
(ii) Tremors produced by the passage of vibratory waves through the rocks of the earth
(iii) A vent through which molted substances comes out
(iv) Excess rain and uneven distribution of water

Codes:	A	B	C	D
(a)	(iv)	(i)	(ii)	(iii)
(b)	(ii)	(iii)	(iv)	(i)
(c)	(iii)	(iv)	(ii)	(i)
(d)	(iv)	(iii)	(i)	(ii)

19. Which of the following is characteristics of producers?
(a) They stored chemical energy in the food
(b) They produce oxygen to be utilized the consumers
(c) They are at the bottom of the food chain
(d) All of the above.

20. The precipitation reaching the ground distribute in different ways as
1. evaporate and reach the atmosphere
2. infiltrate the soil
3. detained in catchment area
4. become a form of run-off

Select the correct answer from the codes given below:

Codes:

(a) 1, 2 and 3
(b) 2, 3 and 4
(c) 1, 3 and 4
(d) 1, 2, 3 and 4 are correct.

21. Metal oxides constitute a major class of inorganic particulate pollutants because
(a) they easily give up their valence electrons
(b) they are formed whenever fuels containing metals are burned
(c) their vapours are injurious to health
(d) None of the above

22. Any part of the earth's crust in which plants root is the definition of
(a) climate (b) soil
(c) atmosphere (d) water

23. Herbivores are also known as
(a) tertiary consumer
(b) primary consumer
(c) secondary consumer
(d) autotrophs

24. Alluvial soils are found mostly in which area of the country?
   (a) Indo-gangetic plains
   (b) Deccan plateau
   (c) North-East Himalayas
   (d) Western Ghats

25. The texture of an igneous rock
   (a) determines the colour of the rock
   (b) refers to the shape of the rock body
   (c) is controlled by the chemistry of megma
   (d) records the rock's cooling history

26. Water vapours present in unit volume is known as
   (a) relative humidity
   (b) absolute humidity
   (c) Both (a) and (b)
   (d) None of these

27. Which one of the following statement is not correct?
   (a) Clouds are the most variable factor influencing the earth's radiation budget
   (b) Clouds have moderate influence on temperature
   (c) Cloudy weather produces lower daily maximum
   (d) Cloudy weather produces higher night minimum

28. ______ zone in atmosphere are common in winter
   (a) Low pressure (b) High pressure
   (c) Medium pressure (d) None of these

29. Which of the following pairs with respect to soil particles and their size is correctly matched?
   (a) Silt 0.01 mm
   (b) Gravel 5.0 mm
   (c) Clay 2.0 mm
   (d) Coarse sand 0.2 mm

30. The atmospheric pressure in aeroplanes can be measured by
   (a) aneroid barometer
   (b) anemometer
   (c) manometer
   (d) barometer

31. Floating generators are used in the sea to harness
   (a) tidal energy
   (b) wave energy
   (c) hydel energy
   (d) energy from OTEC power plant

32. **Assertion (A):** Geothermometers are plant, animal or mineral indicators.
   Reason (R): Whose indicators changes in rock temperature.
   Codes:
   (a) Both (A) and (R) are true and (R) is the correct explanation of (A).
   (b) Both (A) and (R) are true, but (R) is not the correct explanation of (A).
   (c) (A) is true, but (R) is false.
   (d) (A) is false, but (R) is true.

33. Which of the following is the deficiency disease of cadmium?
   (a) Itai-itai
   (b) Tuberculosis
   (c) Brain cancer
   (d) None of the above

34. Automobile exhaust is the major source of carbon monoxide, it also produces in
   (a) photochemical reaction
   (b) depletion of ozone
   (c) reaction of acids
   (d) wild fires and fossil fuel burning

35. Hardness is commonly measured in term of
   (a) $CaSO_4$ equivalents
   (b) $CaCO_3$ equivalents
   (c) $MgSO_4$ equivalents
   (d) $MgCO_3$ equivalents

36. Ground level ozone is not emitted directly into the atmosphere, but is a secondary

pollutant produced (photochemically) by reaction between
(a) NO_2, HCs and sunlight
(b) NO_2, CO_2, and sunlight
(c) CO_2, HCs and sunlight
(d) H_2O, CO_2, SO_2, HCs and sunlight

37. Cd, Pb and Hg are nephrotoxic metals as they can harm of humans.
(a) lungs (b) liver
(c) kidney (d) neurons

38. Match the following:
List I (Pesticides)
A. Herbicides
B. Molluscicides
C. Nematicides
D. Virucides

List II (Used)
(i) Control of viruses
(ii) Control of weeds
(iii) Control of nematodes
(iv) Control of snails

Codes:	A	B	C	D
(a)	(iv)	(i)	(ii)	(iii)
(b)	(iv)	(iii)	(ii)	(i)
(c)	(ii)	(iii)	(i)	(iv)
(d)	(ii)	(iv)	(iii)	(i)

39. In heterotrophic succession, in the beginning
(a) values of R and equal to P
(b) values of R are greater than P
(c) values of R are less than P
(d) R and P behave in an unpredictable manner

40. What happens to the amount of available energy at each level of a food chain?
(a) The amount of available energy increases at each level
(b) The amount of available energy decreases at each level
(c) The amount of available energy remains the same at each level
(d) The amount of available energy changes depending upon number of organisms in the level

41. Physiogamy is the study of
(a) seasonal change in vegetation
(b) general appearance of vegetation
(c) effect of light on flowering of plants
(d) distribution of vegetation is relation of climate

42. Phenograms are used to study
(a) vegetative growth in plants
(b) events in life history of plants
(c) effects of light on vegetative growth in plant
(d) distribution of vegetation in relation to climate

43. Which one of the following sequence is correct in food chain?
(a) Fallen leaves → bacteria → insect larvae → birds
(b) Grasses → fox → rabbit
(c) Phytoplankton → zooplankton → fish
(d) Grasses → chameleon → insect → birds

44. Which one of the following statements is correct
(a) There is very high mixing of gases between troposphere and stratosphere
(b) In thermosphere there is steady decrease in temperature with the increase in height
(c) Temperature decrease with increasing height in troposphere
(d) The first layer of air mass above troposphere in stratosphere

45. Which one of the following types of soil is considered to be the best for plant's growth?
(a) Prism-like (b) Platy
(c) Spheroidal (d) Block-like

46. Among the following, which one has the highest porosity?
(a) Silt (b) Clay
(c) Gravel (d) Sand

47. CAM photosynthesis is found in
(a) blue-green algae
(b) succulent plant
(c) lichens
(d) submerged aquatic plant

48. Pyrology is the study of
(a) role of fire in ecology
(b) variation in species distribution in relation to ambient temperature
(c) distribution of animals in relation to temperature
(d) variation in species distribution in relation to ambient temperature

49. Which compound were used by Miller in experiment for obtaining amino acids and ot organic matter?
(a) Carbon dioxide
(b) Ammonia
(c) Methane and ammonia
(d) Methane, ammonia, water vapour and hydrogen

50. F H C Crick regarding origin of life has written which among the following books?
(a) Origin of life
(b) Life itself! Its origin and nature
(c) Origin of species
(d) Genera Planterum

ANSWERS SHEET

PAPER—I

1. (b)	2. (c)	3. (d)	4. (d)	5. (a)
6. (c)	7. (d)	8. (c)	9. (c)	10. (b)
11. (b)	12. (b)	13. (a)	14. (b)	15. (b)
16. (c)	17. (d)	18. (b)	19. (a)	20. (c)
21. (a)	22. (c)	23. (c)	24. (b)	25. (b)
26. (b)	27. (d)	28. (d)	29. (b)	30. (c)
31. (c)	32. (b)	33. (b)	34. (c)	35. (a)
36. (b)	37. (a)	38. (c)	39. (a)	40. (c)
41. (b)	42. (b)	43. (c)	44. (b)	45. (c)
46. (c)	47. (b)	48. (b)	49. (d)	50. (b)

PAPER—II

1. (b)	2. (b)	3. (a)	4. (d)	5. (a)
6. (a)	7. (b)	8. (a)	9. (b)	10. (b)
11. (a)	12. (b)	13. (d)	14. (a)	15. (d)
16. (a)	17. (a)	18. (b)	19. (b)	20. (a)
21. (a)	22. (d)	23. (d)	24. (d)	25. (d)
26. (d)	27. (d)	28. (d)	29. (a)	30. (c)
31. (b)	32. (b)	33. (a)	34. (b)	35. (d)
36. (c)	37. (c)	38. (c)	39. (b)	40. (b)
41. (a)	42. (b)	43. (a)	44. (b)	45. (a)
46. (b)	47. (a)	48. (b)	49. (a)	50. (a)

PAPER—III

1. (d)	2. (a)	3. (a)	4. (b)	5. (a)
6. (d)	7. (a)	8. (d)	9. (a)	10. (a)
11. (d)	12. (a)	13. (d)	14. (d)	15. (c)
16. (b)	17. (d)	18. (a)	19. (d)	20. (c)
21. (a)	22. (b)	23. (b)	24. (c)	25. (c)
26. (b)	27. (a)	28. (b)	29. (b)	30. (a)
31. (b)	32. (a)	33. (a)	34. (d)	35. (b)
36. (a)	37. (c)	38. (d)	39. (b)	40. (b)
41. (b)	42. (b)	43. (c)	44. (c)	45. (c)
46. (c)	47. (b)	48. (a)	49. (d)	50. (b)

MOCK TEST–5
PAPER–I

1. Which among the following gives more freedom to the learner to interact?
   (a) Small group discussion
   (b) Lectures by experts
   (c) Use of film
   (d) Viewing country-wide classroom program on TV
2. While designing communication strategy feed-forward studies are conducted by
   (a) Media (b) Audience
   (c) Communicator (d) Satellite
3. A theory is correct because
   (a) its derivations match with most observations
   (b) its advocate has written a big volume to establish it
   (c) it is supported by a large number of scholars
   (d) it has a large number of followers
4. Which of the following are true about the concepts?
   I. Concepts have different meanings in different contents.
   II. Concepts are the blocks from which theories are built.
   III. Concepts are ideas, abstractions, that do not have meaning in themselves.
   (a) Only II (b) I and III
   (c) I and II (d) All of these
5. The most sensible idea about teaching and research is that
   (a) they interfere with each other
   (b) they are two entirely different kinds of activities
   (c) they cannot go together
   (d) they are two sides of the same coin
6. Which of the following is quality of a teacher?
   (a) He should know the child psychology
   (b) He should evoke curiosity of the pupils by presenting the subject matter in an effective manner with clear explaining leading to better under-standing of the matter
   (c) He should be trained in various teaching methodologies
   (d) All of these
7. Which of the following is/are true about research?
   (i) Gives emphasis to the development of theories, principles and generalisation, which are very helpful in accurate prediction regarding the variable understudy.
   (ii) It is always directed towards the solution of a problem.
   (iii) It is always based upon empirical or observable evidences.
   (a) Both (i) and (ii)
   (b) Both (i) and (iii)
   (c) Both (ii) and (iii)
   (d) All of the above
8. Which of the following methods of teaching encourages the use of maximum senses?
   (a) Team teaching method
   (b) Problem-solving method
   (c) Laboratory method
   (d) Self-study method
9. A non-fictional literary composition that forms an independent part of a publication, as a newspaper or magazine is known as
   (a) Symposium (b) Paper
   (c) Article (d) None of these
10. Photo bleeding means
   (a) Photo placement
   (b) Photo cropping
   (c) Photo colour adjustment
   (d) Photo cutting

11. Attitudes, concepts, skills and knowledge are products of
(a) Explanation (b) Learning
(c) Research (d) Heredity

12. To study the relationship of family size with income a researcher classifies his population into different income slabs and then takes a random sample from each slab. Which technique of sampling does he adopt?
(a) Systematic Sampling
(b) Random Sampling
(c) Stratified Random Sampling
(d) Cluster Sampling

13. In business communication, the major obstacles arise because of the
(a) psychological barriers
(b) physical barriers
(c) organisational barriers
(d) mechanical barriers

14. The most important question that a researcher is interested to use statistical techniques in his problem then he has to see
(a) whether worthwhile inferences could be drawn
(b) whether the data could be quantified
(c) whether appropriate statistical techniques are available
(d) whether analysis of data would be possible

15. How can the objectivity of the research be enhanced?
(a) Through its validity
(b) Through its impartiality
(c) Through its reliability
(d) All of these

16. Which one of the following is not correct? A belief becomes a scientific truth when it
(a) can be replicated
(b) is established experimentally
(c) is arrived by logically
(d) is accepted by many people

17. **Statement:** All cars are ducks. All ducks are birds.
Conclusions:
(i) All birds are cars.
(ii) All cars are birds.
Choose the correct one.
Codes:
(a) Only conclusion (i) follows
(b) Only conclusion (ii) follows
(c) Both (i) and (ii) follow
(d) Neither (i) nor (ii) follows

18. Research can be conducted by a person who
(a) is a hard worker
(b) has studied research methodology
(c) holds a postgraduate degree
(d) possesses thinking and reasoning ability

19. Action-research is
(a) A longitudinal research
(b) An applied research
(c) A research carried out to solve immediate problems
(d) All of the above

Read the following passage and answer the questions 20 to 24:

The genesis of service tax emanates from the ongoing structural transformation of the Indian economy, whereby presently more than one-half of GDP originates from the services sector. Despite the growing presence of the services sector in the Indian economy it remained out of the tax net prior to 1994-95, leading to a steady deterioration in tax-GDP ratio. The service tax was introduced in 1994-95 on a select category of services at a low rate of five percent. While the service tax rate and the coverage of services being taxed have increased ever since, the combined tax-GDP ratio of the Centre and States, nevertheless, deteriorated from 16.4 percent in 1985-86 to 14.1 percent in 1999-2000. It may be noted that between 1990-91 and 1998-99, the share of industrial sector in GDP dropped by 6.4 percentage points whereas almost 64 percent of the tax revenue was generated by indirect taxes for which industrial sector continues to be the principal tax base. On the other hand, during the same period, the share of services sector in GDP has increased by 10 percentage points and this sector has still remained poorly taxed.

The rationale for service tax, therefore, lies not only in arresting the falling tax-GDP ratio but also in *ipso facto* improving allocative efficiency in the economy as well as promoting equity. Against this backdrop, the service tax needs to be designed taking into account the fact that (i) the share of services in GDP is expanding; (ii) failure to tax services distorts consumer choices and encourages spending on services at the expense of goods; (iii) untaxed service traders are unable to claim Value Added Tax (VAT) on service inputs, which encourages businesses to develop in-house services, creating further distortions; and (iv) most services that are likely to become taxable are positively correlated with expenditure of high-income households and, therefore, service tax improves equity.

In the Indian context, taxation of services assumes importance in the wake of the need for improving the revenue system, ensuring a measure of neutrality in taxation between goods and services and eventually helping to evolve an efficient system of domestic trade taxes, both at the Central and the State levels.

20. What, according to the passage, was the impact of exclusion of service tax till the first half of the last decade of the past century?
   (a) Service sector used to flourish exorbitantly
   (b) There was no impact as there was no service tax
   (c) There was a steady deterioration in the GDP
   (d) Tax-GDP ratio had steadily and gradually aggravated

21. Levying service tax is most likely to achieve which of the following?
   (i) Promoting equity.
   (ii) Check on reducing tax-GDP ratio.
   (iii) Enhancement in allocative efficiency.
   (a) Both (ii) and (iii)
   (b) Both (i) and (iii)
   (c) Both (i) and (ii)
   (d) All the three

22. The origin of service tax is attributed to
   (a) metamorphosis of our country's economy
   (b) increase in Gross Domestic Product (GDP)
   (c) existence of service sector
   (d) tax of the future

23. Which of the following factors helps service tax to improve fairness across different economic strata of society?
   (a) It improves revenue system
   (b) Taxable services are mostly those that are utilised by the rich
   (c) Untaxed service traders are prevented from claiming value added tax
   (d) Encouragement to in-house services is effected

24. Which of the following is most likely to provide neutrality to various economic activities?
   (a) Consistency in tax structure and revenue buoyancy
   (b) Increase in revenue buoyancy
   (c) Fairness in tax administration
   (d) Equity and efficiency in various activities

25. Which of the following is classified in the category of the developmental research?
(a) Descriptive research
(b) Philosophical research
(c) Action research
(d) All of the above

26. The education aims at the fullest realisation of all the potentialities of children. It implies that
I. it is necessary that their attitudes are helpful, encouraging and sympathctic.
II. teacher and parents must know what children are capable of and what potentialities they possess.
III. they should provide suitable opportunities and favourable environmental facilities which are conducive to the maximum growth of children.
Choose the correct one.
Codes:
(a) II and III (b) I and III
(c) I and II (d) All of them

27. How many times has the preamble of Indian constitution been amended so far?
(a) Once (b) Twice
(c) Thrice (d) Never

28. The relationship between earth, mountains and forests can be represented as

(a)  (b) 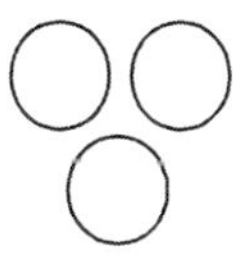

(c)  (d) 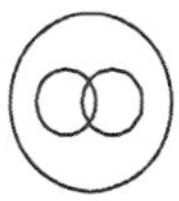

29. Central Fuel Research Institute is situated in
(a) Pune (b) Jadugoda
(c) Lucknow (d) Kolkata

30. The letters in the first set have certain relationship. On the basis of this relationship what is the right choice for the second set?
AST : BRU :: NQV : ?
(a) OPW (b) ORW
(c) MPU (d) MRW

31. The number of students in four classes A, B, C, D and their respective mean marks obtained by each of the class are given below:

	Class A	Class B	Class C	Class D
Number of students	10	40	30	20
Arithmetic mean	20	30	50	15

The combined mean of the marks of four classes together will be
(a) 15 (b) 32
(c) 50 (d) 20

32. Communication with oneself is known as
(a) Organisational communication
(b) Interpersonal communication
(c) Intrapersonal communication
(d) Grapevine communication

33. The number system which is not a positional notation system is
(a) Binary (b) Octal
(c) Roman (d) Decimal

34. Which of the following options will complete the series?
AZ, GT, MN, ?, YB.
(a) TS (b) KF
(c) RX (d) SH

35. If '367' means 'I am happy'; '748' means 'You are sad' and '469' means 'Happy and sad' in a given code, then which of the following represents 'and' in that code?

(a) 4 (b) 6
(c) 3 (d) 9

36. What is the excess 3 code?
(a) self-algebraic code
(b) cyclic complimenting code
(c) cyclic algebraic code
(d) self-complimenting code

37. Which of the following is not created by the Act of Parliament?
(a) Railway Board
(b) Atomic Energy Commission
(c) Backward Class Commission
(d) University Grants Commission

38. Which of the following is radioactive pollutant?
(a) Nickel (b) Iron
(c) Chlorine (d) Thorium

39. The first Indian experimental geostationary communication satellite was
(a) Skylab (b) Apple
(c) INSAT-1A (d) INSAT-1B

40. Which one of the following is a research tool?
(a) Diagram (b) Questionnaire
(c) Graph (d) Illustration

41. Which article of the constitution provides safeguards to Naga Customary and their social practices against any act of Parliament?
(a) Article 371 B (b) Article 371 A
(c) Article 263 (d) Article 371 C

42. **Statement:** Although the city was under kneedeep water for a week in this monsoon, there is no outbreak of any water borne disease.

Assumptions:
(i) Waterborne disease usually spreads in monsoon.
(ii) Water concentration at a place leads to waterborne disease.

Choose the correct option.
(a) Only assumption (i) is implicit
(b) Only assumption (ii) is implicit
(c) Both (i) and (ii) are implicit
(d) Neither (i) nor (ii) is implicit

43. Books and records are the primary sources of data in
(a) laboratory research
(b) historical research
(c) participatory research
(d) clinical research

44. The Kothari Commission's report was entitled on
(a) Learning to be adventure
(b) Education and National Development
(c) Education and socialisation in democracy
(d) Diversification of Education

45. What is the term used for a half byte?
(a) word (b) bit
(c) nibble (d) bug

46. C-band transponder in satellites uses the frequency range
(a) 12 GHz to 14 GHz
(b) 4 GHz to 6 GHz
(c) 2 GHz to 4 GHz
(d) None of these.

47. Which of the following water pollutants is the cause of sterility in human beings?
(a) Manganese (b) Mercury
(c) Arsenic (d) None of these

48. Controlled group condition is applied in
(a) Descriptive Research
(b) Survey Research
(c) Experimental Research
(d) Historical Research

49. Match List I with List II and select the correct answer using the codes given below.
List I (Institutes)
(A) Central Arid Zone Institute
(B) Space Application Centre

(C) Indian Institute of Public Administration
(D) Headquarters of Indian Science Congress

List II (Cities)

(i) Kolkata (ii) New Delhi
(iii) Ahmedabad (iv) Jodhpur

Codes:	A	B	C	D
(a)	(iv)	(iii)	(ii)	(i)
(b)	(iv)	(ii)	(i)	(iii)
(c)	(iii)	(i)	(ii)	(iv)
(d)	(i)	(ii)	(iv)	(iii)

The total CO_2 emissions from various sectors are 5 mmt. In the Pie Chart given below, the percentage contribution to CO_2 emissions from various sectors is indicated.

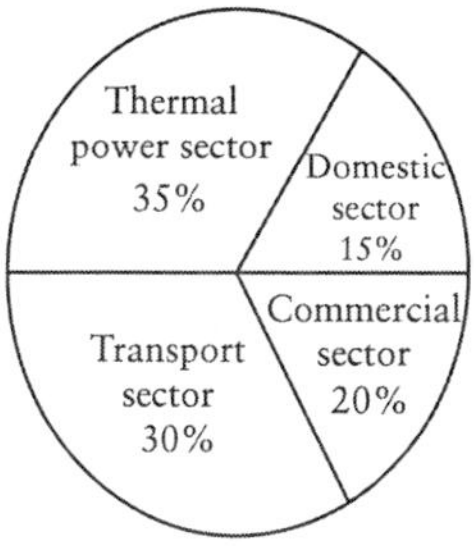

50. What is the absolute CO_2 emission from domestic sector?
(a) 1.75 mmt (b) 0.75 mmt
(c) 1.5 mmt (d) 2.5 mmt

PAPER–II

1. **Assertion (A):** CFCs destroy ozone molecules in stratosphere
Reason (R): CFCs have very high global warming potential
Codes:
(a) Both (A) and (R) are true and (R) is the correct explanation of (A).
(b) Both (A) and (R) are true but (R) is not the correct explanation of (A).
(c) (A) is true, (R) is false.
(d) (A) is false, (R) is true.

2. Which of the following pairs is not correctly matched:
(a) Tropical zone – Hot, winterless
(b) Sub-tropical zone – Hot with cool winter
(c) Temperate zone – Warm summer with pronounced winter
(d) Alpine zone – Long summer with short severe winter

3. To establish wind mill for commercial production of electricity, the optimum range of wind speeds required is:
(a) 4-10 m/sec (b) 20-30 m/sec
(c) 35-45 m/sec (d) > 100 m/sec

4. Which is the correct chronological order (oldest to youngest) in which the following were formed:
(I) Atlantic Ocean
(II) Indian Ocean
(III) Pacific Ocean
(IV) Mediterranean sea
Select the correct answer using the codes given below:
Codes:
(a) III, I, IV, II (b) III, I, II, IV
(c) I, III, II, IV (d) I, III, IV, II

5. **Assertion (A):** The ozone layer absorbs UV radiations.
Reason (R): Part of the UV flux is used up in the formation of ozone in stratosphere.
Codes:
(a) Both (A) and (R) are true and (R) is the correct explanation of (A).
(b) Both (A) and (R) are true and (R) is not the correct explanation of (A).
(c) (A) is true, but (R) is false.
(d) (A) is false, but (R) is true.

6. Match List I and List II and select the correct answer choosing the codes given below the lists:

List I	List II
A. Chain silicates	(i) Quartz
B. Tekto silicates	(ii) Beryl
C. Phyllo silicates	(iii) Augite
D. Cyclo silicates	(iv) Muscovite

Codes:	A	B	C	D
(a)	(i)	(ii)	(iii)	(iv)
(b)	(i)	(ii)	(iv)	(iii)
(c)	(iii)	(i)	(ii)	(iv)
(d)	(iii)	(i)	(iv)	(ii)

7. Precipitation of $CaCO_3$ may occur when
   (a) Sea water is shallow and CO_2 is lost.
   (b) Sea water is warm and CO_2 is being lost.
   (c) Sea water is cold and CO_2 is being lost.
   (d) Sea water is deep and CO_2 is being added.

8. Bowen's law basically tell us
   (a) How a sedimentary rock is formed
   (b) How various igneous minerals are formed
   (c) How some economic minerals are formed
   (d) Both (a) and (b) are correct

9. Match the following List I and List II and select the correct answer using the codes given below:

   List I
   A. Public hearing is required
   B. Public hearing is not required
   C. Baseline air quality data is collected
   D. Baseline noise level data is collected

   List II
   (i) Modernisation of existing irrigation projects
   (ii) Highway projects
   (iii) Once in each season
   (iv) 24 hourly twice a week

Codes:	A	B	C	D
(a)	(i)	(iv)	(ii)	(iii)
(b)	(ii)	(i)	(iv)	(iii)
(c)	(iii)	(i)	(iv)	(ii)
(d)	(iv)	(iii)	(i)	(ii)

10. The first National Park established in India is
    (a) Indira Gandhi National Park
    (b) Indravati National Park
    (c) Corbett National Park
    (d) Kaziranga National Park

11. In a vertical section across a sulphide deposit, the site representing the best situation for supergene enrichment would be
    (a) above the water table
    (b) below the water table
    (c) in the oxidation zone
    (d) in the zone rich in humus

12. If nocturnal animal in the light dark cycle of 12 h light and 12 h darkness kept in constant darkness for 10 days, then what will happen to the onset of its daily activities
    (a) start earlier than what was before
    (b) start later than what was before
    (c) no change in the activity time
    (d) activities remain on throughout the dark period

13. Separation of compounds in Gas Chromatography (GC) depends upon
    (a) Molecular weight
    (b) Solubility in carrier gas
    (c) Solubility in stationary phase
    (d) Solubility in carrier gas and liquid phase

14. Which of the following instrument is most suitable to estimate heavy metals from the effluent?
    (a) Chromatography
    (b) Atomic Absorption spectrophotometer

(c) Flame photometer
(d) Electrophoresis

15. For a Binomial distribution if p is the probability of happening of an event and q = 1 – p, then the variance in a sample of N observations would be:

(a) Npq (b) $\sqrt{Npq}$

(c) $\sqrt{N}/pq$ (d) $pq/\sqrt{N-1}$

16. **Assertion (A):** Sustainable production of hay or green fodder is essential for uninterrupted supply of animal products.
Reason (R): Environmental concerns are detrimental for sustainable production of hay or green fodder.
Codes:
(a) Both (A) and (R) are true but (R) is not the correct explanation of (A).
(b) Both (A) and (R) are true and (R) is the correct explanation of (A).
(c) (A) is true, and (R) is false.
(d) (A) is false, and (R) is true.

17. The proteins in the cell walls of microorganisms have an overall net negative charge at pH of most soil environments, because
(a) the pH of the environment is greater than the pI
(b) the pH of the environment is less than the pI
(c) the pH of the environment is the same as pI
(d) None of the above

18. Match the List I and List II in respect of the geochemical affinity of the elements:

List I	List II
A. Chalcophile	(i) Carbon
B. Lithophile	(ii) Nitrogen
C. Siderophile	(iii) Sulphur
D. Atmophile	(iv) Oxygen
E. Biophile	(v) Iron

Codes:	A	B	C	D	E
(a)	(v)	(iv)	(iii)	(i)	(ii)
(b)	(iii)	(iv)	(v)	(ii)	(i)
(c)	(iv)	(v)	(i)	(ii)	(iii)
(d)	(iii)	(i)	(ii)	(iv)	(v)

19. $PM_{2.5}$ refers to:
(a) mass of particles of size less than 2.5 μm.
(b) mass of particles of size greater than 2.5 μm.
(c) number of particles of size less than 2.5 μm.
(d) number of particles of size greater than 2.5 μm.

20. In a simple regression model $Y = \alpha + \beta X + \in$ (Y = dependent variable, X = independent variable, α, β are regression coefficients, $\in$ = random error), the variance of $\in$ is:
(a) 0
(b) $\frac{\alpha^2}{\beta^2}$
(c) $\frac{\beta^2}{\alpha^2}$
(d) α^2; (σ = standard deviation)

21. Which one of the following statements regarding ELNINO is not true?
(a) It is an extension of equitorial current towards the western coast of South America.
(b) It is an occasional warm current leading to an increase of about 10°C in subsurface water temperature.
(c) It develops as temporary replacement of usual cold Peruvian Current.
(d) It causes an increase in plankton thriving in cold Peruvian current.

22. Match the items in List I with List II and select the correct answer using codes given below:
List I
A. The audible frequency range is
B. The audible sound level pressure is
C. Ratio of Intensity to a reference
D. Energy content for varying sound

List II

(i) 20μPa to 200Pa
(ii) 20 – 20,000 Hz
(iii) Equivalent continuous sound Intensity of sound expressed in level (Leq) log scale is
(iv) Decibel levels

Codes:	A	B	C	D
(a)	(ii)	(i)	(iv)	(iii)
(b)	(i)	(ii)	(iii)	(iv)
(c)	(iv)	(iii)	(ii)	(i)
(d)	(iii)	(iv)	(ii)	(i)

23. Ecologically sensitive and important areas, breeding and spawning grounds of marine life, etc., are categorized in coastal Regulation Zone as
(a) CRZ-IV (b) CRZ-II
(c) CRZ-III (d) CRZ-I

24. Land use pattern is usually studied by the following technique
(a) Aerial photography
(b) Satellite imaging
(c) Satellite imaging and G.I.S.
(d) Satellite imaging, G.I.S. and G.P.S.

25. Particle size in soil can be classified as Clay: 1-4 micron. Silt: 4-62 micron. Sand: 62-1000 micron ; Boulder: >1000 micron. It is hence correct to suggest that in nature particle size distribution follows
(a) Binomial distribution
(b) Lognormal distribution
(c) Linear distribution
(d) Normal distribution

26. *Deinococcus* and *Deinobacter* are radiation resistant bacteria because
(a) They have effective repair mechanism for damaged DNA and have high concentration of carotenoids
(b) They do not absorb radiations
(d) They have RNA instead of DNA
(d) They grow in ice

27. Suppose the number of individual prey population is N_1 and their intrinsic rate of population increase N_1, where:

$r_1 = b - m$

b = birth rate per individual

m = mortality rate per individual, then the rate of change of the prey population (dN_1/dt) (without immigration and emigration) is as below:

(a) $\frac{1}{2}r_1N_1$ (b) r_1N_1
(c) $(r_1N_1)^2$ (d) $(r_1N_1)^{1/2}$

28. Suspended sediment load is that part of the sediment load which is transported within the main body flow. The primary mechanism of maintaining the sediment particles in suspension is
(a) Channel flow
(b) Particle size
(c) Turbulent diffusion
(d) Dissolved gasses

29. A noise signal can be characterized through its amplitude/energy content in the signal. The signal can be expressed in various forms like root mean square value, given as

(a) $\left[\frac{1}{T}\int_0^T a^2(t)dt\right]^{1/2}$ (b) $\left[\frac{1}{2T}\int_0^T a^2(t)dt\right]^{1/2}$

(c) $\left[\frac{1}{T}\int_0^T |a| \cdot dt\right]$ (d) $\left[\frac{1}{2T}\int_0^T |a| \cdot dt\right]$

30. A ship (X) moving due North with a velocity (v) observes that another ship (Y) is moving due west, the actual velocity of (Y) is
(a) (ν) is due East
(b) ($\sqrt{2}\nu$) is towards North West
(c) (ν) is towards South East
(d) ($\sqrt{2}\nu$) is towards North East

31. Polychlorinated biphenyls (PCBs) which cause environmental exposure risk have these important properties
    (a) Very high volatility in air
    (b) Chemically unstable and highly reactive
    (c) Heat stable and have no flash or fire point
    (d) Highly soluble in water and poorly soluble in oils and organic solvents

32. The mass of the earth's mantle is approximately
    (a) 2×10^{25} g (b) 8.1×10^{17} g
    (c) 4.05×10^{27} g (d) 3.1×10^{22} g

33. Eutrophication of water bodies is triggered by
    (a) Excessive growth of phytoplanktons
    (b) Excessive growth of fishes
    (c) Excessive inflow of nutrients
    (d) Bright sunlight

34. **Assertion (A):** Geothermal reservoirs with temperatures above 180°C are useful for generating electric power.
    Reason (R): High temperature steam can be used to drive turbines to generate electricity.
    Codes:
    (a) Both (A) and (R) are true and (R) is the correct explanation of (A).
    (b) Both (A) and (R) are true but (R) is not the correct explanation of (A).
    (c) (A) is true, but (R) is false.
    (d) (A) is false, but (R) is true.

35. For aerosol particles of size comparable to wavelengths of either short-wave radiation or infrared radiation, the following type of scattering takes place
    (a) Rayleigh scattering
    (b) Mie scattering
    (c) Raman scattering
    (d) Brillouin scattering

36. The mass of 1 mole of electron is equal to
    (a) $9.1094 \times 6.16 \times 10^{-28}$ g
    (b) $9.1094 \times 10^{-31} \times 6.023 \times 10^{23}$ kg
    (c) $(9.1094 \times 10^{-31}) / 6.023 \times 10^{23}$ kg
    (d) $(6.023 \times 10^{23}) / 6.1094 \times 10^{-28}$ g

37. For the precipitation of $CaCO_3$ from water
    $Ca^{+2} + CO_3^{-2} - CaCO_3$
    the equilibrium constant K is $10^{-8.3}$. This indicates that
    (a) Ca^{+2} & CO_3^{-2} concentration are equal in water
    (b) $m_{CO_3^{-2}} \gg m_{Ca^{+2}}$
    (c) $m_{Ca^{+2}} < m_{CO_3^{-2}}$
    (d) $m_{Ca^{+2}} = \dfrac{1}{m_{CO_3^{-2}}}$

38. Which one of the following is not a biofertilizer?
    (a) Aquatic ferns
    (b) Blue-green algae
    (c) Phosphate-Solubilising micro-organisms
    (d) Vermicompost

39. CITES has following schedules in order of priority to protect animals and plants from trade
    (a) Schedule I, II, III
    (b) Schedule I, I, III
    (c) Schedule III, III, I
    (d) Schedule II, I, III

Read the following passage carefully and answer the questions (40 to 45):

The Taj Mahal has become one of the world's best known monuments. This domed white marble structure is situated on a high plinth at the southern end of a four-quartered garden, evoking the gardens of paradise, enclosed within walls measuring 305 by 549 metres. Outside the walls, in an area known as Mumtazabad, were living quarters for attendants, markets, serais and other structures built by local merchants and nobles. The tomb complex and the other imperial structures of Mumtazabad were maintained by the income of thirty villages given specifically for the tomb's support. The name Taj Mahal is unknown in Mughal chronicles, but it is used by contemporary Europeans in India, suggesting that this was the tomb's popular name. In contemporary texts, it is generally called simply the Illuminated Tomb (Rauza-i-Munavvara).

Mumtaz Mahal died shortly after delivering her fourteenth child in 1631. The Mughal court was then residing in Burhanpur. Her remains were temporarily buried by the griefstricken emperor in a spacious garden known as Zainabad on the bank of the river Tapti. Six months later her body was transported to Agra, where it was interred in land chosen for the mausoleum. This land, situated south of the Mughal city on the bank of the Jamuna, had belonged to the Kachhwaha rajas since the time of Raja Man Singh and was purchased from the then current raja, Jai Singh. Although contemporary chronicles indicate Jai Singh's willing cooperation in this exchange, extant *farmans* (imperial commands) indicate that the final price was not settled until almost two years after the mausoleum's commencement. Jai Singh's further cooperation was insured by imperial orders issued between 1632 and 1637 demanding that he provide stone masons and carts to transport marble from the mines at Makrana, within his "ancestral domain", to Agra where both the Taj Mahal and Shah Jahan's additions to the Agra fort were constructed concurrently.

Work on the mausoleum was commenced early in 1632. Inscriptional evidence indicates much of the tomb was completed by 1636. By 1643, when Shah Jahan most lavishly celebrated the 'Urs ceremony for Mumtaz Mahal', the entire complex was virtually complete.

40. Marble stone used for the construction of the Taj Mahal was brought from the ancestral domain of Raja Jai Singh. The name of the place where mines of marble is
    (a) Burhanpur (b) Makrana
    (c) Amber (d) Jaipur
41. The popular name Taj Mahal was given by
    (a) Shah Jahan
    (b) Tourists
    (c) Public
    (d) European travellers
42. Point out the true statement from the following
    (a) Marble was not used for the construction of the Taj Mahal.
    (b) Red sand stone is non-visible in the Taj Mahal complex.
    (c) The Taj Mahal is surrounded by a four-quartered garden known as Chahr Bagh.
    (d) The Taj Mahal was constructed to celebrate the 'Urs ceremony for Mumtaz Mahal'.
43. In the contemporary texts the Taj Mahal is known
    (a) Mumtazabad
    (b) Mumtaz Mahal
    (c) Zainabad
    (d) Rauza-i-Munavvara
44. The construction of the Taj Mahal was completed between the period
    (a) 1632 – 1636 A.D.
    (b) 1630 – 1643 A.D.
    (c) 1632 – 1643 A.D.
    (d) 1636 – 1643 A.D.
45. The documents indicating the ownership of land, where the Taj Mahal was built, known as
    (a) Farman
    (b) Sale Deed
    (c) Sale-Purchase Deed
    (d) None of the above

46. **Assertion (A):** A large number of districts in States of India have become water stressed.
Reason (R): The population in India has increased appreciably since independence.
Codes:
(a) Both (A) and (R) are true and (R) is the correct explanation of (A).
(b) Both (A) and (R) are true, but (R) is not the correct explanation of (A).
(c) (A) is true, but (R) is false.
(d) (A) is false, but (R) is true.

47. Under the Climate Change Action Plan of Government of India which of the renewable source of energy has been identified as a priority for exploitation?
(a) Solar energy
(b) Wind energy
(c) Tidal energy
(d) Geothermal energy

48. Lotka-Volterra Model deals with
(a) Prey-Predator interactions
(b) Predicting CO_2 concentrations
(c) Study of pollutant concentration in river streams
(d) Study of pollutant concentration in atmospheric environment

49. Consider the following statements:
(i) Entropy in a spontaneous reaction increases
(ii) Free energy in a spontaneous reaction increases
(iii) Free energy remains constant when reaction is in equilibrium
(iv) Free energy increases in a reverse reaction
Which of these are correct:
Codes:
(a) (i) and (ii) (b) (ii) and (iii)
(c) (i), (iii) and (iv) (d) None of these

50. **Assertion (A):** 'Hot spots' are the region showing richness of endemic species.
Reason (R): The distribution of endemic species are confined to a specific region.
Codes:
(a) Both (A) and (R) are true and (R) is correct explanation of (A).
(b) Both (A) and (R) are true but (R) is not the correct explanation of (A).
(c) (A) is true, but (R) is false.
(d) (A) is false, but (R) is true.

PAPER–III

1. Stratosphere is devoid of weather phenomenon because
(a) all the atmosphere ozone is present in this layer
(b) it is free from moisture and dust
(c) it has a maximum temperature of –2°C
(d) the harmful radiations are absorbed by ozone in this layer

2. Match the List I and List II and select the correct answer from the codes given below the lists:
List I
A. Hekistotherms B. Mesotherms
C. Megatherms D. Microtherms
List II
(i) Cannot tolerate high temperature
(ii) Require high degree of heat throughout the year
(iii) Require moderate temperature for their growth
(iv) Require very low temperature and can stand very severe long winters

Codes:	A	B	C	D
(a)	(iv)	(iii)	(ii)	(i)
(b)	(ii)	(iii)	(iv)	(i)
(c)	(iii)	(iv)	(ii)	(i)
(d)	(iv)	(iii)	(i)	(ii)

3. Water is the most common and the most important chemical compounds for the livings for which of the following reasons?
   1. The life has been originated in the waters of the oceans.
   2. It makes a large proportions of the animal tissues.
   3. Livings use aqueous solutions like blood and digestive juices as media for carrying out their biological functions.

   Select the correct answer using the codes given below:

   Codes:

   (a) 1, 2 and 3 (b) 1 and 2
   (c) 1 and 3 (d) 2 and 3

4. The source of carbon dioxide in the atmosphere is
   (a) respiration and incomplete burning of carbon-containing compounds
   (b) respiration, burning of fossil fuels, converting limestone into cement
   (c) burning of fossil fuels and incomplete industrial burning processes
   (d) None of the above

5. The plants use nitrogen in which of the following forms?
   (a) Molecular nitrogen
   (b) Nitrates
   (c) Nitrogen monoxide
   (d) Nitrogen dioxide

6. Which of the following formula is used to measure the pressure above and below the atmospheric pressure?
   (a) $P = (h + \Delta h)\rho g$
   (b) $P\sqrt{M} = a + \frac{b}{t}$
   (c) P = 101.3 (0.0226 × H) 5.255
   (d) $\left(P + \frac{a}{V^2}\right)(V - b) = nRT$

7. Match the List I and List II and select the correct answer from the codes given below the lists:

   List I

   A. Alkali Metals
   B. Group III Elements
   C. Group V Elements
   D. Germanium

   List II

   (i) Have three electrons in their outer orbital
   (ii) Has the characteristics of both metals and non-metals
   (iii) Metals of main sub-group of Group I of Periodic Table
   (iv) Exhibit –3, +3 and +5 oxidation states

Codes:	A	B	C	D
(a)	(iii)	(iv)	(i)	(ii)
(b)	(ii)	(iii)	(iv)	(i)
(c)	(iii)	(iv)	(ii)	(i)
(d)	(iv)	(iii)	(i)	(ii)

8. Which of the following is the characteristics of Alkaline-Earth Elements?
   (a) Atoms of these elements have one electron in their outer orbital
   (b) They are extremely electropositive and form divalent ionic salts
   (c) They exhibit an oxidation state of +2 in their compounds
   (d) None of the above.

9. The carbon monoxide concentration in the troposphere varies
   (a) 50 ppbv to 100 ppbv
   (b) 10 ppbv to 100 ppbv
   (c) 75 ppbv to 100 ppbv
   (d) 100 ppbv to 1000 ppbv

10. The dissolved oxygen in water body affected by
    (a) inflow and outflow conditions of the water body
    (b) physical, chemical and biologic nature of the water body

(c) geographical terrain
(d) All of the above

11. **Assertion (A):** The radioactive decay such as β- and γ-rays can damage the human body.
Reason (R): β- and γ-rays consist of high energy photons.
Codes:
(a) Both (A) and (R) are true and (R) is the correct explanation of (A).
(b) Both (A) and (R) are true, but (R) is not the correct explanation of (A).
(c) (A) is true, but (R) is false.
(d) (A) is false, but (R) is true.

12. Which of the following is a density dependent effect?
(a) Epidemics in human population
(b) Zero population growth in yeast colony
(c) Sexual reproduction
(d) Sexual dimorphism.

13. Which of the following pairs regarding the National Parks and its location is correctly matched?
(a) Bandhavgarh.........Rajasthan
(b) Nagarahole............Maharashtra
(c) Kaziranga..............Assam
(d) Dudhwa..................Madhya Pradesh.

14. Ecosystem has two components
(a) plants and animals
(b) weeds and trees
(c) biotic and abiotic factors
(d) None of the above

15. Biotic components include
(a) producers, consumers and decomposers
(b) consumers only
(c) producers only
(d) producers and consumers

16. What is the position of man in ecosystem?
(a) Man has nothing to do with the ecosystem.
(b) Man may be necessary in an ecosystem.
(c) Man is most important in an ecosystem.
(d) None of the above is correct.

17. Which of the following is the characteristics of ocean ecosystem?
(a) They are the largest and most stable ecosystem
(b) They occur in the regions with less than 10″ of annual rainfall
(c) The succulent plants are found in the ocean ecosystem
(d) None of the above.

18. The process of interception means
(a) holding of precipitation on different parts of the plants
(b) running of precipitation from the earth surface to lakes, rivers and marshes
(c) the condensation of water vapours
(d) None of the above

19. The earth system is highly
(a) dynamic (b) static
(c) complex (d) None

20. The atmosphere is essential in maintaining the heat balance of the earth as
1. it helps to trap the heat of the sun
2. it absorbs radiation coming from the sun
3. it acts as the prime heat exchanger
Of these
(a) only 1 is correct
(b) 1, 2, and 3 are correct
(c) 2, 3 and 4 are correct
(d) None of the above

21. What is considered to be the approximate difference in average temperature between the "little ice age" and today?

(a) 1 to 3 degrees centigrade
(b) 5 to 8 degrees centigrade
(c) 10 to 12 degrees centigrade
(d) 15 to 20 degrees centigrade

22. Which of the following pairs with respect to soil particles and their size is correctly matched?
(a) Silt 0.01 mm (b) Gravel 5.0 mm
(c) Clay 2.0 mm (d) Co

23. Which of the following best describes the effect of a mountain range on the climate of a region?
(a) The coastal side of the range usually has high levels of rain.
(b) A desert is often found on the inland side of the range.
(c) Average temperatures are lower at high elevations than at the base of mountains.
(d) All of the above.

24. Consider the following statements regarding atmosphere:
1. The atmosphere around the earth is due to force of gravity.
2. The composition of gases in the atmosphere is a result of various chemical reactions occurring through millions of years.
3. The ozone is a short-lived constituents of atmosphere.

Of these statements
Codes:
(a) only 1 is correct
(b) 2 and 3 are correct
(c) 1 and 3 are correct
(d) All are correct.

25. With an increase in altitude, the temperature generally
(a) increase (b) decrease
(c) Both (a) and (b) (d) None

26. The process of interception means
(a) holding of precipitation on different parts of the plants
(b) running of precipitation from the earth surface to lakes, rivers and marshes
(c) the condensation of water vapours
(d) None of the above

27. According to the modern theory of origin of living which one of the following is necessary to be president for the origin of life?
(a) Amino acid
(b) Nucleic acid
(c) Protein
(d) Carbon dioxide

28. Direct nutrient cycling that is from plant back to plant is seen in
(a) mangrove forests
(b) pyruvate
(c) deciduous forests
(d) tropical evergreen forest

29. **Assertion (A):** Ecesis is a step in succession.
Reason (R): Establishment of a species in a new area.
Codes:
(a) Both (A) and (R) are true and (R) is the correct explanation of (A).
(b) Both (A) and (R) are true, but (R) is not the correct explanation of (A).
(c) (A) is false, but (R) is true.
(d) (A) is true, but (R) is false.

30. Although the use of DDT was banned in the United States in 1972, a test of the body tissue of an average United States resident today would most likely reveal the presence of DDT because
(a) DDT is the breakdown product of some newer pesticides on the market
(b) DDT is water soluble
(c) other countries that export produce to the United States still use DDT
(d) many farmers in the United States are still using DDT illegally

31. Consider the following statements regarding the chemical composition of air:
    1. Four fifths of all the components of air are metals.
    2. The water vapour in the air is usually 1-3% by volume.
    3. Seeds, spores and pollen grains are important ingredients of air composition.

    Of these statements
    (a) Only 1 is correct
    (b) 2 and 3 are correct
    (c) 1 and 3 are correct
    (d) All are correct

32. The primary indicators of the quality of urban air are
    (a) atmospheric oxidants
    (b) atmospheric reductant
    (c) Both (a) and (b)
    (d) None of the above

33. The humus in the soil is the
    (a) organic portion of the soil remaining after prolonged microbial decomposition
    (b) heterogenous mixture of products resulting from the microbial and chemical transformation of organic materials
    (c) complex of organic compounds, living organisms, water and included gases
    (d) All of the above

34. Methemoglobinemia is a condition in which
    (a) nitrite ion enters in the liver of hue
    (b) nitrite ion reacts with calcium of bones
    (c) nitrite oxidises the haemoglobin
    (d) nitrite reduces the haemoglobin

35. Match the following:

    List I

    A. Microtherms B. Mesotherms
    C. Megatherms D. Hekisiotherms

    List II

    (i) Require very low temperature and can stand very severe long winters
    (ii) Require high degree of heat throughout the year
    (iii) Cannot tolerate high temperature
    (iv) Require moderate temperature for their growth.

Codes:	A	B	C	D
(a)	(iii)	(iv)	(ii)	(i)
(b)	(iv)	(i)	(ii)	(iii)
(c)	(i)	(iv)	(ii)	(iii)
(d)	(i)	(iii)	(ii)	(iv)

36. In the soil profile A_0 layer is the
    (a) uppermost zone of soil consisting of decomposed matter
    (b) uppermost zone of soil devoid of humus
    (c) lowermost zone of soil, which is devoid of humus
    (d) lower zone of A-horizon consisting of humus

37. The most important form of water to plant is
    (a) capillary water
    (b) hygroscopic water
    (c) gravitational water
    (d) combined water

38. **Assertion (A):** At present in India, the use of solar energy is rather limited.

    Reason (R): Large scale use of solar energy has uncertain environmental implications.
    (a) Both (A) and (R) are true and (R) is the correct explanation of (A).
    (b) Both (A) and (R) are true, but (R) is not the correct explanation of (A).
    (c) (A) is true, but (R) is false.
    (d) (A) is false, but (R) is true.

39. Which of the following statements is correct?

(a) Smog occurs when high concentration of moisture is combined with smoke and oxides of nitrogen
(b) Free cyanides are toxic pollutants
(c) Combustion of natural fuels and roasting of iron produce sulphur dioxide
(d) None of these

40. Match the List I and List II and select the correct answer from the codes given below the lists:

List I (Element)

A. Aluminium B. Copper
C. Cobalt D. Nickel

List II (Function in the Body)

(i) Needed for normal growth
(ii) Metabolism of Vitamin B12
(iii) Electron transport enzyme complex
(iv) Protein transferin in serum

Codes:	**A**	**B**	**C**	**D**
(a)	(i)	(ii)	(iii)	(iv)
(b)	(ii)	(iv)	(i)	(iii)
(c)	(iii)	(iv)	(ii)	(i)
(d)	(iv)	(iii)	(ii)	(i)

41. Darwin noted that the Patagonian hare was similar in appearance and had a niche similar to the European hare. However, the Patagonian hare is not a rabbit. It is a rodent related to the guinea pig. This example illustrates the principle known as
(a) allopatric speciation
(b) adaptive radiation
(c) divergent evolution
(d) convergent evolution

42. Populations of organisms living in life zones may be limited by
(a) access to light.
(b) nutrient availability.
(c) dissolved oxygen.
(d) All of the above.

43. Commensalism is a term which characterises
(a) living together of two or more different kinds of animals
(b) organisational relationship between two or more different animals
(c) a group of two or more different animals which cannot exist without the help of one another
(d) the association between two or more different animals where one may sometimes be harmful to the other

44. Which of the following statements is/are true?
1. A community and its habitat mutually interact
2. A community and its habitat are interdependent
3. A community and its habitat exist independently

Of these statements
(a) Only 1 is correct
(b) 2 and 3 are correct
(c) 1 and 2 are correct
(d) All are correct.

45. The interrelationship of all the organisms belonging to producers, consumers and decomposers classes in a given habitat is called
(a) food chain (b) food web
(c) food cycle (d) ecosystem

46. Which of the following pairs regarding the airborne disease and their causative agent is incorrect?
(a) Measles.................... Rubella
(b) Meningitis .... Neisseria
(c) Smallpox .... Variola
(d) Pneumonia .... Rubeola

47. DDT poisoning causes thin and fragile eggshells in birds such as

(a) brown pelican
(b) ospreys
(c) falcons
(d) All of the above

48. A simple matrix is assembled by displaying various components of a project
(a) on the same axis
(b) along one axis and the predicted impact on environmental parameter on the other axis
(c) on the vertices of a triangle
(d) None of the above

49. Forest Conservation Act was amended in the year
(a) 1978 (b) 1988
(c) 2000 (d) 1999

50. The value of x obtained from the equations $x + y + z = a$, $x^2 + y^2 + z^2 = a^2$ and $x^3 + y^3 + z^3 = a^3$ will be
(a) 0, a and 0 (b) 0, 0 and a
(c) a, $-a$ and $-2a$ (d) 0, $\frac{a}{2}$ and a

ANSWERS SHEET

PAPER—I

1. (a)	2. (c)	3. (a)	4. (d)	5. (d)
6. (d)	7. (d)	8. (c)	9. (b)	10. (c)
11. (b)	12. (c)	13. (c)	14. (b)	15. (d)
16. (b)	17. (a)	18. (d)	19. (c)	20. (d)
21. (d)	22. (a)	23. (b)	24. (a)	25. (d)
26. (d)	27. (a)	28. (d)	29. (b)	30. (a)
31. (b)	32. (c)	33. (c)	34. (d)	35. (d)
36. (d)	37. (a)	38. (d)	39. (b)	40. (b)
41. (b)	42. (c)	43. (b)	44. (b)	45. (c)
46. (b)	47. (a)	48. (c)	49. (a)	50. (b)

PAPER—II

1. (a)	2. (d)	3. (d)	4. (a)	5. (c)
6. (d)	7. (a)	8. (d)	9. (b)	10. (c)
11. (b)	12. (d)	13. (d)	14. (b)	15. (b)
16. (a)	17. (b)	18. (b)	19. (c)	20. (a)
21. (a)	22. (a)	23. (d)	24. (b)	25. (d)
26. (b)	27. (b)	28. (a)	29. (c)	30. (c)
31. (d)	32. (d)	33. (a)	34. (b)	35. (a)
36. (b)	37. (c)	38. (a)	39. (d)	40. (b)
41. (d)	42. (c)	43. (d)	44. (c)	45. (a)
46. (a)	47. (a)	48. (a)	49. (b)	50. (b)

PAPER—III

1. (b)	2. (a)	3. (a)	4. (b)	5. (b)
6. (a)	7. (a)	8. (b)	9. (b)	10. (d)
11. (c)	12. (b)	13. (c)	14. (b)	15. (a)
16. (c)	17. (a)	18. (c)	19. (a)	20. (a)
21. (a)	22. (b)	23. (d)	24. (d)	25. (b)
26. (a)	27. (b)	28. (d)	29. (b)	30. (c)
31. (b)	32. (a)	33. (d)	34. (c)	35. (a)
36. (b)	37. (b)	38. (c)	39. (b)	40. (d)
41. (d)	42. (d)	43. (a)	44. (c)	45. (d)
46. (d)	47. (d)	48. (c)	49. (b)	50. (d)

F105

ATLANTIC TITLES FOR UGC-NET/SLET AND OTHER COMPETITIVE EXAMINATIONS

Commerce: For UGC-NET/SLET and Other Competitive Examinations (Objective Type Questions), *Atlantic Research Division*

Economics: For UGC-NET/SLET and other Competitive Examinations (Objective Type Questions), Third Revised and Enlarged Edition, *K.R. Gupta*

CAT Cracker: Quantitative Aptitude, *K.R. Gupta*

Education: For UGC-NET/SLET, (Objective Type Questions), 2nd ed., Revised, Updated and Enlarged, *Atlantic Research Division*

English: For UGC-NET/JRF/SLET (Paper II and III) and Other Competitive Examinations, (Objective Type Questions), Third Edition Revised, Updated & Enlarged, *R.S. Malik*

History: For UGC-NET/SLET and Other Competitive Examinations (Objective Type Questions), 2nd ed., & Enlarged Edition, *Atlantic Research Division*

Library and Information Science: For UGC-NET/SLET and other Competitive Examinations (Objective Type Questions), *D.K. Pandey*

Management: For UGC-NET/SLET and Other Competitive Examinations (Objective Type Questions), Second ed., Revised, Updated & Enlarged, *Atlantic Research Division*

Mass Communication and Journalism: For UGC-NET/SLET (Objective Type Questions), 2nd ed., Revised, Updated and Enlarged, *Atlantic Research Division*

Political Science: For UGC-NET/SLET (Objective Type Questions), *Atlantic Research Division*

Public Administration: For UGC-NET/SLET (Objective Type Questions), *Atlantic Research Division*

Sociology: For UGC-NET/SLET and Other Competitive Examinations (Objective Type), *Atlantic Research Division*

PREVIOUS YEARS' SOLVED PAPERS

Commerce: For UGC-NET/SLET/JRF Paper I, II, and III, Previous Years' Solved Papers, *Atlantic Research Division*

Education: For UGC-NET/SLET/JRF Paper I, II, and III, Previous Years' Solved Papers, *Atlantic Research Division*

English: For UGC-NET/SLET/JRF Paper I, II, and III, Previous Years' Solved Papers, *Atlantic Research Division*

Geography: For UGC-NET/SLET/JRF Paper I, II, and III, Previous Years' Solved Papers, *Atlantic Research Division*

Graduate Aptitude Test in Engineering (GATE): Mathematics, Previous Years' Solved Papers, *K.R. Gupta*

Graduate Aptitude Test in Engineering (GATE): Physics, Previous Years' Solved Papers, *Atlantic Research Division*

History: For UGC-NET/SLET/JRF Paper I, II, and III, Previous Years' Solved Papers, *Atlantic Research Division*

Home Science: For UGC-NET/SLET/JRF Paper I, II, and III, Previous Years' Solved Papers, *Atlantic Research Division*

Library and Information Science: For UGC-NET/SLET/JRF Paper I, II, and III, Previous Years' Solved Papers, *Atlantic Research Division*

Management: For UGC-NET/SLET/JRF Paper I, II, and III, Previous Years' Solved Papers, *Atlantic Research Division*

Political Science: For UGC-NET/SLET/JRF Paper I, II, and III, Previous Years' Solved Papers, *Atlantic Research Division*

Public Administration: For UGC-NET/SLET/JRF Paper I, II, and III, Previous Years' Solved Papers, *Atlantic Research Division*

Sociology: For UGC-NET/SLET/JRF Paper I, II, and III, Previous Years' Solved Papers, *Atlantic Research Division*

Hindi: For UGC-NET/JRF, Paper I, II, and III, Previous Years' Solved Papers, *Atlantic Research Division*

Law: For UGC-NET/JRF, Paper I, II, and III, Previous Years' Solved Papers, *Atlantic Research Division*